Foundations of Lodging Management

Second Edition

Foundations of Lodging Management

David K. Hayes, Ph.D.
Jack D. Ninemeier, Ph.D.
Allisha A. Miller

Prentice Hall
Boston Columbus Indianapolis New York San Francisco Upper Saddle River
Amsterdam Cape Town Dubai London Madrid Milan Munich Paris Montreal Toronto
Delhi Mexico City Sao Paulo Sydney Hong Kong Seoul Singapore Taipei Tokyo

Editorial Director: Vernon Anthony
Senior Acquisitions Editor: William Lawrensen
Editorial Assistant: Lara Dimmick
Director of Marketing: David Gesell
Campaign Marketing Manager: Leigh Ann Sims
Curriculum Marketing Manager: Thomas Hayward
Senior Marketing Coordinator: Alicia Wozniak
Marketing Assistant: Les Roberts
Production Project Manager: Debbie Ryan
Production Editor: Alexis Biasell
Art Director: Jayne Conte
Cover Designer: Suzanne Behnke
Cover Art: Fotolia
Media Editor: Michell Churma
Lead Media Project Manager: Karen Bretz
Full-Service Project Management: Kailash Jadli, Aptara®, Inc.
Composition: Aptara/Falls Church
Printer/Binder: Edwards Brothers
Cover Printer: Lehigh-Phoenix Color/Hagerstown
Text Font: Garamond

Credits and acknowledgments borrowed from other sources and reproduced, with permission, in this textbook appear on appropriate page within text.

Library of Congress Cataloging-in-Publication Data
Hayes, David K.
Foundations of lodging management / David K. Hayes, Jack D. Ninemeier, Allisha A. Miller.—2nd ed.
p. cm.
Includes bibliographical references and index.
ISBN-13: 978-0-13-256089-4 (alk. paper)
ISBN-10: 0-13-256089-5 (alk. paper)
1. Hospitality industry—Management. I. Ninemeier, Jack D. II. Miller, Allisha. III. Title.
TX911.3.M27H3879 2011
647.94'068—dc22

2011003017

10 9 8 7 6 5 4 3

Prentice Hall
is an imprint of

www.pearsonhighered.com

ISBN 10: 0-13-256089-5
ISBN 13: 978-0-13-256089-4

To our parents:

M.D. and Pauline, whose support and encouragement have been as greatly appreciated as they have been unwavering.

Lorine and Ralph, who emphasized the importance of education and purposeful endeavors balanced with time to "smell the roses."

Laura and David, who demonstrate every day that through humility, hardwork, and perseverance our efforts can reveal the diamonds within ourselves and others.

CONTENTS

PREFACE

Lodging is one of the most exciting and rapidly changing segments of the hospitality industry. Hoteliers operate hotels, and today's hoteliers face challenges unmatched in recent history. Changing consumer demands, global recessions, the continued expansion of the Internet and social networking as major factors in the marketing and selling rooms, advanced operational technology at the front desk, and even the threat of global terrorism all continue to have a significant effect on the day-to-day activities of those who work in and manage hotels.

Like the first edition, *Foundations of Lodging Management, Second Edition* is unique in its simple recognition that the hotel industry consists of far more small hotels than large ones. Today's lodging industry is typified by increasing numbers of smaller, limited-service, franchised hotels and a declining number of larger, full-service, independent hotels. While this change results in more properties and more management opportunities, some might think these smaller operations are less challenging to operate than a larger and full-service hotel. The authors disagree. Limited-service hotels can be very challenging to operate because individual hotel employees, supervisors, and managers are often required to multitask. Therefore, many employees must be intensively cross-trained, and thus they must bring great flexibility and talent to their jobs. The importance of training employees is a fundamental theme throughout this book, and readers will find that the information provided about one department is plainly enough presented that it can serve as an orientation to employees in other hotel departments. In fact, the authors believe that *Foundations of Lodging Management, Second Edition* should be required reading for all hoteliers regardless of the size of their hotel(s) or the departmentally specific position(s) they hold because it will help them better understand the complexity of their entire property.

It is interesting to note that, in the past, if a hotel manager wanted to know about how to manage a housekeeping, front office, or sales and marketing department, it was fairly easy to find a recently published book on these departmental specific topics. The same was true about all of the other individual operating departments in a hotel. If, however, the hotelier's goal was to understand the workings of the entire hotel, as well as how its departments interconnected, little published material was available. The authors directly addressed this need for a comprehensive approach in the first edition and, like that edition; the primary focus of *Foundations of Lodging Management, Second Edition* has been to again provide an accurate and foundational, yet all-inclusive, examination of management in the lodging industry.

INSTRUCTOR RESOURCES

To access supplementary materials online, instructors need to request an instructor access code. Go to **www.pearsonhighered.com/irc**, where you can register for an instructor access code. Within 48 hours after registering, you will receive a confirming e-mail, including an instructor access code. Once you have received your code, go to the site and log on for full instructions on downloading the materials you wish to use.

NEW TO THIS EDITION

Much has changed in the lodging industry since the publication of this book's first edition just a few years ago. The emergence of "green" initiatives in lodging, the changing role of online travel agents (OTAs), and the explosive impact of social networking on hotel room sales are just a few of the lodging-related factors and trends incorporated in this new edition.

The authors have also benefited greatly from the helpful feedback of users. This feedback allowed us to identify selected chapters in the book that would benefit from revision and restructuring where it was clear that doing so would enhance their readability and clarity. As a result of a constantly changing lodging management environment and the insightful advice of our readers, we are pleased to make the following enhancements in this edition:

1. Addition to the author team of Allisha A. Miller, who co-authored the original and revised versions of the internationally adopted Pearson Education *Front Office Management Simulation (FOMS)* online training program. Her operational experience in rooms division management as well as in sales and marketing helped ensure content relevance in many chapters
2. Revised content presentation that resulted in the consolidations of several chapters and the addition of one new chapter as well as an update of all industry-related financial and statistical data
3. Inclusion of the new "Lodging Goes Green" feature
4. Incorporation of the newest legislation regarding employee selection and retention
5. Re-examination of all "Lodging Online" Web site links to ensure functionality, the addition of new sites selected to enhance the relevance of the text, and the deletion of those sites now considered dated or whose information is obsolete
6. Expanded discussion of revenue optimization, rooms pricing, and inventory management
7. Incorporation of the effects of the 2008-2010 worldwide recession on the lodging industry
8. Examination of the real threat to hotels and their guests of domestic and international acts of terrorism
9. The addition of critical food safety temperatures in the first of the book's two food and beverage management-related chapters
10. Inclusion of extensive material about the importance of social media sites such as Facebook and Twitter, as well as user generated content (UGC) sites such as Trip Advisor
11. The addition of detailed information for users of the online version of the Pearson-Prentice Hall *Front Office Management Simulation (FOMS)*

With these modifications, the authors are convinced that *Foundations of Lodging Management, Second Edition* continues to meet its original goal of presenting important hospitality industry information in a way that is easy to read, easy to understand, and easy to remember.

Foundations of Lodging Management, Second edition is the first book exclusively designed to make it easy to incorporate the use of this increasingly popular learning tool for those instructors who wish to do so. For information on adopting the FOMS with this text, go to http://www.prenhall.com/foms/.

ABOUT THE FRONT OFFICE MANAGEMENT SIMULATION (FOMS)

In the past, no effective simulation tool existed to assist instructors in helping students learn how to manage a hotel's front office. The Pearson Education *Front Office Management Simulation (FOMS)* 2nd edition is designed to solve this training dilemma. The FOMS is an online training tool consisting of 24 individual lessons in the following areas of Front Office administration:

- Revenue Management
- Reservation Management
- Guest Stay Information
- Guest Departure and Payment
- Accounting and Financial Summaries

INTENDED AUDIENCES

Instructors

Instructors adopting this book for their classes will again find a basic yet comprehensive text that addresses, in simple language, all of the operating departments of a hotel. In addition, it contains information about the history of the hotel industry as well the role of hotels within the larger hospitality industry. It is appropriate both for those just beginning to study the hotel industry and for those currently working in the industry who seek to advance their careers by continuing their education.

The Supplemental Teaching materials developed for this text are vast and have been extensively reviewed and edited by the authors. The PowerPoints (available on the book's companion Web site at www.prenhall.com/hayes) enhance student learning by making the text material easy to understand and easy to remember.

Students

Serious hospitality students want to understand how an entity as large and complex as a hotel actually operates. *Foundations of Lodging Management, Second Edition* provides that information in an easy-to-read format. Regardless of their specific area of interest in the hotel industry, readers will soon learn how all of a hotel's departments (and employees!) can work together to ensure that guests are treated in a manner that consistently exceeds expectations.

A basic understanding of the hotel industry is critical for those who are committed to hospitality as a career, as well as those who are simply considering such a career. The book's Chapter 14 "Careers in the Lodging Industry," will be of great interest to these students. In addition, readers working in related businesses, such as travel agencies, convention and visitors bureaus, and other travel-related areas, will benefit from understanding how the component parts of the lodging industry fit together.

In most cases, students who work in the lodging industry will start in one of the functional areas of a hotel. As their careers progress, they will gain added expertise and additional responsibilities. This book will be of immediate assistance because it will help these students understand immediately how what they are doing in a hotel will affect the work of other employees and ultimately their guests' overall experience. Therefore, it is an important addition to any hotelier's professional library.

Industry Professionals

Many people are interested in how hoteliers do their jobs. Hotel investors need to understand what hoteliers can be expected to do to help ensure the quality and growth of their hotel investments. Employees look to the hotel's leadership to make decisions that benefit their short-term occupational goals and long-term employment interests. Guests, of course, rely upon professional hoteliers to ensure that they receive value and quality for their lodging expenditures. Finally, professional hoteliers, because they are professionals, seek to better understand how their own efforts complement those of the entire hotel staff. In any hotel, department heads, supervisors, and hourly employees all benefit when they understand how each meshes with the other. *Foundations of Lodging Management, Second Edition* is a valuable text for all of these readers.

CHAPTER ORDER AND CONTENT

To truly understand lodging, one must first understand its history (Chapter 1) as well as its structure (Chapter 2). Because hotels ultimately must provide exceptional service to be successful, that topic is fully addressed (Chapter 3). Exceptional guest service is the result of excellent hotel management, thus that topic is addressed next (Chapter 4), followed by a thorough examination of the important role played by supervisors and hourly staff (Chapter 5).

While there is no universal agreement on the best order in which to study the operational functions of a lodging facility, the authors elected to begin with the Front Office

(Chapter 6), followed by Sales and Marketing (Chapter 7). Housekeeping (Chapter 8) and Maintenance (Chapter 9) are next addressed because they are so important to an understanding of how guests' needs are met by these critical functional areas.

An examination of the food and beverage areas found in limited-service hotels (Chapter 10) as well as full-service hotels (Chapter 11) is included because of the unique role food and beverage services play in a lodging facility. Accounting is addressed next (Chapter 12), followed by the vitally critical areas of lodging safety and security (Chapter 13). The book also includes a chapter that has been carefully designed to allow readers to examine, in detail, the career opportunities available to those who are skilled in lodging management (Chapter 14).

New to this edition, the book concludes with a section (Chapter 15) describing the use of the Pearson Education *Front Office Management Simulation Second Edition* (FOMS), especially for those students who will be utilizing its 24 hands-on lessons and activities to better understand important aspects of managing a hotel's Front Office.

CHAPTER FUNDAMENTALS

The lodging industry is an exciting one, and the authors sought to convey its excitement through a text that would be, first and foremost, user-friendly. To that end, each chapter in *Foundations of Lodging Management Second Edition* includes these instructional elements.

Chapter Outline

Each chapter's tiered outline has been carefully developed to provide the maximum ease in finding important information.

Chapter Overview

Each chapter begins with a short narrative summary that describes what will be presented in the chapter, as well as why the information is important to know.

Chapter Objectives

Each chapter begins with a number of specific learning objectives. These one-sentence objectives help students know exactly what they should learn by reading the chapter.

Lodging Language

As is true in many professional fields, hoteliers often speak their own unique language. Thus, for example, *RevPar* will be analyzed, the *GDS* will ensure reservation connectivity, *DNDs* will instruct housekeepers to clean a room at a later time, and a *recodable lock* will help ensure guest safety. When lodging-specific terms are used in the book (and they are used extensively), they are defined at the time of first usage, often with direct-use examples that help to further clarify their meaning. Unique vocabulary is such an important part of this book and the industry that the glossary contains more than 400 lodging-industry-specific definitions.

Lodging Online

In many cases, the amount of additional information a specific website could provide was significant and particularly useful. Where that was the case, the Web site was presented under the heading "Lodging Online." In these cases, the addition of Web resources enhanced the book's own content. The Web references in this book are purposely extensive and are found in every chapter.

All in a Day's Work

Hoteliers routinely face unique problems and situations that require outstanding decision-making skills. The "All in a Day's Work" element of this text poses a true-to-life lodging problem as well as one possible solution to it. These vignettes make for excellent classroom discussion topics, and, new to this edition, they have been numbered by chapter for ease of identification.

Lodging Goes Green

Also new to this edition, this feature addresses the lodging industry's increasing level of consciously committing to environmentally friendly business practices. The adoption of sustainable business practices by lodging managers is not just good for the environment, it is good for business. This element, present in each chapter, explores how lodging managers are addressing an area of increasing concern to their businesses and to their guests.

Lodging Language Glossary

At each chapter's end, a complete listing of the industry-specific terms defined in the chapter is presented. As a result, readers can quickly review these terms to ensure that they are understood and can be used in their proper context. They will also find this glossary to be a helpful reference as they encounter industry terms and jargon in their other readings.

For Discussion

This extensive feature (10 discussion questions per chapter) encourages students to think and talk about specific issues related to the material they have mastered in each chapter. Many of these questions can serve as excellent homework, writing assignments, or in-class discussion material.

Team Activities

This chapter-concluding feature encourages students to work together to seek information, solve problems, or address lodging industry issues in a group setting.

The authors believe that *Foundations of Lodging Management Second Edition* continues to fill a need in the hospitality industry literature. Its up-to-date and comprehensive but clearly presented coverage of all areas of the lodging industry makes it an essential addition to the professional library of the serious hospitality student.

It is our hope that students, instructors, and industry professionals will find it to be a significant contribution to the field of hospitality management. It has been our honor for a combined 80+ years to work in this exciting field and to contribute, through the publication of learning materials such as this book, to the professional development of our fellow hoteliers and future industry leaders.

David K. Hayes, Ph.D.
Jack D. Ninemeier, Ph.D.
Allisha A. Miller

ACKNOWLEDGMENTS

The production of a book like this one is truly the culmination of the efforts of many. The authors' thanks go to Vernon Anthony, Editorial Director at Pearson Education, for his long-standing support of the authors and belief in this project. We would also like to recognize the efforts of William Lawrensen, our editor, for his outstanding assistance in this text's development, as well as Alexis Biasell and the entire production staff at Pearson Education for their tireless efforts.

Also of tremendous assistance were our text reviewers, Lynn Woods, Northwestern University; Maryam Khan, Howard University; R. Thomas George, the Ohio State University; Susan West, Arkansas Tech University; Heather Biagas, Austin Community College; and Ning-Kuang Chang, Kent State University, who added much to improve the structure and content of the text. For their efforts, we are truly grateful.

PHOTO CREDITS

Chapter 1

Page 2: Thinkstock/Jupiterimages/Comstock. *Page 5:* Thinkstock/Jupiterimages/Comstock/Getty Images. *Page 11:* Thinkstock/Jupiterimages/Photos.com/Getty Images. *Page 12:* Thinkstock/Brand X Pictures.

Chapter 2

Page 23: Thinkstock/Goodshot. *Page 24:* Thinkstock/BananaStock. *Page 32:* Thinkstock/Comstock/Getty Images. *Page 40:* Shutterstock/Chubykin Arkady.

Chapter 3

Page 49: Thinkstock/Comstock. *Page 53:* Shutterstock/Alexandru Axon. *Page 60:* Thinkstock/Digital Vision.

Chapter 4

Page 67: Thinkstock/Stockbyte. *Page 70:* Thinkstock/Comstock. *Page 72:* Thinkstock/Digital Vision. *Page 76:* Shutterstock/tonobalaguerf. *Page 84:* Thinkstock/Lifesize/K-King Photography Media Co. Ltd./Getty Images.

Chapter 5

Page 91: Thinkstock/Pixland/Jupiterimages. *Page 93:* Shutterstock/Konstantin Chagin. *Page 100:* Shutterstock/Yuri Arcurs. *Page 103:* Thinkstock/BananaStock. *Page 114:* R. Shutterstock/Gino Santa Maria.

Chapter 6

Page 123: Thinkstock/Comstock. *Page 125:* Thinkstock/Brand X Pictures. *Page 130:* Shutterstock/Fernando Blanco Calzada. *Page 134:* Thinkstock/Stockbyte.

Chapter 7

Page 148: Shutterstock/Andre Blais. *Page 160:* Thinkstock/Polka Dot/Jupiterimages/Getty Images. *Page 167:* Shutterstock/Dmilriy Shironosov.

Chapter 8

Page 177: Thinkstock/Brand X Pictures. *Page 181:* Thinkstock/Digital Vision/Darrin Klimek. *Page 189:* Thinkstock/Digital Vision/Michael Blann. *Page 193:* Thinkstock/Goodshoot/Jupiterimages/Getty Images. *Page 196:* Thinkstock/Comstock Images.

Chapter 9

Page 205: Shutterstock/Lisa F. Young. *Page 213:* Shutterstock/males. *Page 220:* Shutterstock/Kacso Sandor. *Page 221:* Shutterstock/Nagy Jozsef—Allila.

Chapter 10

Page 230: Shutterstock/studiogi. *Page 233:* Thinkstock/Comstock. *Page 244:* Thinkstock/Creatas.

Chapter 11

Page 252: Shutterstock/Tiut Vlad. *Page 254:* Thinkstock/Comstock/Jupiterimages/Getty Images. *Page 257:* Thinkstock/Digital Vision/Michael Blann. *Page 262:* Thinkstock/Valueline/Steve Mason. *Page 267:* Thinkstock/Comstock/Jupiterimages/Getty Images. *Page 273:* Thinkstock/Comstock/Jupiterimages/Getty Images.

Chapter 12

Page 280: Thinkstock/Stockbyte/John Foxx. *Page 283:* Thinkstock/Photodisc/Keith Brofsky. *Page 286:* Thinkstock/Goodshoot/Jupiterimages/Getty Images. *Page 297:* Thinkstock/Photos.com/Jupiterimages/Getty Images. *Page 302:* Shutterstock/sjgh.

Chapter 13

Page 309: Thinkstock/Photodisc/Jack Hollingsworth. *Page 313:* Thinkstock/Comstock. *Page 319:* Thinkstock/Lifesize/Ryan McVay. *Page 324:* Shutterstock/Rosil Olhman.

Chapter 14

Page 334: Thinkstock/Photos.com/Jupiterimages/Getty Images. *Page 337:* Thinkstock/Stockbyte. *Page 346:* Thinkstock/Comstock Images/Getty Images. *Page 350:* Thinkstock/Stockbyte/Jack Hollingsworth. *Page 356:* Thinkstock/Photos.com/Jupiterimages/Getty Images.

Chapter 15

Page 370: Thinkstock/Medioimages/Photodisc. *Page 372*: Thinkstock/Pixland/Jupiterimages. *Page 378:* Shutterstock/Andresr.

Chapter **1**

Introduction to the Lodging Industry

Chapter Outline

The Early Lodging Industry
United States Lodging Industry: 1900–2010
Lodging Industry Segments
Measuring Hotel Performance
- ADR
- Occupancy
- RevPAR
- GOPPAR

Lodging and the Hospitality Industry
Lodging and the Travel and Tourism Industry
- Leisure Travelers
- Business Travelers

Partners in the Lodging Industry
- Transportation Services
- Travel Agents
- Online Travel Agents
- Tour Operators

Industry Trade Associations

Chapter Overview

The lodging industry has a long history. Travelers have always desired a safe and restful place to spend the night. Today, more and more people travel; and as a result, a large industry has developed to meet their diverse needs.

People travel for many reasons, including sight-seeing, vacations, business, and personal trips. Different types of lodging properties are available to meet the different needs of these travelers, and there are several approaches to classifying the wide range of hotel alternatives available. The most important of these classification systems are presented in this chapter.

It is also important to know how the lodging industry measures its success in meeting the needs of guests. In this chapter, you will learn about four different methods lodging industry professionals use to determine their effectiveness. These measures will help you better understand the types of concerns hoteliers have as they manage their properties and will provide you a preview of how they evaluate the performance of their staff and their hotels.

In this chapter, you will also learn that the lodging industry is considered part of the larger hospitality industry. Hospitality includes all of those businesses designed to offer lodging and food and beverage services to travelers and non-travelers alike.

You will also learn that the hospitality industry is part of the even larger travel and tourism industry. Travel and tourism includes all of those industries developed to serve those who travel for recreational, leisure, or business purposes. For example, people who travel must be transported to the places where they will stay. Thus, the travel and tourism industry includes the airline, bus, train, and rental car businesses whose employees work with their lodging counterparts to help make travel safe, fast, and easy.

Travel agents are an important part of the travel industry because they help people who need travel-planning assistance. Tour operators also have a significant impact on travelers. For example, they work with travel agents to offer attractive vacation packages that make it easy and cost-effective to travel.

Today, the emergence of the online travel agency (OTA) means increasing numbers of travelers reserve (book) their hotel rooms and other travel services online. In the final portion of this chapter, you will learn about these partners of the lodging industry as well as learn about the role of important trade associations that work to improve the lodging, hospitality, and travel and tourism industries.

Chapter Objectives

1. To describe how the lodging industry has developed over its long history.
2. To explain how individual hotel properties in the lodging industry are classified.
3. To explain how the lodging industry measures its success.
4. To describe how the lodging industry is related to the larger hospitality and travel and tourism industries.
5. To identify and explain the importance of industry trade associations.

THE EARLY LODGING INDUSTRY

The **lodging industry** consists of all the **hotels** and other businesses that provide overnight accommodations for guests. Many **hoteliers** also provide food, beverages, and even entertainment for the guests in their **market**.

LODGING LANGUAGE

Lodging industry: All the businesses that provide overnight accommodations for guests.

Hotel: An establishment that provides sleeping rooms as well as various services to the traveling public.

Hotelier: The owner/manager of one or more hotels.

Market: The potential customers for a business's products and services.

In the earliest days, people traveled for religious or business reasons. Inns could be found on the roads leading to religious shrines or temples as well as along significant trade routes. These establishments were often operated by families that offered travelers very basic food and shelter in their homes.

The hotel industry is one of the nation's largest.

Sometimes they were operated by a church or other religious organization. As travel became more popular and less dangerous, people began to travel for more personal reasons, such as to see foreign lands or to experience foreign cultures.

In very popular travel locations, the lodging industry is usually large and well developed. Locations of this kind include areas near beaches, ski resorts, historic settings, or other tourist destinations and in cities with large populations. However, even rural settings and small communities that are less popular with **tourists** require a lodging industry large enough to meet the travel needs of people who visit for business, personal, or other reasons.

LODGING LANGUAGE

Tourist: A person who travels for pleasure.

UNITED STATES HOTEL INDUSTRY: 1900–2010

The lodging industry has changed since its early beginnings and will no doubt continue to do so. This is one reason why it is an exciting and vibrant industry. To understand the modern hotel industry, it is helpful to examine hotels in the United States because they are, in many cases, worldwide leaders. American lodging facilities have evolved to include a tradition of innovation and orientation to guest service that is well worth noting. Highlights of the growth of the hotel industry in the United States since 1900 are shown in Figure 1.1.

1900 Fewer than 10,000 hotels 750,000 to 850,000 rooms	**1900** A typical first-class hotel offers steam heat, gas burners, electric call bells, baths and toilet closets on all floors, billiard and sample rooms, barbershops, and carriage houses. **1904** New York City's St. Regis Hotel provides individually controlled heating and cooling units in each guest room. **1908** The Hotel Statler chain begins in Buffalo. All guest rooms have private baths, full-length mirrors, and telephones, serving as the model for hotel construction for the next 40 years.
1910 10,000 hotels 1 million rooms 300,000 employees Average size: 60–75 rooms	**1910** Electricity is beginning to be installed in new hotels for cooking purposes, as well as for lighting. However, most hotels place candlesticks, new candles, and matches in every room—electric light bulb or not.
1920 Occupancy: 85% Hotel construction reaches an all-time high as rooms are added along the new state and federal highways	**1920** Prohibition begins. **1922** The Treadway Company has some of the first management contracts on small college inns. **1925** The first roadside "motel" opens in San Luis Obispo, California, for $2.50 a night. **1927** The Hotel Statler in Boston becomes the first hotel with radio reception; rooms are with individual headsets to receive broadcasts from a central control room. **1929** The Oakland Airport Hotel becomes the first of its kind in the country.
1930 Occupancy: 65% AHA's *Hotel Red Book* lists 20,000 hotels Typical hotel: 46 rooms Average room rate: $5.60	**1930** Four out of five hotels in the United States go into receivership. **1933** Due to the Great Depression, hotels post the lowest average occupancy rate on record (51%). Construction grinds to a halt. **1934** The Hotel Statler in Detroit is the first to have a central system to "air-condition" every public room.
1940 Occupancy: 64% Average room rate: $3.21	**1940** Air-conditioning and "air-cooling" become prevalent. **1945** Sheraton is the first hotel corporation to be listed on the New York Stock Exchange. **1946** Westin debuts first guest credit card. The first casino hotel, the Flamingo, debuts in Las Vegas. **1947** Westin establishes Hoteltype, the first hotel reservation system. New York City's Roosevelt Hotel installs television sets in all guest rooms. **1949** Hilton becomes the first international hotel chain with the opening of the Caribe Hilton in San Juan, Puerto Rico.
1950 Occupancy: 80% Typical hotel: 17 rooms Average room rate: $5.91	**1951** Hilton is the first chain to install television sets in all guest rooms. **1952** Kemmons Wilson opens his first Holiday Inn in Memphis, Tennessee. **1954** Howard Dearing Johnson initiates the first lodging franchise, a motor lodge in Savannah, Georgia. Conrad Hilton's purchase of the Statler Hotel Company for $111 million is the largest real estate transaction in history. **Mid-1950s** Atlas Hotels develops the first in-room coffee concept. **1957** J.W. Marriott opens his first hotel, the Twin Bridge Marriott Motor Hotel, in Arlington, Virginia, and Jay Pritzker buys his first hotel, the Hyatt House, located outside the Los Angeles Airport. Hilton offers direct-dial telephone service. **1958** Sheraton introduces Reservation, the industry's first automated electronic reservation system, and the first toll-free reservation number.
1960 Occupancy: 67% $3 billion in sales Total hotel rooms: 2,400,450 Typical hotel: 39 rooms, independent and locally owned Average room rate: $9.99	**Early 1960s** Siegas introduces the first true minibar (a small refrigerator displaying products). **1964** Travelodge debuts wheelchair-accessible rooms. **1966** Inter-Continental introduces retractable drying lines in guest showers, business lounges, ice and vending machines in guest corridors, and street entrances to hotel restaurants. **1967** The Atlanta Hyatt Regency opens, featuring a 21-story atrium and changing the course of upscale hotel design. **1969** Westin is the first hotel chain to implement 24-hour room service.

FIGURE 1.1 Highlights in the Modern History of the United States Hotel Industry Courtesy of Panda Professional Hospitality Education and Training

1970 Occupancy: 65% $8 billion in sales Total hotel rooms: 1,627,473 Average room rate: $19.83	**1970** Hilton becomes the first billion-dollar lodging and food-service company and the first to enter the Las Vegas market. **1973** The Sheraton-Anaheim is the first to offer free in-room movies. **1974** The energy crisis hits the industry. Hotels dim exterior signs, cut heat to unoccupied rooms, and ask guests to conserve electricity. **1975** Four Seasons is the first hotel company to offer in-room amenities such as name-brand shampoo. Hyatt introduces an industry first when it opens a concierge club level that provides the ultimate in VIP (very important person) service. Cecil B. Day (Day's Inn) establishes the first seniors' program.
1980 Occupancy: 70% $25.9 billion in sales Total hotel rooms: 2,068,377 Average room rate: $45.44	**1983** Westin is the first major hotel company to offer reservations and checkout using major credit cards. VingCard invents the optical electronic key card. **1984** Holiday Inn is the first to offer a centralized travel and commission plan. Choice Hotels introduces the concept of market segmentation and no-smoking rooms. Hampton Inns is the first to offer a set of amenities. **1986** Teledex Corporation introduces the first telephone designed specifically for hotel guest rooms. Days Inn provides an interactive reservation capability connecting all hotels. **1988** Extended-stay segment introduced with Marriott's Residence Inns and Holiday Corporation's Homewood Suites. **1989** Hyatt introduces a chainwide kids program for ages 3–12 and a business center at the Hyatt Regency Chicago. Hampton Inns is the first hotel chain to introduce the 100 percent satisfaction guarantee.
1990 Occupancy: 64% $60.7 billion in sales Total hotel rooms: 3,065,685 45,020 properties Average room rate: $58.70	**1990** Loews Hotels' Good Neighbor Policy becomes the industry's first and most comprehensive community outreach program. **1991** Westin is the first hotel chain to provide in-room voice mail. Industry sees record losses. **1992** Industry breaks even financially after six consecutive years of losses. **1993** Radisson Hotels Worldwide is the first to introduce business-class rooms. **1994** First online hotel catalog debuts—TravelWeb.com. Promus and Hyatt Hotels are the first chains to establish a site on the Internet. **1995** Choice Hotels International and Promus become the first companies to offer guests "real-time" access to their central reservations system. Choice and Holiday Inn are the first to introduce online booking capability. **1999** Choice Hotels International is the first chain to test making in-room PCs a standard amenity for guests (they decide against it).
2000 Occupancy: 63% $97 billion in sales	**2000** Hilton unveils plans for the first luxury hotel in space. **2001** September 11 destruction of the World Trade Center in New York causes city occupancy rates to plummet. **2002** Travel industry slowly recovers from terrorist attacks amid heightened airport security. **2004** In-room high-speed Internet (HIS) access becomes a necessary amenity to attract business travelers.[1] **2005** Condo-hotels forecasted to be the hotel model of the future. **2009** Onset of the "Great Recession" causes RevPAR to decline 15%-20 % nationally. Market for condo-hotel rooms collapses.
2010 Occupancy (forecast) 55.5% Average Room Rate (forecast) $93.00	**2010** Recovery for the hotel industry is forecasted to be slow but steady for the next five years.[2]

[1]http://www.ahma.com/infocenter/lodging_history.asp
[2]www.pandapros.com

FIGURE 1.1 ***(Continued)***

LODGING INDUSTRY SEGMENTS

Today's lodging industry seeks to provide products and services to a variety of travelers. People seeking lodging accommodations almost all have several needs in common: safety, cleanliness, preferred location, and **value**. In addition, different types of travelers also desire specific features in their overnight accommodations. For example, affluent travelers frequently desire up-scale accommodations, long-term guests may want kitchen facilities, and business travelers may need a business center in their hotel.

LODGING LANGUAGE

Value (lodging accommodations): The price paid to rent a room relative to the quality of the room and services received.

There are more than 49,500 hotels in the United States with more than 4,600,000 sleeping rooms. Therefore, the "average" U.S. hotel has fewer than 100 rooms (4,600,000 rooms/49,500 hotels = 92.9 rooms per hotel), and together these hotels achieve room revenues of more than $140 billion per year.

When most people think about "hotels," they think about a building with guest rooms suitable for sleeping. In its narrowest sense, this definition is correct. However, there are several other ways to classify hotels. For example, they can be classified by size. Small hotels (under 75 rooms) make up 52 percent of all hotels. Medium-sized hotels (75–150 rooms) make up 33 percent of all hotels. Large hotels (150–300 rooms) make up 10 percent of all hotels, and those larger than 300 rooms comprise 5 percent of all hotels. Using these definitions, approximately 85 percent of all U.S. hotels are either small or medium-sized. For this reason, this book will examine the operations of small and medium-sized hotels very closely.

Another useful way to classify hotels relates to the services offered. Some travelers desire food and beverage services in addition to sleeping rooms. Properties that offer travelers food, beverages, and, in most cases, meeting space are classified as **full-service hotels**.

Full-service hotels typically offer more amenities, such as room service and meeting space, than limited-service hotels.

LODGING LANGUAGE

Full-service hotel: A lodging facility that offers complete food and beverage services.

The largest full-service hotels often have banquet rooms, exhibit halls, and spacious ballrooms to accommodate conventions, business meetings, wedding receptions, and other social gatherings. Conventions and business meetings are major sources of revenue for these properties. As you will learn, some full-service hotels are specifically designed for large-scale meetings, conferences, and conventions. A full-service hotel has a restaurant and lounge. In addition, many offer **room service** to guests.

LODGING LANGUAGE

Room service: The delivery of food and beverages to a hotel guest's sleeping room.

As the name implies, a **limited-service hotel** offers very limited food and beverage service. In some limited-service hotels, no food or beverages are offered to guests.

LODGING LANGUAGE

Limited-service hotel: A lodging facility that offers no, or very restricted, food and beverage services. Also known as a "select-service hotel."

Limited-service hotels are free-standing properties that do not have on-site restaurants. They usually offer a complimentary breakfast, vending machines or small packaged food items, Internet access, and sometimes unattended game rooms or swimming pools in addition to daily housekeeping services. These hotels typically provide little, if any, space for group meetings. The majority of hotels in the United States are limited-service hotels, and the numbers of limited-service properties have been growing faster than full-service hotels because these properties are less costly to build and maintain than full-service hotels. They appeal to budget-conscious family vacationers and travelers who are willing to sacrifice extensive food and beverage services for lower priced rooms. You will learn much about the operation of these properties in this book, including details about the food, beverage, and meetings services they do offer.

Figure 1.2 identifies various types of organizations that offer lodging accommodations for travelers. In this chapter, you will learn that the lodging industry is part of the larger hospitality industry that is part of the even larger travel and tourism industry.

The lodging segment of the hospitality industry markets to travelers whose primary purpose for staying at a property is to secure lodging services. When reviewing Figure 1.2, note that the lodging segment of the hospitality industry includes hotels, **bed and breakfast inns** and **camps/park lodges**.

LODGING LANGUAGE

Bed and breakfast inns: Very small properties (one to several guest rooms) owned or managed by persons living on-site; these businesses typically offer one meal a day; also called B&B.

Camps/park lodges: Sleeping facilities in national, state, or other parks and recreational areas that accommodate visitors to these areas.

Figure 1.2 identifies five types of hotels. You have already learned about full-service and limited-service hotels. Now we will define the other basic types of hotels in the lodging segment. These are **extended-stay hotels**, **convention hotels/conference centers**, and **resorts/timeshares**.

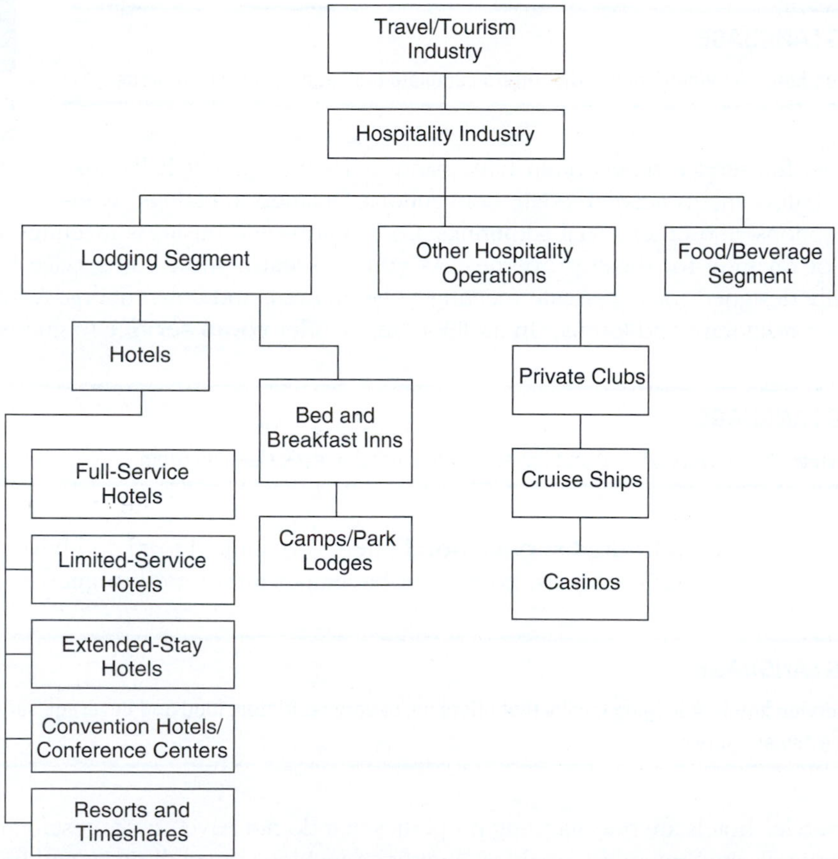

FIGURE 1.2 Overview of Hospitality Industry (Lodging Segment)

LODGING LANGUAGE

Extended-stay hotels: A moderately priced, limited-service hotel marketing to guests desiring accommodation for extended time periods (generally one week or longer).

Convention hotel: A lodging property with extensive and flexible meeting and exhibition spaces that markets to associations, corporations, and other groups bringing people together for meetings.

Conference center: A specialized hospitality operation specifically designed for and dedicated to the needs of small- and medium-sized meetings of 20 to 100 people.

Resort: A full-service hotel with additional attractions that make it a primary destination for travelers.

Timeshare: A lodging property that sells its rooms to guests for use during a specific time period each year; also called vacation ownership property.

Figure 1.2 also identifies other hospitality operations that offer sleeping accommodations. These operations, however, are not generally thought of as lodging properties because of the popularity of their other amenities. The organizations identified are **private clubs**, **cruise ships**, and **casinos**. They are examples of enterprises in the lodging industry that exist for reasons other than to provide sleeping accommodations, but which do so as a service to their members, passengers, or guests.

LODGING LANGUAGE

Private clubs: Membership organizations not open to the public that exist for people enjoying common interests. Examples include country (golf) clubs, city clubs, university clubs, yacht clubs, and military clubs. Some private clubs offer sleeping rooms for members and guests.

Cruise ship: A passenger vessel designed to provide leisure experiences for people on vacation at sea.

Casino: A business operation that offers table and card games along with (usually) slot operations and other games of skill or chance and amenities that are marketed to customers seeking gaming activities and entertainment. Many casinos offer lodging accommodations for their visitors.

To this point, we have been examining lodging operations that are generally available to all of the traveling public. Other types of facilities offer sleeping accommodations for specific types of individuals who spend one or more nights way from their homes. These include noncommercial operations, such as schools, colleges, and universities offering residential services, health care (hospital and nursing homes) facilities, correctional institutions (prisons), and military bases. The material in this book was written for those who work in the hotel industry, but the information it contains applies to many of the lodging facilities mentioned in this chapter.

MEASURING HOTEL PERFORMANCE

Owners and managers of all sizes are interested in how best to evaluate their effectiveness in meeting the needs of their guests. One way to evaluate effectiveness is to measure the amount of money guests are willing to pay to rent a room for one night.

Room rental charges for guest rooms are based, in large measure, upon what guests are willing to pay. If a city (or an area within a city) has too few overnight accommodations for the number of people traveling to it, the prices charged for sleeping rooms will likely be high. Alternatively, if too many sleeping rooms are available, the prices charged for a room will likely be low.

ADR

Average Daily Rate (ADR) is the term used by hoteliers to indicate how expensive sleeping rooms are in a specific hotel or area.

LODGING LANGUAGE

Average Daily Rate (ADR): The average (mean) selling price of all guest rooms in a hotel, city, or country for a specific period of time.

The computation of ADR is very simple. It is computed as:

$$\frac{\text{Total Revenue from Room Sales}}{\text{Total Number of Rooms Sold}} = \text{ADR}$$

If, for example, a hotel sells 150 rooms on one night, and if the total revenue from the room sales for that night is $18,750.00, the hotel's ADR would be $125.00:

$$\frac{\$18{,}750}{150 \text{ rooms sold}} = \$125.00 \text{ ADR}$$

Hotels can be classified by their rate structures. For example, some hotels are very elegant and can charge high rates. Other hotels offer more modest accommodations for budget-minded travelers. As a result, hotels are sometimes classified as budget or economy (very low ADR), midscale (moderate ADR), or luxury (very high ADR). ADR can be calculated for a specific hotel, but it can also be computed for a town or other geographic area.

Assume that a town has several hotels with a total of 1,000 sleeping rooms available. Assume further that on a specific night, 750 rooms in the town were sold, and the revenue generated from these room sales was $93,750.00. The ADR for the town on that date would also be $125.00:

$$\frac{\$93{,}750}{750 \text{ rooms sold}} = \$125.00 \text{ ADR}$$

The ADR of a hotel, city, or region is one indicator of the strength of the hotel business in that location.

Occupancy Rate

Occupancy rate is another widely used measure of hotel performance.

LODGING LANGUAGE

Occupancy rate: The ratio of guest rooms sold (or given away) to the number of guest rooms available for sale in a given time period and expressed as a percentage.

The computation of occupancy percentage rate is also simple:

$$\frac{\text{Total Rooms Sold}}{\text{Total Rooms Available}} = \text{Occupancy Rate}$$

If a hotel has 200 rooms and on a given night sells 150 rooms, the occupancy rate would be 75 percent.

$$\frac{150 \text{ rooms sold}}{200 \text{ rooms available}} = 75\%$$

Hoteliers can compute the occupancy rate for a hotel, a city, or a larger region. It is also possible to compute an occupancy percentage for a period longer than one day. Assume that a town has several hotels with a total of 1,000 sleeping rooms available. During June (30 days in the month), the total number of rooms sold in the town was 18,000. The occupancy rate for that town in June would be 60 percent.

$$\frac{18{,}000 \text{ rooms sold in June}}{30 \text{ days } (\times) \text{ } 1{,}000 \text{ rooms}} = \text{Occupancy }\%$$

Or

$$\frac{18{,}000 \text{ rooms sold in June}}{3{,}000 \text{ rooms available}} = 60\%$$

RevPAR

It is possible for a hotel to have a very high ADR and a very low occupancy rate. Alternatively, it is possible to have a very high occupancy rate and a very low ADR. Revenue Per Available Room, or **RevPAR** is the measure hoteliers use to combine ADR and occupancy rate into one measurement.

LODGING LANGUAGE

RevPAR: The average revenue generated by each guest room available during a specific time period. RevPAR combines the information from ADR and occupancy rate into a single measure.

RevPAR can be calculated in several ways. An easy way to calculate RevPAR is:

$$\text{ADR}(\times)\text{Occupancy Rate} = \text{RevPAR}$$

Thus, for example, if a hotel had an ADR of $90.00 and an occupancy rate of 70%, the hotel's RevPAR would be:

$$\$90.00(\times)\ 0.70 = \$63.00$$

Like ADR and occupancy rate, hoteliers can compute RevPAR for a hotel, a city, or a larger region. It is also possible to compute RevPAR for a period longer than one day. Most hoteliers would agree that an assessment of RevPAR gives a clearer picture of the success of a hotel than does ADR or occupancy rate alone.

GOPPAR

Of course, selling hotel rooms is not the same thing as selling hotel rooms in a profitable way. For that reason, hoteliers also regularly calculate their **gross operating profit per available room (GOPPAR)**. **Gross operating profit** is defined as a hotel's revenue minus the amount of its management controllable expenses.

LODGING LANGUAGE

GOPPAR: The amount of profit made from room sales divided by the number of rooms available to sell.

Gross operating profit: The amount of revenue generated in a defined time period minus its management controllable expenses for that same period.

GOPPAR is a convenient way for hoteliers to assess the amount of profit they make from each room made available for sale. Its calculation is

$$\frac{\text{Gross Operating Profit}}{\text{Rooms Available to Sell}} = \text{GOPPAR}$$

Thus, for example, if a hotel had a gross operating profit of $600,000 and 7,000 rooms available to sell, the GOPPAR would be:

$$\frac{\$600{,}000}{7{,}000} = \$85.71$$

ADR, occupancy rate, RevPAR, and GOPPAR are terms all lodging managers must know and understand because they are useful indicators of the strength of a specific hotel or a larger area's lodging business. When business is good, average room rates, occupancy percentages, and RevPars are high. When hotels are managed well, GOPPARs are high as well. When these indicators are low, knowledgeable hoteliers recognize that business is not as good as when they are higher.

LODGING AND THE HOSPITALITY INDUSTRY

As you learned by examining Figure 1.2, lodging is part of the larger **hospitality industry**.

LODGING LANGUAGE

Hospitality industry: Organizations that provide lodging accommodations and food services for people when they are away from home.

You have learned that full-service hotels generally provide their guests with lodging, meeting, and foodservice products while limited-service hotels primarily offer lodging services. Because hotel managers may, at various times in their careers, work in both full-service and limited-service hotels, knowledge of the food and beverage industry can be very important to hoteliers.

It is important to understand that both hoteliers and restaurateurs are professionals who seek to provide quality products and services to guests. For that reason, many lodging managers study and learn how to provide quality food and beverage services to guests. In this book, you will learn some of the critical aspects of foodservice lodging managers must know.

LODGING AND THE TRAVEL AND TOURISM INDUSTRY

As you have learned, the lodging industry is not only part of the hospitality industry, it is also part of the even larger travel and tourism industry or, simply, the tourism industry.

Regardless of the term used, it refers to those businesses designed to serve the traveling public. Figure 1.3 illustrates the components of the tourism industry, including the lodging segment. The tourism industry consists of:

Hospitality: The food and beverage and lodging operations (including hotels) that house and feed travelers.

Retail (Shopping) Stores: Stores and shops that appeal to travelers.

Transportation Services: Businesses such as bus lines, airlines, and rental car companies that help move travelers from place to place.

Destination (Activity) Sites: Locations offering activities and attractions enjoyed by travelers. Examples include amusement parks and ski resorts as well as other indoor and outdoor activities.

Tourism is the third largest industry in the United States. It is surpassed in size only by the automotive and grocery industries. It is also one of the nation's largest employers and is the second or third largest employer in 30 of the 50 states.

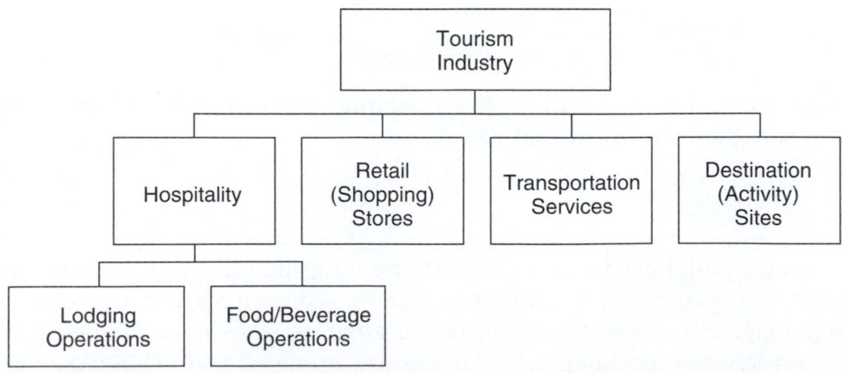

FIGURE 1.3 Components of the Tourism Industry

In its studies on travel, the American Hotel and Lodging Association (AH&LA) has found that of those who stay in hotels,

25 percent are attending a conference or group meeting

29 percent are business travelers

24 percent are on vacation

22 percent are traveling for other reasons (e.g., personal, family, or to attend a special event)

There are a variety of ways that these travelers could be classified—for example, as male or female or as young or old. They can arrive by car or plane, be free-spending or thrifty, and can vary in any number of other ways. The most common distinction made in the lodging industry, however, is between those who are leisure travelers and those who are business travelers.

Leisure Travelers

Leisure travelers enjoy travel. In the hotel business, the term "leisure traveler" refers to persons who travel because they like the experience of visiting new places, are returning to places they have previously visited, or are participating in some leisure activity.

Leisure travelers include vacationers and people traveling to shop, sightsee, attend concerts, and for a wide range of other activities. Leisure travelers may be groups, families, or individuals. They can be senior citizens riding a motor coach on a guided tour of historical sites and youngsters traveling with their families to participate in a regional soccer tournament. Leisure travelers often travel on the weekends, but, especially in the summer, they also travel through the week.

Depending upon its location, a hotel may find that the great majority of its guests are leisure travelers. A hotel on a Florida beach, for example, may attract guests primarily because of the beach. However, hotels that attract leisure travelers may still attract business travelers. The opposite is also true. Hotels primarily designed for business travelers may also host large numbers of leisure travelers.

Business Travelers

Business travelers make up a large and extremely important portion of the travel business. As noted in the preceding section, people attending conferences/meetings (25%) or traveling or business reasons (29%) comprise more than half of travelers. Business travelers include those who attend work-related meetings, seminars, and conferences. Salespersons for business must travel to meet clients, demonstrate new products, and learn new skills.

Business travelers tend to spend more money for their overnight stays and also look for **amenities** and guest services not always offered at hotels geared toward leisure travelers.

A guest who stays at a hotel is commonly classified as either a transient traveler or a group traveler.

LODGING LANGUAGE

Amenities: Hotel products and services designed to attract guests. Examples include Internet access and copying services, in-room hair dryers, irons, ironing boards, and microwave ovens, as well as indoor pools, exercise rooms, and in-room movies.

Much business travel involves trips to large cities; however, even the smallest of towns and the hotels located in those towns attract business travelers who are driving through a smaller town on the way to a city.

PARTNERS IN THE LODGING INDUSTRY

Many organizations, groups, and even entire industries assist hoteliers in serving overnight guests. The transportation industry helps guests travel to and from hotels. Travel agents assist travelers to select a mode of transportation and give advice about which hotels are best for a specific traveler's needs, and tour operators assist travel agents in their work. Increasingly, the Internet has influenced the way travel industry services are marketed and purchased, and the role of Web site operators is, therefore, of increasing importance.

Transportation Services

When a traveler decides to take a trip, one of the first and most important decisions concerns the kind of transportation to be used. Accessibility, speed, comfort, and cost all influence the choice. Generally, the fastest transportation methods also tend to be the most expensive. Historically, stagecoaches, steamships, and railroads developed travel routes that accommodated mail, freight, and passengers. Today, some businesses in the transportation industry, such as the United Parcel Service (UPS) and Federal Express (FedEx), specialize in transporting freight only. Others emphasize passenger transportation, and still others provide both. In the United States, the most popular forms of passenger transportation are airplanes, buses, trains, and automobiles, and these are the businesses most likely to work closely with hoteliers.

Hospitality spans much more than just hotels. Other partners include airlines, car rental companies and travel agents.

AIRLINES

Airline travel is the preferred method for the majority of leisure and business travelers whose destinations are far from their origination point. Airline travel is fast, and its popularity continues to grow. As a result, U.S. airlines carry well more than 500 million passengers per year.

The airline industry is a partner with the hotel industry because many travelers fly into an airport, are picked up there by a hotel-owned and operated **hotel shuttle**, and are then driven to the hotel, where they can check in to their room. In these cases, the shuttle also returns the travelers to the airport when they are ready to depart.

LODGING LANGUAGE

Hotel shuttle: A vehicle used by a hotel to transport guests to and from such destinations as airports, restaurants, and shopping.

In the United States, there is a constant demand for air service, and the airline business is very competitive. This demand is met by airports of many sizes, including those large enough to serve as an airline **hub**.

LODGING LANGUAGE

Hub: Typically, a big-city airport within a short driving distance of a very large population center. These mega-airports are used to economically connect travelers with flights to their desired departure and arrival cities.

BUS LINES

Buses are an important part of the travel industry and can have a substantial effect on a hotel's occupancy. Their use for long-distance transportation by individual travelers is much less than that of airplanes and automobiles. However, buses are used by economy-minded travelers and by travelers being shuttled from airports, train stations, and parking areas. For many hoteliers, the most important role played by the bus lines is that of transporting **charter** travel groups.

LODGING LANGUAGE

Charter: A form of transportation rented exclusively for a specific group of travelers. Planes and buses are often chartered for group travel.

ALL IN A DAY'S WORK 1.1

THE SITUATION

It was 4:00 o'clock in the afternoon. Dani, the general manager of the Day's Sleep Hotel, looked out her office window. "The snow is really coming down," she said.

"I know," replied her assistant manager. "We have already had a lot of travelers pulling off the Interstate to ask for rooms so they don't get stranded on the highway after dark. I think we will easily sell every room we have tonight."

"We need to call the airport and check flight status," said Dani, "or we could have some real problems tonight."

A RESPONSE

As this lodging manager realizes, if the local airport closes because of the snowstorm, hotel occupancy for the area will be greatly affected. Hotel managers must know about industry partners who can help them make good business decisions when necessary. In this case, the closing of the airport would probably mean stranded airport travelers who will require accommodations (increased occupancy) and fewer incoming passengers who will not arrive if the airport is closed (decreased occupancy). The possible closure of the airport will have a big impact on this hotel manager's decision to sell (or not to sell) many rooms to highway travelers. Developing a personal contact at the local airport to help obtain up-to-date and accurate airport information is a good idea for hotel managers.

Charter buses often transport groups of travelers for less money than they would have to pay if they flew to the same destination. In some cases, chartered bus routes operating regularly between cities within 100 or 200 miles of each other may actually be faster than air travel, especially with new airport security measures. Therefore, bus travel can often be inexpensive and rapid.

The federal government defines a bus as a passenger-carrying vehicle designed to seat at least 16 people including the driver. While there are no universal definitions, bus industry professionals generally recognize the following bus types:

Economy: School-type buses are the lowest-cost option for group travelers. These vehicles typically are arranged with bench (not individual) seating and contain no restroom facilities.

Deluxe Motor Coach: This tour-type bus is the most selected for longer trips or for groups seeking more comfort than is available on an economy bus. The typical seating is 40 to 55 individual seats with VCR/DVD capability, multiple monitors, advanced sound systems, and restroom facilities.

Executive Motor Coach: This top-of-the-line bus is chosen by those who prefer extra-luxurious bus travel. Executive coaches are custom-made. Options vary, but typically include full bedrooms, showers, kitchens, and social and meeting spaces. The maximum capacity for buses of this type ranges from 5 to 20 persons.

Buses are generally welcomed by restaurant and hotel managers who want to attract bus operators for the increased business they can generate.

TRAINS

Passenger train transportation was critical to the early expansion and development of the United States. However, today the number of people who prefer to travel by train is much less than those who travel by airplane or automobile. In some areas, especially those that are densely populated, trains still play a major role in public transportation.

Historically, hotels were often built within a short distance of the train station. Today, while trains still move freight cost-effectively, it is generally unprofitable to operate trains for passenger transportation. Why? Public dollars are used to build airports, and airline companies utilize their profit from doing so. The automobile industry has benefited from the immense investment in public roads and highways as the federal government developed the Interstate highway system. Newly built hotels are often located near interchanges

LODGING ONLINE

Amtrak works very hard to attract passenger travel. To see the passenger routes it operates, go to:

www.Amtrak.com

Does Amtrak service your town?

Do you think it should?

or exits on these highways. In addition, state and local governments annually invest significant tax dollars in road construction and maintenance projects.

The average American citizen has been less enthusiastic, however, about using public dollars to purchase the land, track, and equipment needed for a reliable passenger rail system. An exception is the nationwide passenger rail routes operated by Amtrak.

The name "Amtrak" results from the blending of the words "American" and "Track." Its official name is the National Railroad Passenger Corporation. Amtrak is not a part of the federal government, but since its inception in 1971, it has been dependent upon the federal government (and some state governments) for grants that allow it to continue operations.

The Amtrak system carries more than 65,000 passengers per day. New York, Philadelphia, and Washington are the areas where trains are most used and reflect the use of rail for large-city commuting rather than long-distance travel. Hotels located near train stations along these routes can generate substantial revenue volumes from these passengers.

RENTAL CARS

Automobiles are the most popular method of travel in the United States, and the impact of their drivers and passengers on the hotel business is tremendous. Many American families own one or more cars, and use them extensively for short-distance travel. People who travel by air will frequently rent a car or other vehicle upon arrival at their destination.

The car rental business is an important part of the transportation industry and consists of all business that rent or lease passenger cars, vans, trucks, and utility trailers. Some of these businesses offer only short-term rental, others only longer-term leases, and some provide both services.

California, Florida, and Texas have the greatest number of car rental outlets and the largest number of vehicles rented. Hoteliers who enjoy a close association with their local car rental businesses often find that travelers renting cars ask for advice about where to stay when they pick up their cars. Therefore, hotels can gain business from rental agency referrals.

Travel Agents

Assume that you were going to take an auto trip to a town 50 miles away. If you had previously driven there several times, you probably would not need help planning your trip. Now assume that even though you have never been there, you must plan a trip to Europe for 21 days for yourself and five other people. In this case, you are likely to want the services of an experienced **travel agent**.

LODGING LANGUAGE

Travel agent: A professional who assists clients in planning and purchasing travel.

For many travelers, the knowledge and skill of professional travel planners are important to the success of the trip. Constantly changing airfares and schedules, thousands of available vacation packages, and the vast amount of information available on the Internet can make travel planning frustrating and time-consuming. To sort out their travel options,

LODGING ONLINE

The mission of the American Society of Travel Agents (ASTA) is to enhance the professionalism and profitability of member agents through effective representation in industry and government affairs, education and training, and by identifying and meeting the needs of the traveling public. To learn more about ASTA, go to:

http://www.asta.org/

When would you consider the use of a travel agent if you were planning a long trip?

many leisure and business travelers seek the advice of a travel agent. According to a 2008 PhoCusWright survey, travel agents booked:

85 percent of all cruises

70 percent of all tour packages

50 percent of all airline tickets

30 percent of all hotel rooms

25 percent of all car rentals

Many Americans use travel agents to book business or leisure trips, flights, hotel rooms, rental cars, and tours, but travelers are increasingly using the Internet to learn about and purchase travel services, and as a result the use of travel agents has declined somewhat. Older consumers are more likely to use travel agents than younger ones. Travelers who use travel agents tend to be wealthier, take longer trips, and travel more frequently.

Travel agents offer their clients individual tickets or **packages** and organize tailor-made travel on request.

LODGING LANGUAGE

Package: A group of travel services, such as hotel rooms, meals, and airfare, sold for one price. For example, a Valentine's Day Getaway package to Las Vegas suggested by a travel agent might include airfare, lodging, meals, and show tickets for two people at an all-inclusive price.

Travel agents generally advise about and sell vacation packages, air tickets, cruises, hotel bookings, car rentals, and other services. Many corporations have their own in-house travel agents. This is especially true when many members of the company do a lot of traveling to visit their own clients, make sales presentations, or attend meetings and conferences. The Association of Corporate Travel Executives (www.acte.org/) was formed to meet the needs of this important group of travel professionals. Whether retained by individuals or working for corporate employers, travel agents inform and advise travelers about the best ways to maximize their experiences and minimize their expenses.

In the hospitality industry, hotel managers interact with travel agents on a daily basis because in most hotels a large percentage of the reservations will be made by travel agents using the **Global Distribution System (GDS)**, which electronically links travel agents worldwide to individual hotel reservation systems.

LODGING LANGUAGE

Global Distribution System (GDS): Commonly referred to as the GDS, this computer system connects travel professionals worldwide for the purpose of reserving hotel rooms and other services for their clients.

Travel agents have historically worked on a commission basis for the hotel room and airline services they sold. In 2002, however, most large airlines eliminated travel agent commissions. Today, over 90 percent travel agents charge for their travel planning services. Hotels, however, still typically pay commissions to travel agents who book rooms for clients. This commission is usually 10 percent of the hotel room's price.

Regardless of how they are paid, travel agents contract for travel services on behalf of their clients. As a result, they have a legal responsibility to act in the best interests of their clients. Hoteliers should remember that while travel agents collect commissions from hotels, they actually work for the traveler. Wise hoteliers know that a good working relationship with local and national travel agents and the groups to which they belong is vital to their success.

Online Travel Agents

People and companies operating Web sites that allow travelers to reserve (book) hotel rooms online are increasingly important partners to hoteliers. These **online travel agent (OTA)** sites are increasingly popular with travelers.

LODGING LANGUAGE

Online travel agent (OTA): An organization that provides travel booking services on the Internet.

Hotel managers can create their own Web sites and sell their rooms directly to consumers who use the Internet to reserve rooms. Many hotels, however, also utilize intermediary Web site operators, such as Expedia and Travelocity, which sell hotel rooms online for numerous hotel companies.

Consumers like to visit these sites to compare prices, hotel features, and locations before they make their hotel selections. Just as hotel companies have historically relied upon travel agents to "sell" hotel rooms, hoteliers now rely on OTAs to do so. Rather than working for a commission as travel agents have traditionally done, OTAs charge hotels a fee for each room sold. These fees are often negotiable. They are based upon the number of rooms the OTA books for the hotel, the hotel's room rates, and the favorable positioning of the hotel on the OTA's Web site.

There are two main models OTAs use to partner with hotels:

> ***Opaque Rate Model.*** In this model, room rates are not seen by guests until they have successfully "bid" for a room. Guests decide the amount they will pay. Then the OTA matches the guest's request with hotels willing to sell rooms at that price. Priceline.com is, perhaps, the most well-known OTA using this approach.
>
> ***Merchant Model.*** In this model, room rates (often heavily discounted) are readily viewed online by potential guests. They book their rooms through the OTA, who then charges the hotel a fee for each reservation made. Examples include Hotels.com, Travelocity.com, and Expedia.com.

The sale of travel services on the Internet is big business, and it is anticipated that it will continue to grow. While the recession of 2008 and 2009 slowed the online purchase of travel services somewhat, experts predict that in the 2010s, more than 50 percent of all hotel bookings will be completed on the Internet. Therefore, the partnership between hoteliers and OTA operators will continue to be critical to a hotel's success.

Tour Operators

Tour operators are another important part of the travel industry. These travel professionals work closely with travel agencies but are, from a legal perspective, distinctly different.

LODGING LANGUAGE

Tour operator: A company or individual who plans and markets travel packages.

While travel agents work directly for their clients and have a legal responsibility to act in their best interests, tour operators create packages that are designed to make a profit for the tour operator.

A tour operator can be any of a varied group of companies that purchase travel services in large quantities and then market the same services directly or through travel agents to individual travelers. A travel agent may recommend that a traveler buy a specific travel package. However, it is the tour operator who must develop the package, market it, and sell it to travel agency clients.

Assume that a tour operator wants to create a tour package of a trip to New Orleans. The tour operator would select an airline to provide transportation from various starting points to transport travelers to New Orleans. A charter bus would pick up the members of the tour group at the airport and transport them to the hotel preselected by the tour operator. Restaurants to be used and group activities to be undertaken would also be preplanned by the tour operator, as would the selection of tour guides to escort the travelers to the sites included in the package.

The tour operator would market the New Orleans package to travel agents throughout the country. They, in turn, might recommend the trip to their clients. If the package offered attractive prices and activities, clients might purchase it. The result: travelers from around the country will buy the tour operator's New Orleans package. If it is profitable, the tour operator might offer it again.

Because they purchase travel services in large quantities, tour operators can often obtain a significant discount, add a mark-up that represents their profit margin, and still offer lower prices than travelers could negotiate individually.

Large travel agencies may also assemble their own packages; however, when they do so, they take a risk because tour operators do not work on commission, as do travel agents. The tour operator's profit comes only from the sale of travel services previously purchased. Assume that a tour operator purchases 100 tickets to the MTV Video Awards show with the intention of packaging them with airfare and overnight accommodations to create an "MTV Awards" travel package. The tour operator will have incurred the cost of the awards tickets regardless of whether the package sale is successful. Therefore, a travel agent will fail to earn a commission when a vacation package offered for sale does not sell. By contrast, the tour operator who has assembled the unsuccessful package is likely to face real, and sometimes substantial, monetary losses.

Tour operators can offer a variety of services. They may only sell self-guided trips, such as airline tickets to a large city, hotel reservations at a specific hotel, and tickets to the theater at a specific date and time. In this case, it is not a **guided tour**, nor is it directly managed by the tour operator. Any buyer could purchase the package, travel on the plane, stay in the hotel, and visit the theater.

LODGING LANGUAGE

Guided tour: A group tour package that includes the services of one or more tour guides.

Alternatively, a tour operator might decide to offer a full-service guided tour that includes transportation, hotel rooms, meals, activities, and the use of tour guides to serve as the travelers' escorts.

LODGING ONLINE

The National Tour Association (NTA) has approximately 2,700 members. Its membership includes tour operators, travel suppliers, and individuals representing many destinations and attractions. To learn more about the NTA, go to:

http://www.ntaonline.com/

What types of travelers do you think prefer guided tours? Which types would prefer self-guided tours?

Hoteliers interact with tour operators in several ways:

- Negotiating hotel rates offered to tour operators
- Hosting tour-package buyers within their hotels
- Assisting travelers who experience difficulties with one or more features of the tour related to the hotel's services
- Working with travel agents to market tours that include the hotelier's hotel(s)
- Providing hotel service at levels high enough to ensure a continued positive relationship between the tour operator and the hotel

INDUSTRY TRADE ASSOCIATIONS

You have learned that hoteliers work with other professionals in the tourism industry to meet the needs of the traveling public. In many cases, hoteliers work with their peers to meet their own **professional development** needs and to communicate their viewpoints to the public, to government, and to other policy-making entities that affect their industry.

LODGING LANGUAGE

Professional development: The process by which hoteliers continue to improve their knowledge and skills.

Trade associations typically hold monthly and annual gatherings and, in conjunction with these meetings, may offer educational seminars/workshops to improve the knowledge and skills of their members. As well, most trade associations invite companies that sell products and services of interest to the membership to participate in a **trade show** held in conjunction with their annual meeting. These shows attract **vendors** interested in showcasing their latest products and services. Trade shows are an extremely efficient way for show attendees to quickly learn about new products and services. Many associations also have both state- and local-level chapters, some of which also host their own trade shows.

LODGING LANGUAGE

Trade shows: An industry-specific event that allows suppliers to an industry to interact with, educate, and sell to individuals who are part of the industry; also called an exhibition.

Vendors: Those who sell products and services to hoteliers.

There are several trade associations that assist and represent the lodging industry:

- ***American Hotel & Lodging Association.*** Formerly known as the American Hotel and Motel Association, this is the largest and oldest national hotel trade association in the country. Founded in 1910 and now based in Washington, D.C., it is a collection of state-level hotel associations working together to meet the educational, social, and legislative needs of its members.

  The organization is overseen by a board of directors consisting of a chairperson, vice-chairperson, secretary/treasurer, directors (elected by their respective states), an allied member, a corporate board director, and a representative from the National Restaurant Association. To learn more about this group and its goals, go to www.ahla.com/.
- ***Asian American Hotel Owners Association.*** The stated purpose of this group is to provide "an active forum in which Asian American Hotel Owners, through an exchange of ideas with a unified voice, can communicate, interact, and secure their proper position within the hospitality industry, and be a source of inspiration by promoting professionalism and excellence through education and community involvement." AAHOA is a rapidly growing group that strongly advocates the interests of individual hotel owners. To learn more about this group, go to http://www.aahoa.com/AM/Template.cfm.

LODGING GOES GREEN!

The Green Hotel Association is one of the newest trade associations in the lodging industry. "Green" hotels are environmentally friendly properties whose managers are eager to institute programs that save water, save energy, and reduce solid waste—while saving money—to help protect the earth and the environment.

The "Green" Hotels Association's® purpose is to bring together hotels interested in environmental issues. To learn more about this emerging and very important association, go to:

www.greenhotels.com

- ***International Hotel & Restaurant Association.*** This group, based in Paris, France, is an international association exclusively devoted to promoting and defending the interests of the worldwide hotel and restaurant industry. It is a non-profit membership organization that helps its members achieve their business objectives and prepare for the future. To learn more about this association, go to www.ih-ra.com/.
- ***Educational Institute (E.I.) of the American Hotel & Lodging Association.*** While not technically a separate trade association, this group, located in Orlando, Florida, is affiliated with the American Hotel & Lodging Association. It creates and markets professional development and training programs for the hotel industry. The mission of E.I. is to help hotel owners and managers become better trained and to provide resources that allow them to upgrade the knowledge and job skills of their own hotel staff members. Hoteliers can join E.I. by becoming certified in a variety of specific hotel operating areas, including sales and marketing, food and beverage, and housekeeping and security. For more information on this organization, go to www.ei-ahla.org/.

ALL IN A DAY'S WORK 1.2

THE SITUATION

It was early evening, and Ethan was puzzled and frustrated. He was sorting through a pile of papers on his desk. Each was from a magazine, newspaper, or e-mail he had received at his hotel within the past few weeks. Each summarized the predictions of a local, regional, or national industry forecaster. Some said business conditions would improve and others said they would not; while still others said they would likely stay the same.

"Loni," called Ethan to his assistant in the office next door, "given what we experienced in ADR and occupancy last year, what do you think our hotel will do this coming year? I have to make the annual budget and every forecaster seems to think something different."

"Me?" replied Loni, "You know what I always say, predictions are pretty tricky, especially when they are about the future."

"Be serious," said Ethan, "How can we predict what we should spend if we can't predict what we will bring in? I don't know exactly what to expect next year, but I do know the boss expects a budget from me, and soon!"

A RESPONSE

Estimating future business conditions and travel trends is a common part of every hotel manager's job, and it can be difficult. To obtain the information needed to make accurate estimates, hoteliers must have a good source of up-to-date information. To get that information, they join industry associations that provide up-to-date information, read monthly or weekly hotel publications, and consider the opinions of knowledgeable industry leaders.

Lodging Language

Lodging Industry
Hotel
Hotelier
Market
Tourist
Value (Lodging Accommodations)
Full-Service Hotel
Room Service
Limited-Service Hotel
Bed and Breakfast Inns
Camps/Parks Lodges
Extended-Stay Hotel
Convention Hotel
Conference Center
Resort
Timeshare
Private Clubs
Cruise Ship
Casino
Average Daily Rate (ADR)
Occupancy Rate
Revenue Per Available Room (RevPAR)
GOPPAR
Gross Operating Profit
Hospitality industry
Amenities
Hotel Shuttle
Hub
Charter
Travel Agent
Package
Global Distribution System (GDS)
Online Travel Agent (OTA)
Tour Operator
Guided Tour
Professional Development
Trade show
Vendors

For Discussion

1. Think about the last time you spent the night in a hotel or other lodging facility. What were your specific reasons for selecting that property?
2. Make a list of several hotels in your area. What different types of travelers is each of these properties trying to attract?
3. What are some factors that could cause a hotel's revenue to increase or decrease at various times of the year?
4. What are some factors that could cause the occupancy rate for a hotel in a specific location to increase or decrease at various times of the year?
5. Think about your own hometown. Do you think the majority of visitors to its hotels are leisure or business travelers? List the reasons for your answer.
6. What is your favorite method of travel for a short trip? For a long trip?
7. Have you ever used a travel agent? What types of trips do you think most require the help of a travel agent?
8. When you visit a Web site to reserve a hotel room, what Web site features are most important to you? How do you select the Web site that you visit?
9. Trade associations want to meet the needs of their members, including those that are social in nature. Identify some activities that you believe would be fun to do with others working in the same field as yourself.
10. Do you think hotels will change in the next 10 years? In what specific ways?

Team Activities

TEAM ACTIVITY 1

List the most popular attractions within a 50-mile radius of your location. For each, describe the type of person(s) who are drawn to the attraction. How might hoteliers best market to these people to inform them of their hotel's features?

TEAM ACTIVITY 2

Go online and attempt to make a reservation at three different, but similarly priced, hotels in your local area. For each OTA site selected, evaluate:

1. The attractiveness of the Web site
2. The ease with which a room reservation could be made
3. The quality of the information on the site for a:
   a. Leisure traveler
   b. Business traveler

Chapter

2

The Structure of the Lodging Industry

Chapter Outline

Chapter Overview

The best way to understand how hotels operate is to start with an understanding of who owns them, who manages them, and finally, who franchises them. Many individuals and companies invest in hotels. Some investors are experienced in the ownership of hotels, while others are new to the business. An investor may own all or part of a hotel. Some individual investors own many hotels and some hotels are owned by multiple investors. In some cases, investors plan to take an active role in how the hotels they own are managed. In other cases, investors purchase hotels strictly as a financial investment and have neither the interest nor the experience required to run a hotel. These owners need an individual or a company to operate their hotels for them.

Hotel management companies are businesses that operate hotels for owners who do not wish to manage their own properties. A hotel management company may consist of one, a few, or many individual hoteliers. Technically, a single hotel manager, operating a hotel for a single hotel owner, could be considered a hotel management company. In other cases, management companies can be extremely large, employ hundreds or thousands of people, and operate hundreds of hotels for many different owners. Knowing the ways hotel management companies actually run hotels for owners and about how the management contracts both parties implement to set the rules for operating these hotels is important in understanding the lodging industry.

Increasingly, franchise lodging companies, called franchisors, are playing a large role in the development, marketing, and operation of hotels. This is especially true in the United States. Knowing how franchisors and their franchisees work together to advance the standing of a hotel brand, and thus increase its value, is also critical to knowing how the lodging business operates. In this chapter, you will learn how an understanding of franchise agreements, the legal document that defines the roles of the two partners in a franchise relationship, is essential to your knowledge of the lodging industry.

Chapter Objectives

1. To inform you about the different types of investors who own hotels.
2. To tell how hotel management companies help hotel owners operate their hotels.
3. To describe the importance of management contracts in the operation of hotels.
4. To teach you about the impact of franchisors in the lodging industry.
5. To explain how franchisors and franchisees work within a franchise agreement to assist each other in promoting a hotel brand.

HOTEL OWNERS

Hotels are typically operated for two reasons. The first, as you learned in the previous chapter, is to meet the needs of the traveling public. Over the long run, however, this goal can only be achieved if the hotel also meets the hotel owner's **return on investment (ROI)** goals. Thus, both serving guests and doing so profitably are important concerns for hotel owners.

LODGING LANGUAGE

Return on investment: The percentage rate of financial return achieved on the money invested in a hotel property.

Different hotel owners may seek different ROIs depending upon their specific goals. In all cases, however, the ROI is computed using the following formula:

$$\frac{\text{After tax profits}}{\text{Total hotel investment}} = \text{ROI\%}$$

For example, consider a hotel where, in one year, the owner generated after-tax **profit** of \$600,000. If that owner had invested \$5 million in the property, the ROI, for that year, would be computed as:

$$\frac{\$600{,}000}{\$5{,}000{,}000} = 12\%$$

LODGING LANGUAGE

Profit: The money remaining after all the expenses of operating a business have been paid.

Sizeable ROIs are not easy to achieve. They require wise hotel selection and investment, aggressive sales efforts, and professional hotel operations management. When the owner's ROI expectations are met, funds will be sufficient to maintain the hotel in a manner that appeals to guests and, as a result, helps ensure the continued success of the hotel.

It is important to understand that the owner of a hotel actually owns two distinctly different assets. The first asset is the real estate involved. This includes the land, building(s), and furnishings that make up the hotel. The second asset involved in owning a hotel is the operating business itself. For example, in a hotel that is currently operating, the value of the hotel consists of both its real estate value and the profits (if any) made by operating the hotel. For a hotel that has yet to be built, the value of the real estate may be known and building costs can be estimated, but the value of the operating business must be projected. This means that it is usually easier to establish the worth and purchase price

Owners and managers will meet regularly to discuss the financial performance of their operations.

of a hotel that is operating than of one that has yet to be built. A hotel that is performing well will most likely have a sales price that reflects its performance. A hotel that is under-performing will generally be sold for less on a per-room basis because there is no guarantee, even with the proper investment and management, that it will be able to perform better than it does currently.

Individuals can own hotels, and so can legally formed partnerships and corporations. REITS (Real Estate Investment Trusts) are public, stock-issuing companies that can own and (since 1991) operate their own hotels. In some cases, hotel owners share ownership with their customers by "selling" the right to occupy a room for a specific amount of time each year (timeshare). Individuals and companies of many different kinds invest in and own hotels. A convenient way to view this diverse group is by their participation in the actual operation of the hotel. Using this approach, hotel owners can be categorized either as investors or as owner/operators.

Investors

Those who invest in hotels do so for many reasons, including the favorable tax status resulting from the hotel's **depreciation**, the long-term effects of real estate **appreciation**, and the profits that can be made from the hotel's annual operation.

LODGING LANGUAGE

Depreciation: The reduction in the value of an asset as it wears out. This noncash expense is often termed a "tax write-off" because the decline in the value of the asset is tax deductible.

Appreciation: The increase, over time, in the value of an asset. The amount of the increased value is not taxed unless the asset changes hands (is sold).

Regardless of the motivation for buying a hotel, an investor, as defined here, is not typically active in the management of a hotel. The investor can be an individual, a corporation, a governmental entity, or any other entity that funds or seeks to acquire a hotel for its own purposes. Depending on the investment level, the investor may own all or part of the hotel. In some cases, several investors will pool their funds to purchase a hotel that is larger or more expensive than any one of them could have purchased individually.

Owner/Operators

An **owner/operator** is an individual or company that both owns and operates (manages) the hotel in which it has invested.

LODGING LANGUAGE

Owner/ operator: A hotel investor who also manages (operates) the hotel.

Owner/operators can be individuals and their family members, some of whom may work in the hotel every day, or very large multinational hotel companies with offices all over the world. In both cases, the characteristic that distinguishes owner/operators from other hotel investors is their responsibility for the management of the hotel they own.

MANAGEMENT COMPANIES

Because hotel investors, as defined in this chapter, do not typically operate the hotels they own, they must employ a manager to run the hotel. In such situations, if there is only one hotel to manage, a single **General manager (GM)** could be hired and given the responsibility of operating the hotel.

LODGING LANGUAGE

General Manager (GM): The traditional title of the individual at a hotel property who is responsible for final decision-making regarding property-specific operating policies and procedures. Also, the leader of the hotel's management team.

An investor who owns many hotels, however, is likely to employ the services of a **management company**. A management company is an organization formed for the express purpose of managing one or more hotels.

LODGING LANGUAGE:

Management company: An organization that operates a hotel for a fee. Sometimes called a "contract company."

Hotel owners oftentimes rely on management companies to oversee the operational aspect of their investments.

The Role and Structure of Management Companies

The financial success of any lodging facility is dependent, in large measure, upon the quality and skill of its on-site management. Before the mid-1950s, the owners of a hotel typically hired the best general manager they could find to operate the hotel(s) they owned. If they needed a manager with a specific level of skill or experience, they would try to find one. Even talented general managers, however, may not have had the experience desired by the owner. When that was the case, the result was often less than satisfactory for both the owner and the hotel's general manager.

In the 1950s and later, hotel owner groups began to purchase ever larger numbers of hotels, and they could not recruit, train, and supervise the many general managers they required. This resulted in the growth of companies formed simply to manage hotels under ordinary as well as out-of-the-ordinary circumstances. Today, with the growth of large (and small) management companies, owners often find that a hotel management company, with its wide range of personnel, can provide managers with the exact experience they are looking for.

In many cases, owners face special problems in the operation of the hotels they own. Some of these special situations include:

- Managing/directing a major (complete) renovation of a hotel
- Operating a hotel in a severely **depressed market**
- Bankruptcy/**repossession** of the hotel
- Managing a hotel slated for permanent closing
- Managing a hotel because of the unexpected resignation of its general manager
- Managing a hotel for an extended period of time for owners who elect not to become directly involved in the day-to-day operation of the property

---

LODGING LANGUAGE

Depressed market: A hotel market area where occupancy rates and/or ADRs are significantly below their historical levels.

Repossession: The taking back of a property by a seller or lender, usually in response to nonpayment by the buyer.

Under the standard financial arrangement between a management company and a hotel's ownership, the management company receives a predetermined fee for its services. The fees charged by management companies to operate a hotel vary, but commonly range between 1 and 5 percent of the hotel's monthly revenue. Thus, regardless of the hotel's operating performance, the management company is paid the fee for its services, and the hotel's owners receive the profits (if any) after all expenses are paid.

Sometimes, the hotel owner negotiates an agreement that ties the management company's compensation, at least to some degree, to the hotel's actual operating performance. In some cases, this is acceptable, especially with hotels that demonstrate proven profitability. In other cases, however, it can take months or even years to turn an unprofitable hotel into a profitable one. Often, it is the owners of unprofitable or distressed market hotels that seek the assistance of management companies. Understandably, however, few hotel management companies are willing to enter into risky management agreements that may result in their financially subsidizing investors who own a hotel that either has been poorly managed in the past or is not likely to be profitable in its current condition.

As you have learned, some of the people who invest in hotels do not want to manage them. Many of these nonoperating hotel owners choose to hire management companies because they have absolutely no interest in managing the property, or even in their continued ownership of it.

For example, assume that a bank has loaned money to a hotel investor to develop a property. The owner opens the hotel, but, over time, fails to make the required loan repayments. As a result, the bank is forced to repossess the hotel. In this case, the bank, which is now the owner, will likely seek a management company that specializes in

LODGING ONLINE

In the early 2010s, White Lodging Services, Sunstone Hotels, and Interstate Hotels and Resorts (IHC) were among the largest hotel management companies. To review management services offered by IHC, go to:

www.ihc.com

When you arrive, click on "Management Services."

If you were a hotel owner looking for a management services partner, which company characteristics would be most important to you?

distressed properties. The management company would manage the hotel until it is put up for sale and purchased by a new owner.

The hospitality industry, because it is cyclical, sometimes experiences falling occupancy rates and ADRs while at other times these two hotel measures can increase significantly. In some cases, these cycles can result in properties that cannot pay back the money borrowed to purchase them, and the lenders then become involuntary owners through repossession. This was true in the United States in late 2009 and 2010 when many hotels could not pay back the money lent to build or buy them. In such cases, effectively managing a hotel simply meant optimizing the property's value while offering it for sale.

Management companies that specialize in helping lenders maintain repossessed properties until they can be resold will generally:

- Secure and, if it has closed, reopen the hotel
- Implement sales and marketing plans to maximize the hotel's short- and long-term profitability
- Generate reliable financial data about the hotel
- Establish suitable staffing to maximize guest and employee satisfaction
- Show the hotel to prospective buyers
- Report regularly to the owners about the hotel's physical and financial condition

Clearly, in the situation above, a management company provides a vital service to the lender. While an individual general manager might be able to provide the same services (and usually at a lower initial cost), many hotel investors who unwillingly acquire control of a hotel hire management companies to operate their properties until they can be sold or closed.

Of course, management companies can also operate hotels for investors who want to keep their ownership in their hotels. The services of good management companies are always in demand because investors seek them out in an effort to maximize the ROIs of their hotels.

The structure of hotel management companies can be examined from many different viewpoints. One way is to consider whether they are **first-tier** or **second-tier**.

LODGING LANGUAGE

First tier (management company): Management companies that operate hotels for owners using the management company's trade name as the hotel brand. Hyatt, Hilton, and Sheraton are examples.

Second tier (management company): Management companies that operate hotels for owners and do not use the management company name as part of the hotel name. American General Hospitality, Summit Hotel Management, and Winegardner and Hammons are examples.

The term "tier" refers simply to whose name is on the hotel the management company is operating. Tiering does *not* refer to the skill or quality of the management company or of the general managers working for it.

In a first-tier management company, the management company's name is also the name of the hotel. Examples include Hyatt, Sheraton, and Hilton. Second-tier management

LODGING ONLINE

Hotel Business is one of the industry publications that regularly supply information and statistics about the size of companies in the lodging business. To create an account that allows you to view this type of data, go to:

www.hotelbusiness.com

companies can operate many different brands of hotels because the management company's name is not the name used on the hotel.

Another way to examine management companies is by their size. Size can be measured several ways, for example, by the number of hotels operated or the amount of revenue generated. It is important to recognize that a management company operating one large hotel may generate more revenue than another hotel management company that operates three small hotels. Because this is true, hotel management companies are often ranked in size) by the number of rooms they manage rather than by the number of hotels they manage. The hospitality trade press periodically publishes rankings of the largest hotel management companies based upon the number of rooms managed.

While the size of a hotel management company may imply something about the company's success, it is often more useful to segment hotel management companies by the manner in which they participate, or do not participate, in the actual risk and ownership of the hotels they manage. As a result, these companies can be examined based upon their participation in one or more of the following arrangements:

- ***The management company is neither a partner in nor an owner of the hotels it manages.*** In this situation, the hotel's investors hire the management company. This is common, for example, when lenders involuntarily take possession of a hotel. In other cases, the management company may, for its own business reasons, elect to concentrate only on managing properties and will not participate in hotel investment (ownership).
- ***The management company is a partner with others in the ownership of the hotels it manages.*** A common arrangement in the hotel community is that of a management company collaborating with an investor(s) to jointly own and manage one or more hotels. Frequently, in this situation, the management company either buys or is given a share of hotel ownership (usually 1-20 percent) and then assumes the management of the property. Those hotel owners who prefer this arrangement feel that the partial ownership enjoyed by the management company will result in better performance. If the hotel experiences losses, they will be shared by the management company, and this can serve as a motivator for the management company to do well.
- ***The management company only manages hotels it owns.*** Some management companies are formed simply to manage the hotels they actually own. These companies want to participate in the hotel industry as both investors and managers. A clear advantage of this situation is that the management company will benefit from its own success if the hotels it manages are profitable. If the company is not successful, however, it will be responsible for any operating losses incurred by its hotels.
- ***The management company owns some of the hotels it manages and none or only a part of others it manages.*** Some management companies vary their ownership participation depending upon the hotel involved. Therefore, a given management company may:
  - Own all of a specific hotel as well as manage it
  - Manage and be an owning partner in another hotel
  - Manage, but not own any part of, yet another hotel property

Each of the above structures has advantages and disadvantages both for the management company and for those with whom it partners.

ALL IN A DAY'S WORK 2.1

THE SITUATION

"You made the loan to Tillman," said Cynthia Pearson, the president of Equity Bank, to John Gaylon, the vice president of Equity Bank.

"Yes, I know," replied John, "but I didn't know that two new hotels were going to open across the street from Tillman's within 24 months of granting the loan and that the bottom was going to drop out of the market at the same time!"

"Well," said Cynthia, "Tillman is no longer making enough profit to repay his loan. And now that his company has filed bankruptcy, we have a problem. We can extend the loan and pretend everything will be O.K., but I'm not sure it will be."

"Extend and pretend," replied John, "was not what I intended."

A RESPONSE

Lenders to hotel owners may, for one reason or another, find themselves in a position where they must assume operational responsibility for a hotel. The recession of 2008-2009 caused massive hotel foreclosures. In such cases, rarely will the lender seek to run the hotel. Instead the lender will likely hire a management company to operate the asset (hotel) until an orderly sale of it can be arranged. The role of a management company in these cases is to protect the value of the asset while minimizing additional losses to the lender.

Management Contracts

The management of a hotel by an entity that does not own the property can, for many reasons, become a very complex process. For example, assume that a guest slips and falls in the parking lot of a hotel owned by an investor but managed by a management company. Who might be held legally responsible for the guest's injuries? Similarly, if an employee of the hotel charges unfair treatment by management, will it be the management company or the owner who hired the management company that will be held **liable** for any resulting damages?

LODGING LANGUAGE

Liable: Legally bound to compensate for injury or loss.

To address these and numerous other issues, hotel owners and management companies sign a **management contract**. The contract clearly establishes the fees, operating responsibilities, and length of time for which the management company will operate the owner's hotel.

LODGING LANGUAGE

Management contract: An agreement between a hotel's owners and a hotel management company under which, for a fee, the management company operates the hotel. Also sometimes called a "management agreement," or an "operating agreement."

There are as many different contracts between hotel owners and the management companies they employ as there are hotels under management contract. Every hotel owner, depending upon the management company selected, will have a unique management contract for each hotel owned.

In some cases, the contract may include preopening services that are provided even before the hotel is officially open. Preopening activities may include hiring and training staff, purchasing inventories, and other operational activities that must be done before the first overnight guest can be served. While each management contract is different, major elements of management agreements typically include:

- The length of the agreement
- Procedures for early termination by either party
- Procedures for extending the contract
- Contract terms in the event of the hotel's sale
- Basic management fees to be charged
- Incentive fees earned or penalties assessed related to operating performance
- Management company investment required or ownership attained
- Exclusivity: can the management company operate competing hotels in the area?
- Reporting relationships and requirements (how much detail is required, and how frequently will reports be produced?)
- Insurance requirements of the management company (who must carry insurance and how much?)
- Status of employees (are the hotel's employees employed by the owner or by the management company?)
- The control, if any, that the owner has in the selection or removal of the general manager and other managers employed by the management company who work at the owner's hotel.

Management Company Pros and Cons

A variety of benefits can accrue to hotel owners who select a qualified management company to operate their hotels. Among these are:

- ***Improved management quality.*** In some cases, a management company is able to offer talented hotel professionals a better employment situation than an individual hotel owner. A hotelier's opportunities for advancement, increased training prospects, and employment security are frequently enhanced by working for a management company. As a result, owners benefit from the efforts of professional staff who are highly skilled. In addition, a management company may have specialists on staff who can assist the property general manager in areas such as hospitality law, accounting, and food and beverage management. In many cases, the hotel's owners could not supply these additional resources.
- ***Documented managerial effectiveness is available.*** Banks, mortgage companies, and others who are asked to supply investment capital to owners want to know that the hotel for which loans are sought will, in fact, be operated with professional hotel managers. The selection of an experienced management company with documented evidence of the past success in operating hotels similar to the one for which investment is requested adds credibility to a loan application submitted by the hotel's owners.
- ***Payment for services can be tied to performance.*** Most management companies charge a revenue-based fee to operate a hotel. Owners can negotiate additional payment incentives based on meeting profit objectives. These incentives can help ensure that the management company's performance is as strong as possible. Good management companies welcome such arrangements because they allow for above-average fees to be earned in exchange for above-average management performance.
- ***Partnership opportunities are enhanced.*** Many hotel owners are involved in multiple properties. When that is the case, an established management company and an ownership entity can work together in many different hotels. The management company will become knowledgeable about the owner's goals. The owner will become familiar with the abilities as well as the limitations of the management company. In such cases, a long-term partnership can be helpful to both parties.

Despite the many advantages, hotel owners face some potential drawbacks when they use a management company. These include:

- ***The owner cannot generally control selection of the on-site general manager and other high-level managers.*** When using a management company, the hotel's owner may be allowed some input but will not typically select the hotel's general manager. As a result, the quality of the general manager may be related more to the choice of general managers available who are currently employed by the management company than to the quality needed by the hotel. Experienced owners know the importance of quality on-site management and insist upon the best general manager (as well as other managers) that the management company can provide.
- ***Talented managers leave frequently.*** Assume that you were the owner of a hotel management company. You have contracts to operate large hotels that pay you large fees, and smaller hotels where the fees you earn are less. One of your general managers shows considerable talent operating a smaller hotel. The owner of the property is very happy with her. An opening for general manager arises at one of your larger hotels. Do you move the general manager? In many cases, the answer is probably "Yes!" In such cases, a hotel owner may experience frequent turn-over of general managers, especially if the hotel owned is smaller, is in a less popular geographic location, or for some other reason is not viewed as desirable by general managers in the management company that operates it.
- ***The interests of hotel owners and the management companies they employ sometimes conflict.*** On the surface, it would seem that the interests of a hotel owner and the management company selected to operate the hotel would always coincide. Both are interested in operating a profitable hotel. In fact, disputes arise because hotel owners typically seek to minimize the fees they pay to management companies (because lower fees yield greater profits), whereas management companies seek to maximize their fees. As a result, hotel owners who hire management companies often have serious disagreements with them over whether the hotels are indeed operated in the best interest of the owners.

ALL IN A DAY'S WORK 2.2

THE SITUATION

"You see," said Dan Segola, salesperson for Clarkson Foods, "since this hotel is managed by the Freeport Management Company, you qualify for our Breakfast Bonus program."

Dan was telling Shana Alexander, an employee of the Freeport Management Company, and the general manager of the Poplar Tree Hotel, about a special rebate program offered through Clarkson Foods.

"If you buy just five cases per month of Fruity brand orange juice for use on the Poplar Tree's continental breakfast bar, Fruity will write a monthly check to your company. It's their way of rewarding high-volume customers like Freeport."

"But the Poplar Tree is a pretty small hotel," replied Shana. "We only have 70 rooms."

"That's O.K.," said Dave. "Because Freeport manages hotels all over the country, your hotel still qualifies for the volume discount."

If Shana participates in the program, should it be her management company or the Poplar Tree's owners who receive the money paid by Fruity?

A RESPONSE

Despite the logic presented by the Clarkson Food salesperson, benefits such as rebates for purchases made by a hotel should accrue to the hotel's owners, not the management company. The only exception would be if a specific section in the management contract allows the management company to accrue such benefits, and from the perspective of the hotel's investors, that is rarely, if ever, advisable. Shana should participate in the Breakfast Bonus program, accept the check, and deposit it in the hotel owner's bank account, but only when it is clear that doing so would be in the best interests of the hotel's owners, as well as the hotel's guests.

LODGING GOES GREEN!

Management companies in the hospitality industry are increasingly concerned about sustainable operations. Investors Hospitality Management (IHM) was one of the very first hotel management companies to offer hotel owners a customized "Green Plan" for each property IHM agreed to manage. This plan detailed the specific sustainability steps and procedures IHM would undertake if they were selected to manage the property.

For hotel management companies, a commitment to manage properties in an environmentally conscious manner can include implementing practices that range from simple recycling programs to the implementation of energy saving procedures, and the use of eco-friendly cleaners, soaps, lighting, recycled building products, linen use, and even hypo-allergenic fabrics.

To learn more about IHM and its philosophy of social responsibility in hotel operations, go to:

www.investorshm.com/

- ***The costs of management company errors are borne by the owner.*** Under most management contracts, the owner, not the management company, is responsible for all the costs associated with operating the hotel. As a result, any unnecessary costs incurred as a result of any errors in marketing or operating the hotel must be paid by the hotel's owner.
- ***Transfer of ownership may be complicated.*** The length of a management contract, especially if the hotel is large, can be several years. As a result, if the owner decides to sell the hotel during the life of the contract, potential buyers who either operate their own hotels or use a different management company may not be interested in buying. Even if the contract includes a **buy-out** clause, the cost of the buy-out may be so high that the owner can only sell to a buyer who is willing to pay the very highest price for the property, a fact that can limit the number of potential buyers.

LODGING LANGUAGE

Buy-out: An arrangement in which both parties to a contract agree to end the contract early as a result of one party paying the other the agreed-upon financial compensation.

FRANCHISING AND THE LODGING INDUSTRY

To truly understand the lodging industry in the United States, and in the rest of the world as well, you must first understand the **franchise** concept. In a franchise arrangement, one party (the **franchisor**) allows another party (the **franchisee**) to use, for a specific amount of time, the name, operating procedures, and systems developed by the franchisor. In exchange for the right to use these things, the franchisee pays a fee to the franchisor. Franchising allows one business entity to use the logo, trademarks, and operating systems developed by another business entity for the benefit of both. As a result, franchising creates a network of independent business owners sharing a **brand** name.

LODGING LANGUAGE

Franchise: An arrangement whereby one party (the franchisor) allows another party to use its logo, brand name, systems, and resources in exchange for a fee.

Franchisor: An organization that manages a brand and sells the right to use the brand name.

Franchisee: An individual or company that buys, under specific terms and conditions, the right to use a brand name for a fixed period of time and at an agreed-upon price.

Brand: The name of a specific hotel group. For example, Holiday Inn and Comfort Inn are two different brands. Additional examples of brands include Hyatt, Hampton Inn, Super 8, and Radisson.

Many guests recognize name brand hotels because they advertise so well.

Hotel Franchisors

To see the effect of franchising in the hotel industry, assume that a motorist is driving along a highway and sees the name of a popular hotel. The name is easily recognizable due, in part, to an extensive nationwide advertising campaign. In all probability, the driver will suppose that the hotel company purchased some land and built another hotel to operate in this location. In fact, that is not likely to be the case. It is much more likely that an independent investor has built the property and agreed to purchase a franchise from a hotel franchisor.

Many in the hotel industry believe that the first significant hotel franchising arrangements began in the 1950s with Kemmons Wilson and his Holiday Inn **chain**.

LODGING LANGUAGE

Chain: The hotels operated by a group of franchisees who have all franchised the same hotel brand name. Also called a "brand" or "flag."

In a combination of what may well be part historical fact and part hotel lore, the story is told about how, in 1951, Wilson, a resident of Memphis, Tennessee, loaded his wife and five children into the family car and drove to Washington, D.C., for a vacation. He was quite unhappy with the motel accommodations he found along the way. The rooms he encountered were, he believed, too small, too expensive, and in many cases, not clean.

Wilson returned to Tennessee convinced that he could build a chain of hotels across the country that would operate under the same name and provide the traveling public with a lodging experience they could count on to be clean, comfortable, and moderately priced. He hired an architect to draw up the plans for a prototype hotel. The architect, according to legend, was watching the 1942 Bing Crosby movie titled *Holiday Inn* while working, and sketched that name on the top of the plans he was drawing. Wilson, upon seeing the plans, liked them and the name at the top as well. As a result, the Holiday Inn chain was born.

The first Holiday Inn opened in Tennessee in 1952, and the four-hundredth Holiday Inn franchise began operation in December of 1962. Today, Holiday Inns franchises its name as part of the InterContinental Hotels group, which consists of more than 1,500 hotels

LODGING ONLINE

The InterContinetal Hotels Group (IHG) is a good example of a company that franchises multiple brands, including Holiday Inns. To see their Web site and list of managed brands, go to:

http://www.ichotelsgroup.com/

How many different brands are currently managed by IHG?

Why do you think they offer these multiple brands?

worldwide, including the brands Inter-Continental Hotels, Holiday Inn, Holiday Inn Select, Holiday Inn Express, Holiday Inn Crown Plaza, and Staybridge Suites.

In most cases today, a single hotel franchisor has the ability to grant franchises for many different brands or flags. As a result, a hotel investor could, for example, elect to enter into a franchise relationship with Holiday Inn or Holiday Inn Express, two different brand names, both franchised by the InterContinental Hotels group. Alternatively, the investor could choose to franchise a Hilton Hotel, an Embassy Suite hotel, or a Hampton Hotel. The Hilton Hotels company franchises all three of these brands and more as they seek to offer different hotel types that appeal to a variety of travelers. Today's hotel owners are free to choose the brand with which they wish to affiliate, but from an increasingly small number of franchisors. A variation of the franchise arrangement is that of "membership" hotels made up of independent hotel owners who band together to create their own brand. Best Western is the largest of the membership groups, but from a guest's viewpoint, it operates essentially the same way as a chain.

The actual brands managed by any single franchisor change as brands are bought and sold among them. Figure 2.1 shows the 10 of the largest hotel brands currently operating in the United States.

Each brand will, depending upon the franchisor's structure, have a brand manager or president responsible for expanding the number of hotels in the brand and maintaining the quality standards established for it. In the overwhelming majority of cases, franchise companies do not actually own the hotels operating under their brand names. They only own the right to sell the brand name and to determine the standards that will be followed by the hotel owners who elect to affiliate with their brands.

The greatest advantage to a franchisor of entering into a franchise relationship with a hotel owner is the fee payments to the brand that will result from the agreement. Like all businesses, franchise companies desire growth. In general, the greater the number of hotels that operate under a single brand name, the greater the value of the name and thus the fees that can be charged for using it. In addition, each additional hotel that affiliates with a hotel brand helps to pay for marketing and advertising the brand. Additional hotel

Franchisor	Brand	Number of Properties
Best Western International	Best Western	4,065
Wyndham Worldwide	Super 8	2,125
InterContinental Hotels Group	Holiday Inn Express	2,047
Choice Hotels International	Comfort Inn	1,997
Wyndham Worldwide	Days Inn	1,851
Hilton Hotel Corporation	Hampton Inn	1,717
Choice Hotels International	Quality Inn	1,336
InterContinental Hotels Group	Holiday Inn Hotel and Resort	1,321
Accor	Motel 6	983
Wyndham Worldwide	Ramada Inn	895

FIGURE 2.1 Top 10 Hotel Brands Courtesy of Panda Professional Hospitality Education and Training

properties operating under the same brand name typically mean greater profits for the franchise company. As a result, franchisors are aggressive in soliciting agreements with hotel owners who are already affiliated with another brand. In such cases, the franchisor is hoping that the hotel owner will agree to a **conversion** to a new brand name.

LODGING LANGUAGE

Conversion: The changing of a hotel from one brand to another. Also known as "re-flagging."

Conversions can be beneficial to a brand because they allow it to grow more quickly. They can harm the brand, however, if the converted properties do not have the features and quality levels of the hotels already in the brand. Of course, franchisors also actively pursue owners developing new hotels who have not yet selected a franchise brand.

The franchise arrangement in the hotel industry is very popular. In most cities in the United States, nearly all of the medium- to large-sized hotels will be affiliated with a brand.

Hotel Franchisees

Franchising has been of great benefit both to hotel investors and to the owners of brand names. The primary advantages to a hotel investor of buying a franchise are that doing so allows the hotel to acquire a brand name with regional or national recognition and connects the hotel to the Global Distribution System (GDS). As you learned in Chapter 1, connectivity to the GDS is a necessity in today's hotel market. An independent hotel can also purchase this connectivity, but it is costly.

Affiliation with a strong brand will also typically increase the hotel's sales and, therefore, its profitability. The total fees paid by the hotel owner to the brand managers are related to the strength of the brand name and to the revenue the name will bring to the hotel. While the fees related to a franchise agreement are negotiable, they will, on average, equal from 3 to 15 percent of the revenue the hotel generates from selling rooms.

In addition to increased revenue levels, affiliation with a brand often affects the ability of hotel owners to secure external financing. When owners seek financing from banks or other lending institutions, they most frequently find that these lenders, almost without exception, will require an affiliation with an established brand before they consider the loan request.

Additional advantages, depending upon the franchisor selected, may include assistance with on-site training, advice on purchasing hotel furnishings, reduced operating costs resulting from vendors who give brand operators preferred pricing, and free interior and exterior design assistance.

For a hotel's owners, purchasing a hotel franchise is actually very much like purchasing the long-term services of other professionals, such as attorneys or accountants, who help the owner maximize the value of an asset. For example, when selecting a franchise, there will be a number of companies (franchisors) offering the service. These service providers offer a variety of experience, skills, and knowledge. In addition, the prices they charge for their services will vary. Lastly, as is true in many relationships, the franchisor is likely to have a unique "style" of doing business that attracts (or repels) potential franchisees.

Factors that hotel franchisees look for prior to agreeing to affiliate with a specific hotel brand include:

- ***Perceived quality/service level of the brand.*** Travelers associate some brands with higher quality, service levels, and costs than other brands. A Doubletree hotel, for example, will probably be perceived by most travelers as having more services (and charging a higher ADR) than a Hampton Inn even though both brands are franchised by Hilton hotels.

  In most cases, franchisors, in an attempt to offer a franchise product that appeals to hotel owners at a variety of desired investment levels, will offer brands with a range of services, perceived quality, and guest amenities provided. Hotel owners who elect to operate the highest-quality brand offered by a franchisor will spend, on average, more to build or renovate each of their hotel rooms than if they selected a lower-quality level brand. In addition, total operating costs are likely to be higher with brands that offer guests more services (although ADRs are also likely to be higher in these cases). Of course, a well-managed, lower-cost limited-service brand can be more profitable for an owner than a poorly managed, limited-service brand property with a higher **system-wide** ADR. Hotel owners who seek to maximize their ROI must select a brand that is both well managed and appropriate for the travelers to which the hotel is marketed.

LODGING LANGUAGE

System-wide: The term used to describe a characteristic of all hotels within a single brand. Used, for example, in: "Last year, the system-wide ADR for our brand was $99.50."

- ***The quality and experience of the brand managers.*** Brand management, like hotel management, is complex. Brand managers who are experienced in their work will operate the brand better than those who are not. In addition, brand managers who are experienced can show the hotel's owners a track record of their success (or failure).

  It is important to recognize that, despite franchisor claims to the contrary, the relationship between a franchisor and a franchisee is not a true partnership because the brand and its managers are not financially responsible for any losses incurred by the hotel. In fact, no brand available today bases the fees it collects on the profits achieved by its franchisees. Fees, instead, are based upon achieved revenue. As a result, it is the hotel owners, not the brand managers, who bear the financial risk of poor brand management. This makes it critical for the brand managers to be experienced and talented and to demonstrate great integrity in dealings with their franchisees.
- ***The amount of fees paid to the franchisor.*** Far too many hotel owners, when evaluating alternative franchisors, focus only on the fees the hotel will pay to the brand. While the fees paid to a franchisor are certainly one important factor to be considered, they are not the only factor, nor even the most important. Nearly all hotel owners feel that the franchise fees they pay are too high; conversely, nearly all franchisors feel that what their franchisees receive in exchange for their fee payments is a great value to the hotel. In fact, the fees paid to a franchisor are a negotiable part of the franchise arrangement and should be considered seriously only after the hotel owner has narrowed down the list of potential franchisors to those that meet other selection factors.
- ***Direction of the brand.*** By far the most important factor in the long-term success of the franchisor/franchise relationship is the future direction of the brand. Obviously, it is impossible to predict the future, yet knowing how the public is likely to perceive a brand in 5, 10, or 20 years is very important when signing a franchise agreement for the same number of years. Hoteliers can detect clues to the future success of the brand if they examine:
  - The number of hotels currently operating under the brand name
  - The percentage of hotels that have elected to leave the brand in each of the past five years
  - The number of new properties currently being built under the brand's name
  - The number of existing hotels converting to the brand (if conversions are allowed)
  - The ADR trend for the last five years in comparison to the ADR trend for other hotels with which the brand competes
  - The occupancy rate trend for the last five years in comparison to the occupancy rate trend for hotels with which the brand competes
  - The percentage of total hotel room revenue contributed by the brand's reservation system and the percentage of hotels within the brand that achieve the average rate of contribution

Franchise Agreements

When a hotel owner decides to affiliate with a brand, the hotel owner and the brand managers sign a **franchise agreement**.

LODGING LANGUAGE

Franchise agreement: A legal contract between a hotel's owners (the franchisee) and the brand managers (the franchisor) that describes the duties and responsibilities of each in the franchise relationship.

Unlike the practice in some other franchise industries, the majority of hotel brand managers (franchisors) do not operate hotels. They operate franchise companies. Hotel owners (the franchisees) are the operating entities in nearly all hotel franchise relationships. This is especially true of limited-service hotels. The publicly traded Choice Hotels International (NYSE:CHH), for example, is one of the lodging industry's largest franchisors. It franchises more than 6,000 hotels under the Comfort Inn, Comfort Suites, Quality, Sleep Inn, Clarion, Cambria Suites, MainStay Suites, Suburban Extended Stay, EconoLodge, Rodeway Inn, and the Ascend Collection brands, yet it operates none of its own hotels. Its revenue is derived from franchisor fees, not hotel operating profits.

With the ownership of a hotel vested in one business entity and the responsibility for brand management the responsibility of another business entity, it is not surprising that conflict can arise between the hotel's owners and the brand managers. For example, assume that the managers of a specific brand decide that the exterior building signage identifying the brand to the traveling public has become dated and is in need of modernization. The brand managers may have the authority to require franchisees to update their hotel signage. The owners, however, may resist the change because of the significant purchase and installation costs they will incur replacing signs that are in perfectly good working order even if they are "dated" in the opinion of the brand's managers. In fact, the hotel owners may disagree with the brand managers about this and numerous other operating issues.

Conflicts between brand managers and owners are sometimes based on honest disagreements about how to best promote the brand and the best interests of each party. Unfortunately, sometimes franchisors have been known to promote their own interests more than those of their franchisees. Unlike what has happened in some other industries, the history of hotel franchising does not include widespread cases of franchisor fraud or deception. Nonetheless, hotel franchise relationships are subject to the same federal and state laws that protect franchisees from dishonest franchisors in all industries. The most important franchise-related law is the one enforced by the **Federal Trade Commission (FTC)**.

LODGING LANGUAGE

Federal Trade Commission (FTC): Government agency that enforces federal antitrust and consumer protection laws. It also seeks to ensure that the nation's business markets function competitively and are free of undue restrictions caused by acts or practices that are unfair or deceptive.

To ensure fairness in franchising, the FTC, in 1979, issued regulations with the full force of federal law. This set of laws is titled "Disclosure Requirements and Prohibitions Concerning Franchising and Business Opportunity Ventures." Commonly referred to as the "Franchise Rule," it spells out the obligations of franchisors when they attempt to sell franchises to potential franchisees.

Essentially, the Franchise Rule requires that franchisors:

- Supply potential franchisees with a disclosure document at the first face-to-face meeting or 10 business days before any money is paid by the franchisee to the franchisor, whichever is earlier
- Provide evidence, in writing, of any profit forecasts made by the franchisor

LODGING ONLINE

To review the entire Franchise Rule developed by the FTC and to learn about the requirements placed upon those who sell franchises, go to: www.ftc.gov/bcp/franchise/16cfr436.shtm

- Disclose the number and percentage of franchisees achieving the profit levels advertised in any promotional ads that include profit claims
- Provide potential franchisees with copies of the basic franchise agreement used by the franchisor
- Refund promptly any deposit monies legally due to potential franchisees that elect not to sign a franchise agreement with the franchisor
- Not make claims orally or in writing that conflict with the written disclosure documents provided to the franchisee

In addition to federal laws and regulations, most states have franchise investment laws that require franchisors to provide a presale disclosure document known as a **Franchise Offering Circular (FOC)** to potential franchisees.

LODGING LANGUAGE

Franchise Offering Circular (FOC): Franchise disclosure document prepared by a franchisor and registered and filed with the state governmental agency responsible for administering franchise relationships.

These states prohibit the sale of a franchise inside their borders until the franchisor's FOC has been filed with the proper state authorities. Despite their disclosure requirements, neither the FTC nor the states verify the accuracy of the information in the disclosure documents. Verification of a franchisor's claims is the responsibility of the buyer (franchisee). For example, a hotel franchise company can claim that its franchisees make, on average, a 10 percent annual profit. This claim will *not* be verified as accurate by either the FTC or the state in which the franchisor files an FOC. Thus, owners considering a franchise should seek verification of any item in the FOC that is questionable prior to signing a franchise agreement.

Despite the relatively good relationships between franchisors and franchisees in the hotel industry, some owners feel that franchisors have too much power to set **brand standards** and to control the terms and conditions of the franchise agreements.

LODGING LANGUAGE

Brand Standard: A hotel service or feature that must be offered by any property entering or remaining in a specific hotel brand. Used, for example, in: "*The franchisor has determined that free wireless Internet access in all guest rooms will become a new brand standard effective on January 1st. next year.*"

LODGING ONLINE

Owners of hotels can learn a great deal about buying and operating a franchise by joining the International Franchise Association (IFA). To review the type of information this association provides to its members, go to:

www.franchise.org/

LODGING ONLINE

The Asian American Hotel Owners Association (AAHOA) has been at the forefront of promoting fairness in hotel franchising. Its associate members interact with many brand-management companies. To learn more about AAHOA and to review its 12 Points of Fair Franchising, go to:

www.aahoa.com

When you arrive, click on "Advocacy" to review the 12 Points of Fair Franchising.

ALL IN A DAY'S WORK 2.3

THE SITUATION

"We had to make the change," said Jim Pratt to Andrew Haywood. "Today's business traveler is demanding it." Jim was one of the brand managers for the franchise company that Andrew had affiliated with when he purchased his first hotel.

"If I had known about this before, I might have chosen a different franchise company. This change will cost me thousands of dollars!" replied Andrew.

The two men were discussing the franchisor's recent decision to mandate that all rooms in the brand, and all of the rooms in Andrew's hotel, would become nonsmoking effective January 1st.

A RESPONSE

In nearly all cases, franchise agreements give brand managers the right to modify brand standards as they see fit. In most cases, significant brand standard changes will be discussed in great detail with franchisees prior to implementation. It is unlikely, however, that any brand standard change proposed by a franchisor would be supported by every one of a brand's franchisees. In this case, despite the owner's objections, the hotel will, in fact, be required to comply with the new standard.

Groups of outspoken owners, led chiefly by the **Asian American Hotel Owner's Association (AAHOA)**, have recently proposed, and actively campaigned for, fundamental changes in the basic franchise agreements that have long been in use in the lodging industry. The proposed changes seek to give hotel owners more control over the content of franchise agreements and a more equal say in the operation of their hotels.

LODGING LANGUAGE

Asian American Hotel Owners Association (AAHOA): An association of hotel owners who, through an exchange of ideas, seek to promote professionalism and excellence in hotel ownership.

Franchise agreements are complex as well as increasingly important. Relatively few independently operated hotels can survive without a nationally recognized brand name. As a result, owners, management companies, and franchisors must all understand their roles in the hotel franchising environment and work together for the good of guests and the hotel industry.

OWNERSHIP AND MANAGEMENT ALTERNATIVES

As you have learned, owners of hotels may operate the properties themselves, hire a management company to operate them, and then, regardless of that decision, may elect to affiliate or not to affiliate with a hotel brand. Owners of both large and small hotels

Rank	Hotel	City/ Location	Number of Rooms
1.	First World Hotel	Malaysia	6,118
2.	MGM Grand	Las Vegas	5,690
3.	Luxor	Las Vegas	4,408
4.	Mandalay Bay (Inc. TheHotel)	Las Vegas	4,341
5.	The Venetian	Las Vegas	4,027
6.	Excalibur	Las Vegas	4,008
7.	Bellagio	Las Vegas	3,993
8.	Circus Circus	Las Vegas	3,774
9.	Planet Hollywood	Las Vegas	3,697
10.	Shinagawa Prince Hotel Tokyo	Tokyo	3,680

FIGURE 2.2 Ten of the World's Largest Hotels[1]

must make these same decisions. Figure 2.2 lists 10 of the world's largest hotels. Note that some are independent (not affiliated with a franchise brand) and others have an affiliation. Note also that several of the world's largest hotels are in Las Vegas, a very popular destination for leisure travelers and a major convention center.

Hotel investors have many options when considering the operation of the properties they own. This is true because there are a variety of ways that hotels can be owned and managed, including:

- ***Single-unit property not affiliated with any brand.*** Some single-unit properties have been in business for many years, are extremely successful, and may be the best-known hotel in their community or area. In such cases, the hotel's owner may choose to operate as a completely independent property. This situation, however, is fairly uncommon in the United States. Single-unit properties have been historically capturing an ever-smaller **market share** in the lodging industry nationwide.

LODGING LANGUAGE

Market share: The percentage of a total market (typically measured in dollars spent) captured by a property. For example, a hotel generating $200,000 in guest room rental in a market where travelers spend $1,000,000 per year would have a 20 percent market share ($200,000/ $1,000,000 = 20%).

- ***Single-unit properties affiliated with a brand.*** Individually owned properties that are part of a hotel chain are the most common arrangement in the United States today. American-based hotel brands are expanding rapidly internationally. Brand affiliation, whether international, nationwide, regional, or located within an even smaller area, is successful because of name recognition, and because it is often easier to obtain financing for businesses affiliated with a brand.

LODGING ONLINE

The Independent Hotel in Philadelphia, PA, is an excellent example of a successful single-unit hotel that has elected not to affiliate with a brand. To learn about this unique property, go to:

www.theindependenthotel.com/

Do you think potential guests visiting this hotel's Web site would be concerned that it is not affiliated with a known hotel brand?

LODGING ONLINE

While brands managed by U.S. companies such as Marriott and Hilton are most familiar to Americans, there are also very large brands operated by non-U.S. companies. One of the largest of these manages the Pullman, Ibis, Sofitel, All-Seasons, and Novotel brands among several others. To see the Web site of Accor, the French company that owns these brands, go to:

www.accor.com/en.html

When you arrive, click on "Our Hotels" to review a list of their currently managed brands.

Of course, some owners own more than one hotel. When they do, they have a variety of options available to them. These include:

- ***Multiunit properties affiliated with the same brand.*** Some owners own several hotels and affiliate them all with the same brand or the same franchisor. This often makes operating them easier because the brand's managers are well known to the owner. In a large city, an individual owner could operate two or more hotels, within the same brand, and in fairly close proximity to each other. In a smaller city, of course, doing so would run the risk of the two properties competing directly for the same type of guest. In many cases, this model works well for owners who own multiple properties in multiple cities.
- ***Multiunit properties affiliated with different brands.*** Some multiproperty owners elect to affiliate with several brands. Sometimes they do this because they own more than one hotel in a market area and feel that two hotels with the same brand would not be best. In other cases, the owners may have some limited-service and some full-service hotels, and the same brand name would not fit both types of properties equally well.
- ***Multiunit properties operated by a management company or the brand.*** You have learned that management companies will, for a fee, operate a hotel for an owner. Some brands will also, for a fee, offer management services to hotel owners.
- ***Single or multiunit properties owned by the brand.*** Some brands do actually own some of their own hotels. Independent (not owned by the brand) ownership and affiliation with a brand is, by far, however, the most common hotel arrangement in the United States.

Owners must decide whether their individual hotels will be operated as an independent or a franchise hotel.

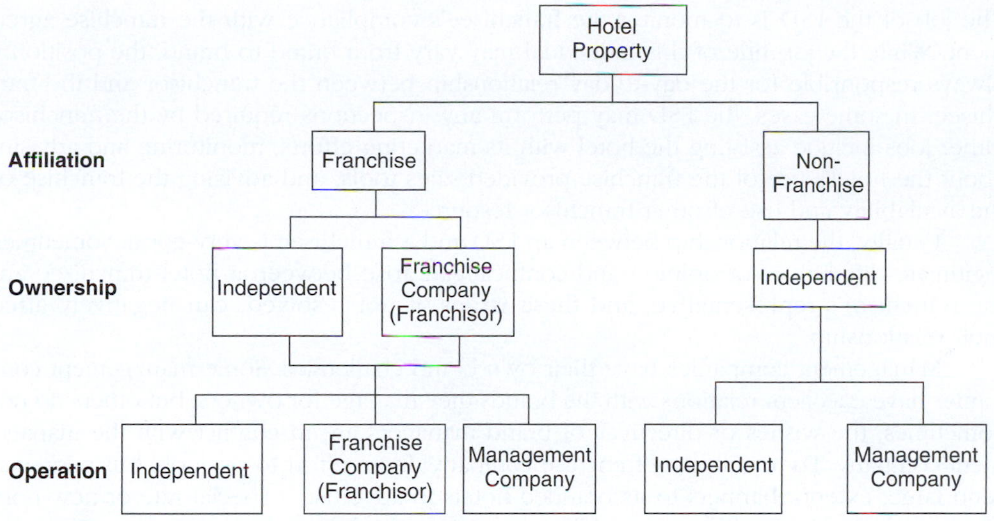

FIGURE 2.3 Hotel Ownership/Management Alternatives

Figure 2.3 is a summary of the possible ownership/management arrangements available to hotel owners. It confirms that the ownership/management issues of a hotel can be complex because of the many possible operating alternatives available to hotel owners.

OWNERSHIP AND OPERATIONAL CHALLENGES

Understanding the specific ownership, management, and affiliation of a hotel is critical to understanding the decision-making involved in operating it. For example, in a hotel operated by a management company, the business interests of hotel's owners may sometimes conflict with the business interests of the management company. Consider the situation in which a contract for managing a hotel is up for renewal. Most neutral observers would maintain that it is in the best interest of the hotel's owners to negotiate as short a contract length as possible and one that holds the management company responsible for the financial results they achieve. The same observers would very likely state that it is in the best interest of the management company to negotiate as long a contract as possible and one that holds the hotel's owners, not the management company, financially responsible in the event that hotel operating performance does not meet anticipated levels. Likewise, hotel owners like to keep the fees they pay management companies low while the management company, in most cases, would prefer higher fees.

It is a simple fact that hotel owners often find themselves in conflict or disagreement with brand managers about how to best operate the brand, as well as how to operate the individual hotels that make up the brand. Assume, for example, that the brand managers for a hotel have, as a brand standard, established breakfast hours for the hotel's complimentary continental breakfast to be from 6:00 a.m. to 9:00 a.m.

A particular hotel owner, however, may prefer to begin the breakfast at 7:00 a.m., rather than 6:00 a.m. on weekends to reduce labor costs. The change in starting times would violate the brand standard. When owners violate or ignore brand standards, the resulting influence on the hotel's relationship with the brand can be very negative and damaging.

In most cases, a hotel owner's relationship with a brand is developed with the brand's **franchise service director (FSD)**.

LODGING LANGUAGE

Franchise Services Director (FSD): the representative of a franchise brand who interacts directly with a hotel franchisee. Different brands may title this important position somewhat differently, but each will have a comparable position.

The job of the FSD is to monitor the franchisee's compliance with the franchise agreement. While the job title of this individual may vary from brand to brand, the position is always responsible for the day-to-day relationship between the franchisor and the franchisee. In some cases, the FSD may perform any inspections required by the franchisor. Other jobs include assisting the hotel with its marketing efforts, monitoring and advising about the hotel's use of the franchise-provided sales tools, and advising the franchise on the availability and use of other franchisor resources.

Usually, the relationship between an FSD and a franchisee is very good. Sometimes, legitimate differences of opinion and conflicts can arise between a hotel franchisee and the franchisor's representative, and these issues, if not resolved, can negatively affect their relationship.

Management companies have their own brand challenges. Some management companies have excellent relations with the brands they manage for owners, but others do not. Sometimes, the wishes or directives of brand managers are in conflict with the management company. For example, a franchise company, in an effort to promote business, may send large, exterior banners to its branded hotels to advertise a special rate or new hotel feature. Obviously, the brand would like these signs displayed on the property. The management company's sales philosophy, however, may not include hanging exterior banners because it believes that they cheapen the image of the hotel. As a result, the banners are not displayed. It is likely that the FSD, upon learning the banners are not used, will see the management company as acting in a way that hurts the hotel while the management company would feel the same way about the brand's directive that the banner be displayed.

Hotel owners, management companies, and franchisors must all work together to further the hotel industry. There are some areas of their relationship where hotel owners and brand managers as well as owners and management companies can honestly disagree about what is fair, what is best to do, or what has, in fact, been contractually agreed to. Despite some areas of conflict, however, the relationships developed among these three major groups strongly and favorably affect today's lodging industry as well as the hoteliers working in it.

Lodging Language

Return on Investment (ROI)
Profit
Depreciation
Appreciation
Owner/Operator
General Manager (GM)
Management Company
Depressed Market
Repossession
First-tier
Second-tier
Liable
Management Contract
Buy-out
Franchise
Franchisor
Franchisee
Brand
Chain
Conversion
System-wide
Franchise Agreement
Federal Trade Commission (FTC)
Franchise Offering circular (FOC)
Brand Standard
Asian American Hotel Owners Association (AAHOA)
Market Share
Franchise Service Director (FSD)

For Discussion

1. Hotel investors seek strong ROIs through increases in the value of their hotel's real estate, operating profits, or both. What factors in a geographic area do you think make the real estate value of hotels increase or decrease?
2. What career advancement advantages might a GM who works for a management company have, compared to a GM working for an individual hotel owner? What advantages might the GM gain by working for an individual hotel investor?
3. Not all hotel owners enter into franchise agreements. Why do you think a hotel owner might choose not to affiliate with a franchise brand?
4. Brand managers work hard to establish an image for their brand. Consider a hotel brand that is associated with rooms that sell for a high price. What factors might make a traveler want to choose that brand?
5. Brand managers for economy or budget hotels also work hard to establish their brand image. Consider a hotel brand that is associated with rooms that sell for a very low price. What factors in addition to price might make a traveler want to choose that brand?
6. Different brands enforce different brand standards. Name three brand standards that would likely vary significantly based upon the system-wide ADR of a brand.

7. What is your favorite hotel brand? Why?

8. Some lodging industry professionals feel there are now too many different brands. Explain why you do or do not agree with them.

9. Many guests believe that the brands actually own hotels, when in almost all cases they do not. How does this relationship affect the hoteliers who actually operate hotels?

10. In the past, brand names helped travelers feel confident about the quality of hotels they chose. Today, hotel Web sites provide the same type of help. Visit the Web site of one higher and one lower-priced hotel. Do you think the Internet has helped lower-cost brands compete more equally for guests? Explain your answer.

Team Activities

TEAM ACTIVITY 1

Identify the 25 hotels nearest to you. List their brand names, and identify the corporations that own those brands. How many different brands were identified? How many different corporations that own the brands were identified?

TEAM ACTIVITY 2

Many students hoping to work for first-tier management companies believe that these companies own the hotels using their names. Identify five first-tier hotels in your area or a nearby city. Find out how many of these are actually owned and operated by the first-tier management company.

[1]Compilation Sources

1. Compiled from: *Wikipedia* . [Online] 09 20, 2010. [Cited: 09 20, 2010.] http://en.wikipedia.org/wiki/List_of_largest_hotels_in_the_world#3.2C000_or_more_rooms.
2. Compiled from: Insider Viewpoint of Las Vegas. [Online] December 16, 2009. [Cited: 09 20, 2010.] http://www.insidervlv.com/hotelslargestworld.html.
3. Compiled from: *Hotelier Middle East* . [Online] ITP Publishing Group Ltd. All rights reserved. [Cited: 09 20, 2010.] http://www.hoteliermiddleeast.com/pics-7733-top-10-largest-hotels-in-the-world/0.

Chapter

3

Guest Service in the Lodging Industry

Chapter Outline

Chapter Overview

There are a wide range of organizations in the hospitality industry. Many offer lodging accommodations, and they are the focus of this book. Others offer food and beverage products. Still others are part of the recreation, leisure, or meetings segments of the industry. To be successful, all of these organizations have one thing in common: they must consistently provide quality guest service.

Lodging operations are part of the hospitality industry. A popular name for the segment of hospitality offering food and beverage products is "food services." People purchasing lodging, food and beverages consider *service* to be a very important element in the experience they are buying. At its most basic level, every hospitality organization must focus on providing its guests with friendly and accommodating service. It is more often the service, not the product (food, beverage, or sleeping room), that most influences guests' perceptions about their experience and their interest in returning to the property or to another property in the chain.

How would you treat a special friend or a relative whom you invite into your home for a meal? The answer to this question can help to define how guests visiting a lodging operation should be treated. After all, the earliest travelers were offered meals and a safe night's rest by families living near trade routes and were invited into the family's home for today's equivalent of lodging and food services.

It is true that guests in your home would not be presented with a bill covering the charges at the end of their visit. By contrast, those visiting a hotel must pay for the products and services they receive. However, the policies and procedures, the training activities, and the basic vision and mission of the organization can be developed with an emphasis on serving guests just as you would host your friends and family.

Customers are guests. Do the terms "customer" and "guest" mean the same thing? Perhaps they do in a dictionary; however, in the real world of hospitality, the manager who treats a visitor as a guest will likely be more successful than competitors treating the visitor merely as a customer.

In this chapter, we will emphasize the principle that a service philosophy is important, and, as is true in so many other areas of lodging management, that "it all begins with the manager." We will define quality, review how it impacts the service provided by a hotel, and discuss what must be done to develop quality as a standard and to then keep that standard enforced.

A second major focus of the chapter will review the concept of "moments of truth," and we will discuss the procedures needed to maintain the vision that service must be an ongoing priority. A third major emphasis of the chapter focuses directly on employees. You will learn about your employees' role in delivering guest service and see that they are, indeed, service professionals. Finally, we will explain benchmarking, using, as an example, the Ritz-Carlton Hotel Company.

Chapter Objectives

1. To define quality and review its impact upon the level of service provided by a lodging property.
2. To describe the concept of "moments of truth" in guest service.
3. To explain the important role of employees in consistently delivering guest service.
4. To explain the tactics managers use to help ensure guests receive quality service.
5. To present the basic guest service philosophy of the Ritz-Carlton Hotel Company.

THE IMPORTANCE OF QUALITY SERVICE IN LODGING

The concept of **quality** is widely discussed in the world of hospitality management. Unfortunately, it is much easier to talk about quality than to effectively implement and consistently deliver it in a hospitality operation.

LODGING LANGUAGE

Quality: The consistent delivery of products and services according to expected standards.

In this book, quality is defined as "the consistent delivery of products and services according to expected standards." Note that guest **service**—the topic of this chapter—is specifically noted in the definition.

LODGING LANGUAGE

Service (guest): The process of helping guests by addressing their wants and needs with respect and dignity and in a timely manner.

This is important because the guest renting a room at a hotel or purchasing a meal at the hotel's restaurant is buying, and wants to receive, an anticipated standard of service in exchange for the payment. Increasingly, guests are willing to pay more when they visit hospitality properties offering service that meets or exceeds their service expectations. The level of service quality is an important factor in the experience that guests receive during their visits to lodging operations.

Service Concerns

Our definition of service focuses on basic concerns, and we must emphasize two important points. First, service is not the same as servility (to assist someone who is of a better social class). The Ritz-Carlton Hotel Company, which will be discussed later in this chapter, emphasizes this point in an exceptional way with its corporate mantra stating that all its employees are "Ladies and Gentlemen Serving Ladies and Gentlemen." This company knows that the best hospitality employees are those who genuinely enjoy working with others on their team and helping guests. They do so with respect and dignity.

Second, the definition of service emphasizes helping guests by addressing their wants and needs. What do guests want? A business traveler person and a family on vacation are two very different types of hotel guests, but at the most fundamental level, they want the same things. Among these basics are a clean room in a safe environment and courteous, respectful treatment from the property's staff members.

All lodging properties must, at the very least, meet these basic expectations for a price that represents **value** in the eyes of its guests. Then, as guest expectations increase (e.g., the desire for more luxurious guestrooms and for more personalized service that may require a greater **employee-to-guest ratio**), the hotel can increase its prices to meet these higher-level expectations.

LODGING LANGUAGE

Value: The relationship between price paid and the quality of the products and services received.

Employee-to-guest ratio: The number of employees relative to the number of guests. In the lodging industry, this is typically expressed in terms of employees per room; a 500-room luxury, full-service property may have 500 employees: a 1:1 employee-to-guest ratio. A 100-room limited-service property may have 25 employees: a 1:4 employee-to-guest ratio.

If you were a guest in a hotel, would you want to be checked into a dirty room (as a result of the actions and inactions of management and staff who don't really care)? Would you want to be "greeted" by a front desk clerk making a personal telephone call while you waited to check in? Would you want to be told that problems in your room, which could have been avoided (e.g., a poorly functioning television or inoperable heating and cooling unit), can't be fixed until tomorrow, and there are no other rooms available to which you can be moved? You would answer these questions with a No! Guests will answer the questions exactly the same way; will probably not return to the property; and today, may be quick to use the Internet to post comments that tell their friends, family, and many more about their unacceptable visit.

Experienced hoteliers know that quality service is critical to success, and, fortunately for lodging professionals, its delivery involves an attitude and philosophy that is within their control.

Service Expectations

In the preceding section, we asked whether you would be pleased if basic service concerns were not addressed during your visit to a hotel. Your response was probably no, and you realized that hotel guests encountering these levels of service would likewise be displeased.

It is often helpful to think about your own service expectations and use them to plan service experiences and to evaluate service procedures. Consider the guest check-in process. Guests will have formed some impressions about the property before they arrive to get their room. For example, they will have seen the building's exterior and its lobby or registration area, and they may have had contact with representatives of the organization when reservations were made. However, first impressions about the guest service they will receive during their stay are formed during the check-in process. If you were an arriving guest, what would you want to occur during your own check-in? Your responses probably include:

- Minimal waiting time to check-in
- A friendly welcome, including eye contact, a smile, and acknowledgment of your name (e.g., "Good afternoon. Welcome to our hotel, Ms. Gonzalez.")
- Accurate information about your reservation and the price you will pay for your room
- The proper type of room immediately available for you
- Answers to your questions about the hotel and its services
- Directions to your room

Not surprisingly, your guests are likely to have the same expectations. Your own service desires can help you establish check-in procedures and implement the staff training required to check-in guests according to your own standards. Your own expectations are also likely to suggest how evaluation of check-in services should be done. That is, you can use your own expectations to determine the extent to which your own front desk staff demonstrates the desired service standards when guests check in.

AVOIDING THE COMMODITIZATION OF LODGING PRODUCTS AND SERVICES

A **commodity** is a widely available and unspecialized product that is difficult or impossible to differentiate from similar products offered by competitors. Pencils, grain, metals, and light bulbs are examples of commodity products.

LODGING LANGUAGE

Commodity: A commonly available and most often unspecialized product.

When buyers consider an item to be a commodity, the item's price becomes its most important characteristic. In such cases, lowest price means best; and as a result, downward price pressure means the providers of the commodity often struggle to maintain profitability. This is especially true when there are many providers of the commodity.

Hospitality managers routinely sell both products and services. Thus, for example, a restaurateur sells a steak (the product) and the manner in which it is cooked and served (the service). Hoteliers sell the overnight use of a room (the product) and the manner in which guests are treated during their stay (the service). In the hospitality industry, service providers who over-emphasize the *price* of the products they sell, rather than quality of service they deliver to guests, risk the commoditization of their services.

In many cases, the Internet has, because of its emphasis on room prices rather than service levels, pushed hotels toward product commoditization. It is important for hoteliers to remember, however, that quality services provide intangible benefits to buyers. The benefits are intangible because they cannot be held, touched, or even seen before they are purchased. In most cases, a service is a performance rather than a product. As a result, hoteliers face unique challenges in communicating the benefits of the services they provide guests. This communication dilemma is captured in the tongue-in-check lodging industry observation that "when their eyes are closed, all rooms look the same to our guests." Because hotel rooms within the same price range can indeed look very similar (when the guest is awake or asleep!), experienced hoteliers know they must rely on providing quality service to prevent commoditization.

To avoid product commoditization and its accompanying downward pressure on selling prices, hoteliers recognize the significant impact of service inconsistency and inseparability. Inconsistency of service simply means that differently skilled employees may provide guests different levels of service. Well-trained staff, for example, clean rooms properly, and the result will be guests who are pleased with their stays. Poorly trained staff do not clean rooms well, and the result may be very unhappy guests. Recognizing this, hoteliers strive to hire and train qualified employees so that inconsistency is eliminated.

Service inseparability refers to the tendency of guests to associate the quality of service provided with the actual person who provides it. As a result, an inattentive or rude desk clerk will be perceived by guests as providing poor guest service, while a smiling and cheerful desk clerk is perceived as providing good service—*even when the precise tasks performed by the two are similar or identical.*

Service providers should never let their products and services become commodities. Providing quality guest services by eliminating service inconsistency and recognizing the concept of inseparability helps ensure that guests will not view product and services offerings as commodities. As a lodging professional seeking to avoid commoditization of your own lodging products and services, it will be your job to ensure that when guests arrive at your property:

- They feel important
- They feel special
- They are comfortable
- If service expectations of guests have not been met, they are corrected promptly and with a positive attitude

INGREDIENTS IN A QUALITY SERVICE SYSTEM

The hospitality industry's emphasis on quality service is not just a passing fad that will go away to be replaced by the next fad. Quality service is so important that entire books have been written about quality in the hospitality industry.[1] There are six ingredients in a "recipe" that can be used to develop and implement a quality service system. These are shown in Figure 3.1.

We'll look at the "ingredients" in the recipe for quality guest service in this section.

Consider the Guests Being Served

Some lodging operations serve a narrow range of guests. Consider, for example, a small rooms-only lodging property with a strategic location at a busy interchange on an interstate highway. Most of its guests probably desire the same thing—a relatively inexpensive, safe, and clean sleeping room at a price representing a value to the traveler.

Other lodging properties may serve a more diverse range of guests. Consider, for example, an upscale restaurant in a hotel that is serving, at the same time, busy executives conducting business over dinner, a couple celebrating a wedding anniversary, a group of senior citizens enjoying their once-monthly dining-out social event, and a young couple on their first date.

What exactly do these seemingly diverse groups of diners have in common? While it is up to the hotel's management team to determine this precisely, a possible answer is: freshly prepared food delivered by servers who are attentive to their guests' unique needs in a special environment at a price that represents a value for the products purchased and the services received.

Consider two other examples of hospitality properties serving diverse guest groups. First, a downtown hotel may serve business guests during the week and other guests visiting the downtown area for shopping and social reasons during the weekend. Second, a small hotel in a tourist destination may serve numerous groups of guests depending upon the convention and group meetings in the city at that specific time. For the first three days of the week, the hotel may be occupied primarily by a senior citizens group; during the next four days of the same week, most of the guests could be attending a high school sports tournament. It is important for managers to know as much as possible about all of the guests being served. They do this by using marketing

Ingredient 1:	Consider the guests being served.
Ingredient 2:	Determine what the guests desire.
Ingredient 3:	Develop procedures to deliver what guests want.
Ingredient 4:	Train and empower staff.
Ingredient 5:	Implement revised systems.
Ingredient 6:	Evaluate and modify service delivery systems.

FIGURE 3.1 Six Components of Quality in the Hospitality Industry

[1]See, for example, John King and Ronald Cichy, *Managing for Quality in the Hospitality Industry*. (Upper Saddle River, N.J.: Pearson Education, 2006.)

Guests expect to receive professional and courteous service during their arrival and stay.

tactics (see Chapter 7) and by recognizing that basic service expectations are integral to the guests' experiences.

Determine What the Guests Desire

A questioning process is a good way to determine guests' wants and needs. Questions such as "What did you like about your visit?" and "What would make your visit more enjoyable?" can help a manager determine guests' needs. These and related questions can be asked of guests by managers as they "manage by walking around" or by a simple online questionnaire or comment card provided to guests as they check in or out.

In well-managed properties, top-level managers routinely talk with guests as they check in or out to learn anything that can be helpful about what they like and would want during their visit. Feedback from guests does not simply tell what guests want; the information helps managers evaluate service systems.

Every lodging manager has another way to collect information about the guests—by asking the hotel's employees. It is ironic but true that employees often know more about the likes and dislikes of guests than do their **supervisors** or even the property's **manager**.

LODGING LANGUAGE

Supervisor: A staff member who directs the work of line-level (nonsupervisory) employees.

Manager: A staff member who directs the work of supervisors.

Regular staff members frequently have more extensive guest contact than any other employees in the property. Consider, for example, a guest complaining to a front desk clerk about the long line at the time of check-in or a food server receiving compliments (or complaints!) about the food in the hotel's dining room. When managers want to know about what guests desire, one good way to find out is to simply ask the employees who provide products and services to them.

Develop Procedures to Deliver What Guests Want

After the types of guests to be served, and their desires are known, the next ingredient in a quality service system is to develop procedures that will consistently deliver what guests want. Two of the best ways to make procedures more guest-friendly are to **benchmark** and to utilize **cross-functional teams** of employees.

LODGING ONLINE

Hoteliers can learn much about what guests think about their property by utilizing the services of a shopping service. To learn what a shopping service (also called "mystery shopper") does, and to see a sample of a great shopper's report form, go to:

www.satisfactionservicesinc.com/

When you arrive, click on "On Services." Also, click on "Sample Reports" then "Hotel Evaluation" to note the information gathered about many aspects of a guest's stay at the hotel.

Are there additional aspects that you think are important and should be included?

LODGING LANGUAGE

Benchmark: The search for best practices and an understanding about how they are achieved in efforts to determine how well a hospitality organization is doing.

Cross-functional teams: A group of employees from each department within the hospitality operation who work together to resolve operating problems.

Benchmarking is the process of understanding exactly how your property does something and, additionally, determining how it is done by your competition. If, for example, guests desire fast check-in, as most guests do, it is important to know your property's current procedures to speed up the check-in process and, as well, to determine what other properties do to minimize guest check-in times. Studying available industry training resources, discussions with other hoteliers at professional meetings, reviewing articles in trade magazines, and careful observation when visiting other properties are among the benchmarking tactics that can be used.

Experienced lodging managers know the benefits of asking employees for advice about ways to improve work methods. Cross-functional teams are made up of staff members from each area in the hotel who meet, brainstorm, and consider ways to improve work methods. This contrasts with the more traditional alternative of utilizing only employees from the same department to address a problem. The disadvantage of having only members of the same department meet is illustrated by a front office staff addressing a slow check-in problem and concluding that the problem doesn't rest with them because it is caused by the housekeepers who don't get rooms ready for reuse quickly enough. Alternatively, if employees from the front office, housekeeping, and even maintenance areas address the problem, all areas can work together to solve the problem. For example, a team may determine that the check-in process is slowed by guests asking about meeting room locations. A large map posted near the check-in area and/or small maps given to guests when they check in may reduce the need for busy front desk clerks to provide this detailed and time-consuming information.

Train and Empower Staff

Hotel employees are critical to the consistent delivery of quality service. When new procedures are implemented to better meet the guests' service expectations, employees must learn new work methods. New or additional tools or equipment may also be necessary. After staff members are trained in revised work tasks, they can also be given the opportunity to make decisions about the unique needs of the guests they are helping. **Empowerment** is the act of granting authority to employees to make key decisions.

LODGING LANGUAGE

Empowerment: The act of granting authority to employees to make key decisions within their areas of responsibility.

For example, service employees have a responsibility to please guests. Empowered staff members are allowed to make decisions about how this is to be done as they interact with guests with differing wants, needs, and expectations.

Before staff members can be empowered, they must be trained and provided with the tools and other resources needed to do their jobs. They must also be well aware that their primary responsibility is to serve the guests. Consider, for example, a limited-service property whose complimentary breakfast ends at 10:00 a.m. At 2:30 p.m. a couple with a young child check in to the hotel, and a parent asks if the child can have a glass of milk. If this first service request is answered by the front desk clerk with the comment, *"I'm sorry; we have no food service available after 10:00 in the morning"* (in other words, No!), the guest's first request for special service has been denied.

Contrast the above situation with this possible response: *"I'll check to see if we have a carton of milk in our breakfast area. I am pretty sure we do, and I will get it for you now. Or we can bring it to your room if you would prefer that."* This is the response of a front desk clerk who is empowered to make reasonable decisions that please the guests. In this situation, an inexpensive carton of milk is all that it will cost the hotel to begin delivering on its service promise. This, in turn, can yield a satisfied guest who knows that the hotel staff genuinely wants to help, commoditization of product is avoided, and the guest will return frequently to the property and to other units of the chain and tell others about the great service at the property.

Implement Revised Systems

To undertsand the way managers can work together to revise and improve operating procedures, assume a hotel has received numerous guest complaints about room cleanliness. The hotel manager and the housekeepers may work together to develop improved room-cleaning procedures. The new work methods could be tried in selected rooms to test and further refine the more guest-friendly processes before they are rolled out to the entire property. Here's an example: Hotel guests desire a clean room, preferably one that looks as if they are the first person to ever sleep in it. In the traditional housekeeping model, a guest room is cleaned by a single housekeeper. Then, after the room is cleaned, it may be checked by a housekeeping supervisor to make sure that it has been properly prepared for the next guest. What if, instead, a cross-functional team determined that two housekeepers could clean a guest room together and do an effective self-inspection at the end of the cleaning process?

The manager might decide to try this approach and work with the two-person teams and the head housekeeper to study and plan how to do it. Then the new method could be used for several days with two housekeepers in rooms on a single floor or wing of the hotel. After close evaluation, the plan might then be expanded to other teams of housekeepers cleaning other rooms, including any needed changes made to the procedure as the process is implemented.

Evaluate and Modify Service Delivery Systems

Over time, guest preferences are likely to change. In addition, technologies will evolve, and new and improved work methods may become useful. These can impact what guests desire and what products and services can be most effectively delivered. Problems can also arise in service delivery systems. All these events provide examples of the need to evaluate and, if necessary, modify procedures in current use.

Hotel managers cannot address problems unless they are aware of them. While this seems obvious, some hoteliers do not take advantage of a simple customer feedback system. It is much easier to retain existing guests than to continually find new ones. Comment card systems can address the concerns of current guests with the goal of identifying problems and resolving them (hopefully while the guest is still at the property!)

Hotels increasingly provide online comment cards for use by guests who prefer to supply their e-mail addresses and respond in that way. As well, hard copy comment cards may be placed in each guest room or presented to guests at check-in (or check-out). Regardless of the method used, information such as that found in Figure 3.2 (Sample Guest Comment Card) is extremely helpful in ensuring that quality guest service is delivered consistently.

What Do You Think about Our Hotel?

Your time is very important and so are your thoughts about your stay at our hotel. We would sincerely appreciate knowing your thoughts about your visit. Will you please complete this survey and place it in the Guest Comments box at the front desk (or e-mail it to us)? Thank You!

While You Are Here

We want you to be 100% satisfied about every experience you have during your visit. If there is anything we can do, please let us know. If you experience any problem, ***we guarantee we will correct it***. Please call the hotel operator or contact our Front Desk and tell our staff what we can do to make your stay with us more enjoyable.

We are committed to making your visit enjoyable and hassle-free; please tell us how to do so.

Welcome and Thank You!

FIGURE 3.2a Guest Comment Card (front/ outside)

	Exceeded Expectations	Met Expectations	Missed Expectations
Front Desk Staff	❑	❑	❑
Housekeeping Staff	❑	❑	❑
Restaurant/Lounge Staff	❑	❑	❑
Your Guest Room	❑	❑	❑
Restaurant and Lounges	❑	❑	❑

During your visit, did you have any problems? ❑ Yes ❑ No

If so, please tell us about them . . .

____

____

____

Was the difficulty reported?
❑ Yes ❑ No

To whom did you report it? ______________

____

Was it resolved to your complete satisfaction?
❑ Yes ❑ No

If not, what could we have done differently to satisfy you?

____

____

Overall, did we exceed your expectations?
❑ Yes ❑ No

If not, what could we have done better?

____

____

____

If you visited this area again, would you select our hotel?
❑ Yes ❑ No ❑ Undecided

How many times have you stayed at our hotel during the last year? ______________

Date of this stay? ______________

Your Room Number: ______________

Name: ______________

Address: ______________

____

City: ______________

State: ____________ Zip: ____________

Telephone: ______________

E-mail: ______________

Would you like to be contacted about promotional offers? ❑ Yes ❑ No

Other Comments:

____

____

____

____

Was any specific employee(s) especially helpful to you? ❑ Yes ❑ No
If so, who: ______________

Thank you for helping us to serve you better.

FIGURE 3.2b Guest Comment Card (reverse/ inside)

Many guests desire and use amenities, such as a pool or meeting space, offered by hotels.

Note that the sample comment card asks guests to notify hotel staff about problems so that they can be corrected before the guests depart. This is done because the hotel manager wants the guests to know about the hotel's sincere interest in addressing problems to their satisfaction. Prompt attention to problems dramatically increases the likelihood of **repeat business**.

LODGING LANGUAGE

Repeat business: Guests who return to the property for additional visits after their first visit.

Increasingly, hoteliers are using advanced technology to obtain guest comments and suggestions. In-room surveys using the television set are just one example. Creative cell phone apps are another. Online surveys sent to guests' e-mail addresses after their stay are another. Information generated by these methods enables managers to quickly and accurately determine guest opinions. Continually monitoring guest reviews and comments on consumer generated media sites such as TripAdvisor.com, Facebook, My Space, and others also help managers better understand what their guests have experienced during their stays.

Careful analysis of guest feedback helps to identify problems. Perhaps resolution will involve a new policy, training, purchase of tools or equipment, and/or changes in operating procedures. Perhaps the manager alone or all of the property managers working together will decide what to do and other people on the team may be asked for advice. Will a cross-functional team be needed for careful study and analysis? An effective hotelier will know the best approach to address the problem. Then, as problems are researched, no matter how small they may appear to be, the property will have taken another step on its journey toward consistently meeting required quality standards.

As you have learned, the process of maintaining quality guest service is cyclical. It is driven by changes in (a) the guests being served, (b) their wants and needs, and (c) the work methods implemented to yield products/services meeting quality standards desired by the guests.

SERVICE AND "MOMENTS OF TRUTH"

"Moments of truth" are opportunities for guests to form an impression about a lodging organization. While a moment of truth may involve an employee (e.g., excellent or rude service), there need not be any human interaction. Consider, for example, the negative impressions formed by a guest who has to enter a hotel by first walking through a trash-

LODGING ONLINE

Guests increasingly share their travel experiences on social network sites. TripAdvisor is the largest site devoted to the sharing of travel experiences. Posting reviews on the site is free to the reviewer. The Web site is financially supported by advertisers. To see examples of the type of reviews posted, go to:

www.tripadvisor.com/

When you arrive, enter the name of a hotel you have used in the past or hope to visit in the future.

What should managers of lodging facilities do when they discover negative reviews of their properties have been posted online?

littered parking lot. Contrast this with the positive first impression created by the large vase of fresh, beautiful flowers at the check-in desk. Consider also the **wow factor** when one of these fresh flower stems is given to the guest as part of the registration process!

LODGING LANGUAGE

Moments of Truth: Any (and every) time a guest has an opportunity to form an impression about the hospitality organization. Moments of truth can be positive or negative.

Wow Factor: The feeling guests have when they experience an unanticipated and positive "extra" as they interact with a hospitality operation.

THE EVOLUTION OF SERVICE

Today's requirements for quality service have evolved from a past emphasis on commodities/products and are being incorporated into something that guests increasingly expect: an experience. This shift in expectations can be illustrated using something very basic: a place to sleep.

As seen above, long ago a traveler slept on a blanket on the ground or in a bed in a house along the road. "Yesterday" guests had access to a private room in a lodging property. "Today" the guest expects friendly service from the hotel's staff. In the future, lodging guests will enjoy an "experience." They will receive great service and will stay in a room which technology enables them to "design" for themselves. Do they want a certain "view" from the windows or the world's most famous paintings on the wall? (Plasma screen technology can provide them.) Do they want firm or soft pillows or black or blue ink in their pens? What foods do they want to eat in the morning? This personal preference information will be available, and hotel staff will have their preferences ready for them at check-in time.

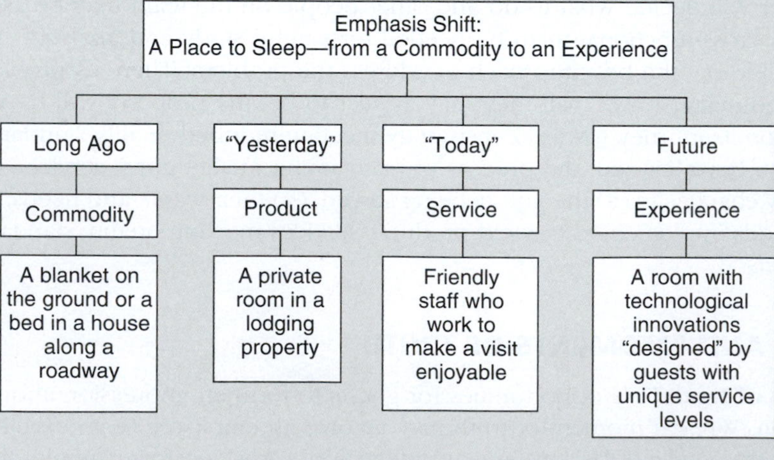

Hoteliers want their guests to have positive moments of truth. These occur through planning (e.g., an efficient guest check-in process), but they can also be spontaneous, such as those that occur when an empowered staff member pleases a guest who has made an out-of-the-ordinary request. Unfortunately, negative moments of truth can occur in some hotels. Many of these can be anticipated. For example, a hotel manager who permits housekeepers to spend only a short amount of time cleaning each room in order to reduce labor costs should not be surprised about guest room cleanliness complaints. Others are unanticipated. Consider, for example, a guest's reactions to a front desk clerk after a wake-up call is received one hour later than expected.

Lodging managers plan many aspects of a guest's experience at their properties. Through an organized planning process, they have a system in place for guest reservations and registration, for luggage transport to the room, for guest security and safety while guests are on-site, for guest check-out, and for other guest/property interactions. However, guests in these managers' hotels will probably encounter (sometimes by chance alone) other moments of truth that can be favorable or unfavorable and, in the process, influence their total perception of the visit. **Word of mouth advertising** occurs when previous guests tell others in person or via the Internet (word of mouse!) about their experiences during a visit to the property. Unfortunately, guests with negative impressions after a visit are likely to tell many more people about their problems than are guests who have just enjoyed a pleasing visit. To make matters even worse, readers will pay closer attention to negative comments posted online than they will to positive comments.

LODGING LANGUAGE

Word of Mouth Advertising: The favorable or unfavorable comments made when previous guests of a hospitality operation tell others about their experiences.

Our examination thus far shows that the simple definition of "quality" at the beginning of this chapter (i.e., the consistent delivery of products and services according to expected standards) can, in fact, be very difficult to attain. For example, if a lodging property serves 125 guests each day for several years, some guest-related problems are to likely occur re-

MANAGING THE MOMENTS OF TRUTH

Assume that a restaurant manager in a hotel determines that there are at least 42 opportunities (moments) when a guest can form an opinion of the operation. These include such things as when the guest enters the restaurant, receives the initial "meeting and greeting" by the receptionist, is escorted to the table, is seated, given a menu, and the lapsed time until the server's first visit to the table. Assume also that the restaurant is open for lunch (100 guests are typically served) and dinner (150 guests are served on an average shift). The number of *planned* moments of truth is significant:

Number of moments of truth per lunch period	= 100 guests (×) 42 moments of truth =	**4,200**
Number of moments of truth per dinner shift	= 150 guests (×) 42 moments of truth =	**6,300**
Number of moments of truth per day	= 4,200 + 6,300 =	**10,500**
Number of moments of truth per week	= 10,500 moments of truth (×) 6 days of weekly operation =	**63,000**
Number of moments of truth per year	= 63,000 moments of truth per week (×) 52 weeks per year =	**3,276,000**

The manager in this example has 3,276,000 formal (planned) opportunities each year to make a good impression. Unfortunately, there are also a (seemingly) infinite number of *informal*, or unplanned, occasions when guest opinions can be formed. These include encounters with other employees, the perceived levels of cleanliness, and the guests' enjoyment of the food/beverage products served in the hotel's restaurant.

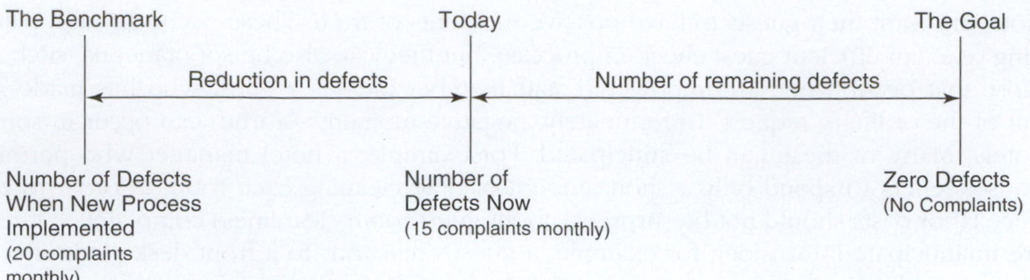

Assume that guest complaints are used to measure service defects. Process changes have reduced the number of defects from 20 complaints monthly (the benchmark) to 15 monthly complaints today. The measurement of success should focus on the reduction in complaints (5) rather than on the remaining number of existing complaints (15). Then revisions to systems and procedures can continue on the hotel's journey towards zero defects.

FIGURE 3.3 The March Toward Zero Defects

gardless of the extent to which a service attitude exists and guest-friendly processes are in place. However, the hotel's managers must make certain that effective plans are in place to minimize the number of service failures, and to correct the problems that do arise.

Some lodging managers establish a goal of **zero defects** when quality service processes are implemented. In other words, it is their goal that there will never be any guest-related complaints.

LODGING LANGUAGE

Zero defects: A goal of no guest-related complaints established when guest service processes are implemented.

However, a goal of zero defects may be frustrating, because even with the best intentions and most effective processes in place, mistakes, and thus defects, inevitably occur. Managers can and should, however, establish a goal of zero defects and measure their progress toward that goal. Figure 3.3 illustrates how a decline in defects can be measured.

SERVICE DELIVERY BY EMPLOYEES

After viewing a video emphasizing quality service, one manager was heard saying to another, "I'd give anything to have service staff like those shown in the video." What the manager had seen was a series of situations in which a trained employee (a) provided a hospitable greeting, (b) practiced the "art and science" of suggestive upselling to provide a guest with a wider awareness of the property's products and services, (c) utilized product knowledge, (d) answered all guest questions, (e) helped other employees when they became especially busy during the work shift, and (f) consistently met or exceeded the guests' service expectations.

Why couldn't (didn't) that manager employ, train, and enable staff members who consistently did these relatively simple and commonsense things? What kind of service was this manager's staff providing to guests if they did not do what was emphasized in the training video? Unfortunately, many people considering a recent experience in a lodging operation might also be asking, "What was wrong with the staff? What was wrong with their supervisors for allowing these things to happen? If I can see the negative impact a staff member's actions or inactions have on business," they may ask themselves, "why can't the managers who work here everyday see it as well?"

The quality of service provided to guests in any type of hospitality operation is influenced most by the staff members providing the service and by the processes they use to provide the service. If this is true, and the employee is a key element in service delivery, what role, then, does the manager play?

It has been said that the vast majority of all problems in most lodging operations are caused by the manager. The observation runs contrary to the thinking of the manager who believes, "If only I could find good employees, my operating problems would be solved, my guests would be happy, and my business would be profitable!" In fact, it is the manager who effectively or ineffectively recruits, trains, and empowers staff members to serve the guests. It is the manager who does, or does not, serve as a role model to emphasize the importance of guest service in the hospitality organization. Managers cannot delegate the **accountability** that they receive from their own boss to their subordinates. Instead, managers are held responsible for the extent to which the property is successful. In the next chapter, we will examine exactly how this is done. As emphasized throughout this chapter, service is an essential ingredient in the success of managers and all lodging organizations.

LODGING LANGUAGE

Accountability: An obligation created when a person is delegated duties/responsibilities by higher levels of management.

MANAGEMENT TACTICS FOR SUPERIOR GUEST SERVICE

How can managers ensure that their employees know and consistently practice superior guest service skills? What tactics can they implement to make service a top priority of all the staff members in a hotel operation? Some popular and helpful tactics are listed in Figure 3.4.

Lodging managers must understand their role in establishing and maintaining quality service as a top priority. They must recognize that what they do, and don't do, as well

ALL IN A DAY'S WORK 3.1

THE SITUATION

"Well Cyndi, good luck," said Mr. Patel. "I know you will do a great job!"

Cyndi was the new general manager in a limited-service hotel that was not doing well. In the not so distant past, the hotel had been very successful. Employee turnover was very low, and staff members gave a high priority to meeting and exceeding the expectations of the guests who stayed at the property. Sharon, the previous manager, had been there for many years. She emphasized guest service as a key to success, and she was proven correct each year as business volume and profits increased. But Sharon retired. Alan, the manager who succeeded her, emphasized cutting costs instead of providing value for the guests. Staffing patterns were cut until employees had no extra time for even the simplest interactions with guests' needs. The business suffered, and Mr. Patel, the hotel's owner, replaced Alan with Cyndi, who was instructed to "turn the business around."

It was Cyndi's first job as a hotel general manager. With so many issues demanding her attention, she wasn't sure where to start.

A RESPONSE

Cyndi needs to understand that any hotel's greatest asset is its staff. They are the team that will produce success or failure. She should meet with all the staff members to obtain feedback about the operation: What do they like? Dislike? What do the guests like? Dislike? How do they respond to the guests' needs? The hotel's team should work together to formulate a plan that focuses on serving the guests. The team should define who the guests are and what they want, and should commit, as a team, to consistently move toward the goal of providing superior guest service.

Cyndi can train the staff and empower them to be "ambassadors" to please the guests. They can be given the authority and power to respond to guests' needs in unique ways so as to meet the guests' expectations when the hotel falls short in some way. She must realize that these changes will not occur overnight because it will take time for the staff to begin to respect and trust her. Ultimately, employees who are satisfied and happy will provide quality products and services to the guests. Repeat business will result, the financial performance sought by Mr. Patel will be achieved, and Cyndi will know she has been successful.[2]

[2]The authors acknowledge the assistance of Ms. Nancy Bacyinski, Regional Director of Operations, HDS Services, Ohio/Kentucky Market, for developing this solution.

- ☑ Recruit and select service-minded staff.
- ☑ Provide effective orientation and training.
- ☑ Supervise with a service emphasis.
- ☑ Empower staff with decision-making authority for service.
- ☑ Emphasize continuous quality improvement.

FIGURE 3.4 Checklist to Maintain a Service Priority

as what they say, and don't say, are the biggest factors in determining the extent to which service is emphasized in their operations. Let's review the items in the Figure 3.4 service priority checklist.

Recruit and Select Service-Minded Staff

With proper management, a lodging property can be considered an **employer of choice** in its community. Its **turnover rate** can be relatively low, and experienced staff members can understand and consistently apply quality service principles. However, applicants will still need to be recruited and selected.

LODGING LANGUAGE

Employer of choice: The concept that the hospitality operation is a preferred place of employment in the community for applicants who have alternative employment opportunities.

Turnover rate: A measure of the proportion of a work force that is replaced during a designated time period (month, quarter, or year). It can be calculated as: Number of Employees Separated (÷) Number of Employees in the Workforce = Turnover Rate.

One technique managers use is to hire only applicants who give good answers to open-ended questions like "What would you do if a guest waiting behind other guests to check in came to the front of the check-in line to ask a question?" or "What would you do if a guest wants help with a specific item on the limited-service breakfast buffet, and you are busy helping another guest at that moment?"

LODGING GOES GREEN!

Increasingly, hotel guests view a hotel's commitment to "Green" practices as a sign of commitment to quality guest service. As a result, the following "Green" trends are clearly emerging in the lodging industry:

- Consumers have been asking for green products, thus there has been a clear increase in demand for such products.
- Businesses have evaluated their "Green" commitments, generating corporate goals, monitoring and evaluating their "Green" performance and improving their corporate images.
- The demand for "Green" products has increased competition among suppliers, thus increasing the availability of more environmentally friendly products.
- Local, state, and Federal governments have taken measures and passed legislation that supports those properties committed to "Green" practices.

Hotel guests, and society at large, will continue to seek many things from the businesses they support. Today, a commitment to sustainable practices is one of their emerging concerns. Increasingly, businesses in the lodging industry are recognizing and responding to these important "Green"-influenced trends.

In addition to asking questions to learn about applicants' service initiatives, managers should emphasize the importance of service. They can, for example, discuss the property's **mission statement** with its service focus. They can also review how the position for which an applicant is applying directly relates to serving guests.

LODGING LANGUAGE

Mission Statement: A planning tool that broadly identifies what a hospitality operation would like to accomplish and how it will accomplish it.

Provide Effective Orientation and Training

Management's emphasis on quality guest service continues at the time of new employee orientation. During their orientations, staff members should be reintroduced to the property's mission statement, which should emphasize the critical importance of guest service. They must be trained in guest-friendly procedures. As well, they must be given adequate time to obtain the required knowledge and skills they must possess before they have significant guest contact.

Because all employees must know the importance of guest service and how to deliver it, an extensive program on this topic should be presented as an integral part of the hotel's orientation program.

Many managers make at least two mistakes when planning and presenting training programs. First, they emphasize skills, such as how to check in a guest and how to a clean a room, and do not give enough attention to developing a service attitude and teaching how to effectively serve guests. They often shortchange the length of training because they believe that it is more important to get the staff member into the position quickly, or that "Everything that must be learned can be taught on the job." In fact, providing effective guest relations training during the orientation process and taking the time to properly deliver basic knowledge and skills training before new staff members have guest contact is very important.

Supervise with a Service Emphasis

Employees, like everyone else, normally do what they are rewarded to do. If service is important, lodging managers should emphasize this. They should thank staff members when exceptional guest service is rendered. Note, for example, that the guest feedback card illustrated in Figure 3.2 allows guests who complete a comment card to name a staff member who was especially helpful to them during their visit.

Managers should discuss service-related problems, if any, with employees and mutually agree upon corrective actions during performance appraisals. Employee compensation decisions should be based, in part, upon the consistency of quality service delivery.

Effective lodging managers practice the delivery of superior service themselves. In other words, they "walk the talk" and do what they tell their employees to do. Imagine the opportunity to role-model service when a lodging manager greets a guest at the

LODGING ONLINE

The number of businesses that help managers learn more about how to deliver superior guest service is growing. To view one such company's site, go to:

www.businesstrainingworks.com/

When you arrive at the site, review the services offered.

Can you recognize how the service-related information provided by companies such as this could be directly applied to developing and practicing superior guest service skills in the lodging industry?

Professional hoteliers are trained to provide professional and quality guest service.

hotel's front door and carries the luggage to the front desk. How about the manager who walks with guests to the front door as they leave, wishes them a safe journey, enthusiastically thanks them for their business, and asks them to return?

Empower Staff with Service Authority

The importance of employee empowerment has been noted throughout this chapter. Lodging managers should facilitate—not merely direct—the delivery of superior service. Staff members who are in contact with guests require the ability to make quick decisions that focus on guest needs as they arise.

Because it is not possible to anticipate what every guest wants all of the time, it is not possible to develop and teach procedures that recognize how to consistently meet or exceed the expectations of every guest. Lodging managers must empower their staff as they (a) share their service mission, (b) provide the training and other resources required to meet the needs of the majority of guests, and (c) encourage staff members to help guests with out-of-the-ordinary service requests.

Emphasize Continuous Quality Improvement

Guests and the lodging operations that serve them constantly change. As a result, lodging properties become either better or worse. They rarely stay the same. Today's emphasis on

LODGING ONLINE

In addition to those companies providing general service training, a number of businesses provide hospitality-specific service training. To view one such company's site, go to:

www.hospitalityexcellence.com/

When you arrive at the site, review the services offered.

Can you recognize the advantages of using industry-specific training materials to help employees develop and practice superior guest service skills in the lodging industry?

"better, faster, cheaper" is important. However, the first two factors just noted (better and faster) should be developed with the guests' needs in mind. The third factor (cheaper) is also a meaningful goal as long as it involves taking error out of the products and service rather than reducing value delivered to guests.

The concept of **continuous quality improvement (CQI)** relates to the journey that the manager and staff take to reduce defects; or in other words, to get better.

LODGING LANGUAGE

Continuous Quality Improvement (CQI): Ongoing efforts within a hospitality operation to better meet (or exceed) guest expectations and to define ways to perform work with better, less costly, and faster methods.

Whenever a problem is identified, it should be resolved and corrected in such a way that it will not reoccur. CQI means that managers and their employees address both the largest (e.g., guest complaints about service or value) and the smallest (e.g., replacing a light bulb in a lobby area lamp) problems. In both cases, procedures are put in place to recognize and resolve problems, and defects are removed from the hotel's work methods. This is quality service improvement in action. As this happens, the improvement results in fewer defects, and another step has been taken on the lodging property's journey toward zero defects and excellence.

LODGING PROPERTY STAFF ARE SERVICE PROFESSIONALS

Professionals are people working in an occupation that requires extensive knowledge and skills. Medicine, law, accounting, and teaching are all occupations that satisfy this definition. People in these occupations have formal education in a specialized body of knowledge with a common base of information. In addition, membership in their profession is controlled by **licensing** or **registration** procedures that require the demonstration of effective knowledge and performance.

LODGING LANGUAGE

Professional: People working in an occupation that requires extensive knowledge and skills in a specialized body of knowledge.

Licensing: Formal authorization to practice a profession that is granted by a governmental agency.

Registration: Acceptance for one to work within a profession that is (typically) granted by a nongovernmental agency such as an association.

Hospitality service personnel should also be thought of as professionals because they too must possess specialized knowledge and skills to be effective. Furthermore, a common base of information relating to guest service is an integral part of every job in the hospitality industry. Certification rather than registration or licensing is available from professional associations serving the hospitality industry, including the American Hotel and Lodging Association and the National Restaurant Association.

Certification processes typically identify the competencies required for job success, make available training resources that provide the knowledge and skills required for competency, and test to measure competencies. For example, the Educational Institute of the American Hotel & Lodging Association (EI of AH&LA) offers two certification designations for managers of lodging properties: Certified Hotel Administrator (CHA) for those affiliated with full-service properties and Certified Lodging Manager (CLM) for managers of limited-service hotels. The Certified Lodging Owner (CLO) program has been developed for those who own hotels. In addition, EI offers several certification programs of interest to those with managerial responsibilities. These include Certified Hospitality Housekeeping Executive (CHHE), Certified Hospitality Trainer (CHT), Certified Hospitality Supervisor (CHS), Certified Revenue Manager (CRM), and Certified Lodging Security Supervisor (CLSS).

WHAT MAKES SERVICE SUPERIOR?

Service is an attitude as much as it is a skill. Lodging employees provide superior service to their guests when they:

- acknowledge guests and thank them for visiting
- smile
- maintain eye contact
- reflect a genuine interest in providing quality service
- consider every guest to be unique
- create a warm environment of hospitality
- strive for excellence in guest service skills
- are courteous, polite, and attentive
- determine what guests *really* want and need, and then provide products and services that address these wants and needs
- pay more attention to guests than to machines and coworkers
- invite guests to return

Entry-level personnel also have opportunities to obtain professional recognition from the EI of AHLA. There are programs available for a variety of important lodging positions, including front desk representative, bell attendant, guestroom attendant, laundry attendant, and security officer.

Each of the above designations requires experience and knowledge. The ability to consistently provide effective guest service is an important skill required for effectiveness in any hospitality position from those at the top of the organization to those with entry-level responsibilities.

There are many fine hotel companies, operating large and small hotels, that excel at providing superior service to their guests. The Ritz-Carlton Hotel Company is widely known for its emphasis on quality. It has twice won the prestigious **Malcolm-Baldrige National Quality Award**, which is administered by the federal government (National Institute of Standards and Technology, Commerce Department). The Ritz-Carlton Company is just one example of the use of service excellence in the establishment of a reputation for quality. Hotel companies of all sizes that are committed to quality service share similar philosophies. Among these are commitments:

- To welcome all guests
- To provide the finest service for every guest
- To treat all guests with respect and dignity
- To maintain a positive attitude in all dealings with guests
- To maintain the highest standards of cleanliness
- To protect the safety of guests and the security of their possessions
- To look and act professionally at all times

LODGING LANGUAGE

Malcolm-Baldridge National Quality Award: Award granted to U.S. businesses that demonstrate successful quality-related strategies relating to leadership, information/analysis, strategic planning, human resource development/management, process management, business results, and customer focus/satisfaction.

LODGING ONLINE

To learn about the certification programs offered by the Educational Institute of the American Hotel & Lodging Association, go to:

http://www.ahlei.org/

When you arrive at the site, click on "Certification."

Does EI offer a certification program for the position you seek in the lodging industry?

LODGING ONLINE

The corporate motto of Ritz-Carlton is: "*We are Ladies and Gentlemen serving Ladies and Gentlemen*." Check out its Web site at:

http://corporate.ritzcarlton.com/en/Default.htm

When you arrive at the site, click "Corporate Site," then click "The Ritz-Carlton Leadership Center" to review this company's own certification program.

Do you think this company is committed to excellence in the area of staff training?

ALL IN A DAY'S WORK 3.2

THE SITUATION

"Hey, Mr. Jamison, can I ask you something?" said Travis, a front desk clerk at the Seaside Hotel, when he saw Mr. Jamison crossing the lobby in front of the front desk. Mr. Jamison was the general manager of the 85-room limited-service property.

"Not right now, Travis; I'm very busy. I have three things to do in the next five minutes, and I am supposed to be at a Chamber of Commerce luncheon at this very moment." With that, Mr. Jamison continued walking without allowing Travis time to ask his question.

"Well," thought Travis, "I guess Mr. Jamison remembers that there is a tour bus scheduled to stop here mid-afternoon with about 45 guests who will need to be checked in. The schedule shows that I am the only one here until 3:00 o'clock, when Latoya comes in. I'm sure he has scheduled an additional front desk clerk but just didn't post the new shift on the schedule. That must be it. Or maybe he planned to work at the front desk himself."

At about 2:00 p.m., the tour bus arrived. Mr. Jamison had not returned from his lunch meeting, and there was no one available to help Travis with check-in, so it went very slowly. Members of the tour group complained loudly to their tour guide. The tour guide was not pleased about that, and at 2:30 p.m. she demanded to speak to the hotel's manager. Travis replied that the manager was still at lunch.

A RESPONSE

Do managers ever create problems? Yes, they do, and the problem just described is an example. Perhaps Mr. Jamison was busy, but he should not be too busy to listen to his staff. Apparently he did forget to schedule additional front desk assistance. Perhaps he planned to work the front desk himself along with Travis. Regardless of the plan (if there was one), he forgot. Fortunately, Travis is an excellent employee and wanted to remind him, but Mr. Jamison "doesn't have time to listen." As a result, the guests were delayed at check-in. Managers must always take the time to listen to staff members.

This is also important because of the image projected by the manager. Mr. Jamison would not want Travis or any other hotel employee to ignore guest's needs because they are "too busy." In fact, Mr. Jamison would expect staff members to give the highest priority to addressing guests' needs. Why should the employees expect anything less in their interactions with Mr. Jamison? If the hotel manager disregards employees' questions and concerns, staff members may feel it is O.K. to treat guests the same way. In this case, Mr. Jamison was too busy to do his job properly.

Lodging Language

Quality
Service (Guest)
Value
Employee-to-Guest Ratio
Commodity
Supervisor
Manager
Benchmark
Cross-Functional Teams
Empowerment
Repeat Business
Moments of Truth
Wow Factor
Word of Mouth Advertising
Zero Defects
Accountability
Employer of Choice
Turnover Rate
Mission Statement
Continuous Quality Improvement (CQI)
Professionals
Licensing
Registration
Malcolm-Baldridge National Quality Award

For Discussion

1. What do you think would be the definition of excellent service at time of check-in (a) at a motel on the highway and (b) at a full-service Ritz-Carlton hotel? In what ways would they be similar?
2. Review the six ingredients necessary to develop a quality service system that were presented in this chapter. Assume that you are the manager of a hotel property where guests must very frequently wait in line a long time to check in. Work through a potential solution to this problem utilizing the six-step method discussed in this chapter.
3. Think about the last time you visited a hotel or restaurant as a guest; what moments of truth do you recall? What impact did they have on your overall impression of the hospitality operation?
4. Consider the following statement: "The vast majority of all problems in a lodging property are caused by the manager—not by the employees." Do you agree? If you currently hold a job in the hospitality industry, what would your manager think about this statement?
5. Do you believe that line-level staff members in hospitality positions, such as front desk clerk and housekeeper, are professionals? Why or why not?
6. Review the Ritz-Carlton Hotel Company's motto "We are Ladies and Gentlemen serving Ladies and Gentlemen." What impact would that philosophy likely have on the company's line-level employees?
7. Hoteliers are concerned about commoditization of products and services. What are three things you learned in this chapter that can help you avoid commoditization in a hotel you would manage?
8. Assume that you are a hotel manager who is very concerned about providing quality guest service. List three critical topics you would discuss in a guest service training session presented to all new employees at the time of their orientation.
9. Sometimes even very good employees are reluctant to change. Assume, for example, that a specific housekeeping procedure had been utilized for many years at a property. A change is necessary because of numerous guest complaints. What tactics could you, as a manager, use to reduce the employees' resistance to change as the new procedures are implemented?
10. Determining what guests want while they are staying at your lodging property and the extent to which they are satisfied during their visit are important steps in delivering superior service. Assume that you are a guest in a lodging property. Would you want to provide information to its manager(s) about your likes and dislikes? Do you think other guests would feel the same?

Team Activities

TEAM ACTIVITY 1

Make a list of things you would like and dislike if you were a guest in a limited-service property. What are some tactics that the property's manager could use to ensure that your likes were more consistently met and that your dislikes were more consistently avoided?

TEAM ACTIVITY 2

Review the Web sites of three hotels in your area. To what extent do they emphasize service on their sites? What suggestions could you make to these organizations to improve their emphasis on service?

Chapter

4

Managing Lodging Operations

Chapter Outline

The Role of Lodging Managers

Management Functions

Planning

Organizing

Directing

Controlling

Management Principles

Management: Science and Art

Lodging Management Structure

Larger Hotels

Smaller Hotels

The Role of the Hotel General Manager

Owner Relations

Staff Development

Property Management

Brand Affiliation Management

Community Relations

The Role of the General Manager's Supervisor

Management Company Supervision

Property Owner Supervision

Chapter Overview

In every business, managers are responsible for providing the quality products and services customers and guests are looking for. The duties and responsibilities of managers can be viewed in several ways. One way to examine managers and their role in operating a business is to study the four major functions of management: planning, organizing, directing, and controlling. Planning involves setting goals and deciding what to do as well as when to do it. Proper organizing of the available resources can help managers reach the goals the business has established. Because most businesses rely upon employees to help accomplish organizational goals, these staff members must be directed, or led, in a way that ensures quality service. Finally, managers are responsible for monitoring and controlling the costs associated with operating a business.

Hotel managers are primarily responsible for the day-to-day activities of a hotel. Some hotels need only a few managers; others need a good many managers. In a large hotel, the organizational structure must accommodate many managers; while in a smaller, limited-service hotel, there may be only one manager. In hotels of all sizes, the managers will have certain tasks and responsibilities that must be accomplished. In this chapter, we will examine the five major responsibilities of a hotel's general manager in great detail.

In the hotel business, a general manager's supervisor could be a representative of a management company hired to operate the hotel, or the owner of the hotel. Both of these possibilities will be explored in this chapter.

Chapter Objectives

1. To explain to you the four major functions of management.
2. To show the organizational structure of different-size hotels.
3. To describe in detail the five major parts of a hotel general manager's job.
4. To describe how managers function when they are employed by a management company.
5. To describe how managers interact with their hotels' owners.

THE ROLE OF LODGING MANAGERS

If you are reading this book, it is likely that you are now managing a hotel, or hope to manage one someday. Regardless of the industry in which they work, all managers share some common responsibilities. In fact the word **management** itself gives clues about what managers actually do at work.

LODGING LANGUAGE

Management: The coordination of individual efforts to achieve established goals.

Management is the process of coordinating the many efforts required to achieve goals set by an organization. In the hotel business, the goals might include opening or remodeling a hotel, increasing an existing hotel's revenue, maintaining a swimming pool, cleaning rooms, or improving the overall quality of a guest's experience. It is important to understand that management is necessary anytime the goals of an organization require the efforts of more than one person. Certainly, that is the case in the hotel business.

Management Functions

Managers are the people in an organization who are responsible for coordinating the group efforts required to achieve goals. To see exactly how managers do their jobs, it is helpful to examine the four basic functions of management. While management has existed for centuries, in 1916 Henri Fayol, a French manager in the mining industry, first described these four management functions in detail. As shown in Figure 4.1, these are:

- Planning
- Organizing
- Directing
- Controlling

Many modern writers and speakers on management have added to Fayol's original observations. His view that the four basic functions are the building blocks of management is

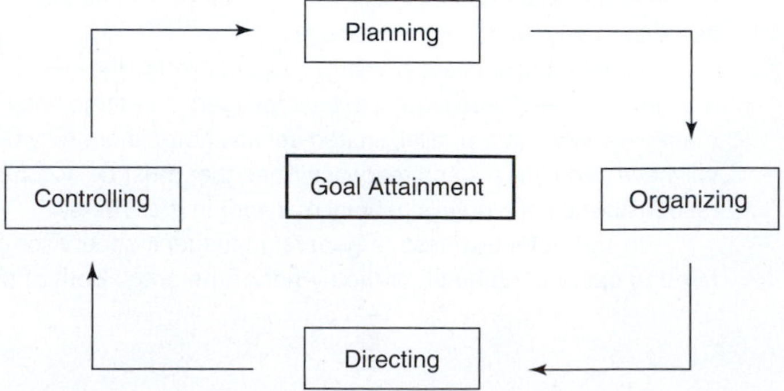

FIGURE 4.1 The Four Functions of Management

still held to be true, however, and it is still very useful in examining the concept of management in detail.

PLANNING

Planning is the process of looking into the future in order to establish goals for an organization. Planning exists, to some degree, in every human activity.

LODGING LANGUAGE

Planning: The process of considering the future and establishing goals for an organization.

Whether you manage a factory, a church, a university, a hospital, an entire government, or a hotel, you must decide on the goals you want to achieve. When planning is done properly, it consists of an honest assessment of the current state of an organization as well as a realistic prediction of what the organization can achieve in the future. When planning, managers establish **short-range goals** and **long-range goals**.

LODGING LANGUAGE

Short-range goals: Goals that are to be achieved in the very near future (usually less than one year). Sometimes called "short-term goals."

Long-range goals: Goals that are to be achieved over an extended period (usually longer than one year). Sometimes called "long-term goals."

In order for lodging managers to achieve their hotels' goals, they will need to implement the four management functions: planning, organizing, directing, and controlling.

In the hotel business, a short-range management goal might be to interview and select a local company to service the hotel's office computers when they are in need of repair. A long-term goal might be to plan for the eventual replacement and upgrade of the computers in all managers' offices within the hotel.

ORGANIZING

After managerial planning has identified goals, managers must be concerned about **organizing** the resources of the organization to achieve these goals.

LODGING LANGUAGE

Organizing: Actions designed to bring together and arrange the resources of a group to help it achieve its goals.

The resources available to managers include people, facilities, equipment, and money. When management is effective, these resources are arranged in a way that maximizes the organization's chances of achieving its goals.

When managers organize resources, they answer questions such as:

- Who will be responsible for making organizing decisions?
- Which managers will be in charge of meeting specific goals?
- Who will determine the number of additional workers needed to achieve our goals?
- Who will identify other additional resources needed to achieve our goals?
- What organizational business structure will best help us meet our goals?

The organizational structure of a business is a very important factor in its ability to meet its goals. The specific structures commonly used in the hotel industry will be examined later in this chapter.

DIRECTING

It is important to remember that management is an activity performed by people and with people. As a result, an important part of management is the creation of an environment that encourages workers to want to do their best work. **Directing** people in a way that results in their best work effort can be challenging. It involves leading and inspiring others, teaching new skills and attitudes, helping workers develop through their own efforts, and creating pay systems that compensate workers fairly.

LODGING LANGUAGE

Directing: The process of supervising staff members in the workplace.

It is wrong to see a manager as simply a taskmaster responsible for "forcing" others to work. The best managers lead their organization's workers by helping them do their best work. Effective managers "lead" their workers in a direction that is good for the organization and for the workers. When this happens, guests, employees, and the business all benefit.

CONTROLLING

Good managers know that it is necessary to check up or follow up on assigned tasks to ensure that the work of those managed is progressing toward the achievement of the organization's objectives. Even with proper planning, appropriate organizing, and good direction, some goals may not be achieved. This is so because misunderstandings, unexpected obstacles, or changes in the business environment can affect workers' efforts and thus result in unmet goals. The process of **controlling** is one of comparing actual results with planned results. It involves comparing the progress of the organization in meeting its goals with its original projections, and eliminating the obstacles that hinder goal achievement.

Key Activities	Management Function			
	Planning	Organizing	Directing	Controlling
Activity 1	Determine objectives	Clarify workers' assignments	Communicate organizational objectives	Compare actual results with planned results
Activity 2	Identify the tasks to be completed to meet objectives	Select appropriate employees	Lead and challenge employees to do their best	Suggest corrective action where appropriate
Activity 3	Establish operating policies, procedures, and standards	Assign duties and authority for each employee	Reward workers by recognition and appropriate pay	Utilize information gained in the control process to improve the organization's planning process

FIGURE 4.2 Key Activities in Management Functions

LODGING LANGUAGE

Controlling: The process of comparing actual results to planned results and taking corrective action as needed.

Some managers think that accountants and other financial managers are the only ones responsible for the controlling function. In fact, all managers, when evaluating their own efforts as well as those of their own employees, can take steps that can lead to improved organizational performance and efficiency.

Figure 4.2 summarizes some of the major activities managers undertake when they perform the four functions of management.

MANAGEMENT PRINCIPLES

The most important thing managers can manage is their own time. This is so because the effective use of your time, more than any other factor, is likely to lead to success in your management position. While education is important, there are many educated managers who do not consistently utilize what they know. Similarly, there are experienced and well-intentioned managers who have difficulty making the most productive use of their time at work. The best managers know that "time is money"—for themselves and for their workers. As a result, effective managers look for methods and procedures designed to save time for their organization and themselves.

One concept that managers have found to be time-saving is that of identifying and following established managerial principles. These principles save time because they supply time-tested solutions to the questions and issues that often arise at work. For example, one managerial principle is that each worker should have only one immediate supervisor. Thus, if employees need to know where to obtain their daily work assignments, they will know exactly who will provide it. Also, the managers in this situation know exactly who they must supervise.

It is sometimes difficult to identify managerial principles that work in every situation. As a result, managers often use principles as a guide, and then determine, based upon specific circumstances, whether the principle appropriately applies. In most cases, however, managers will find that some universal managerial principles can be identified and will be helpful in managing any organization while other principles can be identified or created for a specific work group, hotel, or hotel company.

It is important to understand that a managerial principle is different from a company policy, but policies typically result from belief in a managerial principle. For example, a hotel manager might decide that new employees hired for a specific type of work are to

As you progress throughout your hospitality career, your own management principles will evolve based on your experiences.

be paid a predetermined starting wage. In this case, the hotel policy was used to establish the wage. The managerial *principle* this policy would be founded upon is:

Pay rates within any organization should be established fairly.

Consider two hotel organizations. In the first, the managers believe in the above principle and create pay policies based upon it. In the other organization, the managers either do not know or do not follow the principle. It is easy to see which organization will, in the long run, attract and retain better employees.

As your own career evolves, you will develop your own set of tested managerial principles. These are statements about management that you believe to be true and on which you will base your own managerial policies. Some management principles that experienced managers have found to be true are included in Figure 4.3.

1. The good of the organization must be put before the good of the organization's individual members.
2. The responsibility to achieve organizational goals should be accompanied by the authority to do so.
3. Discipline in an organization is necessary but must be impartially applied.
4. A worker should have one (and only one) immediate supervisor.
5. Pay rates within an organization should be established fairly.
6. There should be clear lines of **authority** for use in achieving organizational goals.

FIGURE 4.3 Sample Management Principles

LODGING ONLINE

The American Hotel and Lodging Association (AH&LA) is a major hotel industry trade association. Its members utilize association resources to stay abreast of advances in hotel management that affect the hotels they manage and their own management careers. To learn about the educational services available through AH&LA, go to:

www.ahla.com/

Do you agree that it is in the best interest of lodging industry professionals to continue their learning even after their formal schooling has been completed?

LODGING LANGUAGE

Authority: The power or right to direct the activities of others and to enforce compliance.

Your own list of managerial principles will evolve as your career develops. It is important to remember that managerial principles such as these provide organizational direction and, as a result, free a manager's time to focus on the necessary management tasks of planning, organizing, directing, and controlling.

MANAGEMENT: SCIENCE AND ART

You have learned that management consists of certain processes and the application of certain principles. A question often considered by those who manage is simply this:

Is management a science or an art?

Some people believe that managers can only learn by doing. They wrongly believe that management is not a science. In their view, one cannot learn to manage by studying managerial processes and principles. There is in fact a science of management when "science"

ALL IN A DAY'S WORK 4.1

THE SITUATION

"But Beth told me to vacuum the third floor hallways right away," said Mark Bell, the hotel employee responsible for keeping the hotel's carpeted hallways neat and clean. "She is my boss, after all."

"Well, I'm telling you that I was just down to the second floor and its hallway is really dirty. It should be vacuumed first," said Walter, the man responsible for maintaining the hotel's plumbing, heating, and cooling systems. Walter was an important member of the hotel's management team, and now Mark was not sure whether he should do as Beth, his immediate supervisor, had asked, or whether he should follow Walter's instructions. He certainly did not want to get into trouble with either one!

A RESPONSE

Some principles of management are so universally true that managers who violate them will nearly always find problems arising. In this case, the employee's frustration and confusion are the direct result of management's violation of the principle that a worker should have only one boss. Despite his good intentions, Walter has placed Mark in a very unfortunate situation. If you were Walter's boss, you would need to explain to him the importance of involving Beth in any reassignment of her employee's tasks, with emphasis on the principle that workers should have only one boss directly responsible for their activities.

This is not simply a matter of one manager being courteous to another; it is a critical managerial principle and one that is necessary to follow if employees are to be clear about their duties and responsibilities.

Management is both an art (an individual's creativity and skill) and science (large body of knowledge and information).

is defined as a large body of knowledge and information about management. This information represents the best thinking on the process of management. The science of management, however, is not as comprehensive or accurate as mathematics or physics. The reason for this is simple. Management is a process that involves humans and human behavior. Humans are not always consistent. While the behavior of many people can be predicted to some degree, employees, supervisors, and managers often react differently when faced with the same situation. That is why that the art aspect of management is also important.

The art of management consists of an individual manager's creative power and personal skills. Creative power is evident when a manager contemplates problems, events, and possibilities. Some managers are very good at finding creative solutions to new problems. The personal skills of managers develop through practical experience and study. The best managers know that a life-long study of their management field and the continual updating of their knowledge base is an important part of maximizing their personal management skills.

While the science of management teaches a manager to know, the art of management teaches a manager to do. To illustrate the relationship in another area, consider the sailors of years gone by who used the stars to guide their ships. Astronomy was the science the sailors used, and navigation was the art they employed to sail the ships. In a similar manner, physicians will use their knowledge of the field of medicine (science) when treating a newly discovered disease (an art).

A good manager, then, is both a scientist and an artist. Hospitality managers rely on both science and creative talent to do their jobs. In this book, you will discover information related to both the science and the art of hospitality management. Because the hospitality field continues to develop, you will sometimes face problems for which there is no "known" scientific solution. When that is the case, your personal problem-solving creativity will be utilized. Your creativity will be greatly influenced, however, by your knowledge of management science. When you apply the facts, principles, and rules of management to new situations, you will find that your managerial creativity is enhanced, and your skill as a management artist will continue to develop.

LODGING MANAGEMENT STRUCTURE

If a hotel is to meet its service and profit goals, everyone in the organization must know the jobs for which they are responsible. **Organizational charts** help make those responsibilities clear.

LODGING LANGUAGE

Organizational chart: A visual portrayal of the jobs and positions of authority within an organization.

Properly organizing a group's work efforts leads to the achievement of goals. A well-developed organizational chart is the result of management's thoughtful structuring of resources to meet its stated objectives.

Organizing work has always been an important part of management. Governments, businesses, armies, and institutions of higher education are all examples of organizations that carefully structure their human resources in a way that achieves maximum efficiency. This is also true in the hotel industry. Knowing the objectives of the hotel, breaking down work into its logical components, assigning qualified personnel, and informing group members about their expected accomplishments enhance the hotel's ability to meet its objectives.

Larger Hotels

In a large hotel, the organizational chart will also be large because there are so many employees in so many different positions. From the guest's perspective, however, the primary functions of hotel personnel remain the same regardless of property size. Guests want to be checked into a safe and clean room and expect to be charged the correct amount upon departure. As the number of rooms in a hotel increases, so too does the number of staff employed, and the staff members work in increasingly more specialized positions. Figure 4.4 is an organizational chart that illustrates the departments and functions that would likely be found in a larger hotel.

Smaller Hotels

Smaller, limited-service hotels perform most of the same functions as larger properties but must do so with fewer employees. Figure 4.5 illustrates an organization chart for a smaller, limited-service hotel. It shows the most common organizational structure for a limited-service hotel with 75-100 rooms, the most widespread type of hotel being built in the United States in the 2010s.

Note that the number of positions in this hotel is much smaller than in a full-service hotel. In fact, as you learned in Chapter 2, the owner of a limited-service hotel often may be its general manager. It is important to understand that in many ways the operation of a limited-service hotel is just as complex as that of a full-service property. This is because, with the exception of extensive food- and beverage-related services, all of the guest-related activities found in a full-service hotel are also found in a limited-service hotel. As a result, most of the employees in a limited-service hotel must be multiskilled and able to perform several tasks well.

A larger limited-service hotel, of necessity, will probably have an individual in charge of maintenance, as well as maintenance support staff, an executive housekeeper who supervises the hourly employees who clean the hotel's rooms and public spaces, and a front office manager who supervises the front desk staff.

Unlike a larger full-service hotel, there may or may not be a designated individual specifically responsible for increasing the hotel's sales. A bookkeeper/accountant (typically part-time) is often retained to prepare financial reports and tax returns.

We will continue our management study by examining the role of the general manager, the individual most responsible for providing management leadership at the property

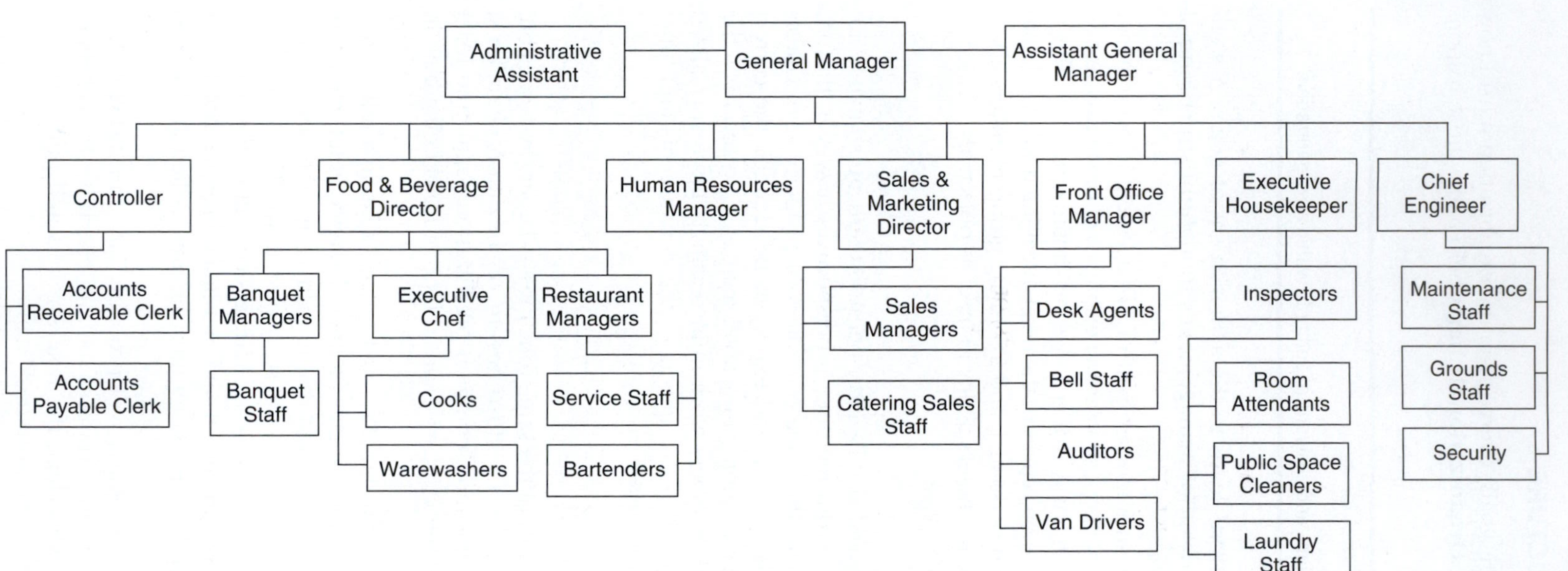

FIGURE 4.4 **Organization Chart for Large (350-room), Full-Service Hotel**

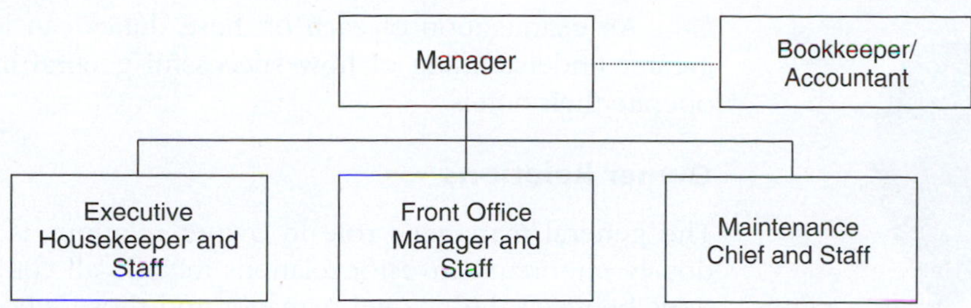

FIGURE 4.5 Organization Chart for Small (75–100 Rooms), Limited-Service Hotel

level. Hotel management companies and owners strongly influence the managerial actions of general managers so that their roles will be examined as well. It is important to recognize that your career in lodging management may take you to a large or a small hotel. You may serve as a department head, general manager, or hotel owner. You may choose to work for a franchisor and monitor franchisees or even in the management of one of the brand's hotels. Regardless of your management career choices, however, you will find lodging management to be challenging, exciting, and rewarding.

THE ROLE OF THE HOTEL GENERAL MANAGER

A hotel can be viewed from a variety of perspectives. Guests, of course, will see the hotel through their own eyes, as will the hotel's employees, its owners, and its management team. To understand fully the operational requirements of a small to mid-sized hotel, it can be helpful to consider it from the perspective of its management team. This is not to imply that the managers and supervisors in a hotel are more important than the hotel's guests, other employees, or owners. However, those who operate the hotel on a day-to-day basis take the actions and make the managerial decisions that most directly affect all of these groups and other groups as well.

Recall from Chapter 1 that the general manager is the leader of the on-site management team. In most hotels, the general manager is likely to be the single most important human variable affecting the hotel's short-term profitability and success. Hotel general managers "wear many hats" in the fulfillment of their duties. It is not possible to identify any one role that is most important because the responsibilities involved in any specific general manager's position will vary based upon many factors, including the hotel's ownership structure, the location of the hotel, its size, and the services it offers to guests.

In some hotels, the general manager may be very guest-oriented and spend a great deal of time with them. In others, the general manager may be primarily a staff development specialist who guides the professional growth of other hotel employees. Still other general managers find that many of their duties take them away from the hotel itself. Figure 4.6 lists the five most important duties for which general managers are responsible.

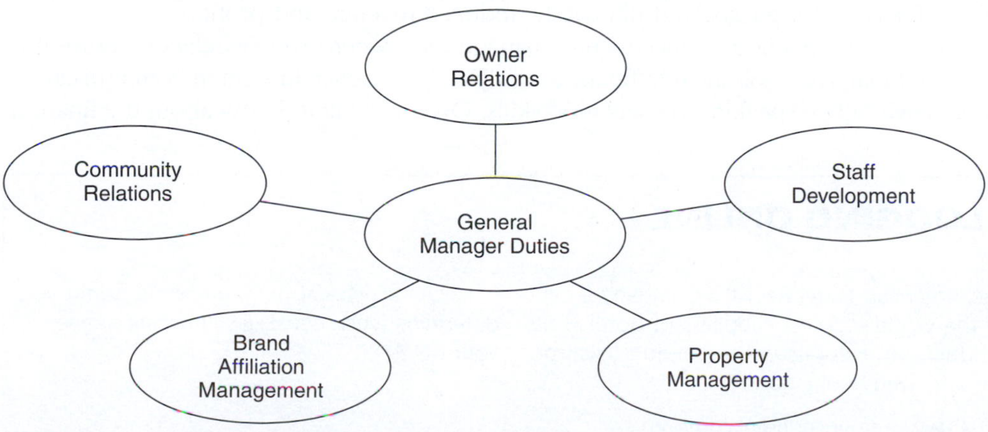

FIGURE 4.6 Duties of a Hotel General Manager

General managers have many roles. They are leaders of employees and their communities as well as the voice of the property to its owner(s).

An examination of each of these duties can lead to a greater understanding of how successful general managers operate their hotels.

Owner Relations

The general manager's role in owner relations is tremendously important. Investor relations include all communications between the general manager and those who own or invest in the property. As you have learned, property ownership can take many forms. A hotel may be owned and operated by a general manager. More often, however, the general manager is employed either directly by the hotel's owners or by a management company that operates the hotel for the owner.

Individuals or corporations who own or invest in a hotel property look to the general manager to have a positive influence on the hotel's standing in the market, its physical condition, and its profitability. A hotel consists of two distinct components. The first is that of an operating hotel business. A hotel generates revenue, incurs expenses, and seeks to realize a profit. However, a hotel is also a piece of real estate that has a distinct value. The land the hotel is located on and the hotel building itself will be worth a specific dollar amount. Some owners will view their hotel primarily in terms of its operating business success, whereas others will focus on the real estate value of the hotel. The general manager must continually inform ownership about the condition of both.

If the hotel requires additional investment in either the business (such as additional employees or more spending on advertising) or the real estate asset (such as new **FF&E**), roof repair, parking lot resurfacing, and the like), it is most often the general manager who will communicate that information to the hotel's ownership.

LODGING LANGUAGE

FF&E: The furniture, fixtures, and equipment used by a hotel to service its guests.

Hotel owners are usually willing to make additional investments in a hotel property when doing so makes good economic sense. However, they generally must be presented with a persuasive business case that additional investment is, in fact, a worthwhile course of action. It is an important part of the general manager's job to help make that case. If this is not done, the hotel building may deteriorate to the point that it results in a declining quality of service for guests, and ultimately, reduced revenue and profits.

The talents required to successfully manage the owner/investor relations portion of the general manager's job include financial analysis, proficiency in written communication, and effective public speaking/presentation skills. Owners want to know about the financial

LODGING ONLINE

The American Hotel Register Company is one of the world's largest suppliers of hotel FF&E products. To view its online catalog (click on the displayed book), go to:

www.americanhotel.com/

As a general manager, how could you determine when new FF&E items are needed in your hotel?

LODGING GOES GREEN!

Advancements in energy-related technology are an excellent example of the inherent advantages of direct contact between a hotel's general manager and its owners.

To better understand why, consider an environmentally friendly supplemental power source such as the ClearEdge5 (www.clearedgepower.com). The ClearEdge5 is a combined heat and power (CHP) unit that efficiently converts natural gas or propane into energy using fuel cell technology.

The device converts natural gas into ultra-clean hydrogen through a catalytic process. The hydrogen is then processed to create direct current (DC) electricity used to provide power. The power is then stored until needed. It makes an effective source of backup power when energy needs temporarily spike. In a hotel this could be when, for example, extra hot water is needed in the morning as guests take showers or when air-conditioning loads are high in the middle of hot days.

In this case, and many more like it, general managers can best understand the genuine intentions of owners who elect to install such devices. Will it provide energy cost savings, a commitment to the reduction of the hotel's carbon footprint, or a part of an overall "Green" marketing effort? When managers have direct access to owners and thus an understanding of their goals, they can then do their best to help their property's owners achieve those goals.

performance of their hotel properties. No one is likely to have a better idea of how the hotel is performing than the general manager. The ability of a general manager to effectively inform investors and owners about the current performance and future needs of their hotels will be critical to the property's long-term success.

Staff Development

Regardless of a hotel's size, the general manager of a property will play a major role in the professional development of the hotel's key staff members. In this regard, general managers can be considered the teachers in a hotel. This is true even when the staff members to be taught by the general manager have greater technical expertise in a specific area of hotel operations, such as maintenance or accounting, than does the general manager.

In today's world of rapid technological advances, it is unlikely that the general manager will be the most knowledgeable expert in every functional (departmental) area of the hotel. For example, the general manager will probably know less about how the electronic lock system operates than the person assigned to perform routine maintenance on the locks. However, the general manager is still the ultimate supervisor of this employee and as a result will be responsible for his or her growth and development as a hotel professional. In this example, the general manager is not the person who changes the batteries in the locking device but may instruct the individual(s) who are responsible for doing this about the best way to replace the batteries with a minimum amount of disruption to guests. In addition, teaching supervisors and staff members how to establish systematic records (in this case, to record which lock batteries were changed as well as when they were changed) is another way general managers can help staff improve at their jobs.

Perhaps the best way for managers to teach those with whom they work is to serve as a **role model** for them.

LODGING LANGUAGE

Role model: An individual who displays positive personal and professional characteristics that others find desirable.

An effective role model consistently displays the guest-service-oriented characteristics needed for success in the hotel industry.

Managers sometimes complain, "My staff doesn't pay attention to me." This statement is typically made when an employee does not complete an assigned task, completes the task in a different manner than that which was recommended, or completes the work but does so poorly. In fact, the problem is typically *not* that employees pay too little attention to managers but, rather, that they pay intensely close attention.

Every managerial action observed by an employee either adds to the manager's stature as a role model or detracts from it. When management, for example, insists that each guest room be cleaned perfectly every time, that is how the rooms will be cleaned. When management consistently greets each guest in a warm manner, employees will do the same. As role models and leaders, general managers greatly influence those who look to them to set the standard of excellence for their hotels.

If you become a general manager you may, in some cases, find that you will serve as a **mentor** for some of your staff.

LODGING LANGUAGE

Mentor: To serve as a personal teacher. Also known as a guide or coach.

In a mentor relationship, the mentor, or teacher, serves both as a role model and as a private tutor. In your own career, you are likely to have a mentor (as your career begins) and also to serve as a mentor (as your career advances and you begin to teach others).

Property Management

The actual operation of a hotel property is the activity most people think of when they consider the job of the hotel manager. It is true that there are a variety of jobs within the hotel that must be completed properly if guests are to have a satisfactory stay. It is also true that the ultimate completion of these tasks is the responsibility of the hotel's general manager working with the hotel's staff. On any given day, for example, a hotel general manager must know or be able to readily determine:

- The number of guests that will be arriving
- The number of guests that will be departing
- The total number of rooms to be sold
- That a record of each arriving guest's name has been created and is readily available
- The room rate to be paid by each guest
- That all room amenities promised by the hotel will be provided
- That all services typically provided by the hotel will be available
- That each room to be used has been thoroughly cleaned
- That the hotel's physical plant will supply the necessary heating or cooling of air, water (at the proper temperature and in sufficient quantity), and power required by guests
- That the hotel's guests and their property will be safeguarded during the guest's stay
- That proper procedures are in place to record the daily financial activity of the hotel and safely secure its money

Clearly, it is not possible for the hotel's general manager to personally complete all of these or the hundreds of other tasks that must be done daily. For example, the general manager of a limited-service hotel would not, on a daily basis, check each hotel room to be sold that night to ensure that cleanliness standards have been met. That is the job of the employees assigned the task of cleaning and inspecting guest rooms. What the general manager can and should know, however, is that the proper number of staff have been assigned to the job of cleaning rooms, that these staff have been thoroughly trained, that they have the necessary equipment and supplies to properly clean the rooms assigned to them, and that there is a qualified individual responsible for regularly checking the cleanliness of the rooms to be sold

LEGAL ASPECTS OF LODGING MANAGEMENT

There is no doubt that hotel managers must be multitalented individuals. In addition to knowing about their own specialty areas such as food and beverage, marketing, accounting, or rooms management, managers may play specialized roles such as employee counselor, interior designer, contractor, or information systems analyst. An additional role assumed by most general managers is that of the hotel's on-site legal expert.

Hotel managers frequently make decisions that impact the legal standing of their hotels owners. Some managers estimate that 60 to 70 percent of the decisions they make on a daily basis involved some type of legal issue. Of course, hotel managers are not attorneys. But the decisions they make daily about employee hiring, food and liquor liability, harassment, guest's civil rights, and federal regulations related to wages and salaries (to name just a few areas) are among those that may or may not increase their organization's chances of needing the services of an attorney.

Experienced hotel managers know that lawsuits can damage the reputation of a business, are expensive, and can be very time-consuming. Because that is true, avoiding lawsuits is among a lodging manager's most important goals. Fortunately there are a large number of law-related training resources available to lodging managers who do assume the role of their properties' on-site legal expert.

To effectively manage their hotels, general managers count on the help of the supervisory staff they have directly trained and developed, as well as the efforts of the **line-level** employees trained by the supervisory staff.

LODGING LANGUAGE

Line-level: Employees whose jobs are nonsupervisory. These are typically positions where the employee is paid a per-hour wage (not a salary) and performs a recurring and specific task for the hotel. Sometimes referred to as an "hourly" employee.

While successful hotel managers do not perform every routine task in their hotels, the best managers always know what needs to be done in their properties. As a result, they can identify needed improvements in the hotel's operation. For example, effective general managers, through observation, can identify that:

- cleaning procedures used in the breakfast area must be improved
- the maintenance-tool storage area should be reorganized
- room attendants must be better trained in the proper disposal of hypodermic needles found in guest rooms
- the guest room preferences of the hotel's best clients should be kept in a location easily accessible to the front desk staff
- "**comp**" room reports need to be recorded, with a justification for each comp, on a daily basis

LODGING LANGUAGE

Comp: Short for "complimentary" or "no-charge" for products or services.

Rooms, food, beverages, or other services may be given to guests by management if, in their opinion, the "comp" is in the best interests of the hotel.

The term can be used either as an adjective (e.g., "I gave them a comp room") or a verb (as in "I told the front desk agent to comp the room").

Knowing what needs to be done is actually an easy part of the management process. Knowing how to get the employees in each functional area to consistently address the tasks in their respective areas of responsibility is the hard part. It is here that the general manager demonstrates real leadership and, often through sheer will power, motivates a hotel staff to achieve things that were never before considered possible.

Property management, while only one of the five major tasks of the general manager, is a task critical to the hotel's success. It is also one of the most exciting. The talents required to successfully handle this part of the job include organizational and coaching skills, analytical and financial analysis skills, ability to anticipate guest needs, competitive spirit, and tremendous attention to detail. In addition, a truly effective general manager has the near-magical ability to inspire staff members to make guests feel truly welcome when they stay at the property.

General managers must be careful not to overmanage their properties. It may seem somewhat odd to warn an aspiring general manager about spending too much time managing the property, but this can happen. Remember, it is the manager's well-trained staff who provides guests with consistently excellent service. After all, no general manager can be on the property 24 hours a day, seven days a week.

General managers must do many things while they are at work. One important task that must be accomplished is that of managing the brand affiliation of the hotel.

Brand Affiliation Management

In the United States, it would be difficult to overestimate the importance of brand affiliation in today's hotel environment or in the daily activities of a hotel general manager. This is especially true in the limited-service segment of the industry. Most guests are unaware of the fact that the great majority of hotels are not operated by the brand whose name is on the hotel, but rather by hoteliers employed by the hotel's owners or their chosen management company.

As a hotelier, it is important to understand that if you are operating a branded hotel, you have a responsibility to your employer, but you also have a responsibility to comply with the franchise agreement (see Chapter 2) signed by your hotel's owners. The agreement will always include a section that requires your best efforts in maintaining the established standards of the brand. In addition, the general manager of a branded property will be responsible for communicating effectively with franchise brand officials about marketing and sales programs offered by the brand that can improve the profitability of the hotel.

Conflicts can and do arise between hotel owners, hotel managers, and brand managers. For example, assume that the brand managers for a hotel chain have established, as a brand standard, that three varieties of fresh fruit (apples, oranges, bananas, etc.), and two varieties of bread for toasting are to be offered on the hotel's complimentary continental breakfast buffet. The hotel's owners, however, as a cost-cutting measure, instruct the hotel manager to offer only two types of fruit and one type of bread for toasting anytime hotel occupancy falls below 25 percent.

A manager who follows the directive of the brand managers will violate the owner's wishes but following the instructions of the hotel's owner would be in violation of a brand standard. When owners instruct general managers to violate or ignore brand standards, this can adversely influence the hotel's relationship with the brand. When brand managers seek the general manager's compliance with acts that may be in the best interest of the brand managers but not the hotel's owners, difficulties may also arise. Issues always arise regarding loyalty to owners/employers and ethical standards for functioning as a professional general manager, but they take on extra complexity when a hotel is operated as part of a franchised chain.

For most general managers operating franchised properties, contact between themselves and the brand managers actually occurs through the hotel's franchise service director (FSD) described in Chapter 2.

Legitimate differences of opinion and conflicts can arise between a hotel general manager and a franchisor's representative. The personal relationship, however, that ultimately develops between the franchise service director and the general manager is an important one. When the relationship is good, the franchise service director is seen as a valuable resource. When it is not good, conflicts between the franchise service director and the manager can escalate to the point where they negatively affect the manager's ability to effectively operate the hotel.

For example, assume that a hotel's owners elect to affiliate with a specific brand. Assume also that after one year of operation the hotel's sales revenues are not as high as the owners had projected. The owners complain to the brand managers that the brand is at fault for the lower-than-desired sales. In cases such as these, it is not unusual, and in fact is most likely, that the brand managers and the franchise service director will claim that it is the general manager, other managers in the hotel, or the hotel's operational methods that are the cause of the sales shortfall. Not surprisingly, if you were the hotel's general manager, you would be unlikely to agree with this assessment. The potential for conflict in this case is clear.

As a general manager, one of your chief responsibilities is to balance the legitimate interests of your hotel and the brand in a manner that reflects positively on your own professionalism. To illustrate one (of many) additional aspect of brand affiliation management, consider the **Quality Inspection Scores** (sometimes called Quality Assurance [QA] scores) regularly given to properties by the franchise brand.

LODGING LANGUAGE

Quality Inspection Scores: Sometimes called Quality Assurance (QA) scores, these scores are the result of annual (or more frequent) inspections conducted by a franchise company to ensure that franchisor-mandated standards are being met by the franchisee. In some cases, management companies or the property itself may also establish internal inspection systems. In general, however, it is the franchise company's quality inspection score that is used as a measure of the effectiveness of the general manager, the hotel's management team, and the owner's financial commitment to the property.

Quality Inspection Scores are the result of annual, or even more frequent, inspections conducted by a franchise company to ensure that mandated standards are being met by the franchisee. In the typical case, a franchise brand inspector (who may be the FSD) arrives at the hotel property (either with or without prior notification to the hotel) and, accompanied by the general manager, undertakes a complete property inspection. The property then receives a score or grade based on its compliance with established brand standards that have previously been communicated to the hotel.

If a hotel consistently scores too low on these inspections, it runs the risk of being dropped as a franchisee by the brand's managers. Properties that consistently score high on the inspections may be rewarded by the brand managers in a way that allows the hotel to use its high score in its promotion and advertising. Choice Hotels, for example, designates franchise partners that score very well as "Silver" award winners, those that score even better as "Gold" award winners, and the very highest scorers are designated as "Platinum" award winners. Other franchise companies employ similar awards or classifications for affiliated hotels scoring well on inspections.

In some cases, the property itself may establish standards and inspection/rating systems in addition to, or in preparation for, the brand inspection. Often, the resulting scores of brand inspections are used in property ratings, marketing efforts, and even to partially determine the general manager and other hotel managers' compensation/bonuses. Therefore, Quality Inspection Scores become an important example of how the general manager interacts with franchisors and/or management companies. The talents required to successfully address the brand affiliation management portion of the general manager's job include well-developed interpersonal skills, persuasive ability, listening skills, and often the ability to write effectively.

General managers who have worked with various franchise companies will verify that different brands have differing "personalities." Some brands attempt to exert extreme influence on day-to-day property operations; others take a more hands-off approach. In either case, it is up to you as a general manager to manage the franchise relationship for the good of your hotel's owners, investors, community, employees, and most importantly, your guests.

ALL IN A DAY'S WORK 4.2

THE SITUATION

"I'm sorry Jim," said Sharon, the franchise service director for Better Stay Hotels. Sharon had just completed her biannual inspection of the Better Stay Hotel in which Jim was the manager. "Your quality assurance score went down from the last time I was here, and it actually went down quite a bit in the area of guest room cleanliness."

"We have a new person in charge of that," replied Jim. "She is just getting used to the job. It's only her second month at the hotel. I think that's why our scores were lower. I know she will get better."

A RESPONSE

Despite knowing why his inspection scores were low, Jim has clearly neglected staff development: an important aspect of his job. When it is known that a key staff member (in this case the person in charge of guest room cleanliness) needs extra assistance or supervision, the manager's job is to provide that added attention. Jim obviously did not and his hotel's quality inspection scores will reflect that fact. While a manager has many tasks, perhaps none is as important as developing an adequately trained staff to ensure the cleanliness of guest rooms.

Community Relations

While it might at first appear that hotel managers have plenty to do simply contending with owner relations, staff development, property management, and brand affiliation issues, today's hotel managers have an additional and important role to play in their local communities.

In many communities, a hotel is more than merely another service business. In fact, the hotels in an area, collectively, can dictate in large measure how those outside the community view the area. There is no doubt, for example, that the hotels located in and around the French Quarter of New Orleans lend ambiance to the entire area. In a similar manner, the style of the hotels located along a specific stretch of beach will provide much of the character of that beach area. This is just as true of business-traveler oriented hotels in nontourist areas. Therefore, local government and community leaders often look to local hotel general managers to become leaders in efforts to attract new businesses, expand tourism opportunities, and provide input as to the needs of the local business community. All of these tasks are important because the financial health of any local hotel industry is partially dependent on the health of the entire local economy.

The opportunities for a general manager to assist the local community will be varied and significant. Consider, for example, the hotel general manager who gets a call from the local mayor asking if the hotel can assist in hosting a small gathering for the representatives of a manufacturing business that is considering building a new factory in the community. The manufacturer's decision to do so would mean many jobs for the local community as well as the opportunity for increased guest room sales by the hotel. Obviously, the general manager in this case would want to assist and, in fact, be a very visible host and community representative.

LODGING ONLINE

One of the most famous tourism areas in the United States is the section of Miami, Florida, known as South Beach. It also provides an excellent example of how hotels help establish the ambiance of an area. To see a brief description of some Art-Deco limited-service and full-service SoBe (South Beach) hotels, go to:

www.sobenightsonline.com/

If you were the general manager of a SoBe hotel, how important would it be for you to participate in the marketing of the entire SoBe area?

Additional community efforts that often involve a general manager include hosting and attending charity events, assisting with community fund-raisers held at the hotel, and interactions with community organizations seeking support from area businesses.

The talents required to successfully perform the community relations segment of the general manager's job include an outgoing personality, well-developed social skills, and, very often, effective public speaking and presentation skills.

THE ROLE OF THE GENERAL MANAGER'S SUPERVISOR

While the typical hotel organizational chart shows the general manager to be the highest-level on-property manager, all hotel managers, unless they are also the owners, have a person or group to whom they report. This reporting and the resulting supervision, if properly done, are critical to the long-term success of the hotel property as well as to the continued professional development of the general manager.

As the highest-level manager at the hotel property, the general manager will be supervised by one of the following:

Management company

Property owner

These two entities may have their own views of what a successful general manager should know and do. Because their views on satisfactory performance can vary, it is good for you to know about each of them.

Management Company Supervision

Some general managers are directly supervised by a member of the management company that employs them. As you learned in Chapter 2, management companies operate hotels for owners. As a result, many lodging industry managers are employed not by the owners of a hotel, but by the management company operating it. Sometimes a management company may also own all, or part, of a hotel it is operating. In most cases, however, the management company does not own the hotel it operates. When that is so, the general manager is not supervised directly by the hotel's owners, but rather is employed and thus supervised by the management company.

A general manager who works for a management company advances in the company by helping that company meet its own goals. These goals may not necessarily be the same as those of hotel owners. One might think that a hotel management company and a hotel's owners would always seek to reach identical goals, but that is not always the case.

For example, assume that you are the very talented manager of a 75-room hotel. Your management company has just entered into a 10-year contract to operate a 150-room hotel in your hometown. That 150-room hotel needs a new general manager, and it is a position you would very much like to assume. However, the owners of your current hotel (located in another city) are adamant that they want you to remain and have even threatened the management company that they will not renew the management contract when it soon expires if you are allowed to transfer. This problem (and it is a good one for you!) as well as others like it can occur when long-term career advancement with in your management company conflicts with the desires of the hotel owners for whom you are currently managing. In a situation such as this, your company will evaluate your long-term employment prospects. You will likely do the same. Just as you must evaluate what is best for you, your management company will assess the course of action that is best for the long-term growth of the *management company.* In this case, however, it will not likely be possible to simultaneously satisfy your desire for a promotion and a return to your hometown and the desire of your current hotels' owners that you stay at their hotel.

When a management company operates a hotel, it impacts the supervision of a general manager, but it can also affect the supervision of other managers at the hotel. Consider, for example, a hotel in which the owner is considering replacing the management company. If the change takes place, it is likely that the general manager and, in a larger property, the person responsible for hotel sales will be replaced. Other managers, however, such as the persons responsible for rooms cleaning and the maintenance of the facility, are much less likely to be replaced. This is true because a management company winning a new contract does not, as some believe, replace every employee at the hotel. In fact, to do so would disrupt the hotel tremendously. As a result, a general manager may supervise some lower-level managers whose loyalty will primarily be to the management company, while some other managers may be more loyal to a specific hotel and its owners.

Hotel general managers employed by a management company are typically supervised by a district, or **regional manager**. While the specific title will vary by company, a regional manager is the person in a management company who has a direct **line of authority** over general managers in individual properties.

LODGING LANGUAGE

Regional Manager: The individual responsible for the operation of multiple hotels in a designated geographic area. In some companies, the person's title may be area or district manager.

Line of Authority: A direct superior-subordinate relationship in which one person (the superior) is completely responsible for directing and exercising control over the actions of another (the subordinate).

Depending upon the size of the management company and the number of hotels it manages, the regional manager may supervise a few or many individual general managers. It is the primary job of the regional manager to supervise hotel general managers and, in many cases, to serve as the management company's contact with the managed hotels' owners or investors.

Property Owner Supervision

Not all general managers work for management companies. Those that do not are typically employed and supervised directly by their hotels' owners. In smaller, limited-service hotels, the general manager may report directly to the property's owner. In some cases, this may be a single individual. This is especially true with hotels consisting of 75 rooms or less because it is very possible and common, for one individual or family to purchase such a property.

General Managers either report to their management companies or directly to their hotel's owners.

LODGING ONLINE

The Small Business Administration helps individuals and small companies develop and expand. It has played a major role in assisting individual hotel owners in the purchase of their hotel properties. To review some of the many services offered by this agency, go to:

www.sba.gov/

When you arrive at the site, click on "About SBA"

Would you like to own your own hotel? Would you also want to manage it?

The Small Business Administration is a division of the federal government that helps small business owners (such as those buying smaller hotels) to finance the purchase of their businesses. While many small owners serve as general manager of their hotel, the most successful of them will buy additional hotels and then seek professional managers to assist in the operation of these additional properties.

Regardless of a hotel's size, when a general manager reports directly to the hotel's owner, there can be significant advantages and some disadvantages. The advantages can include:

- ***Better understanding of ownership goals and objectives.*** As you have learned, hotel owners can have unique objectives for the operation of their properties. Some are most concerned about preserving the value of the hotel as a real estate asset while others put more emphasis on the operational profitability of the hotel. A general manager who reports directly to the hotel's owner will be most familiar with the owner's goals and, therefore, can make better managerial decisions about how to achieve them.
- ***Direct access.*** Often it is important for a general manager to get a rapid answer to an important operational question. For example, assume that a general manager is considering the repair of a major piece of heating equipment in the hotel. The repair would cost $3,000, and a complete replacement of the equipment would be $10,000. Assume also that the piece of equipment provides the power to heat the hotel's hot water, and while it is out of service, the hotel will not have hot water for guest rooms. In this case, the owner may decide to spend the additional money to completely replace the faulty piece of equipment. If the general manager reports directly to the owner, the owner can often be asked quickly about a repair vs. replacement preference, and the proper management decision can be made promptly.
- ***Clear lines of authority.*** It might seem obvious that a general manager should perform in a way that serves the best interests of the hotel's owners. However, there are times, (e.g., when the general manager is employed by a management company) when the interests of the owners can conflict with those of the management company or the brand with which the hotel is affiliated. When the general manager reports directly to the hotel's owners, these conflicts are most often reduced or eliminated because the line of authority is very clearly understood by both the general manager and the owners. In such a situation, the owner takes the role of superior while the general manager will most often take a subordinate decision-making position.

Despite these advantages, working directly with the hotel's owners also may have some disadvantages. These can include:

- ***Lack of owner experience in hotel operating methods.*** For most hoteliers, the management of a hotel is their profession, whereas the owners of hotels may be in a different profession. The hotel owner's profession may be banking, real estate development, law, or any number of other occupations. Thus, the owner may know very little about hotel operations but nonetheless, in most cases, will have a line of authority over the general manager. The result can sometimes be frustration and misunderstanding on both sides.

  For example, assume that Roger T., the owner of a hotel, also owns several restaurants. In the restaurant business, any charges incurred by a restaurant's guests are traditionally collected at the time of the guest's departure, and in line with this practice, Roger instructs his restaurant managers not to extend credit to any guests. In the hotel business, however, many guest charges, especially for the hotel's best customers, will be treated as a **direct bill**. Unless Roger understands that there is a fundamental difference between the way hotels determine the creditworthiness of guests and the way restaurants approach the same issue, conflict could occur between Roger and his hotel managers.

LODGING LANGUAGE

Direct bill: A financial arrangement whereby a guest is allowed to purchase hotel services and products on credit terms.

- ***Multiple lines of authority.*** When a single individual owns a hotel, the line of authority between the owner and the general manager is typically quite clear. When the ownership of a hotel is held by two or more partners, however, or by a company with many owners, the question of precisely who the general manager reports to can be quite complex. For example, in a small company that owns a hotel, the hotel's general manager may report to the company's president regarding operational issues but to the company's chief financial officer on matters of money. Because operational issues and financial issues will often be interrelated, the potential for conflicting advice and direction in such cases is clear.
- ***Issues of multiple loyalties.*** Professional hoteliers have loyalties to their families, their vocation, their employees, their guests, and of course their immediate employers. General managers operating branded hotels have responsibility to the

ALL IN A DAY'S WORK 4.3

THE SITUATION

"We'll just see about that!" said Mrs. Kaufield. "I've never heard of such a rule, and I stay in Best Sleep hotels all over the country. But I'll never stay at one again. I don't think your bosses at Best Sleep will be so happy with you when I tell them that! I want the telephone number to your company's headquarters right now!"

Brenda Kaufield was a guest at the Best Sleep Inn at the local city airport. She had been complaining loudly to Sylvia Johnston, the hotel's general manager, about the hotel's policy of requiring each guest to present a valid credit card at the time of check-in. Brenda Kaufield did not have such a card. When the employee at the front desk refused to waive the policy and assign her a room, Brenda had demanded to see the hotel general manager. Sylvia had politely explained the hotel's policy but continued to enforce it. No card. No room. That's exactly the policy the owners of the hotel had instructed Sylvia to implement, and she had carefully followed their directive.

A RESPONSE

The owners of franchised hotels are free to set many of their own operational policies. It is the general manager's job to enforce these policies. In this case, a guest is unhappy with a locally instituted payment policy and wants to complain to the general manager's "Boss." The guest has demanded the telephone number to "Company headquarters." Of course, despite confusion by guests, franchisors are not the "Boss" of hotel owners. Guests typically can and do take their concerns to a hotel's brand managers however. In a franchised hotel, this typically takes the form of calling a toll-free number supplied by the franchisor. The franchisor would take the complaint and in most cases simply relay the complaint back to the hotel for resolution.

As the general manager of a franchised hotel, Sylvia should, of course, provide the guest with the brand's complaint-line number if she cannot resolve the guest's issue. The hotel's owners may eventually decide to modify or eliminate the payment policy if enough guests complain about it. While it is in effect, however, it is this general manager's job to enforce the policy, despite the guest complaints that may result. In this case, Sylvia has done that very well.

> brand's managers as well. When the owner of a hotel places demands on the general manager that cause any of these interests to get out of balance, conflict can result.
>
> For example, assume that a hotel manager is operating a franchised property where the brand standard for light bulbs placed in the sleeping area of a guest room is a 100-watt bulb. The hotel owner, in an effort to reduce the property's utility costs, instructs the general manager to replace the 100-watt bulbs with 75-watt bulbs. In a situation such as this, the manager faces a direct conflict between the instructions of the owner and those of the brand managers. Unfortunately, the hotel manager may not be able to appeal the owner's directive to another authority figure, and thus the result is likely to be a violation of the brand standard as well as a reduction in guest satisfaction.

Many hotel managers find that they prefer to work directly for the owners of a hotel. They cite the ease of accessibility to ownership and the clear lines of authority that generally result from such an arrangement. In many cases, such managers may themselves someday become hotel owners. Still other managers prefer, for a variety of reasons, to work for a professional hotel management company or other entity responsible for successfully operating hotels.

In all cases, general managers should operate their hotels in a way that maximizes the benefits to its owners and its guests. In the remainder of this book, you will learn how managers can do just that!

Lodging Language

Management	Directing	FF&E	Quality Inspection Scores
Planning	Controlling	Role Model	Regional Manager
Short-Range Goals	Authority	Mentor	Line of Authority
Long-Range Goals	Organizational Chart	Line-Level	Direct Bill
Organizing		Comp	

For Discussion

1. Some managers specialize in one of the four functional areas of management. In which functional area do you think you would do best? Why?
2. When managerial principles are violated, problems at work often result. Consider the last time you had a work-related problem. Was it the result of a managerial principle being violated? What principle do you think was violated?
3. The science of lodging management can be studied and learned. The art of lodging management can be practiced. Which do you think would be most important to your own development as a hotel manager?
4. Think about a skill you now have. Did you learn the skill by yourself, or did you have a teacher? Did that teacher serve as a role model, a mentor, or both?
5. Some general managers prefer to manage smaller properties. Other general managers prefer to work in large properties. Which would you prefer? Why?
6. Some industry experts say the best general managers have a sales and marketing background. Others believe accounting, front office, food and beverage, or housekeeping experience is most important for a general manager's success. What are two important characteristics you believe successful general managers possess? Why must they possess those characteristics?
7. Hotel managers in franchised hotels often find the desires of their property owners are in conflict with the desires of their brand managers. What personal skills would general managers in such situations need if they hoped to satisfy both their owners and the brand's managers? How could they obtain such skills?
8. Excelling at community relations typically requires managers to promote their local geographic areas as well as their hotels. What possible conflicts could you see resulting from such efforts?
9. Hoteliers who work for a management company often find, as they advance in the company, that they are selected to be promoted to new hotels that are larger or more complex to operate than their current hotel. How do you think the management company would decide which hoteliers within the company are ready for such a promotion?
10. Some hotel owners manage the hotel they own. What are some advantages you would gain by operating a hotel you owned personally? What are some possible disadvantages?

Team Activities

TEAM ACTIVITY 1

Assume that your team is in the beginning stages of establishing a new hotel brand. Identify three characteristics you would want every person responsible for operating one of your branded hotels to possess. How could you as brand managers help ensure that all of the owners of your branded hotels, as well as their property managers, possessed these essential characteristics?

TEAM ACTIVITY 2

Some managers feel they are too busy managing their own properties to become active in their local business communities. Identify three areas in which community service could be very good for a hotel's business and explain the revenue potential that could result from an involvement in each area.

Chapter

5 Staffing the Lodging Operation

Chapter Outline

The Importance of Teamwork in Lodging Operations
The Role of Supervisors
- Responsibilities
- Leadership Styles
- Communication
- Motivation

The Role of Entry-Level Employees
- Responsibilities
- Career Tracks

Choosing and Keeping the Right Staff Members
- Recruitment
- Selection
- Orientation
- Training
- Workplace Fairness
  - *Employee Discipline*
  - *Performance Appraisal*
- Retention

Worker Safety and Health
Legal Aspects of Supervision
- Employee Selection and the Law
- The Employer-Employee Relationship
- Additional Legal Issues in the Workplace

Diversity in Staffing

Chapter Overview

Today's lodging managers must recognize the importance of every staff member working in their hotels. This chapter explains the unique roles played by a hotel's supervisors and its entry-level staff.

Supervisors, as well as managers, are leaders in their hotels. In this chapter, you will learn about their job responsibilities as well as the various leadership styles they can use to accomplish their property's goals. This chapter also focuses on entry-level employees because, if a hotel is to be successful, it requires the best efforts of every supervisor and every other employee.

In this chapter, you will learn about the traits supervisors seek in guest-oriented lodging employees. The ways in which supervisors recruit, select, and orient new employees are critical to the success of workers as well as the hotels where they work. Therefore, these important activities are examined in detail in this chapter.

Employees must be selected in a way that is legally permissible, but there are other human resource oriented legal issues related to workers, and some of the most important of these are addressed in the chapter. Most managers agree that employees who are treated equitably perform better. Work teams that reflect the rich diversity of the lodging industry perform better as well. Because that is true, the chapter examines the many advantages that accrue when supervisors embrace diversity in the workplace.

The supervisor's duty toward workers does not end when the hiring process has been completed. In fact, after employees have been selected and hired, management's responsibility toward them increases. Effectively planning and delivering training programs is one of those responsibilities. Training in job-specific tasks is especially critical because it benefits both the hotel's staff (because they will feel more comfortable doing their jobs) and its guests (who will benefit from employees doing the right things in the right ways). Encouraging outstanding performance; ensuring that employees are treated fairly in matters of compensation, discipline, and performance appraisal; and exhibiting genuine concern for workers' safety and health are additional responsibilities of all successful lodging managers and are addressed in detail.

The management of human resources is always challenging. The chapter concludes by addressing some of the human resource-related issues you are likely to encounter when you become responsible for assembling and successfully leading your own lodging team.

Chapter Objectives

1. To show how lodging supervisors and entry-level staff work together in successful hotels.
2. To present to you some of the processes managers use to screen and select high-quality lodging employees.
3. To examine some of the important issues related to training and retaining staff.
4. To explain the role of supervisors in maintaining workplace safety and employee health.
5. To describe some of the advantages to a hotel of embracing a diverse workforce.

THE IMPORTANCE OF TEAMWORK IN THE LODGING INDUSTRY

Which member of the hotel's team is more important: the manager or the housekeeper? Front office clerks or maintenance employees? One does not have to think very long to realize that these questions have little meaning because the answers are so simple: All staff members in a hotel are integral to its success. From the perspective of the guest, of course, the employee cleaning rooms is just as important as the hotel's general manager. Management and non-management staff must cooperate and work together as a **team** if the hotel and its staff members are to be successful.

LODGING LANGUAGE

Team: A group of individuals who work together and place the goals of the group above their own.

Effective work teams have a clear goal: their organization's success. Every member of the team is encouraged to participate in decisions that affect the team. When possible, decisions are made by agreement among the team members. Individual team members have a clear idea about their role and their work assignments, and if there is disagreement, it leads to discussions and consensus about the property's goals and/or the best ways to attain them.

At its most basic level, a hotel constitutes a work group that includes of all its employees. At the same time, a hotel is organized into departments that include only part of the group. Within each department, work may be divided into very small units. For example, large hotels may have employees in the front office department who only check guests in and out while others in that department are responsible for making guest reservations. In smaller properties, one person may perform both of these front office activities.

In addition to formal work groups, one or more informal groups may develop within a hotel for reasons including:

- the common interests of group members
- the desire to be close to other employees in a similar situation
- economic concerns
- a desire to satisfy personal needs that are common to other workers

Managers use participative leadership to promote teamwork and ensure employees are part of the problem solving process.

When the supervisor believes that the members of an informal group want to achieve the hotel's goals, efforts can be made to work with the group. "Friendly" groups can be strengthened by increasing their status, reacting favorably to group members, and by ensuring that no obstacles hinder the group's continuation.

If supervisors are confronted with an informal group that works against the hotel's goals, they should attempt to (a) modify the attitudes of group members, (b) redirect the group toward more useful goals, and (c) address issues causing the group members' negative attitudes.

Effective supervisors can use the same basic principles to effectively work with formal and informal groups. Hotel managers can help build teams by using a **participative management**, or shared leadership style.

LODGING LANGUAGE

Participative management: A leadership style that emphasizes seeking out and considering group input before making decisions that affect the group.

When managers use a participative management leadership style, their entire team (not just the manager) assists with problem-solving and decision-making. Although the manager remains responsible for the effectiveness of the decision-making process, employee ideas are solicited before decisions are made.

LODGING ONLINE

There are numerous Web sites that will help you learn more about teamwork. A very good one is:

www.ravenwerks.com/teamwork/teamwork.htm

When you reach the site, you can click onto articles relating to global business, leadership, teamwork, best practices, marketing, customer service, and technology.

Do you think lodging industry work teams operate differently in different parts of the world? Why?

When managers facilitate teamwork, they are practicing a different leadership style than the one traditionally used in the lodging industry. They have moved away from the philosophy that "I am the leader, and everyone must do things my way" to "We will all benefit when we work together as a team." Perhaps effective supervisors should really be called "team leaders" or "team facilitators" to emphasize their ongoing interactions with team members whose work they supervise. The best team leaders recognize that:

- Each member of the team must know the importance of the work to be done and must be given the training and other resources required to work effectively.
- Teams must know that they have the full support of upper management.
- Teams can be used in all areas of the lodging organization.

The success of any hotel is tied to the ability of all its employees to perform as members of a team whose ultimate goal is guest-satisfaction.

THE ROLE OF SUPERVISORS

Before examining the role of effective supervisors, it's important to understand three key employee groups. These are managers, supervisors, and **entry-level employees**.

LODGING LANGUAGE

Entry-level employees: Staff members working in positions that require little previous experience and who do not direct the work of other staff members. Sometimes called "hourly" employees.

Figure 5.1 displays these three groups and indicates that a hotel's general manager supervises the work of department heads (in large hotels) and managers (in smaller and limited-service properties). Department heads direct the work of managers who, in both large and small hotels, direct the work of supervisors who are then responsible for the performance of entry-level employees.

Responsibilities

Supervisors have responsibilities to their own boss, to their management peers, and to their employees. Figure 5.2 lists many of these supervisory responsibilities.

When reviewing Figure 5.2, note that many of a supervisor's responsibilities relate to interpersonal relationships, such as showing respect, working as a member of the team, and treating all employees fairly.

Leadership Styles

Supervisors demonstrate effective **leadership** traits.

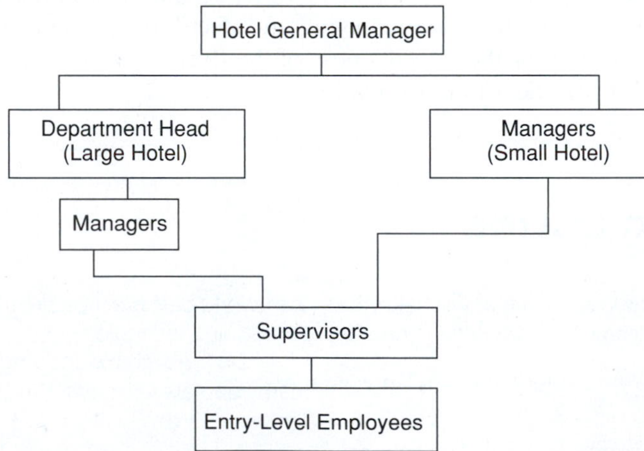

FIGURE 5.1 Hotel Managers, Supervisors, and Entry-Level Employees

To Superiors	To Peers	To Entry-Level Employees
• To respect them • To serve as a linking pin between higher and lower organizational levels • To help them be successful • To operate within budget restraints • To comply with applicable policies and procedures • To promote the hotel's goals • To provide proper reports and other information on a timely basis • To work effectively and efficiently • To use the hotel's limited resources as wisely as possible • To work with all staff as members of a team	• To respect them • To recognize them as individuals • To help them with job-related problems • To work with all staff as members of a team	• To respect them • To safeguard their health and well-being • To understand their problems and concerns • To help them be successful in their job • To support them • To treat them fairly • To recognize them as individuals • To help them find pride and joy in the workplace • To work with all entry-level employees as members of a team

FIGURE 5.2 A Supervisor's Responsibilities

LODGING LANGUAGE

Leadership: Accomplishing goals by working with others while gaining their respect, loyalty, and enthusiastic cooperation.

Supervisors must combine their own knowledge, skills, attitudes, and abilities with those of their employees to accomplish work assignments. They know that leadership is an art that involves the use of common sense and insight to interact with their staff and, at the same time, it is a science that uses proven managerial principles and procedures.

tics
Using effective lead yees
to communicate wit reach
will motivate them
the hotel's goals.

To be an effective leader, supervisors must:

- have the knowledge and skill to do or understand the technical aspects of the work performed by those they supervise
- be confident about their own abilities
- care about those they supervise
- provide information to employees to help them participate in the decision-making process
- do what they expect employees to do
- consistently ensure that every task done by every staff member is understood, appropriately supervised, and accomplished on time
- train staff members to work as part of the hotel's team
- make appropriate and timely decisions
- help employees to develop an attitude of responsibility for the work they do
- seek responsibility (and take it) for their actions
- be involved in an ongoing professional development program

Supervisors can utilize four basic styles of leadership. These are shown in Figure 5.3.

Supervisors should understand each of these leadership styles.

An **autocratic leadership style** is most effective when a supervisor interacts with inexperienced staff members who must learn proper work procedures. It may also be appropriate when there is an emergency situation or little time to perform a task (e.g., when a tour bus arrives earlier than expected because of a reservations misunderstanding). An autocratic leadership approach can yield employees who produce short-run, high-quality output. However, it is not likely to yield team players and can sometimes cause resentment between the supervisor and employees.

LODGING LANGUAGE

Autocratic leadership style: Leadership approach that emphasizes a "do it my way or else!" philosophy.

The **bureaucratic leadership style** relies upon rules, regulations, policies, and procedures to control employee behavior. It may be effective when new equipment/procedures are

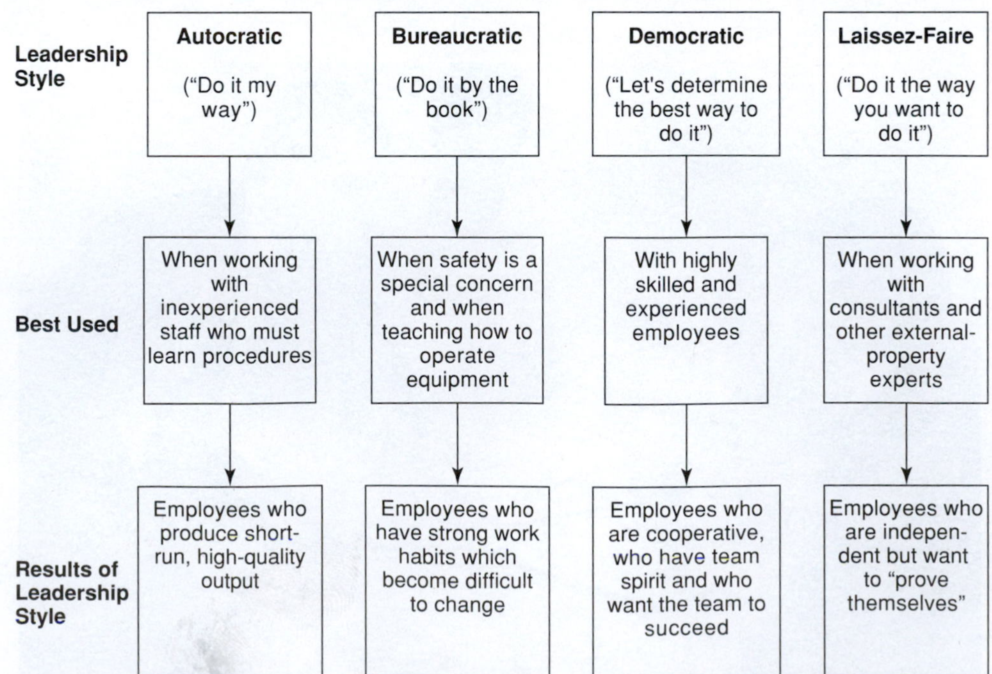

FIGURE 5.3 Styles of Supervisory Leadership

being implemented and when there is a safety concern. However, the style does not usually help to motivate employees to be creative in problem solving and can create strong employee resistance when future changes are required.

LODGING LANGUAGE

Bureaucratic leadership style: Leadership approach that emphasizes a "do it by the book" philosophy.

The **democratic leadership style** is most effective when used with highly skilled and experienced employees. Appropriate use of this style leads to cooperation and group spirit because the supervisor is centered on staff members rather than on the work to be done.

LODGING LANGUAGE

Democratic leadership style: Leadership approach that emphasizes a "let's work together and determine the best way to do it" philosophy.

The **laissez-faire leadership style** removes the supervisor from the decision-making process and is best used with very highly skilled, experienced, and educated employees and/or when working with outside experts, including consultants.

LODGING LANGUAGE

Laissez-faire leadership style: Leadership approach that emphasizes a "do it the way you feel it can best be done" approach.

Which supervisory leadership style is best? Ideally, supervisors would assess the teams they are assigned to lead and adapt the leadership style most helpful for the specific circumstances. Experienced lodging supervisors know that, in most hotels, there are two groups of employees. One is the group whose members are interested in a long-term lodging career while the other group's members are not. Effective supervisors might choose to use an autocratic leadership style as new employees in either group learn how to do their jobs. Then, depending upon each staff member's own personality and abilities, a democratic or laissez-faire approach may be best for long-term staff members and an autocratic or bureaucratic approach might be best for those who are less interested in a long-term relationship with the property.

Communication

Supervisors in any organization, including hotels, must be effective communicators. Have you even heard of a problem that was caused by a misunderstanding or a communication glitch? Communications problems can easily occur even when both the sender and the receiver of the information speak the same language. Additional communications challenges arise when, as is often the case in the lodging industry, employees in entry-level hotel positions whose native language is different from that of their supervisors.

Supervisors who wish to minimize communication difficulties are careful to avoid:

- The use of unfamiliar words or symbols. Terms such as "ADR" (average daily rate) and "RevPar" (revenue per available room) are unique to the hotel industry and must be explained if are used when training new employees.
- Poor communications timing. For example, trying to communicate a very detailed message when the recipient is too busy to pay attention is poor approach.
- Background disturbance. A supervisor trying to speak to an employee in a noisy area may have communication problems. Interviewing an applicant while being interrupted with telephone calls or by staff members entering the office is another example of background disturbance.

- An overemphasis on personal considerations. The meaning of messages can sometimes be influenced by one's feelings about the other person. "I don't like him, and what he is saying is wrong or untrue" is an example. The opposite ("I like her; so what she is saying must be true") also can occur and also should be avoided.
- Failure to recognize personal differences. Different educational levels, cultures, experiences, and perceptions can impact the effectiveness of communication. Young supervisors attempting to direct the work of older employees and college-educated supervisors interacting with high school-aged employees are possible examples.

Unintended communication. Words are not the only way we communicate. Consider, for example, the message given by a smile or a frown. People also communicate with **body language**. For example, when their arms are at their side, they may be "saying" that they are receptive to a message, and conversely, when their arms are crossed in front of them they are not welcoming the message.

LODGING LANGUAGE

Body language: The concept that one communicates by the way one's arms, hands, and/or legs are positioned during a conversation or presentation.

Good supervisors seek to avoid communication misunderstandings and always work hard to improve their verbal and written communication skills. One additional skill common to effective supervisors is their ability to motivate others.

Motivation

Attitudes held by employees have a dramatic impact upon their job performance and their interest in remaining with the hotel. In most cases, attitudes reflect the way people feel about the other people and events around them. Positive attutides lead to positive outlooks, and negative attitudes generally lead to negative outlooks.

An employee's attitude about many things, such as an interest in having a job, interacting with people, and living a healthy lifestyle, is formed long before the employee begins working at the hotel. Other attitudes, such as doing the best job possible, attempting to consistently meet the needs of guests, and following reasonable work procedures, may be formed or, at least, influenced by what does (and does not) happen in the workplace. Assume, for example, that a job applicant has no knowledge about the hotel as an employer. The new employee's experiences during the application and selection process and early job activities, including orientation and training, will help establish an attitude that sets the stage for that staff member's relationship with the property.

Many supervisors believe they have a personal responsibility to motivate their employees. **Motivation** is an internal force that drives employees to do something to reach a goal. Therefore, since motivation involves a force that must be developed within an employee, other supervisors believe it is not actually possible for them to motivate their team members.

LODGING LANGUAGE

Motivation: An internal force that drives employees to do something to reach a goal.

Can supervisors motivate their work teams? A popular and widely accepted motivation theory defines five basic human needs and suggests that people must reach a self-determined level of satisfaction with a lower-level need before having a desire to attain higher-level needs.[1] While no need may ever be completely satisfied, the basic need most unfulfilled provides the strongest motivation at any given point in time.

[1]Abraham Maslow, *Motivation and Personality* (New York: Harper & Row, 1964).

Human Needs	How Met on the Job
• Physical Needs	• Rest breaks, increased compensation, work bonuses
• Safety and Security Needs	• Consistent application of work rules and policies, nonthreatening work environment, availability of proper working equipment
• Social Needs	• Committee assignments, friendships with other employees, participation in social activities sponsored by the hotel, availability of an employee newspaper
• Ego (self-esteem)	• Awards such as employee of the month or year, service pins, paid attendance at external-property training sessions, recognition, personal letters from one's boss.
• Self-fulfillment (Knowing that one is doing the very best one can do)	• Involvement in planning goals, objectives, and budgets and by participating in creative special projects

FIGURE 5.4 Basic Human Needs Can Be Met on the Job

Figure 5.4 reviews each of these needs and shows how they might be addressed on the job. Another motivation theory was advanced by different researcher at about the same time as the theory just presented.[2] It considers two sets of factors necessary in the workplace to promote employee motivation. One set is referred to as maintenance factors; the second set is called motivation factors. Details about this popular needs-related theory are listed in Figure 5.5.

Maintenance Factors	
Factor	Examples of Concerns
• Economics	• Wages, salaries, fringe benefits
• Security	• Procedures for handling grievances, reasonable work rules and policies, employee discipline programs
• Social	• Chance to interact with other employees on and off the job
• Working Conditions	• Proper levels of heat, light, ventilation, and number of working hours
• Status	• Job titles, work privileges, other signs of position or rank
Motivational Factors	
• Challenging work • Feelings of personal accomplishment • Recognition of achievements • Opportunities to participate in the decision-making process • Increased job responsibilities • Feeling important to the hotel • Having access to information	

FIGURE 5.5 Maintenance and Motivational Factors

[2]Frederick Herzberg et al., *The Motivation to Work* (New York: Wiley, 1964).

According to this theory, maintenance factors do not motivate employees. However, if they are not present in the workplace, employee dissatisfaction will result. By contrast, the second set of factors identified in Figure 5.5 is called motivational factors, and they provide the conditions necessary to motivate employees. Experienced supervisors know that employees interested in their work are likely to have an internal drive (motivation) that will benefit the employee, the guest, and the hotel. They also understand that staff members who believe in the hotel's goals will be more willing to help the hotel than will other staff members motivated only by punishment and reward. These supervisors do not become overly concerned about whether it is the employees or their leaders that actually "provide" motivation. Rather they work hard to ensure that their team members are working in an atmosphere that encourages high levels of performance from everyone.

THE ROLE OF ENTRY-LEVEL EMPLOYEES

Entry-level hotel employees in the hotel industry should be considered professionals. They deserve and desire this respect and will earn it when those managing their efforts utilize positive leadership tactics.

Professionals are proud, know the correct way to do their job, try to do it better, and make the profession better in the process. Professional entry-level employees "go the extra mile," are part of the hotel's team, try to put forth the best possible efforts to meet the guests' needs and the hotel's goals, and are genuinely interested in helping other employees.

ALL IN A DAY'S WORK 5.1

THE SITUATION

"I guess I am doing okay," said Raoul, a front office clerk at the Edgemont Inn, in response to a question posed by Nancy, a housekeeper at the property.

"Well," said Nancy in reply, "we housekeepers are not doing okay. In fact, we never do anything right! We never receive a sit-down evaluation from our supervisor." She continued, "Whenever there is a problem, we hear about it, and, of course, it's always our fault! The boss never accepts responsibility for lack of clear direction, never shares information with us, and never thanks us for showing up and doing a good job. No wonder another housekeeper quit this week, and you can bet that I'll be gone as soon as I find another job!"

"I know that things must be bad," said Raoul. "The grapevine says that housekeeping is a tough place to work. That's interesting, because we at the front office have the opposite problem: we hear nothing from our boss so we don't know when there is a problem except when the guests tell us about issues that affect them. We don't have formal performance evaluations either, and even though our boss spends most of the day only a few feet from us, we really don't know how things are going.

A RESPONSE

Even though Raoul and Nancy are employed in two different departments with two different supervisors, they share some things in common: their supervisors are not utilizing proper leadership techniques.

Their frustration affects their performance and, ultimately, their employment with the hotel. Both of their supervisors should respect their staff members, provide input about employee performance, provide job-related information that affects their staff, and recognize that they—not their staff members—are likely to be the root cause of the problems that are occurring.

When Raoul and Nancy were hired, they probably wanted to do a good job. They may have been hoping for a long-term employment relationship with the property. Unfortunately, that has now changed. The hotel's managers should know about the turnover rates in these two departments and be concerned by it. The general manager should also recognize other problems that may indicate ineffective supervision. These can be dealt with by meeting with all the property managers to plan and implement an effective employee appraisal program. Along the way, the use of cross-functional teams (teams that include members of two or more different departments) to identify other problems and generate resolution alternatives can help to define where problems originate and what might be done to resolve them.

Responsibilities

Entry-level employees have important jobs. If they did not, they would not be employed by the hotel. They know what is expected of them because their supervisor tells and shows them, and they consistently meet these standards. They have effective ways to communicate with their supervisor, and they do so often. Professional employees are courteous and are concerned about the problems that they and other staff members have on the job.

How employees get along with their supervisor will impact their success. In the best of circumstances, there will be mutual respect and understanding between both parties. Perhaps a good relationship will arise naturally and will be easy to build upon. However, this may not be the case. Sometimes friction occurs between leaders and work teams. When that happens, it can be more difficult, but in such cases, it is even more important to work hard to develop, maintain, and improve the relationship. Good employees recognize that their boss will not likely be their close personal friend; however, both employee and boss can respect each other. Respect is necessary in every relationship, and it is necessary for success on the job. Respect is most likely to occur when the staff member:

- cooperates and complies with reasonable requests made by the supervisor
- consistently attains standards of quality and quantity output
- is dependable; actually does what he/she says will be done
- has good manners and is respectful of guests, coworkers, supervisors, and others
- works well with others
- shows an interest in the job and in the work to be done
- demonstrates ambition and is willing to work hard to be successful
- shows loyalty by publicly supporting the hotel, their supervisor, and their coworkers
- is creative, generates ideas, and sets a good example for others

By doing the things mentioned above, employees show respect for their peers and supervisors. In turn, they gain the respect of others.

Supervisors of entry-level employees should expect certain things of their staff members. Examples of reasonable expectations include:

- belief in and compliance with the hotel's policies and regulations
- their best efforts in providing quality products and services to guests
- suggestions about better ways to do assigned work
- maturity—keeping promises, meeting work obligations, and a serious attitude about the job to be done
- speaking positively (or not all) about the hotel and its managers
- a recognition that purposeful change is inevitable and cooperating with it rather than resisting it
- taking responsibility for their own on-the-job behavior
- consistently working to the best of their abilities
- serving as a contributing member of the hotel's guest service team

Many employees must work together to make a hotel successful. Supervisors must have the philosophy that work is accomplished with employees rather than in spite of them. Supervisors and their staff must work together in a cooperative, win-win relationship. As they do so, they help to best serve their guests and also help to meet their own best interests.

Career Tracks

Some entry-level employees working in hotels do not desire a long-term career in the lodging or hospitality industry. They may be students working their way through school or older people working at a part-time job to supplement their retirement income. Other staff members may have initially accepted a job at the property and because they liked the work became interested in a career in the lodging industry. Still others began working at a hotel already knowing that it was a first step in their lodging hospitality career. There is a place for all of these staff members in the hotel.

Treating entry-level employees with respect and keeping them involved are key components of a successful team.

WHAT SHOULD EMPLOYEES EXPECT FROM THEIR SUPERVISOR?

The staff members of a hotel have a right to expect certain things from their supervisor. These expectations include:

- fair compensation for the jobs they perform
- safe working conditions
- the training needed to perform their current job well
- additional training for advancement if that is possible
- help to ensure that all employees work well together
- a full explanation of policies, rules, and regulations that affect them
- a fair evaluation of their work
- recognition for a job well done
- the use of a leadership style appropriate for each employee
- effective role-modeling; the supervisor sets a good example of professional behavior

LODGING ONLINE

Some Internet Web sites provide a wide range of information about the management of people. For example, go to:

www.managementhelp.org/

When you reach the site, click on a management topic of interest to you.

Do you see why many lodging industry professionals believe the study of management is an on-going and life-long process?

Hotel employees, like everyone else, tend to do what is in their best self-interest. If, for example, they perceive it to be beneficial to remain employed at a lodging property, they will do so. The reverse is also true, and they will leave for another opportunity that they believe to be better.

It is the supervisor's challenge to make the hotel workplace compatible with their interests because there are many things that supervisors can do to promote careers in the hotel and the lodging industry. Supervisors can:

- Show excitement—find opportunities to discuss the many benefits and rewards of working in the hotel industry.
- Begin with an emphasis on career rather than job at the time new employees are recruited.
- Explain how career advancement can happen. Consider the following statement made to a new employee during orientation: "Here is our hotel's organization chart. You are beginning in this entry-level position. People in these upper-level positions began where you are now, and they have advanced to positions of greater responsibility."
- Provide opportunities for all employees who master their current job to receive training and professional development opportunities applicable to other positions if they wish to do so.
- Serve as a mentor by making suggestions where appropriate and answering questions when asked.
- Serve as a role model. Be positive and upbeat about the property and the lodging industry; actively participate in their personal development and training programs.
- Help interested employees plan a personal **career ladder**.

LODGING LANGUAGE

Career ladder: A plan that details successively more responsible positions within an organization or an industry. Career ladders allow one to plan and schedule developmental activities necessary to assume more responsible positions.

The hotel's organization chart is a simple career ladder and suggests successively more responsible positions in the property. For example, in a large hotel one may begin as a front office clerk, advance to become a front office supervisor, and then move to front office manager. Alternatively, in a limited-service property, some staff members may wish to transfer between departments to gain a better understanding of how the entire hotel works. In both examples, the organization chart suggests advancement opportunities.

The challenge of every supervisor is to help employees find pride and joy in their work. For many, this involves a future of more responsible challenges. Supervisors help their employees by encouraging advancement for every employee who demonstrates the ability to advance.

CHOOSING AND KEEPING THE RIGHT STAFF MEMBERS

Managers and supervisors in every department in hotels of every size must be genuinely concerned about finding and keeping quality employees. Large hotels typically have a **human resources** department that helps managers in each functional area to more effectively (and legally) manage employees. The human resources department is typically staffed with one or more employees who help other hotel managers and supervisors deal with human resources concerns, including recruitment, selection, orientation, training, compensation, legal, safety and health, and perform a wide range of other specialized tasks.

LODGING LANGUAGE

Human resources (department): The functional area in a hotel with the responsibility to assist managers in other departments with employee-related concerns. Also known as "HR"

Historically, the terms "Personnel" and "Personnel management" have been used to describe the discipline of human resources management. However, these terms are not really appropriate because the human resources function involves much more than just managing or directing employees at work. Many other behind-the-scenes activities that support the property's employees are part of the larger scope of human resources.

No hotel can be successful unless its human resource activities are effectively managed. In most limited-service and smaller full-service properties, there is neither a human resources department nor a full-time human resources director. These responsibilities may become part of the work of the general manager and in some cases, a support person who performs clerical and record-keeping tasks related to human resources as well as other tasks.

Alternatively, some of the responsibilities for human resources may be decentralized. For example, the general manager may perform activities relating to property-wide concerns. Examples include ensuring that the application form complies with current employment law and that those responsible for specific hotel functions (e.g., the front office or housekeeping) undertake other activities including recruitment, selection, and orientation for their areas of responsibility.

Regardless of whether human resources activities are performed by a general manager with numerous other responsibilities, decentralized throughout the property, or undertaken by one or more human resource staff specialists, the same basic issues must be addressed if hotel employees are to be effectively managed. These issues include:

Recruitment
Selection
Orientation
Training
Workplace Fairness
Retention

Because of their importance, hotel managers must be knowledgeable about each of these.

Recruitment

The high turnover rate incurred by some hotels makes employee **recruitment** a seemingly never-ending but absolutely critical management task.

LODGING LANGUAGE

Recruitment: Activities designed to attract qualified applicants for the hotel's vacant management and non-management positions.

Recruitment can be especially difficult in locations where qualified workers are scarce. This can be the case because of a common misconception that entry-level positions in the hospitality industry pay poorly and provide few opportunities for advancement.

Hotel managers must recognize that the need to recruit for vacant positions is directly related to their hotel's turnover rate because if fewer current staff members leave their jobs, the need to recruit for vacant positions is reduced. There are many things that a hotel's managers can do to influence turnover rates. The development of policies, procedures, and standards to help make the hotel the employer of choice within the community is a good place to start. If these succeed, the need for recruitment activities is reduced.

What are the best tactics to use when new staff members must be recruited? Human resources managers in large properties and department managers in smaller hotels can utilize the same methods. Often, a good mix of **internal recruiting** and **external recruiting** techniques is best.

LODGING LANGUAGE

Internal recruiting: Tactics to identify and attract staff members who are currently employed at the hotel for vacancies that represent promotions or transfers to other positions.

External recruiting: Tactics designed to attract persons who are not current hotel employees for vacant positions at a property.

As the names imply, internal recruiting focuses on employees who are currently employed at the hotel (internal applicants). External recruiting focuses on searching for applicants who are *not* currently employed at the hotel.

The human resources tool known as a **job description** is useful for both internal and external recruiting. People thinking about applying for a job want to know what the job involves. A job description identifies the tasks in a job. It is important that job descriptions be kept current so that there are no surprises after employees are hired.

LODGING LANGUAGE

Job description: A list of tasks that an employee working in a specific position must be able to effectively perform.

Many hotels emphasize promotion from within, and this is an example of an internal recruiting technique. Managers in these properties look first to high-performing current staff members when higher-level managerial or supervisory positions become vacant. Promotional opportunities provide incentives for employees to remain with the hotel and to excel in their current positions. Some staff members may want to transfer to other positions in the hotel for professional development, personal interests, or other reasons. They should always be allowed to do so if the transfer is in the best interest of the hotel.

Alerting friends and relatives of current employees about position vacancies is another example of internal recruiting. Sometimes, bonuses are paid to staff members who nominate applicants who are selected and then employed at the hotel for a specified time period. An advantage of this tactic is that current employees know what it is like to work at the hotel. If they like their job, they can be excellent recruiters within their circle of friends and families.

There are many external recruitment tactics that may be effective. The well-known ones include Internet job-posting sites, Twitter, Craigslist, newspaper and other media advertisements, student job fairs, use of employment and executive search firms for managerial positions, and recruiting at colleges.

All employees, by what they do or fail to do, make an impression on their fellow employees. This, in turn, affects the hotel's turnover rate. Employees can also influence the perceptions of applicants who may, for example, talk with current employees about how great or terrible it is to work for a specific hotel. Managers who seriously consider their recruitment strategies

Selecting the right employees and providing them with the proper training will improve retention and provide long-term benefits for both the hotel and the employees.

LODGING ONLINE

One of the most popular job search sites for hourly and managerial positions is Hospitality Careers.com. To view its Web site and jobs in your area, go to:

www.hcareers.com/

Do you think most people who apply for hotel jobs seek long-term or short-term employment? What do you think would most influence their decisions?

LODGING GOES GREEN!

Increasingly, hotels that go green find they attract better quality candidates for their job openings. That's because workers are increasingly aware that companies that show their concern about the well-being of the environment most often share that same concern for the well-being of their workers. As a result, prospective workers increasingly seek out those companies that openly demonstrate their health, social, and environmental interests and priorities. More and more workers live their lives in a way that values health, the environment, social justice, personal development, and sustainable living. They prefer to associate with companies that share those values.

A hotel need not implement every possible green program to attract this new breed of socially conscious worker, but neither can they simply "pretend" to be green. Today's sophisticated workers can easily see beyond false claims of care, and they will not hesitate to share what they find out about their companies freely and easily via Web pages, blogs, tweets, and chat rooms.

If your organization decides to implement environmentally friendly programs, let your current and your prospective employees know about them, because workers at all levels care about their world and they want to associate with employers who show they also care.

and solicit input from their staff members may discover tactics that will increase their hotel's share of available job applicants.

Selection

Selection is the process of evaluating applicants for positions in order to choose those most qualified and those most likely to be successful.

LODGING LANGUAGE

Selection: The process of evaluating job applicants to determine who is most qualified for and likely to be successful in a vacant position.

A **job specification** is a human resource tool that can help with employee selection. It identifies the personal qualities judged necessary for successful job performance. Within the limitations imposed by the law, examples of appropriate qualifications can include education, work experience, past performance, and physical abilities.

LODGING LANGUAGE

Job specification: A list of personal qualities or characteristic necessary for successful job performance.

Who should make employee selection decisions? Even in properties with human resources departments, the selection decision should be made by the appropriate department manager. Prior to selection, information about each applicant's eligibility for a position must be gathered. This may be done by using a variety of procedures, including:

Preliminary screening. This includes filing out an application form

Employment interview(s). If the hotel has a human resources department, a preliminary interview will probably be conducted by an HR staff member. Applicants successfully completing this screening interview will then be referred to a manager in the department recruiting the staff member for a second interview. In smaller properties, the initial and follow-up interviews may be conducted by the person who will be the immediate supervisor of the employee.

Typically the interviewer should use a mix of open-ended questions (e.g., "What tactics do you use to interact with the strangers who are our guests?") and more structured performance-related questions (e.g., "What are the most important concerns when cleaning the condenser coils on a refrigeration unit?") if an experienced maintenance technician is being recruited.

Employment tests. Applicants are most frequently tested when experience or specific knowledge is required. For example, an applicant may be given a paper-and-pencil test that addresses the arithmetic involved in cashiering skills required for a front office clerk.

Reference checks and recommendations. After an applicant has given approval to do so, past employers may be contacted to confirm employment dates and previous positions held.

Physical exams and drug testing. Physical exams may be useful for some positions such as swimming pool lifeguards as long as they do not discriminate. Drug testing, while controversial, is legal under specialized situations in many states.[3]

Applicants judged by the screening process to be most qualified for the vacant position will usually be offered a job with the property. If the applicant accepts the job offer, the next tasks involve helping the new employee prepare for success in the newly filled position.

Orientation

Orientation is the process of providing basic information about the hotel that must be known by all of its employees. Effective orientation is critical because it helps to establish the relationship between the hotel and its employees.

LODGING LANGUAGE

Orientation: The process of providing basic information about the hotel that must be known by all of its employees.

Orientation programs must be well thought out. They should not be presented inconsistently and haphazardly. Managers show concern for new employees by ensuring that the orientation program is organized, consistently comprehensive, and professionally well done.

Goals of orientation include:

- Reducing anxiety. New staff members are looking for reinforcement that their employment decision was a good one.
- Improving morale and reducing turnover. Orientation programs should establish a good foundation for the relationship between the new employees and the hotel.
- Providing consistency. An effective orientation process yields a team of employees who are more likely to be aware of and believe in the property's goals. They will know what to do, for example, in case of a fire or other emergency, and they will have a correct understanding of the hotel's personnel policies, including vacation, personal days, sick leave, and other benefits.
- Developing realistic expectations. New employees want to know what their managers expect of them. Orientation programs should provide this information.

Since the orientation process involves informing employees about general information applicable to all hotel employees, human resources personnel in large properties normally perform this function. In smaller hotels, the general manager, department head, or supervisor should assume this responsibility. General topics to be covered in a comprehensive orientation program may include:

- Hotel overview, including its mission statement, the importance of effective guest service, and the emphasis on teamwork.
- Review of important policies and procedures.

[3]An experienced, licensed attorney should be contacted for state/local regulations applicable to all selection tools.

- Detailed discussion of compensation, including fringe benefits.
- Safety and accident prevention concerns.
- Employee/union relations (if applicable).
- Physical facility, including a tour of all areas. A meal in the hotel's restaurant may be included as part of the tour.
- Other topics of priority to the hotel, such as its emphasis on quality, empowerment, and professional development opportunities.

Many hotels provide an **employee handbook** during orientation. Its purpose is to provide details about the basic subject matter presented during orientation.

LODGING LANGUAGE

Employee handbook: Written policies and procedures related to employment at the hotel, sometimes called an "employee manual."

In large properties, a personal introduction by the hotel's general manager can have a significant impact on the relationship between the employee, the hotel, and its staff members. New employees will be impressed that the general manager cares enough to welcome them to the hotel's team. In some hotels, a second follow-up orientation is held several weeks or months after the initial orientation session. This allows employees to provide input about their initial job experiences and to ask questions based upon their experience in the workplace. The session can also be used to reinforce the most important aspects of the orientation program.

Training

Newly selected employees must be trained, but all employees—both those newly hired and with experience—benefit from effective training. Training is necessary for all staff members regardless of how much experience they have in a position. New employees must be trained to perform their jobs so that quality and quantity standards can be consistently attained. However, even experienced staff members need training, as, for example, when new equipment is purchased or as new work procedures are implemented. Even general managers will require training as new operating techniques and managerial approaches evolve in response to advances in technology, modifications in company goals, and changes in guests' expectations.

In larger properties, HR personnel may develop programs designed to teach managers how to train. In smaller properties, the general manager may decide who will be responsible for conducting training and in what areas. In some hotels, a departmental trainer may be responsible for all of the training required for new staff members in that department. Other hotels may utilize several trainers, each of whom is responsible for conducting on-the-job training in specific areas.

LODGING ONLINE

The Educational Institute of the American Hotel & Lodging Association offers an extensive array of educational programs and independent learning formats for hoteliers and for hospitality management students. Go to:

http://www.ahlei.org/

Note that courses of study are available for staff members working in almost any lodging department and position, and that programs are available for employees working in large and small lodging properties.

Why do you think most experienced hoteliers consider learning a lifelong undertaking? Do you?

ALL IN A DAY'S WORK 5.2

THE SITUATION

Sylva Cooper was the general manager of the Sunshine Springs Inn, a limited-service property with 65 rooms. She was facilitating the weekly meeting with her department managers. "You know," said Sylva, "I'm convinced that we can gain a competitive edge over the chain properties in this area if we can increase our emphasis on guest service. I think we already do a pretty good job. We occasionally get complaints about poor guest service, but we usually receive positive feedback. What do you think about training all of our staff to excel in guest service, to consistently deliver quality service, and then try to market our guest service attitude?"

"I think it's a good idea," said Jerome, the front office manager.

"Me too," said Vanessa, the housekeeping manager. "But who is going to develop our training program? And who will present it? For that matter, when do we find time to bring our employees together for the training? After all, we're really busy now. Maybe there will be more time to do this later in the year."

A RESPONSE

A small lodging property like the Sunshine Springs Inn will not likely have a human resources department to develop and deliver training programs. But busy lodging managers cannot continue doing what they have always done just because they lack the time, money, or other resources to update their skills. Fortunately, in the hospitality industry, many training programs have already been developed and are readily available. Some are specific to the industry, while others are generic and can be used by any organization dealing with the public. In this case, Sylva and her department heads must recognize that their attitude about guest service is the most important factor in implementing a guest service emphasis and keeping it going. Creative scheduling can allow all staff members to participate in the training. Costs for wages paid to trainees and to purchase materials can be budgeted, and other hurdles can be overcome if managers are truly committed to staff training.

BENEFITS OF TRAINING

Experienced hoteliers know that training can make a positive influence on a number of important areas in a lodging property. These include:

- productivity
- quality
- guests' perceptions about the hotel
- attainment of financial goals
- improved job skills
- employee job satisfaction
- help with employee recruitment efforts
- improvement in employee attitudes
- reduction in turnover
- improved teamwork

Training new employees is not difficult, but planning and delivering training takes time and effort. In business, time costs money, so training is, initially, more expensive than the alternative of not training. However, since trained employees are more productive, are better able to meet quality requirements, feel better about the work they do, and are more likely to remain with the hotel, it becomes easy to justify training time and expenditures.

Staff members can be trained on an individualized (one-to-one) basis or in a group with other trainees. A four-step process can be used with either method. These steps are shown in Figure 5.6.

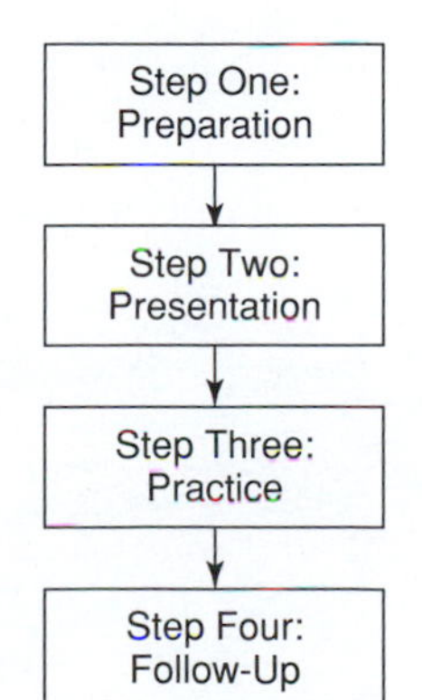

FIGURE 5.6 Four-Step Training Method

Let's look at how supervisors apply the Four-Step Training Method when training new or more experienced employees.

Step One ***Preparation.*** To begin, the trainer must develop and consistently pursue definable training objectives. Before teaching a **job task**, the trainer should know exactly why and how it should be done.

To prepare for training, trainers should

1. Work out a time schedule indicating when the training will take place.
2. Gather all needed training equipment, tools, and materials.
3. Select and properly arrange the training location.
4. Identify the specific job tasks the trainee must learn.
5. Put the trainee(s) at ease.
6. Find out what the trainee already knows about each task.
7. Explain what the trainee should expect to learn in the session.
8. Set a good example for the trainee.
9. Tell "what's in it" for the trainee.
10. Plan to deliver the training at the trainees' language level.

FIGURE 5.7 The Four-Step Training Method: Preparation

LODGING LANGUAGE

Job task: An activity that an employee working in a specific position must know how and be able to do. For example, a front office agent in a hotel must be able to properly check in an arriving guest.

Decisions about the time needed for training and its location along with the assembly and set-up of all necessary materials and equipment must also occur before training begins. It is also important to explain, from the trainee's point of view, why the training is important and how the trainee will benefit from it. Figure 5.7 lists the activities required to properly prepare for training.

Step Two ***Presentation.*** After the training session is prepared, presentation issues become important. Specific work procedures become the foundation for presenting the training. Each training activity should be designed to illustrate and emphasize the correct way to do each job task.

After the trainer reviews how a task should be done, employees should demonstrate the correct way to do it. The demonstration should involve as much repetition as necessary to make sure that the trainee understands how the activity is done and fits into the entire job. Figure 5.8 lists the activities required to properly prepare for the presentation of training.

After the training has been presented it is time for the trainee to practice.

Step Three ***Practice.*** After the trainer has explained and demonstrated the job task, the trainee should perform the task alone. Repetition is an important way to be certain that the trainee knows how to do the work and can begin to acquire the necessary skills and speed. While the trainee practices, the trainer can make suggestions about ways to do the work better and, at the

To present the training, trainers should:

1. Explain and demonstrate job tasks to the trainee.
2. Maintain a patient and appropriate pace throughout the training.
3. Make sure that the trainee understands each job task and procedure.
4. Encourage the trainee to ask questions.
5. Check for understanding by asking open-ended questions.
6. Take up only one point at a time.
7. Follow an orderly sequence by teaching tasks in the order they will be done on the job.
8. Provide only information or instruction that can be mastered at one session.
9. Make all instructions clear, concise, and complete.
10. Make the session interesting.
11. Have all equipment/tools available.
12. Show the trainee how to do the task correctly.
13. Remind the trainee to look at effectiveness from the perspective of guests and other hotel staff.

FIGURE 5.8 The Four-Step Training Method: Presentation

As the trainee practices the task, trainers should:

1. Test the trainee by asking him/her to perform the task in the required way within a specified time frame.
2. Ask the trainee to explain the "hows and whys" of the task on a point-by-point basis.
3. Carefully note and correct any improper or substandard actions.
4. Make sure that the trainee understands requirements by asking questions such as: "Why is it best to do it this way?"
5. Tell the trainee when he or she did well.
6. Correct errors during the training so trainees can immediately learn from their mistakes.
7. Allow extra time for private (personal) practice if needed.
8. Encourage the trainee to ask questions.

FIGURE 5.9 The Four-Step Training Method: Practice

same time, compliment the trainee for mastering the information or skill needed to do the job properly. Figure 5.9 presents specific suggestions for this important training step.

Step Four ***Follow-Up.*** At some point after the trainer has allowed the trainee to practice, the trainee should be able to do the work without constant supervision. The trainer should, however, continue to monitor the trainee just in case any problems arise. At this time, **reinforcement** becomes important.

LODGING LANGUAGE

Reinforcement (training): Use of encouraging words and actions that re-emphasize the proper way to do a job task.

If follow-up is effective, the trainee will develop a continued positive attitude about the training and, at the same time, will learn how to do the job correctly. Figure 5.10 presents specific follow-up training activities.

LODGING ONLINE

At the most basic level, some principles for training entry-level employees in the lodging industry are the same as those for training entry-level staff members in other service organizations. To see a resource focused on training, go to:

www.trainingmag.com/

When you arrive, take special notice of any generic training tools that could be used in the hotel industry.

The importance of teamwork is an example of a training topic that would be needed in every service organization. What are some others?

To follow-up after training, trainers should:

1. Allow the trainee to work independently in the appropriate work area.
2. Encourage the trainee to ask for help whenever it is needed.
3. Tell the trainee who to ask for help in the future.
4. Check the trainee's performance frequently.
5. Let the trainee know how he or she is doing.
6. Help the trainee correct mistakes.
7. Make sure that the trainee learns from mistakes.
8. Ask the trainees for suggestions about better ways to do the job and encourage them to improve on existing standards.
9. Reward good performance with positive feedback, including a sincere "Thank You" for the trainee's best effort.

FIGURE 5.10 The Four-Step Training Method: Follow-Up

Workplace Fairness

Even the most carefully selected and trained employees will not stay in their jobs if they feel they are mistreated. For that reason, helping to ensure workplace fairness is an important part of every supervisor's job. Employees seek equitable treatment in a variety of employment areas, including pay, work schedules, and daily work assignments. Two critical areas in which supervisors must be especially sensitive to charges of favoring one worker or group over another are employee discipline and performance appraisal.

EMPLOYEE DISCIPLINE

When some hotel supervisors think about employee **discipline**, they think of it only in terms of punishment for wrongdoing.

LODGING LANGUAGE

Discipline: Corrective actions designed to encourage employees to follow established policies, rules, and regulations.

To help ensure workplace fairness, a better approach is to view discipline as a variety of techniques supervisors use to improve an employee's on-the-job performance. Many factors influence a hotel employee's job performance. These include:

- Hotel-related factors, including the property's orientation and training programs, the leadership style(s) of the employee's supervisor, and the organization's policies and procedures.
- Personal factors, including ethics, integrity, and level of commitment to the hotel and its success.
- Union contracts.
- The influences of other employees.

When employees believe disciplinary actions are intended to help point out areas for improvement, fewer accusations of unfairness in the use of discipline are likely to arise. When there is a good relationship between the supervisor and the employees, the supervisor's instructions, suggestions, role-modeling, and other reinforcement tactics will encourage desired performance. It is only when this does not occur that disciplinary actions should be applied. If supervisors find they must discipline employees, they should recall that:

- Reprimands should be done in private.
- Any information leading to the decision should be available to the employee and be factual.
- The discipline should be based on what the employee did, not who he or she is.
- The disciplinary action should be undertaken as promptly as possible.
- The severity of the punishment should be in keeping with the seriousness of the problem.
- A **progressive disciplinary program** should be used. For example, one or more oral warnings followed by a written reprimand, followed, if appropriate, by suspension, transfer, or another action including, as the final action, termination of the employee.

LODGING LANGUAGE

Progressive disciplinary program: A carefully planned series of corrective actions, each increasing in its severity and designed to encourage employees to follow established policies, rules, and regulations.

Employees react unfavorably to disciplinary actions they perceive to be unfair. This can be the case, for example, when an employee is disciplined for an action that other employees do, but for which those employees are not disciplined. Supervisors seeking to ensure fairness in the use of disciplinary actions should always remember that the disciplinary actions they undertake should be immediate, consistent with the treatment of other employees, and impersonal. That is because it is the employee's behavior and performance, not the employee's personality, which must be made to conform to work standards.

PERFORMANCE APPRAISAL

Students in hospitality management programs like to know how well they are doing and are anxious for their instructors to evaluate their progress in class.[4] For example, they want to learn their test scores as soon as possible after taking a test. In the same way, hotel employees want to know how well they are doing and want their supervisors to evaluate their on-the-job efforts. A **performance appraisal** system that has been fairly designed and that is equitably applied should be in place to do this.

LODGING LANGUAGE

Performance appraisal: A periodic formal evaluation of an employee's job performance, including a discussion of professional development goals, also called "performance evaluation."

Well-designed performance appraisal systems help supervisors measure past employee performance, assist them to plan and develop activities for professional and personal improvement, and establish goals and procedures to guide improvement efforts.

Although the goals of performance appraisal are so significant, many hotels do not have formal appraisal processes in place. Some of those that do, unfortunately, utilize programs that are flawed and viewed as unfair by employees. For example, some formal evaluation systems require evaluators to compare employees against one another. As a result, some employees must be classified as "very good" and others must be "very bad" even though, in fact, all of them may be consistently meeting or exceeding job standards.

Ideally, a performance appraisal answers two questions: How well does the staff member being evaluated perform the job, and, if performance inadequacies do exist, what corrective actions can be taken to improve the employee's performance? For an employee appraisal system to be viewed as fair, supervisors must recognize their responsibility to identify job tasks, train new and existing employees to meet quality standards, and provide the workplace tools and equipment necessary for job success.

Some supervisors do not like to confront employees or point out performance shortcomings. These supervisors tend to rate all employees as "average," or all of them as "above average" to minimize the time they spend on performance evaluations. They may be unwilling to share negative appraisal results with employees who are not performing well. Employees will not view such supervisors as fair.

It is important to recognize that performance appraisals do not need to be done only when formally required by hotel policy. Instead, some appraisal systems allow for informal conversations that can occur at any time and that are designed to give supervisors an opportunity to improve employee performance. Regardless of the specific characteristics of their property appraisal program, effective supervisors design fair systems, explain them fully to the hotel's employees, and then apply them justly every time.

Retention

Hoteliers in all types of properties and in all areas of the country often voice concerns about a labor shortage because they cannot recruit all of the staff members they would like to employ. A partial solution to this challenge is simply that of retaining existing employees. It is not necessary to continually recruit, orient, and train new staff members if existing staff members remain with the organization.

---

[4]This section and the one that follows are adapted from Jack Ninemeier and David Hayes, *Restaurant Operations Management* (Upper Saddle River, NJ: Pearson Education, 2006).

Hotel employees can leave their jobs for a variety of reasons. Retirement, moving out of the area, and completing their education are among the reasons currently employed staff members might leave a property. In each of these cases, there may be little, if anything, hotel managers can do to retain the employee. Some **turnover** is good for a hotel because new employees with diverse attitudes and ideas are brought into the organization. However, the extensive turnover rates experienced by some properties seriously hinder their ability to maintain quality standards and meet financial goals. High levels of turnover are not good, and to some degree, those levels can be controlled by effective managers and supervisors.

LODGING LANGUAGE

Turnover (employee): The replacement of employees needed in an organization or a position as other staff members leave.

Some hoteliers resign themselves to a belief that high turnover is an unavoidable cost of doing business in the lodging industry. They believe that little or nothing can be done about it. As a result, these managers continue the cycle of recruitment–turnover–recruitment that causes significant problems for themselves and their hotels.

A better alternative is to work hard to become an employer-of-choice (see Chapter 3) within their communities. Many of the tactics needed to achieve this status involve care and common sense. The supervisor should ask, "How would I like to be treated if I were an entry-level employee?" The answers to this basic question will suggest the actions supervisors and managers can take to reduce excessive turnover rates, improve employee retention, and thus reduce costs related to high employee turnover. The good news is that the implementation of tactics designed to make a hotel an employer-of-choice is usually not very expensive. They involve activities that recognize the worth and dignity of individual employees and allow them to find pride and joy in their jobs and experience fairness in their workplace. Some of these tactics are noted below.

Tactic 1: Demonstrate Leadership to Your Staff

- Select the best employees possible, train them well, provide the work resources they need to be effective, and treat them fairly.
- Comply with all employment laws: Employ only those legally allowed to work.
- Eliminate employees who don't contribute their fair share to the achievement of the hotel's goals. Avoid favoritism.
- Recognize that the "customers" (your guests) are **not** always right. Guests who abuse employees are not right. Employees need to be supported when interactions involving uncivil guests occur.

Tactic 2: Prepare Each Staff Member for Success

- Share your vision about the hotel's future and the way it affects the future success of each staff member.
- Inform employees about professional development opportunities with the organization; take the responsibility to help them progress within their careers to the extent they wish to do so.
- Develop and consistently implement high-quality orientation and training programs.
- Be certain that employees with training responsibilities know how to effectively train.

Tactic 3: Supervise the Way You Would Want to Be Supervised

- Develop and enforce on-time policies for all employees.
- Provide employees with a personal copy of their work schedule.
- Know about and refer staff members to employee assistance programs if you become aware that they have personal problems.
- Invite selected staff members to attend management meetings; allow talented employees to begin supervisory training before they are promoted to a supervisory position.

LODGING ONLINE

Want to learn more about managing turnover by retaining employees? If so, go to:

www.highretention.com/

Think about your desired position in the lodging industry. What factors would cause you to stay in your job with a specific hotel? What factors might cause you to leave?

Tactic 4: Create a Positive Workplace

- Conduct regularly scheduled meetings for all staff members to keep them infomed and to allow for their input.
- Celebrate employees' birthdays and other special occasions.
- Utilize creative employee-recognition programs.
- Praise staff members when praise is due.
- If practical, allow employees to share scheduling responsibilities, if applicable.
- Provide incentives for employees who work on nonscheduled shifts.
- Invite family members of new employees to visit the hotel.

Tactic 5: Celebrate Successful Employees

- Reward positive employee accomplishments each time you observe them.
- Don't reward your best employees by giving them more work to do just because they can do it.
- Assist employees in successfully meeting their work responsibilities by identifying child care and elder care options.
- Identify public transportation system options for those needing these services.

WORKER SAFETY AND HEALTH

All hoteliers, including the general manager, department heads, supervisors and the employees themselves, must be concerned about **safety hazards** and **health hazards**. Most hotels are not perceived as unsafe or unhealthy, but problems can arise, especially when certain jobs are performed incorrectly.

LODGING LANGUAGE

Safety hazard: Conditions in the workplace that can cause immediate harm. Examples include unsafe equipment, accidents, and the improper use of chemicals.

Health hazard: Aspects of the workplace that can lead to a decline in an employee's health. Examples include stressful working conditions and exposure to toxic chemicals.

Many work-related accidents and illnesses in hotels relate to:

- ***The work that must be done.*** For example, housekeepers may need to use hazardous chemicals when cleaning guest rooms. Without proper training, very serious accidents can result.
- ***Working conditions.*** For example, slippery sidewalks or wet interior lobby floors can cause accidents for anyone who walks on them.

Managers in every hotel department should be responsible for maintaining their workplaces and working conditions to minimize accidents. They should also be responsible for safety and other training for staff members. The general manager plays an important role by maintaining the philosophy that safety is the highest-priority concern. The general manager can carefully observe the facility, equipment, and work procedures in use; note any problems; and follow up to ensure that they have been corrected. The manager is responsible for the budget; if funds for problem correction and training materials programs are needed, for example, they should be allocated.

Employees should be trained to minimize safety and health hazards.

Effective hotel managers and supervisors implement safety programs of two types. The first addresses property-wide issues, such as fire safety, guest security, and response to natural disasters. The second type is department-specific. Thus for example, in this type of safety program, housekeepers will be trained in areas of safety important for their jobs (such as the safe use of chemical cleaners) while food and beverage employees will be trained in topics important to their jobs (such as storing and serving food safely). Hotels have other workplace safety issues that should be addressed by effective supervisors. These include:

- Workplace stress
- Violence in the workplace
- Disease prevention (e.g., preventing the contracting of human immunodeficiency virus (HIV; the virus that causes AIDS)
- Reptitive motion injuries such carpal tunnel syndrome

A genuine concern for workers in all aspects of their jobs is a characteristic of successful hotel managers and those who effectively select and retain talented staff members.

LEGAL ASPECTS OF SUPERVISION

Many legal issues affect the interactions that hotel managers have with their staff as they select, train, and retain their employees. These issues impose significant restraints on what managers can and cannot do. Hotel managers who know about and keep current with information about legal aspects of managing staff can avoid costly and time-consuming disputes, grievances, and lawsuits.

Employee Selection and the Law

An employer's legal responsibilities toward employees begin even before potential workers have been selected for an interview. You have learned that managers and supervisors should use written job descriptions to identify the knowledge and skills prospective employees must possess to do their jobs properly. Legally, however, only **bonafide occupational qualifications (BOQs)** may be used to screen out unqualified applicants.

LODGING LANGUAGE

Bonafide occupational qualifications (BOQs): The skills and knowledge to perform a job that are necessary to safely and adequately perform all the tasks required by the job.

Managers should carefully review job descriptions with the appropriate department managers to assess whether the tasks listed are necessary and whether they can be modified in a way that might accommodate additional qualified workers. In all cases, BOQs should not unfairly or illegally eliminate otherwise qualified candidates. Legitimate BOQs might include language skills (e.g., front office clerks may be required to speak English to communicate with guests) and minimum age requirements (e.g., in many areas, minors are not permitted to work during certain late-night hours or to serve alcoholic beverages).

The federal, state, and local employment laws affecting hoteliers are significant. In those hotels with a designated HR department, the responsibility for knowing and following these laws will typically rest with that department. In smaller hotels that do not have a designated HR staff, responsibility for knowing and following employment laws rests with general managers and their staffs.

The Employer-Employee Relationship

After employees have been legally selected, hoteliers have the basic right to terminate them if needed because, in most states in the United States, the employer's relationship with the employee is one of **at-will employment**.

LODGING LANGUAGE

At-will employment: The employment relationship that exists when employers can hire any employee they choose and dismiss an employee with or without cause at any time. Employees can also elect to work for the employer or to terminate the relationship anytime they desire to do so.

Assuming that no laws are violated, at-will employment means that an employer can hire or dismiss an employee at any time if it is in the best interests of the business to do so. Similarily, employees can elect to quit their job if they feel it is in their best interest to do so.

Additional Legal Issues in the Workplace

There are numerous laws or legal issues that have a significant effect upon the management of staff members during their employment. Some examples of employment-related legal issues include.

SEXUAL HARASSMENT

The laws in this area are designed to ensure that a manager or supervisor cannot ask a subordinate for sexual favors in exchange for employment benefits, nor can an employee be punished if an offer is rejected. Sexual harassment also includes the use of improper language or conduct.

THE FAMILY AND MEDICAL LEAVE ACT (FMLA)

Hotels that employ 50 or more persons are required to provide up to 12 weeks of leave (unpaid) to an employee if the time is needed for the birth, adoption, or, in some cases, the foster care of a child. The act also applies when an employee or a member of an employee's immediate family has a serious illness. The term "immediate family," for the purpose of this law, has been defined as a parent, spouse, or child.

MINIMUM WAGES AND OVERTIME PAY

The Fair Labor Standards Act (FLSA) is federal law that addresses the employment of minors. It also established a **minimum wage** to be paid to covered employees and pay rates for **overtime** work.

LODGING LANGUAGE

Minimum wage: The lowest amount of compensation that an employer may pay to an employee covered by the FLSA or applicable state law. Most hotel employees are covered by minimum wage provisions; however, exceptions can include youthful employees being paid a training wage for the first 90 days of employment and tipped employees (if reported tips plus wages received at least equal the minimum wage).

Overtime: The number of hours of work after which an employee must receive a pay premium (generally one and one-half times the normal hourly rate).

Another provision of the FLSA relates to equal pay. This portion of the law states that, regardless of gender, employees holding essentially the same job must be equitably compensated with financial and nonfinancial rewards.

In addition to these examples, there are numerous additional laws relating to the employment status of workers, payroll-related taxes that must collected from or paid on their behalf, and tax credits offered to employers for hiring disadvantaged workers. The provisions relating to these type issues are complicated and change frequently. As a result, someone on the hotel's staff must understand these laws and must keep up with them as they change. This staff member may be the human resources director in a large property and will usually be the general manager in smaller hotels. If the property employs an HR staff, the general manager should regularly ask for guidance about the hotel's policies/practices and when external legal assistance is warranted.

DIVERSITY IN STAFFING

The concept of **diversity** in the workforce receives much attention in the hospitality industry and especially in the hotel industry.

LODGING LANGUAGE

Diversity: The range of differences in attitudes, values, and behaviors of employees relative to gender, race, age, ethnicity, physical ability, and other personal characteristics.

The United States has historically been a "melting pot" of people from many different countries. The culture of the United States has always been diverse and is becoming even more so. One result is that the composition of the workforce, including employees in the hotel industry, is increasingly female, African American, Hispanic, and Asian. The percentage of Anglo-American males who make up the hotel industry's workforce will likely continue to decrease in coming years.

You have learned that it is illegal for employers to discriminate against employees or others on the basis of race, color, religion, sex, or national origin. You also know that people with disabilities who are seeking employment cannot be discriminated against. Therefore, the hotel industry will have an increasingly diverse workforce—first, because the employee market itself is diverse, and second, because it is illegal to exclude people from employment consideration.

Historically, the hotel industry has employed many women and other minorities for entry-level positions. Some are promoted and assume very responsible and well-paying positions at the highest level of hotel properties and in multiunit hotel organizations, including service on boards of directors. However, as a percentage of the total positions at these levels, the number of women is still relatively small. Increasingly, hotel organizations are developing and implementing diversity programs because it is the right thing to do, and because it makes good business sense.

What are the advantages to a lodging organization that actively recruits and promotes employees with diverse backgrounds? Proponents of diversity initiatives frequently cite the following benefits:

- The organization's corporate culture is more open to change. It is, therefore, better able to recognize the need for changes required by the ever evolving marketplace.
- A larger base of potential employees and more success in recruiting qualified applicants.
- Better relationships with guests and more opportunities for increased business—more guests of diverse backgrounds will be able to identify with employees, and staff members can more effectively interpret their needs and deliver a wider range of the products and services they desire.
- Higher retention rates for employees.
- Decreased guest complaints.
- Improved decision-making due to a more diverse range of creative alternatives generated to address operating challenges.
- Improved hotel reputation and image within the community and, for multiunit organizations, within all of their operating locations.

Properly planned valuing-diversity efforts are not programs; rather, they are basic, ongoing changes in the hotel's organizational culture that are integrated into "the way things are done" at the property or company. Strategies that can be useful in developing and implementing diversity initiatives include those relating to:

- Educational programs at all employee levels, including the highest in the organization, which address valuing-diversity issues.
- An emphasis on employing, training, and promoting the best employees from the diverse groups of staff members who work at the hotel.
- Emphasizing ownership by minority franchisees in multiunit companies. This can include offering financial assistance to new minority franchisees and helping to match new franchisees with potential lenders.
- Advertising and marketing efforts directed toward minority markets.
- Interactions with minority vendors to increase the amount the hotel buys from them.
- Including minority organizations in the charitable activities of the hotel.

Diversity training activities are an integral part of a hotel's implementation efforts and must be developed for each specific organization. All employees at all organizational levels should participate in the training. For example, entry-level staff should know the basics of equality and develop respect for diverse cultures. Managers must know about diversity details when hiring employees and understand the basics of equal employment opportunity laws.

Hotels with a successful diversity emphasis establish measurable goals, reward staff for attaining them, and continually improve their diversity implementation efforts because they know it is good for their staff, their business, and their community.

Lodging Language

Team
Participative Management
Entry-level Employees
Leadership
Autocratic Leadership Style
Bureaucratic Leadership Style
Democratic Leadership Style
Laissez-faire Leadership Style
Body Language
Motivation
Career ladder
Human resources (department)
Recruitment
Internal recruiting
External recruiting
Job description
Selection
Job specification
Orientation
Employee handbook
Job Task
Reinforcement (training)
Discipline
Progressive disciplinary program
Performance appraisal
Turnover (employee)
Safety hazard
Health hazard
Bonafide Occupational Qualification (BOQ)
At-will employment
Minimum wage
Overtime
Diversity

For Discussion

1. Give an example of a time in your own travel experience when teamwork (or lack of teamwork) by employees in different departments of a hotel directly affected the quality of your stay.
2. Assume that you are a supervisor and direct the work of several teen-aged employees who have worked for you for a few months and the work of several older employees who have worked at the property for several years. What are examples of differences in the way you would provide leadership to these different groups of employees?
3. Assume that you were a new entry-level employee in a hotel. What are some things that you would want your supervisor to do for you during your first few weeks on the job?
4. Assume that you are the general manager at a hotel. What are five things you would want all recently hired staff members to know regardless of their specific job or department?
5. Have you ever been treated unfairly in a job that you have held? How did that experience influence how you felt about staying in that job?
6. In the same geographic area, most hourly hotel employees who are skilled at performing a task in a hotel (i.e., a housekeeper or a front office agent) will be paid fairly similar wages at each of various hotels that seek to employ them. In addition to hourly pay, what factors do you think would make an employee initially choose to work at one hotel rather than another?
7. The costs related to employee turnover are significant, and managers should do what they can to minimize those costs. In addition to hourly pay, what factors do you think most often make an employee leave one employer and seek identical work with another employer? Do you think hotel managers can influence the factors you identified?
8. Some people consider entry-level positions in the hotel and hospitality industry to be dead-end jobs. What is the difference between a dead-end job and an entry-level position in a well-managed hotel? How would you respond to someone who stated that all beginning jobs in the hotel and hospitality industry are dead-end jobs?
9. There was a brief examination of the legal aspects of managing hotel staff in this chapter. What can you as a hotel manager do to help keep your hotel in compliance with all of the changing laws and regulations that would apply to your staff and your property?
10. Workplace diversity is a reality in most hotels. What are some specific benefits guests gain from experiencing that diversity? What are some specific benefits gained by the hotel?

Team Activities

TEAM ACTIVITY 1

Have each team list 10 creative tactics that a general manager or department head in a smaller property could use to recruit high-quality entry-level employees for their hotels. Assess the potential effectiveness of the items on each team's list.

TEAM ACTIVITY 2

It is often said that the best employees are given a disincentive to do good work because, in return, they are given more work! If, for example, a new staff member must be trained, a good employee, not a bad one, will be assigned this task. What are some practical things you as a manager can do to reward rather than punish your good employees who assume training duties? Consider what can be done before, during, and after these good staff members undertake training responsibilities.

Chapter

6

The Front Office Department

Chapter Outline

Front Office Responsibilities
- The Property Management System
- Guest Services
- Guest Accounting and Data Management

Forecasting Demand
- The Effect of Demand on Room Rates
- Estimating Demand
- Use of the PMS in Forecasting Demand

Establishing Room Rates
- Revenue Management
- Transient Rates
- Group Rates
- Contract Rates

Reservations
- Hotel Direct Inquiries
- Central Reservation Systems
- Internet Booking Sites

Reception and Guest Service
- Pre-arrival
- Arrival and Stay
- Departure

Guest Accounting
- Data Management
- Night Audit

Chapter Overview

The front office area in a hotel includes a registration desk or area where front office staff members assist arriving and departing guests, but the managers and staff of the front office department do much more than that. They assist in, or are responsible for, several important hotel functions, each of which is analyzed in detail in this chapter.

For many guests, the only person they will actually see when they arrive or depart from a hotel is a member of the front office. For that reason, the employees who work at the front office are critical to a hotel's long-term success.

Because the rooms sold by a hotel are extremely perishable (i.e., a guest room left unsold on one night can never again be sold on that night), it is very important that hotels do the best job possible in matching guest room availability with guest room demand. In addition, since it is not possible to increase or decrease the number of rooms available to sell each day (because a hotel is constructed with a fixed number of rooms), an important responsibility of the front office is to sell rooms at prices that management feels will optimize total revenue. An aggressively managed and talented front office staff will do this well.

Making guest reservations is often the first thing that comes to mind when one considers the main functions of a front office, and this is an essential and often complex aspect of its role. In addition to reservations, however, it is up to front office personnel to assign arriving guests to specific rooms and to respond to their needs during their stay. These needs can include anything from transportation and information to medical assistance. In all of these situations and many others, the unwavering role of the front office is to make the guest's stay as comfortable and as welcoming as possible.

In addition to servicing guests, another essential task of the front office is its responsibility for collecting the money guests pay for their rooms. This means that the individual responsible for the front office must devise and administer revenue management systems that charge guests the right amount for the services they use, and that the hotel collects in full, and keeps secure, all the money it has earned.

When forecasting room demand, accommodating guests, and collecting money for services rendered, the front office generates a large amount of information, much of which is critical for management decision-making. It is the role of the front office to collect, sort, and maintain this information and data in ways that assist in management decision-making. In this chapter, you will learn how that is done.

Chapter Objectives

1. To explain the main activities that occur in a hotel's front office.
2. To describe the process of forecasting hotel demand and establishing room rates.
3. To review the major sources of hotel reservations.
4. To explain the role of the front office before, during, and after a guest arrives at the hotel.
5. To examine how the front office manages guest and hotel data, including performance of the night audit.

FRONT OFFICE RESPONSIBILITIES

The **front office** is often referred to as the **front desk**, but its operation involves much more than simply the activities that occur at a hotel's front desk. In a smaller, limited-service hotel, the front office may consist, physically, of only the area used for guest registration. In a larger property, the front office may include numerous staff members, each responsible for a portion of this important department's management or operation.

LODGING LANGUAGE

Front Office: The department within the hotel responsible for guest reservations, registration, service, and payment.

Front Desk: The area within the hotel used for guest registration and payment.

In a small hotel, the front office may be managed directly by the general manager or, in larger properties, by the **FOM** (front office manager).

LODGING LANGUAGE

FOM: The hotel industry term for a front office manager.

The front office is responsible for managing three very important areas:

- The **Property Management System (PMS)**
- Guest Services
- Guest Accounting and Data Management

LODGING LANGUAGE

Property management system (PMS): The industry term for the computerized system used to record guest reservations, financial information, and other data related to the operation of a hotel's front office.

In smaller properties, responsibility for these areas will overlap. In fact, in a very small limited-service property, one person may perform all of these tasks and more. It is important that hotel managers understand the basic purpose of each front office responsibility.

The Property Management System

The PMS is the heart of the front office. Its effective management is critical to a well-run property. The PMS is the computerized system used by a hotel to manage its **central reservations system (CRS)**, rooms revenue, room rates, reservations and room assignments, guest histories, and accounting information as well as other selected guest service and management information functions.

LODGING LANGUAGE

Central reservations system (CRS): The industry term for the computerized program used to record guest room reservations.

A simple PMS will have limited features while more extensive (and expensive) systems offer hoteliers a wide range of management information features. Essentially, however, every PMS records (a) who is coming to the hotel and when, (b) what the guests spend when they are there, and (c) the approved form of payment used and the amount paid upon departure.

The management of a PMS entails understanding and using the system's preprogrammed features. The individual responsible for maintaining the PMS should be knowledgeable about all of these. When a hotel is not affiliated with a franchisor, it selects and maintains its own PMS. In such cases, training on the system is often provided by the manufacturer of the PMS. When a hotel is franchised, the franchisor most often mandates the PMS to be used, updates its programs periodically, and conducts regular training sessions about its operation.

PMS systems, like any other piece of electronic equipment, require care and maintenance. If they are not properly maintained, the results of a malfunction can be devastating to a hotel. Imagine for example, the problems that would occur if, one hour before many guests were to arrive on a sold-out night, the PMS crashed, making it impossible for the front office staff to ascertain the names of the guests who were coming to the hotel, the room types these guests had requested, and the room rates they were to pay. It does happen, but it can often be avoided by proper PMS maintenance. Because a PMS consists of a hardware component and a software component, the proper maintenance of both is a primary concern of the FOM and front office staff.

Management of the hardware requires that the front office staff keep the computer equipment clean and free of dust. Cables connecting PC workstations to the main computer should be examined periodically and replaced as needed. The source of power to the system should be managed and surge-protected so that unanticipated power surges or outages do not affect the continued operation of the system. Any installed **back-up system** hardware related to the PMS should also be inspected and tested on a regular basis.

LODGING LANGUAGE

Back-up system: Redundant hardware and/or software operated in parallel to the system it serves. Used in times of failure or power outages, such systems are often operated on batteries. For example, a back-up system to the hotel's PMS would enable continued operation even in the event of a power failure.

While hardware problems sometimes occur, most frequently it is a software-related problem that causes PMS difficulties. Often, because the PMS is connected by a modem to the PMS's software support organization, repair can be achieved simply by calling PMS software support. In fact, one of the primary features separating outstanding PMS systems from less effective ones is the system's level and availability of software support.

Guest Services

The front office is responsible for a variety of guest services. These include the welcome guests receive when they arrive at the hotel to check in, as well as hotel services related to their stay. Remember that for most guests the front office staff may be their only contact with hotel employees. The employees of the front office must be highly trained and ready to assist in a variety of guest-related requests for services. Some of these services can be:

- Transportation to and from an airport or other transportation terminal
- Handling luggage
- Providing directions to attractions within the local area
- Conveying information about available hotel services
- Taking messages for guests
- Routing mail
- Newspaper delivery
- Management of safety deposit boxes
- Arranging for wake-up calls
- Providing for guest security by the careful dissemination of guest-related information
- Handling guests' concerns and payment disputes

Depending on the location of the hotel and the services it offers, these guest service functions may be attended to by any of the individuals employed at the front office. In a larger property with more activity, guest services may have a specific individual assigned only to that task. In all cases, guests will return to a hotel with a friendly helpful staff, but may not return to a hotel with poorly trained or indifferent front office staff.

Guest Accounting and Data Management

The front office is an important area within a hotel that is responsible for gathering and reporting financial information. In Chapter 12, we will examine hotel accounting functions in detail. In this chapter, we will review the front office responsibilities for managing important financial and personal data related to guests. This data includes reservations, charges, payments, and money due to the hotel. In addition, you will learn about the importance of the **night audit** and the work of the hotel's **night auditor**.

LODGING LANGUAGE

Night audit: The process of reviewing for accuracy and completeness the accounting transactions from one day to conclude, or "close," that day's sales information in preparation for recording the transactions of the next day.

Night auditor: The individual who performs the daily review of all the financial transactions with hotel guests recorded by the front office.

Some hotels maintain a great deal of information (data) about their guests while others do not. The nature of the hotel business, however, requires that the front office personnel be skilled in their work because the intricacies of the financial transactions that must be recorded by the front office can be complex. For example, assume that four men traveling to a hotel to attend a softball tournament share a room for two nights. Upon departure, each wants to pay his share of the **folio** balance.

LODGING LANGUAGE

Folio: Detailed list of a hotel guest's room charges as well as other charges authorized by the guest or legally imposed by the hotel.

One man wishes to pay with cash, one with a check, one with a credit card, and another with a debit card. As can be seen, even the simplest of transactions can get complex, but the front office must ensure that all guest folios are properly processed and maintained. Additional accounting or data management tasks that must be completed by the front office include maintaining an accurate list, by room number, of guest room occupants, verifying the accuracy of the room rates charged to guests, and confirming departure dates.

Data management is an extremely important front office function. Some of this data relates to guests, and some relates to the management of the hotel. The amount of data processed in a hotel is large and growing larger each year. An effective FOM in a U.S. hotel in the pre-computer 1930s would, very likely, have kept a record of a specific guest's preferences for room location, type of bed (double or king-sized) preferred, and the like. This information would have been written down by hand and referred to when that specific guest reserved a room or arrived at the hotel. Today's professionally managed front office would have such information, and much more, available through the features of the hotel's PMS. Today, even the smallest hotel's PMS would keep a record of:

One of the front office's most important responsibilities is to ensure charges and payments made by guests are accurate.

- The name of the guest staying at the hotel
- The date of the guest's last stay
- The guest's address, telephone number, and credit or debit card information
- The room rate paid and **room type** occupied by the guest during his or her last stay
- A history of the guest's prior folio charges
- The form of payment used by the guest to settle his or her account with the hotel
- The guest's membership in groups receiving a discount from the hotel
- The guest's company affiliation
- The guest's room-type preferences

Depending upon the sophistication of the PMS, even more data on individual guests may be secured and maintained by the front office staff.

LODGING LANGUAGE

Room type: Specific configurations of guest rooms. For example, king-sized bed vs. double-sized bed, or parlor suite vs. standard sleeping room. Commonly abbreviated (K for king, D for double bed, etc.), reserving of the proper room type is often as important to guests as whether the hotel, in fact, has a room available for them.

In addition to maintaining data on individual guests, the front office collects and evaluates information related to the entire hotel's operation. Some guest-related examples include the tracking of guest telephone calls (including those that are complimentary and those for which the hotel imposes a charge), the viewing of in-room movies for which there is a charge, and updating the clean or dirty status of rooms. This is necessary to ensure that a guest checking into the hotel is assigned a room that has been properly cleaned.

FORECASTING DEMAND

One of the most important questions an effective front office staff must be able to answer is, upon first examination, very simple. That question is:

How many rooms will the hotel sell tonight?

The question is much more complex than it appears. For example, assume that a hotel with 100 rooms available to sell forecasts all 100 rooms will be sold on a given night. It would seem that this hotel is prepared to house the guests it anticipates. If, however, the hotel has only 50 rooms with king-sized beds, and if 60 rooms of this type have been reserved, the front office staff will not be able to accommodate all of the guests who reserved a room with a king-sized bed.

Before any guest can be properly checked into a hotel the front office staff will have accomplished many important tasks. The most critical of these, however, are forecasting the demand for guest rooms, establishing room rates, and making guest reservations.

The Effect of Demand on Room Rates

In Chapter 1, we examined briefly how the number of guests requesting hotel rooms affects a hotel's selling prices and its resulting average daily rate (ADR). As the demand for guest rooms in a given area increases, the prices charged for rooms typically increases as well. As a result, one of the most important roles played by the front office is that of maximizing the hotel's revenue per available room, commonly known as RevPAR. As you learned in Chapter 1, RevPAR is a simple computation that can be expressed algebraically as A (×) B = C

Where:

A = Occupancy %

B = Average Daily Rate (ADR)

C = Revenue Per Available Room (RevPAR)

Thus:

Occupancy % × Average Daily Rate = RevPAR

For example, in a hotel with an occupancy rate of 70 percent, and an ADR of $90, the RevPAR would be calculated as:

(70%) (×) ($90) = $63

Stated another way, each of the hotel's available rooms generated, on average, $63 each day for the period being evaluated. RevPAR can be computed on a daily, weekly, monthly, or even annual basis. Mathematically, when a hotel's occupancy rate increases, RevPAR increases. In a similar manner, when ADR increases, RevPAR also increases. Thus, to improve RevPAR, the goal must be to increase the occupancy rate and/or the ADR. It is the job of the front office to help the hotel achieve one or both of these goals.

Properly forecasting guest demand for hotel rooms is important for two reasons. The first is that hotel rooms can typically be sold for a higher price when the hotel knows that demand for its rooms will be greater. Second, increased demand for rooms means that more rooms will be sold and that fact affects hotel staffing and the need for available room supplies. Typically, both occupancy and ADR for a hotel will increase during a time of heavy demand for rooms. When this occurs, RevPAR for the hotel will increase, and most often, so will the hotel's profitability.

Estimating Demand

The daily demand for hotel rooms, even in the same geographic area, can vary greatly. This is a reality and the challenge faced by all hotel managers. Imagine, for example, the difference in demand for hotel rooms in Indianapolis, on the day before the Indianapolis 500 race (traditionally a **sell-out** period for the entire Indianapolis area) and on the Wednesday night before Thanksgiving (traditionally a very slow day for business travel of all types).

LODGING LANGUAGE

Sell-out: (1) A situation in which all available rooms are sold. A hotel, area, or entire city may, if demand is strong enough, sell out. (2) A period of time in which management must attempt to optimize ADR.

The point to remember is that the FOM must know when there is strong demand for the hotel's rooms—that is, what special events, group activities, holidays, or other factors will influence room demand. To maximize RevPAR, the hotel's management staff must attempt to drive (increase) ADR when the demand for rooms is high and to increase occupancy (by offering lower rates) when demand is low. Both of these strategies, if

Managers use forecast demand techniques, such as tracking historical data and researching upcoming events, to predict the hotel's occupancy and revenue levels.

successfully implemented, will have the effect of increasing RevPAR, and both strategies depend on the ability of the front office team to forecast room demand.

To illustrate the importance of forecasting demand, imagine a hotel in a college town. Five times per year, the college's football team plays a home game. Traditionally, attendance at the games enables all area hotels to sell-out at a high ADR. The importance of knowing the dates of these games as far into the future as possible, so that sales-related hotel staff will not inadvertently sell rooms on those dates for a low rate is evident.

Many hotels find that the demand for their rooms varies through the week, regardless of special events that may be held in the area. Hotels that primarily service business travelers, for example, generally find that Tuesday or Wednesday is the day when demand for their rooms is greatest. Hotels that service leisure travelers will likely find that weekends generate the most business. To summarize, the proper forecasting of room demand requires that the front office:

1. Keep accurate historical records to understand past demand and its possible impact on future demand
2. Know about special events or circumstances that will affect future room demand

In all cases, the front office must be able to forecast the demand for rooms well enough to allow the hotel to effectively price its rooms and maximize its RevPAR.

Use of the PMS in Forecasting Demand

Forecasting future hotel demand accurately is very difficult without the use of an up-to-date PMS. For some hotels, the date of an annual occasion such as a holiday, sporting event, graduation, or concert may be known well in advance. The staff of the front office, by reviewing past hotel records, can estimate the demand for guest rooms during these events. Details of past guest demand, however, are only readily accessible by using a computerized PMS. As stated earlier in this book, most franchise companies mandate that their franchisees use the franchisor-approved PMS. For independent hoteliers, there are a variety of PMS systems on the market. In all cases, if a PMS is effective:

1. ***Information will be easily accessible.*** This is an absolute necessity. It has been said that there are managers who know what happened in the past and others who know what is happening now. The best front office management staff, however, must also know what will happen in the future. The ability of a hotel to forecast is greatest when those responsible for the front office know about the past, present, and future demand for their rooms.

   To compete effectively in today's hotel environment, all front office staff members must have the ability to rapidly access the **historical data** they need to forecast properly. In addition, the **guest history** of individual guests must be easily accessible. When a PMS is too advanced or complicated for easy use by the hotel employees who will be using it, problems related to the inability to acquire timely data will occur.

LODGING LANGUAGE

Historical data: Information related to the stays of past guests. Collectively, this information details the history of all past hotel guests.

Guest history: Information related to the past stay(s) of one guest.

   The readily accessible historical data in a PMS should include:
   - How many rooms were sold during a specific date or time period(s)?
   - Who stayed at the hotel during that time?
   - What room types did they occupy?
   - What room rates were they charged?
   - When did they make their reservation?

   Unless front office staff members can rely on the PMS to quickly supply answers to questions such as these, the hotel's forecasting ability will be greatly reduced.
2. ***Its information is readily compatible with Windows Office products.*** This is related to the preceding item. Most of the computer-literate staff members employed by hotels today will be familiar only with the Microsoft Corporation's automated office products, including Word for word processing and Excel for the creation of spreadsheets. Because Microsoft commands 90 percent or more of the office products market, the use of a PMS that reports data to the front office in these familiar forms is essential.

   Most hotels today use Microsoft Word for mailing correspondence, including marketing letters, Microsoft Excel for financial and spreadsheet analysis, and Microsoft Access for data base management.
3. ***Internet connectivity will be easy and dependable.*** If they are not directly connected, the ability to easily connect the PMS and CRS to the Internet is a critical requirement. There is so much data on the Internet, and its use is so pervasive, that all PMS equipment and software must provide dependable access to it if a front office is to forecast room demand properly.

LODGING ONLINE

Microsoft Office products in the Windows format have become the standard in the hotel industry. To view the wide range of these business tools available to hoteliers, go to:

www.microsoft.com

When you arrive, click on "Office" to review a list of the tools available in this product line.

If you were the FOM at a middle-sized hotel, how would you teach the use of Microsoft Excel to a new staff member who had never used that program?

ALL IN A DAY'S WORK 6.1

THE SITUATION

"I can't believe it!" said Mike Rice, the general manager of the hotel, as he reviewed the report.

"Believe it," replied Dani Pelley, front desk clerk on the a.m. shift.

It was 9:30 a.m. and Dani had printed, as she always did, a reservation activity report for the prior 24 hours. The PMS provided such reports easily, and upon further investigation Dani had discovered that Karl (a desk agent working the night audit shift) had sold 75 of the hotel's 90 rooms to one guest, for a Saturday night date nine months in the future. Because the guest had wanted to buy so many rooms, Karl had given the guest a 20 percent discount on each room reserved.

"That's the day State University holds its graduation this year," said Mike.

"Right," replied Dani. "We've sold out the hotel every State University graduation for the past four years . . . and always at a rate much higher than our normal ADR. This year, Karl has basically sold out the hotel already, but our ADR compared to last year will be awful!"

A RESPONSE

It is too late for Mike to do now what should clearly have been done earlier. As soon as management is aware that a specific future date is both a high-demand date and is available for staff members to sell, room rates for that date should be adjusted in the PMS to reflect the desired rate. In addition, during high-demand date such as the one identified here, normally allowable discounts for room purchases should be reduced or eliminated. In this case, unfortunately, the hotel will be legally required to honor the guest's reservations, but in the future, it must improve the timeliness of its demand forecasting process.

4. ***A strong revenue management component will be included.*** An effective PMS will include an advanced **revenue management (RM)** program. This program is used to help the hotel forecast room demand and establish appropriate pricing because it is designed for that very purpose. Some property management systems have very sophisticated and detailed features that can readily be used by a **revenue manager** while others take a less complex approach. While there is sometimes a fine line between having enough options and having too many, the power of the revenue management component of a PMS must at least be equal to the forecasting abilities of the front office staff.

LODGING LANGUAGE

Revenue Management (RM): The process and procedures used to optimize RevPAR.

Revenue Manager: An individual whose major task consists of forecasting room demand so that the hotel can maximize RevPAR. In larger hotels, this will be a full-time position. In a smaller, limited-service property, the general manager or FOM will have this responsibility.

ESTABLISHING ROOM RATES

Perhaps no task of the front office is more important than the timely establishment of room rates that help the hotel to optimize RevPAR. In a larger hotel, this task may be assigned to a director of sales and marketing, a revenue manager, or some other staff person or team. In a limited-service hotel, however, the task will generally fall to the general manager or the FOM.

After a hotel has done a good job of identifying when demand for its rooms will be greatest, management can implement yield management (revenue management) strategies to establish both transient and group room rates.

Revenue Management

Revenue management, or revenue optimization management, is also referred to by some in the lodging industry as yield management because its goal is to "yield" as much income for the hotel as possible. Regardless of the term used, yield management is a revenue enhancement concept that originated in the airline industry. Today its principles are used by the car rental, cruise line, and lodging industries as well as other industries that sell perishable items, such as hotel rooms, that cannot be carried over in inventory if they remain unsold on a given day.

The actual methods utilized to forecast demand and thus establish revenue management strategies are many and are as varied as the individuals operating hotels. To illustrate the revenue management concept, assume that a hotel's **rack rate** is $150 per night.

LODGING LANGUAGE

Rack rate: The price at which a hotel sells its rooms when no discounts of any kind are offered to the guest. Often shortened to "rack."

It is appropriate to sell rooms at their rack rates when the hotel is confident that the demand for hotel rooms will be greater than the supply. In other words, when the forecast says that all, or nearly all, rooms will be sold, it is not necessary to discount the rooms to help ensure their sale. When demand for rooms is less than the number of rooms available to sell, discounts are typically offered.

To illustrate, assume the hotel with a $150 rack rate routinely offers discounts plans of 10 percent, 20 percent, and 30 percent off the rack rate based on forecasted demand. When demand is very light, discounts as high as 30 percent off rack are offered to maximize occupancy rates. When demand is stronger, the hotel only offers discounts of 20 percent, 10 percent, or, in cases where the demand for rooms equals or exceeds supply, no discount at all.

In a high demand period, guests requesting reservations originally designed to offer a 30 percent discounts are told that such discounts are not available, and the hotel cannot accept that type reservation request. On another, lower demand date, however, the same request for a reservation at the 30 percent discount rate would, indeed, be accepted. The opening and closing of discounted rates is the core activity of yield management, and a person who does it well is effective in this task.

Figure 6.1 illustrates one discount strategy that might be employed by a hotel's revenue manager.

Sophisticated revenue managers are likely to employ highly advanced and often mathematically complex methods of managing yield. Some techniques for this purpose may be included in a property's PMS, but individuals operating a specific hotel may develop their own techniques as well.

Just as RevPAR maximization is related to managing room rates and their resulting ADRs, it is also related to managing occupancy percentage. Revenue managers can manage occupancy as well as rate. Perhaps the most well known, but least understood method of managing occupancy is the practice of **overbooking** the hotel. Any discussion on overbooking must begin with a simple truth. That truth is: *No experienced hotelier would (or should!) ever knowingly take a reservation for a room that is not going to be available for the guest upon arrival.*

LODGING LANGUAGE

Overbook(ed): A situation in which the hotel has more confirmed guest reservations than it has rooms available to lodge those guests. Sometimes referred to as "oversold."

Forecasted Room Demand	Rate Strategy
90–100 % occupancy	Offer no discounts
70–90 % occupancy	Offer discounts up to 10%
50–70% occupancy	Offer discounts up to 20%
Less than 50% occupancy	Offer discounts up to 30% or more

FIGURE 6.1 Yield Management Strategy Based on Room Demand

While PMS systems vary somewhat, front desk staff should be instructed on the proper procedure for billing a no-show guest. In general, the following steps are required:
- Create or select a "room" in the PMS called "No Show"
- Check the no-show guest into that room
- Charge one night's room charge to the room
- Charge the room payment to guest's credit or debit card
- Finalize payment and ensure that a zero balance is now due
- Check the guest out of the room
- Record the no-show charge

FIGURE 6.2 Charging a No-Show

There are at least two reasons this is true. First, in an overbooked situation, a guest with a reservation who arrives to find that the hotel has no room available is inevitably, and correctly so, angry. No professional hotelier wants to make guests angry! Second, from a financial point of view, it will be expensive to relocate the guest. This is true because, in most cases, the hotel that has **walked** a guest will incur the following expense:

- Transportation of the walked guest to and from an alternative property
- Telephone calls made by the guest to inform those who need to know about the alternative lodging accommodations
- The cost of the first night's room charges at the alternative hotel
- The cost related to the loss of good will on the part of the walked guest

LODGING LANGUAGE

Walk: A situation in which a guest with a reservation is relocated from the reserved hotel to another hotel because no room was available at the reserved hotel.

Why then do hotels overbook? Sometimes it is an error on the part of the hotel. This would be the case, for example, if a guest reservation was made, but mistakenly not recorded in the PMS. Sometimes it is due to a maintenance or housekeeping-related issue resulting in the unavailability of a room that had been forecast to be available for sale. Sometimes, however, an experienced manager, applying a revenue optimization strategy, intentionally accepts more reservations than the hotel can accommodate because the manager wants to completely fill the hotel and anticipates that one or more of the guests who have reservations will cancel it or will be a **no-show**.

LODGING LANGUAG

No-show: A guest who makes a room reservation but fails to cancel it or does not arrive at the hotel on the date of the confirmed reservation. (See Figure 6.2)

For example, assume a 100-room hotel typically experiences a 5 percent no-show rate each day. Assume further that, on a given day, 101 rooms have been sold. While it might appear to be overbooked, the hotel is not likely to walk any guest. This is so because on an average sold-out night, 5 percent (or 5 rooms) of guests who were supposed to arrive will not do so. Since the hotel only overbooked by 1 percent (1 room), the number of no-shows (5) will, on average, exceed the number of rooms overbooked.

LODGING ONLINE

Each of the major credit/ debit card issuers helps businesses with issues like no-show charges. To review one such company's resources, go to:

http://www.mastercard.com/us/merchant/

When you arrive, select "Solutions," then select "Industry Solutions," then "Travel and Tourism," to see how these cards are utilized by businesses such as individual hotels.

Successful revenue management means selling the right room to the right person, at the right price and at the right time.

No-shows are not unique to the hotel business. Restaurants, airlines, and rental car agencies are just a few of the businesses that must also manage their reservations while knowing that a certain percentage of those reserving will not show up to claim their product or service. If the hotel's total reservation management plan is too conservative (e.g., it does not factor in no-shows), rooms will go unsold even on sell-out nights. If it is too aggressive (it factors in too many no-shows), too many guests with confirmed reservations will arrive at the hotel. These guests will, inevitably, need to be walked and, just as inevitably, will be upset. Therefore, this situation should be avoided whenever possible.

Transient Rates

While much has been written about yield management, some of what is said is overly simplistic. It implies that hoteliers can charge high rates in response to temporary spikes in customer demand with no long-term impact on a hotel's regular guests or the reputation of the industry. That is simply not true. Consider, for example, the case of Hosea Gamez. Mr. Gamez stays every Tuesday through Thursday at the Sleep Well Hotel. The price he pays for his room is the hotel's normal **corporate rate**.

LODGING LANGUAGE

Corporate rate: The special rate a hotel charges to its typical business traveler. For example, a rate that is 5–20 percent below the hotel's rack rate might be designated as the hotel's corporate rate.

One week, the hotel's staff forecasts great demand for rooms and decides to eliminate all discount programs (including corporate rates) and will sell its rooms only at rack rate for that week. Understandably, Mr. Gamez may be quite upset with the hotel's decision. In fact, if he is charged a higher than (his) normal rate for his room during this busy week, he may decide to look elsewhere for a room in future weeks when the hotel is not forecasted to be so busy.

If, in fact, he stays at another hotel and likes it, the Sleep Well may have lost a good customer. If Mr. Gamez is very upset by the hotel's attempt to charge him a higher rate, a posting on one or more Web-based social networking sites (such as Facebook, Google Buzz, or Tripadvisor.com) could make his complaint known to hundreds and even thousands of travelers. The lesson here is clear; hotels must practice revenue management but must also be aware that there may be some individual, regular guests whose room rates must be considered on a case-by-case basis.

While the rates for **transient** travelers can indeed be yield-managed, care must be taken when yield-managing the rates of corporate travelers as well as some other large-volume room buyers. This concept is so important that some franchisors do not allow their affiliated hotels to eliminate the discounts offered to corporate travelers (and selected others) except in the rarest of cases.

LODGING LANGUAGE

Transient: Individual guests who are not part of a group or tour booking. Transient guests can be further subdivided by traveler demographics to obtain more detailed information about the type of guest staying in the hotel (e.g., corporate, leisure, and government).

Good front office employees are well-trained in knowing which of the hotel's transient travelers retain their regular room rates or **negotiated rates** even during very busy times for the hotel.

LODGING LANGUAGE

Negotiated Rate: An agreed upon rate that is offered by a hotel but is subject to room availability. Also referred to as a volume rate or volume discount rate.

A rate agreed to by a hotel and a large company that does significant business with the hotel is an example of a negotiated rate.

Group Rates

Perhaps the most important distinction to be made in the area of establishing demand forecasts, and thus room rates, is that of transient rates vs. **group rates**. Many people who do not understand the hotel industry believe that the great majority of the rooms sold in a hotel are sold to individual transient travelers.

LODGING LANGUAGE

Group rate: Special discounted room rates given to customers who agree to buy a large number of room nights for their group. In smaller hotels, any customer buying 10 or more room nights would likely qualify for a group rate. In larger hotels, the number of rooms required to qualify can vary to a greater number.

Examples of those qualifying for group rates include leisure tour buses, wedding parties, sports teams, business meetings and conventions.

This is certainly true in some hotels, but in others, such as convention properties, hotels located close to demand generators that attract groups, and hotels that actively seek group business, the vast majority of rooms are sold to guests traveling as a group or attending a group event.

LODGING ONLINE

The nearly 3,000-room Opryland Hotel in Nashville, Tennessee, is an example of a property that relies very heavily on group and group meeting business.

To review this impressive property, go to:

http://www.gaylordhotels.com/gaylord-opryland

What property characteristics do you think are most important to large groups choosing a hotel?

LODGING GOES GREEN!

Increasingly, those hotels that specialize in group meetings are finding that their customers are interested in sustainability. Environmental sustainability has been defined as meeting the needs of the present without compromising the ability of future generations to meet their own needs. For those involved in the meeting industry, a commitment to sustainability increasingly takes the form of membership in the Green Meeting Industry Council (GMIC). The GMIC is a 501(c)(6) nonprofit organization. It is a membership-based professional organization that provides educational resources to planners, suppliers, and hotels seeking to meet the ever-rising standards consumers set for sustainable meetings. The GMIC promotes green practices globally by offering educational programs in the form of training workshops and online resources.

GMIC is the premier global community solely dedicated to sustainability in the meetings and events industry, not only through education but also by spearheading research, policy, and standards. The group has developed standards in nine meetings-related areas. These are:

Accommodations, Audio Visual, Communication, Exhibits, Food and Beverage (On-site), Office, Destinations, Meeting Venue, and Transportation. To learn more about this group and its standards, visit its Web site at www.greenmeetings.info/

In most cases, group room rates are 100 percent yieldable; that is, the price to be charged to the individual travelers in the group should be based on the hotel's forecasted demand for a given time period. This is true even in times of normal business volume. Consider the case of a hotel that has been invited to bid on a piece of tour group business consisting of one tour bus carrying 40 individual travelers. The travelers would stay one night and then go on their way the next morning.

The week in which the tour bus has requested rooms is a very typical one for the hotel: demand is forecasted to be about the same as in any other ordinary week. In this case, however, if the tour bus is scheduled to arrive on Sunday (traditionally a very slow night for the hotel), a much lower room rate might be offered to attract the bus tour than if the same bus operator requested rooms on Tuesday night (consistently a very busy day for this hotel). This is so because the hotel is unlikely to sell the 40 rooms on Sunday night but is likely to sell all or some of them on Tuesday night.

The point to remember, then, is that while a hotel should implement demand forecast systems that support yield management efforts, care must be taken to consider the total impact of revenue management decisions on selected corporate and transient rates while leaving group rates highly yieldable, even during periods of normal hotel occupancy.

Contract Rates

In addition to the rates charged to its transient and group customers, many hotels elect to offer special **contract rates**.

LODGING LANGUAGE

Contract rate: A fixed term room rate that is agreed to in advance and for the length of the contract agreement. For example, the agreement by a hotel to provide five rooms every Sunday through Thursday night for one year for an out-of-town road construction crew working on a nearby highway project.

Offering contract rates affects demand forecasts because, when a contract for rooms is signed, a hotel's revenue manager knows a certain number of rooms will be sold for a defined period of time. This predictability can have positive benefits for both parties to the contract. For example, many hotels located near airports offer contract rates for the airline crews that will consistently, and for a long period of time, need overnight accommodations. In such an arrangement, the hotel knows it will sell a predetermined number of rooms nightly for a predetermined period of time. The airline knows its crews will be assured accommodations regardless of how busy the hotel may be, and at a rate they are guaranteed in advance. While contract rates are typically lower than transient or group rates, the predictability of these rooms's sale can make them attractive to hoteliers seeking to optimize RevPAR.

RESERVATIONS

The effective management of guest reservations is one of the most complex tasks undertaken and achieved by a successful front office. This is so because the hotel's revenue is dependent, in large measure, on the front office's ability to effectively forecast demand, establish rates, and then take the proper number of reservations effectively. Reservations can be made for hotel rooms in a variety of ways, and the hotel front office must be trained to respond properly to each reservation source. For purposes of examining precisely how a hotel receives and records its guest reservations, reservations may be viewed as coming either from:

- Hotel Direct Inquiry
- Central Reservation System
- Internet Booking Site

Hotel Direct Inquiries

In many cases, guests who wish to stay at a hotel will simply place a telephone call directly to the hotel when they want to make a transient or even group reservation. The manner in which these calls are handled by the front office staff can make a tremendous difference in the hotel's ability to capture the business. Compare, for example, the two alternative telephone greetings below that might be used by a front office staff member responsible for simply answering the telephone. If you were a hotel owner, which response would you prefer to be in use at your hotel?

Front Office Agent A: *Clarion Hotel*

Front Office Agent B: *It's a great day at the Clarion Hotel! This is Kimberly. How may I assist you today?*

Most hoteliers would agree that the greeting of front desk agent B would result in a better image for the hotel, and, therefore, that more room reservations will be made. It is important to realize that any telephone call made to the hotel could potentially be a guest requesting to make 1, 100, or even 1,000 reservations! Therefore, every telephone call is important and should be answered professionally and promptly.

To check the effectiveness of the telephone sales effort, some hotels use outside parties to "shop" the hotel. These individuals call the hotel for the purpose of making a reservation (later they will call back to cancel the reservation and evaluate how well the hotel handles cancellations). How the hotel processes the reservation request is evaluated in detail, with a written summary provided to the hotel's management. These evaluations can identify areas of the front office that could use improvement.

The art of selling rooms by telephone is highly developed, and there are excellent tools available to hoteliers wanting to improve their own and their staff's effectiveness. Critical areas that should be examined for training needs include:

- Telephone etiquette
- Qualifying the guest
- Describing the property
- Presenting the rate
- Overcoming price resistance
- **Upselling**
- Closing the sale
- Recapping the sale

LODGING LANGUAGE

Upselling: Tactics used to increase the hotel's average daily rate (ADR) by encouraging guests to reserve higher-priced rooms with better or more amenities than are provided with lower-priced rooms (e.g., view, complimentary breakfast and newspaper, increased square footage).

Those responsible for the management of the front office should know whether the individuals answering the telephone and selling rooms by phone are effective in that task. If they are not, sales will suffer until staff training improves. A periodic review of front office telephone skills and training methods is critical if this important area is to receive the attention it deserves.

In addition to telephone calls made directly to the hotel, in nearly all properties **walk-ins** occur on a regular basis.

LODGING LANGUAGE

Walk-in: A guest seeking a room who arrives at the hotel without an advance reservation.

For any number of reasons, some travelers find themselves in need of a hotel room but without a reservation made in advance. Travelers whose plans are variable may not know where they will be at the end of the day. Other travelers find that their plans change during the day, and still others simply prefer not to make advance reservations. Walk-ins can very positively affect the overall profitability of a hotel. In some properties, particularly those in highway locations, walk-ins can account for as much as 30 percent or more of total rooms sold. On bad-weather days, such as those with snowstorms or heavy rains, a highway hotel may completely sell out to drivers who elect to stop for the night until the weather improves. To sell large numbers of rooms to walk-ins, excellent **curb appeal** as well as a friendly initial greeting from the front office staff is needed.

LODGING LANGUAGE

Curb appeal: The initial visual impression the hotel's parking areas, grounds, and external buildings create for an arriving guest.

Franchised hotels receive increased reservations because their franchisors operate call centers that book reservations for guests who call the hotel's toll-free reservation number.

Central Reservation Systems

Franchised hotels of the type examined most closely in this text are entitled to use the services of the central reservation system (CRS) operated by their franchisor. Generally, this central system is accessed by guests who call a toll-free number (no charge to the caller) when they want a hotel reservation. Historically, a significant number of transient room reservations come from this toll-free number. Today, increasing numbers of individual and group travelers access the CRS through the Internet.

Whether calling a toll free number or using an Internet access site, potential guests make their reservation request known and receive rate and availability information about the desired hotel(s). After they complete the reservation process, they are given a **confirmation number**, or if they are canceling a reservation, they are given a **cancellation number**. In some cases, group rooms are also sold by the toll-free number or on the Internet, but these sales usually account for a fairly small amount of the total rooms sold.

LODGING LANGUAGE

Confirmation number: A series of numbers and/or letters that serve to identify a specific hotel reservation.

Cancellation number: A series of numbers and/or letters that serve to identify the cancellation of a specific hotel reservation.

Depending on its location, in some hotels an effective franchise toll-free number can deliver between 5 percent and 40 percent of the total transient **room nights** sold.

LODGING LANGUAGE

Room night: The number of rooms used times the number of nights they are sold. For example, a guest who reserves two rooms for five nights each has made a reservation for 10 room nights (2 rooms × 5 nights = 10 room nights).

A transient hotel near a city may receive only 10–20 percent of its volume from the franchisor, but a resort location will be much higher. Generally, the better-known the franchisor, the larger the contribution of room nights sold by its CRS. Just as important, the better-known franchisors most often deliver reservations sold at rates higher than those achieved by the hotel's own front office reservationists.

Since the reservation agent accepting telephone calls in a national reservation toll-free call center is not likely to be familiar with each specific hotel in the franchise system, it is critical that the information available to the agent about the hotel is 100 percent accurate. In general, a toll-free number call center will request that the hotel supply as much information as possible on a variety of topics, including:

- Room availability
- **Black-out dates**
- Room rates
- Seasonality of rates
- Room types
- Distances to local attractions
- Hotel amenities and services offered
- Directions to the property

LODGING LANGUAGE

Black-out date: Specific day(s) when the hotel is sold out and/or is not accepting normal reservations.

In addition to taking telephone calls, a franchisor's central reservation system personnel will also manage the hotel's connection to the Global Distribution System (GDS).

LODGING ONLINE

Navigating a hotel brand's Internet site to make reservations has become increasingly easy for consumers. To see what the traveler sees, select either of the following hotel sites:

www.choicehotels.com or:

www.marriott.com

Find the rates and availability of rooms for your next birthday at a hotel near your hometown or school.

The GDS was discussed in Chapter 1. It is a vehicle by which travel agents and other quantity room buyers reserve rooms. This approach is much preferable to calling a hotel brand's central reservation system or calling the hotel directly because the GDS allows hotel room rates to be quickly compared between brands. For example, assume that you are a travel agent. A client wants you to reserve a hotel room in Oklahoma City for a specific Friday evening. You could place calls to the central reservation systems of several different brands (if you knew which brands were represented in that city), compare rates, and then make the reservation. By connecting to the GDS, however, you would quickly be able to:

- Identify all the hotels located in the city
- Select those with rooms available on the requested night
- Compare room rates charged by competing hotels
- Evaluate each hotel's location and features
- Make the reservation
- Receive a confirmation number

The advantages of using the GDS are clear, and its popularity continues among those who are full-time travel professionals. As a result, it is important for the front office staff to make sure that the information about the hotel displayed in the GDS is accurate and up-to-date.

Internet Booking Sites

The Internet has become the single most popular way for individual travelers to serve as their own travel agents and book room reservations with hotels without having to contact them directly. Today there are literally hundreds of Internet sites at which an individual can make a hotel room reservation. This is possible because these Internet booking sites are connected to the GDS or to CRSs operated by hotel franchisors. As a result, virtually anyone with a computer and Internet access is able to select an Internet booking site, enter dates on which a room reservation is desired, read (or view) information about the hotels that have availability on those dates, and then reserve a room online.

Hotel brands want individual consumers to use the Internet to make reservations because, unlike travel agents, individual travelers do not charge the hotel a fee for making the reservation. As a result, all hotel brand managers include an Internet booking site as part of their central reservation system. The result has been a decline in the number of reservations made through the GDS by travel agents, but a tremendous increase in the number made by individual travelers. As more consumers use the Internet and as more

LODGING ONLINE

An advantage to travelers of using a non brand-specific Internet booking site (sometimes called third-party booking sites) is that they can view competing hotel brands at the same time. To see several competitive brands at the same time, select either of the following online travel agent (OTAs) booking sites:

www.travelocity.com

Or

www.hotels.com

Find the lowest rate available for the night of your next birthday at a hotel near your hometown or school

LODGING ONLINE

Some hotels are very creative in developing their own special Web sites. To view one such site, go to:

www.orleanscasino.com/

Note how the hotel uses the site to advertise package specials by choosing "Accommodations" on the drop-down menu.

hotel companies embrace the Internet as a significant marketing tool, this source of transient reservations will continue to grow.

In addition to Internet booking sites operated by hotel franchise companies and independent site operators, many independent hotels, as well as hotels affiliated with chains, have developed their own Web sites. These technologically savvy hotels often link their sites with those of local area attractions, businesses, nonprofit organizations, and other enterprises that are likely to need guest rooms on a regular basis.

RECEPTION AND GUEST SERVICE

While the front office is not, by itself, responsible for the entire experience of hotel guests, it is an area that is especially visible to guests. Because of its responsibility for providing so many guest services, it is important that the front office be properly trained, staffed, and managed. When a guest arrives at a hotel, it the responsibility of the front office staff to greet them and take care of them. Actually, the role of the front office begins even before guests arrive. The front office staff will interact with guests prior to their arrival, during their stay, and at the time of their departure.

ALL IN A DAY'S WORK 6.2

THE SITUATION

"Listen here," said Mr. Zollars, "I booked a room at this hotel, and I'm staying here tonight!"

"Sir," replied Chuck Lee as politely as he could, "I'm sorry, but we don't have your reservation or any available rooms!"

When Mr. Zollars had arrived at the hotel, Chuck looked for the reservation Mr. Zollars was given when he had booked online at www.buyaroom.com/.

The problem, Chuck realized, was that buyaroom.com was not directly interfaced (connected) with the hotel's PMS or CRS. When a reservation was made through buyaroom.com's Web site, buyaroom.com would manually fax or e-mail the reservation information directly to the hotel. In Mr. Zollars's case, unfortunately, the information from buyaroom.com had never come, and thus the reservation had never been made. Since the hotel had sold out and now had no available rooms, it was impossible to accommodate Mr. Zollars.

A RESPONSE

Hoteliers participating with Internet booking sites not directly interfaced with their CRS, or that of their franchisor, must be very careful. Unless a reservation is immediately entered into a hotel's PMS at the time it is made, errors such as this one with Mr. Zollars can occur. An added problem is that it will be difficult to explain to Mr. Zollars that any complaints about his "reservation" must be directed to buyaroom.com because the purchase was made from that company and not directly from the hotel.

In this case, Chuck, the front office staff member, should be courteous, help Mr. Zollars find the nearest hotel that can accommodate him for the night, and then report the guest's difficulty to the hotel's FOM. The manager, as promptly as possible, should contact buyaroom.com to devise a plan to eliminate future reservation transmittal issues. If these issues cannot be resolved, the hotel should seriously consider not participating with (i.e., accepting reservations from) that specific Internet booking site. Otherwise it risks many more Zollars-type incidents.

Pre-arrival

Guest services at the front office actually begin at the time the guest makes an advance reservation. On the night before a guest's arrival date, the front office staff, as part of their nightly duties, requests the PMS to physically print, or store in its memory for retrieval, a **registration (reg) card** for all guests scheduled to arrive the next day.

LODGING LANGUAGE

Registration (Reg) card: A document that provides details such as guest's name, arrival date, rate to be paid, departure date, and other information related to the guest's stay. In conversation, most often shortened to "reg" card, as in: "Where is the signed Reg card for room 417?"

The registration card is important because it forms the basis for the legal contract between the hotel and the guest. In this contract, the hotel agrees to supply a room, and the guest agrees to pay for it. While the procedures of the hotel and the features of the hotel's PMS dictate some of the information contained on a registration card, all such cards should accurately contain:

- Guest name
- Guest address/contact information
- Guest telephone number
- Arrival date
- Departure date
- Number of adults/children staying in the room
- Room rate to be paid
- Room type requested
- Form of payment (payment card) used to reserve the room

When a guest arrives at the hotel, an accurate registration card should be readily available for guest signature. If not, that could mean the hotel's front office staff, CRS, or Internet booking site is not obtaining complete information at the time of reservation. It is the job of the front office staff to obtain any missing information at the time of the guest's arrival. The front office staff must also secure a signed registration card from every arriving guest. In older PMS systems, the registration cards were pre-printed and held for the guest's arrival. Any changes to the registration card were then initialed by the guest at the time of arrival. In most modern systems, the PMS simply holds the registration card information in computer memory. It is revised, as needed, upon guest arrival, with a corrected copy printed (if requested) for the guest.

Creating accurate registration cards is more than simply a matter of good record-keeping. When guests arrive at the hotel, announce that they have a reservation, and state that they are ready to check in, a front office staff member should be able to quickly retrieve a copy of the guest's registration information. Travelers arriving at a hotel to find that their reservation has been lost are likely to be very upset, especially if the hotel is sold out and has no acceptable hotel alternative available. Similarly, a registration card that contains a misspelled name, erroneous room rates, or incorrect room types will create negative first impressions for the guest and extra work for the front office.

Arrival and Stay

When guests arrive at the hotel, the role of the front office is to take care of their needs during the stay. During pre-arrival, registration information will have been properly recorded. The next important function provided by the front office staff is that of correctly registering guests. This five-step process consists of:

1. ***Greeting the guest.*** When guests arrive at the front office, a professionally dressed, well-trained staff member should greet them in a friendly way. Because most hotel guests arrive in the late afternoon or evening and check-in time can be very busy, it may not always be possible to avoid the need for guests to wait in line for registration.

Proper staffing, however, should minimize the wait. When it is their turn to be registered, guests should, above all else, be made to feel welcome!

2. ***Confirming the information on the registration record.*** It is critical that all of the information on a registration card be accurate. This includes the spelling of the guest's name, the arrival and departure dates, room rate, room type, and any other information related to the specific guest. Accuracy in departure date and room rate information is so important that hotels often require both areas of the registration document be initialed by the arriving guest. Since the registration card will serve as the record of the guest's stay, it must be complete and precise. In addition, misunderstandings regarding room rate (one of the most frequent causes of guest dissatisfaction) can be minimized if the room rate is clearly communicated and understood by both the hotel and the guest. Most hotels require a guest signature on the registration record and, in many cases, the guest's initialing of the room rate to be charged, prior to the guest's room assignment.
3. ***Securing a form of payment.*** In most hotels, guests must either pay for their room in advance or provide a valid source of credit at registration. While some hotels accept checks, the most prevalent source of credit provided by guests is a credit or debit card. These cards must be legitimate, however, before they represent an acceptable form of payment. To establish the card's legitimacy, the front office agent should **authorize** the card at the time of guest registration.

LODGING LANGUAGE

Authorize: To validate or confirm. When used in reference to a credit card offered by a guest at the time of check-in, the term "authorize" refers to the office agent's validation of the card. A hotel's front office validation means: (A) The card is being used legally. (B) The card has sufficient credit remaining to pay for the guest's estimated charges. (C) A hold for a dollar amount determined by front office policy has been placed on the card to ensure the hotel's payment.

Used as in "Lisa, please authorize Mr. Patel's MasterCard for $1,000."

Hotels use a verification service to authorize credit cards. The front office staff member who is registering the guest enters the information from the card (account number and expiration date) as well as the dollar amount to be authorized by keypad or magnetic swipe. If the card is valid, the verification service issues an authorization code using a combination of numbers and/or letters that lets the hotel know it can accept the card for payment.

Effective front office personnel always authorize the credit cards they accept as a promise of guest payment. In fact, one objective measure of how well a front office is managed is its consistency in securing and authorizing valid cards.

4. ***Room assignment.*** After a guest's registration information has been confirmed and an acceptable form of payment has been offered, the guest should be assigned to a specific guest room. In some hotels, all guest rooms are identical, and room assignment is of little consequence. In other hotels, the room types may vary greatly in perceived quality and/or rate based on one or more of the following room characteristics:
   - Location
   - View
   - Bed type
   - Amenities or features

   Whenever possible, a guest's room preferences should be accommodated. In most cases, room assignment is a simple task. There will be times, unfortunately, when a guest cannot be accommodated. This can be the case, for example, when the hotel is overbooked and must walk the guest. Recall that a guest who must be walked is one who has a confirmed reservation but cannot be accommodated by the hotel. When this occurs, it is imperative that the front office staff carefully follows the hotel's established policies for walking a guest. In all cases, when confronted with the task of walking a guest, the front office staff should:

- Apologize for the inconvenience.
- Clearly explain the hotel's walk policy.
- Offer any reasonable assistance possible to minimize the difficulty of the situation.

5. ***Issuance of room keys.*** The final step in the registration process is the issuance of room keys. The actual number of keys to be issued is a matter of hotel policy and guest preference. It is important, however, that guest room keys be tightly controlled because the theft, loss, or unauthorized duplication of keys could seriously threaten guest safety. Upon receiving room keys, the guests are either escorted or directed to their rooms.

According to various court rulings, a guest who has been assigned to and enters a hotel room enjoys many of the same constitutional rights in that room that he or she would enjoy in his or her own home. Protecting the privacy rights of guests is not simply the legal thing to do; it is also a courteous and considerate policy.

A professionally managed front office is one where guests are confident that their privacy is protected by all hotel staff members. This includes maintaining a guest's anonymity. To that end, front office staff should:

- Never confirm or deny that a guest is registered in the hotel without the guest's express permission to do so.
- Never provide information related to a guest's stay (e.g., arrival, departure, or room number) to anyone without the guest's express permission to do so.
- Never perform registration tasks in such a way as to allow guest room information to be overheard by others in the front office area. For example, for a front office staff member to say aloud, "Here is your key to room number 416, Mr. Franken," would be inappropriate because the guest's privacy would be violated by such a comment.
- Never mark room numbers directly onto keys.
- Never issue a duplicate room key to anyone without confirming by positive identification that the person is the room's properly registered guest.

Guests should be confident that personal details of their stay will remain confidential, that information the hotel may have about them, including their address, telephone number, e-mail address, and credit card, is secure, and that no unauthorized person can gain access to their room.

One of the most challenging aspects of providing excellent guest service at the front office relates to ensuring that guests are satisfied during their stay. When guests experience difficulties in the hotel, they will most likely turn to the front office and its staff for assistance. During their stay and during the departure process, guests are likely to bring up any issues that detracted from their experience. It is the responsibility of the front office staff to address these guest issues and to correct them if it is possible to do so.

Departure

Some hotels provide guests the option of using self-check-out systems when they conclude their stay. In all of these systems, a copy of the guest's folio is made available prior to check-out, and if the guest has no objection to the items on the bill, the guest is charged the amount listed on the folio. In these cases, the guest does not have to physically visit the front office to check out of the hotel. These systems are designed to save the guest time during the departure process. In the normal case, however, when guests come to the front office to check out, the hotel staff must perform two important tasks. The first is the actual settlement of the guest's bill, which is a several-step process that includes:

- Confirmation of the guest's identity
- Presentation of a copy of the bill for the guest's inspection
- Processing the guest's payment
- Revising the room's status in the PMS to designate the room as vacant and ready to be cleaned

In most cases, the departure process is a relatively straightforward process. This is especially true if the guest's form of payment was properly confirmed at check-in. In some cases, however, guests will have experienced a difficulty with their stay and an adjustment of their bill may be in order. In such cases, it is important that front office staff know the limits of their authority to make adjustments. That is, an employee may be authorized to make folio adjustments up to a predetermined dollar amount, with a supervisor or manager required to authorize adjustments exceeding that amount.

The second essential task to be accomplished by the front office agent when a guest checks out is the possible rebooking of the guest for a future stay. If the guest's stay has been a positive one, it is appropriate and simply good management to ask guests if a future reservation can be made for them at the hotel or at another hotel in the chain. This is a selling opportunity that experienced lodging managers do not overlook.

GUEST ACCOUNTING

Accounting for guest purchases, while less visible than providing guest services, is another critical responsibility of the front office. During their stay, guests are likely to purchase a variety of hotel goods and services in addition to renting their rooms. Accounting for guests simply means that all data related to a guest's use of the hotel is accurately generated and recorded, and that guests are properly charged for their purchases. Depending on the services and amenities offered by the hotel, there can be many sources of guest charges. The following list of products and services is not all-inclusive but represents some of the many possible charges that hotel staff must accurately identify and then **post** to the guest's folio:

- Guest room charges, including appropriate taxes
- In-room safe charges
- In-room mini-bar charges
- Pay-per-view movies/games
- Internet access charges
- Restaurant or bar charges
- Resort or spa charges
- Telephone tolls
- Gift shop purchases
- Laundry charges
- Parking charges
- Meeting room charges
- Audiovisual equipment rental
- Banquet food or beverage charges
- Business center charges

LODGING LANGUAGE

Post: To enter a guest's charges into the PMS to create a permanent record of the sale. Used as in "Please post this meeting room charge to Mr. Walker's folio."

Effective guest accounting in a hotel, as it relates to the front office, consists of two different but important tasks. The first is that of information (data) management, and the second is the completion of the night audit.

Data Management

The front office is the center for the hotel's data-management systems. These systems identify charges to be posted to guest folios. At the front office, the PMS and other accounting systems also maintain the hotel's financial and operational records. In most cases, these systems are extensive and complex. Their management requires a talented and technologically well-informed staff because an increasing number of important data-generating systems are, or should be, directly **interfaced** with the hotel's PMS.

LODGING LANGUAGE

Interface: The process in which one data-generating system automatically shares all or part of its information with another system.

The process of interfacing two data-management systems can be challenging because in many cases the systems will have been manufactured by different companies. For example, the company that produces the hotel's PMS will not be the same as the company providing the hotel with its electronic guestroom door locking system. Clearly, however, the guest who is checked into room 101 by the PMS should automatically be issued a key for room 101 (not for room 102!) by the electronic locking system. When the PMS and lock system are interfaced, this happens automatically. When they are not, a hotel staff member must produce the key separately, and this introduces the possibility of an error.

To complicate matters further, in many cases multiple system interfaces are required, but not all are completely under the control of the hotel. For example, a hotel that wishes to improve its **call accounting** system will find that a new system must be interfaced with the existing telephone system, the local telephone call provider's system, the long-distance call provider's system, and the hotel's PMS. The many challenges of implementing such an integrated system fall primarily to the front office.

LODGING LANGUAGE

Call accounting: The system used by a hotel to document and charge guests for the use of their in-room telephones.

Telephones are one of the most complex data- and equipment-management areas in a hotel. Even the smallest of hotels is large enough to have its own private branch exchange, or **PBX**.

LODGING LANGUAGE

PBX: Short for "Private Branch Exchange." The system within the hotel used to process incoming, internal, and outgoing telephone calls.

Today's hotel PBX is highly automated, as it must be because of the significant use of telephones in the typical hotel. The PBX is the hotel's telephone system, and it is maintained by the front office. It includes the call-accounting system used to charge guests for telephone calls. For example, if a registered guest directly dials a person in another state from the guestroom, the hotel will actually be billed for the call. Of course, the hotel would want its cost for the call to be as low as possible while still providing that guest with quality long-distance service. The hotel will, depending on the distance and length of the long-distance call, post a charge to the guest's folio to offset the cost of the call. The call-accounting system records the time, length, and the number called for every telephone call made in each guest room (as well as those made from administrative phones). These call records must be accurate if guests are expected to pay for the calls they initiate.

LODGING ONLINE

Mitel is one of the best and most popular makers of hotel telephone systems. To view its site, go to:

www.mitel.com/PortalController?country=US

When you arrive, click on "Solutions," then "Hospitality."

Given the increased popularity of cell phones, why do you think hotels have continued to provide in-room telephones?

LODGING ONLINE

For a sample of the type of movies shown to guests on a pay-per–view system, review the offerings of Lodgenet, one of the largest pay-per-view movie and services providers. You can do so at:

www.lodgenet.com/Pages/Home.aspx

Why do you think in-room movies are so popular with travelers?

It is important to know that even local calls are not free for the hotel. Proper operation of the call-accounting system is critical because, in the past, telephone tolls (charges) were a significant source of revenue for many hotels. Telephone revenue, as a percentage of total hotel revenue, has been declining in recent years due to the increased use of cell phones; however, a properly managed call-accounting system is still important because telephone revenue that goes uncollected due to an improperly managed system negatively affects the hotel's bottom line.

In addition to telephone-related information, the front office must manage the guest data and charges that result from a variety of in-room services. Increasingly, guests can use the televisions, telephones, and/or hotel-provided keyboards in their rooms to access products and services sold by the hotel. This trend will no doubt continue and expand. Currently, some of the most popular products and services guests can purchase from their rooms include movies, games, safes, and Internet equipment and connections.

MOVIES

Pay-per-view movie systems have long been a popular feature offered to hotel guests. Essentially, these systems offer guests the opportunity to view movies that are currently, or have just recently finished, showing in theaters. In addition, most pay-per-view providers offer a variety of adult-oriented movies. Guests pay the hotel for viewing the movies. Then, at month's end, the movie provider charges the hotel based on the number of movies viewed as well as for any equipment charges included in the hotel's pay-per-view contract.

Today's in-room movie services include enhanced features that allow guests to access the Internet, review their folios on their television screens, and even to check out of the hotel using a PMS-interfaced pay-per-view system.

GAMES

Many hotels offer guests the chance to play video games on the television screens in their rooms. The games are typically accessed in the same manner as pay-per-view movies. While these game services are very similar to pay-per-view movies (they are pay-per-play), some can be played using the TV remote control, while others require the use of an in-room joystick, mouse, or keyboard to play the game. This means that the hotel must provide these electronic devices and keep them secure in the rooms. The front office is not responsible for the security of the in-room devices, but it is responsible for maintaining an effective PMS data interface so that all games played are, in fact, charged to the proper guest folio.

SAFES

Recently, more hotels have begun offering in-room safes for guests' use. These safes are electronic and can be opened only by the guest and the hotel's own staff. Charges for the use of the safe, if any, are typically posted to the guest's folio through a PMS interface.

INTERNET EQUIPMENT AND ACCESS

At many hotels, wireless Internet access is now offered as a free service. At those hotels that do still charge for it, access, connection equipment (such as wireless routers, adapters, and the like), and all usage fees must be properly identified and posted to the appropriate folio.

The management of data related to guest charges is important to a hotel's profitability. Each hotel will offer some free services and establish charges for other products and services. Purchases by guests must be identified and posted to the proper folio. The night auditor who performs the night audit has the final responsibility for completing this task.

Night Audit

Hotels must account for every guest's charges every day. An interesting accounting issue arises, however, because hotels are open seven days a week, 24 hours a day. The issue is this: When do one day's hotel sales end and another day's sales begin?

To illustrate the issue, assume that a hotel on an interstate highway accepts an arriving guest at the following times: 11:00 p.m., midnight, 1:00 a.m., 2:00 a.m., 3:00 a.m., 4:00 a.m., and 5:00 a.m.

At what point are these guests considered that night's guests, and at what point should they be considered the next day's guest? Traditionally, the end of the day (and, therefore, the beginning of the next day) is not a fixed time at all. Rather, it is designated as the time at which the night auditor concludes (closes) the night audit. The night audit could, theoretically, be performed at any time during the day or night. Traditionally, however, it is performed in the very late evening/ early morning hours when the hotel's overall activity is at its slowest because most guests have, at that point, gone to sleep for the night and, therefore, will not be purchasing additional hotel products or services.

The night audit function is important for many departments in the hotel. Completing it consists of the following eight key items:

1. Posting the appropriate room and tax rates to the folios of the guests currently in the hotel.
2. Verifying the accurate status of all rooms recorded in the PMS.
3. Posting any necessary adjustments to guest folios.
4. Verifying that all legitimate non-room charges have been posted throughout the day to the proper guest folio.
5. Monitoring guest account balances to determine whether any are over the guest's established credit limit.
6. Balancing and reconciling the front office's cash bank.
7. Updating and backing-up the electronic data maintained by the front office.
8. Producing, duplicating, and distributing all management-mandated reports, such as those related to room and non-room related revenue, ADR, occupancy percentage, source of business, and in-house guest lists.

A modern PMS will complete many of these essential tasks automatically. In most hotels, the night auditor completes the audit between 1:00 a.m. and 4:00 a.m. It is important for this task to be completed correctly and on time because some guests will begin to check out of the hotel very early in the morning, and their folios must be as up-to-date as possible at that time. In a well-run front office, properly prepared and up-to-date folios will await these guests upon check out.

LODGING ONLINE

Front office management is a specialized and rapidly changing area of hotel operation. To purchase a complete and up-to-date text about professional procedures and methods used in front office management, go to

www.amazon.com/

When you arrive, enter "Professional Front Office Management" to view a selection of current texts.

Do you think Front Office Management would be an area in which you might like to begin your lodging industry career?

ALL IN A DAY'S WORK 6.3

THE SITUATION

"I just want to go to sleep," said Mr. Rosenbloom, the guest in room 205. "Tell those people next door to quiet down. It's 2:30 in the morning!"

"Those people," as Shingi, the hotel night auditor, knew well, were in room 207.

Mr. Rosenbloom had first called the front office at 1:00 a.m. that night, asking Shingi if she could do something about the noise and loud music coming from room 207. Shingi had promptly called room 207 to say, politely, that there had been a guest complaint and to request that the room hold down the noise level.

The occupants of 207 quickly assured Shingi that they would keep it down; however, Mr. Rosenbloom called the front office again at 1:45 a.m. saying that the noise and loud music coming from 207 had resumed.

After that call, Shingi had visited room 207, personally heard the loud noise and music, knocked on the door, and when the occupants answered, she again asked them politely to hold down the noise level, but also informed them if they did not, they would be asked to leave the hotel. The guests in 207 then assured Shingi that they would quiet down.

Now it was 2:30 a.m. and it appeared that the "party" in 207 was starting up again.

A RESPONSE

Hotels should, of course, respect the privacy of guests in their rooms, but guests must also respect the rights of other guests. In this case, the rights of guests in room 207 are unreasonably infringing on the rights of the guest in room 205. In most hotels, front office policy stipulates that after two warnings the hotel's own security staff or the local police are to be summoned to warn and/or remove unruly guests. Front office staff (or hotel security satff) should never physically confront unruly guests, but they must always maintain control over inappropriate behavior occurring in their hotels. The hotel's management must implement policies designed to guide front office staff when faced with such situations.

Lodging Language

Front Office
Front Desk
FOM
Property Management System (PMS)
Central Reservation System (CRS)
Back-up System
Night Audit
Night Auditor
Folio
Room Type
Sell-out
Historical Data
Guest History
Revenue Management (RM)
Revenue Manager
Rack Rate
Overbook(ed)
Walked
No-show
Corporate Rate
Transient
Negotiated rate
Group Rate
Contract rate
Upselling
Walk-in
Curb Appeal
Confirmation Number
Cancellation Number
Room Nights
Black-out Date
Registration (Reg) Card
Authorize
Post
Interface
Call Accounting
PBX

For Discussion

1. Hotels are not the only businesses that must employ talented employees who are oriented to guest service. Identify three other businesses that employ individuals in a significant guest service role. Could these businesses be a source of employees for a hotel's front office?
2. Some individuals are better than others are at providing quality guest service. Name five personal characteristics you would seek in a person who wanted to be employed at a front office you managed.
3. Some guests do not understand the need for hotel managers to adjust room rates to meet forecasted demand. How would you respond to a guest who complained about paying more than the average room rate on a night all the hotels in your area forecasted to be a sell-out situation?
4. Many factors can influence demand for hotel rooms. Identify three events or times of the year in your area that you believe would heavily increase room demand. Why would these events increase room demand?
5. Some hotels have greatly expanded the amount of information about guests they maintain in guest histories or profiles. Identify five items of information about a guest that you believe hotels have a legitimate purpose in securing. What

information might you, if you were a guest, not wish to share with a hotel?

6. Interestingly, the restaurant business does not typically offer discounts for large groups. That is, a restaurant generally charges the same prices to those at a table for two as it would for those at a table of 22. In the hotel business, discounts are typically given for group sales of 10 room nights or more. Why do you think these two related industries approach pricing so differently?
7. Some Internet booking sites operate by letting guests bid for hotel rooms at whatever price the guest is willing to pay. In such cases, guests may not know the hotel they will be reserving at the time of their bid. If the guest's bid is successful (i.e., if a hotel is willing to sell a room for the suggested bid price), a nonrefundable reservation is made. If you were managing a front office, would you want your hotel to participate in such an arrangement? Explain your reasoning.
8. Some hotels believe that self check-in and self check-out by guests will be appealing because it will save the guest time. Other hoteliers believe that guests desire contact with hotel staff during registration and departure. Which position do you take? Does the type of hotel involved help determine your view?
9. When guests register at a hotel, they must supply information such as their name, address, and telephone number. Do you believe that hotels have the right to share this data with others, such as with direct mail or advertising companies without the express approval of the guest? Should such data be shared with the hotel's franchise company?
10. The night audit position in a hotel is an important one. What personal characteristics do you believe are necessary for an employee to enjoy the late night/early a.m. work shifts required of such a position?

Team Activities

TEAM ACTIVITY 1

There are a large number of PMS systems on the market. Search the Internet with your team to identify three such systems. Each of them will promote its own features and advantages. Select two features or advantages for each PMS system you identified. Why would it be important for a hotelier to have the advertised feature or benefit?

TEAM ACTIVITY 2

One of the most important tasks facing FOMs and employees is that of monitoring demand for guest rooms and then managing rates to optimize the hotel's RevPAR. Identify an event in your area that greatly affects hotel demand (or use a national event, such as the Indianapolis 500 or Mardi Gras). Use the Internet to check the price of five different hotels affected by the event one week before, during, and one week after the event. What can you determine about the room rate strategy of each hotel you exa

Chapter

7

The Sales and Marketing Department

Chapter Outline

Chapter Overview

The economic health of a hotel depends upon securing its fair share of the hotel rooms sold in a viable market. If a hotel does not do a good job of selling rooms, it will not acquire its fair share and as a result will not be as profitable as it should be. Ultimately, a well-run hotel must attract, maintain, and expand a strong guest base. This is the goal of all sales and marketing efforts.

The hotel sales and marketing effort takes place both inside and outside the hotel. Within the hotel, those responsible will establish a budget, create a marketing plan, and implement it. The marketing plan will detail what is to be done internally and externally to maximize hotel sales.

As you learned in the previous chapter, on-site sales efforts are important. In addition to efforts that take place within the hotel, hotel properties also rely on their own outside activities as well as those of other entities such as their area's convention and visitor's bureau to assist in marketing their properties. In a franchised hotel, the franchisor will also assist in property sales and marketing, and in this chapter you will learn about the resources they contribute to the sales effort.

While every hotel guest is a unique individual, hotels have traditionally viewed guests as falling into one or another of two broad categories: individual travelers and members of a group. In this chapter, we will closely examine these two segments to understand better how to effectively market and sell to each of them.

In very small hotels, the general manager may be entirely responsible for sales and marketing. In larger hotels, the effort may be divided among many people. In both types of properties, however, there are common sales and marketing tools that are used to increase a hotel's sales effectiveness. In this chapter, we will examine the most popular of these tools and see how hoteliers utilize them to increase hotel revenues.

The sales effort of a hotel is so important that its owners and managers will carefully and continually evaluate it. There is a clear relationship between effort and success in sales and marketing, but evaluating that relationship can be complex because a strong effort in a weak hotel market may actually yield less business than a weak sales effort in a strong market. Because this is true, evaluations of a hotel's sales efforts must be carefully done. In this chapter, you will learn about the methods used in the hotel industry to fairly evaluate the staff members responsible for a hotel's sales and marketing effectiveness.

Chapter Objectives

1. To define the terms "sales" and "marketing" and to explain the relationship between a hotel's sales and marketing effort and its financial success.
2. To describe to you a hotel's internal and external sales and marketing activities.
3. To identify the two major hotel markets and describe how each can be solicited to help optimize revenues.
4. To teach you about the major sales and marketing tools used by sales and marketing professionals.
5. To explain how professional hoteliers evaluate a hotel's sales and marketing efforts.

THE IMPORTANCE OF SALES AND MARKETING

Very few hotels operate in a noncompetitive environment. In most cases, a guest chooses a hotel after considering several alternative properties. Not all hotels appeal equally to all guests. For example, a couple with children looking for a nearby weekend getaway may want to stay only at a hotel with a swimming pool their children can use. A business traveler may consider a free in-room high-speed Internet connection to be a very important feature. In both cases, the guest has needs, and the hotel has facilities that may, or may not, meet those needs.

In its simplest form, the goal of a hotel's sales and marketing effort is to identify and communicate with guests whose needs match the services and facilities offered by the hotel. When this is done well, the hotel will sell its fair share of rooms to these guests, and its profitability will be enhanced.

While every employee in a hotel may have an impact on a guest's experience, it is the job of sales and marketing personnel to attract potential guests. In smaller hotels, the

Effective hotel sales and marketing means matching a hotel's amenities with guests' lodging and events needs.

LODGING ONLINE

Hotel managers who work full-time or part-time in the area of sales and marketing can benefit tremendously from membership in Hospitality Sales and Marketing Association International (HSMAI). To view this organization's Web site, go to:

www.hsmai.org/

Do you think membership in professional associations such as HSMAI helps hoteliers improve their job skills?

general manager may be the person most responsible for selling the hotel's rooms. In larger hotels, a **Director of Sales and Marketing (DOSM)** will be responsible for the sales and marketing effort.

LODGING LANGUAGE

Director of Sales and Marketing (DOSM): The person responsible for leading a hotel's marketing efforts. Job title variations include DOS (director of sales) and DOM (director of marketing).

The hotel professional responsible for sales and marketing must identify and cultivate clients, plan the hotel's marketing efforts, provide input on appropriate room rates, negotiate sales contracts, and serve as a leader and mentor to the hotel's entire sales and marketing team.

The marketing of hotels can be very complex. In fact, entire books are devoted to the topic of hotel sales and marketing. There are also many different opinions about how it is best done. There are nearly as many approaches to the sales and marketing of hotels as there are people working in the area. On reason is that each hotel is unique, and as a result, how each hotel should best be sold and marketed may be unique.

Even the precise definitions of the terms **sales** and **marketing** are often debated in the hotel industry. In fact, there is no universally accepted definition for these terms as they relate to the hotel business.

LODGING LANGUAGE

Sales: Activities directly related to a client's purchase (booking) of hotel rooms or services.

Marketing: Activities directly related to increasing a potential guest's awareness of a hotel.

For purposes of this text, we will consider "marketing" to be all activities designed to increase consumer awareness and demand by promoting and advertising the hotel, and sales to comprise activities related directly to **booking** guests.

LODGING LANGUAGE

Booking: A confirmed sale, such as a reservation (individual or group) or an event. Used as in: "What is the current level of group bookings for the month?" or "How many out-of-state tour buses did Monica book last month?"

A sale, or booking, is typically the result of effective marketing. That is, a potential guest sees or hears information about a particular hotel and then decides to utilize (book) the hotel's guest rooms or other services. As Figure 7.1 illustrates, when executed properly, increased marketing activities will lead to greater hotel profitability.

When not done, or when done poorly, hotel marketing activities may not lead to greater consumer awareness. When that happens, the anticipated increases in sales levels

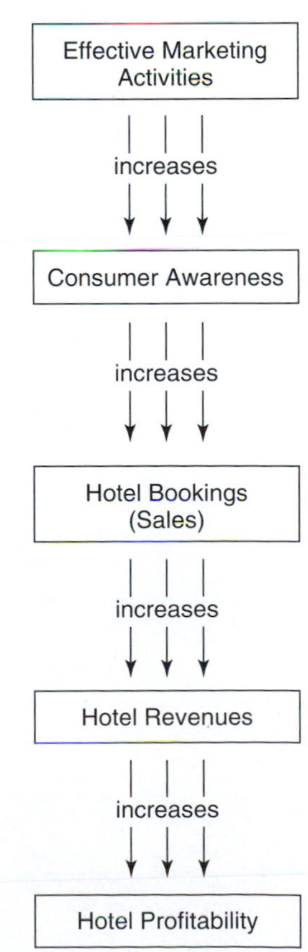

FIGURE 7.1 The Goal of Marketing Is Increased Profitability

> **LODGING ONLINE**
>
> Hotel brand Web sites are increasingly utilized by consumers who want to book a hotel room. To see the level of quality in these sites, type the name of a city you would like to visit and the word "hotel' in the search cell of:
>
> www.google.com
>
> When you get the results, choose hotels from two different brands and compare their Web site's "look."
>
> Did you find one site more appealing than the other? Why?

may not occur. Sometimes a marketing activity increases consumer awareness at so a high cost to the hotel that total profits actually decrease. This can occur, for example, when a hotel pays excessively high rates to advertise in a magazine or on a Web site but does not receive sales increases sufficient to pay for the ads.

The distinction between sales and marketing activities is sometimes clear-cut but more often is somewhat uncertain. For example, designing a hotel advertisement and placing it in the local Yellow Pages telephone directory is clearly a marketing activity designed to inform potential guests about the hotel. Typing the final contract document for a group reserving 100 sleeping rooms is clearly a sales activity. Representing the hotel at a trade show whose attendees are professional meeting planners, however, can be considered either marketing (an activity related to increasing awareness) or sales (activities directly related to booking business) or both. The way sales or marketing is defined is less important than knowing that both activities must be planned and executed well if the hotel is to achieve its desired ADR, occupancy rate, and profit goals.

SALES AND MARKETING ACTIVITIES

The goal of all hotel sales and marketing activities should be to increase sales and, therefore, revenues. One way to examine the sales and marketing efforts of hotels is to consider the activities involved before, during, and after a sale, as illustrated in Figure 7.2.

Not all sales involve each of the three activities we will examine, but each is part of the sales cycle. At every phase in the sales cycle, hotel employees must perform well or risk losing the sale to another hotel. The following events are typical of the actual hotel sales process:

Pre-Sales Phase

- Laura Grades, a manager at the Best Sleep Hotel, meets Mr. Jacobs at a community golf outing held to raise funds for the American Cancer Society. Mr. Jacobs mentions that he is this year's state chapter president of the Society of Antique Furniture Appraisers.
- At the dinner following the golf outing, Laura inquires about any meetings held in the city by the society. Mr. Jacobs replies that the group meets annually in the area for three days, and that its board of directors votes each year on which hotel to select. In the past, he says, the group has always stayed at the Altoona Hotel (a competitor of the Best Sleep Hotel), and that the members seem relatively happy with that hotel.

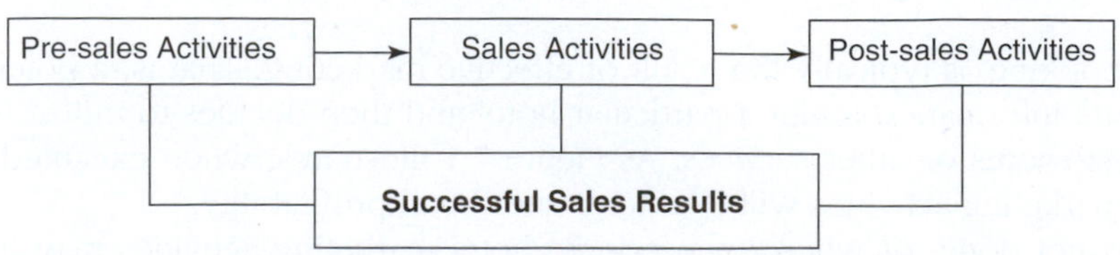

FIGURE 7.2 Three Types of Activities in the Sales Cycle

- After dinner, Laura invites Mr. Jacobs to come to the Best Sleep Hotel for a **site tour**. Based primarily on the friendship established on the golf course, Mr. Jacobs agrees to the meeting.

LODGING LANGUAGE

Site tour: A potential customer's physical visit to a hotel that is hosted by a member of the hotel's staff.

- During the site tour, Laura points out the Best Sleep's most significant features and subtly contrasts them to the Altoona Hotel (but without criticizing the competitor). At the conclusion of the tour, Laura asks Mr. Jacobs if he could arrange to include the Best Sleep Hotel on the list of hotels allowed to submit a **bid** for hosting the society's next meeting. Mr. Jacobs agrees to do so.

LODGING LANGUAGE

Bid: An offer by a hotel to supply sleeping rooms, meeting space, food and beverages, or other services to a potential client at a stated price. If the bid is accepted, the hotel will issue the client a contract detailing the agreement made between the hotel and the client.

Sales Phase

- The Best Sleep's bid is carefully prepared and submitted before the deadline established by the society. Room rates to be charged are based upon the hotel's estimate of the society's actual sleeping room **pickup** as well as other revenue they will generate.

LODGING LANGUAGE

Pickup: The actual number of rooms purchased by a client in a specific time period. Used as in: "What was the Florida Furniture Society's total room pick-up last week?"

- Based on the bids received, the society's board narrows its choice of hotels to two, one of which is the Best Sleep Hotel. The board, following a site tour, and with the personal support of Mr. Jacobs, selects the Best Sleep Hotel for its next meeting.
- Laura prepares a **group contract** for the society detailing the agreement with the hotel and specifically mentioning any **attrition** and cancellation penalties.

LODGING LANGUAGE

Group contract: A legal document used to summarize the agreement between a hotel and its group client.

Attrition: The difference between the original request of group rooms and the actual pickup of a group. For example, a group might reserve 100 rooms but actually use only 50 rooms. Because the room rate quoted to the group was based upon the revenue generated from the 100 rooms, the hotel's standard group contract may require, in such a case, that the group pay a penalty for its failure to purchase the number of rooms it originally agreed to purchase.

- Laura next establishes a group **block** for the society to ensure that sleeping rooms are reserved for its meeting.

LODGING LANGUAGE

Block: Rooms reserved exclusively for members of a specific group. Used as in, "We need to create a block of 50 rooms for May 10th and 11th for the Society of Antique Furniture Appraisers."

- Laura or other hotel staff member monitors the society's block to ensure that the hotel meets its contractual terms. That is, it holds (reserves), for the group's purchase only, the required number of rooms for the length of time stipulated in the group contract.
- Laura attends a pre-event sales meeting of her hotel's staff. The staff reviews the needs and special requests of all the groups that will be coming to the hotel in the next week. One of these groups is the society, and Laura reviews its contract terms with the staff.
- Laura is present on the first day of the society's meeting to welcome the board members, Mr. Jacobs, and others. Periodically, during the society's stay, Laura meets with the group's main contact person(s) to make sure that all is going well.

Post-Sales Phase

- Laura writes to each member of the society's board thanking them for choosing the Best Sleep Hotel. The letter is co-signed by the general manager. Laura hand-delivers a special token of appreciation gift to Mr. Jacobs and thanks him for his assistance in securing the society's business.
- The society is added to a preferred client list. This means that it will be contacted and recognized in some manner by the hotel on a regular basis.
- Entries made in the sales activity calendar ensure that the hotel sales team will begin the bid process with the society next year in ample time to retain the business.
- All written records related to the society's event are properly filed.

There are many activities that must be performed flawlessly to succeed in the highly competitive hotel sales arena. People skills, organizational skills, and conflict-management abilities are essential characteristics of sales and marketing professionals. Many of the sales activities identified above are complex, and all are vitally important. Errors made in any of the processes required for a successful sale could cause as much client dissatisfaction as would errors in any of the hotel's other operating departments.

The marketing activities of a hotel typically draw a great deal of attention. However, it is important to recognize that sales execution is just as important as the marketing activities. It makes little sense to expend significant resources attracting new clients (marketing) if the sales processes involving the hotel's current clients are not properly managed. In fact, until a hotel's sales efforts are smooth and efficient, it is probably best not to risk permanently alienating potential clients by attempting to make sales to them in a manner that is unprofessional.

The number of marketing and sales activities that *could* be undertaken by a specific hotel is immense. Before any such activities are contemplated, however, it is important to establish who on the hotel staff will be responsible for the property's sales and marketing efforts and how much money can be spent to support the efforts.

The process of assembling a sales and marketing team, establishing a budget, and identifying the sales and marketing activities to be carried out by the team are all measures undertaken inside (on) the hotel property. There are also significant efforts undertaken outside (off) the hotel property. These sales and marketing activities may be performed on the hotel's behalf by its staff, its franchisor, the area **convention and visitor's bureau (CVB)**, and others.

LODGING LANGUAGE

Convention and Visitors' Bureau (CVB): An organization, generally funded by taxes levied on overnight hotel guests, which seeks to increase the number of visitors to the area it represents. Also called the "CVB" for short.

On-Property Activities

On-property sales and marketing activities will be varied but are best begun by establishing a sales and marketing team, developing a budget to support the sales and marketing effort, and then creating and following a **marketing plan**.

LODGING LANGUAGE

Marketing Plan: A calendar of specific activities designed to meet the hotel's revenue goals.

SALES AND MARKETING TEAM

Perhaps the most important task related to sales and marketing is determining who on the hotel staff will be responsible for these activities. The answer should be "Everyone!" Every hotel employee who comes into contact with guests, or whose work in some way affects a guest's experience, is involved with sales and marketing. Therefore, in one sense, all on-property employee activities, from cleaning guest rooms to trimming the grass to picking up discarded bottles and cans in the parking lot, are sales and marketing activities because all of these activities affect a guests' perceptions of a hotel and thus his or her willingness to stay there.

In larger hotels, the DOSM heads a sizable staff of professional salespeople. In a smaller, limited-service hotel, sales duties may be shared by the general manager and the front office manager, or may be performed only by the general manager. Even the smallest hotels, however, can benefit from the development of a **sales and marketing committee**, chaired by the hotel's general manager or DOSM.

LODGING LANGUAGE

Sales and Marketing Committee: The team of employees responsible for coordinating the hotel's sales and marketing efforts.

A sales and marketing committee is important because many areas of a hotel are affected by the sales effort. For example, assume that the general manager or director of sales and marketing wishes to create and promote a couples' **inclusive**-priced weekend getaway package that includes a room at the hotel, chocolates and roses delivered to the room prior to arrival, a complimentary pay-per-view movie, and a late check-out the next morning. The impact on the hotel's entire operation can be significant.

LODGING LANGUAGE

Inclusive: A single price that includes all charges.

In this example, an employee has to place the chocolates and flowers in the proper room before the guests arrive. In addition, the PMS and the night auditor must be aware that the guest's first pay-per-view movie is included in the price of the package and thus the guests should not be charged for it (but they should be charged for additional movies). The housekeeping staff must be informed that rooms reserved for this package will have to be cleaned later than usual because of the late check-out. In this example, a coordinated effort is clearly required. It is the role of the sales and marketing committee to provide the coordination, and to do so it should include representatives from all areas of the hotel.

SALES AND MARKETING BUDGETS

As is true in all areas of a hotel, the costs of sales and marketing efforts must be known or estimated if they are to be properly managed. When developing a sales and marketing budget, hoteliers must first establish their hotel's estimated or budgeted revenue levels. They then calculate the projected sales and marketing costs necessary to generate these revenues.

Annual sales and marketing budgets are typically prepared in advance of the coming year. Therefore, a sales and marketing budget for the period January through December of a year might be prepared in September or October of the previous year. The budget is developed by projecting revenue and expenses on a monthly basis and then combining this information for the year. As the budget year evolves, adjustments can be

LODGING ONLINE

Budgeting is a skill that can be learned, and there are tools to help managers do just that. To review the features of one such tool, go to:

www.centage.com/

When you arrive, try the free "Test Drive."

Why do you think forecasting revenue such an important part of a DOSM's job?

made to the sales and marketing budget to account for changes in actual hotel revenue or in the sales and marketing expenditures. Typical expenses in the sales and marketing area include staff salaries and wages as well as the funds required to support the activities in the hotel's marketing plan.

THE SALES AND MARKETING PLAN

Effective hotel marketing begins with the development of a marketing plan, which is simply a list of activities designed to meet the sales goals of the hotel. Activities often included in a marketing plan involve analysis of the hotel's competitors, the establishment of prices, and a calendar of specific tasks and expenditures to be made by the hotel's staff throughout the year.

The physical format of marketing plans can vary greatly, but most include the following:

- An overview of the area in which the hotel competes, including
  - Occupancy trends
  - ADR trends
  - Performance of the hotel in the market
- Competitive analysis, including a review of each competitor's:
  - Strengths
  - Weaknesses
  - Price structure
- Comprehensive self-assessment of the property, including a review of its:
  - Strengths
  - Weaknesses
  - Price structure
- Forecast of future market conditions, including:
  - Estimates of market growth or contraction
  - Performance goals and objectives for the hotel
  - Timeline for achieving these goals and objectives
- Plans relating to specific marketing strategies and activities designed to meet the hotel's goals and objectives, including those related to:
  - **Advertising**
  - Promotions
  - **Publicity**
- Development of a marketing budget to support the identified strategies and activities
- Selection of measurement and evaluation tools to help assess the marketing plan's effectiveness and to allow for needed modifications

LODGING LANGUAGE

Advertising: Information about a hotel that the hotel pays a fee to distribute.

Publicity: Information about a hotel that is distributed by the media but for which the hotel does not pay a fee.

In addition to advertising activities, an effective sales and marketing plan includes promotion and publicity-generating activities. These three terms are closely related, sometimes overlap, and are often confused; however, each plays a part in the successful sales and marketing of a hotel.

Advertising. Hotels have numerous opportunities to advertise their products and services. The best advertising is clearly directed at the hotel's identified target markets, and it should be cost-effective because advertising, by definition, must be paid for by the hotel.

Promotions. In the hotel industry, the term "promotion" most often refers to a special packaging of products or services. For example, a hotel in a cold climate may create a "Summer Getaway" promotion to be marketed in the winter. The inclusive package might include a sleeping room, the use of the hotel's pool, a special "beach theme" dinner party, and complimentary rum-based drinks to remind guests of being at a beach. Specially priced, this package would be promoted through advertising and publicity. Similarly, a franchise company may offer, as a special promotion, triple airline (frequent flier) miles for all stays completed between two idientified dates. Again, information about this promotion would be disseminated through advertising and, possibly, publicity.

Publicity. Publicity refers to information about the hotel that is distributed free of charge by the media. The good news is that publicity costs the hotel nothing. The bad news is that the publicity may be either good or bad. The news media is, of necessity, an independent force in the shaping of public opinion. Cultivating good relationships with the media is an important part of a hotel manager's job. When a good relationship exists, it may be easier for the hotel to achieve positive publicity. If, for example, the governor of the state is visiting your hotel, and this fact is mentioned in the newspaper, the publicity value is good. However, even with good media relationships, a highly publicized fire in a nearby hotel carrying the same brand affiliation as your hotel could be widely reported and might reflect poorly on your own property.

An annual marketing plan is essentially a blueprint or recipe for the sales and marketing effort. The sales and marketing committee should be carefully monitored to make sure

ALL IN A DAY'S WORK 7.1

THE SITUATION

Darnell Claxton, the manager at the Best Sleep hotel, was listening carefully as Wanda McInty, the advertising sales representative, finished her presentation. It was Wednesday afternoon. Wanda had arrived unannounced at the hotel 15 minutes earlier, and because she was associated with the local university, Darnell had agreed to see her without an appointment.

"So you see," said Wanda, "it's the actual football program that will be sold during the big State University homecoming football game next month. We're going to print thousands of copies. Advertising in it will give great exposure to your hotel. And best of all, the cost is only $2,000 for a full-page ad. All the local hotels are participating. Can we count on the Best Sleep to buy an ad? I have to turn in all the ad requests by this Friday, so I really need your answer today."

A RESPONSE

Hotel sales and marketing plans should always allow some room for unanticipated activities and expenditures. Hoteliers responsible for managing sales and marketing efforts know, however, that literally hundreds of advertising and promotional opportunities are presented to them annually. In the great majority of cases, the hotel should pursue only planned (and budgeted-for) activities, and not those that are undertaken as an impulsive reaction to a persuasive sales pitch.

If advertising in the local university football program is indeed a part of Best Sleep's total marketing plan this year, then the advertising opportunity should be explored. If not, Darnell can politely reply that while such an expenditure is not in the budget this year, the sales and marketing team of the hotel will seriously consider it for next year, and he should see that they do so. True professionals who are selling advertising understand the hotel budgeting process, and they will appreciate Darnell's time and polite consideration of their proposal regardless of his final decision about the ad.

that it undertakes and implements the activities and expenditures proposed in the plan. The plan should be evaluated regularly to ensure that the activities yield the results anticipated by the hotel.

Off-Property Activities

In addition to the external sales and marketing activities implemented by a hotel, there will also be off-property sales efforts undertaken by others. Several groups may benefit from increased room sales activity at a hotel and, therefore, have an interest in assisting with its sales and marketing efforts. Chief among these groups in a franchised hotel is the hotel's franchisor. In addition, the local CVB and others can benefit when hotels do a good job selling their products. Understanding the role each of these groups plays is essential to effective hotel marketing.

FRANCHISOR'S EFFORTS

Franchisors charge their franchisees monthly fees based upon the sales levels achieved by the franchisee's hotel. When the revenue achieved by a hotel increases, so do the fees collected by the franchisor. As a result, franchisors work hard to promote the sale of rooms represented by their brands. Some significant efforts include

National call centers. Many travelers prefer a certain hotel brand but may not know whether it is represented in specific geographic areas. For example, a traveler in Florida may enjoy staying at Best Sleep brand hotels but does not know if there is a Best Sleep property in Denver. If Best Sleep advertises that travelers can call a toll-free number to learn about its locations and to make reservations, the Florida traveler might make the telephone call and, utilizing the information given by the national call center, reserve a Best Sleep room in Denver. Despite the increased popularity of booking rooms via the Internet, all national hotel brands still maintain a toll-free call center. Hotel managers should periodically call the national call center to carefully monitor the information about their hotel that the agents answering calls give to potential guests. Information about the hotel should be kept up-to-date and accurate to maximize the chances for the call center to sell its rooms.

Brand-specific Web sites. Hotel brands understand that using the Internet is a favorite way for many travelers to get information about hotels. The best brands have created easily usable, highly informative Web sites that allow travelers with Internet access to make reservations and receive confirmation numbers.

Other Web sites. Many travel-related Web site operators seek an association with hotels because of their own for-profit structure. Individual hotels seek the association to sell more rooms. In many cases, franchisors can help negotiate lower fees and better placement on these travel sites than could an individual hotel property.

National advertising. Most hotels are too small to advertise on national television or take out an ad in a national newspaper such as the *Wall Street Journal, New York Times,* or *USA Today*. Collectively, however, the advertising fees collected by a franchisor can make such ad placement possible. When a brand develops a nationally recognized name and logo, it can be used in advertisements directed toward the brand's target customers. The result is national exposure and effective advertising for even the smallest of hotels affiliated with the brand.

Brand-specific promotions. Earlier in this chapter you learned that hotels can create promotions to offer special services or packages of services designed to attract travelers. Brand managers also create and market special promotions. These can include special rates, room amenities, or upgrades given to members of the brand's **frequent guest program**.

LODGING LANGUAGE

Frequent Guest Program: A promotional effort administered by a hotel brand that rewards travelers every time they choose to stay at the brand's affiliated hotels. Typical rewards include free-night stays, room upgrades, and complimentary hotel services.

PMS training and support programs. Because the PMS is so important to a hotel's ability to sell rooms effectively, most franchisors offer training programs related to its operation as well as technical support in times of hardware or software glitches or failure. These programs are typically free to franchisees or are supplied to them at a nominal fee.

Sales training programs. The effective selling of hotel rooms is a skill that can be taught and learned. Well-managed hotel brands offer their franchisees frequent and inexpensive or free-to-attend classes and seminars and may distribute training materials to help managers teach rooms-selling skills to employees who need training of this type.

CVB EFFORTS

In addition to the sales and marketing efforts of a hotel and its franchisor, the local convention and visitor's bureau may help to market the hotel. Professional hoteliers, whether their properties are large or small, are active members of their CVBs. By participating, they can influence the CVB in ways that increase business opportunities for their hotels. Not every effort by a CVB will result in additional room nights sold in an area, but the mission of any CVB is to increase the number of visitors to the area it represents, and of course, some of these visitors will require overnight accommodations.

CVBs are also known as Tourism Boards or Tourism Bureaus in some areas. In all cases, however, they are not-for-profit organizations that represent a specific destination such as a city, region, or country. They serve as the major point of contact for their destination for meeting professionals and tour operators as well as individual visitors.

CVBs should offer accurate and unbiased information about an area's lodging and entertainment facilities. They save visitors time and energy because they are a one-stop "shop" for local tourism information. They provide a full range of information about a destination and do not charge for their services because they are funded by a combination of taxes and membership dues. The advantages of a hotel enjoying a positive working relationship with its local CVB are clear.

A CVB may be operated as an independent entity or may be affiliated with a local area **chamber of commerce**.

LODGING LANGUAGE

Chamber of Commerce: An organization whose goal is the advancement of all business interests within a community or larger business region. Sometimes called "the chamber" for short.

OTHER EFFORTS

Many individuals, businesses, and other entities profit when hotels sell more hotel rooms. Some of the most important of these are the travel agent and travel advisory groups. As you learned in Chapter 1, travel agents assist transient and group travelers who come to a hotel for a variety of reasons, such as vacations, weddings, visiting friends and family in the area, or any number of other work- and non-work-related reasons. Unlike the corporate traveler who

LODGING ONLINE

Professionally managed convention and visitors bureaus work hard to promote the areas they represent. One of the very best is the CVB of New York City. To view its Web site and explore the ways a CVB can help promote tourism-related and other visitors to a business community, go to:

www.nycgo.com/

Did the efforts of this group increase your own interest in visiting New York?

LODGING ONLINE

Chambers of commerce exist in nearly every community. There are also regional, state, and national chambers. Go to:

www.2chambers.com/

What is the official name of the Chamber of Commerce that includes your hometown?

may return to the same geographic area frequently, leisure travelers tend to visit a specific area or hotel less often. As a result, leisure travelers have traditionally relied very heavily on the advice of travel agents and other travel advisory groups to recommend hotels. A travel agent who books a client into a hotel is usually paid a commission for the booking. A large travel agency can influence a great many travelers to use a specific hotel. That is why contact with travel agents can be an important tactic in a hotel's sales and marketing efforts.

In addition to travel agents, many travelers are members of one or more travel advisory groups. These groups consist of individuals who share useful travel information, including information about hotels, with other members. One of the largest and most popular travel advisory groups is the American Automobile Association (AAA). AAA is a not-for-profit membership organization of over 80 motor clubs, with more than 1,000 agency offices serving more than 44 million people in the United States and Canada.

AAA publishes a tour book that rates hotels for travelers. Its evaluators visit hotels without announcing that they are coming (but at the hotel's specific request). They rate hotels on a variety of characteristics, including:

- Exterior, grounds, and public areas
- Guestroom sleeping and bath areas
- Housekeeping and maintenance
- Room décor, ambiance, and amenities
- Management
- Guest services

Based on the evaluator's assessment, the hotel is assigned an overall property rating consisting of one to five diamonds as shown in Figure 7.3.

Historically, **AAA ratings** were heavily relied upon to inform (or warn!) travelers about the level of quality they could expect at a specific hotel. Today's travelers rely more on social network sites such as TripAdvisor.com, Facebook, and others as they research hotels on the Internet. Thus, while rating organizations such as AAA do continue to play an important role in hotel assessment for many travelers, it is a role that has been reduced by the ascent of the Internet as a travel tool.

One Diamond: Essential, no-frills accommodations. These hotels meet basic requirements related to comfort, cleanliness, and hospitality.
Two Diamonds: Modest enhancements to the one-diamond type property are required. Moderate prices prevail, and amenities and design elements are modest as well.
Three Diamonds: These properties appeal to travelers with greater needs than those provided by two-diamond hotels. Marked improvements in physical attributes, amenities, and level of service above the two-diamond properties are evident in these hotels.
Four Diamonds: These hotels are upscale in all areas. Accommodations are refined and stylish. The hallmark of a four-diamond hotel is its extensive array of amenities and a high degree of hospitality, service, and attention to detail.
Five Diamonds: This highest level reflects a hotel of the first class. The physical facilities are extraordinary in every manner. The fundamental hallmarks at this level are meticulous service and the ability to exceed all guest expectations while maintaining an impeccable standard of excellence and personalized service.

FIGURE 7.3 What the AAA Diamond Ratings Represent

LODGING ONLINE

AAA ratings are important to travelers as well as to hoteliers. To learn more about how to promote a hotel by working with this membership travel organization, go to its Web site at:

www.aaa.com

When you arrive, click on "About AAA" then click on "Doing Business with AAA."

Why do you think AAA has so many members?

HOTEL MARKETS

The types of travelers who visit hotels are as varied as the hotels serving them. While travelers can be segmented in a variety of ways, most hoteliers consider travelers to be either transient or part of a group. Therefore, "transient" and "group" are the two major hotel markets. Recall that transient travelers are individual hotel guests who are not part of a group or tour booking. Transient guests can be further subdivided by traveler demographics to gain more detailed information about them. For example, they can be considered corporate, leisure, or government travelers. The group market, on the other hand, refers to guests who are a part of a larger, multiple-traveler booking, such as those in a tour bus, wedding party, visiting sports team, or corporate training session. To understand how sales and marketing efforts can effectively target these two traveler markets, they will be examined in detail.

LODGING LANGUAGE

LEED: Short for "Leadership in Energy and Environmental Design." LEED promotes practical and measurable green building design, construction, operations, and maintenance solutions.

LODGING GOES GREEN!

While Stars and Diamonds have historically been used by rating agencies to assess the quality of hotels and restaurants, increasingly, it may be the "Color" of a facility that will communicate important information to potential guests. Today, a hotel's Platinum, Gold, or Silver **LEED** status is becoming a significant marketing tool aimed toward the ever-growing number of guests who prefer to do business with environmentally friendly hotels.

LEED stands for Leadership in Energy and Environmental Design. Developed by the U.S. Green Building Council, LEED provides building owners and operators a concise framework for identifying and implementing practical and measurable green building design, construction, operations, and maintenance solutions.

The LEED certification system provides third-party verification that a building was designed and built using strategies aimed at improving performance across all the metrics that matter most: energy savings, water efficiency, CO_2 emissions reduction, improved indoor environmental quality, and stewardship of resources and sensitivity to their impacts.

Hotels can receive certifications based on the number of points they earn (as a percentage of all possible points) during an official LEED assessment. Currently, the LEED certification levels are:

LEED Certified	37% of maximum points
LEED Certified Silver	47% of maximum points
LEED Certified Gold	56% of maximum points
LEED Certified Platinum	75% of maximum points

As increasing numbers of guests inquire about a hotel's LEED status, they expect DOSMs to make their hotels' "Green" performance and LEED certification levels an important part of their overall advertising and promotion programs.

A hotels sales and marketing team will market to both transient (individual travelers) and group guests (those staying because of an event or function).

Transient Travelers

Individual transient travelers are important to nearly all hotels, but they are especially important to limited-service properties. This is so because limited-service properties are not typically built with as much meeting space as is often requested by groups and do not generally offer extensive food services. Transient travelers generally do not require meeting space or food services, and, therefore, they can freely choose between limited-service and full-service properties.

Transient travelers can be segmented, or categorized, in a variety of ways. The best segmentations for a specific hotel to use depend upon the make-up of its own unique transient market. In many hotels, the following transient categories are considered to be significant enough to **track**.

LODGING LANGUAGE

Track: To maintain extensive information on a specific type of traveler. For example, a hotel may wish to track the ADR, rooms used, and arrival patterns of transient military travelers to learn more about this specific type of traveler.

Corporate

This segment consists of business travelers. It is a very important segment because the room rates paid by business travelers are among the highest the hotel will receive. Business travelers have special needs, and the members of the sales and marketing team who sell to them must be keenly aware of both the source of these travelers and the hotel services they desire. Business travelers make up a large portion of the traveling public. This segment is increasingly changing from one dominated by male travelers to one divided more evenly between male and female travelers. Business travelers are a demanding group, but one that pays well for what it wants.

Groups of corporate travelers sometimes come together to form a **consortia**. Consortia are simply multiple large buyers of hotel (or other hospitality) services that join forces to obtain lower prices for their members.

LODGING LANGUAGE

Consortia: Groups of hotel service buyers organized for the purpose of reducing their clients' travel-related costs. A single such group is a consortium.

For example, a consortium representing dozens of large corporate travel departments may request that a hotel offer significant discounts if any of the corporate travelers represented by the consortium stay at the hotel. A hotel that agrees to work with the consortium will evaluate the potential volume level of this client, establish a contracted rate (see Chapter 6), identify any blackout dates that apply, and then track the consortium's pick-up. The corporate market is large, and as a result, many hotels assign their very best salespersons to this transient segment.

Leisure. Leisure travelers are also an important market segment for many hotels. In some resort areas, they may constitute nearly 100 percent of all hotel guests. As mentioned earlier in this chapter, leisure travelers visit an area for a variety of personal and recreational reasons, and this group must be directly addressed in any successful sales and marketing plan.

Government. Local, state, and federal government workers (including military personnel) are a large part of the clientele of many mid-priced full- and limited-service hotels. Government travelers typically are allowed a **per diem** for their hotel stays, and this amount, for some hotels, represents an ADR attractive enough to aggressively seek their business.

LODGING LANGUAGE

Per Diem: A daily, fixed amount paid for a traveler's expenses. Established by companies, government agencies, or other entities, the per diem amount for a traveler will be based upon the costs associated with the area to which the individual travels.

For example, the per diem for food and lodging for a traveler spending the night in New York City will be higher than for a traveler spending the night in a less expensive area of the country.

Long-term stay. In some cases, when guests check in to a hotel they plan to stay for a very long time. These long-term or extended-stay guests are a significant market segment. In fact, some entire hotel brands have been designed to appeal specifically to them. Not all hotels appeal to long-term stay guests, but most hotels have some clients who fit this category. At the less expensive end of the room rate scale, some properties that attract extended stay guests do so by providing larger rooms (or suites), cooking facilities, and refrigerators. At the higher end of the room charge scale, hotels have always appealed to some wealthy clients who prefer to live in an environment that provides food, security, and cleaning services rather than in an apartment. Long-term-stay guests come to hotels for a wide variety of reasons and include individuals working on construction projects, those seeking permanent housing in the area, and those whose homes are temporarily uninhabitable. This is a highly desirable market segment for several reasons, including the guaranteed occupancy

LODGING ONLINE

The federal government establishes per diem rates to help control its travel costs. To view the rates established for travelers by the General Services Administration, go to:

www.gsa.gov

When you arrive, enter "per diem" in the search window.

What is the current GSA per diem for the area in which you are located?

the guests bring to the hotel, the ease of cleaning their rooms, and their relatively uncomplicated billing. A disadvantage is that these rooms are often sold at very low daily rates. Despite that fact, some hotels assign specific sales and marketing team members specifically to this segment and have great success with it.

Group Travelers

For many hotels, 50 percent or more of their business is the result of providing lodging for group travelers. In fact, in some large hotels built primarily to house groups holding conventions, nearly 100 percent of their entire business may be group-related.

The actual definition of what constitutes a group varies by hotel. For example, two people traveling together are not likely to be considered a group by any hotel, whereas nearly all hotels would consider 100 people traveling together a group. For many hotels, the purchase of 10 or more rooms constitutes a minimum-sized group sale, but this can vary somewhat depending upon the hotel manager and the size of the hotel. Since there is no universally accepted definition of group, the hotel's manager determines when a proposed sale is considered a group sale and thus will be issued a group contract.

A group contract details the responsibilities of each party in the purchase of a large number of hotel rooms. This special arrangement lets the hotel know how many rooms the group wishes to purchase and identifies a deadline date by which the purchase must be made.

Typically, a group contract will include information related to the group's:

- Name
- Billing address
- Arrival date
- Departure date
- Requested room types
- Requested number of rooms
- Room rate(s)
- Date by which the requested rooms must be reserved
- Requests for additional hotel services such as meeting rooms and meals
- Form of payment
- Time of payment
- Authorized representative(s) for the group

Group contracts can be lengthy and detailed because groups often make extensive use of hotel services in addition to sleeping rooms. These services can include:

- Welcome receptions
- Catered meals
- Meeting space
- Audiovisual equipment
- Registration services
- Transportation
- Baggage handling
- On-site leisure activities
- Off-site leisure activities

The needs of a specific group often depend upon the reasons for their travel. Thus, for example, the needs of a seniors group touring for leisure and stopping for one night on their way to a final destination will be different from the needs of a future bride wishing to secure weekend sleeping rooms for her wedding guests as well as the food and beverage services needed for her wedding banquet.

An effective sales and marketing plan will include significant efforts to attract the **SMERF** market and other groups that are potential clients of the hotel.

LODGING LANGUAGE

SMERF: Short for "Social, Military, Educational, Religious, or Fraternal groups" and organizations.

LODGING ONLINE

Meeting Professionals International (MPI) is the world's largest association of meeting planning professionals.

www.mpiweb.org

When you arrive, click on "Education" to review the large number of educational services it offers its members.

What skills do you think it would take to succeed as a meeting planner?

This is so because the market segment for this type of group is of significant size. Group members hold organizational meetings, may travel as a group, and frequently hold conferences and conventions. Additional market groups that may, depending on the hotel, deserve special marketing plan attention include sports teams, government workers, tour bus, or any other defined group large enough to be worth soliciting. This can be more effectively done if the hotel begins by identifying the **meeting planners** used by the groups the hotel has targeted for solicitation.

LODGING LANGUAGE

Meeting planner: A professional employed by a group to negotiate the group's contract with a hotel.

Professional meeting planners annually buy large numbers of sleeping rooms and reserve significant amounts of meeting and catering space. They may do so on behalf of many different groups and organizations as well as some corporations. Sophisticated buyers of hotel products, they often use comparison-shopping techniques, and can heavily influence a hotel's reputation based on their experience with it.

SALES AND MARKETING TOOLS

Regardless of whether they seek to attract transient business, group business, or both, the sales and marketing team will utilize a variety of sales tools. The type of tool selected and its effectiveness depends, in many cases, upon the skill of the person developing and using the tool as well as the appropriateness of the tool for the market segment sought by the hotel. Among the many available selling tools, the seven listed below are used by most hotels:

- In-person sales calls
- Print and direct mail
- Telephone
- E-mail
- Traditional internet sites
- User generated content (UGC) internet sites
- Client appreciation activities

In-Person Sales Calls

For most hotels, guests who stay are new guests. While some guests do return week after week or year after year, most hotel guests do not. Because that is true, a hotel must continually seek new clients. Identifying and soliciting new clients is, arguably, the single most important task of a sales team. A sales **lead** can come from many sources.

LODGING LANGUAGE

Lead: Information about a transient or group rooms prospect who is likely to buy products and services from the hotel.

When the sales and marketing team believes a lead represents strong potential for a sale, the lead will be followed, if possible, by a pre-arranged and in-person **sales call**.

LODGING LANGUAGE

Sales call: A pre-arranged meeting held for the purpose of explaining and selling the hotel's products and services.

Networking can create leads. Leads can come from a convention and visitors bureau, from a referral by a current guest, from employees, or simply from a prospect's telephone call to the hotel.

LODGING LANGUAGE

Networking: The development of personal relationships for a business-related purpose. For example, an area's chamber of commerce–sponsored breakfast open to all community business leaders interested in improving local traffic conditions would be a networking opportunity for a member of a hotel's sales team.

A sales team's ability to seek out and cultivate quality leads is critical to its success. An effective sales and marketing team structures its work in a way that provides adequate time to follow up leads with a sales call and reserves adequate time for **cold calling**.

LODGING LANGUAGE

Cold calling: Making telephone contact with, or an in person sales visit to, a potential client without having previously set an appointment to do so.

Effective salespeople seek opportunities to cold call whenever they can. The objective of this type of sales call is to qualify prospective clients by identifying those with a high likelihood of using the hotel's rooms or services. Of course, the most likely prospects are further cultivated until a sale is made. Outstanding sales teams actively seek out and create sales opportunities by following up on sales leads and by making a predetermined number of in-person sales calls and cold calls each week. Such calls can be followed up with a thank-you note or letter, e-mail, voice mail, or text thanking the prospect for the meeting and inviting the prospect to the hotel for a site tour.

In addition to arranging meetings with potential clients outside of the hotel, sales and marketing teams should always be prepared to host a **drop in**.

LODGING LANGUAGE

Drop in: A potential buyer of a significant number of rooms or hotel services who arrives at the hotel without an appointment.

A drop in is potential buyer who arrives on the property and requests a site tour of sleeping rooms, meeting rooms, or banquet facilities. If a member of the hotel's staff is not available to meet with these prospects when they arrive, a sales opportunity may be lost. Drop ins are a reminder to management that some member of the hotel's sales team should be available at the hotel for the maximum number of reasonable hours per day to conduct site tours if needed.

Print and Direct Mail

Not every potential client can be contacted by a personal sales call. Print material delivered by direct mail can be an effective sales tool for potential clients located far away from the hotel or for times when a hotel sales team is attempting to determine the quality of a potential sales lead prior to arranging a sales call. For example, assume that a hotel's sales team first identified and then sought to advertise its rooms and services to the

100 largest group tour bus companies in the country. While it is unlikely that a member of the hotel's sales team could visit 100 tour bus locations, the team could develop a **direct mail** advertising piece that could be sent to all of them.

LODGING LANGUAGE

Direct Mail: The process of sending an advertisement to clients by U.S. mail service. The total cost of a direct mail piece includes the expenditures for the advertisement's design, printing, and mailing.

Direct mail can be viewed as an indirect sales call. A sales and marketing team can set a goal for the number of direct mail pieces to be mailed each month. If the number of direct mail pieces drops below established goals, the hotel's sales and marketing team leader should discuss the need to maintain appropriate direct mailing levels. This can be done simply by explaining that direct mail pieces can "visit" prospects when a direct sales call is not possible. Just as increasing personal cold calls will most often increase hotel sales, the greater the number of high quality direct mail pieces sent out, the more likely is the hotel to achieve its sales goals.

Of course, like direct sales calls, these indirect sales calls must be effective in the selling mission. The rules for effectiveness in direct mail are similar to those for in-person sales. The best direct mail pieces:

- Are eye-catching
- Reflect positively on the hotel's image
- Are easy to read, brief and to-the-point
- Introduce relevant hotel features and benefits
- Support the offered benefits with proof statements
- Are cost-effective
- Ask for the sale (order) or a site visit

If possible, the direct mail piece should also include an incentive designed to encourage the person receiving it to book the hotel now rather than postpone the decision. An effective direct mail piece could be a skillfully created postcard, a well-written first-class letter, or even a cleverly fashioned package. In all cases, it should be designed to expand the sales reach of a hotel. It must do so in a cost-effective way, and it should result in measurable increases in the hotel's visibility and revenue.

Telephone

Even in this day of increasingly advanced technology, the ordinary telephone call still presents an excellent selling opportunity for most hotels. Many incoming calls to a hotel will be from potential guests and, therefore, should be answered and responded to in a prompt and professional manner. In addition, outgoing telephone calls should be used extensively by the sales and marketing team to identify prospects, set appointments, and solicit room sales.

When trained properly, the sales and marketing team can use the telephone to:

- Make transient reservations
- Answer questions about group reservations and bids
- Find prospects who may be interested in a site tour
- Identify prospects and arrange dates and times for in-person sales calls
- Increase the speed and accuracy of information transmitted to the caller
- Overcome resistance to sales barriers (e.g., room rate too high or the hotel's lack of specific amenities)
- Improve total hotel revenue generated by telephone

When potential guests call a hotel directly, the employees answering the telephone must be knowledgeable and confident from the first moment they pick up the phone. The caller will form an instantaneous impression not only of the hotel representative, but also of the hotel itself from the representative's demeanor on the phone. To make a sale or

LODGING ONLINE

The Educational Institute of the American Hotel and Lodging Association (AH&LA) produces up-to-date training material about how to effectively utilize the telephone as a sales tool. To view its most recent videos and other telephone skills-related products, go to:

http://www.ahlei.org/

When you arrive, enter "Telephone" in the site's search engine to review their product offerings.

Have you ever experienced poor guest service during a telephone call you made to a business?

provide information professionally, it is important that inside sales representatives have effective telephone skills. They must use their voices to increase trust and project a favorable personal impression. They must use positive and proactive language to handle a variety of situations effectively. Because answering machines are so prevalent in today's business world, the hotel sales staff must also have the ability, when necessary, to leave clear, concise voice mail messages.

E-Mail

Today's active business person answers telephone calls and text messages, reviews the daily mail, and checks e-mail continually throughout the day. The most effective hotel sales efforts recognize this fact and use it, as well as other more traditional forms of client communication, to improve hotel revenues.

Hotels have long communicated with guests by means of direct mailings, the telephone, fax, and more recently by text message. Today, e-mail systems are increasingly used. Hotel salespersons should include their e-mail addresses on their business cards. Since most hotel guests do so as well, an effective, up-to-date e-mail list is today's equivalent of traditional systems of manually filing business cards. Unlike direct mail, e-mails can be inexpensively sent to hundreds of clients and potential clients in a matter of seconds. While each hotel must decide how best to use e-mail in its selling efforts, there are some general principles related to the use of e-mail.

An effective sales and marketing team will:

- Maintain an up-to-date list of e-mail addresses
- Create e-mail sales messages that are short but effective
- Send e-mails at the proper frequency (too many will be perceived as spam, yet too few will not be as effective)
- Provide a convenient way for recipients to be removed from your e-mail list

In addition to its usefulness in communicating a sales message directly to clients, e-mail is increasingly the preferred method of attaching and exchanging documents such as sales proposals, menus, and contracts. Most e-mail systems automatically update the user's database whenever an e-mail is received, thus helping to keep e-mail addresses current.

Properly used, an e-mail database can be accessed whenever the hotel wishes to innovatively communicate a special rate, promotion, or new hotel feature to its client list. Improperly used, e-mails can irritate potential guests. They may become so annoying that the recipients simply delete them almost as quickly as they are sent! Well-designed e-mail communication systems will continue to play an important role in a hotel's sales and marketing effort and should be utilized to their fullest potential.

Traditional Internet Sites

Recognizing the popularity of the Internet, most large hotels have created their own Web sites to help increase revenues. In addition, large and small hotels affiliated with a brand often share Web sites with other brand franchisees. In this way, even small hotels can

With more travelers using the Internet to book their travel needs, it is important for hoteliers to consistently monitor traditional Internet sites (www.google.com) and UGC Internet sites (www.twitter.com).

achieve some level of visibility on their own Web page. While the Internet is, in many respects, simply another marketing tool used by a hotel, its significance, growth, and potential require special attention.

When properly utilized and managed, the Internet is an excellent vehicle for communicating with current and potential clients. An important point for hoteliers to remember is that the Internet allows smaller hotels to compete on an equal footing with larger ones. The Internet, at this point in its development, delivers just three media components: audio, text, and images. Each can be just as good on a small hotel's Web site as on a larger competitor's site (or even better!). An effectively designed Web site allows a hotel to take advantage of an inexpensive direct line to consumers.

Before the Internet came into wide use and hotels began to create their own Web sites, a sales team that wanted an individual consumer or travel agent to "see" and experience the hotel had to do a direct mail piece or arrange for site visits. Both of these strategies can be expensive. With a Web site, potential clients can "see" and virtually tour the hotel immediately and at a typical cost to the hotel of only a few hundred dollars per month.

Web sites can easily generate in-person and telephone sales opportunities. Consider, for example, that drop-ins, callers, meeting planners, travel agents, and consortium members may all learn about a specific hotel by surfing hotel Web sites on the Internet. Individual transient guests can reserve rooms via the Internet, and meeting planners can view a hotel's rooms and meeting space through the hotel's online brochure or, more recently, streaming video tours. In addition, many travel wholesalers sell on the Internet, and technology-savvy hotels can connect their own Web sites to wholesale sites likely to draw potential guests.

The appearance of a hotel's own Web site has become increasingly important and will continue to be even more so. The placement of text, images, and other media and white space on a Web page makes a strong statement about the quality of a hotel's products and services. Despite this fact, many hotels do not have the in-house ability to create an effective Web page, nor do they have the technical skill required to evaluate the site's effectiveness.

Evaluating the quality of a Web site can be complex; however, there are some characteristics that all effective hotel Web sites have in common. These are identified in Figure 7.4.

LODGING ONLINE

Some companies specialize in providing Web site design and other technology application solutions to hotels. To view one such company's product offerings, go to:

www.acromarketing.com/

How would you go about locating a Web site designer for a hotel you managed?

LODGING LANGUAGE

Link: Short for *Hyperlink.* A relationship between two Web sites. If a Web site chooses to link itself with another Web site, the link, when activated, will direct the user to the linked Web page. An external link leads to a Web page other than the current one; an internal link leads to another section of the current Web site.

Some hotels do not obtain the results they seek from their Web sites because they do not link their sites properly and do not take full advantage of Internet search engines to identify the sites to which they should link. Effective Web sites should be linked in a manner that maximizes their sales potential. For example, assume a hotel is located near the stadium of a professional sports team. Internet users who enter the name of the team in a search engine (e.g., Bing, Excite or Yahoo) are probably looking for information about the team such as its roster, won/lost record, and schedule. They are not necessarily seeking hotel rooms. Therefore, linking with sites that appear on a search for the team's name may not be effective for the hotel despite the high number of hits to these sites. Alternatively, however, consumers who search for driving directions to the stadium are likely to be:

- Attending one or more of the games
- Unfamiliar with the area
- Potentially seeking a place to dine or stay overnight

In this example, Web sites that appear when "Stadium," "Stadium Driving Directions," and similar entries are entered into search engines are likely to produce guests for the hotel even though the number of hits from these sites may be smaller. With which sites should a hotel link? The answer is: all of the sites affiliated with the hotel's major **demand generators**.

LODGING LANGUAGE

Demand generator: An organization, entity, or location that creates a significant need for hotel services. Examples in a community include large businesses, tourist sites, sports teams, educational facilities, and manufacturing plants.

Once guests arrive at a hotel Web site through effective link development, the site can be used to promote the hotel's packages, guest rooms, and other services. There are significant

- The site is easy to navigate.
- The site has some level of interactivity.
- The site is connected (has a **link**) to appropriate companion sites.
- The site allows for the online booking of a reservation.
- The site balances guest privacy needs with the hotel's desire to build a customer database.
- Updating and revising room rates on the site is easy.
- The site includes a virtual tour of the property (with at least enough pictures or streaming video to provide an accurate image of the hotel).
- The site complements the hotel's other marketing efforts.
- The site is in the language(s) of the hotel's major clients.
- The site address is easy to remember.

FIGURE 7.4 Characteristics of Effective Hotel Web Sites

marketing cost savings when discounts on hotel products and services are offered on a Web site. Spending money on regular advertising means that a hotel must pay for everyone who sees (and doesn't see) the advertisement, regardless of whether a purchase is made. By contrast, when marketing dollars are spent by charging less for products purchased online, the hotel must only pay for the people who actually place orders. As a result, the hotel is charged for this form of advertising only when it is effective.

Many Web shoppers are looking for the best quality of hotel they can select at the lowest price available, and Web advertising makes it easy for them to identify which hotel offers a low price. For many hotels, selling rooms on the Web for a reduced price makes good economic sense because it is often a much less expensive sales method than in-person sales calls or a direct mail campaign. Because of the increasing importance of the Web to total sales and marketing efforts, a hotel should always promote its Web site to current clients and contacts by including the hotel's Web site address on staff business cards as well as on all advertising and promotional materials.

User Generated Content (UGC) Internet Sites

The Internet's biggest recent change has been the explosion of social networking sites, video sharing sites, blogs, tweets, and an ever-changing number of **user generated content (UGC) sites**.

LODGING LANGUAGE

User Generated Content (UGC) site: A Web site designed to host forums, blogs, or other reviewer submitted information allowing those seeking information to read the comments of other consumers prior to making their buying decisions. UGC sites are sometimes referred to as Web 2.0

In the hotel industry, UGC sites are important because travelers like to share their travel experiences with others. Increasingly, these shared experiences impact potential buyers as much or more than traditional advertising.

DOSMs have always been aware of the importance of word-of-mouth advertising. Positive word of mouth costs nothing, and its impact is significant. In today's world, word of "Mouse" is even more critical than word of mouth because of the large number of potential customers who will read positive (or negative) reviews of a hotel on UGC sites. As a result, effective sales teams continually monitor UGC sites such as Tripadvisor.com and Travbuddy.com and learn how to respond to both positive and negative reviews.

Client-Appreciation Activities

Experienced hoteliers know that making a sale is only the beginning (and not the end) of the client/hotel relationship. Too many hotels lose clients simply because they did not let the client know how much their business was appreciated. Client-appreciation activities allow the hotel to express its gratitude to clients for their current business. These activities can include anything from inviting a client or group of clients to join the hotel manager for dinner or drinks, to organizing an elaborate, once or twice a year gala client-appreciation event.

LODGING ONLINE

Online hotel reviews are estimated to influence more than 85 percent of travel site visitors' buying decisions. These sites publish traveler reviews that are fairly written as well as those that are not. To review one of the most popular UGC sites, go to:

www.tripadvisor.com/

What specific steps would you encourage DOSMs to take if past guests of their hotels posted reviews that were inaccurate and highly unfair?

Golfing and sporting events, concerts, and theater tickets are all ways to express a genuine appreciation for business received. Gift giving is another traditional way to express appreciation to a hotel's best clients. Gifts given to clients as tokens of appreciation can range from the simple to the elaborate. It is, of course, important to first determine whether the client's employer permits the acceptance of gifts. In all cases, the goal of a successful client-appreciation event or activity is to solidify the business relationship with current clients and to communicate to potential clients the seriousness with which the hotel views the hotel–client relationship. On a regular basis, hotels must objectively review and evaluate the quantity and quality of their client-appreciation activities.

EVALUATION OF SALES AND MARKETING EFFORTS

Evaluating sales and marketing efforts is one of the most difficult tasks faced by hoteliers. Reduced sales and guest counts, for example, are not always the result of ineffective sales and marketing. As the U.S. recession of 2008–2010 reminded the industry, revenues may decline for a variety of reasons totally beyond the control of a hotel's sales and marketing department.

Consider, for example, that even in good economic times a hotel with stagnant or declining revenues may not be providing good guest service. If so, it may well be the poor service, not poor selling efforts, that keeps sales from increasing. This could also be true when housekeeping, maintenance, food and beverage, or other staff members do not perform well. In other cases, the hotel may face lowered sales levels if the property is older or if newer competitors are capturing more of the market. Also, if the total market size declines, it is reasonable to expect that revenue levels, at least in the short run, will decline also.

Despite the difficulty of measuring and evaluating the efforts of the sales and marketing team, it must be done. Fortunately, there are a variety of tools available to help make this job easier. Certainly a hotel owner or general manager can subjectively evaluate the professionalism and appearance of the sales and marketing staff, their diligence at work, and their creativity in presenting the hotel's best features. Also, in some cases, the presence of increasing occupancies may indicate good efforts by the sales and marketing team, as may increases in ADR. It is important to remember, however, that both types of increases could result from an increase in guest demand and thus could actually mask a decline in the quality of sales and marketing efforts.

Fortunately, there are industry standardized and quantitative reports designed to help measure the actual end results of the sales and marketing effort. These include an evaluation of the hotel's Performance to Sales and Marketing Plan and the **Smith Travel Accommodations Report (STAR report)**.

LODGING LANGUAGE

STAR report: Short for the "Smith Travel Accommodations Report." Produced by the Smith Travel Research (STR) company, this report is used to compare a hotel's sales results to those of its selected competitor.

Performance to Sales and Marketing Plan

One valuable way to evaluate a hotel's sales and marketing effort is to compare the property's accomplishments to those originally identified in its Sales and Marketing Plan. Recall that the Sales and Marketing Plan identifies specific marketing strategies and activities designed to meet the hotel's revenue goals. Therefore, hotel owners and managers can compare the specific advertising, promotion, and publicity efforts originally planned by the sales and marketing team with the work this group actually completed.

In addition to evaluating what was done, the timeliness of efforts and conformity to established budgets can also be reviewed. To illustrate, assume that a hotel had intended, as part of its sales and marketing plan, to create a New Year's Eve package designed to attract local transient guests on the night of December 31. The package was designed to include, for one special price, a guest room, champagne, party favors, and a complimentary in-room movie. Advertisement of the package was to begin in mid-November, with a total established advertising budget of $5,000.

If, as planned, advertising for the package really did begin in mid-November, and if the total amount spent on advertising was approximately $5,000, then the sales team has likely performed well. If, alternatively, the advertisement for the package was initiated four weeks late (mid-December), and if, as a result, the hotel could only sell out its rooms by spending substantially more on advertising than was originally planned, the team has not performed as well in terms of timing or adherence to budget. In this case, the team's efforts should be closely examined to identify why the advertising was delayed and how the team responded to the delay.

In evaluating the sales and marketing team's overall performance in implementing the sales and marketing plan, there are four important areas to consider:

What. This simply means comparing what was planned to be done with what was actually done. "Plan your work, then work your plan" is an often-repeated phrase in the hotel business. Even the best sales and marketing plans will be ineffective if they are not implemented.

Who. Even if a sales or marketing activity has been fully completed, the quality of accomplishment is typically dependent upon the expertise of the employees doing the work. It is important that the hotel assign employees skilled at sales and marketing to its essential sales and marketing activities. These activities are too important to be delegated to unskilled employees.

How Much. Given a large enough marketing budget, virtually any hotel sales and marketing team could achieve improvements in hotel revenues. Realistically, however, marketing resources, like all resources in a hotel, are limited. It is important to undertake activities designed to improve revenues, but it is just as important to complete these activities in a cost-effective manner. By comparing actual marketing expenditures to the expenditures in the budget section of the sales and marketing plan, the cost-management abilities of the sales and marketing team can be properly assessed.

How Effective. The most important evaluation of a sales and marketing plan is based on its ultimate effectiveness. Following implementation of the sales and marketing plan, did revenues go up, go down, or stay the same? Even the best plans are sometimes affected by unanticipated events, and these must be considered. Nonetheless, if specific target goals of occupancy level and ADR have been established in a sales and marketing plan, it is reasonable to compare them with actual results to evaluate the overall effectiveness of the sales and marketing effort.

STAR Reports

While an assessment of the "Performance to Sales and Marketing Plan" tells the hotel's owner and management what has been done by the sales team, it does not, by itself, assess the relative quality of the results achieved. If a hotel has followed its sales and marketing plan, and is experiencing a 60 percent occupancy rate, it is difficult to know whether that level of occupancy is good or bad unless the occupancy level of competing hotels is also known. If, for example, your hotel is averaging a 60 percent occupancy and your direct competitors are averaging 50 percent, you may be pleased with the performance of the sales and marketing team. If, on the other hand, your direct competitors are averaging a 70 percent occupancy, it is clear that you are not achieving your fair share of the business available in your market.

Similarly, if your ADR is $100, and your direct competitors' ADR is $80, your sales team is likely showing success in selling at a good rate. If your direct competitors' ADR is $120, however, you are comparatively less successful.

The hotel industry's most widely accepted means of assessing the comparative strength of a property's sales and marketing staff is the STAR report prepared by Smith Travel Research (STR). It is by far the most credible independent measure of a hotel's comparative revenue generation. A STAR report details, among other information, a hotel's daily, weekly, monthly, or annual ADR, occupancy percentage, RevPAR, and relative share of the market. It also reports this same data on a hotel's **competitive set**.

LODGING LANGUAGE

Competitive set: The group of competing hotels to which an individual hotel's operating performance is compared. Sometimes referred to as a "Comp Set."

The STAR report is important because unbiased occupancy rate, ADR, RevPAR, and resulting market share comparisons are important to a wide range of interest groups. These include:

Hotel Owners. Hotel owners and investors want to know if the management team they have put in place is competing effectively in the marketplace. Managing the asset (hotel) to maximize its financial potential is an important goal, and the STAR report indicates, in many ways, how well this goal is being achieved.

Management Companies. These companies know that their effectiveness as managing consultants will be based, to some degree, on how well they perform on the STAR report. Good results are used to demonstrate the value of these companies to owners.

Property Managers. General managers and DOSMs want to know the effectiveness of their marketing plans and sales efforts as well as those of their competitors.

Franchisors. Brand managers want a measure of how well their brands compete in the marketplace. Strong brand performance helps sell additional franchises. Weak performance helps indicate where brand managers can better assist current franchisees.

Real Estate Appraisers. These professionals interpret STAR report results to assist in establishing the financial value (worth) of a hotel. This information is useful when establishing the selling price for a hotel.

The Financial Community. Prospects asked to invest in or lend money to buy or renovate hotels want to know about the sales strength of the hotel seeking funding. Good relative performance (a strong STAR report) helps persuade lenders to lend, while a weak STAR report indicates potential problems and will make it more difficult to secure funding.

A variety of other groups may be interested in the STAR Report for specific hotels or specific geographic areas. Many general managers and sales and marketing directors see the STAR report as the primary measure used to judge their own performance. STAR reports can provide a wealth of information to those sophisticated enough to read and analyze the data they contain. Fortunately, STR produces excellent materials that teach managers how to fully interpret their STAR reports.

STR produces a variety of comparative reports on a daily, weekly, monthly, and annual basis. Hotels voluntarily submit financial data to STR. In return, STR maintains the confidentiality of the individual hotel data it receives. By combining the operating data submitted by selected competitors, an individual hotel's operating performance can be compared to that of its competitive set.

Understanding the competitive set is a key component of understanding the STAR report. Essentially, a competitive set consists of a group of hotels used to establish a performance benchmark. To illustrate, assume that you manage a 100-room limited-service property in a large city. You compete for most of your customers with five

LODGING ONLINE

STAR Report interpretation and analysis is an important and often complex activity. To request instructional information on interpreting STAR reports, and to see the wide variety of benchmarking products produced by STR, go to:

www.strglobal.com/

Why do you think managers want to compare the operating results of their hotels against those of their competitors?

other hotels in your area, each of which has approximately the same number of rooms, services, approximate ADR, and quality as your own property. Assume also that you have identified these same five properties to STR as the group you wish to consider as your competitive set. In nearly all cases, each of these hotels will, as you did, voluntarily submit sales data to STR. This data is then tabulated and returned to your hotel in the form of a STAR report. STR will only report the aggregate results of the competitive set. The company never releases or divulges information on an individual property.

Operating comparisons produced by STR can be customized, but popular comparison categories include those related to:

- Occupancy
- ADR
- RevPAR
- Market share
- Historical trends
- Monthly and year-to-date performance
- City, region, or state performance

The STAR report assesses hotel performance and then assigns a score (index) that directly reflects a specific hotel's performance relative to its competitive set. An index of 100 means that, on a selected operating characteristic such as ADR or occupancy percentage, a hotel has performed exactly equal to its competitive set. An index score above 100 means the hotel has outperformed its competitive set, and an index below 100 means the competitive set has outperformed, on that characteristic, the specific hotel being scored.

To accurately gauge the overall effectiveness of a hotel's management, a property's STAR report must be examined in its entirety. When it is, a hotel's sales and marketing performance can be directly compared to the sales and marketing efforts of its competitors. As a result, STAR performance goals can be established for any operating factor, including occupancy rate, ADR, RevPAR, market penetration, or growth.

When STAR performance does not reach the goals set by the hotel's owners or managers, there can be a variety of problems, not all of which can be easily solved by the general manager or the sales and marketing team. Some of these include:

- Poor public perception of the franchise (brand) name
- Poor signage
- Poor property access by car
- Poor **room mix** for the market
- Substandard furnishings or décor
- Marketing/ advertising budget too small
- Marketing staff too small
- Marketing staff ineffective

LODGING LANGUAGE

Room mix: The ratio of room types in a hotel. For example, the number of double-bedded rooms compared to king-bedded rooms, the number of smoking-permitted rooms to no-smoking rooms, or the number of suites compared to standard rooms.

Some hotel managers dislike STAR reports because they view them as an objective measure (score or index) of a subjective activity (management). Despite their limitations, however, STAR reports are perceived by many in the hotel industry as the best indicator of sales and marketing effectiveness.

STAR reports and others like them, when properly interpreted, are valuable tools for assessing the performance of a sales and marketing team as well as the entire property. Serious hoteliers should learn to analyze them and to review them regularly.

ALL IN A DAY'S WORK 7.2

THE SITUATION

"But I thought you said we did great," said Lance to Sabrina Davis, the general manager of the Crawford Hotel. "We must have done well, because we were packed during the Classic Car Convention! What did we do wrong?"

The Crawford was a limited-service property not affiliated with a brand. Lance, the property's front office manager, and Sabrina were reviewing the hotel's latest monthly STAR report. It showed that occupancy at the Crawford had increased 12 percent (from 60% to 67.2%) when compared to the previous year, and ADR had increased 3 percent. That brought the RevPAR increase for the property to approximately 15 percent when compared to the previous year.

"We did do well," replied Sabrina, "but our competitive set increased their occupancy by 12 percent, and they also increased their rate by 15 percent. They must have increased their rates during the car show a lot more than we did!"

A RESPONSE

Managing room rates during high-volume demand periods can be difficult. In this case, a high-demand period (the Classic Car Convention) was evidently used by the competitive set to drive rates higher than those achieved by the CrawfordHotel. The resulting "underselling" by the Crawford shows up in the STAR report as poor performance, despite RevPAR increases for the hotel.

Careful examination of the monthly STAR report, as is the case here, can provide valuable guidance to hotel managers. It is as important to independent hotels as it is to those that are franchised. In future high-demand periods, both Lance and Sabrina should closely monitor the rates charged by their competitors to ensure that the Crawford's rates stay in line with those of their competitive set.

Lodging Language

DOSM
Sales
Marketing
Booking
Site Tour
Bid
Pickup
Group Contract
Attrition
Block
Convention and Visitor's Bureau (CVB)
Marketing Plan
Sales and Marketing Committee
Inclusive
Advertising
Publicity
Frequent Guest Program
Chamber of Commerce
LEED
Track
Consortia
Per Diem
SMERF
Meeting Planner
Lead
Sales Call
Networking
Cold Calling
Drop In
Direct Mail
Link
Demand Generator
User Generated Content (UGC) site
STAR Report
Competitive Set
Room Mix

For Discussion

1. Effective marketing increases consumer awareness of a hotel. Selling relates to the personal aspect of client relations. Which of these two activities do you believe is more important in the long-term success of a hotel? Explain your position.
2. You have learned that every employee in a hotel is responsible for sales and marketing. Identify three specific activities that each hourly hotel employee can be instructed to undertake to assist in the hotel's sales and marketing effort.
3. Convention and visitors bureaus (CVBs) receive most of their funding from special taxes levied on hotel guests. What other businesses in a city or region benefit from the efforts of a CVB? Why do you think most communities refrain from assessing a CVB tax on those businesses?
4. Some hoteliers believe that the Internet will eliminate the need for travel agents. Do you agree? Explain your position.
5. UGC sites can include postings that unfairly or inaccurately represent a guest's experience at a hotel. What specific steps could you take if you were a hotel DOSM whose property was on the receiving end of an unjustified negative review posted on such a site?
6. Those who purchase group rooms from a hotel often want to do so at a discount price. Identify three factors that an hotelier

might consider before agreeing to give a significant discount for a group room purchase.

7. In large hotels with a full-time sales staff, hotel salespersons are typically paid a salary and (if their work is superior) a bonus for their work. In many other industries, salespersons are only paid the commissions they earn. Why do you think hotel salespersons are rarely, if ever, paid "commission-only" for their efforts?

8. The Internet has had a significant impact on how hotel rooms are sold. As a traveler, do you prefer to book your rooms online? Explain your answer.

9. The properties selected to be a part of a specific hotel's competitive set will strongly affect how the hotel's sales performance is assessed. Identify at least three hotel characteristics that should be considered when selecting the properties to be included in a hotel's competitive set.

10. Some in the hotel industry believe that too heavy an emphasis on the STAR report to evaluate a hotel's sales effort has a negative effect. Others defend the STAR report as the only independent way to evaluate a sales team's effectiveness. Identify two positive and two negative aspects of STAR report utilization in an assessment of a hotel's sales effort.

Team Activities

TEAM ACTIVITY 1

The distinctions between the terms "sales" and "marketing" are as many as there are authors writing about the topics. Identify at least three books, or book chapters, devoted to hospitality sales and marketing, and compare the definitions of these two terms in each reference.

What were the similarities among the definitions? What were the differences? Why do you think that the Hospitality Sales and Marketing Association International (HSMAI) has chosen that name rather than the "Hospitality Marketing and Sales Association International

TEAM ACTIVITY 2

The rapid expansion of hotel brands has made it much more difficult for consumers to differentiate among them. Choose from the following segments of the lodging industry:

- Full-service
- Limited-service
- All-suite

Then select two from among the largest franchise brands in the segment selected and consider each brand's marketing efforts. What feature(s) have the brand's managers chosen to emphasize? Do you think most consumers are aware of the distinctions advertised by the brand managers? What would you suggest the brand managers do differently?

Chapter

8 The Housekeeping Department

Chapter Outline

Chapter Overview

For hoteliers working in a lodging facility, no one area within the hotel is more important than the others. For example, the sales and marketing or front office areas already reviewed in this text are no more important than housekeeping, the subject of this chapter. In virtually every industry survey, however, guests rate room cleanliness as the single most important feature affecting their decision to choose or not choose a specific hotel.

Guests want, first and foremost, a clean room. It is the role of the housekeeping department to provide that clean room as well as to clean most other areas of the hotel. For this reason, it is difficult to overestimate the importance of a well-managed and properly staffed housekeeping department.

In this chapter, we will examine the responsibilities of a hotel's housekeeping department and how the work of its employees affects the front office, maintenance, and food and beverage departments.

You will learn that hoteliers who manage housekeeping must select and properly train their staff, manage product inventories, and also protect guest property accidentally left behind when guests check out. This chapter examines all of these functions and the importance of safety training for everyone working in housekeeping. Training can be especially challenging if, as is often the case, the staff of the department is multinational and, therefore, multilingual.

The job of the housekeeping department is complex and becomes more so every day. Properly cleaning a hotel requires knowledge of the many available tools and chemicals that make cleaning jobs easier. In this chapter, we will closely examine how to use a checklist to evaluate the results of the housekeeping department's cleaning efforts.

In addition to cleaning rooms, the housekeeping department in most hotels is responsible for cleaning the sheets, towels, and other items processed in the hotel's laundry area. While some hotels do not do their own laundry on-site (on-premise), in most hotels the on-premise laundry (OPL) is a significant part of the housekeeping department's daily activities. In this chapter, we will examine the steps utilized to process laundry in an OPL, as well as the unique features of on-premise guest-operated laundry facilities.

Chapter Objectives

1. To identify the areas of responsibility assigned to the housekeeping department of a lodging facility.
2. To explain how hoteliers should manage property left by guests.
3. To show the importance of safety training for employees working in housekeeping.
4. To teach you, in detail, how housekeepers should clean guest rooms and public space areas in a lodging facility.
5. To explain the processes required to clean the laundry generated by a lodging facility.

THE ROLE OF HOUSEKEEPING

The housekeeping department in a hotel is responsible for the hotel's cleanliness. Because that is true, every guest or visitor to the hotel will readily be able to see the results of the housekeepers' work. When a hotel's housekeeping staff is effective, guest satisfaction is high, employee morale is good, and ultimately the hotel is profitable. When the quality of the housekeeping staff's work is below industry standards, guest complaints soar, employees at the front desk and in other departments of the hotel become disillusioned about management's commitment to quality service, and profits suffer due to increased allowances and adjustments made at the front desk to compensate guests for poor experiences. In addition, guests who feel the hotel was not clean simply do not return.

Areas of Responsibility

The number of areas in a hotel that must be cleaned is so large that the housekeeping department will nearly always be the hotel's largest department in terms of number of employees. Depending on the type and size of the hotel, the housekeeping department will generally be responsible for cleaning and maintaining all of the following:

Public Spaces
- Lobby areas
- Public restrooms
- Front desk areas
- Management offices
- Game rooms
- Exercise areas
- Pool and spa areas
- Selected meeting and food service areas
- Employee break rooms and locker rooms

Guest Areas
- Elevators
- Corridors
- Stairwells
- Guest rooms
  - Sleeping areas
  - Bath areas
  - Kitchen areas

Laundry Areas
- Laundry preparation areas
- Laundry supply closets
- Guest linen and supplies storage areas

Housekeeping is an important department at every hotel because it ensures guests receive a clean and comfortable room each and every time they stay.

Decisions about the number of employees required to clean these areas and frequency of cleaning are the responsibility of the **Executive Housekeeper**.

LODGING LANGUAGE

Executive Housekeeper: The individual responsible for the management and operation of a hotel's housekeeping department.

It may sometimes be unclear whether a space in a hotel is the cleaning responsibility of the housekeeping or another department. A good example is the dining area in a full-service hotel. In some hotels, the general manager may decide that housekeeping staff clean the dining room while in other hotels this would become the responsibility of the food and beverage department. The important rule is that every department must know and carry out its cleaning responsibilities.

There will always be some areas in a hotel that call for a management decision about who should clean those areas. The general manager, in conjunction with the executive housekeeper, must make these decisions so that the cleaning of every area of the hotel is assigned to a specific department. To facilitate this process, many hotels use a color-coded map of the entire property. Areas of cleaning responsibility are assigned to departments by color code. Each department is responsible for cleaning and maintaining the areas that match its assigned color. With this system, the department head assigned to the area knows the responsibility for the cleaning of every area in the hotel, and accountability can be ensured.

Interactions

Providing perfectly cleaned guest rooms is a top priority for any well-run hotel. The cleaning of guest rooms is always the responsibility of the housekeeping department and must be executed flawlessly. The specifics of guest room cleaning are examined later in this chapter. What is less well known, but of utmost importance, is the communication role the housekeeping department must play in relaying **room status** information to the front desk staff and room maintenance issues to those responsible for room repairs. In a hotel with a food and beverage department, housekeeping must also interact with that important area. You will learn about these interactions in this section.

LODGING LANGUAGE

Room status: The up-to-date (actual) condition of each of the hotel's guest rooms (e.g., occupied, vacant, or dirty).

FRONT DESK

No front office manager wants to assign arriving guests to a dirty room. In fact, in a well-managed hotel, there is a strict policy not to assign a guest to a room unless:

- It was properly cleaned by the housekeeping department
- It was verified as clean by a second member of housekeeping
- Its clean and vacant status has been correctly reported to the front desk

While this might, at first glance, appear to be a simple process, it is quite complex and, if not managed properly, contains the potential for a variety of miscommunications.

To illustrate the importance of maintaining accurate guest room status, let's examine the stay of Mr. and Mrs. Flood. This couple checks into a room at the Best Sleep Hotel at 4:00 p.m. on Monday afternoon and are assigned to a room that the housekeeping staff has reported to the front desk as "clean and vacant." That is, housekeeping personnel have communicated that the room has been cleaned and inspected for cleanliness and that no other guest is occupying it.

If, in fact, the room was properly cleaned and no other guest is assigned to it, the Floods, upon arriving at the room, should have no housekeeping-related complaints. Consider, however, the problems that could occur if the room, instead of being clean, was

Term	Meaning
Clean and Vacant	The room is vacant, has been cleaned, and can be assigned to a guest. In some hotels, the designation used is "*Clean and Ready*"
Occupied	The room is registered to a current guest
On-Change	The room is vacant but not yet cleaned In some hotels, the designation used is "*Vacant and Dirty*"
Do Not Disturb (DND)	The room is occupied but has not been cleaned due to the guest's request not to be disturbed
Sleep-out (sleeper)	The room is reported as occupied but was not used (bed not used; no personal belongings in room), and the guest is not present
Stay-over	The guest will be staying in the room at least one more night
Due-out	The guest(s) have indicated this is the last day they will use the room
Check-out	The guest(s) have departed
Out of Order	The room is unrentable and thus is unassignable at this time
Lock out	The guest has items in the room, but will be denied access until management approves re-entry
Late Check-out	The guests have requested and been given an extension of the regular check-out time

FIGURE 8.1 Common Room Status Terms

scheduled for cleaning but the cleaning had not yet occurred. In this case, the couple would have been checked into a dirty room and, of course, will return to the front desk area unhappy and concerned about the overall quality of their stay.

Similarly, if the room is cleaned but the Floods, upon their arrival, discover someone's possessions, (or someone!) in the room, they will again be upset and return to the front desk area unhappy and concerned about the quality of the hotel's management staff as well as their own safety.

From these examples, you can see that it is critical for a housekeeping staff to continuously and accurately maintain the room status of all guest rooms in the hotel. Figure 8.1 lists the room status definitions commonly used in U.S. hotels. Specific companies or areas of the country may vary the terms and/or the abbreviations used to designate them; however, these terms or their equivalents must be used in the hotel if housekeeping is to accurately represent room status to the front desk.

It is easy to see that the housekeeping department must carefully report the status of rooms. The process of communicating room status between housekeeping and the front desk begins each morning when the housekeeping department receives an updated occupancy report from the front desk.

This occupancy report will detail, for each room, the room status displayed by the property management system (PMS) for front office agents. If there are no discrepancies, the report will accurately show which rooms are **stay-overs**, occupied, clean and vacant, on-change, or out of order. It is up to the housekeeping department to take this report and communicate room status changes to the front desk as they are made, just as the front desk should communicate its known room status changes to housekeeping.

LODGING LANGUAGE

Stay-over: A guest who is *not* scheduled to check out of the hotel on the day his or her room status is assessed. That is, the guest will be staying at least one more day.

If both the front office and housekeeping perform their jobs well, an accurate, up-to-date room status is maintained in the PMS throughout the day. Generally, the front office notifies the housekeeping department of check-outs and other room status changes throughout the day by:

- calling or texting the executive housekeeper or a housekeeping supervisor
- updating the PMS (when the housekeeping department has easy access to seeing updates and changes)
- using another communication tool, such as a telephone, two-way radio, or paging device

Changes in room status made by housekeeping staff can also be communicated to the front office in a variety of ways, including:

- having a housekeeper or housekeeping supervisor contact the front office by telephone (from each room as its status changes) to inform the desk of the change
- via radio or handheld computer
- by using the hotel's guest room phone interface with the PMS (if available) to make the changes directly via codes entered into the telephone in the affected room

At the end of the housekeeping shift, the housekeeping personnel will prepare a final and up-to-date room-status report based on a physical check of each room. This report is then compared to the updated PMS occupancy report to identify any discrepancies. If there are any, the front office manager must investigate them. A discrepancy could occur if, for example, a front office agent is fraudulently selling rooms to guests (assigning the guests to a room but not recording the income in the hotel's PMS). In this case, the discrepancy report would uncover the activity because the guest room, reported as "vacant" in the PMS, would show as "occupied" on the housekeeping room status report.

MAINTENANCE

An additional and absolutely critical communication line must exist between the housekeeping and **maintenance** departments of the hotel. Repairs and replacements will inevitably be needed due to the wear and tear caused by guests using hotel rooms.

LODGING LANGUAGE

Maintenance: The activities required to keep a building and its contents in good repair. Also, the department or area of a hotel responsible for these activities.

For example, when light bulbs burn out in a guest room, they must be replaced. This simple task may be assigned to housekeeping. If, however, a guest accidentally breaks the leg off of a chair in the room, or if a toilet is running constantly, housekeeping must request a repair. The ability of the housekeeping department to aggressively identify and then quickly report needed room repairs will make a significant difference in the satisfaction level of guests. The actual method used by housekeeping to report room issues to the Maintenance department is detailed in Chapter 9 (The Maintenance Department).

A critical point to remember is that the housekeeping department because its staff members are in the rooms most frequently, plays a crucial role in maintaining room quality by reporting room defects quickly and accurately to the hotel employees responsible for eliminating them. Maintenance department employees then make the repairs and clean up their work or, if appropriate, contact housekeeping to retidy the room prior to renting it to a guest. When communications between housekeeping and maintenance personnel are good, the rooms, hotel guests, and the property itself will all benefit.

FOOD AND BEVERAGE

Some hotels have extensive food and beverage departments. When they do, linens, tablecloths, and napkins may be cleaned and pressed in the hotel's **on-premise laundry (OPL)**.

LODGING LANGUAGE

On-premise Laundry (OPL): The area within the hotel where the cleaning of fabrics takes place.

When a hotel offers guests the choice of in-room dining, the housekeeping department may be responsible for returning used dishes and glassware to the food and beverage dish-washing area. Alternatively, housekeeping staff may simply remove these items from the guest room and place them in the hotel's hallways for pick-up by a food and beverage staff member.

In addition to providing laundry service and providing for in-room dining dish return, the housekeeping department in a larger property may be responsible for maintaining employee uniforms for food and beverage (and other departments). In a smaller property, the housekeeping department may be responsible for cleaning all or part of the lobby foodservices area in which complimentary beverages, breakfasts, or other meals are served.

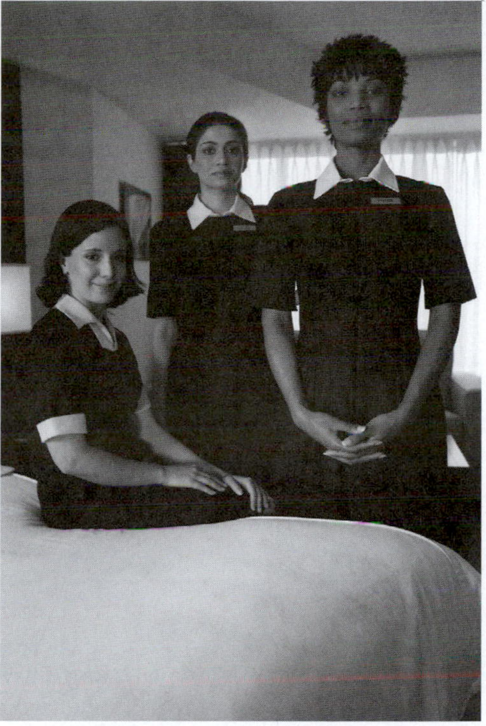

An effectively managed housekeeping department will consistently produce clean and comfortable guest rooms.

MANAGING HOUSEKEEPING

The executive housekeeper in a hotel has the responsibility for the cleanliness of the entire facility. He or she must know about personnel administration, budgeting, laundry sanitation, fabrics and uniforms, room-cleaning chemicals and routines, and of course, be guest-service-oriented.

Managers in the housekeeping department must be among a hotel's most talented. The challenges of keeping a hotel clean are many, as are the special issues faced by the executive housekeeper and the housekeeping staff. The unique issues faced by the department may pertain to staffing, inventory control, and the management of guest property accidentally or purposely left behind.

Staffing

It is usually very difficult to staff a hotel housekeeping department. This is because of the large number of housekeeping staff needed, the difficulty of the work, and unfortunately, in some cases, a wage structure that does not induce the best employees to seek or progress in hotel housekeeping careers.

Properly approached and fairly treated, however, this department can be well staffed with stable, highly professional employees who add tremendously to the success of the hotel. In most hotels, the key staff positions are the executive housekeeper, inspectors, room attendants, and, in some cases, housepersons.

ALL IN A DAY'S WORK 8.1

THE SITUATION

"It isn't fair," Jenna Walbert, the executive housekeeper, said to Basil Josiah, the hotel's general manager. "My staff cleans the men's employee locker room every day, but just look at this!"

Basil carefully inspected the area. Ashtrays overflowed, food was left on benches, dirty uniforms littered the floor, and newspapers were strewn about. It was a mess.

"The guys in food and beverage and maintenance do this every day," continued Jenna angrily. "Our houseperson is too busy trying to keep the lobby carpets sharp to spend an hour a day down here cleaning up after our own staff. I think you should make the food and beverage and maintenance departments keep this place clean. *They* are the ones who are messing it up."

A RESPONSE

Accepting Jenna's suggestion may be tempting to Basil, but the solution to this problem is probably not the reassignment of cleaning responsibilities. The housekeeping department is typically responsible for cleaning the entire hotel (including employee locker rooms). In this case, however, the male employees in some departments are abusing the system. Fairness in this case requires that the departmental managers supervising the employees responsible for the mess correct their behavior, and this situation, immediately. Basil can and should end Jenna's difficulty by using his authority as general manager to enforce their compliance.

LODGING ONLINE

The International Executive Housekeepers Association (IEHA) is the professional association for managers working in housekeeping. With more than 6,000 members, the IEHA offers educational programs and certification and publishes a monthly magazine. To view its Web site, go to:

www.ieha.org/

What do you think is an executive housekeeper's most important personality trait? Do you have it?

EXECUTIVE HOUSEKEEPERS

A hotel with a well-trained, motivated, and professional executive housekeeper has a tremendous advantage over those establishments that do not employ such a person. An effective executive housekeeper is not only a valuable member of the hotel's management team, he or she is also an effective administrator, department motivator, and team player.

At many hotels, the executive housekeeper has worked up from an entry-level housekeeping position. In other hotels, the executive housekeeper may not have held any entry-level housekeeping positions. In either case, the skills required to be an effective executive housekeeper, like the skills needed by all managers, are related to planning, organizing, directing, and controlling the activities of the department. Executive housekeepers must have an unquestioned commitment to cleanliness, impeccable standards, on-going dedication to their area, and human resource-related skills well above the average for managers. It is only with these characteristics that a hotel's executive housekeeper will provide the departmental leadership required in today's competitive hotel environment.

INSPECTORS

The housekeeping departments of many hotels include one or more people in the position of **inspector (inspectress)**. These employees report directly to the executive housekeeper.

LODGING LANGUAGE

Inspector (Inspectress): Employee responsible for physically checking the room status of guest rooms and performing other tasks as assigned by the executive housekeeper.

Regardless of a hotel's size, it is important that someone verify the actual readiness of guest rooms before they are listed in the PMS as clean, vacant, and available to sell. This job falls to the inspectors. An inspector physically enters and checks a guest room after it has been cleaned to determine whether any areas that should have been cleaned have been missed or if there are other defects in the room that require further attention.

In a very large hotel, there may be several inspectors working at the same time. The primary responsibility of the inspector is to assess the quality of room cleanliness, but it is equally important to point out deficiencies to **room attendants**, assure that they are corrected, and report revisions in room status to the executive housekeeper or the front desk.

LODGING LANGUAGE

Room attendant: Employee responsible for cleaning guest rooms. Also referred to as "housekeeper." Sometimes called "maids" by guests, but that term is *never* used by professional hoteliers.

An effective inspector has high standards of cleanliness and the ability to point out deficiencies in rooms reportedly cleaned by room attendants in a way that motivates the attendants to do their very best work—in other words, without appearing overly critical of sincere efforts to do a good job. Inspectors are truly a hotel guest's best friend because their sharp eyes enforce the standards of cleanliness established by the executive housekeeper.

ROOM ATTENDANTS

Highly skilled and motivated room attendants are incredibly vital to a hotel's success. Yet many hotels find it difficult to recruit, select, and retain a sufficient number of room attendants to adequately clean the number of rooms sold. As a result, the hotel operates shorthanded, and room cleanliness suffers. In addition, managers and other non-housekeeping staff end up cleaning rooms, and inspectors sometimes are not able to inspect because they are too busy helping to clean rooms.

When executive housekeepers are asked why these problems occur, their answers include:

- We don't pay enough to attract the right people.
- The work is too hard.
- There is a labor shortage.
- Today's workers simply won't work.
- Not enough people like to do the work a housekeeper is required to do.
- Workers don't care about doing a good job anymore.

It is sometimes tempting to accept such statements as the truth. You should not, however, because in nearly all cases they are simply not true. Interestingly, the best executive housekeepers not only have adequate numbers of room attendants on staff, they have a waiting list of room attendants from other hotels in the area hoping to join their staff. Remember that strategies designed to properly recruit and retain room attendants must be put in place if a hotel is to be perceived as the employer of choice for the area's best room attendants.

Properly cleaning guest rooms can be hard and physically demanding work. Some larger hotels used to employ male **housepersons** to perform the very labor-intensive tasks, such as carrying heavy loads of laundry and moving furniture within rooms.

LODGING LANGUAGE

Houseperson: Housekeeping employee responsible for assisting room attendants with their work.

Today, such employees are just as likely to be female as male, and, as is true with laundry workers and **public space** cleaners, they comprise an integral part of the overall housekeeping department.

LODGING LANGUAGE

Public space: Areas within the hotel that can be freely accessed by guests and visitors. Examples include lobby areas, public restrooms, corridors, and stairwells.

Entry-level housekeeping wages are often among the lowest in the hotel. Nonetheless, it is possible and critical to build a highly motivated, dedicated staff of room attendants. The approaches to doing so are many but at minimum include:

- Treating room attendants with the respect they deserve at all times
- Ensuring that room attendants are supervised by excellent supervisors
- Maintaining room-cleaning assignment policies that are perceived as fair by the room attendants
- Providing excellent, ongoing training

- Providing a realistic career ladder for room attendants
- Enforcing housekeeping department policies that affect room attendants consistently and without favoritism
- Providing for room attendant safety through training and appropriate hotel policies
- Providing benefit packages that are competitive for the area
- Paying fair wages to all part-time and full-time housekeeping staff

Reasonable hotel managers may disagree about what constitutes fair wages for room attendants. Some simply pay room attendants an hourly wage. Others add incentives for extra effort, such as meeting established quality levels. Still others pay a designated dollar amount for each room cleaned. Regardless of the payment approach, it is important to treat room attendants fairly. Some hoteliers treat room attendants as if they are not important. Hotels that do this will, inevitably, lose their best room attendants to hotels that demonstrate real concern for these crucial staff members.

OTHER HOUSEKEEPING STAFF

In addition to the executive housekeeper, inspectors, and room attendants, the housekeeping department will, depending upon its size, employ one or more staff members to clean public spaces, maintain departmental records or serve as administrative assistants to the executive housekeeper.

The OPL in a hotel is often a hot and physically demanding place to work. Employees needed in this area include those actually moving items to be washed from the guest rooms to the laundry area, those loading and unloading washers and dryers, and those responsible for folding and storing the cleaned items as well as transporting them to carts or storage areas located near guest rooms. In some special cases, seamstresses or tailors may be employed to care for uniforms and guest clothes.

Inventory Management

The housekeeping department maintains a large number of products used in the cleaning and servicing of rooms. In addition, a large number of inventory items are required each time a room is cleaned. The following partial list gives some indication of the number of guest-room-related inventory items that must be maintained by the executive housekeeper:

Sheets (all sizes)	Acid-based cleaners
Pillowcases	Glassware
Bedspreads	Cups
Bath towels	Coffee/coffee filters
Hand towels	Laundry bags
Washcloths	Laundry tags
Soaps	Clothes hangers
Shampoos	In-room literature and signage
Conditioners	Television viewing guides
Sewing kits	Telephone books
Glass cleaner	Pens
Furniture polish	Paper/pads/stationery

If too many units of any item are kept in storage, the hotel may have committed money to housekeeping inventory that could be put to better use elsewhere in the hotel. Alternatively, if too few items are kept on hand, housekeepers may not have what they need to properly clean and re-stock rooms. Therefore, the executive housekeeper must know how much of each item is in use or in storage, as well as any items that have been ordered but not yet received.

Purchasing and receiving replacements for some items, such as custom bedspreads, drapes, or logo items, may take weeks or even months. In light of this, experienced

Department: Housekeeping		Item: King-size Sheets	
Prepared By:		Date:	
For Period:		to	
Count on: January 1		850 units	
	Plus		
Purchased in month		144 units	
Total in service		994 units	
	Less		
Count on: February 1		877 units	
Total Monthly usage		**117**	

FIGURE 8.2 Best Sleep Hotel Product Usage Report

executive housekeepers know that an actual monthly (or more often) count of all significant housekeeping supplies is essential to maintaining an adequate level of them.

A second reason for regular supply inventories is that they allow the executive housekeeper to compile **product usage reports**.

LODGING LANGUAGE

Product usage report: A report detailing the amount of an inventoried item used by a hotel in a specified time period (week, month, quarter, or year).

Figure 8.2 shows a monthly product-usage report for king-sized bed sheets. It is completed using actual product counts taken at the beginning of each month by the housekeeping staff. The same format can be used to compute product usage in any department and for any product in the hotel.

When determining the count of products in housekeeping, it is important to count the total number of products on hand, whether they are in use, in storage, or in reserve. To accurately determine the total number of king-sized bed sheets actually on hand, for example, physical counts would need to be taken in:

- Guest rooms
- Room attendant cleaning carts
- Soiled linen areas (including inside washers and dryers)
- Clean linen storage areas
- New product (unopened cases) storage areas

Note in Figure 8.2 that 117 bed sheets were used in the month. This may mean that the sheets were taken out of service because they were too badly stained to continue using, that they had become torn or frayed beyond use, and/or that they were stolen. Regardless of the reason, if the physical count of the king-sized bed sheets is accurate, management knows the number used and can easily compute the cost of king-sized sheets taken out of service in January. Experienced executive housekeepers ensure that their department computes monthly product usage rates on all significant housekeeping items so that per-room cleaning costs can be accurately calculated.

Managing Lost and Found

Guests often either intentionally or accidentally leave valuable items in their rooms when they check out. These items are commonly referred to as those that have been "lost and found." As a result, the housekeeping department in a hotel must have specific and written lost and found procedures in place. This is because it is often difficult to know what to do with property whose ownership is unknown.

In most states in the United States, the law makes a distinction between three types of property whose ownership is in doubt. Each of the three types of unclaimed property requires a different response by the housekeeping staff. The three property types are **mislaid property**, **lost property**, and **abandoned property**.

LODGING LANGUAGE

Mislaid property: Items the owner has unintentionally left behind. Common examples include laptop computers, jewelry, and clothing.

Lost property: Items the owner has unintentionally left behind and then forgotten. Common examples include robes, slippers, hairdryers, and cosmetics.

Abandoned property: Items the owner has intentionally left behind. Common examples include newspapers, magazines, foods and beverages.

The laws in most states require hotels to safeguard mislaid property until the rightful owner returns. For example, a notebook computer left by a guest in a guest room, *after* the guest checks out, is to be protected by the hotel until its owner returns. To throw or give the computer away on the same day it was discovered in the room would be illegal.

In fact, if the hotel were to give it away to someone other than its rightful owner, the hotel would be responsible to the owner for the value of the computer. Executive housekeepers must make sure that a policy is in place requiring that employees discovering mislaid property identify it as such to their supervisor and then place it in safe keeping (in most states 60–90 days).

In the case of a misplaced notebook computer, it is very likely that the guest who mislaid it will contact the hotel to arrange for its return. For a variety of reasons, however, the guest may never contact the hotel. If the hotel is not contacted in a reasonable period of time (in most states 60–90 days) the mislaid property would then legally be considered lost property, or property that its owner has forgotten.

A hotel is required to hold lost property until the rightful owner claims it. In many states, the item's finder must even make a good faith effort to return the lost item to its owner. For example, if a leather jacket is left in a guest room, and the hotel staff discovers the owner's name and telephone number sewn into the lining, they must attempt to reach the jacket's owner. Due to privacy concerns, some hotels are hesitant to directly contact those guests who have left items in their rooms. Regardless of the aggressiveness with which hotels seek to return lost items to their rightful owners, hotel employees who find lost property in the course of their work should always be required to turn the found property over to their employer.

How long a hotel must hold lost property depends upon the value of the property. In general, the greater value, the more reasonable it is to hold the item for an extended period. The executive housekeeper, in consultation with the general manager, should establish the length of time mislaid and lost property will be held before the hotel disposes it of. In most cases, 90 days is a reasonable time to hold those mislaid or lost items found in a hotel.

In the case of abandoned property, the owner has no intention of returning to retrieve the item(s). Interestingly, the law does not require a hotel to attempt to find the owner of abandoned property. Many of the guest items left in hotel rooms fall into this category. Magazines, worn-out clothing, personal toiletry items such as combs and razors, and a variety of grocery items are often abandoned.

It can be difficult for executive housekeepers and their staffs to know if an item has been abandoned rather than misplaced or lost. When in doubt, property left behind in a room or found in a lobby area should be treated as either mislaid or lost. After it is held for a reasonable period, the hotel should dispose of it. Some hotels give such items to local charities; others give them to the hotel employee who found them.

Regardless of the hotel's abandoned property policy, it is the job of the executive housekeeper to have a written lost and found procedure in place that protects guest property until it is claimed or declared abandoned. In large hotels with designated safety and security departments, the head of that department may develop this policy and may even be responsible for safekeeping misplaced or lost items.

LODGING ONLINE

A number of companies sell complete "lost and found" documentation packages that include forms, log books, and software. The American Hotel Registry is a full-service hotel products supplier. To view this innovative company's lost and found (and other) product offerings, go to:

www.americanhotel.com/

Have you ever forgotten an item when checking out of a hotel? Did you return for it?

Because of the importance of securing the property of guests, hotels should document their lost and found efforts. Pre-printed forms on which to record information about lost and found items are readily available from many business stationery sources and can be useful. Regardless of the form(s) used, the executive housekeeper should protect the hotel with a written record of:

- The date the item was found
- A brief description of the item
- The location where the item was found (e.g., the number of the hotel room)
- The name of the finder
- The name of the supervisor who received the item

When the item is returned to the rightful owner or disposed of, the written record should include:

- The date the item was returned to the owner
- Owner's name, address, and contact information
- The name of the housekeeping manager returning the item
- The method of return (e.g., by mail, or in person)
- The method of disposal (e.g., thrown in the trash)
- The date the property was declared to be abandoned
- The date the property was disposed
- The name of hotel employee (or charity) receiving the abandoned property

SAFETY TRAINING

Employee accident rates in the housekeeping department are often among the highest in the hotel. There are two reasons for this. The first is the simple fact that the housekeeping department is usually one of the hotel's largest in terms of the number of workers employed. The second reason, however, relates to the physical nature of the job. Housekeepers often work with equipment and supplies that must be very carefully handled if accidents are to be avoided. The right housekeeping tools and equipment help improve productivity. They also improve safety and reduce accidents. Therefore, these items should be provided to each housekeeper and placed, where appropriate, on every**room attendant cart**. If they are not, unnecessary on-the-job injuries will result, and medical costs related to accidents will increase.

LODGING LANGUAGE

Room attendant cart: A wheeled cart that contains all of the items needed to properly and safely clean and restock a guest room. Also referred to as a "room attendant's cleaning cart or a housekeeping cart."

Training the housekeeping staff properly is just as important as providing them with the necessary tools and supplies to do their jobs. Employee training is always a crucial aspect of the executive housekeeper's job, and safety training is the most essential element of training. The executive housekeeper must make sure that the department has the necessary training programs in place to minimize threats to worker safety.

Housekeepers' jobs often require the use of machines, such as vacuum cleaners, washers, dryers, high-capacity linen ironing and folding apparatus, and other equipment. Workers should never be allowed to operate these until they are fully trained. Supplies used by housekeepers in the completion of their daily tasks include powerful cleaners and chemicals. Properly used, they make the workers' jobs easier. Improperly used, the same chemicals and cleaners can cause nausea, skin rashes, lung damage, vomiting, blindness, and even death. Because this is true, effective executive housekeepers ensure that housekeeping employees handle only the machinery and supplies they have been trained to handle.

All hotel employees require both general and department-specific training, and the housekeeping department is no exception. In housekeeping, specific areas of training concern most often include:

- Handling chemicals
- Cleaning procedures
- Proper lifting techniques
- Properly entering guest rooms
- Contending with guest rooms containing:
  - Firearms
  - Uncaged pets/animals
  - Guests perceived to be threatening
  - Guests who are ill/unconscious
  - Drugs and drug paraphernalia
  - Blood and **blood-borne pathogens**
  - Unsafe (damaged) furniture or fixtures
  - Bed bugs
- Guest service
- Guest room security
- Lost and found procedures

LODGING LANGUAGE

Blood-borne pathogen: Any microorganism or virus that is carried by blood and that can cause a disease.

The special training required by housekeeping staff in regard to blood-borne pathogens and lost and found items deserves special attention.

Blood-borne pathogen training is especially important for room attendants because they may come into contact with body fluids and/or bloody sheets, towels, or facial tissues while cleaning guest rooms. Employees who are not trained in the proper procedures for such situations could become infected.

Hypodermic needles left by intravenous drug users or guests with medical conditions requiring the use of these needles may also threaten the safety of room attendants. Human immunodeficiency virus (HIV) and Hepatitis B are two well-known and very serious diseases

LODGING ONLINE

In the United States, the federal government's Occupational Safety & Health Administration (OSHA) is very involved in the development of standards, education, and training materials for workers who could be exposed to blood-borne pathogens. To view information related to blood-borne pathogen and needle stick prevention training, go to:

www.osha.gov/SLTC/bloodbornepathogens/index.html

How important do you think it would be to implement room attendant training programs emphasizing personal safety?

spread by blood-borne pathogens. Health threats such as these as well as other threats must be addressed through proper training, and it is the responsibility of the hotel's managers to ensure that such training takes place.

Because housekeepers face so many safety-related risks in their jobs, it is important for all hotels to have an effective safety-training program in place.

CLEANING RESPONSIBILITIES

Because it is responsible for cleaning so many different areas, an effective housekeeping department must have a flexible, talented staff who must implement detailed procedures for cleaning and inspecting guest rooms as well as the hotel's public spaces. While it is beyond the scope of this book to detail the specific how-tos of guest room and public space cleaning, it is important to know that employees must be carefully scheduled to clean these areas and that standards of cleanliness for all areas must be established and enforced.

Enforcement of cleaning standards generally takes the form of the systematic inspection of guest rooms and public spaces by the department's inspectors, the executive housekeeper, and even the hotel's general manager. As mentioned earlier in this text, however, in some hotels effective inspection programs utilize the hotel's room attendants and other non-supervisory housekeeping staff in the role of inspector. The front office manager can also be a valuable resource in the inspection/quality control programs initiated by the executive housekeeper. This is so because it is often the front desk area of the hotel that receives, directly from guests, any negative comments about guest room or facility cleanliness.

Employee Scheduling

Properly scheduling employees in the housekeeping department requires skill on the part of the manager making the schedule and flexibility on the part of the staff. Depending upon the size and occupancy rate of the hotel, it is not unusual to find housekeeping staff working at any time of the day or night. Public space cleaners may find that late night or early morning hours are best for completing their work. To complete the number of laundry loads needed to support the hotel's occupancy levels, laundry staff may find that they too may have to work very late at night or very early in the morning.

Room attendants' work schedules are generally less flexible with regard to when they can work. This is because guests in stay-over rooms will expect their rooms to be cleaned between the time they leave them in the morning and the time they are reasonably likely to return after their day's activities. Therefore, unless the guest requests alternative times, stay-over rooms in the typical hotel are generally cleaned between 8:00 a.m. and 3:00 p.m. In addition, the housekeeping staff must have cleaned enough rooms to allow front office staff to assign cleaned and vacant rooms to guests at the arrival time established by the hotel. Thus, if the advertised arrival time 3:00 p.m., enough rooms must be ready to allow guests to be assigned one promptly upon their 3:00 p.m. arrival. If this is not done, and a front office agent greets a guest with the words, "*Your room is not ready yet; housekeeping is still cleaning rooms*" the guest is very likely to be dissatisfied.

The number of room attendants that should be scheduled to work on any given day depends upon several factors, including the size of the guest rooms, the amenities in the rooms, the number of rooms to be cleaned, and the amount (if any) of **deep cleaning** taking place.

LODGING LANGUAGE

Deep cleaning: Intensive cleaning of a guest room. Typically includes thorough cleaning of such items as drapes, lamp shades, carpets, furniture, and walls. Regularly scheduled deep cleaning of guest rooms is one mark of an effective housekeeping department.

Larger guest rooms generally take more time to properly clean than smaller ones, and rooms with special amenities, such as refrigerators, microwaves, stoves, and dining areas, require more of an attendant's time than those without these features.

The actual number of rooms to be cleaned is the variable that is most critical to effective scheduling, and this number is subject to normal, but rapid, fluctuation. Assume, for example, that an executive housekeeper wishes to inform employees one week ahead of time about next week's work schedule. For example, if Monday is the first day of the month, the executive housekeeper would like to post, on the first, the room attendants' work schedule for the 8th through the 15th of that month.

Based upon the room sales forecast provided by the general manager or front office manager, the executive housekeeper determines how many room attendants are needed and then posts the schedule. If, however, on the 5th day of the month the sales and marketing team makes a large last-minute sale (e.g., 75 rooms per night) to a group of guests arriving on the 7th and staying through the 10th, more room attendants will be needed than on the original schedule. Alternatively, if a significant numbers of transient or group reservation cancellations occur, fewer room attendants will be needed and the schedule will need to be modified. This can be the case when inclement weather, airport closings, or other unusual events cause major disruptions in typical travel patterns.

Some inexperienced executive housekeepers, in an attempt to firmly quantify the number of workers needed on a given day, rely exclusively on a **minutes per room** target to establish the room attendants' schedule.

LODGING LANGUAGE

Minutes per room (guest room cleaning): The average number of minutes required to clean a guest room.

Average (cleaning) minutes per room is calculated by managers by using the following formula:

$$\frac{\text{Total number of minutes needed to clean guest rooms}}{\text{Total number of guest rooms cleaned}} = \text{Minutes per room}$$

For example, in a hotel where 100 rooms were cleaned, and the total number of minutes paid to full- and part-time room cleaning staff was 2,500, the formula would be calculated as:

$$\frac{\text{2,500 minutes used}}{\text{100 rooms cleaned}} = \text{25 minutes per room}$$

Managers then use the minutes per room formula to help develop the room attendant work schedule.

For example, if a thorough cleaning typically takes 30 minutes, and an estimated 100 rooms will be cleaned, the two-step formula used to compute the number of room attendant work hours that should be scheduled is:

Step One

$$\text{30 minutes per room cleaning time} \times \text{100 rooms to be cleaned} = \text{3,000 minutes}$$

Step Two

$$\frac{\text{3,000 minutes}}{\text{60 minutes per hour}} = \text{50 hours of room attendant time needed}$$

The actual number of employees an executive housekeeper would schedule in this example would be dependent on the number of full-time and part-time room attendants employed by the hotel.

Experienced housekeepers rely on both rooms per minute computations *and* information about the hotel's guests to determine the actual number of room attendant hours that should be scheduled on a specific day. For example, executive housekeepers know that it takes more minutes to clean a room in which the guest has checked out than one in which the guest is a stay-over. As a result, as the percentage of guest rooms that are stay-overs increases, the number of room attendant minutes (and therefore the total number of hours) required to clean those rooms declines.

Likewise, when a room has multiple occupants, it is more likely to take longer to clean it than a room housing only a single guest. With experience, executive housekeepers can develop a hotel-specific formula that uses both minutes per room and the unique characteristics of the hotel's guests and sales patterns to determine achievable productivity levels that are reasonable for the hotel and its housekeepers.

Guest Room Cleaning

Effective guest room cleaning is the heart of the housekeeping department and also of the entire hotel operation. In most hotels, this activity, more than any other, will determine the long-term success or failure of the property. It must be done extremely well. A motivated executive housekeeper and well-trained staff are required, but so too are regular inspections that identify areas for improvement and reinforce good practices.

Some hoteliers evaluate the effectiveness of a hotel's housekeeping department only by computing its labor, cleaning, guest supplies, or **cost per occupied room (CPOR)**.

LODGING LANGUAGE

Cost Per Occupied Room (CPOR): Total costs incurred for an item or area, divided by the number of rooms occupied in the hotel for the time period examined.

The total cost per occupied room is calculated as a time period's total expenditures for an area such as labor or supplies, divided by the number of rooms occupied during that same time period. For example, in a hotel that spent \$7,000 on room attendant wages in a week that it sold 1,000 rooms, the cost per occupied room for room attendants would be computed as:

$$\frac{\$7{,}000 \text{ room attendant cost}}{1{,}000 \text{ rooms sold}} = \$7 \text{ room attendant cost per occupied room}$$

It would be wrong to think that achieving lower costs per occupied room or spending fewer minutes cleaning each room is always better. In fact, spending too little money supplying a room or spending too little time cleaning each guest room is as bad, or worse, than spending too much. The proper approach is to inspect the guest rooms and then determine whether the hotel is maximizing the effectiveness of the housekeeping department. If it is not, more staff training or additions to staff may be required to maintain established standards, and management must address these issues.

It is a good idea to develop inspection sheets that identify areas to be evaluated during routine inspections of public spaces, guest bathroom and sleeping room areas, and the laundry. They can focus attention on every area affecting guest satisfaction. Of course, the property inspection sheets a hotel develops should consider the hotel's specific needs and characteristics. Inspection checklists, however, can provide an excellent starting point for examining the cleaning process.

SLEEPING AREA

The sleeping area of a guest room is typically the first part seen by the guest when entering the room. It must be absolutely clean. Figure 8.3 is an example of an inspection sheet that could be used to inspect the sleeping area of a guest room.

Recall that the actual inspection sheet used would, of course, be developed specifically for the hotel inspected.

BATHROOM AREA

The bathroom area of a guest room is very closely inspected by guests for cleanliness. Inadequate cleaning of this area by the housekeeping staff will inevitably result in guest dissatisfaction and complaints. Like the sleeping area of the guest room, the bathroom area must be absolutely clean. Figure 8.4 is an example of an inspection sheet that may be used to inspect the bathroom area of a guest room.

GUEST ROOM SLEEPING AREA INSPECTION

Date: ______________________________ *Inspected by:* ______________________

Room Number: ______________

ITEM/AREA	OUTSTANDING	ACCEPTABLE	UNACCEPTABLE	COMMENTS
All light bulbs functioning	❑	❑	❑	
Lamps clean/functioning	❑	❑	❑	
Carpet unspotted	❑	❑	❑	
Drapes/cords/hooks in place	❑	❑	❑	
Outside windows/ ledges clean	❑	❑	❑	
Bedspread clean	❑	❑	❑	
Pillows in good condition	❑	❑	❑	
Pictures straight/ dusted	❑	❑	❑	
Air vents dusted	❑	❑	❑	
Mirrors clean	❑	❑	❑	
TV clean/ dusted	❑	❑	❑	
Counters/ furniture dusted	❑	❑	❑	
Guest amenities (iron/boards, etc.) in place	❑	❑	❑	
Guest literature in place	❑	❑	❑	
Telephone clean	❑	❑	❑	
Telephone handset clean	❑	❑	❑	
Night stand clean	❑	❑	❑	
Furniture dusted	❑	❑	❑	
Closet doors clean	❑	❑	❑	
Closet shelf clean	❑	❑	❑	
Proper number/ type hangers	❑	❑	❑	
Laundry bags in place	❑	❑	❑	
Extra pillows/ blankets in place	❑	❑	❑	
Refrigerators/ microwaves clean	❑	❑	❑	
Dresser top clean	❑	❑	❑	
Dresser drawers clean	❑	❑	❑	
Area under bed or bed box clean	❑	❑	❑	
Coffee pot clean	❑	❑	❑	
Coffee items stocked	❑	❑	❑	
Waste basket in place	❑	❑	❑	
Logo items in place	❑	❑	❑	
Inside of corridor door clean	❑	❑	❑	
Print material posted on door	❑	❑	❑	
Evacuation sign in place	❑	❑	❑	
Do Not Disturb sign in place	❑	❑	❑	
Other ________________	❑	❑	❑	
Other ________________	❑	❑	❑	
Other ________________	❑	❑	❑	
Other ________________	❑	❑	❑	
Other ________________	❑	❑	❑	

FIGURE 8.3 Sample Guest Room Sleeping Area Inspection Sheet

LODGING ONLINE

Bed bugs are small parasitic insects that live by feeding on the blood of humans and warm-blooded animals. Bed bugs were largely eradicated in the United States by the mid-1940s, but have recently re-emerged in significant numbers. The exact source of the re-infestations is not known, but is ascribed to an increase in travel from areas where the bugs are prevalent as well as the absence of employee training programs aimed at bed bug detection and prevention.

Even in very clean hotels, bugs can crawl out of a traveler's suitcase and establish themselves in guest rooms. The process of eliminating bed bugs from guest rooms can be time-consuming, expensive and lead to bad publicity, litigation, and loss of business. For those reasons, every housekeeping department should implement a comprehensive employee training program designed to detect and eliminate bed bugs. One such training program is available from the Educational Institute of the American Hotel and Lodging Association. To review it, go to:

www.ahlei.org/

When you arrive, enter "bed bug training" in the search field.

How important do you think it would be to implement room attendant training programs emphasizing prevention and detection of bed bugs?

Essential duties of the housekeeping department include the care of linens and other bedding supplies.

GUEST ROOM BATH AREA INSPECTION

Date: ______________________ *Inspected by:* ______________________

Room Number: ______________

ITEM/AREA	OUTSTANDING	ACCEPTABLE	UNACCEPTABLE	COMMENTS
Lights working	❑	❑	❑	
Light fixtures clean	❑	❑	❑	
Fans working	❑	❑	❑	
Air vents clean	❑	❑	❑	
Telephone clean/functioning	❑	❑	❑	
Shower head clean	❑	❑	❑	
Bathtub fixtures clean	❑	❑	❑	
Tile and tub clean	❑	❑	❑	
Safety handles clean	❑	❑	❑	
Shower rod clean/all hooks in place	❑	❑	❑	
Shower curtain clean	❑	❑	❑	
Toilet free of water stains inside	❑	❑	❑	
Toilet exterior and back clean	❑	❑	❑	
Sink fixtures clean	❑	❑	❑	
Sink and stopper clean	❑	❑	❑	
Mirror(s) clean	❑	❑	❑	
Counter tops clean	❑	❑	❑	
Hair dryers/other amenities clean	❑	❑	❑	
Floor tiles clean	❑	❑	❑	
Soaps/amenities in place	❑	❑	❑	
Electrical switches/outlets clean	❑	❑	❑	
Towel bars clean	❑	❑	❑	
Proper terry in place	❑	❑	❑	
Tissues in place	❑	❑	❑	
Toilet paper holder clean	❑	❑	❑	
Toilet paper and replacement roll in place	❑	❑	❑	
Wall coverings clean	❑	❑	❑	
Inside door clean	❑	❑	❑	
Locks polished/ working	❑	❑	❑	
Exterior of bath door clean	❑	❑	❑	
Other ______________	❑	❑	❑	
Other ______________	❑	❑	❑	
Other ______________	❑	❑	❑	
Other ______________	❑	❑	❑	
Other ______________	❑	❑	❑	

FIGURE 8.4 Sample Guest Room Bath Area Inspection Sheet

KITCHEN AND SUITE INSPECTION

Date: ______________________ *Inspected by:* ______________________

Room Number: ______________

ITEM/AREA	OUTSTANDING	ACCEPTABLE	UNACCEPTABLE	COMMENTS
Range top clean	❑	❑	❑	
Oven clean	❑	❑	❑	
Refrigerator clean	❑	❑	❑	
Freezer empty	❑	❑	❑	
Ice trays available	❑	❑	❑	
Microwave clean	❑	❑	❑	
Dishwasher empty/ clean	❑	❑	❑	
Appropriate glassware in place	❑	❑	❑	
Appropriate flatware in place	❑	❑	❑	
Appropriate dishware in place	❑	❑	❑	
Appropriate pots/ pans/ cooking utensils in place	❑	❑	❑	
VCR/ DVD in working order	❑	❑	❑	
High-speed Internet in working order	❑	❑	❑	
Sofa-bed clean/ easily pulled out	❑	❑	❑	
Other ______________	❑	❑	❑	
Other ______________	❑	❑	❑	
Other ______________	❑	❑	❑	
Other ______________	❑	❑	❑	
Other ______________	❑	❑	❑	
Other ______________	❑	❑	❑	
Other ______________	❑	❑	❑	
Other ______________	❑	❑	❑	

FIGURE 8.5 Sample Kitchen and Suite Inspection Sheet

The actual inspection sheet used would be tailored specifically for the bathroom area inspected.

KITCHEN AREAS AND SUITES

Many hotels have guest rooms that include in-room kitchen facilities for guests. In addition, all-suite hotels may include kitchens, living room areas, and equipment and features that require separate inspection. Figure 8.5 is an example of an inspection sheet that could be modified for use in guest rooms that include kitchen facilities or in suites.

Public Space Cleaning

The public space in a hotel is one of the first areas seen by the guests. In a larger hotel, the efforts of one or more full-time employees will be required to maintain proper cleanliness levels. The importance of guest room cleanliness is a consistent theme in this chapter because it is very critical to the long-term success of the hotel. Public spaces, however, are equally important because they form the basis for a guest's and the public's initial impressions of the property. It is essential, therefore, that the goals for all public space areas include excellent appearance and impeccable cleanliness. Every hotel will have its own requirements for public space cleaning based on its size and product offerings. For example, in a smaller limited-service hotel that offers a complimentary breakfast, the breakfast area may become part of a public space cleaner's daily cleaning assignment. In a larger full-service hotel, the food and beverage department might assume the responsibility for cleaning dining areas.

Figure 8.6 is an inspection checklist designed to help examine some public spaces common to many hotels. It should be modified to reflect the needs of the hotel using it.

PUBLIC SPACE INSPECTION

Date: ______________________ *Inspection assisted by:* ______________________

ITEM/AREA	OUTSTANDING	ACCEPTABLE	UNACCEPTABLE	COMMENTS
Lobby/Front Desk				
Entrance door/ glass clean	❑	❑	❑	
Ashtrays clean	❑	❑	❑	
Front Desk counter area clean	❑	❑	❑	
Drapes/ window treatments clean	❑	❑	❑	
Decorative pieces dust-free	❑	❑	❑	
Carpets, floors clean	❑	❑	❑	
Furniture straight/clean	❑	❑	❑	
Pictures straight/dusted	❑	❑	❑	
Lobby telephones clean	❑	❑	❑	
Ceiling/wall vents clean	❑	❑	❑	
Pool/ Spa/ Exercise Areas				
Wet terry collected	❑	❑	❑	
Terry supplies adequate/properly placed	❑	❑	❑	
Carpet unspotted/clean	❑	❑	❑	
Floors clean	❑	❑	❑	
Windows/ledges clean	❑	❑	❑	
Exercise equipment clean	❑	❑	❑	
Wall coverings clean	❑	❑	❑	
Public restrooms clean	❑	❑	❑	
Air vents dusted	❑	❑	❑	
Safety equipment clean/in place	❑	❑	❑	
Administrative Areas				
Light bulbs/lamps clean and functioning	❑	❑	❑	
Telephones clean	❑	❑	❑	
Carpet unspotted	❑	❑	❑	
Windows clean	❑	❑	❑	
Upholstered furniture clean	❑	❑	❑	
Furniture/desks dusted	❑	❑	❑	
Waste containers clean/in place	❑	❑	❑	
Pictures, wall hangings straight/ dusted	❑	❑	❑	
Vents dusted	❑	❑	❑	
Wall coverings clean	❑	❑	❑	

FIGURE 8.6 Sample Public Space Inspection Sheet

ALL IN A DAY'S WORK 8.2

THE SITUATION:

"Your maids are thieves," said the very angry middle-aged woman standing at the front desk to Levine Parsons, the hotel's front office manager.

"I'm in room 253," the woman continued, "and when I left my room this morning I put my diamond earrings on the night stand. When I got back to my room this afternoon they were gone! I want you to call the person who cleaned my room right now and tell them to give me back my property. If you don't I'm going to sue you and your hotel! My husband is a lawyer!"

A RESPONSE

Unfortunately, hotel guests accusing room attendants of theft is a fairly common occurrence in the lodging industry. For this reason, it is very important for hoteliers to be familiar with their state's innkeeper liability laws. A hotel is not a bank. In most states, the guest in this situation would not be able to recover the cost of the earrings from the hotel, nor would she have grounds for a lawsuit if the hotel routinely informed all its guests that they had access to no-cost safety deposit boxes for the safekeeping of their valuables.

To assist Levine in this situation, however, the hotel must have written procedures in place so that she can investigate accusations of theft and, in the proper manner, talk with involved employees about their alleged actions. In most cases, accusations against room attendants will be spread somewhat equally among all room attendants. When they are not (e.g., when one specific room attendant is accused much more frequently than others), managers must take the appropriate actions to protect guests' property.

While an accusation of theft is certainly not proof of wrongdoing, a reasonable manager would not continue to allow one employee with multiple accusations to be in a position to continue to cause potential harm to the hotel's reputation.

A housekeeping department must carefully manage its linen supply level to ensure it is adequate to meet guest needs.

LAUNDRY OPERATIONS

Hotels sell overnight rooms, and as a result, the sheets, towels, pillows, blankets, and other fabric items used by guests must be professionally cleaned and disinfected. Some fabric items are cleaned daily; others are cleaned on a systematic schedule determined by the executive housekeeper. Still other items, such as shower curtains, may be made of vinyl or plastic, yet these too must be cleaned regularly. Processing these items and others is the job of the hotel's laundry staff, which is an important division of the housekeeping department.

Hotels have traditionally been designed with space for processing their own laundry; but more recently, as extended-stay hotels have gained popularity, some are also providing laundry areas inside the hotel so that guests can do their own personal laundry. In this section, we will examine both the processing of a hotel's laundry and the unique features of a guest-operated laundry.

Laundry Processing

Hotels generate a tremendous amount of laundry. Some hotels, especially very small ones, may not actually clean their soiled laundry on-site. Most hotels, however, will do their own laundry. Significant time, space, equipment, and expertise are required to properly wash, dry, and fold the large amount of dirty **linen** and **terry** products generated by a hotel. Table linens, including the tablecloths and napkins used in the food and beverage department, employee uniforms, and other laundry items must also be processed. Not surprisingly, laundry represents one of the hotel's major expenses, and an OPL must be managed properly if the hotel is to control this important cost.

LODGING LANGUAGE

Linen: Generic term for the guest room sheets and pillowcases (and food and beverage department tablecloths and napkins) washed and dried in the laundry area.

Terry: Generic term for the bath towels, bath mats, hand towels, and wash cloths washed and dried in the laundry area.

A hotel's laundry needs vary with its size and product offerings. A smaller extended-stay or limited-service property (100 rooms or less) may do less than 500,000 pounds of laundry per year. At this volume level, the hotel may use linens that are wrinkle-free, and the OPL may consist simply of washers and dryers. Larger, full-service hotels with extensive food and beverage volume have expanded laundry needs because of the tablecloths and napkins to be processed and the increased linen and terry needs that occur when there are more guest rooms. These properties may require additional equipment to press and fold laundered items.

In very large hotels, the OPL may process well over 1 million pounds of laundry per year and employ dozens of workers. It will also maintain a substantial number of pieces of high-volume laundry-related equipment. Regardless of its size, the OPL is a major responsibility of the housekeeping department and the executive housekeeper.

LODGING ONLINE

Large-volume OPLs require large-volume equipment. One of the hotel industry's leading suppliers of large-volume laundry equipment is the Pellerin Milnor Corporation. To review some features of its "tunnel washer" designed specifically for OPLs processing laundry for hotels of 500 rooms or more, go to:

www.milnor.com/

How important do you think clean linen is to the success of a hotel?

When most people think of a laundry they think of clothes washers and dryers. In an OPL, the process is more complex, involves more equipment, and actually begins not in the laundry area but in the guest rooms, pool area, dining rooms, and meeting spaces. It is in these areas that room attendants collect the soiled linen and terry that is to be cleaned by the OPL. Operating an effective OPL is a multistep process that includes:

- Collecting
- Sorting/Repairing
- Washing
- Drying
- Finishing/Folding
- Storing
- Delivering

COLLECTING

Room attendants collect soiled linen from guest room sleeping areas and used terry products from guest room bath areas, spa areas, and pools. In the guest rooms, room attendants strip beds and put dirty linens directly into laundry bags attached to their cleaning carts. When full, these laundry bags are either hand carried or carted to the OPL. Dirty linen and terry should never be used as rags to clean a guest room because doing so could damage them. Sometimes laundry is presorted in the guest room before it reaches the OPL. This is the case when linen or terry is blood-stained and must be placed separately into a **biohazard waste bag** to help OPL workers avoid exposure to blood-borne pathogens. Bags of this type should be placed on every housekeeping cart, and room attendants should be required to use them.

LODGING LANGUAGE

Biohazard Waste Bag: A specially marked plastic bag used in hotels. Laundry items that are stained with blood or bodily fluids and thus need special handling are put into these bags for transport to the OPL.

The food service department generates tablecloths and napkins to be cleaned, and in larger hotels, employee uniforms may be processed in the OPL. As a result, the executive housekeeper must also have efficient methods in place to collect these items from their various locations and deliver them to the OPL.

SORTING/REPAIRING

Once in the OPL, laundry is sorted both by fabric type and by the degree of staining. Different fibers and colors require different cleaning chemicals in the wash and, in many cases, different water temperatures or length of washing. Linens made of 100 percent cotton, for example, are washed in a different manner than an employee uniforms with a high polyester content. Similarly, a white terry wash cloth used by a guest to polish black shoes would not be washed in the same load as the regular terry collected in the hotel because the heavily soiled cloth would need special prewash stain removal treatment to come completely clean. In some hotels, an item like this may be laundered in a special washer designated only for heavily stained laundry. In some cases, a tear or rip in a cloth item may mean that it must be discarded, but in other cases, it can be repaired. These repairs are typically made prior to washing. Discarded terry and linen items may be placed in a trash bin or cleaned and donated to an employee or local charity.

WASHING

Washing is the most complex part of the laundering process. Today's laundry items are made from very durable fabrics, and washers can be preset to dispense cleaning products into the water at the right time and in the right amounts. Even so, executive housekeepers must still teach laundry workers to monitor washing times, wash temperatures, chemicals, and **agitation** when washing laundry.

LODGING LANGUAGE

Agitation (washing machine): Movement of the washing machine resulting in friction as fabrics rub against each other.

Length of washing time is a key factor because heavily stained items need to be washed longer than lightly soiled items. Too long a washing cycle may waste time, water, energy, and chemicals. If the washing cycle selected is too short, the laundry may not be cleaned. Wash water temperature is important because some fabrics can handle exposure to very hot water whereas others cannot. Generally, hot water cleans better than cold, but fabrics washed in water too hot for their fiber type can be damaged.

The chemicals used to wash items are determined by the type of fabric. Chemicals used in the laundry area include detergents, bleaches, heavy stain removers, and fabric softeners. The amount of each to be used should maximize the cleanliness of the fabric washed and control the cost of chemical usage.

Lastly, agitation time and strength must be determined for each fabric type. Agitation is the friction of the laundry against itself during the wash cycle. With too little agitation (caused when the washer is packed too full), items washed will not be cleaned properly. With excessive agitation, the fabrics washed will wear out too rapidly because of the damage done to their fibers.

Some large and small hotels have begun using an **ozone system** for washing laundry items.

LODGING LANGUAGE

Ozone system (laundry): A method of processing laundry that utilizes ozonated cold water rather than hot water to clean and sanitize laundry items.

Ozone is an extremely powerful oxidant that is 150 percent more effective than chlorine bleach. It destroys bacteria, deactivates viruses, and controls odors. An ozone system replaces the hot water normally used for washing with highly ozonated cold water. The result is better cleaning, reduced energy costs, and longer fabric life.

The next step in the wash cycle is water extraction. Removing as much water as possible makes the washed laundry lighter and easier for laundry workers to handle. In addition, items that require drying will do so more quickly. When the water has been extracted from the cleaned fabrics, the wash cycle is complete.

In today's modern washing machines, the time, temperature, chemical input, and agitation levels can be preset. These must first be determined, however, in consultation with the washing equipment manufacturer and the chemical supplier if wash results are to be maximized and OPL costs are to be controlled to the greatest degree possible.

DRYING

Some fabrics do not need to be dried after they are washed. This is the case with some linens that are removed from the washer and then immediately ironed. Terry, however, as well as most other fabrics, must be properly dried before folding or ironing. Drying is the

LODGING ONLINE

Ozone laundry systems have become increasingly popular in hotels. To learn about these low-temperature washing systems, go to:

www.ozonelaundrysystems.com

How important to you would it be to operate an environmentally friendly OPL in a hotel you managed?

process of moving hot air (140–145 degrees F) through the fabrics to vaporize and remove moisture. Fabrics that have been dried must go through a cool-down period in the dryer before they are removed from it. This minimizes any damage to the fabric and helps prevent wrinkling. Once removed from the dryer, however, these items should be immediately finished.

FINISHING AND FOLDING

The finishing of fabrics is important because washers and dryers should not produce more clean laundry than workers can readily process by ironing and/or folding. Since hotels increasingly use wrinkle-free fabrics, finishing work today involves more folding than ironing. Regardless of how much ironing is done, the space required for finishing laundry must be adequate. In larger hotels, the folding of linens and terry may be done by machine while in smaller properties it is generally done by hand. The finishing area must be very clean so that the finishing process itself does not soil the laundry. Once the laundry has been finished, it moves to the storage area(s) of the housekeeping department.

STORING

The storage of linens is important because many fabrics must "rest" after washing and drying if the damage to them is to be minimized. Most laundry experts suggest a rest time of 24 hours for cleaned laundry. Therefore, the housekeeping department should strive to maintain **laundry par levels** of three times the hotel's normal usage.

LODGING LANGUAGE

Laundry Par Levels: The amount of laundry in use, in process, and in storage.

For example, in a 150-room hotel, there should be enough linen and terry to have:

- One set in the rooms
- One set in the laundry (being washed and dried)
- One set in storage

In this manner, the hotel will have adequate products for guests and enough reserve to permit the laundry to rest before being put back into the rooms.

If laundry par levels are too high, storage may be difficult and too much money will have been committed to laundry inventories. If laundry par levels are too low, guests may not receive the items they need. As well, room attendants may not be able to complete their work in a timely manner because they must wait for laundry products before they can finish cleaning the rooms. In addition, fabrics may not be allowed to rest properly if they are needed immediately to make up rooms that must be sold.

DELIVERING

In smaller hotels, room attendants may go to laundry storage areas in the OPL to pick up linen and terry items. In larger properties, these items may be delivered to housekeeping storage areas located in various parts of the hotel. Because linens and terry are frequent targets of theft by hotel guests and staff, the storage areas containing them should be kept locked, and the housekeeping staff should inventory them on a regular basis.

As with guest rooms, management should inspect OPL areas on a regular basis. Figure 8.7 is a sample inspection sheet that can be modified and used. Note the specific reference to **material safety data sheets**.

LODGING LANGUAGE

Material Safety Data Sheets (MSDS): Written statements describing the potential hazards of, and best ways to handle, chemicals or toxic substances. An MSDS is provided to the buyer by the manufacturer of the chemical or toxic substance used by the hotel and must be posted or made readily available in a place where it is easily accessible to those who will actually handle the product.

LAUNDRY AREA INSPECTION

Date: ______________________ Inspection by: ______________________

ITEM/AREA	OUTSTANDING	ACCEPTABLE	UNACCEPTABLE	COMMENTS
Bags and carts used to collect laundry are clean and in good condition	❑	❑	❑	
Area used to sort laundry is clean/ uncluttered	❑	❑	❑	
Washers clean inside and out	❑	❑	❑	
Washing instruction signs easily read	❑	❑	❑	
Area around washers clean/ free of clutter	❑	❑	❑	
Chemicals properly labeled and stored	❑	❑	❑	
Material Safety Data Sheets (MSDS) readily available	❑	❑	❑	
Dryer temperatures controlled, posted	❑	❑	❑	
Folding area adequate, clean of all debris	❑	❑	❑	
Storage areas clean, labeled	❑	❑	❑	
Other ______________	❑	❑	❑	
Other ______________	❑	❑	❑	
Other ______________	❑	❑	❑	
Other ______________	❑	❑	❑	
Other ______________	❑	❑	❑	

FIGURE 8.7 Sample Laundry Area Inspection Sheet

Guest-Operated Laundry

Guest-operated laundry equipment is very common in apartments, condominiums, and college residence halls. In hotels, guest-operated laundries are popular with families traveling on vacation, long-term-stay guests, and even business travelers who like to travel with as few clothing items as possible. The ability to do one or more loads of laundry at their own convenience and within the hotel is increasingly appealing to many travelers. Some all-suite hotel chains (e.g., Hawthorn Suites) have mandated that all of their hotels have an on-premise guest-operated laundry facility.

Most guest-operated laundry facilities consist of a room with one or more coin-operated home-style washers and dryers. Ample space is typically provided for the sorting, folding, and ironing of laundry. Most guest-operated laundries also contain vending machines where detergents, bleach, and fabric softeners may be purchased. Large-screen televisions and/or background music or even exercise equipment can help to make these areas a pleasant hotel amenity.

LODGING GOES GREEN!

Many hotels utilize environmentally friendly conservation efforts in their guest rooms. Figure 8.8 illustrates the type of information that can be used to convey the program's intentions to hotel guests and to solicit their participation. As you'll note, guests are invited to help reduce detergent, water, and environmental pollution by allowing housekeeping staff to reuse their bed and bath linens.

Green hotels can do much more than invite guests to participate in guest-room conservation efforts. For example, non-synthetic (botanical) cleaning chemicals including cleansers and disinfectants can be used. Newly developed botanical products work very well. They leave a pleasant aroma and help to eliminate the microorganisms with which they come in contact. Some housekeepers report, as well, that they do not suffer from the allergies and headaches that can arise when more harsh synthetic products are used.

Help Us Conserve Our Natural Resources

We at the _____ Hotel want to do our fair share to help conserve our country's limited natural resources. Want to help?

If your bed and bath linens are reused during your stay, water and energy consumption can be reduced, as will the amount of detergent waste water that must be recycled.

If you would like your sheets and pillowcases replaced, just leave this card on the pillowcase. If you would like your bath linens replaced, simply leave them on the floor.

Thanks! for helping to conserve our environment.

FIGURE 8.8 Linen Change Request Form

Hotels may develop and maintain their own guest-operated laundry areas, but in many cases, the hotel will enter a partnership with a company whose business is the management of coin-operated laundry facilities. These companies typically provide and maintain the laundry equipment, fill vending machines with needed cleaning products, and share with the hotel, on a predetermined basis, the revenue generated by the laundry's operation. The hotel, in return, maintains the cleanliness and security of the laundry area. The many advantages of this partnership to a hotel include monthly commission checks and the elimination of the costs associated with buying, installing, and maintaining guest laundry equipment.

Lodging Language

Executive Housekeeper
Room Status
Stay-over
Maintenance
On-premise laundry (OPL)
Inspector (Inspectress)
Room Attendant
Houseperson
Public Space
Product Usage Report
Mislaid Property
Lost Property
Abandoned Property
Room Attendant Cart
Blood-borne Pathogen
Deep Cleaning
Minutes Per Room (guest room cleaning)
Cost Per Occupied Room (CPOR)
Linen
Terry
Biohazard Waste Bag
Agitation (washing machine)
Ozone System (laundry)
Laundry Par Levels
Material Safety Data Sheets (MSDS)

For Discussion

1. Many hotels find it difficult to hire and retain housekeeping staff. Identify three reasons you believe contribute to this difficulty. What could the general manager of a hotel do to help overcome these obstacles?
2. Some hoteliers feel that room attendants must be able to fluently speak the language of the majority of the hotel's guests to do their jobs effectively. They feel that guest contact is an important role of the room attendant's job, and to converse with guests they must have strong language skills. Other hoteliers feel that a command of the principal language used by guests is not required. If the hotel you managed was in the United States, would you require room attendants at the hotel to be fluent in English? What are some factors that would influence your decision?
3. Housekeeping is one of the departments in the hotel that must work every holiday because the hotel is open and can be very busy. Assume that you have a housekeeping department with 12 employees and your hotel recognizes New Year's Day, Memorial Day, Fourth of July, Labor Day, Thanksgiving, and Christmas as paid holidays. Also assume that at least one-half of your housekeeping employees need to work each holiday. What factors would influence you as you develop a scheduling system that fairly assigns holiday work days and off days to these employees?
4. Increasingly, some hotel chains (e.g., Hyatt, Lowes, and Accor) are outsourcing their housekeeping operations. What would likely be some advantages of taking such an approach to room cleaning? What are some potential disadvantages of taking such an approach?
5. In some hotels, abandoned property found by employees is given to the finder after an established period of time. In other hotels, such property is given to designated charities. Identify an advantage and a disadvantage of utilizing the charity approach.
6. Some hotels allow, and even encourage, the tipping of room attendants. This is typically done through the placement of a "tip" envelope with the employee's name on it in the guest room. Identify three factors that you believe would encourage a guest to tip a room attendant. Are these factors influenced

most by the hotel's management or by the hotel's individual room attendant(s)?

7. Housekeeping employees (especially room attendants) often have easy access to guests' personal belongings. As a result, some hotels require applicants for a room attendant position to undergo a criminal-background check. Would you implement such a policy at a hotel you manage? Would you require that all hotel employees (or just room attendants) undergo such a background check? Explain your decision.
8. Housekeeping is a very physically demanding work. Identify five things a hotel's executive housekeeper or general manager could do to make the work of housekeeping employees as physically light (less strenuous) as possible.
9. Some hotels do an excellent job of maintaining public space cleanliness yet do not maintain back-of-the-house areas (which cannot be seen by guests) in a similar manner. How do you think such an operating standard would be viewed by employees of the hotel?
10. In an effort to conserve natural resources and reduce costs, many hotels change sheets and towels in stay-over rooms only when requested to do so by the guest. Identify a positive and negative aspect of this policy.

Team Activities

TEAM ACTIVITY 1

Housekeeper safety and security should be the most important factor to consider when developing room-cleaning procedures. Identify a step-by-step procedure to be used when a hotel housekeeper encounters blood or body fluids on linens or terry found in a guest room.

TEAM ACTIVITY 2

In the normal course of their jobs, housekeeping employees often recover abandoned property. Assume that your team is the supervisory staff of a housekeeping department and you have been asked by your general manager to draft a hotel policy regarding the finding of cash. In your policy, detail what is to happen when cash is found, how long it will be held, and what will happen to it after the holding period has ended.

Chapter

9 The Maintenance Department

Chapter Outline

Chapter Overview

Hotel guests have expectations about their hotel stays that simply must be met. These include such basic items as ample hot water for baths and showers, guest room lights that work, and comfortable temperatures in the hotel's public spaces and guest rooms. Employees working in a hotel expect that the tools and equipment they need to do their jobs will be safe and in good condition. In addition, the owners of a hotel have expectations. Among other things they expect that the building and its contents will be correctly repaired and maintained to protect the value of their investments in them. The hotel's maintenance department meets and fulfills all of these expectations and more.

In some hotels, the maintenance department is known as the maintenance and engineering department or as the engineering and maintenance department. For that reason, the head of the maintenance department is commonly referred to as the chief engineer. Regardless of the name used to identify the department, the chief engineer and the department's staff are responsible for properly maintaining the hotel's building and grounds.

A well-run maintenance department assists the hotel's sales effort by providing guests with the very best experience possible as it relates to the appearance and functioning of the building's exterior and interior. This makes it easier for the sales and marketing team to sell rooms in the hotel. In this chapter, you will learn about the major areas of responsibility of the maintenance department and how it interacts with the hotel's front office, housekeeping, and food and beverage departments.

Chief engineers and their staff members are responsible for the routine maintenance of the hotel. This includes such tasks as lawn care and adding appropriate chemicals to the hotel's swimming pool. In addition to routine maintenance, every chief engineer or manager in charge of maintenance should develop an effective preventive maintenance program. These are implemented to prolong the life of a hotel's facilities and equipment and to ensure their peak operating efficiency. It is also important that the department be ready for any emergency maintenance that may be required. In this chapter, you will learn about routine, preventive, and emergency maintenance.

In most cases, a hotel's chief engineer will also have responsibility for helping the hotel's general manager monitor and manage utility usage. When utilities such as water, gas, and electricity are not well managed, and the equipment that utilizes these resources is not well maintained, the hotel's operating costs will be higher than necessary. As a result, profits will be lower than they should be. In this chapter, you will also learn how the maintenance department can effectively oversee this important concern.

Chapter Objectives

1. To identify the areas of responsibility assigned to the maintenance department of a lodging facility.
2. To explain to you the importance of routine maintenance in a professionally managed hotel.
3. To explain the importance of preventive maintenance in a professionally managed hotel.
4. To explain to you the importance of emergency maintenance in a professionally managed hotel.
5. To describe the processes required to properly manage and control utility consumption in a lodging facility.

THE ROLE OF MAINTENANCE

Every hotel has a variety of valuable **assets**.

LODGING LANGUAGE

Asset: The resources owned by an organization. These include cash, accounts receivable, inventories, goodwill, furniture, fixtures, equipment, buildings, and real estate.

Assets include the hotel's staff, its cash in the bank, its customer base, and its reputation. The hotel's grounds, buildings, and equipment comprise the hotel's most visible and usually the most expensive asset, and they directly affect the value of the hotel's other assets. How guests perceive the hotel's facilities impacts its profitability. It is important, then, for the hotel's managers to develop systems to protect its physical assets by performing essential maintenance on the hotel's facilities.

When a hotel's building, equipment, and grounds are properly maintained, guests will be more likely to perceive a positive experience during their stay, and the hotel's ability to increase sales is enhanced. This is the primary job of the maintenance department. When guests experience poor facilities such as potholes in parking areas, leaking faucets, burned-out light bulbs, poor heating/cooling capacities, or insufficient hot water, their dissatisfaction increases, and the hotel's sales potential is diminished. In addition to guest satisfaction, however, an effective maintenance department will achieve many other important goals, including:

- Protecting and enhancing the financial value of the building and grounds
- Supporting the efforts of other hotel departments
- Ensuring maintenance-related adherence to brand standards
- Controlling maintenance and repair costs
- Controlling energy usage
- Minimizing guests' facility-related complaints
- Increasing the pride and morale of the hotel's staff

These goals can be achieved if the maintenance department effectively performs **preventive maintenance**, **routine maintenance**, and **emergency maintenance**, and if it properly manages the hotel's utility usage.

LODGING LANGUAGE

Preventive maintenance: Maintenance activities designed to minimize maintenance costs and prolong the life of equipment.

Routine maintenance: Maintenance activities that must be performed on a continual (ongoing) basis.

Emergency maintenance: Maintenance activities performed in response to an urgent situation.

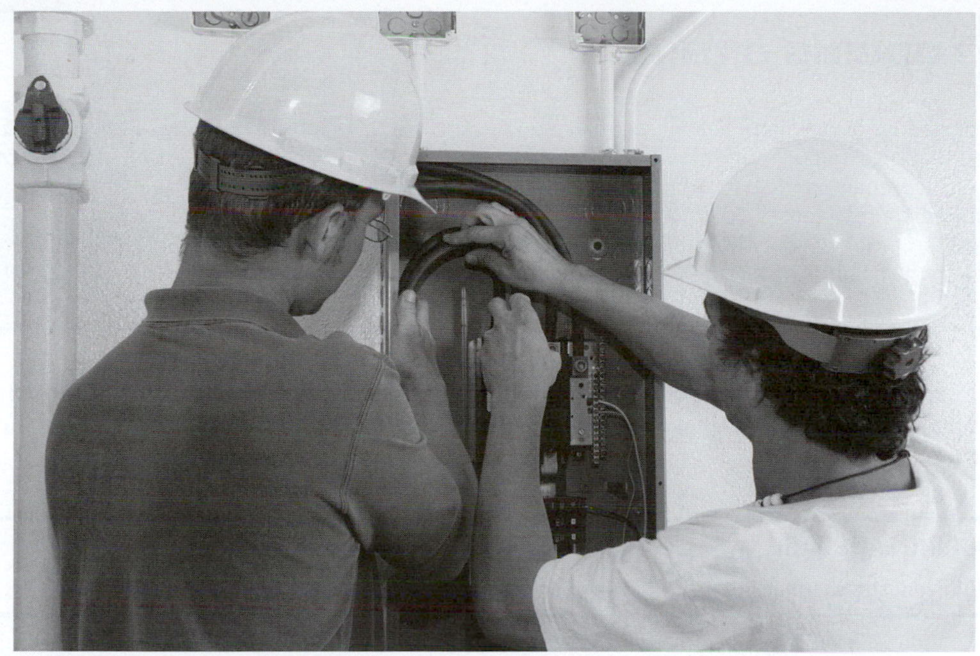

The main role of the maintenance department is to ensure that the property is properly functioning so that guests will enjoy their stay.

Areas of Responsibility

The staff in the maintenance department of a hotel is fully responsible for the facility's upkeep (its maintenance), but it is also responsible for selected **engineering** tasks and, when necessary, specific renovation tasks.

LODGING LANGUAGE

Engineering: Designing and operating a building to ensure a safe and comfortable atmosphere.

These three distinct areas sometimes overlap. To understand the complete role of the maintenance department, we will examine its engineering, maintenance, and renovation activities separately.

ENGINEERING

Some hoteliers use the terms "engineering" and "maintenance" interchangeably. Thus, in some hotel companies, the department responsible for the care of the hotel is just as likely to be called "engineering" as "maintenance," and in some cases, its name will be a combination of both terms (maintenance and engineering). Engineering, as a building specialty, however, is different from maintenance.

The engineering of a building refers to the application of physics, chemistry, and mathematics to design and operate a building that provides a comfortable atmosphere for guests and employees. For example, in a hotel lobby area that must be air-conditioned, the building's engineer calculates the amount of air-conditioned air required to cool it properly. Factors that are considered include the temperature and humidity of the outside air, the desired lobby temperature, the temperature at which air-conditioned air enters the lobby, and the movement of the air once it is inside the lobby. Based on these calculations, the size of the air-conditioning unit required to cool the lobby is determined, as are the optimum number and location of air vents and fans delivering the cold air to the area. The engineering knowledge required to balance these features and make the right decision about air conditioner or heating capacity is significant.

Improperly engineered facilities can result in underpowered or overpowered equipment, increased building deterioration, excessive energy usage, and higher-than-necessary operating costs. In most cases the head of the maintenance department in a hotel will not

LODGING ONLINE

Engineering a building's heating, refrigeration, ventilation, and air-conditioning systems is quite complex, and special knowledge is required to manage it. To familiarize yourself with an organization whose members specialize in this field, review the Web site of the American Society of Heating, Refrigerating, and Air Conditioning Engineers at:

www.ashrae.com/

How important to you is your ability to control the temperature of a room in which you are trying to sleep?

have actually designed the building's **HVAC** systems, but he or she must be thoroughly familiar with them as well as with the engineering of the building's electrical, water, and waste systems.

LODGING LANGUAGE

HVAC: Industry shorthand term for "heating, ventilating, and air-conditioning."

In very small hotels, the entire maintenance department may consist of only one full-time (or even part-time) maintenance staff member. Larger properties employ dozens of maintenance and engineering staff. Whatever a hotel's size, however, there are engineering issues to be addressed because providing a safe and comfortable environment is an ongoing process that must be continually administered.

MAINTENANCE

Maintenance, as the term implies, refers to "maintaining" the hotel's physical property. It has been said that maintenance costs are like taxes; if they are not paid one year, they will be paid the next year—and with a penalty!

The maintenance-related costs of a hotel are often related to the hotel's age. As a building ages, its maintenance costs generally increase. Even brand-new hotels, however, require **POM**-related expenditures. These costs include staff wages and benefits, replacement parts, contract services, and energy costs.

LODGING LANGUAGE

POM: Short for "property operation and maintenance." The term is taken from the Uniform System of Accounts for Hotels and refers to the segment of the income statement that details the costs of operating the maintenance department.

The maintenance department should maintain the property in the most effective manner possible given the budget assigned it. To do so, hotel maintenance must be:

Planned. From routinely changing air filters in heating and cooling units to awarding a contract for tree trimming, the maintenance department performs too many tasks to leave these activities to chance. An effective maintenance manager is a careful administrator who reviews every piece of equipment and required activity in the hotel and then plans what should be done, when it should be done, and who should do it.

Implemented. Some maintenance managers know what *should* be done in their properties and have good intentions of completing all the required tasks, yet do not do them. Shortages of properly trained staff, insufficient budgets, lack of supervisory skills, inadequate tools, and/or underestimation of the time required to perform a given task can all adversely impact the ability of the department to achieve its goals.

Many excellent checklists and suggested activities have been developed for maintenance departments. Virtually every franchisor offers such checklists free of charge to its franchisees because it is in the best interests of the franchisor for every hotel in the system to represent the brand as well as possible.

Checklists and suggested activities that are not properly implemented, however, will not result in an acceptable maintenance program. Thus, when evaluating a maintenance department, the important factor is not whether it has planned an acceptable maintenance program for the hotel, but the degree to which it has effectively implemented or performed the planned program.

Recorded. Record-keeping is an immensely important maintenance function. Routine, scheduled maintenance tasks cannot be properly planned unless maintenance personnel know when these tasks were last performed. For example, if the plan calls for lubricating hot water pumps every six months, a written record must be kept of the last time the pumps were lubricated. Similarly, if a faucet in a guest room is replaced, a record should be kept of when the replacement was made. This will enable the maintenance department to evaluate the quality (length-of-life) of the faucets used and to take advantage of any warranty programs that apply to the replacement parts.

In many cases such as fire-suppression systems, elevators, and other safety-related equipment, local ordinances or laws may require that records documenting the performance of system maintenance be kept on file or displayed publicly. Even when it is not mandated by local ordinance, however, excellent record-keeping in all areas of the maintenance department is a good indicator of overall departmental effectiveness.

The cost of maintaining a building is very closely related to its original design and size as well as to the facilities it includes. Hotels with food service and banquet facilities, swimming pools, and exercise rooms, for example, will experience greater maintenance costs than limited-service hotels that do not have these facilities. High-rise buildings will have elevator systems that must be maintained, while one-story hotels will not. Resort facilities spread over any acres will need more landscape care than those located on smaller parcels of ground.

The materials and construction techniques used in building the hotel will also affect its POM costs. A hotel with an exterior that must be painted will experience exterior painting costs, while a hotel made of masonry will not. Energy costs will also be affected by construction. Hotels built with good insulation and well-made windows will naturally experience lower energy costs than those that are not built this way.

The finishes and interior equipment specified for installation by the hotel's builders have a tremendous impact on long-term POM costs. Durable finishes and high-quality, long-life equipment may initially be more expensive but will generally reduce operating and maintenance costs.

RENOVATION

Even with the very best of maintenance programs, hotel buildings wear out with use and must be renovated to compete well against newer properties. Hotel buildings have a predictable life span that directly affects their maintenance and renovation needs.

Figure 9.1 details the typical life span of a hotel building. As can be seen, the challenges of maintaining a building increase as it ages.

Building Age	Building Characteristics and Requirements
1–3 years	Low maintenance costs incurred
3–6 years	Maintenance costs increase
6–8 years	Refurbishment required; average maintenance costs incurred
8–15 years	Minor renovation and refurbishment required
15–20 years	Major renovation and refurbishment required
20+ years	Restoration required; high maintenance costs incurred

FIGURE 9.1 Hotel Life Span

Because every hotel will at some point need renovation and refurbishment, its owners must take steps to reserve funds for the time when renovation is undertaken. Owners do this by establishing an **FF&E reserve**.

LODGING LANGUAGE

FF&E Reserve: Funds set aside by ownership today for the future "furniture, fixture, and equipment" replacement needs of a hotel.

Generally, FF&E reserves are funded by setting aside 1–5 percent of a hotel's gross sales revenue. If designated funds such as these are not reserved, the hotel may not be able to undertake minor renovations, major renovations, or **restoration** when needed.

LODGING LANGUAGE

Restoration: Returning an older hotel building to its original, or better than original, condition.

Figure 9.2 lists specific items that must be considered when planning a hotel's short- and long-term renovation program.

LODGING LANGUAGE

Case Goods: Non-upholstered furniture such as guest room dressers, tables, end tables, and desks.

Refurbishment and minor renovation is actually an ongoing process in most hotels. Major refurbishment should take place every 6 to 10 years, and the costs associated with doing so are often very high. Extra cleaning costs are likely to be incurred during construction. Moreover, it is almost inevitable that guest services will be disrupted, resulting in unhappy guests who must be satisfied, and in lost revenue from out-of-service areas that normally generate revenue.

Restoration takes place when a hotel undergoes a renovation so extensive that walls are frequently relocated, guest rooms and public space are totally reconfigured, and mechanical systems are replaced with more modern ones. The typical hotel undergoes a restoration every 20 to 25 years. Restorations are a challenging time for management, the maintenance department, and guests. If restoration is not undertaken when needed, however, the revenue-producing potential of the hotel will decline.

	Minor Renovation	Major Renovation
Guest Rooms	Drapes, bedspreads	Bed frames, mattresses
	Lamps, shades	Wall lights
	Carpets	Wall vinyl
	Upholstered furniture	**Case goods**
	Faucets	Sinks, countertops
	Mattresses	Televisions
Food and Beverage	Carpets, chairs, reupholster booths	Decorative lighting
	Table top décor	Tables
	Dishes, flatware	Serving equipment
		Wall coverings
Public Space	Table lamps, lobby furniture	Overhead lighting
	Lobby carpet	Corridor carpet
	Lobby wall coverings	Corridor vinyl
	Meeting rooms	Restrooms

FIGURE 9.2 Selected Hotel Renovation and Replacement Considerations

Interactions

The efforts of the maintenance department affect the guests, the hotel's managers, and even the hotel's line employees. On a departmental basis, maintenance has the most interaction with the front office and housekeeping. In full-service hotels, the food and beverage department will also regularly interact with maintenance.

FRONT OFFICE

The maintenance department interacts with the front office in many ways. Among the most important of these are:

Providing room-status updates. When a room or its contents are damaged and cannot be rented to another guest, the maintenance department will place it in an OOO (out-of-order) status. Front office staff must then be informed about the room's status, including how long it will be unrentable and the date when it is most likely to return to service.

Responding to guest service requests. Guests occupying hotel rooms generate a variety of requests for assistance from the maintenance department. Such requests can include, for example, adjustment of the reception on televisions, replacement of light bulbs, adjustment of in-room heating or cooling (HVAC) units, and the resolution of plumbing complaints. Guests with such needs or concerns will typically call the front office, whose staff must then relay the request for service to a member of the maintenance staff.

Communicating information about specific hotel conditions. The normal maintenance performed in a hotel can result in disruption to regular building functions and/or guest services. When, for example, a swimming pool must be closed for resurfacing, or when water must be temporarily shut off to make plumbing repairs, or when a power outage disrupts electrical service to the entire hotel, the maintenance department must keep the front office well-informed of the status of the repairs or disruption and how these will affect the hotel's guests and employees.

Additional interactions between the maintenance department and the front office can include assisting with guests' needs in meeting rooms, the servicing or repairing of front office equipment and furniture, and carefully coordinating the scheduled maintenance of rooms with the front office manager to minimize disruption to guests and any negative impact on hotel revenues.

Housekeeping: Making minor repairs in guest rooms is a major responsibility of all maintenance departments. Because the housekeeping department cleans the rooms, its staff members play a critical role in identifying major and minor repair issues and reporting them to maintenance. When these two departments work well together, minor issues such as loose handles on dressers and drawers, torn wall vinyl, and leaky faucets can all be quickly identified and repaired.

Food and Beverage: The food and beverage department of a hotel may be very small, as in many limited-service properties, or extremely large, as in a convention or resort hotel. In both cases, however, the normal repair and maintenance on items such as kitchen cooking equipment, refrigerators and freezers, dishwashing equipment, and ice makers may be performed by the maintenance department's staff. Repairs to frequently used items such as dining and meeting room tables and chairs may also be completed by maintenance staff.

MANAGING MAINTENANCE

The job of maintaining a building begins immediately after it is designed, engineered, and built. With a properly trained staff, maintenance tasks can be planned and implemented to maximize the life of the property while minimizing the cost of operating the building. Managing maintenance in a hotel is a process that can be examined in a variety of ways. One helpful way is to consider maintenance as either routine, preventive, or emergency.

In each of these approaches, staffing the department with properly skilled employees is critically important.

Staffing

The talents of the maintenance staff crucially affect a hotel's profitable operation. This is true because so much of a guest's impression of the quality of a hotel is dependent on the work of the maintenance department. The quality of the maintenance staff and the quality of their work will, in the guest's eyes, represent the quality of the entire hotel. When maintenance work is performed poorly or is not undertaken at all, it quickly shows. The solution to this potential problem lies in the selection of an excellent manager to head the maintenance department. In most hotels, there will also be a need for appropriately trained maintenance assistants.

CHIEF ENGINEER

In the hotel industry, the head of maintenance may hold a variety of titles. The most widely used titles are **chief engineer** and **maintenance chief**. Whatever the title, the person with this role is the head of one of the hotel's most important departments.

LODGING LANGUAGE

Chief engineer: The employee responsible for the management of a hotel's maintenance department. Sometimes referred to as "maintenance chief."

Maintenance chief: The employee responsible for the management of a hotel's maintenance department. Sometimes referred to as "chief engineer."

In smaller hotels, the chief engineer may take a very hands-on role in the maintenance effort. This could involve actually performing maintenance and repair tasks. In larger hotels, with a larger staff, the chief engineer serves in an administrative role that consists of planning work, organizing staff, directing and evaluating employee efforts, and controlling the POM budget. Regardless of a hotel's size, the chief engineer must be well-organized, attentive to detail, and a cooperative member of the management team.

MAINTENANCE ASSISTANTS

In addition to the chief engineer, the maintenance department may employ one or more individuals with varying degrees of skill in the areas of:

- Engineering
- Mechanics
- Plumbing
- Electricity
- Carpentry
- Water treatment (for pools and spas)
- Landscaping
- Grounds maintenance

The needs of each specific hotel dictate the actual skills, make-up, and number of maintenance staff required. It would be difficult to find one person skilled in all of the technical maintenance areas needed in a hotel. When the necessary skills or manpower needs exceed the capabilities of the in-house staff, the chief engineer,sometimes in consultation with the general manager, must decide to **outsource** the work. The ability to effectively determine which tasks are best performed by in-house or outsourced staff is a characteristic of an excellent chief engineer.

LODGING LANGUAGE

Outsource: To obtain labor or parts from an outside provider. Typically done to reduce costs or obtain specialized expertise.

ALL IN A DAY'S WORK 9.1

THE SITUATION

"The telephone is ringing off the hook!" Dani Pelley, the front office manager, told Lindsey Noel, the hotel's general manager. "I called maintenance and Ted said they were looking into it."

"It" was a complete outage of the satellite system used to deliver television reception to the hotel. The hotel's pay-per-view features were down and the free-to-guests channels were unavailable. Guests were calling the front desk to complain or to request a repair on their television sets.

"What do we do now?" asked Dani.

Lindsey picked up the walkie-talkie, radioed Ted, the chief engineer, and got the bad news: Satellite reception was indeed down. The hotel's equipment was not at fault, but the satellite service provider was experiencing equipment difficulty due to a heavy rainstorm in the area. The chief had just gotten off the telephone with them to report the problem, and they estimated a repair time of between 2 and 24 hours. Until the problem was fixed, there would simply be no TV reception in the guest rooms.

A RESPONSE

Sometimes hotels experience maintenance or facility problems that are simply beyond their control. In this situation, the most important thing for management to do is inform guests and appropriate hotel employees about the problem, keep them updated as to any changes in the estimated repair time, and be prepared to make room-rate adjustments or provide other compensation as approved by management.

In smaller hotels, calling each room may be appropriate. In larger properties that are so equipped, activating the telephone message light in each room and recording a message explaining the problem may be a good solution.

Routine Maintenance

When managing a hotel's routine maintenance tasks, the chief engineer is simply directing the customary care of the facility. For example, in hotels with lawns and plant beds around entrances or parking areas, it is customary to periodically cut and edge the grass and to maintain the visual integrity of the plant bed by pulling weeds and replacing foliage as needed. If this work is not done, the curb appeal of the hotel suffers. Cleaning interior windows, picking up trash in the parking lot, and shoveling snow in climates that require it are additional examples of routine maintenance. Often, only limited employee training is required to adequately complete routine maintenance tasks.

The chief engineer is generally the person who decides whether to perform routine maintenance work in-house or to pay an outside vendor to perform it. Regardless of the decision, an effective chief engineer must be concerned with both the exterior and interior of the hotel.

EXTERIOR

On the outside of the hotel, tasks such as lawn care, landscaping maintenance, grounds care, and leaf and snow removal are important issues. Just as important is attention to the details required for the care of the hotel building itself. This includes such tasks as routine roof inspection and repair, window cleaning and window seals inspection, and the care and painting, if required, of the building's exterior finishes.

The location of a hotel will dictate, to a large degree, the items that must be considered for routine exterior maintenance. A resort hotel in the Miami, Florida, area will have exterior maintenance needs that are different from those of a downtown high-rise hotel in Chicago, Illinois. Regardless of the setting, however, properly maintaining the outside of the hotel improves curb appeal, decreases operational costs, and ultimately increases the building's value. The maintenance department must ensure that routine exterior maintenance is performed correctly and in a timely manner.

INTERIOR

The chief engineer must also supervise routine maintenance inside the hotel. Some examples of routine interior maintenance tasks include the care of indoor plants, the washing of interior windows (if not assigned to housekeeping), and, in some cases, the care and cleaning of floors and carpets.

One significant task nearly always assigned to the maintenance department is the changing of light bulbs. Regardless of their type, light bulbs will burn out and then must be replaced. In some instances, individual light bulbs are immediately replaced when they burn out. That is, the maintenance department implements a **replace as needed** program for bulbs.

LODGING LANGUAGE

Replace as needed: A parts or equipment replacement plan that delays installing a new part until the original part fails or is near failure. For example, most chief engineers would use a replace-as-needed plan in the maintenance of refrigeration compressors or water pumps.

The cost to a hotel of replacing a light bulb consists of two components. These are the price of the bulb itself and the labor dollars required to change the bulb. Therefore, in special cases, such as the light bulbs in a hotel with high ceilings that require special lifts or ladders for access, the hotel may implement a **total replacement** program that involves changing all bulbs, including those that have not burned out, on a regularly predetermined schedule.

LODGING LANGUAGE

Total replacement: A parts or equipment replacement plan that involves installing new or substitute parts based on a predetermined schedule. For example, most chief engineers would use a total replacement approach to the maintenance of light bulbs in high-rise exterior highway signs.

Using this approach, while it involves discarding some bulbs or lamps with life remaining, may significantly reduce bulb-replacement labor costs and make the hotel's total bulb-replacement costs lower.

Another form of routine interior maintenance involves items related to guest rooms and public spaces. These items must be attended to on a regular basis when they malfunction, wear out, or break and need repair or replacement. For example, a room attendant in a guest room may notice and report that a chair leg is broken or that the tub in the room drains slowly. Similarly, a front office agent may report that a guest has complained about poor television reception or reported a toilet that does not flush properly. When events such as these occur, the maintenance department is notified with a **work order**, or maintenance request. Figure 9.3 shows a sample work order.

LODGING LANGUAGE

Work order: A form used to initiate and document a request for maintenance. Also referred to as a "maintenance request."

In a well-managed hotel, any staff member who sees an area of concern can initiate a work order. Work orders are prenumbered, multicopy forms that, depending on the number of copies preferred by the general manager, are used to notify maintenance, the front office, housekeeping, and others who may need to know when a maintenance request is initiated or completed. In some hotels, blank work order forms are placed in the guest room for guests to initiate. In some cases, these requests can be initiated using the hotel's in-room television system.

Regardless of their original source, the work orders, once received by the maintenance department, are reviewed and prioritized. For example, a work order indicating an inoperable guest room lock would take priority over one addressing a crooked picture in another guest room. A maintenance employee completes the task(s) called for on the

Best Sleep Hotel Work Order

Work Order Number: ________ (Preassigned) ________ Initiated By: ____________

Date: ____________ Time: ____________ Room or Location: ____________

Problem Observed: ____

____

____

Received On: ____________________ Assigned To: ____________________

Date Corrected: ____________________ Time Spent: ____________________

M&E Employee Comments: ____

____

____

____

____

Chief Engineer Comments: ____

____

____

____

____

FIGURE 9.3 Work Order

work order and informs the proper departments, and the information related to the work performed is carefully retained. In a well-run department, the chief engineer keeps a room-by-room record of replacements and repairs that have been made.

Some general managers evaluate the effectiveness of their maintenance department based on the rapidity with which maintenance work orders are completed. While the timely completion of maintenance requests should not be the only factor for judging a maintenance department, it is an important indicator of effectiveness and efficiency. When work orders are not completed promptly (or at all), the maintenance department loses credibility in the eyes of the hotel's staff and guests. An effective chief engineer monitors the speed at which work orders are prioritized and completed and then, if needed, takes corrective action.

Preventive Maintenance

When not performing routine maintenance or responding to work orders, the maintenance department has a good many other maintenance-related tasks to perform. In fact, many hoteliers believe that the most important maintenance performed in a hotel is its **PM (preventive maintenance) program**.

LODGING LANGUAGE

PM (preventive maintenance) program: A specific inspection and activities schedule designed to minimize maintenance-related costs and to prolong the life of equipment by preventing small problems before they become larger ones.

An effective PM program saves money for a hotel by reducing:

- Long-term repair costs (because equipment life is prolonged)
- Replacement parts costs (because purchases of parts can be planned)
- Labor costs (because PM can be performed during otherwise slow periods)
- The dollar amount of adjustments and allowances due to guest dissatisfaction (because guest inconvenience is reduced)
- The costs of emergency repairs (because they will occur less frequently)

A well-managed maintenance program performs routine and preventive maintenance tasks.

LODGING GOES GREEN!

Like the Housekeeping department, the maintenance department in a hotel will purchase and use a variety of chemicals to do its job. This includes products such as general-purpose cleaners, industrial degreasers, carpet cleaners, floor finishes/sealers, and floor finish strippers. Handled improperly, these chemicals can pose a significant threat to the environment and to employees using them. In many cases, these chemicals are sold in concentrated form and thus must be dispensed. As a result, the dispensing equipment used must be carefully maintained and calibrated to ensure the safety of maintenance workers and to minimize the environmental impact of the cleaning product.

The maintenance department in a hotel illustrates the fact that a truly green orientation entails more than the purchase of environmentally friendly products. It requires the right employee practices as well. As a result, those hoteliers who are committed to environmentally friendly operation must also be committed to aggressive "green-practices" employee training programs. This is especially important in a hotel's maintenance department, but it is also true in every department within the hotel.

In addition to saving money, a good PM program reduces guest complaints, eases the job of the sales staff, enhances the eye appeal and functionality of the hotel, and improves employee morale.

Schedules for PM programs can come from a variety of sources. Equipment suppliers often suggest maintenance activities for their products, franchisors may mandate PM schedules, and local ordinances may require specific PM activities (such as boiler equipment or water heater inspection). Most important of all, the chief engineer's skill and experience and knowledge of the hotel's needs dictate PM schedules.

Most PM activities involve basic inspection, replacement, cleaning, and lubrication. PM is not generally considered to be a repair program, nor should it be viewed as one. Repairs must be completed when they are needed, while PM activities should be performed on a scheduled basis.

Some chief engineers design PM programs that are segmented into activities to be performed daily, weekly, monthly, semi-annually, and annually. Others segment the hotel into major areas (e.g., food service and laundry) and then develop area-specific PM schedules. In both cases, the PM program should identify what is to be done, when it is to be done, and how it is to be done. It should also provide an easy method to document the completion of the activity.

Figure 9.4 is a sample of a daily, monthly, and annual PM task list for a dryer in a hotel's laundry area.

PM ACTIVITY: LAUNDRY AREA DRYER

DAILY
- ❑ Clean lint trap
- ❑ Wipe down inside chamber with mild detergent
- ❑ Clean and wipe dry the outside dryer shell

MONTHLY
- ❑ Vacuum the inside of dryer (upper and lower chambers)
- ❑ Check and tighten, if needed, the bolts holding dryer to floor
- ❑ Check all electrical connections
- ❑ Check fan belt for wear; replace if needed
- ❑ Lubricate moving parts

ANNUALLY
- ❑ Check pulley alignment
- ❑ Adjust rotating basket if needed
- ❑ Lubricate motor bearings
- ❑ Lubricate drum bearings if needed

FIGURE 9.4 Sample PM Task List for Laundry Area Dryer

LODGING ONLINE

Carpet and area rug care can be complex, but a variety of resources are available to help determine how to best care for these items. To view one such free resource, go to the Web site of the Carpet and Rug Institute at:

www.carpet-rug.org/

How much do you think hotel managers should know about the proper care and cleaning of commercial carpets? Where should they learn about it?

The chief engineer of a hotel must have a written and complete PM program in place. All of the hotel's equipment, including furnaces, air conditioners, water-heating equipment, and elevators, must have individual PM programs. In addition, the maintenance department must create specific PM programs for the following areas:

- Public space
- Guest rooms
- Food service
- Laundry
- Other equipment

PUBLIC SPACE

Public space PM programs are vitally important but relatively simple to develop. In public spaces such as lobbies, corridors, and meeting areas, PM programs should include such items as windows, HVAC units, furniture, lights, elevators, and carpets. In fact, carpet care is one of the most challenging PM activities of all. Carpet care duties are often shared between housekeeping and maintenance, with housekeeping taking responsibility for minor (spot) cleaning issues, and the maintenance department responsible for long-term carpet PM.

It is important for public space appearances to be well maintained because they significantly influence guest opinions about the entire hotel. Professional hoteliers know that a good first impression goes a long way toward ensuring a satisfactory guest stay.

GUEST ROOMS

The hotel's guest rooms are perhaps the most important and certainly the most extensive area for PM. Despite that, some chief engineers do not implement aggressive guest room PM programs. The guest room PM program is critical to the hotel's sales efforts, to its ability to retain guests, and to the maintenance of the asset's monetary value. In fact, there are few things a chief engineer should pay more attention to than the PM program used for guestrooms.

An effective PM program requires a quarterly, or more frequent, inspection of guest rooms with a careful examination of each item on the guest room **PM Checklist**.

LODGING LANGUAGE

PM Checklist: A tool developed to identify all the critical areas that should be inspected during a PM review of a room, area, or piece of equipment.

The checklist for any PM area is developed to help maintenance staff with their inspections. Figure 9.5 is an example of a PM checklist that can be used for guest rooms.

Note that the extensive checklist in Figure 9.5 can be tailored for each individual property. For example, hotels that have in-room microwaves and refrigerators could add these items to the guest room PM checklist. If some guest rooms contain whirlpool-type tubs, these could be included. It is the responsibility of the chief engineer to develop a custom PM checklist and inspection schedule for guest rooms and then to see that the

	The Best Sleep Hotel Guest Room PM Checklist										
	Place an "x" by any item not meeting hotel standards										
Year__________		Room Number __________									
Area	Item	Quarter				Area	Item	Quarter			
Inspected	Inspected	1	2	3	4	Inspected	Inspected	1	2	3	4
Entrance	Number sign					Bathroom	Floor tile/grouting				
Door	Exterior Finish					continued	Telephone				
	Interior Finish						Blow Dryer				
	Peep hole						GFI plug operational				
	Door closer					Drapes	Drape Hooks				
	Deadbolt						Drape wand				
	Lock/lock plate						Valance				
	Evacuation/fire safety plan						Drape rods and brackets				
	Innkeeper's laws frame					Bedroom	Entrance ceiling				
	Hinges						Room ceiling				
Closet	Shelf Stable						Night Stand				
	Clothes Hooks						Night stand drawers				
	Clothes Rod						Dresser				
	Carpet/Covebase						Dresser drawers				
	Luggage Rack						Headboard				
	Vinyl/Walls						Desk				
	Closet door finish						Desk chair				
	Closet door operation						Upholstered chairs				
	Closet door mirror						Bed frames				
Fixtures,	Entry light						Mattress (condition)				
lights and	Closet light						Mattress (turned)				
bulbs	Swing lamps						Mirrors				
	Dresser lamps						Art work				
	Desk lamp						Wall vinyl				
	Pole lamp						Electrical switches				
	Bathroom					HVAC	Filters changed				
	Smoke Detector						Fan				
	Sprinkler head						Motor				
Bathroom	Door Finish						Controls				
	Door lock						Condensate pan				
	Ceiling condition						Wiring				
	Overhead Fan					TV/Radio	Picture quality				
	Toilet operation						Swivel				
	Toilet caulking						Lock down				
	Tub diverter spout						Volume				
	Tub tile/grouting						Remote control				
	Tub stopper						Cabinet condition				
	Shower head						Connections				
	Curtain rod secure						Video game controls				
	Safety bar secure					Telephone	Line 1				
	Non-skid surface						Line 2				
	Sink Faucet						Jacks secure				
	Sink stopper					Connecting	Interior Finish				
	Piping					Door	Exterior Finish				
	Aerator						Frame				
	Toilet Paper holder						Door Stop				
	Towel rack						Lock(s) operation				
	Mirrors						Door knob				
	Vinyl Walls						Hinges				
						Other					
Inspector initials											
The Best Sleep Hotel, 20XX											

FIGURE 9.5 Guest Room PM Checklist File location

inspections are performed when scheduled. When they are, guest room quality complaints will be minimized and long-term repair costs will be reduced because small problems will be uncovered and attended to before they become big ones.

FOOD SERVICE

There are three major PM concerns in the food service area. The first is back-of-the-house equipment. The ovens, ranges, griddles, fryers, and other production equipment in the kitchen are heavily used and, of course, must be properly maintained. Specialty equipment such as dishwashers, fryers, and convection ovens may require the PM expertise of specifically trained technicians. If so, these outsourced vendors should be selected and their work scheduled by the chief engineer or by the food and beverage director. In all cases, every piece of kitchen equipment as well as all mechanical bar equipment should be included in the PM program.

A second area of PM concern in the food services area is the dining and lounge space used by guests. Included in this program are chairs, tabletops, and bases. An especially annoying PM issue for guests involves table leveling. In a professionally managed hotel, there is simply no excuse for wobbly tables or for foreign objects (such as folded paper napkins and match books) to be placed under tables to make them level. In addition, PM must include all fixed seating, booths, self-serve salad or buffet areas, lighting fixtures, and guest-check processing equipment.

A third area of PM concern in food and beverages, and one that is sometimes overlooked, includes meeting and conference rooms and equipment. Included in this PM program are light fixtures, tables, chairs, and wall coverings within the hotel's meeting rooms. In addition, the PM program must include transport carts and any audiovisual-elated items owned by the hotel. These may include flip chart stands, TVs, overhead projectors, computer projection units, and speaker telephones. In those hotels that have determined that audiovisual-related equipment will be the responsibility of the maintenance department (instead of the banquet area of the food and beverage department), equipment in this area must also be maintained.

LAUNDRY

In the laundry, the washers, dryers, folding equipment, water supply lines, drains, lighting fixtures, and temperature-control units require PM programs. The clothes dryer is an especially important concern because of the potential for fire. Dryer drum temperatures can be very high, and the lint build-up during the natural drying process requires vigilance on the part of the maintenance department as well as housekeeping personnel. Lint traps should be cleaned at least once per day (or more often) and should be thoroughly inspected weekly.

In many cases, the company supplying laundry chemicals to the hotel maintains the equipment used to dispense chemicals into the washers. This does not relieve the maintenance department of that type of responsibility. If chemical usage is too high, this may be because the chemical supplier has adjusted equipment to overdispense chemicals in an effort to sell more products. For this reason and because improperly maintained chemical-dispensing units may result in substandard laundry quality and even cause damage to linen and terry, the maintenance department should make chemical dispenser maintenance an important part of the laundry PM program even if it is performed in conjunction with the dispensing equipment supplier.

LODGING ONLINE

Diversey Inc. is a company that supplies chemicals to hotel laundries. It does an excellent job of PM on its own dispensing equipment. To view the company's Web site, go to:

www.johnsondiversey.com

When you arrive, click "Lodging" under the "Industries" tab.

How important do you think clean sheets and towels are to guests' satisfaction when staying in a hotel?

LODGING ONLINE

A comprehensive PM program for hotels is sometimes easier to maintain than to begin because there are so many pieces of equipment to be included. Today, software exists to help a chief engineer decide what must be maintained and how frequently to schedule PM. To view one software company's hotel-oriented PM program, go to:

www.attr.com/

What are some reasons why it is better to do PM on a piece of equipment rather than repair it when it breaks down?

OTHER AREAS AND EQUIPMENT

Additional areas of concern when developing a PM program can include pools and spas, front office equipment, electronic guest room locks, exterior door locks, motor vehicles such as courtesy vans, and in-hotel transportation equipment including housekeeper's carts and luggage carts, just to name but a few.

A quality PM maintenance program involves a vast number of pieces of equipment and areas of the hotel. An effective chief engineer develops, maintains, and documents an effective and comprehensive PM program that both reduces repair costs and enhances the image of the hotel.

Emergency Maintenance

The strongest rationale for implementing well-designed and aggressive routine and PM programs is the ability to manage and minimize repair costs. Despite the very best routine and PM efforts of the chief engineer and the maintenance staff, however, a hotel sometimes requires emergency maintenance. Emergency maintenance occurrences are generally defined as those that:

- Are unexpected
- Threaten to negatively impact hotel revenue
- Require immediate attention to minimize danger or damage
- Require labor and parts that must be purchased at a premium price

For example, assume that a water pipe bursts in one of the hotel's unoccupied guest rooms in the middle of the night. A short time later, the guests in the room one floor below the room with the broken pipe call the front desk to complain about water coming into their room from the ceiling. Clearly, this situation requires emergency maintenance. If not attended to immediately, extensive repair work to the pipe as well as to the ceilings and walls around the leak may be required.

Hotel managers can encounter a variety of situations that require immediate attention from the maintenance department. Some of these include:

No heat or air-conditioning in room. This is especially an emergency during extremely cold or hot weather, and when the HVAC unit controlling air temperature is not working due to mechanical malfunction.

No electricity in room. Blown electrcial fuses in a hotel are fairly common. Even more common is a blown **GFI outlet**. While these are easy to reset, many guests will not know how to do so. The result can be frequent emergency power outage calls to the front desk, followed by the need for maintenance staff to reset the outlets.

LODGING LANGUAGE

GFI outlet: Short for "Ground Fault Interrupter" outlet. This special electrical outlet is designed to interrupt power (by "tripping" or "blowing") before significant damage can be done to a building's wiring system. These outlets are most commonly installed in the bathroom or vanity areas of a hotel room, where high-voltage usage (such as high wattage hairdryers) or high moisture levels can cause electrical power interruptions.

Gas leaks or smell of gas. This is a very serious situation because sparks from equipment or appliances (and even cell phones) can ignite gas. Immediate shut-off is required in a situation of known gas leakage. If appropriate, the hotel's natural gas provider should also be contacted in such emergencies.

Interior flooding. In most cases, the action required in these emergencies involves shutting off the water at the source of the leak and then making the appropriate plumbing repair. In most cases, repairs of this type must be made quickly to avoid damaging furniture, flooring materials, and other guest rooms or public areas of the hotel.

Toilet stoppage. This extremely common situation always requires prompt maintenance attention. A guest may tolerate a slow drain in a sink or tub, but a toilet stoppage emergency is quite a different matter. To avoid further problems including flooding, these emergencies must be addressed immediately.

While minor maintenance-related emergencies are not typically brought to the attention of the hotel's general manager, the chief engineer should notify the general manager or other appropriate hotel management staff when doing so is necessary to protect the well-being of guests and the reputation of the hotel.

Emergency repairs are expensive. They sometimes require the authorization of overtime for maintenance staff or outside repair personnel. In addition, needed repair parts that might normally be purchased through customary sources may need to be secured quickly (and at a premium price) from non-customary sources. While it is not possible to avoid all emergency maintenance, effective routine and PM programs reduce the number of times emergency maintenance is required and the total cost of property maintenance.

MANAGING UTILITIES

Utility management is an important part of a hotel's overall operation. Utility costs in hotels include expenses for water and sewage, gas, electricity, or other fossil fuel for heating and cooling the building, fuel for heating water, and, in some cases, the purchase of steam or chilled water. Hotels with active programs to conserve energy find that the procedures they use are not only environmentally friendly, but also save money.

Energy-related expenses that were once taken for granted by the public and most hoteliers became very important and costly during the energy crisis of the early 1970s. Since then, these costs have moderated somewhat. When the cost of utilities is relatively low, few Americans, including hoteliers, take strong measures to conserve resources and implement **energy management** programs. Alternatively, when energy costs are high, managers have a heightened sense of awareness about these costs. Every hotel manager, and every hotel staff member, should always practice energy-effective management.

LODGING LANGUAGE

Energy management: Specific engineering, maintenance, and facility-design policies and activities intended to control and reduce energy usage.

It is important to remember that, in most cases, the utilities cost for lighting, heating, and operating hotel equipment will be incurred regardless of occupancy levels. While it is true that higher hotel occupancy will result in some incremental increase in utility costs, (e.g., more rooms sold will result in increased water consumption for bathing), as much as 80 percent of total utility costs for a hotel are actually fixed. A hotel's original design and construction and the age of its buildings significantly affect its energy usage. Its usage is most affected, however, by the regular maintenance and **calibration** of the equipment consuming energy.

Managing and conserving utilities is very important because they represent one of a hotel's largest operating costs.

LODGING LANGUAGE

Calibration: The adjustment of equipment to maximize its effectiveness and operational efficiency.

Depending on the location of the hotel, energy costs can represent as much as 3–15 percent of total operating costs. In addition, energy is a valuable resource, and as responsible members of the hotel industry, all hoteliers should be committed to energy conservation. Because that is true, it is easy to see why an effective maintenance department should be very concerned with conserving energy and controlling utility costs.

Electricity

Electricity is the most common and usually the most expensive form of energy used in hotels. To be effective, the hotel's electrical source must be dependable, and it will be if the maintenance department maintains the hotel's electrical systems in a safe manner. While some hotels have a **back-up generator** for use in an emergency outage situation, most will rely on one or more local power providers to deliver electricity.

LODGING LANGUAGE

Back-up generator: Equipment used to make limited amounts of electricity on-site; utilized in times of power failure or when the hotel experiences low supply from the usual provider of electricity.

In some locations, electric bills account for more than 50 percent (and sometimes as much as 80 percent) of a hotel's total utility costs. Controlling electrical consumption can really pay off for hoteliers interested in lowering utility bills.

Electricity is used everywhere in a hotel. It powers the administrative computers, operates fire safety systems, keeps food cold in freezers and refrigerators, and provides power for security systems, to name but a few uses. When considering the total electrical consumption of hotels, however, the two most important uses of electricity, and, therefore, those the chief engineer must manage most carefully, are related to lighting and HVAC systems.

LIGHTING

The lighting in a hotel is tremendously important for curb appeal, guest comfort, worker efficiency, and property security. Lighting is sometimes referred to as illumination, and light levels are measured in **foot-candles**.

LODGING LANGUAGE

Foot-candle: A measure of illumination. One foot-candle equals one lumen per square foot.

Generally, the greater the number of foot-candles, the greater the illumination. Hotels require varying degrees of illumination in different locations, and the types of light fixtures and bulbs used play a large role in producing the most appropriate light for each hotel setting.

Artificial light is produced to supplement natural (sun) light. Natural light is cost-effective and, when used properly, can reduce utility costs by limiting the amount of artificial light that is needed. When lighting must be supplemented, the hotel can choose from two basic lighting options. The first of these is **incandescent lamps**.

LODGING LANGUAGE

Incandescent lamp: A lamp in which a filament inside the lamp's bulb is heated by electrical current to produce light.

Incandescent lamps are what most people think of when they think of the older style light bulbs used in their homes. Incandescent bulbs have relatively short life spans (2,000 hours or less) and thus must be frequently changed. They are fairly inefficient since they produce only 15–20 lumens per watt. For example, a 100-watt bulb produces 1,500–2,000 lumens. Incandescent lights are popular, however, because they are easy to install, easy to move, inexpensive to purchase, and have the characteristic of starting and restarting instantly. Incandescent lamp bulbs can be made in such a way as to concentrate light in one area (these are known as spotlights or floodlights).

In cases where a conventional incandescent light is not best suited for a specific lighting need, hotels can select an **electric discharge lamp** as a second lighting option.

LODGING LANGUAGE

Electric discharge lamp: A lamp in which light is generated by passing electrical current through a space filled with a special combination of gases. Examples include fluorescent, mercury vapor, metal halide, and sodium.

Electric discharge lamps do not operate directly from electricity. They must use a **ballast**.

LODGING LANGUAGE

Ballast: The device in an electric discharge lamp that starts, stops, and controls the electrical current to the light.

Electric discharge lamps have longer lives (5,000–25,000 hours), and higher efficiency (40–80 lumens per watt) than incandescent lamps. The most common lamp of this type is the fluorescent, and it is frequently used where high light levels and low operating costs are important. If an electric discharge lamp stops working, either the bulb or the ballast may need replacing.

Other types of electric discharge lamps include those for parking areas or security lighting. In cases such as these, sodium lamps are a good choice because they can generate 200 lumens per watt used and have extremely long lives, but the cost of purchasing and installing these lights is also greater than for fluorescent lamps.

In the late 1980s, the compact version of the fluorescent light known as the **CFL** became popular in many hotels.

LODGING LANGUAGE

CFL: Short for "Compact Fluorescent Light." An alternative light source that uses less energy and lasts longer than incandescent light.

Changing the hotel lighting system to utilize CFL bulbs will provide savings because this type of bulb uses less energy and has a longer life than do incandescent bulbs.

These lights are designed to combine the energy efficiency and long life of a traditional fluorescent light with the convenience and ballast-free operation of an incandescent light. For many applications, they provide an excellent blend of operational savings and convenience.

CFLs are increasing in popularity because they are:

Energy-efficient. CFLs use about one-fourth the energy of traditional incandescent light bulbs. For example, a 26-watt CFL produces the same amount of light as a typical 100-watt incandescent bulb.

Cost-effective. Because CFLs use about one-fourth the energy of incandescent bulbs, hotels using them save money on their electric bills. While the initial

LODGING ONLINE

The proper use of indoor and outdoor lighting in a hotel is important in many ways. To obtain a better understanding of how lighting works, visit the General Electric Company's lighting Web site. Go to:

www.gelighting.com/na/

When you arrive, select "Learn about Light," and then select "Facts About Light."

purchase price of a CFL is higher than an incandescent, the bulb lasts about 10 times longer.

Environmentally friendly. Power plants that generate electricity also produce pollution. Since CFLs use less electricity to produce the same amount of light as incandescent light bulbs, reducing the amount of electricity used also reduces the amount of pollution produced.

When selecting lighting, hotels can choose from a wide choice of lamps, bulbs, and light fixtures. The proper type, the color of the light, and the operational costs must all be taken into consideration when selecting lighting fixtures and lamps. In all cases, however, lighting maintenance, including lamp repair, bulb changing, and fixture cleaning, must be an integral part of the hotel's PM program.

HVAC

Another significant user of electrical power is the hotel's HVAC system. Heating, ventilation, and air-conditioning are considered together in the hotel's maintenance program because they all utilize the hotel's air-treatment, thermostats, **duct** and **air handler** systems.

LODGING LANGUAGE

Duct: A passageway, usually built of sheet metal, that allows fresh, cold, or warm air to be directed to various parts of a building.

Air handler: The fans and mechanical systems required to move air through ducts and to vents.

A properly operating HVAC system delivers air at a desired temperature to rooms in the hotel. The efficiency with which a hotel's HVAC system operates, and thus the comfort of the building, is affected by a variety of factors, including:

- The original temperature of the air in the room
- The temperature of the air delivered to the room
- The relative humidity of the air when delivered
- The air movement in the room
- The temperature-absorbing surfaces in the room

HVAC systems can be fairly straightforward or very complex, but all consist of components responsible for heating and cooling the hotel.

Heating Components: While it is possible for all of a hotel's heating components to be operated electrically, this is not normally the case. Heating by electricity, especially in cold climates, is generally not cost-effective. Because of this, hotels heat at least some parts of their buildings using natural gas, liquefied petroleum gas (LPG), steam, or fuel oil although electricity can be used to heat small areas.

In most hotels, the heating of hot water is second in cost only to the heating of air. A hotel requires an effective furnace (or heat pump system) for heating air, and a boiler of the right size for heating water. Regardless of the heat source, fans powered by electricity move warm air produced by the furnace to the appropriate parts of the building.

Similarly, electricity often powers pumps to move hot water produced by the hot water heater. The maintenance of these two heating components can be complex, but an effective chief engineer maintains them in a manner that is safe and cost-effective, performing calibration and maintenance tasks in accordance with manufacturer's recommendations and local building code requirements.

Cooling Components: Just as a hotel must heat air and water, in most cases it must also cool them. The major cost of operating air-cooling or air-conditioning systems is related to electricity usage. Essentially, in an air-conditioning system, electrically operated equipment extracts heat from either air or water and then utilizes the remaining cooled air or water to absorb and remove more heat from the building. The effectiveness of a cooling system is dependent on several factors, including:

- The original air temperature and humidity of the space to be cooled
- The temperature and humidity of the chilled air entering the room from the HVAC system
- The quantity of chilled air entering the room
- The operational efficiency of the air-conditioning equipment

Some cooling systems are designed to produce small quantities of very cold air that is then pumped or blown into a room to reduce its temperature, while other systems supply larger quantities of air that is not as cold but has the same room-cooling affect because the quantity of air supplied is greater.

The ability of a cooling system to deliver cold air or water of a specified temperature and in the quantity required determines the overall effectiveness of a cooling system. Very often, especially in hot humid weather, the demands placed upon a hotel's cooling system are intense. The ability of the maintenance department to maintain cooling equipment in a manner that minimizes guest discomfort (and the resulting complaints) is critical to the success of the hotel. Effective routine and PM maintenance on cooling equipment is a crucial part of the chief engineer's job in climates where air-conditioning is a frequent need.

Natural Gas

In some geographic areas where natural gas is plentiful and cost-effective, hotels use it to heat water for guest rooms and to power laundry area clothes dryers. Natural gas is also used in many hotel HVAC systems to directly or indirectly provide heat to guest rooms and public spaces.

Interestingly, the overwhelming majority of chefs and cooks prefer natural gas when cooking because of its rapid heat production and the amount of immediate temperature control it allows. Cooking with natural gas is also economical. It costs about half as much to cook with a natural gas range as with a similar electric range. Although a natural gas range may cost somewhat more than an electric model, these durable pieces of cooking equipment will pay the hotel back with energy savings and years of reliable service. Many of the new models of natural gas cooking equipment use an electronic spark ignition rather than a continuously burning **pilot light**, thereby saving as much as 30 percent on energy costs when compared to a unit using a pilot light.

LODGING LANGUAGE

Pilot light: A small permanent flame used to ignite gas at a burner.

Managed properly, natural gas is an extremely safe source of energy. If a hotel is using natural gas equipment of any type, each gas hot water heater, furnace, or other piece of equipment should have a PM program designed specifically to minimize operating costs, ensure safety, and maximize the efficiency of the unit. This is especially important because the combustible nature of natural gas requires that gas leaks be avoided at all times. In addition, the calibration of the oxygen and fuel mixture required to maximize the efficiency of the combustion process must be continually and carefully monitored.

LODGING ONLINE

Gas equipment manufacturers are understandably proud of their products. For more information on gas-operated food service equipment as well as managerial tips and restaurant operations information, go to:

www.cookingforprofit.com/

Do you prefer to cook using a gas or an electric stove? Why?

Water

Aggressively managing a hotel's water consumption is very cost-effective because it pays three ways. Conserving water:

1. Reduces the number of gallons of water purchased
2. Reduces the amount the hotel will pay in sewage (water removal) costs
3. Reduces water-heating costs because less hot water must be produced

Water costs can be dramatically reduced if the maintenance department carefully monitors water usage in all areas of the hotel. Figure 9.6 lists just a few of the activities a hotel can undertake to help reduce water-related costs. Working together, the hotel staff led by the chief engineer should implement every water-saving activity that improves the hotel's bottom line and does not negatively affect guest satisfaction.

Managing Waste

Hotels generate a tremendous amount of solid waste (trash). Sources of waste include packaging materials, such as cardboard boxes, crates, and bags used in shipping hotel

Guest Rooms
- Include inspection of all guest room faucets on the PM checklist
- Inspect toilet flush valves monthly; replace as needed
- Consider installing water-saver showerheads
- Investigate earth–friendly procedures designed to enlist the aid of guests in the water conservation process

Public Space
- Include inspection of all public restroom faucets on the PM checklist
- Install automatic flush valves in men's room urinals
- Where practical, reduce hot water temperatures in public restrooms
- Check pool and spa fill levels and water pump operation daily

Laundry
- Include, as part of the PM program, the monthly inspection of water fittings on all washers
- Pre-soak stained terry and linen rather than double washing
- Use the lowest hot water wash setting possible while still ensuring clean terry and linen

Food Service
- Serve water to diners only on request
- Operate dishwashers only as needed
- Use sprayers, not faucets, to prerinse dishes and flatware intended to be machine-washed
- Use chemical sanitizers rather than excessively hot water to sanitize pots and pans
- Use sprayers (not faucets) to rinse/wash produce prior to cooking or storage

Outdoors
- Inspect sprinkler systems for leaking and misdirected spraying daily
- Utilize the sprinkler system only when critically needed. Do not overwater
- Minimize the use of sprayed water for cleaning (driveway and parking areas, for example); sweep and spot clean these areas as needed

FIGURE 9.6 Sample Water Conservation Techniques

ALL IN A DAY'S WORK 9.2

THE SITUATION

"This doesn't make any sense," said Tamara, the hotel's controller. "Occupancy was about the same this month as it was for the same month last year. But our water bill is 40 percent higher than the same time last year!"

Terrell, the maintenance chief, looked at the bill from the hotel's local water company. "I don't know what's happening either," he said. "For the bill to go up that much, something must really be wrong!"

"I'll say it's wrong," said Jack, the general manager of the hotel. "Terrell," continued Jack, "you've got to find out what's going on here. This leak is really affecting our profits!"

A RESPONSE

Unexpected increases in utility costs are always unwelcome. In this situation, a large increase in water costs indicates either a broken water line on the property, defective equipment that has resulted in excessive water usage (e.g., malfunctioning ice machines or equipment with water-cooled motors), or a large number of small waste areas (such as multiple toilets that are leaking water into their overflow valves).

Of course, it is also possible that the meter measuring the amount of water used by the hotel is defective. In all cases, however, it is the responsibility of the maintenance chief to systematically identify and eliminate these potential sources of wasted water and their effect of "draining" the hotel's profits!

supplies, kitchen garbage, guest room trash, and even yard waste generated from the hotel's landscaping efforts. Increasingly, the hotel industry has come to realize that excessive waste and poorly conceived waste-disposal methods are detrimental to the environment and represent a poor use of natural resources. In addition, as landfills become scarce, the cost of solid waste disposal has risen. Because of this, hotels have encouraged manufacturers that ship products to them to practice **source reduction** and have aggressively implemented creative programs to reduce the generation of their own solid waste.

LODGING LANGUAGE

Source reduction: Efforts by product manufacturers to design and ship products in a way that minimizes packaging waste resulting from the product's shipment to a hotel.

Source reduction involves decreasing the amount of materials and/or energy used during the manufacture or distribution of products and packages. Since it stops waste before it starts, source reduction is the top solid waste priority of the U.S. Environmental Protection Agency.

Source reduction is not the same as recycling. Recycling is collecting already used materials and making them into another product. Recycling begins at the end of a product's life, while source reduction takes place when the product and its packaging are being designed.

One way to think about source reduction and recycling is that they are complementary activities: when combined, source reduction and recycling have a significant impact on preventing solid waste and saving resources. Source reduction conserves raw material and energy resources. Smaller packages and concentrated products, such as detergents and other cleaners, typically use fewer materials and require less energy to transport. In addition, source-reduced cleaning products take up less storage space and are easier to use. Recycling, minimizing waste generation, and wise purchasing can all help reduce waste disposal costs and should be implemented wherever possible.

In addition to improving conservation efforts and controlling costs, effective waste management means keeping inside and outside trash-removal areas clean and, to the greatest degree possible, attractive. This can be achieved by proper sanitation procedures and by enclosing the trash-removal areas with fencing or other eye-appealing materials.

Poorly maintained trash-removal areas are unsightly and can attract insects, rodents, and other scavenging animals. The chief engineer should regularly inspect these areas for PM of fencing or other surrounds and for the quality of sanitation in the trash-removal areas.

Lodging Language

Asset	Restoration	PM (Preventive Maintenance) Program	Incandescent Lamp
Preventive Maintenance	Case Goods	PM Checklist	Electric Discharge Lamp
Routine Maintenance	Chief Engineer	GFI Outlet	Ballast
Emergency Maintenance	Maintenance Chief	Energy Management	CFL
Engineering	Outsource	Calibration	Duct
HVAC	Replace as Needed	Back-up Generator	Air Handler
POM	Total Replacement	Foot-candle	Pilot Light
FF&E Reserve	Work Order		Source Reduction

For Discussion

1. Many chief engineers find that maintaining an older hotel is more challenging than maintaining a newer property. Name five areas in a hotel you think might become more difficult to manage as the hotel ages.
2. Many hotel general managers require the entire maintenance staff to go through extensive guest-service training programs. Why do you think they feel this training is important?
3. For many routine maintenance replacement items, a hotel manager has a choice between doing all of the maintenance at once (such as changing air filters in all guest rooms quarterly) and doing it as needed (such as replacing hot water heater pumps when they stop working). In other cases, such as replacing parking lot light bulbs or fan belts on motors, the manager has a choice between systematic total replacement and a "replace as needed" approach. Assume that you were required to decide on a replacement program for exterior parking lot lights in a hotel with parking for 150 cars. What factors would influence your decision?
4. In some hotels the cleaning of exterior sidewalks and parking areas is the responsibility of housekeeping. In others it is the responsibility of maintenance. Name three factors that would influence which department you would assign to this important task.
5. In most hotels, a representative from the maintenance department must be available 24/7 in case of a hotel emergency. How do you think such employees could be fairly compensated for this responsibility?
6. Lawn care is an example of a maintenance task that can be done in-house or outsourced. Assume that you operate a 135-room hotel with three acres of total lawn and landscape area. Identify three factors that might influence your decision to select an outside lawn care service for your hotel's lawn and landscape work as compared to maintaining it in-house.
7. Maintaining food service equipment often requires specialized skill and replacement parts. Name three factors that you would consider before deciding to outsource the preventive maintenance of such equipment rather than performing it in-house.
8. Water conservation is important in a hotel. List three things you could do as a hotel guest to help conserve water. How do you think hoteliers could inform guests about activities like the ones you listed?
9. Maintenance staff are often highly skilled at specific building-related trades (e.g., plumbing, electricity, carpentry, or HVAC repair). What are some steps a maintenance chief could undertake to ensure that the skills of his or her staff were kept up-to-date?
10. Many hotels have implemented aggressive recycling programs. What factors would influence your decision to begin such a program?

Team Activities

TEAM ACTIVITY 1

For major hotel repairs that cannot be done by in-house staff, some hoteliers prefer to establish a relationship with one prime contractor in each field or trade (e.g., plumbing, heating, and electrical) and then employ that contractor as needed.

Other managers prefer to solicit competitive bids for each major project and then select the best bidder. Identify three advantages and three disadvantages to each approach. Which approach would you suggest at a hotel managed by your team?

TEAM ACTIVITY 2

Maintenance staff members must often enter occupied guest rooms to address rooms-related emergency repairs. The result is often interaction with unhappy guests.

Write a script two team members can present in a role-play format. In the role-play, assume it is a hot summer day, and a maintenance staff member is explaining (correctly) to an unhappy guest that the air-conditioning unit in the room is actually working properly. However, the guest continues to complain that the room is too hot and implores the staff member to make the AC work immediately.

Chapter

10

Food Service and Meeting Management in Limited-Service Hotels

Chapter Outline

Chapter Overview

This chapter addresses the food services and meeting space alternatives traditionally offered by limited-service hotels. The subject is important because it represents a significant difference between limited-service properties and their full-service counterparts. It is also important because the number and quality of food and beverage products offered by limited-service hotel brands continues to expand as these products are used in efforts to gain competitive advantage for the brands.

As you have learned, the term "limited-service" has historically indicated a very restricted availability of food services and meeting spaces. By contrast, the term "full-service" designates properties with the availability of more extensive food services and, often, much larger meeting space. Increasingly, however, there are limited-service hotels with fairly extensive product availability and full-service hotels with fewer offerings.

The range of food services available in the limited-service hotel segment varies widely. Some properties offer deluxe hot breakfast buffets that include made-to-order items. Other hotels offer only the most basic continental breakfast with a menu that includes coffee, juice, bread for toasting and, perhaps, a muffin or bagel.

The physical space allocated for food services likewise can vary from hundreds of square feet (or more) to just several square feet. Some limited-service properties also market their public spaces and food services for holiday parties, family occasions, and other events in direct competition with full-service hotels in the area.

Coordinating an effective limited-service hotel's food service program takes real talent, and managers of limited-service hotels utilize the same basic principles to manage their food service operations as do managers in full-service hotels or any other quantity food-production operation. They must begin by planning the menu, and this, in turn, indicates the menu items needed. These products must be purchased, received, and stored. Serving areas must be set up and maintained during times of guest service, and they must be cleaned at the end of the meal period.

Many guests make their hotel selection decision based upon the availability, variety, and quality of the complimentary food services available to them. As a result, marketing concerns that focus on the wants and needs of present and potential guests are very important factors to consider in the planning and delivery of food services.

In most hotels, some guests will be repeat visitors and will know about the food services offered. Other guests may have visited properties of the same brand and will know something about how food service works at the hotel. Still other guests, however, will have no experience with the brand and its offerings. In these cases, it is important to inform guests fully about details of the lobby food services, including the hours of operation and the types of products available. This can be done when they check in and by means of information provided in guest rooms and in public areas.

Limited-service hotels are often excellent choices for small group meetings. Some properties are planned with this market in mind and space is readily available for small meetings. In other cases, managers must be creative in finding ways to make the limited available space useful for accommodating the needs of small groups. Some properties actively seek out small meetings; others have an ongoing meetings business without the need to do so, and still others are less proactive and just accept the business if it comes to them. Likewise, some properties provide no food services for groups staying in the hotel, others help meeting planners obtain food services from outside sources, and still others offer menus and services on-site to accommodate the group's needs.

Extensive food services and meetings business are relatively new features of the limited-service segment, and the best managerial efforts to market and operate these programs are still evolving. One thing appears certain: many members of the traveling public enjoy the food services and meeting alternatives offered by limited-service properties. In the limited-service market, franchised and independent operators alike will no doubt continue to plan and implement ways to stay competitive by offering consistently high-quality food services and meeting alternatives.

Chapter Objectives

1. To explore the range of breakfast options offered by limited-service hotels.
2. To examine additional (non-breakfast) food and beverage services offered by limited-service hotels.
3. To discuss management concerns important when implementing a high-quality and cost-effective hotel lobby-based food service.
4. To explain to you the importance of informing guests about the availability of lobby food services and providing attractive serving and dining areas for their enjoyment.
5. To review alternatives to manage small group meetings, including the provision of food and beverage services for session attendees.

RANGE OF FOOD SERVICES

Throughout this book, we have referred to limited-service hotels as being lodging properties that do not provide extensive food service options for guests. For example, unlike their full-service hotel counterparts, hotel guests in limited-service properties do not have access to à la carte dining or room service delivered by property employees.

LODGING LANGUAGE

A la carte (menu): A menu that lists its dishes separately and individually priced.

As will be seen later in this chapter, the banquet and meeting facilities offered in limited-service hotels are typically modest in terms of the number of guests that can be accommodated and in the type of food services available to meeting attendees. Another difference is that limited-service managers most often do not market their food services to the general public, while managers in full-service properties frequently rely on local residents to visit their dining rooms.

Some full-service properties also offer off-site food services (most limited-service properties do not), and full-service managers aggressively sell meetings with or without assorted food services and banquets. By contrast, limited-service properties with meeting space may market meetings-only business to small groups and typically offer only minimal food services as part of the hotel meeting packages sold.

Historically, full-service hotels offered food services in dining rooms adjacent to or near their lobby areas. Some, especially very large hotels with **atriums** or other large, open lobby areas, may offer à la carte dining in public spaces that are not in separate rooms. Large full-service hotels may also have small retail areas selling coffee, pastries, and sandwiches and even bars dispensing alcoholic beverages in lobby areas.

LODGING LANGUAGE

Atrium: A large, open central space used by some hotels for registration, lobby, retail sales, and food services, among other purposes.

In contrast to full-service hotels, limited-service properties typically offer breakfast and do so in their relatively small lobby/dining areas. Some may offer alcoholic beverages and additional foods items in these same areas later in the day.

Many limited-service properties offer creatively designed multi-purpose spaces with attractive tables and chairs that can be used for food consumption at many times and for many purposes. In most cases, a small kitchen will be located adjacent to the public area, and service counters, storage cabinets, and other space and equipment used for food services are designed to attractively blend into the lobby environment.

Since food services in these properties are most typically offered in the lobby, a new term, **lobby food services**, has come into use in the lodging industry.

LODGING LANGUAGE

Lobby food services: Food services offered in a limited-service hotel's atrium or lobby area.

Figure 10.1 reviews the most common types of food services offered by limited- and full-service hotels. Over time, and with the evolution of lobby food services, the distinction between very minimal food service (in limited-service properties) and very extensive food services (in full-service hotels) is becoming blurred. The reason for this is that both types of hotels are attempting to determine exactly what their guests want and to find ways to cost-effectively meet their guests' expectations.

Breakfast Alternatives

When most people think about food services in limited-service hotels, they think about breakfast, because food and beverages items available during the early morning (breakfast) hours are most commonly offered by these properties. Actually, some limited-service hotels offer other types of food and beverage services, and these will be examined in the next section of the chapter.

Factor	Type of Hotel	
	Limited-Service	**Full-Service**
À la carte dining available	No	Yes
Room service available	No	Sometimes
Banquet capabilities	Modest, if any	Yes
Alcoholic beverages available	Sometimes	Usually
Off-site food services available	No	Sometimes
Offer meetings with limited food services	Sometimes	Yes
Offer meetings with extensive food services	No	Yes
Markets food services to general public	No	Yes
Locations of food services (Dining)	Usually in lobby	Dedicated area(s) in property
Food preparation/storage areas	Minimal	Extensive
Payment for consumed food	Included in room rate	Charges in addition to room rate

FIGURE 10.1 Food Service in Limited- and Full-Service Hotels

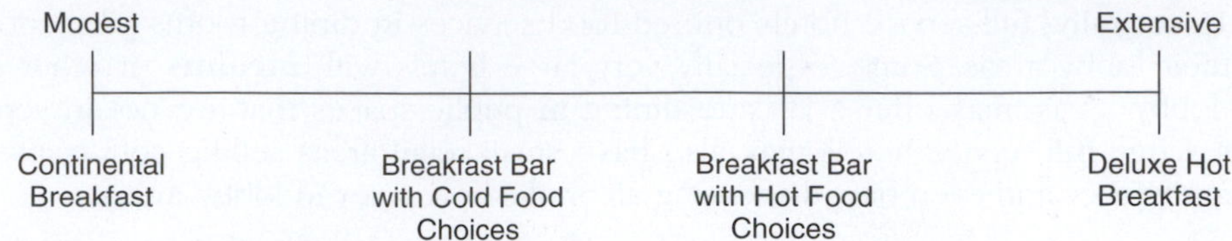

FIGURE 10.2 Range of Breakfast Food Services in Limited-Service Hotels

The range of breakfast alternatives typically offered by limited-service hotels is illustrated in Figure 10.2.

Some properties offer their guests only a very limited **continental breakfast**.

LODGING LANGUAGE

Continental Breakfast: A simple breakfast consisting of fruit juice or fruit, coffee, and toast or a pastry.

The simplest continental breakfast requires no cooking equipment and very little preparation, storage or service space. A simple coffee maker and supplies (disposable cups, napkins, stir sticks, sugar/cream), a pitcher or individual portions of juice (or juice dispenser), a simple bread item with butter and, perhaps, jelly or a pastry (doughnut or sweet roll purchased from a supplier) illustrate the requirements for a limited continental breakfast with very few guest choices.

WHAT'S IN A NAME?

While the term "limited-service" is widely used to represent the segment of the lodging industry without extensive food service capabilities, many owners and managers of properties in this segment do not like the name. They point out that their service to guests is not limited in regard to guest registration, room accommodations, cleanliness, safety, or other non-food-service amenities and is, in reality, equal to that of their full-service peers. Many of these owners prefer the term "select service" to indicate the "selected" but high-quality services they do offer.

The need for hotels of every size or category to consistently deliver service levels meeting the expectations of their guests is standard throughout the industry. In this context, then, limited-service properties actually provide "selected-full-service" to guests who do not require or desire extensive on-site food, beverage, or meetings options.

Hotels often elect to serve a Continental breakfast because of the reduced amount of preparation time and storage space needed to do so.

Some hotel properties enhance their continental breakfast offerings with additional cold food choices. These might, for example, include an expanded selection of juices and several types of breads, rolls, and pastries along with coffee and milk. Other items (i.e., yogurts, fresh fruits, and assorted breakfast cereals) might also be made available.

A breakfast bar with hot food choices expands the variety of menu items available to guests even further. Perhaps, for example, a toaster is available for bread, bagels, and prepared waffles and/or a waffle maker with pre-portioned batter is available in individual portion cups. Note that Figure 10.2 indicates some limited-service properties offer a **deluxe hot breakfast** with numerous food offerings. For example, there may be a buffet to allow guests to self-serve eggs (perhaps several styles), bacon, sausage, ham, potatoes, and other items that are prepared on-site in a small kitchen. In other properties, guests order desired items that have been prepared in advance or, alternatively, are prepared to order. In relatively few properties, a limited table service breakfast is available.

LODGING LANGUAGE

Deluxe Hot Breakfast: A breakfast with hot food choices offered by a limited-service hotel.

As the complexity of the breakfast food services increases, so does the amount of storage, equipment, preparation and service space, number of labor hours required, and skill levels of food service employees. In addition, associated operating expenses can rise dramatically. The decision about the type of food services to offer is critical and is an important part of the package marketed to prospective guests. Consider, for example, a new property being built or an existing facility being renovated. The space and equipment needed to offer a modest continental or a deluxe hot breakfast are vastly different. Including this space if it will not be used or excluding space that will later be required has significant financial consequences. As well, guests looking for value in their room rate will make personal decisions about the worth of the breakfast option they are paying for. It is important to design food service needs into the property at the time it is constructed or when major renovations are undertaken.

Other Food Services

In addition to the breakfasts offered, an increasing number of limited-service hotels offer their guests added food and beverage options. These can include:

All-day hot beverage service. Brewed coffee and hot water for tea along with required supplies may be available at a "help-yourself" beverage station in the lobby 24 hours per day.

Alcoholic beverages and snacks: During a defined time period (e.g., from 5:00 p.m. to 6:30 p.m.) a hotel may invite its guests to a special **manager's reception**. This event is typically held in the lobby or breakfast area of a limited-service hotel. It will be hosted by one or more hotel managers. In addition to wines and beers, the hotel may offer cocktails and complimentary foods, including appetizers, snacks, and **finger foods**. This event originated to provide opportunities for management staff to greet guests. In some properties, however, only the hotel staff person responsible for serving the complimentary foods and beverages hosts the reception.

LODGING LANGUAGE

Manager's reception: A time, usually during the late afternoon/early evening, when complimentary foods and beverages are offered to guests of limited-service properties.

Finger foods: Small sandwiches, salty snacks, sliced vegetables, cubed cheese, and other foods that do not require flatware or other service items for guest consumption.

Meetings-related food services. Some limited-service properties have meeting spaces available for small groups. These properties may offer food and beverage services ranging from simple coffee breaks to entire meals.

LODGING ONLINE

The food and beverage services offered by franchised hotels vary greatly. Homewood Suites, one of the Hilton Hotels brands, offers its guests a deluxe hot breakfast, dinner, and alcoholic beverages on a daily basis. To see more about its extensive complimentary food program, go to:

http://homewoodsuites.com/

When you arrive, click "At Every Homewood Suites" then click "Breakfast and Reception."

Why do you think guests would be attracted to a limited-service all-suites hotel chain offering a complimentary evening dinner reception?

Special-event food services. Some limited-service properties with adequate food preparation and service space market their facilities for small private parties, such as wedding receptions and anniversaries, and for public events, such as New Year's Eve or Mardi gras parties. Just as at their full-service hotel counterparts, these public events are often packaged with a guest room rental.

MANAGEMENT OF LOBBY FOOD SERVICES

Figure 10.3 outlines the process managers use to plan and deliver breakfast in a limited-service hotel.

Examination of the process begins with a close look at Step 1: Menu Planning.

Menu Planning

What items should be offered on the breakfast menu? Several critical factors must be addressed, and Figure 10.4 lists those factors.

Owners and managers of independent hotels can make their own decisions about what to offer to guests. Corporate hotels (those owned by a multi-unit hotel organization) and franchised properties typically impose limitations on planners. In chain hotels, menus are planned to meet brand standards that incorporate the expectations of guests who visit different properties in the chain.

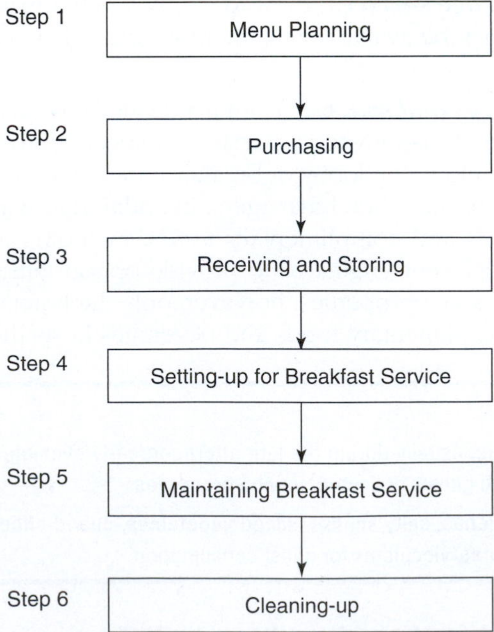

FIGURE 10.3 Managing Breakfast Operations in a Limited-Service Hotel

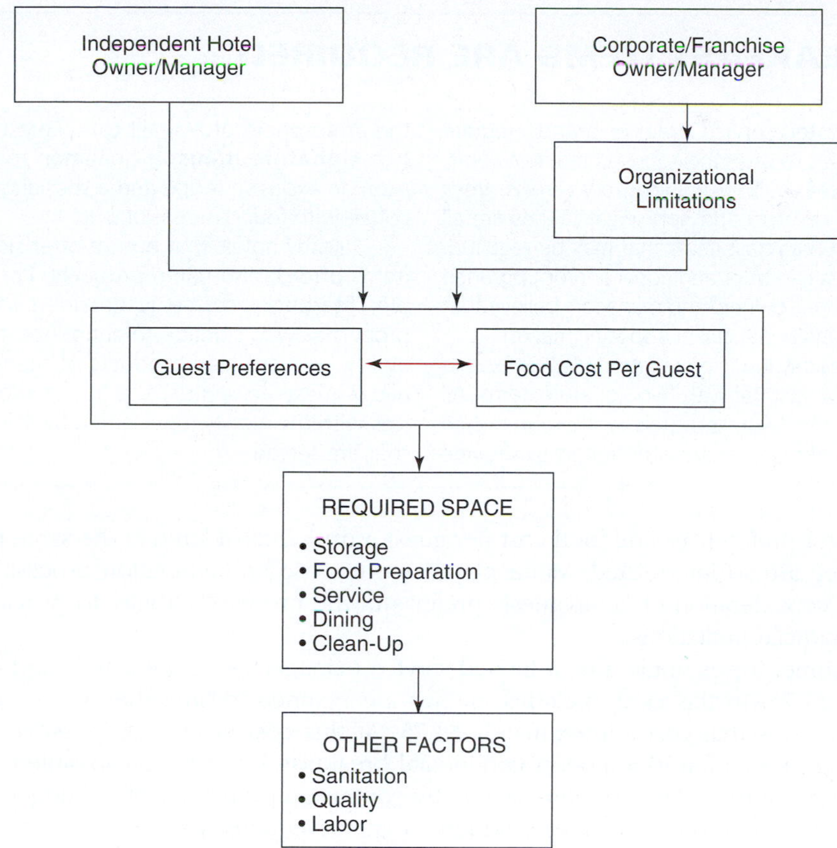

FIGURE 10.4 Menu Planning Factors for Managers of Limited-Service Hotels

Standards may also be established to specify the exact item served, for example, yogurt, fresh orange juice, or cinnamon rolls, and even specific brands of items. In the United States, for example, this could include brands such as Kellogg breakfast cereals or Smucker's jams. Specifying product brand with high levels of name recognition and guest perceptions of quality will reflect positively on the hotel.

Corporate- and franchise-affiliated properties will also mandate the number of hours of breakfast operation, and this, in turn, will impact the equipment and staffing required to provide quality service and products.

Remember when it comes to food service; "It all starts with the menu."

LODGING LANGUAGE

Signature item: Food or beverage products produced by a hospitality operation that are unique to the property and that the general public associates with it.

A franchise company representative will review the hotel's food services operation during inspection visits. Compliance with required standards, cleanliness, and overall attractiveness of the serving and dining areas are all important aspects of the property's evaluation by its franchisor.

As shown in Figure 10.4, two important factors managers must consider when planning breakfast menus are guest preferences and **food cost per guest**.

LODGING LANGUAGE

Food Cost Per Guest (limited-service hotels): The average amount expended for breakfast for each guest served. Food Cost per Guest is calculated as: Total Breakfast Food Cost (÷) Number of Guests Served = Food Cost Per Guest.

BREAKFAST ITEMS ARE REQUIRED

Most limited-service lodging brands require their hotels to offer their guests breakfast items. Coffee, tea, milk, fruit juices, dry cereals, fresh fruits, and sweet and non-sweet breads are all common breakfast items that may be required. Properties can offer additional and/or upgraded items if their owners and managers believe that they will be beneficial in a specific market.

Holiday Inn Express introduced its Express Start Breakfast Bar with two signature items. All Holiday Inn Express hotels were required to have breakfast bar areas designed to provide the atmosphere of a small café. Guests enjoy two **signature items**: a cinnamon roll made from an exclusive recipe and a special gourmet coffee with four different blends.

Many hotels that do not offer signature items offer brand-name products. For example, Starbucks coffee is provided in many properties with signage to announce its availability, and branded products of many types allow guests to identify the hotel's food services with the quality represented by the brands that are served.

Guest preferences and food cost per guest must be considered at the same time because they are so interrelated. Menu planners often use an elimination process that involves a consideration of items guests prefer and the property's ability to provide them within financial limitations.

Assume, for example, that a limited-service manager has a budgeted food cost per guest of $1.75. In this case, breakfast menus are planned to limit the average guest to breakfast items that cost approximately $1.75. At this cost, it may be possible to offer something in addition to a modest continental breakfast, but it is not possible to offer a wide variety of expensive breakfast items. By contrast, a property with a budget of $3.50 per guest is able to offer additional and more expensive items without exceeding its food cost per guest goal. In both cases, the food cost per guest must be considered when calculating room rates to be charged. This is because, while breakfast costs may be complementary to guests, the charges must be borne by the hotel.

Limited-service properties utilizing an **accrual accounting system** calculate breakfast food costs for a fiscal period (typically one month) as follows:

Beginning Inventory of food items
+ Purchases of food items
− Ending Inventory of food items
Food Cost

LODGING LANGUAGE

Accrual Accounting System: An accounting system that matches expenses incurred with revenues generated. In an accrual system, revenue is considered to be earned when products/services are provided, not when money paid for them is received. Expenses are incurred when products, labor, and other costs are expended to generate revenue, not when the expenses are paid.

BREAKFAST COST PER WHAT?

Food cost per guest is one popular way to compute the cost of providing a complimentary breakfast, but there are other ways. Some hoteliers prefer to compute their food cost per occupied room. The formula for food cost per occupied room is similar to the one for food cost per guest. It is calculated as:

Total Breakfast Food Cost ÷ Number of Occupied Rooms = Food Cost Per Occupied Room

The advantage of this method is that keeping count of the number of guests actually consuming breakfasts is not required because it is the number of rooms occupied, not guests served, that is critical to the computation.

Properties using a **cash accounting system** to determine the cost of food consider the amount of money paid during the fiscal period (usually one month) for food, supplies, and related breakfast items.

LODGING LANGUAGE

Cash Accounting System: An accounting system that considers revenue to be earned when it is received and expenses to be incurred when they are paid.

Figure 10.5 indicates that the space needed for storage, food preparation, and dining is another important consideration when menus are planned. New construction that incorporates the space needed for a limited food service operation allows for an ideal design in terms of location within the hotel and the required square footage. By contrast, existing properties that were not designed for extensive breakfast service can face significant challenges. Depending upon the type of breakfast offered, the amount of space required for food storage, preparation, and clean-up can be equal to, if not greater than, the amount of space required for the guest serving area. Additional space is also needed for guest seating and can range from "anywhere there is room for a table and chairs" to well-thought-out, functional, and attractive lobby spaces.

Limited-service properties designed for small business meetings may have a separate room that is used for breakfast service and then becomes available for meeting space after breakfast clean-up is completed. Still other properties use lobby space for service and dining, with an adjacent room that can be used for overflow breakfast service (if the space is not reserved for a meeting) and for meetings held after breakfast service has ended.

Figure 10.5 indicates that still other factors must be considered in planning menus for limited-service hotel breakfasts. For example, sanitation concerns are critical. Equipment is required to keep perishable items such as dairy products at the proper temperature before use and during service. Reusable pitchers, trays, tongs, and other items must be properly washed, rinsed, and sanitized between uses. Refuse from food preparation and after guest use must be quickly removed from the lobby area and properly maintained until it can be disposed of.

SANITATION ESSENTIALS

Foodservice managers have many responsibilities. They hire and train staff, decide what should be on the menu, cost recipes, buy food, and evaluate the effectiveness of their kitchens. All of those jobs are important, but none is *more* important than protecting the health of their guests and employees by serving only food that is safe to eat. It is easy to *say* that kitchen managers must make sure that no one is harmed from eating food made in their kitchens, but every year tens of thousands of cases of food-borne illness are reported. A food-borne illness is a sickness caused by eating food that has been contaminated by germs, chemicals, or physical hazards like glass or metal shavings.

One of the best defenses against food-borne illnesses is the storing of foods at the proper temperature. Recommended temperatures for storing food products are:

- ✓ Refrigerated food storage: 41°F (5°C) or below
- ✓ Frozen food storage: 0°F (-18°C) or below
- ✓ Dry storage foods: 50°F–70°F (10°–21°C)

Germs that are harmful to foods grow best in what foodservice managers call the "Temperature Danger Zone." The temperature danger zone is the temperature range of 41°F–135°F (5°C– 57°C). Professional foodservice managers make every effort to minimize the time potentially hazardous foods are in this temperature range. The total time that foods are exposed to the temperatures in the danger zone (including receiving, storing, preparation, production, and holding) should be less than four hours. An important caution is that the four hours include the time before products reach the hotel's kitchens; and that is why it is important to purchase products only from professional food suppliers.

WHY SO MUCH STORAGE SPACE?

Much less storage space is required for limited-service hotel breakfast operations than for three-meal-a-day à la carte food preparation in a full-service restaurant. Nonetheless, there must be space for refrigerated storage (of milk, butter, and other dairy products), for frozen storage (if frozen juices, waffles, and/or other bread/pastry products are used), and dry storage. Cases of disposable plates, flatware, cups and glasses, napkins, and related items are very bulky. Space may be needed for a coffee maker, small ice bin, sink (many local health departments require a water source in any food preparation area, and this is a good idea even if it is not required), and for storage of serving items such as pitchers, toasters, and serving trays that cannot remain in the lobby. In some cases, lockable storage is provided above or below attractive serving counters that have been built into the breakfast area.

Product quality is another important factor to consider when menus are planned. Earlier in the chapter, we noted that many products are purchased on a brand-name basis to help ensure quality. Items such as fresh fruits, baked goods, and other non-branded items must also be purchased from reputable suppliers.

Labor is another factor that cannot be forgotten even when little or no food preparation is required. It is typically easy to recruit and select applicants for breakfast attendant positions because little or no experience and only minimal culinary skills are required for these jobs. Some applicants may desire a part-time job during the early morning hours so that the rest of their day is free for personal use. Many properties utilize a part-time employee specifically for breakfast service duties. Others combine tasks so that a staff member can be used as a food service worker in the morning and then complete a shift in another department.

In very small properties, the night auditor or front desk clerk may set up the food service. A food service attendant may then arrive to maintain the serving area and to clean up after service concludes. Regardless of the staffing plan, however, food service attendants must be responsible, have a positive guest focus, be able to work quickly, and be able to perform many tasks at the same time.

In a limited-service property, the responsibility for menu planning typically rests with the general manager, who must attempt to meet franchisor standards, please guests, and stay within the budget. It is important to recognize that the availability of complimentary breakfast is a significant factor in the hotel selection decision of many guests. The menu planner must earnestly attempt to determine what the guests prefer, and do not prefer, as part of the ongoing process of menu evaluation and improvement. Despite the fact that franchise brands and their breakfast requirements are national or even international, the food preferences of many guests are regional, and these guest preferences must be addressed when deciding what to offer on the breakfast menu.

Purchasing

After the menu is planned, the items required will be known and can be purchased. Limited-service properties that are part of a multi-unit organization may pool their purchase needs by using a **centralized purchasing** system. For example, assume that independent hotel owners or franchisees with several properties in the same area offer the same or, at least, many of the same menu items on their breakfast menus. These owners can combine the purchase needs for all the properties and than select a supplier to provide all the participating hotels with dairy or food products or disposable supplies for a specified time period such as six months. Savings can result because suppliers frequently quote a lower price per case or unit as the number of units ordered increases.

LODGING LANGUAGE

Centralized purchasing: A purchasing system in which participating properties develop common purchase requirements and combine purchase quantities. Suppliers frequently lower the price per purchase unit (per pound or per gallon, for example) as the quantities of items to be purchased increase.

LODGING ONLINE

Food, beverage, and supply products needed for food services in limited-service hotels can be purchased from large commercial warehouses. To learn how one food service distributor can help with the purchasing task, go to:

www.gfs.com/en

When you arrive at this site, click "GFS market place stores" to see a list of the customer types buying from this company.

Why do you think hotel managers like to purchase wholesale foods in retail settings?

Other hotel managers do not purchase from wholesale suppliers. Instead, they purchase from large retail stores that sell products in large "commercial" sizes and/or from food wholesalers with retail outlets. For example, Gordon's Food Service (GFS) is a very large supplier of food and other products to hotels, restaurants, and institutional purchasers in several Midwestern states. It also has retail outlets offering products sold in bulk to customers coming into their stores.

Managers must determine what quantity of food and supplies should be purchased. To do so, limited-service properties can utilize a **par inventory system** to help manage the purchase of many required items.

LODGING LANGUAGE

Par inventory system: A system of managing purchasing and inventory levels based upon the requirement that a specified quantity of product be available in inventory. For example, if a par of five cases of disposable coffee cups is established, the quantity necessary to bring the inventory level back to five cases is ordered whenever coffee cups are purchased.

Extremely perishable products such as fresh breads and pastries must typically be ordered daily. Other items such as dairy products and fresh fruits may be ordered several times weekly. Still other items such as dry cereals and frozen products may be ordered several times monthly depending upon the amount of available inventory space and the amount of money the manager is willing to commit to inventory. This, in turn, relates to the per purchase unit savings to be realized from purchasing in a larger quantity than needed for immediate use.

Par inventory systems do not work well for perishable foods. Items such as fresh pastries and dairy products are typically purchased in quantities that relate more to forecasted occupancy levels than to par levels. This is so because more of these products are purchased as more rooms are sold, and fewer should be purchased when fewer guests will be in the hotel.

Managers are often confronted with two purchasing challenges regarding the correct amount of food to order. First, low sales forecasts may turn into a busy breakfast if many reservations with short booking times and/or walk-in guests arrive. At times like these, it may be necessary for hotel staff to purchase products from a local retail or wholesale outlet at a higher-than-planned price. Second, it can be difficult to know the guests' selection preferences, and these can change on an almost daily basis. For example, if numerous guest rooms have been reserved for the use of junior sports teams during a specific weekend, more sweet cereals and pastries may be consumed and must be available because younger breakfast eaters may prefer these items.

As food usage rates relative to occupancy levels are analyzed, managers can begin to accurately determine par quantities and the amount to be purchased on a regular basis. Doing so is necessary to control food costs. Money that is wasted when products must be discarded does not benefit the guests or the property. Money saved through effective purchasing and food handling is available to purchase more or better-quality products and, at the same time, provide guests with a better breakfast value. This, in turn, can yield a competitive marketing edge for the property.

Receiving and Storing

After products are purchased, the **receiving** and storing processes become important. If a manager purchases products at a retail or wholesale outlet, there are few, if any, concerns about receiving. What has been purchased can simply be transported to the hotel and put in storage. However, if suppliers deliver products to the hotel, special procedures are in order.

LODGING LANGUAGE

Receiving (food service): The point at which ownership of products being purchased transfers from the seller (supplier) to the hospitality operation.

Often there will not be a food services employee available when orders are delivered. In such cases, other arrangements for receiving must be made. Should receiving be done by the front office attendant (who may be busy) or by the general manager (who may be unavailable)? Each property must address this question with the approach that is best for it. In all instances, however, the employee who does the receiving should be properly trained to do at least four things:

1. Confirm by counting and reading labels that the correct items and quantity of each item noted on the **delivery invoice** were ordered and have been delivered to the hotel.
2. Sign the delivery invoice.
3. Move products that have been received into the appropriate storage area.
4. Retain the signed delivery invoice, and route it to the individual with accounting/bookkeeping responsibilities.

LODGING LANGUAGE

Delivery invoice: A statement from the supplier that accompanies product delivery and provides information to establish the amount of money due to the supplier. This information includes name of product, quantity, and price, and must be signed by a hotel representative to confirm that the products were delivered.

Many of the products that are received will be expensive and could be prone to theft. Many will also be susceptible to quality deterioration or spoilage. Therefore, it is important that products be quickly moved to their proper locked storage areas. If an inventory par level is being maintained, it will be necessary for someone to update inventory records with the quantities of incoming products.

Setting Up Breakfast Service

A significant amount of effort is required to prepare for even a relatively simple breakfast for hotel guests. It is very unlikely that all, or even most, of the hotel's guests will want to have breakfast at the moment service begins. In fact, there may be only a very few guests present at the beginning of service. However, the first guest should be able to select from the full variety of foods that will be available to those having breakfast later in the morning. In other words, all the food items to be offered should be available when the service begins. It is not appropriate to get the coffee ready and then begin preparing breakfast service for later-arriving guests. Hotel managers must carefully consider how long it takes to prepare for breakfast service, determine the most reasonable start and end times for service based upon guest desires, and then schedule labor accordingly.

Hotels offering breakfast will require the efforts of one or more food service attendants to prepare and maintain the breakfast service. The performance of a food service attendant is affected by at least three factors under the hotel manager's control:

Proper Training. Training is just as important for a food service attendant as for any other hotel employee. Training should include such matters as where food and

WHO ATE THE DOUGHNUTS?

Doughnuts and other fresh pastries are delivered daily to many limited-service hotel properties for breakfast use. They may arrive before the food service attendant begins the work shift. Hopefully, these items will be properly received by the food service attendant, front office staff, night auditor, or other responsible employee and will then be quickly moved into a secure storage area. If this does not happen, the opportunity for employees and other non-guests to consume a free breakfast is obvious.

Less-than-careful managers may have the philosophy that "Who cares about a few doughnuts?" In fact, the manager should care a great deal! Why? If each doughnut costs 25 cents and 10 doughnuts are consumed inappropriately each day, a property with a 10 percent bottom line (net income before taxes) must generate $25 each day to yield the $2.50 profit required to purchase the doughnuts.

(10 doughnuts @ $0.25 = $2.50 ÷ .10 profit = $25.00 in revenue)

If this consumption continued each day, the hotel would require revenues of $9,125 each year ($25 per-day × 365 days per-year) just to pay for these unaccounted-for doughnuts. To continue with our example, if the property's ADR was $65, it would need to rent 140 rooms ($9,125 revenue ÷ $65.00 ADR = 140 rooms) just to compensate for the doughnut costs that would otherwise not need to be purchased.

No hotel, or any other business, can afford to throw away more than $9,000 revenue annually on wasted expenses. In fact, doughnut expense and every other expense can add up quickly in the hotel business, where the details are very important.

supply items are located, how to operate coffee machines and other equipment, and where refuse should be placed as waste receptacles become filled.

Development of a Work Task Checklist. Just as cooks need recipes, food service attendants can use a "recipe" or checklist that indicates the tasks to be done as breakfast is readied for service, as guests are served, and as clean-up activities are undertaken. The sequence in which tasks are to be done should be clearly specified.

Serving Diagram. A graphic illustrating "what goes where" can be very helpful in the efficient set-up of a serving area. Figure 10.5 illustrates a sample lobby food services set-up of the type that can be used to train new food service attendants and remind experienced personnel about the proper location of menu items on serving lines.

Maintaining Breakfast Service

Ongoing work will be necessary to replenish the breakfast area and keep it clean and sanitary during service. An efficiently designed storage area and serving kitchen are an important first step in the process of speeding the flow of work in the area and reducing the attendant's travel time between the area and the serving line. The attendant must be able to anticipate when items must be replenished. In addition, some limited-service hotels offer hot beverages 24 hours daily; hopefully, the coffee service station is in a location convenient for breakfast service and for those using the lobby for other purposes during the remainder of the day.

Serving areas must be kept tidy, and spills must be cleaned up immediately and correctly. These tasks can be very difficult when, for example, there are many guests, including families with young children, who are prone to have spills, enjoying the lobby food services at the same time.

Cleaning Up

Clean-up tasks can sometimes begin before breakfast service is completed. For example, equipment and preparation tables in the storage area/serving kitchen can be cleaned as the number of guests being served decreases, and dining tables not in use can be cleaned as well. However, recall our earlier observation about the first guests having access to all of the same meal components as those enjoying breakfast later. The reverse is

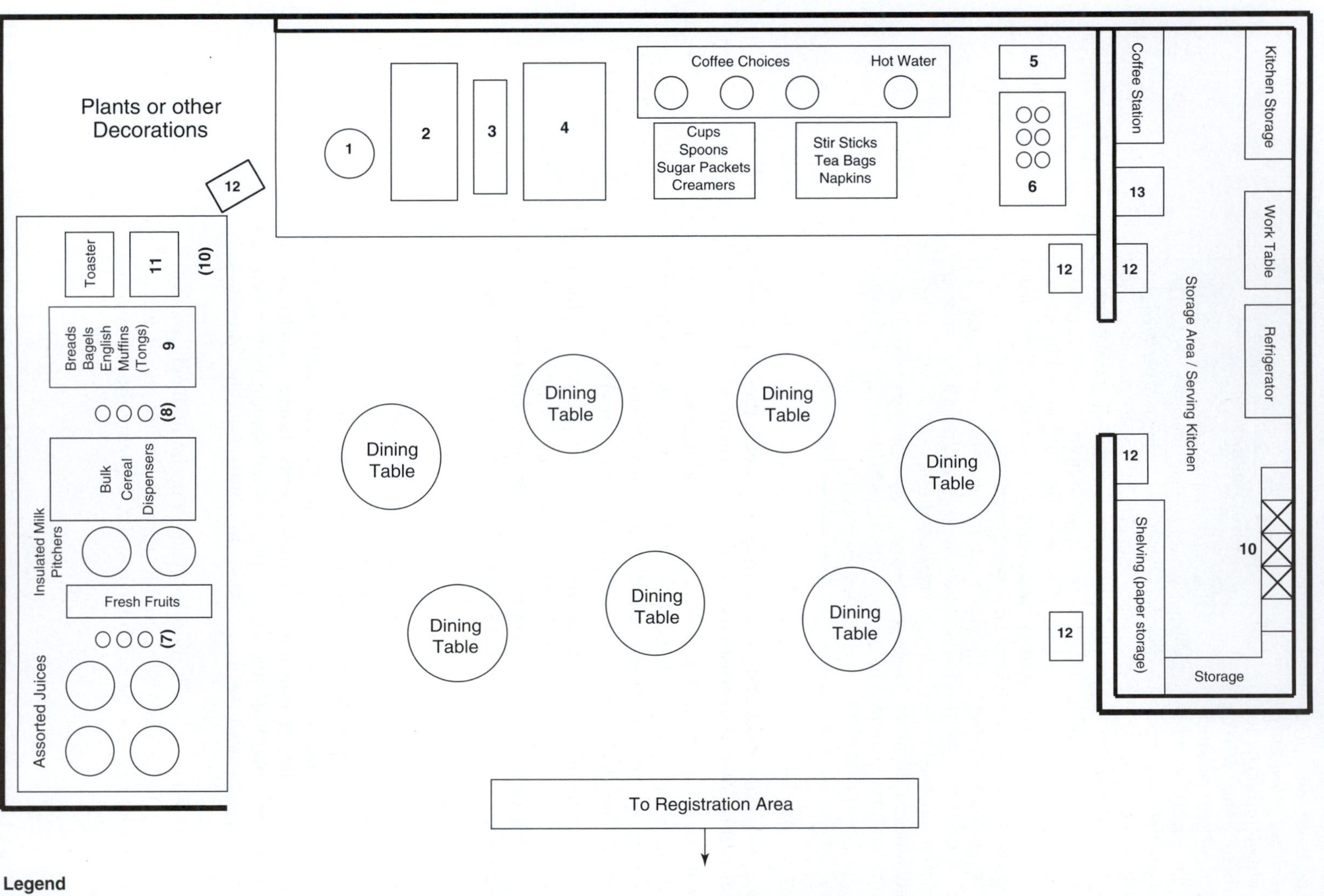

FIGURE 10.5 Sample Layout of Lobby Food Services Showing Placement of Menu Items

WHAT ABOUT FOOD SERVICE TRAYS?

Some guests prefer to pick up breakfast items from the food service area and take them to their rooms. The number of such guests may increase when there is no available dining space. It seems logical, therefore, for hotel managers to anticipate a need for food service trays to accommodate these guests.

However, some managers believe that the availability of trays encourages excess food consumption, waste, and removal from the property for later consumption. These properties may not make food service trays available.

A third group of hotel managers recognize the need to please the guests and also the problems just noted. Their solution: Have trays available but out of sight in case a guest requests one during a slow time and make them readily available during busy serving periods.

There is no easy way to decide on the approach that will please guests the most and at the same time be cost-effective. While it is likely that some guests will take advantage of the property, the vast majority of them will not. Unfortunately, excessive costs must be spread among all guests, and managers have the responsibility to do their best to minimize these costs.

LODGING ONLINE

To learn about coffee-brewing, food-serving, and other equipment useful in serving breakfasts in limited-service hotels, go to:

www.aaacommercialproducts.com/

How important do you think display cases are for the attractive presentation of food?

LODGING GOES GREEN!

The National Restaurant Association (NRA) is an example of a good information source for hoteliers seeking to implement energy conservation and sustainability actions in the area of hotel food and beverage services. The American Culinary Federation (ACF) and the American Dietetics Association (ADA) are additional associations specializing in food services. Hoteliers who are concerned about the impact on the environment of their food operations can check the Web sites of these and other food industry associations regularly for "green" operating tips.

For those hoteliers operating food programs in limited-service hotels, the following green practices (commonly utilized by restaurateurs) can make a significant and positive impact on hotel profits and the environment.

1. **Recycle:** Paper, cardboard, plastics, glass, and aluminum are all common packaging or food preparation materials that that are easily recyclable. Recycling helps save the environment and reduces a hotel's waste disposal costs.
2. **Turn It Off:** Turning off unnecessary interior and exterior lighting, computers, POS systems, refrigerated display cases, hood vents, and coffee machines on a regular schedule saves money and energy. Adding motion detectors to decrease lighting costs in little used food and beverage storage areas can save even more.
3. **Clean It Up:** When food service equipment is properly maintained, its operating costs are reduced. Regularly remove dust from compressors, oil and calibrate equipment, and frequently check refrigeration and cooking equipment for tightness of seals and gaskets. The result is less energy usage, longer equipment life, and a reduced carbon footprint.
4. **Buy Local:** Buying as many food and beverage products as possible from local farmers and processors reduces packaging and shipping costs, enhances the freshness of products served to guests, and helps support the local economy.
5. **Teach and Train:** Inform and train food service employees about all of the energy savings and conservation efforts undertaken by the hotel. Informed employees will want to participate in sustainability efforts when they know exactly what they are expected to do.

NEVER FORGET ABOUT SANITATION!

It is easy to think about the need to consistently use food-handling practices that incorporate sanitation concerns when one works with potentially hazardous foods, such as meats, seafood, and other items that we associate with food-borne illness. However, sanitation is just as important when handling any food products, including those typically available in a limited-service hotel's breakfast offering. It should be obvious that food service attendants should not cough or sneeze around food, handle food products with their bare hands, and touch any food (including foods in individual containers) after handling garbage.

Should the hotel manager assume that staff members employed for these positions know and consistently practice effective food-handling procedures? No! Does the manager have the responsibility to incorporate sanitation information into the training that is provided? Yes! Fortunately, there is excellent information on sanitation training available from the National Restaurant Association and the Educational Institute of the American Hotel & Motel Association. Local health departments may also have information or training programs available. Sanitation training should be incorporated into activities designed to prepare food service attendants for their work. As well, hotel managers should observe the work of food service attendants to make sure that these important procedures are consistently practiced.

also true. The last person enjoying breakfast should have access to the same items as those dining earlier. Clean-up activities, therefore, should not focus on "tearing down" the serving line until a designated time and then only after a **last-call** has been made to guests in the dining area.

LODGING LANGUAGE

Last-call: Notice given to guests that service will end at a specified time. For example, guests in a hotel bar may be notified 20 minutes before closing time that last drink orders must be placed, and guests in a lobby breakfast service may be informed that service will end in 10 minutes.

Removing all food items to their proper storage areas and disposing of items that cannot be reused, such as fresh pastries, frozen waffles (which will have thawed), and coffee cream in serving pitchers, if used, are important tasks. Serving equipment and food/beverage items and supplies should be placed under lock as part of clean-up and closing duties. Clean-up of the equipment, preparation and storage areas, food serving counters, and lobby tables/chairs are among the tasks that are the responsibility of food service attendants in many limited-service properties. In well-managed properties the job descriptions for these employees will specify what other duties, if any, are among their responsibilities; such as cleaning floors and removing food service trash.

LODGING ONLINE

Most limited-service hotels use disposable serviceware because they find this more cost-effective than utilizing reusable items. Dixie is one of the industry's largest suppliers of such products. To learn more about this company, go to:

www.dixie.com/

What concerns might you have about the environment as you select disposable service ware used in your breakfast program?

ALL IN A DAY'S WORK 10.1

THE SITUATION

"I wish our manager was here every time guests complain about our complimentary breakfast," said Caesar, a front office clerk at the Seaside Inn Lodge. He was talking to his friend Romaro, a housekeeper at the 65-room limited-service hotel.

"Lots of guests complain to me," said Caesar, "and I've seen guest comment cards with the same complaints. I know our manager is aware of the problems because I talked to him several times. I guess he is concerned about it, but all he talks about is cost, cost, cost! His idea is to provide large quantities of cheap food."

"Yes, I guess there is a problem," said Romaro, "But, after all, the food is free, and there is plenty of it. I think our prices are lower than some of the other hotels in the area, and if I were the boss, I would do the same thing: try to offer plenty of food as the way to keep guests coming back."

"I don't know," said Caesar, "If I were the boss, I think I would raise the room rate by one or two dollars and put all of that extra money into buying better-quality food."

A RESPONSE

Many guests select a limited-service property, in part, because of the complimentary food services it offers. Guests want to enjoy this amenity, and it is an essential factor in their assessment of value. Simply serving lots of food that guests do not enjoy (the manager's tactic) and charging guests more as the first step in improving food services (Caesar's suggestion) are both likely to be ineffective tactics.

The manager and his staff can determine what guests like and do not like about the food services program. They can do that by observing guests during the serving period and by talking with them. They can carefully analyze guest comment cards or other feedback systems. If they spend less to purchase what guests don't want and spend more to purchase what guests do like, it may be possible to better satisfy guests without the need to raise prices.

MANAGEMENT OF ADDITIONAL FOODSERVICES

Breakfast is the one food service option common to nearly all limited-service hotels. Some limited-service properties offer more options. In most cases, these additional services can be classified as one of the following:

Manager's Reception

Complimentary Dinner

Meetings and Special Events

Because of their importance, each of these expanded options will be examined for its impact on guests and challenges for management.

Manager's Receptions

Many limited-service hotels, and some full-service hotels, offer their guests alcoholic beverages at a hosted manager's reception. These events typically have very defined start and stop times. For example, a hotel may offer its manager's reception from 5:00 p.m. to 7:00 p.m. During these times, complimentary drinks and, in some cases, light snacks or appetizers are typically served.

Manager's receptions are popular with guests but can lead to challenges related to the responsible service of alcohol. This is so because at some manager's receptions alcoholic beverage products are offered on a "serve yourself" basis. When this is the case, the potential for a guests' over-consumption of alcohol can be real.

It is important for hotel managers to recognize that, due to **third-party liability** (dram shop) legislation, hotels can be held responsible for the amount of alcohol served to guests even in a "serve yourself" arrangement. Experienced hoteliers know the importance of implementing service polices during manager's receptions that carefully control and prevent the over-consumption of alcohol by guests.

Some hotels choose to offer guests a complimentary alcoholic beverage as part as of their Manager's Reception.

LODGING LANGUAGE

Third-party liability: A legal concept that can hold the provider of alcoholic beverages responsible for the acts of those who have consumed the alcohol. Also referred to as "dram shop" legislation.

Complimentary Dinners

Those hotels offering complimentary dinner face the same challenges as those hotels that serve breakfast. In nearly all cases, those hotels offering complimentary dinners do so utilizing a serve-yourself food buffet arrangement similar to that offered at breakfast. In most cases, the dinner meal will be offered utilizing the same food display and dining space utilized for the property's breakfast service.

When a hotel elects to offer its guests a full dinner, it does because it believes this amenity will attract large numbers of guests who seek to socialize with other guests or who seek to save minimize their out-of-town meal expenses. When hotels offer guests a complimentary breakfast and dinner, the savings for travelers can be significant.

LODGING ONLINE

Hoteliers can choose from a variety of sources when securing training materials for those employees responsible for serving alcohol. TIPS (Training for Intervention Procedures) is one of the most popular. To learn more about the alcohol service training products offered by this group, go to:

www.gettips.com/

Do you think every hotel employee who serves alcoholic beverages should be trained in responsible beverage service techniques?

LODGING ONLINE

Many limited-service hotel brands aggressively market their complimentary food and beverage offerings. To see how some of them do so, go to one or more of the following sites:

www.marriott.com/fairfieldinn

www.comfortinns.com

www.wingateinns.com

www.ichotelsgroup.com/hiexpress

Do you think large numbers of guests choose their limited-service hotels based upon complimentary food and beverage offerings? Why or why not?

Meetings and Special Events

The opportunities for limited-service hotel mangers to offer meetings and host special events such as dinners, parties, or weddings are as varied as the facilities they manage. For example, some limited-service properties are designed with a lobby or off-lobby dining area and a second area that can be used for meetings. Other limited-service properties are designed with a multi-purpose area that can be used for both small meetings and smaller gatherings held as a special event.

THE SMALL MEETINGS BUSINESS

Some limited-service hotels actively solicit small meetings business from out-of-town groups that will involve the need for some or all of the attendees to rent sleeping rooms as well as from local groups that will require few, if any, guest room rentals. This is the case, for example, when the meeting is held to celebrate a local resident's birthday, wedding, or anniversary.

The idea of marketing to groups may encourage one to think about conventions, conferences, and events attracting hundreds or even thousands of attendees. In fact, however, the average business meeting involves fewer than 25 people. Meetings of this size can be accommodated by many limited-service properties. In many areas, small weddings or other gatherings consisting of 50 or fewer guests are so common that limited-service hotels can host a large number of such small meeting events annually.

The small meetings market is vast. In addition to business groups, it includes numerous other community-based organizations that are looking for a place to meet for just a few hours, a day, or even longer. Families that reserve a large block of rooms sometimes use the meeting room as a during-the-day gathering place. The availability of this space may serve as an incentive for families to use the property. Limited-service hotels and other properties that reach out to these groups and do an excellent job of accommodating their meetings can build a repeat business that may eventually grow to a significant percentage of the hotel's total revenue base.

The hotel's marketing team can identify potential meetings clients through the local chamber of commerce and other community groups and/or contacts. Within-hotel advertising messages can reach existing guests, and advertisements can be placed in community publications. Front office clerks can be trained to route incoming calls requesting information about the hotel as a meeting site to the appropriate person(s) and should obtain a call-back telephone number from the caller if this person is not available.

SMALL MEETINGS MANAGEMENT

In some limited-service hotels, available meeting space is reserved by contacting a front office agent. The front office agents at these properties must be trained in the procedures for selling and reserving meeting space. In addition, they must know about the importance of group meeting business and must follow through, if needed, by contacting the person within the hotel who is responsible for selling the hotel's meeting space. In larger limited-service hotels, a designated sales office is operated and personnel in this office sell and reserve meeting space. In very small hotels, the general manager may be the person responsible for servicing the needs of meetings and event planners.

WHY NOT MARKET THE MEETING ROOM?

Why would some limited-service properties have a meeting room available and not aggressively market it to prospective groups needing space? For some properties, this is not necessary because their meeting space is regularly booked and a concerted selling effort is not required.

Other properties regularly receive referrals from the local convention and visitor's bureau, chamber of commerce, or other organizations. If a property does not have a full-time sales staff, its managers typically set their priorities on generating revenues in the area that is most profitable: rental of guest rooms.

Smaller hotels actively seeking the small meetings' business may have a great competitive edge over larger lodging properties for several reasons. First, planners of small meetings may be looking for smaller spaces and may be more likely to think about small rather than large hotels. Second, many large hotels actively pursue the business of larger groups and do not market as aggressively to small groups. Third, limited-service properties can offer the promise of fewer logistical problems. Parking, an easy-to-find meeting room within the property and the availability of hotel personnel (the front office agent) immediately outside the meeting room door (in many properties) are examples of amenities that could be very attractive to the planners of small group meeting.

LODGING ONLINE

To see how one limited-service hotel chain helps meeting planners, go to:

www.ichotelsgroup.com/

When you reach the site, click on "Meetings and groups." In addition to information about booking a group of rooms, you will find help for professional (meeting) planners and for the occasional (meeting) planner. This site allows planners to find and select a facility and to request a price proposal.

Have you ever attended a meeting or special event held at a limited-service hotel? If so, what did you like and dislike about the facility and its meeting services?

Many limited-service hotels develop a meeting room charge policy that relates to the revenues being generated. If, for example, a specified number of guest rooms are rented, the meeting room fee may be reduced or even eliminated. In other cases, hotels charge a specified amount for each meeting attendee. This charge typically includes the meeting room, audiovisual equipment rental, and refreshment break(s) and/or a light meal. Other properties may charge a flat rate for the meeting space. As with guest room rental charges, rates are often negotiable based in large measure upon the demand for the meeting room at the time for which it is requested.

In many cases, meeting planners may want audiovisual (AV) equipment to project images to the group, show video clips, or simply ensure that all meeting attendees can hear the meeting's speakers. As a result, some properties provide a speaker's podium, a dry erase board, and, perhaps, an overhead projector and microphone at little or no cost. The meeting sponsors bring in or may rent additional equipment as needed. Sometimes this equipment is rented by the hotel with charges passed on to guests at cost or with a **mark-up**. In other properties, meeting planners are given a list of companies in the area that they can contact about the rental of AV equipment.

LODGING LANGUAGE

Mark-up: A fee added to a supplier's charges that the hotel bills a guest or group to compensate for value added by the hotel.

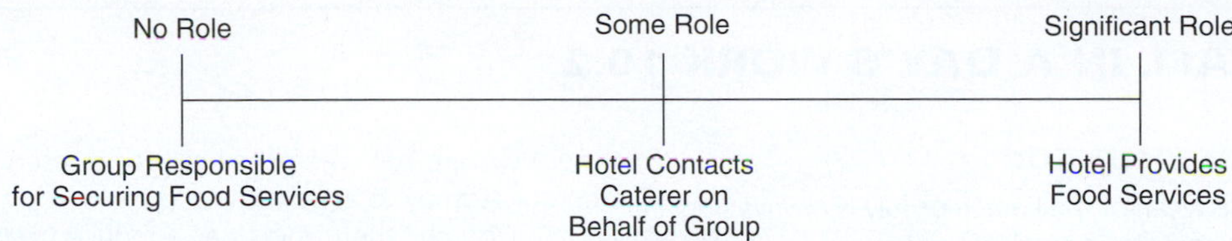

FIGURE 10.6 Role of Limited-Service Hotels in Meetings Food Services

SMALL MEETING FOOD SERVICES

When meetings are held in limited-service hotels, the need for food services can vary from the simple to the very complex. A group meeting at a limited-service hotel for a short period could, for example, request nothing more than that water is made available during the meeting. In other cases, the meeting planner might request the hotel serve one or more full meals. In still other cases, the meeting attendees leave the property for their meals and request only beverage service during their meetings.

Figure 10.6 illustrates the various roles of limited-service hotels in providing food services for on-property meetings.

As you review that figure note that some limited-service hotels have no role in the provision of food services but permit groups to bring in their own refreshment breaks or meals. The meeting planners may make their own contacts with potential caterers, or alternatively the hotel may provide the group with a list of caterers in the area.

If outside caterers are allowed, it is important for hotel managers to contact their local health department to make sure the caterer meets all legal requirements for the service of food to the public. As well, the property's attorney should be contacted to determine the extent, if any, of the property's liability if food-borne illness problems arise from foods brought in by meeting attendees and/or an outside caterer. Figure 10.6 also indicates that limited-service properties may themselves provide food and beverages for group meetings. Some property managers prepare menus to illustrate the range of food and beverage items that can be offered and present these to the meeting planners. The hotel's meetings sales staff can also help potential clients plan other menu items that could be produced with the property's limited facilities.

Some of the items on the property's breakfast menu (e.g., pastries, bagels, juice, and coffee,) may be acceptable for a mid-morning refreshment break. Other food items that do not require extensive on-site preparation (e.g., snack bars, cookies, and fresh fruit) may also be provided to meeting attendees by the hotel's foodservice staff.

In a limited-service setting creative menu planners may be able to offer a lunch of tossed salad, a sandwich deli tray (for example; sliced ham, turkey, roast beef, condiment packets and cheeses with assorted breads and buns), and a baked dessert along with an assortment of hot and cold beverages. These items could be purchased locally and provided to meeting attendees without extensive on-site preparation. Similarly, creative menu planners may be able to plan evening dinner meals that can be produced within the equipment and space confines of their own properties.

When a limited-service hotel property is located very near a restaurant, managers of these hotels may choose to partner with the restaurant in addressing meeting attendee meal needs.

In such a case, the hotelier may make arrangements with the restaurant manager that enable meeting attendees to reserve tables at the restaurant for their meals. Some restaurants even have small private rooms where attendees can sit, eat, and continue their discussions. In some cases, the hotel may receive a referral fee from the restaurant for supplying this added business.

It should be clear to you that, in many cases, the meetings and special events options available to limited-service hotels are not all that limited. Creative limited-service hotel managers can and should carefully assess their own properties' abilities to host onsite meetings and to profit from doing so.

ALL IN A DAY'S WORK 10.2

THE SITUATION

The week of the Fourth of July is always slow in Carsonville, a small town known for its liberal arts college. This year, the Fourth of July is on a Tuesday, and Leilani, the general manager of a 65-room limited-service hotel in the town, had resigned herself to almost no business for the entire week.

She couldn't believe the phone call from a meeting planner who wanted to book 75 percent of her rooms for Wednesday through Saturday of that week. The only problem: a large number of meeting attendees will be driving in, and the hotel's 10-person meeting room will not accommodate the group. There is one option: use the larger room where the hotel's complimentary breakfast bar is typically served.

"It's amazing," thought Leilani "We can book three-quarters of our rooms and, with our normal business, basically have a full house for most of what would normally be one of the slowest weeks in the year."

But what do I do about the guests who will be staying here in the 10 or 15 rooms that are not part of the meeting? I won't have a space to serve them breakfast. Should I tell them we are full when they call for a reservation or stop by to ask about rates?

Do I sell them rooms at a reduced price and indicate that there is no breakfast available that week? Is there something else I could do?

A RESPONSE

If she operates a franchised property, Leilani's franchisor will certainly require that she offer free breakfast to all of her guests. Hoteliers, however, are noted for their creativity. In this case, the ability to provide a breakfast alternative for a few rooms (the non-meeting attendees) might allow Leilani to transform the week from unprofitable to profitable.

In addition to her current ideas, converting the 10-person meeting room or even a vacant guest room into a "private" breakfast area might be an option, as is offering room-service trays to those guests not attending the meeting.

As a last alternative, she may find that contacting a local restaurant and simply arranging to buy breakfast for all of her non-meeting guests could be the most creative and cost effective solution of all!

Lodging Language

A la carte	Manager's Reception	Accrual Accounting System	Delivery Invoice
Atrium	Finger Foods	Cash Accounting System	Last-call
Lobby Food Services	Signature Items	Centralized Purchasing	Third Party Liability
Continental Breakfast	Food Cost per Guest (Limited-Service Hotels)	Par Inventory System	Mark-up
Deluxe Hot Breakfast		Receiving (Food Service)	

For Discussion

1. Name at least three daily sanitation-related concerns that you would have if you were the general manager of a limited-service hotel offering a complimentary breakfast bar.
2. How would you determine the food cost per guest to budget for the operation of your limited-service hotel's breakfast? What indirect costs, if any, such as for lobby cleaning, administrative expenses, and related costs other than food and direct serving labor, would you allocate to the food services operation? Why?
3. What steps should a manager of a limited-service hotel offering complimentary alcoholic beverages during a Manager's Reception take to help ensure that guests do not over-consume these beverages?
4. What types of control do you think could be useful to ensure that only registered hotel guests utilize the free food services that are available at a limited-service hotel?
5. What are the advantages of providing within-the-guestroom information about the complimentary breakfast service in a limited-service hotel?
6. Assume that you observe two children repeatedly coming down to the lobby area during the time that the breakfast bar is in operation, and that each time these two children take very large amounts of food back to their room. Assume also that you know they are guests with their family at the property. What, if anything, would you want the hotel's breakfast attendant to do or say to these guests?
7. What are three alternatives you could give to a meeting planner hoping to provide lunch to meeting attendees in your limited-service hotel's small meeting room?
8. What factors would you consider in deciding whether your hotel should purchase and then rent audiovisual equipment (e.g., a digital projector and screen or specialized video

conferencing equipment) to groups conducting business meetings at your property?

9. Assume that your property offers a fairly comprehensive complimentary breakfast program but does not feature hot foods. What are some steps you could take to minimize the excessive use of disposable paper and plastic products guests use when serving themselves?

10. Identify at least three specific local-area groups that general managers of limited-service hotels could target for small group meetings sales.

Team Activities

TEAM ACTIVITY 1

Select several limited-service properties in your area that offer complimentary food services. Contact these properties and ask about the most significant challenges that arise in the operation of their food service programs. What suggestions can your team make to address these challenges?

TEAM ACTIVITY 2

Have each team member review recent articles in full-service hotel and commercial food services trade magazines. Identify at least one production and one nonproduction issue that would be equally applicable to managers in limited-service hotel properties offering a complimentary breakfast operation. How would these current issues affect managers of the food service program in a limited-service hotel?

Chapter

11

Food and Beverage Operations

Full-Service Hotels

Chapter Outline

Chapter Overview

Full-service hotels offer food and beverage products and services to guests staying at the hotel and to others living in the community or visiting the property. People attending conventions and meetings as well as other groups desiring food and beverage service can also enjoy à la carte or banquet meals at these hotels. As a result, managers at these properties must accommodate the diverse needs of a wide range of guests when planning their food and beverage offerings.

The organization of a hotel's food and beverage department typically depends upon the volume of revenue it generates. Smaller properties may have a food and beverage manager who directs the work of the employees responsible for food production and beverage service. As the department grows in size, specialized positions (e.g., specialized chefs for the dining room, room service managers, beverage managers, and banquet managers) become necessary.

The food management process begins with menu-planning efforts that focus on what guests want to purchase and what the operation can profitably produce. After menus are planned, ingredients must be purchased, received, stored, issued, and produced. Finally, meals must actually be served to guests.

Full-service hotels will typically have one or more dining areas (e.g., a casual coffee shop and a more formal dining room). In addition, other retail sales outlets such as pool snack bars, lobby kiosks offering coffee, and various beverage outlets may be operated to meet the needs of the hotel's guests. Many full-service hotels also offer room service, a distinct type of food service not generally available in limited-service hotels. Because of its complexity, a wide range of menu-planning factors, operating issues, and guest-related concerns must be addressed to effectively manage this unique food service operation.

In most communities, full-service hotels offer the widest range of banquet facilities available to guests. A full-service hotel's banquet room can range from a small space accommodating 50 people or less to large convention/conference facilities that may seat several thousand people. There is significant profit opportunity in banquet operations when hoteliers manage them effectively. As with any other type of food service operation, the first managerial consideration is menu planning driven by the identification of the guests to be served.

A successful banquet event is the result of hard work and coordination of effort. Two tools—*banquet event orders* and *banquet contracts*—help minimize misunderstandings between managers in different hotel departments and with guests. Other banquet concerns, including issues relating to the provision of alcoholic beverages during events, are also very important. These will be addressed in this chapter.

As you read this chapter, you will learn that the food and beverage operation in a full-service hotel is much more complicated than that found in a limited-service property. Food and beverage managers with specialized knowledge of the hotel business, guest relations skills, and food and beverage experience are required. The profitability of food and beverage operations in full-service hotels is a direct result of their efforts.

Chapter Objectives

1. To show the organizational structure used in smaller hotels' food and beverage operations.
2. To show the organizational structure used in larger full-service hotels' food and beverage operations.
3. To examine how hoteliers assess guest needs when planning food and beverage offerings.
4. To review important operating procedures related to purchasing, receiving, storing, issuing, and producing food and beverage products.
5. To present management concerns related to serving à la carte meals, room-service, and banquets in a hotel.

HOTEL FOOD AND BEVERAGE OFFERINGS

Full-service hotels offer à la carte and other food services for travelers who stay at the property and for others, including residents of the local community. Recall from Chapter 10 that the term, "à la carte" refers to items on a menu that are individually priced. Deciding exactly what to offer depends greatly on the hotel's location and goals. Is the hotel attempting to attract motorists on a nearby roadway traveling for pleasure or business? Is the property located in a city's business district? Does it do a large volume of convention business? Is it a resort or vacation property? In all cases, the food and beverage services offered by the hotel must be planned to meet the dining needs of those to whom the property is marketed.

Many full-service hotels also generate revenue from people living in the local community and who enjoy the same types of dining options as the hotel's guests. For example, residents of a rural community may enjoy the value-priced meals offered by a lodging property on an interstate highway exit located near the community. Residents of a large city may like to celebrate special occasions in the dining outlet of a hotel serving upscale business and pleasure travelers. It is a challenge for managers in hotel food services to identify their guests and to understand and consistently provide what they need. If they do not accomplish this, other competitive food service

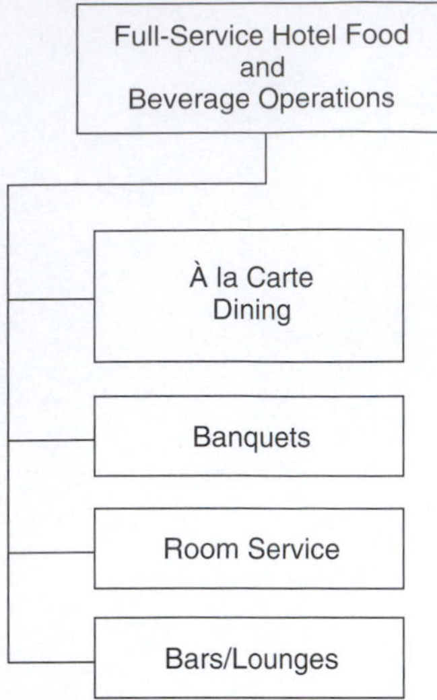

FIGURE 11.1 Food and Beverage Services Offered by Full-Service Hotels

operations, including traditional restaurants, will provide the products and services that guests seek.

Figure 11.1 illustrates the types of food and beverage services typically offered to guests in a full-service hotel.

À la Carte Dining. Depending upon its size, a full-service hotel will have one or more à la carte dining alternatives. For example, a small property might have a coffee and pastry stand or a single dining room. A very large property may have several theme restaurants and other casual dine-in options. It may also offer one or more quick-service outlets in its lobbies and/or in a swimming pool area or other locations around the property.

Banquets. Many hotels offer **banquet** functions for groups of guests meeting at the property and for others celebrating special occasions.

LODGING LANGUAGE

Banquet: A food event held in a hotel's privately reserved function room.

Room Service. Some hotels deliver food and beverage products to guest rooms. This type of food and beverage service is unique to lodging properties.

Bars and Lounges. Some hotels have a bar or lounge located near the à la carte dining room. In some cases, bar and lounge guests may also order food items in these areas. Sometimes all of the hotel's à la carte menu items can be served in the bar or lounge while in other properties a separate and more limited bar menu may be offered.

In addition to its guest-oriented food and beverage operations, some very large full-service hotels provide food services to their employees. Large hotels may employ hundreds or even thousands of staff members. Employee cafeterias are sometimes available for staff use, and a low-cost or even no-cost meal is offered.

Hoteliers must decide what type of food and beverage services to offer, such as à la carte, banquets or room service.

ORGANIZATION OF HOTEL FOOD AND BEVERAGE OPERATIONS

The organization of a food and beverage operation in a full-service hotel depends upon its size and the revenue it generates. Smaller hotels tend to generate lower revenues from food services than their higher-revenue counterparts. In the United States, the average full-service hotel can generate 25 percent or more of its total revenue from food and beverage sales. Some properties, especially those with large-volume convention/meeting/banquet business, can generate food and beverage revenues approaching 50 percent of total hotel revenues. Regardless of a hotel's size, the organizational structure of its food and beverage operation must support its revenue-generating efforts.

Smaller Hotels

Figure 11.2 shows how a food and beverage operation might be organized in a smaller hotel. The hotel's general manager supervises a food and beverage manager who, in turn, manages the work of someone responsible for food production (the head cook/chef), dining room service (the restaurant manager), and beverage production and service (the head bartender).

In a smaller full-service hotel, managerial functions are typically combined into just a few positions. For example, the food and beverage manager

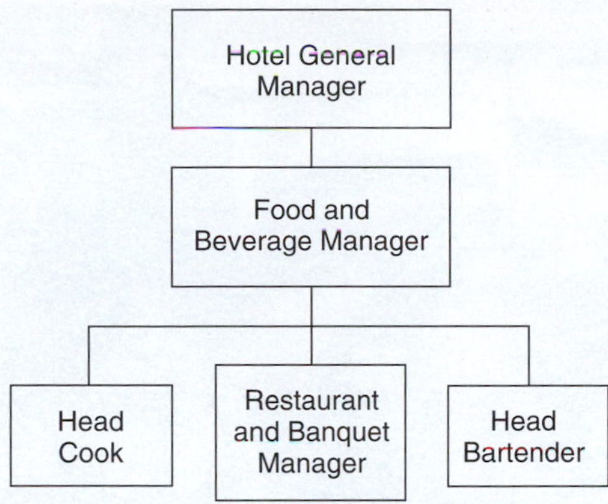

FIGURE 11.2 Organization of Food and Beverage Management Positions in Small Hotels

may be responsible for food and beverage purchasing, some accounting and control activities related to the operating of the department, and the management of banquet operations, among other duties. In hotels with larger food and beverage departments, each of these specialized tasks would be performed by a designated staff member with full-time responsibility for completing them.

Larger Hotels

As a hotel's food service operation becomes larger, additional managerial positions are needed. This is illustrated in Figure 11.3.

Note that in a large hotel, the food and beverage manager's position shown in Figure 11.2 is now titled "Director of Food and Beverage Operations." The individual filling that position supervises the work of an executive chef who, in turn, supervises a sous chef (with responsibility for food production for à la carte dining and room service) and a banquet chef (with responsibility for food produced for group functions). The director of food and beverage operations may also direct the work of a catering manager (who interacts with clients and sells group functions) and a banquet manager (who is responsible for banquet set-ups/tear-downs and service at banquets). Other **direct reports** of the director of food and beverage operations are the restaurant manager (responsible for service in the à la carte dining room[s]), the room service manager, and the beverage manager (who is responsible for the head bartenders at each beverage outlet).

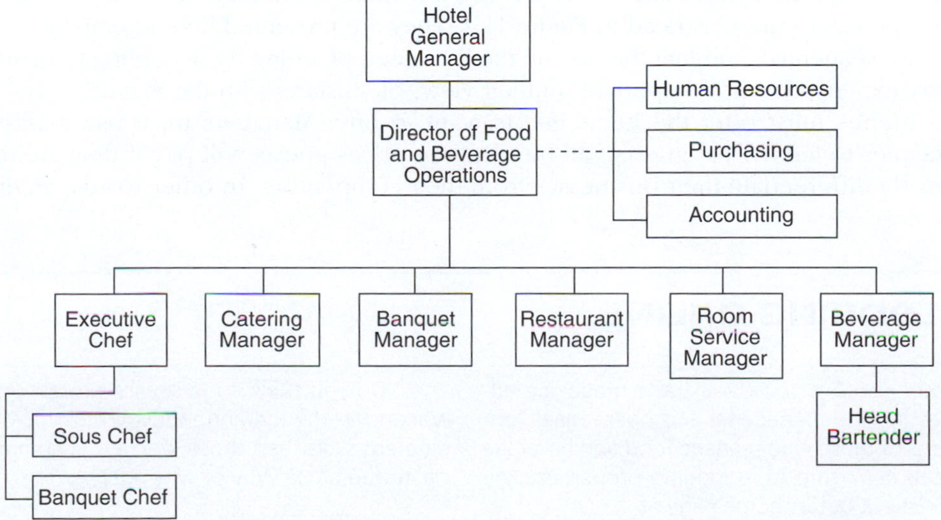

FIGURE 11.3 Organization of Food and Beverage Management Positions in Large Hotels

The size of the food and beverage operation will determine the size of staff and their specific responsibilities.

LODGING LANGUAGE

Direct report: An employee over whom a supervisor has immediate authority. For example, a sous chef is a direct report of the executive chef.

The director of food and beverage operations in a large hotel also has the benefit of technical assistance from personnel whose specialties involve human resources (including recruitment, selection, orientation, compensation/benefits administration, and interpretation/implementation of the ever-expanding body of legal issues relating to employment), centralized purchasing, and accounting/financial management.

MENU PLANNING

Food service managers in a hotel or any other type of organization must be consistently concerned about several important processes if their operations are to be successful. These processes are illustrated in Figure 11.4. They are presented here to emphasize that they are sequential, and that the first on the list, menu planning, is, according to many industry experts, the most important. In their view, "it all starts with the menu!"

Menus must offer the items guests want to buy. Managers must use marketing principles to learn what guests will buy and the prices guests will pay if they are to effectively differentiate their businesses from their competitors. In other words, an effec-

LODGING ONLINE

Hotel F&B Executive is a trade magazine addressing the managerial and operational concerns of those who manage food and beverage (F&B) departments in lodging properties. You can check out its home page at:

www.hotelfandb.com/

Do you think food service professionals working in the lodging industry must possess different skills than those working in commercial restaurants? Why or why not?

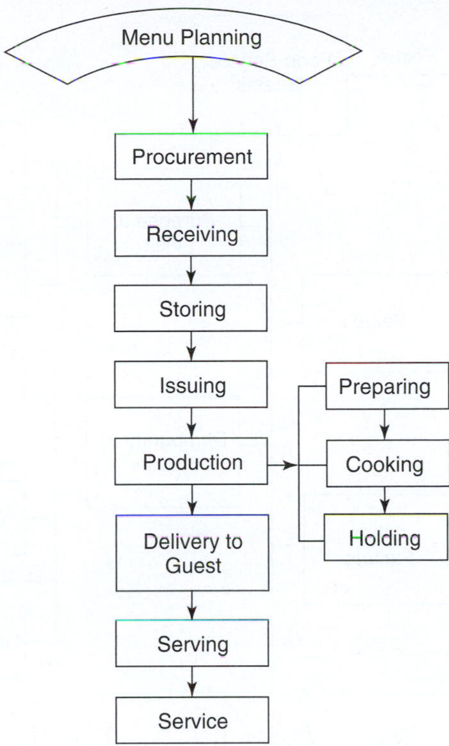

FIGURE 11.4 Overview of Food Service Processes

tive menu focuses on the guests. Entire books have been written on the topic of **menu planning.**[1]

LODGING LANGUAGE

Menu planning: The process of determining which food and beverage items will most please the guests while meeting established cost objectives.

Two of the most important menu planning considerations relate to the guests (what they want and will pay for) and to the resources available to provide menu items that consistently meet established quality standards.

Guest Concerns

The guests are the most important consideration when planning the menu, and it is critical to know what items they will order. What guest-related factors should be considered in planning a menu? Figure 11.5 helps answer this question.

PROBLEMS AND PROFITS IN HOTEL FOOD SERVICES

Food service departments in hotels have some unique challenges. One of the most important is the inability of many to be profitable. At most full-service hotels, food and beverage sales bring in fewer revenue dollars and bottom-line profits than the rental of guest rooms. As a result, financial management concerns create an umbrella under which hotel food services must constantly operate.

[1]See, for example, Jack Ninemeier and David Hayes, *Menu Planning, Design and Evaluation 2nd. Edition.* (Richmond, Calif.: McCutchan Publishing Corp., 2008).

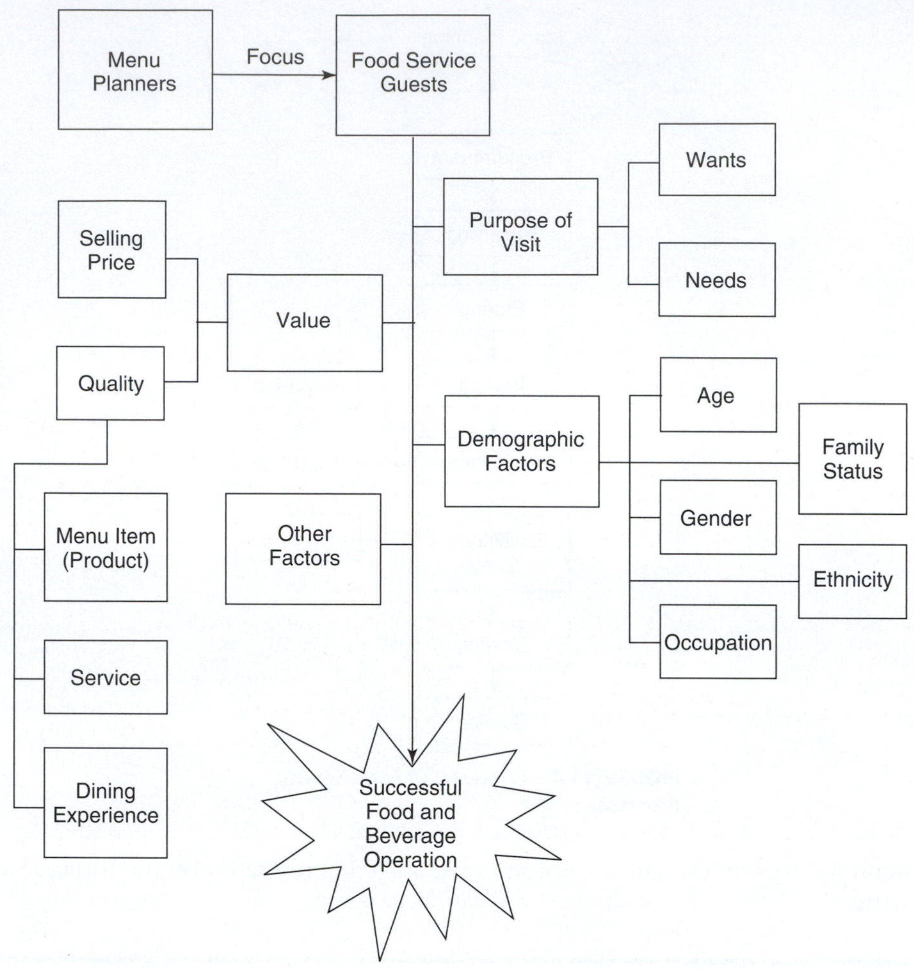

FIGURE 11.5 Menu Planning: Focus on Guests

Figure 11.5 lists many guest-related factors that must be considered when planning menus:

Purpose of Visit. Guests want an experience in line with the purpose of their visit. They may just be hungry (e.g., when travelers on an interstate highway stop at a roadside hotel), they may be discussing business, or they may be a couple or a family visiting an upscale hotel restaurant to celebrate a special occasion.

Value. The concept of **value** relates to a guest's perception of the selling price of an item relative to the quality of the menu item, service, and dining experience. Guests want to get what they pay for; they do not want to feel cheated, and, increasingly, many guests will pay more for a higher perceived quality of dining experience.

LODGING LANGUAGE

Value (foodserivce): The guest's perception of the selling price of a menu item relative to the quality of the menu item, service, and dining experience received.

Demographic Factors. Concerns such as the guests' age, marital status, gender, ethnicity, and occupation are likely to impact menu item preferences. Knowing the answer to the question "Who will be visiting our hotel's restaurant?" will help in planning the menu.

LODGING LANGUAGE

Demographic Factors: Characteristics such as age, marital status, gender, ethnicity, and occupation that help to describe or classify a person as a member of a group.

Other Factors. Social factors such as income, education, and wealth may influence what a guest desires. Other factors, including guests' lifestyles and even their personalities (e.g., the extent to which they like to try "new" foods) can be relevant to menu-planning decisions.

The goal of every menu planner is to offer items that please the guests. When guests are satisfied, they are more likely to provide repeat business. At the same time, they will tell their friends, and word-of-mouth advertising helps the food and beverage operation to remain successful.

Food and beverage operators face many guest-related concerns when planning a menu, such as who will visit their establishments and why.

Operating Concerns

Figure 11.6 highlights some of the ways that the menu, once planned, impacts the food services operation.

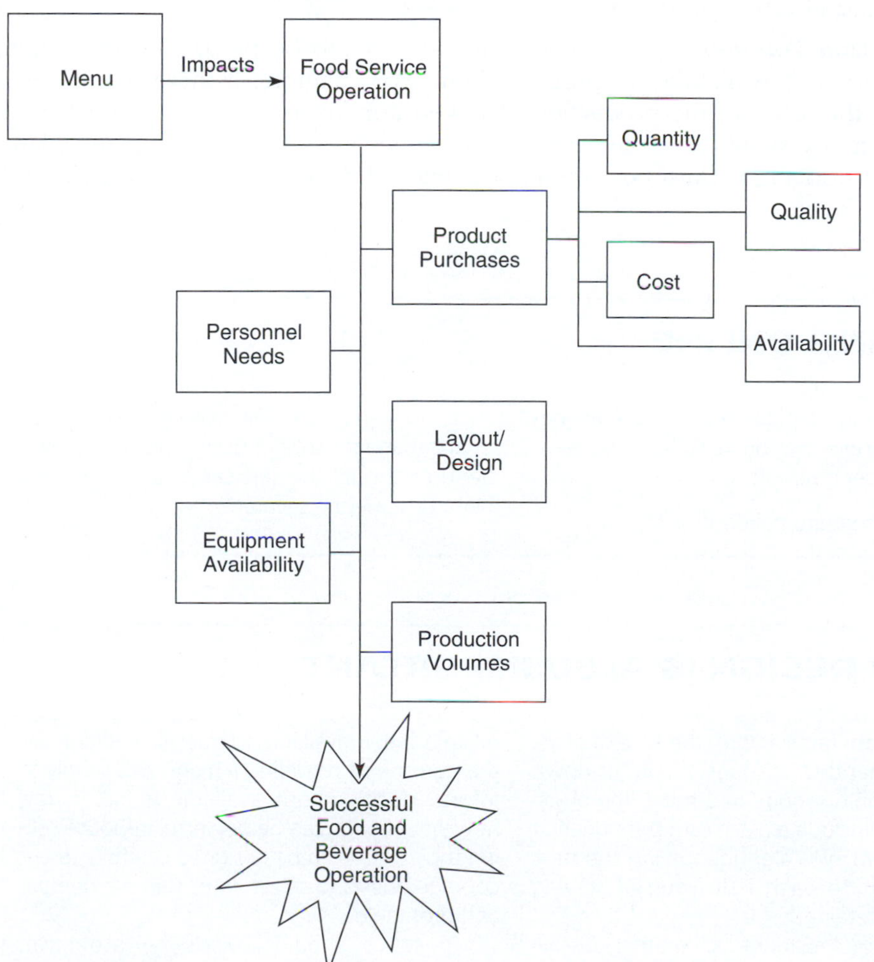

FIGURE 11.6 Menu Planning and Operations

These aspects include:

Product Purchases. All of the ingredients required to produce all the menu items offered must be consistently available in the required quantity and quality and at the right cost. Otherwise, guests may be disappointed because desired items are not available. Moreover, there will likely be significant operational disruptions when alternative menu items need to be produced.

Personnel Needs. Trained staff members must be available to produce and serve the items offered on the menu. Consider, for example, the differences in the experience and skill level necessary for an effective server in a hotel's coffee shop compared to a server preparing **flambé** dishes tableside in an upscale hotel restaurant.

LODGING LANGUAGE

Flambé: A cooking procedure in which alcohol (ethanol) is added to a hot pan to create a burst of flames.

Layout/Design Concerns. If a menu specifies a self-service salad bar, the space must be available for the serving counters and to accommodate guest movement around the salad bar area. A menu featuring fresh-baked breads requires the space necessary for an on-site bake shop or for the placement of specialized baking equipment such as proofers and ovens.

Equipment Availability. If the menu includes fried foods and grilled items, deep-fat fryers and grills will be necessary based upon anticipated business volume. The space needed for the equipment and adequate ventilation as required by fire safety codes must also be considered.

Production Volumes. The volume of menu items to be prepared must match the equipment availability to produce them. For example, if there is only one oven in the kitchen, the production of baked appetizers, entrées, desserts, and breads in any significant volume would be difficult. As a result, the menu planner in this operation must be careful not to exceed the production capacity of the available oven.

LODGING ONLINE

After the menu is planned, it must be designed. An excellent resource to help you learn more about menu design is:

www.themenumaker.com/

Do you think the average hotel food service manager should design his or her own menu or should the services of a professional menu designer be secured?

MENU DESIGN IS ALSO IMPORTANT

Most people are familiar with the type of physical menus handed to guests in a sit-down restaurant's dining room. In a hotel, the physical menu can include a place card positioned at a banquet seat or a sign identifying the item available next to each help-yourself serving dish on a buffet line.

Most hotel restaurants, whether upscale or casual, and most room service operations make a menu available to guests. Traditionally, the purpose of providing a menu was simply to inform guests about available items. Today, however, menus can be powerful in-house selling tools. They can be designed carefully to encourage guests to select items that are popular and profitable.

Menus should always be attractive, clean, and easy-to-read.

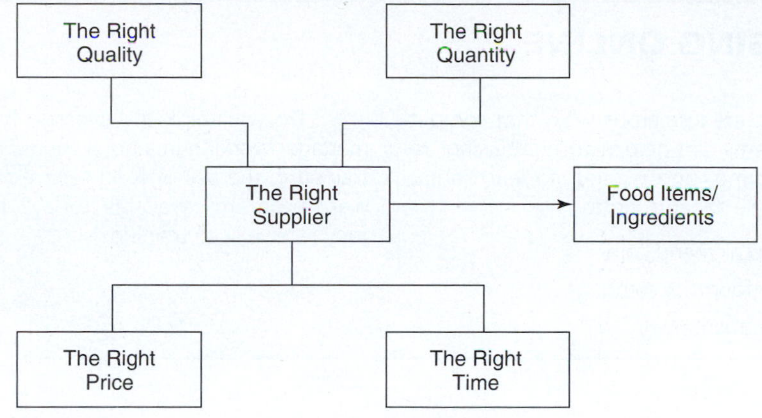

FIGURE 11.7 Five Special Purchasing Concerns

FOOD SERVICE CONTROL POINTS

After the menu is planned, other processes must be effectively managed to help the hotel's food and beverage operation be successful. Figure 11.4 indicates the processes that must occur after the menu is planned. They include:

Procurement

After the menu is planned, the **ingredients** needed to produce the items on it will be known.

LODGING LANGUAGE

Ingredients: Individual components of a food or beverage recipe. For example, flour and sugar are ingredients in pastries.

All ingredients must be procured (obtained) using effective purchasing procedures. Figure 11.7 identifies five special concerns in the food service purchasing process.

Quality is perhaps the single most important concern when purchasing food and beverage items. The purchaser must consider the intended use of the items; the closer an item is to being suitable for its intended use, the more appropriate is its quality.

For example, bright red maraschino cherries might be required at the bar for a drink garnish and in the kitchen as an ingredient in a fruit gelatin salad. A whole cherry with stem (at a relatively higher cost) may be needed at the bar because it is attractive. Cherry halves or chopped cherry pieces (at a relatively lower cost) might be best in a gelatin salad. Quality, in most cases, can best be determined only if one first knows how the product will be used.

Another purchasing factor relates to the quantity of items needed. If too much product is purchased, money that could be utilized for other purposes is tied up in inventory. As well, the quality of some products can deteriorate in storage, space must be available to house excess inventory, and when too much product is held in inventory there could be an increased chance of spoilage, **theft** and **pilferage**.

LODGING LANGUAGE

Theft: Stealing all of something at one time; for example, a thief might steal a case of liquor.

Pilferage: Stealing small quantities of something over a period of time; for example, a thief might steal one bottle from a case of beer.

By contrast, when too little product is available, **stockouts** can occur. Guests may be disappointed because a desired menu item is not available, and operating concerns can arise if substitute items must be produced.

LODGING ONLINE

Today, there are numerous ways that computerized systems can help with purchasing, receiving, storing, and issuing. To learn about some of these systems, go to:

www.calcmenu.com/
www.foodtrak.com/
www.tracrite.net/

Do you think the average food service manager working in a hotel should be specially trained in the use of food service-related software programs available today? How could they receive such training?

LODGING LANGUAGE

Stockout: The condition that arises when a food/beverage item needed for production is not available on-site.

The price is right when the cost of a food item or ingredient provides a good value. Wise purchasers realize that they are buying more than just products from a supplier. They also receive product information and service. The perceived value of these three factors (product quality, information, and service) should most influence the purchasing decision.

The right time for product delivery must also be considered. Suppliers offering a good deal on an item for tomorrow's banquet that is delivered next week are not providing value. Purchasers who frequently have problems securing the right products at the right time should look first at their operation to determine whether there is an internal problem. If not, they should select suppliers who consistently deliver required products on a timely basis.

The right supplier consistently delivers the right quality and quantities of product at the right price and at the right time. Some food services managers like to have only a few suppliers so that they can eliminate paperwork and enhance their relationship with suppliers. Other managers believe that interactions with many suppliers are beneficial to the operation. Whichever of these approaches is used, the importance of professional procurement including supplier selection and purchasing cannot be overlooked.

Receiving, Storing, and Issuing

After products are purchased, they must be received, stored, and issued to production areas. Receiving occurs when products are physically delivered to the operation. Storing is the process of holding products in a secure space with proper temperature, humidity, and product rotation until they are needed. **Issuing** involves moving products from the storage area to the place of production. Basic receiving, storing, and issuing procedures are similar for food and beverage products. These products must be protected until used so that menu items can be produced at the lowest possible cost and highest quality.

LODGING LANGUAGE

Issuing: The process of moving stored products to the place of production.

Production

Production is the process of readying products for consumption. It involves cooks working in the kitchen and bartenders working in bar areas.

LODGING LANGUAGE

Production: All of the cooking and preparation processes used to ready menu items for consumption.

Effective food or beverage production requires the use of **standardized recipes** to indicate the type and quantity of ingredients, preparation methods, and portion tools along with production instructions.

LODGING LANGUAGE

Standardized recipe: A written explanation about how a food or beverage item should be prepared. It lists the quantity of each ingredient, preparation techniques, portion size, and other information production personnel need to ensure that the item is always prepared in the same way.

Some menu items may be produced from **scratch** while others can be purchased in a **convenience food** form.

LODGING LANGUAGE

Scratch (food production): The use of basic ingredients to make items for sale. For example, a minestrone soup may be made on-site with fresh vegetables, meat, and other ingredients.

Convenience food: Food or beverage products that have some labor "built in" that otherwise would have to be added on-site. For example, a minestrone soup may be purchased pre-made in a frozen or canned form.

In many cases, a **make or buy analysis** should be performed to determine which items should be made from scratch and which should be purchased as a convenience food.

LODGING LANGUAGE

Make or Buy Analysis: The process of considering quality, costs, and other factors in scratch production and convenience food alternatives to determine which form is best for the operation.

The production of food items generally requires more elaborate and extensive preparation skills than are needed for beverages. A menu may offer a range of items requiring different levels of preparation skills. For example:

- Hamburger patties that must be grilled or that must be formed and then grilled
- Combination dishes that involve the need to clean, pre-prepare (clean, cut, and chop), and cook a variety of ingredients
- Elaborate sauces that require experience in stock reduction and preparation to prepare a sauce that in itself is an ingredient (**chained recipe**) in another menu item
- Menu items that are produced can be made individually (such as a single broiled steak) or in batches (such as a large quantity of soup).

LODGING LANGUAGE

Chained recipe: A recipe for an item such as a sauce that is itself an ingredient in another recipe (such as a tomato sauce used in a pasta dish).

Serving and Service

When a hotel has a dining room, food items prepared by cooks are transferred to employees who then serve them to guests. Bartenders preparing drinks may also produce the drinks and then transfer them to other employees who actually serve the drinks to guests. The process of moving products from production to service personnel is called

serving. Service personnel then deliver food and beverage products to guests in a process called **service**. Both serving and service procedures must be professionally planned and executed.

LODGING LANGUAGE

Serving: The process of moving prepared food or beverage items from production staff to service personnel.

Service (food and beverage): The process of transferring food and beverage products from wait staff to the guests.

Systems for food and beverage serving must be effectively designed to minimize service bottlenecks that can lower food quality (such as cold food) and lengthen guest waits (e.g., when many slow-to-prepare ice cream drinks containing alcohol hinder the production of other drinks). The speed and manner in which products are delivered to guests is very important because the perceived quality of service is just as important as product quality when guests evaluate their overall food service experiences.

À LA CARTE DINING

À la carte food services allow guests in a hotel's restaurant to order and pay for the specific menu items they desire. These meals are typically served in a designated dining area, such as a dining room, pool snack bar, or coffee shop. There are many activities included in preparing for and providing service to guests in à la carte dining operations. Some of the most important of these activities include getting ready for service and service procedures.

Getting Ready for Service

When food is prepared, it can be served in a variety of styles, including:

American (plated) service is a very common à la carte servicing style. In it, guests place their individual orders, which are prepared in the kitchen and delivered to their tables.

American (Plated) Service. In this serving style, food is pre-portioned onto serviceware (e.g., plates or bowls) in the kitchen and is then served to guests seated at tables in the dining area.

Traditional French Service. In this service style, menu items such as a classic Caesar Salad or a flaming Steak Diane are prepared and cooked at the guests' tables.

Russian (Platter) Service. In this style, food is placed on serviceware in the kitchen, brought to the guests' tables by servers, and individual portions are then placed onto the guests' plates by the servers.

English (Family) Service. In this style, food is brought to the table by the server in serving dishes that are placed on the guests' tables so that they can pass food items to one other.

Buffet (Self-Service). In this popular serving style, guests help themselves to a variety of food items that have been positioned for easy access by guests.

Counter (Bar) Service. In hotels this style of service is most common in bars and lounges. Guests place orders with service personnel behind a counter area who prepare and serve menu items to guests who may be seated at the bar.

Service styles can be combined in the same meal. For example, a Caesar Salad may be prepared tableside (French Service), and the entrée may be pre-plated in the kitchen (American Service).

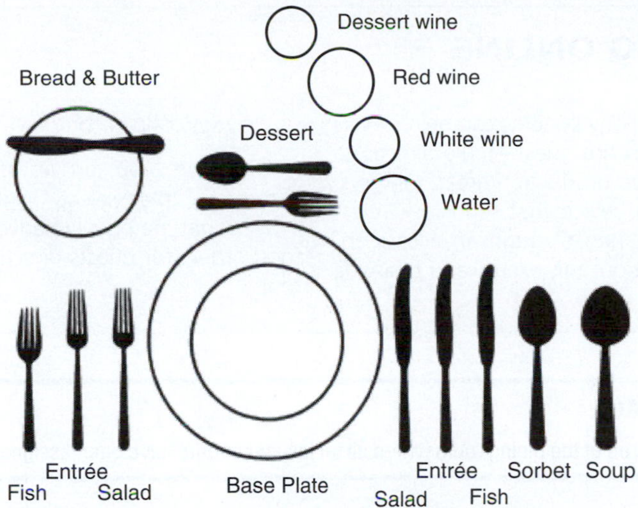

FIGURE 11.8 Example of Place Setting in an Up-Scale Dining Room

Service Procedures

Preparing to serve food properly requires staff to undertake a variety of activities including:

- Ensuring tables, chairs, and booths are clean, safe, and steady
- Checking to assure that tablecloths, if used, are correctly placed and are clean and free of burns, holes, and tears
- Ensuring **place settings** are positioned according to the hotel's standards (see an example in Figure 11.8). Note that serving pieces are typically placed such that guests use the outside items first and then move toward the center of the place setting. When reviewing Figurer 11.8, note the arrangement of the forks. Guests will first enjoy a fish course, followed by the entrée. Since a formal European meal is being served, the salad course is served after (not before) the entrée, so the salad fork is placed closest to the center of the place setting.
- Confirming that there are no water spots or fingerprints on glassware, flatware, or other serviceware.

LODGING LANGUAGE

Place setting: The arrangement of plates, glasses, knives, forks, spoons (flatware), and other service items on a dining table for one guest.

Preparing for service extends beyond checking guest dining areas. Preparing service staff is equally important. Because this is true, many food service managers implement a mandatory staff **line-up** prior to the beginning of service.

LODGING LANGUAGE

Line-up (training): A brief informational training session held before the work shift begins.

Topics discussed in the daily line-up typically include:

- Specific **server station** assignments
- Daily specials
- New menu item introductions (including opportunities to sample new items)
- Estimates of business volume during the shift based upon reservations and/or other information
- A mini-training session on a topic such as procedures to resolve service-related problems

LODGING ONLINE

Advanced technology systems can help servers place orders from the guest's table directly to the food/beverage production areas. One system uses a palm device that sends a wireless signal to the kitchen through an access antenna. To learn about this example of tableside order placement, go to:

www.rmpos.com/

When you arrive at the site, click "Products," then select "Write-On Handheld."

What are possible advantages of placing food orders for guests directly from the dining room?

LODGING LANGUAGE

Server station: An area of the dining room where all tables and booths have been assigned to a specific server.

Many steps are involved in the interaction between wait staff and guests as the dining process evolves. These steps are identified in Figure 11.9.

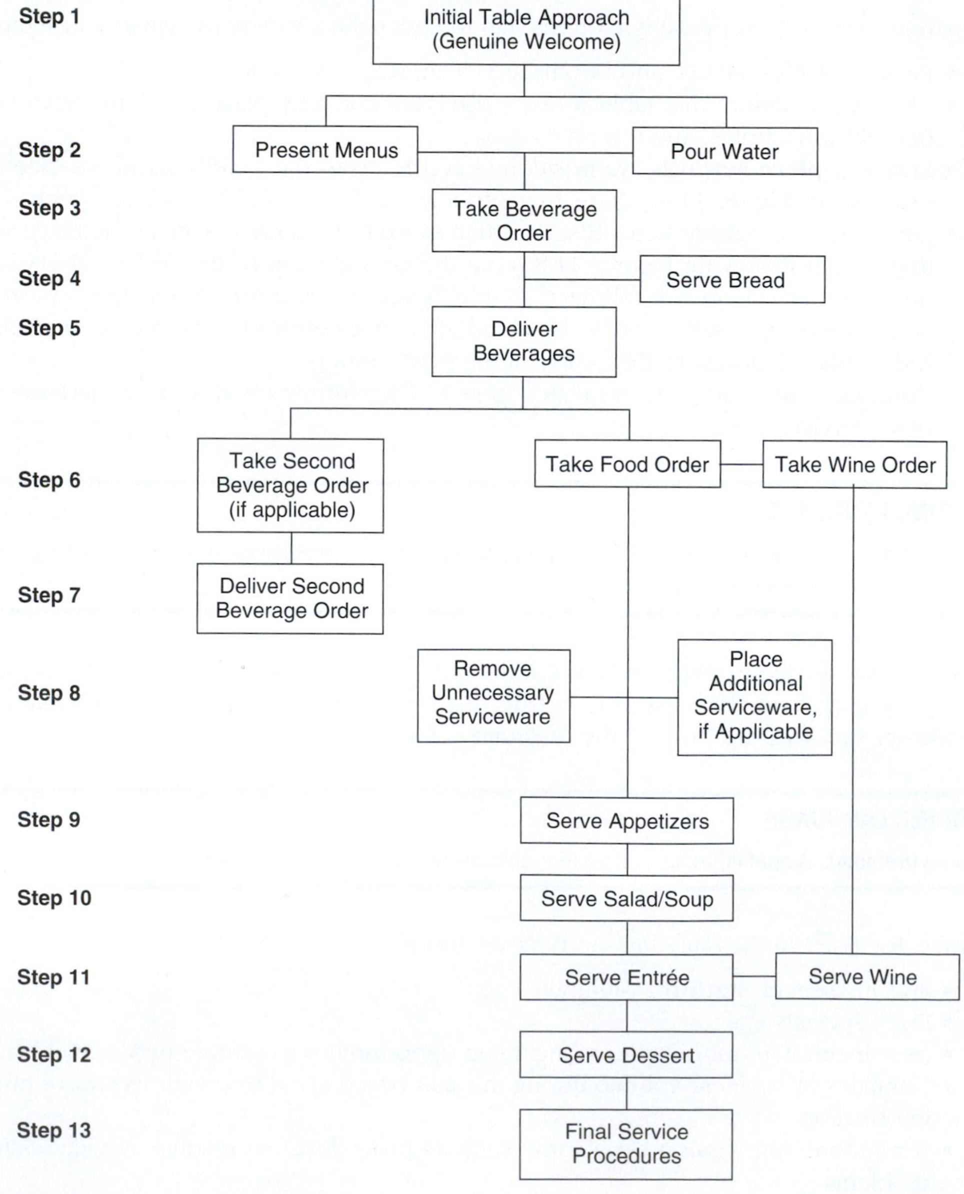

FIGURE 11.9 The Service Sequence

"WHO GETS THE SPAGHETTI?"

"Who gets the spaghetti?" or any other ordered item, is a question that will never need to be asked, and should never be asked, in a well-managed dining area. Servers should use a numbering system so that they know who gets the spaghetti. Each table in the dining room should be assigned a number (this helps with server station assignments), and each table's seats should also be numbered. When that is true, there should be no question about who gets the spaghetti because the server will have written or entered the table and seat number corresponding to the guest ordering the spaghetti on the order pad when the guest's order was placed.

The server's first step is clear; the next several steps may not be. It is important to approach the table as soon as possible after the guests are seated (Step 1).

A hospitable and genuine greeting is important. ("Hello, welcome to Vernon's Restaurant. We are pleased that you're here, and my goal is to make your visit a memorable one.") Eye contact, a feeling of self-confidence, and a genuine spirit of hospitality are helpful in this initial guest contact.

Step 2 in the service sequence will vary by property. Guests may be provided with menus by a host or hostess as they are seated, and a busperson may serve water to them before their server reaches the table. When presenting the menu, the server can mention any specials available in addition to what is listed on the menu.

A beverage order can be taken (Step 3), and bread (if offered) can be brought to the table after the beverage order is taken (Step 4). Trays should be used to carry beverage orders (and everything else!) to the table. If possible, beverages should be served from the guest's right side with the server's right hand. Service trays should not be placed on the guest's table when the server takes or delivers an order.

After beverages are delivered (Step 5), three activities become important (in Step 6) when the server next returns to the table:

- Take a second beverage order (if applicable).
- Take the food order.
- Take a wine order.

As orders are taken, servers should:

- Be thorough and ask questions. If, for example, a guest orders a steak, the server must inquire about the desired degree of doneness. If a guest orders a baked potato, they should be asked about preferred toppings.
- Repeat orders to help ensure accuracy.
- Be alert to guests' needs. For example, if they appear rushed, suggest items that can be prepared and served quickly.
- Pick up the menus after each guest has placed an order, and return them to their proper storage location.

After food/wine orders are taken, a second round of beverage orders can be delivered, if applicable. In Step 7 and Step 8, servers should remove items that will not be needed, such as pre-set wine glasses if no wine is ordered. Additional service items that will be needed after orders are known should be brought to the table. These may include special knives (if steaks are ordered) and special condiments, such as tartar sauce for seafood.

Steps 9–12 review the sequence of serving appetizers, salads/soups, entrées wine, and desserts. In these steps, attention to detail is very important. Does a guest need more water or other beverage, was an item of flatware dropped on the floor and thus needs replacement, or does someone have second thoughts about a condiment not requested earlier?

Step 13 notes the importance of final service procedures. These include:

- Presenting the check
- Assisting the guests with payment
- Ending the meal experience with a sincere "*Thank you; I enjoyed serving you; please visit us again.*"

ALL IN A DAY'S WORK 11.1

THE SITUATION

"Whose job is it, anyway?" asked Francis, a frustrated food server at the Barkley Grill in the Mountain View Hotel, to Louis, the dining room manager.

"I'm glad we're very busy tonight, and I'm working as hard as I can to provide the quality of service that our guests want," Francis continued. "When I go to one table, however, the guests already have a menu. When I go to another, they don't. The same with water. Sometimes guests have their waters before I arrive and sometimes they don't. I'm glad when they have a menu and water; it helps speed service. But, I have to waste a lot of time picking up menus and preparing water glasses to bring to the table because I never know whether guests will have them when I arrive. If they do, I look silly, and I have to return the extra glasses to the server station before I can take the order. I don't save time; I actually waste time, which could be better spent on more productive tasks."

A RESPONSE

Francis is right about the problem. The policy may be that the host or hostess staff should provide menus to the guests and that a busperson should bring water. However, if staff are not properly trained, what actually happens may not be what policy dictates. Louis can confirm the problem ("Let's talk about this at the end of the shift when we are better able to do so. In the meantime, I'll try to help out wherever I can so that you and the rest of the staff will not have to waste time.")

Francis has a legitimate complaint and did the right thing by discussing the problem with his supervisor. Louis should make it a priority to meet with dining service staff and agree upon who does what. Once this is determined, effective training programs can help to implement the agreed-upon procedures.

LODGING GOES GREEN!

What does it really mean to be a green food operation? Much of the focus on green foodservice has been placed on sustainable food options, reducing packaging wastes and emphasizing local food sourcing. Those are all important, but full-service hoteliers must also manage their food service operation in a way that is water use and energy efficient. Interestingly, the views of restaurateurs and consumers toward water have changed substantially over the past decade. In fact, water usage in food service operations serves as one good example why hoteliers must continually monitor their own and their guests' evolving views of acceptable operating practices.

For those hoteliers operating food programs in full-service hotels, the following green practices commonly utilized by restaurateurs can make a significant and positive impact on hotel profits and the environment.

1. Watch the "Bottled" Water: The decade from 2000-2010 saw an explosion in the consumption of bottled water in the United States. Increasingly, however, consumers became aware of the cost to the environment of the millions of used plastic bottles required to meet this increased demand. In hotel meeting rooms across the country, guests began to request that the hotel *not* provide bottled water. Environmentally conscious meeting planners who feel strongly on this and other green practices issues remind hoteliers of the importance of following trends in consumer perceptions of acceptable green practices.

2. Watch the "Tap" Water: Water is the single most important finite resource on earth. Foodservice operations, in general, sometimes do a poor job of water conservation. Water conservation practices along with efficient plumbing fixtures and equipment can save the hotel industry millions of dollars each year. Kitchen water fixtures, aerators, pre-rinse spray valves, urinals and toilets are all areas where tight seals and modern design can yield big savings.

3. Replace Candescent Lights with Light-Emitting Diode (LED) Lighting. The savings to hotels of replacing traditional incandescent lighting with LED or compact florescent lighting (CFL) can be significant. Not only are lighting costs reduced, but the cost of labor required to replace burned out bulbs is also reduced.

4. Check the Label: Buying appliances, electronics, and equipment that have been tested by the Environmental Protection Agency

(EPA) and that display their Energy Star label is a good way to reduce energy costs. The Energy Star label was created as a U.S. government program in 1992. Manufacturers in Canada, Japan, New Zealand, and the European Union have since adopted it. Devices carrying the Energy Star label operate using 20%-30% less energy than required by Federal standards.

5. Think Farm to Fork: Farm to Fork is a way of considering the environmental impact of transporting food from the area in which it is grown or produced to the area in which it is consumed. Minimizing the time from Farm to Fork not only reduces impact on the environment, it helps ensure ingredient quality. For many foodservice operators, a commitment to buy (whenever possible) baked goods, fresh produce, and even meats within a 150-mile radius of their operation is a way to recognize the importance of the Farm to Fork concept.

ROOM SERVICE

Many full-service hotels offer room service. Room service is the hotel term that describes the entire process of delivering menu items to guests in their rooms. Some hotels offer room service 24/7 (24 hours per day, 7 days per week). Guests of all types utilize room service, ranging from the business traveler wanting a quick breakfast, to small groups desiring a lunch during their meetings in guest room suites, to couples wanting to enjoy a romantic meal alone.

Large hotels generally employ a room service manager with total responsibility for this specialized guest offering. In such hotels, room service staff may work in a separate food preparation area designed especially for room service orders. Also, employees in these properties who deliver menu items to guest rooms may do so on a full-time basis.

In smaller hotels, the food and beverage manager will most often plan to have room service items produced by the same cook who produces the restaurant meals. In these smaller properties, room service items are typically delivered to guest rooms by a restaurant server.

Profitability

Guests noting the seemingly high prices on room service menus sometimes think that hotels make a lot of profit on room service. In fact, this is not typically the case.

If room service is not profitable for the hotel, why is it offered? There are several answers. First, it is a service to guests and some guests may select a property based on its availability. Among this type of guests are those arriving on late night airline flights and others wanting food and beverage services for small business meetings in guest rooms.

Providing quality room service requires careful planning and execution.

Secondly, the offering of room service (especially on a 24/7 basis) can add significantly to guests' perceptions of a hotel's exclusiveness and attention toward guest needs. Finally, some hotel rating services, such as the American Automobile Association (AAA), only assign their highest ratings to hotels that offer room service.

Why does room service frequently lose money? High labor costs are one reason. Much time is needed to transport food from the kitchen to guest room areas. The capital costs incurred to purchase equipment, such as delivery carts and warming devices, can be significant. If costs were allocated for elevators to transport items, for staging areas to store room service carts and to prepare them for deliveries, and for similar costs, the expenses would even be greater. Finally, items such as glasses, cups, flatware, and serviceware increase room service costs.

The need to return soiled room service items to kitchen areas often creates other problems. For example, questions of "*whose job is it to return dirty dishware items?*" to the food and beverage area can arise. Unfortunately, while those questions are being addressed, unsightly guest trays may remain in hotel hallways for longer than desirable periods of time, and some serviceware items (which can be costly to replace) may be stolen.

In some hotels, the room service department provides food and beverage service in **hospitality suites** and for other group functions in a guest room. In convention properties, vendors and exhibitors may invite customers to visit hotel rooms for **hosted events**. When these services are provided by room service staff rather than by banquet service staff, the likelihood of room service profitability increases.

LODGING LANGUAGE

Hospitality suite: A guest room rented by a supplier/vendor, usually during a convention/conference, to provide complimentary food and/or beverages to invited guests.

Hosted event: Functions that are complimentary for invited guests; costs are borne by the event's sponsor. A hosted bar may offer free beverages to wedding party guests, and a corporate sponsor may pay for a hosted reception in a hospitality suite.

Menu Planning

Special concerns are important when planning room service menus. As with any other food service alternative, quality is important. Room service menus should only offer items that can be transported relatively long distances from food preparation areas without decreases in quality. Because guests may perceive room service prices to be high, they expect food quality to be high to help justify the prices. Unfortunately, some popular items (fried eggs and french fries, for example) are not ideal room service menu items because of quality problems that can arise when they are held at serving temperatures for long periods of time during transport to guest rooms.

A food and beverage manager in a hotel can easily check food quality in the hotel's restaurant or a banquet setting by sampling various items. However, room service managers have less access to products served in room service. Efforts to solicit feedback from guests are a critical way of seeing whether quality requirements are consistently attained.

Creative hoteliers know that room service menus can be used to sell other hotel products and services. For example, a room service breakfast menu can indicate that the hotel's Sunday brunch in the dining room is very popular. An invitation on the room service breakfast menu to call about daily dinner specials in the dining room can also interest guests in thinking ahead about their evening dinner plans.

Hotels located near some airports and other tourism areas attracting international guests have another room service challenge: language barriers. A non-English-speaking guest alone in a guest room with a menu written in English will have great difficulty in ordering. Alternatives such as pictures and menu item descriptions written in the languages most used by the hotel's international guests may be solutions. If there are minimum order charges, mandatory tipping policies, or other requirements for guest room orders, these should be clearly indicated on the menu and may also be stated by the order taker.

Operating Issues

Trained room service order takers are needed regardless of whether this is full-time position or only one part of many responsibilities. Communication problems occur all too frequently in room service. If the employee fails to take a complete order, guest dissatisfaction is likely. The same types of questions that are asked in an à la carte restaurant must be asked by the room service order taker. For example:

- How would you like your steak prepared?
- Would you like sour cream with your baked potato?
- Would you like a glass of wine to complete your dinner? Tonight's special wines would go well with your entrée, and they are a great value!

It is difficult to correct errors in any food service operation. However, an inaccurate order in the dining room can sometimes be quickly corrected. For example, if catsup for french fries is omitted, it can be immediately provided. However, if catsup is omitted from the room service tray, a relatively long and time-consuming trip back to the kitchen will be necessary. Should the guest wait with cold food as a result? Alternatively, should the guest consume the meal without the desired condiments? Either way, guest dissatisfaction can result, and the negative impression may carry over to other hotel experiences. At the same time, servers who must spend additional time on this work task will be unavailable to serve other guests who, in turn, may become dissatisfied as the wait for their room service order increases. A minor problem, then, can create a ripple effect that impacts the perceptions of many guests about their entire lodging experience.

Opportunities for **suggestive selling** are plentiful in room service. The room service **guest check average** can be increased if guests are informed about items they may not have initially ordered, such as appetizers or desserts because they didn't know or think about them.

LODGING LANGUAGE

Suggestive selling: Information suggested by an order taker (in a room service operation) or by a server (in an à la carte dining operation) to encourage guests to purchase additional items or higher priced items they might otherwise not have ordered. This is commonly referred to as *up-selling.*

Guest check average: The average amount spent by a guest for a room service or dining room order. The formula for calculating Guest Check Average is:

Total Revenue ÷ Total Number of Guests Served = Guest Check Average.

Room service orders, like those in à la carte dining operations, are entered into the operation's **point-of-sale (POS) system**. Orders can then be viewed on a screen or printed on hard copy tickets to be given to the room service cook(s). A copy of the order is also given to the server when the order is transported to the guest room.

LODGING LANGUAGE

Point of Sale (POS) system: A computer system that maintains a record of guests' food and beverage purchases and payments.

In all cases, it is important for the room server to carefully note whether the items that have been plated (portioned) and placed on the room service cart for delivery are, in fact, the ones that were ordered.

POS systems with software applications designed especially for room service have greatly improved room service order taking. Modern systems typically indicate the room number and the name of the guest registered in the room from which the order is placed. Using the guest's name is an effective selling tactic, and it has become easy for the order taker to do so. When orders are placed, these systems provide information about whether

LODGING ONLINE

Significant advances have been made in the development of hotel-specific POS systems. To see one such system, designed by Microsoft, go to:

http://www.micros.com

When you arrive at the site, click on "Products," then select "Hotels and Resorts," and then select "Restaurants."

How can food and beverage managers in the hotel industry be encouraged to stay abreast of rapidly changing POS system technology?

guests are permitted to charge meals purchases to their room folios or if the meals must be paid for at the time of delivery.

In-Room Service

From the guests' perspective, room service does not end when the food and beverage order reaches the guest room. In fact, delivery of the menu items ordered by a guest is just the beginning. Room service attendants must be adequately trained in service procedures that include:

- Asking guests where the room service meal should be placed
- Explaining procedures for retrieval of room service items
- Presenting the guest check and securing signature or payment
- Opening bottles of wine
- Inquiring if the guest needs anything that has not been delivered
- Providing an attitude of genuine hospitality (rather than appearing rushed to make another room service delivery)

Managers must continually assess how room service in their hotels can be improved. Guest feedback is crucial in this effort. Sometimes, a section relating to room service is included in a general guest rating form used to evaluate the entire property. Alternatively, a specific evaluation form provided when room service is delivered can be used.

The results of guest feedback should be randomly requested from the room service manager and reviewed by the property's general manager. When results are favorable, affected personnel should be recognized and rewarded. If challenges arise, the general manager should work with those in the food and beverage department to resolve the issues. Follow-up is important so that the same problem or others related to it do not re-occur.

BANQUET OPERATIONS

The availability of a wide variety of types and sizes of banquet events sold by a hotel's **catering** sales staff is an important factor separating hotel food and beverage departments from many of their counterparts in other segments of the food service industry. The volume of banquet business helps determine whether banquet operations are the responsibility of food production and service staff or, alternatively, whether employees with specialized banquet duties are utilized.

The hotel's marketing and sales staff will normally be responsible for generating banquet business and for negotiating contracts for specific banquet events. The delivery of the promised products and services, however, falls to the food and beverage department.

LODGING LANGUAGE

Catering: The process of selling a banquet event.

Hotels with extensive convention/meeting business have special banquet needs. Large properties often have a separate convention services department whose personnel plan and coordinate all activities (including those that are food- and beverage-related) for the groups visiting the hotel. General managers of smaller hotels in which the food and

ALL IN A DAY'S WORK 11.2

THE SITUATION

Mr. Vuki, the hotel's GM, was chairing the weekly executive committee meeting. The current topic was guest data generated from a newly implemented on-screen feedback system assessing performance in guest rooms, the dining room, and at the front office. Some department heads expressed satisfaction (or at least relief!) because the guest comment scores were 90 percent "Positive," on every factor assessed. "We must be doing a good job," said the food and beverage director. "There are no consistent complaints about anything."

Mr. Vuki, however, had a different thought. "Yes, at least nine guests out of ten think we are doing an excellent job. However, we should not be satisfied until every guest says we are doing a good job. The difference between where we are now and a perfect score represents improvements we can still make."

"Let's look at room service, for example," Mr. Vuki said. "Last week we had two complaints about cold food, and one guest indicated that the order was incomplete. Also, I am carrying more room service trays back to the kitchen that I find in the hallways as I walk around on the guest room floors."

"Yes," said the executive housekeeper. "My housekeepers tell me that they are also making more frequent calls to the kitchen to pick up room service trays left from the night before as well as from breakfast."

Suddenly, the food and beverage director was on the defensive. "We are short of employees in every service position. We have just hired and are now training several waiters and waitresses who, we hope, can work both in the dining room and in room service if we need them. In the meantime, I'm going to need your help in addressing these issues."

A RESPONSE

Mr. Vuki is correct to emphasize the opportunities to improve the operation still further even in times when guest comment scores are relatively high. The executive committee meeting provides an excellent opportunity to discuss issues impacting more than one department. However, the food and beverage director should have explored service staffing issues with affected department heads as soon as he became aware of the problem. It was not necessary to wait until comments were made in the executive committee meeting.

Mr. Vuki should discuss issues of communication, teamwork, and cooperation among all department heads and their employees. He should also facilitate a discussion and agreement about what can be done to address the issues of cold food and unreturned room service trays.

beverage director administers the banquet function and their counterparts in larger properties with specialized banquet managers have something in common: they must all know and understand how banquet functions work, how they can be evaluated, and how banquets can better meet the hotel's profitability and guest-related goals.

Profitability

Banquets are generally more profitable than restaurant (dining room) operations in hotels for several reasons:

- Banquets are frequently used to celebrate special events. This provides the opportunity to sell menu items that are more expensive and, therefore, higher in **contribution margin**.
- The number of meals to be served is known in advance; in fact, there is a formal **guarantee**. Also, the event will have known starting and ending times. This makes it easier to schedule production and service labor and to reduce the "peaks and valleys" in labor requirements that often occur during, respectively, busy and slow periods in à la carte dining room operations. Finally, in a banquet, there is less likelihood of overproduction of food and subsequent waste.
- Banquet planners are frequently able to sell a **hosted bar** or a **cash bar** that enables increased sales of alcoholic beverages to guests desiring them.
- There are opportunities to rent banquet rooms in addition to selling food and beverage products.
- Servers like working banquet events because, typically, mandatory service charges increase their income.

LODGING LANGUAGE

Contribution Margin: The amount of revenue remaining from a food sale after the cost of the food used to generate the sale is paid for.

Guarantee: A contractual agreement about the number of meals to be provided at a banquet event. The event's sponsor agrees to pay for the number of guests served or the guarantee, whichever is greater.

Hosted Bar: A beverage service alternative in which the host of a function pays for beverages during all or part of the banquet event. Also known as an "open bar."

Cash Bar: A beverage service alternative where guests desiring beverages during a banquet function pay for them personally.

The banquet business is very desirable, and hotel managers should do everything possible to gain a significant market share of the community's banquet business for their hotels.

Menu Planning

Most of the factors involved in planning a menu for the hotel's restaurant(s) are important when planning banquet menus. These can include concerns about:

- guest preferences
- the ability to consistently produce items of the desired quality
- the availability of ingredients required to produce the menu items
- production/service staff with appropriate skills
- equipment, layout, or facility design issues
- nutritional issues
- sanitation
- peak volume production capabilities
- the ability to generate required profit levels at the selling prices that are charged

In addition to these concerns, there can be other planning issues related to banquet menus. The menu planner must be confident that the items to be offered can be produced in the appropriate quantity, at the appropriate level of quality, and within the required time schedule. The old saying that "the customer is always right" must be tempered when banquet menus are planned. The hotel, not the banquet buyer, will be criticized if there is a failure to deliver according to anticipated standards. For example, consider a banquet host desiring a flambéed entrée, table-side-prepared Caesar salad, and handmade pastries for hundreds of guests. These items are very labor-intensive, and a large amount of specialized service would be required to deliver the items. Personnel in the sales and marketing department of most hotels would be setting up a no-win situation if they booked this event as described. If the hotel accepts the business and does not effectively deliver the promised banquet event, the guests will be upset. If the banquet buyer could not be convinced to choose a more practical menu, his or her business may be lost. However, it is likely in the hotel's best short- and long-term interest to refuse such banquet business if it cannot be delivered according to high-quality standards.

To ensure the menu items offered to guests are ones the hotel can readily produce, many properties have pre-established banquet menus that take into account the hotel's production limitations and its profitability goals. These menus are an excellent starting point for negotiations with prospective clients. Often these menus can be used without change. In other cases, relatively minor changes, such as the substitution of a specific vegetable or dessert for the ones listed on the banquet menu can be easily made.

On other occasions, a menu designed specifically for a special event is needed. A talented banquet planner, working with the property's executive chef, can develop a menu that meets the guests' expectations and the hotel's financial requirements. By contrast, without close cooperation between the catering sales staff and the food and beverage department, conflict over what can and cannot be profitably offered to guests can easily occur.

LODGING ONLINE

Hotels often market their banquet services as critical part of their larger online presence. To see an example of one hotel's banquet menu marketing efforts, go to:

www.hiltoncs.com/

When you arrive at the site, click "Banquet Menus."

Have you ever attended a banquet event at a hotel? In your opinion, how did the product and service you received at that event compare to what you have experienced at stand-alone restaurants?

Banquet Event Orders and Contracts

Banquet planning involves paying attention to numerous details. Most hotels utilize a **banquet event order (BEO)**. A sample BEO is shown in Figure 11.10. It summarizes banquet details and helps to prevent communication problems between hotel staff and the event's sponsors.

LODGING LANGUAGE

Banquet Event Order (BEO): A form used by sales and food service personnel to detail all the requirements for a banquet event. Information provided by the client is summarized on the form, and it becomes the basis for the formal contract between the client and the hotel.

The information in the BEO describes specific details about the event to be held. In some cases, it is used to form the legal contract between a hotel and a banquet buyer. However, in other cases, a separate document may be used. In either case, it is best to have a written and signed contract that clearly identifies:

Time of Guarantee: The date when an attendance guarantee (guest count) must be received.

Cancellation policies: This should include an explanation of fees to be assessed if the banquet contract is canceled. For example, there may be a cancellation fee of 50 percent of the anticipated billing if the contract is voided 60 or more days before the event was to be held, and a 100 percent fee may apply if a cancellation occurs 60 days or less from the scheduled date of the event.

Guarantee-reduction policy: For example, if the final guarantee is less than a specified percentage of the initial guarantee, an additional per-person charge may be assessed.

Billing: Information about the amount and schedule for guest payment would be addressed in the section of the agreement.

Prior to arrival, service staff should pay careful attention to the details included in a group's BEO to ensure a smooth and successful event.

Other Banquet Concerns

Banquet room setup, service styles, and control of beverage functions are among the other special concerns of hotel banquet managers.

BANQUET ROOM SETUP

A hotel's banquet rooms (also called **function rooms**) must be set up by the hotel's staff to reflect the type and purpose of the event to be held. For example, the room setup required for a business seminar would be very different from that of a formal wedding dinner.

EVENT DATE:	BANQUET EVENT ORDER (BEO) #:
Organization:	
Billing Address:	Business Phone #:
	Business Fax #:
Contact Name:	Business E-Mail
Account Executive:	Room Rental: $
Guaranteed: ( ) persons	
BEVERAGES	**ROOM SET UP**
❑ Full ❑ Limited ❑ Hosted bar ❑ Non-hosted bar	❑ Classroom ❑ Theater ❑ Other: __________
❑ With bartender ( ) bars ❑ Cash bar ( ) cashiers	❑ Diagram below
❑ Premium ❑ Call ❑ House	Need:
( ) per drink ( ) bar package ( ) hours of operation	❑ Registration table / chairs: __________ ❑ Wastebasket
Time: Room:	❑ Easels ❑ Podium: ❑ standing ❑ tabletop ❑ Pads / pencils / pens / mints
Bar Opening/Closing Instructions: Bar to close at: __________ AM / PM Bar to reopen at: __________ AM / PM	❑ Water / glasses Diagram:
Wine with Lunch / Dinner __________ with entrée, __________ servers Time: Location:	
Additional Instructions:	Linen: ❑ White ❑ Other: __________
FOOD MENU	Skirting:
_______ baseplates _______ waterglasses _______ butter rosettes on lemon leaves	Napkin: ❑ White ❑ Other: __________
❑ Introduction ❑ Invocation ❑ Nothing before meal	Music:
First Course Served at: __________ AM / PM Meal Served at: __________ AM / PM	**AUDIO/VISUAL**
	❑ Microphone: __________ ❑ Slide Projector - package: __________ ❑ Overhead Projector - package: __________ ❑ VHS / monitor / package: __________ ❑ Mixer, _______ channel ❑ AV - cart ❑ White board / markers ❑ Screen ❑ Flipchart/pads/tape/pens ❑ LCD projector
	COAT CHECK
	❑ Hosted ❑ Cash: _______ ( ) Attendant(s) ( ) Coat Racks
BEVERAGE MENU	**PARKING**
	❑ Hosted ❑ Cash: $_________ Fee per car: $_________
	BILLING (METHOD OF PAYMENT)
	Deposit received: $__________

FIGURE 11.10 Sample Banquet Event Order (BEO)

LODGING LANGUAGE

Function room: A designated hotel space that can accommodate different types of special events.

In most cases, function room setup is a very straightforward activity. The space assigned for the banquet is normally determined when the banquet event is booked and at the appropriate time the room will be set up as specified. Numerous details are typically involved in setting up a banquet room. The room's size is determined by the number of guests expected (although local fire safety codes or ordinances may also impact this decision). The type (round, square, or rectangular, for example) and size of tables; the number of seats per table; and the required space for aisles, dance floors, head tables, reception/buffet lines, or other purposes should be noted on the BEO and will affect room set up. Timing may also become critical when the same space must be used for different functions throughout the same day or when a very large evening event precedes a very large breakfast event in the same space the following day.

BANQUET SERVICE STYLES

Banquet events can involve numerous ways to serve food and beverage products to guests. Most of these serving styles (American, French, Russian, English, and Buffet) are applicable to dining room service, and several were discussed earlier in this chapter. Another style sometimes used at banquets is called Butler Service: appetizers and pre-poured champagne, for example, can be passed by service personnel circulating among guests standing at a reception. Frequently more than one service style is used during a single banquet event.

Service styles can differentiate an elegant and higher-cost banquet from its less-elegant and lower-priced counterpart. For example, a Caesar salad might be prepared tableside as a demonstration for those seated at a **head table**; then, pre-portioned servings of the Caesar salad could be served to those guests seated at all other tables. Alternatively, vegetables for a soup course could be brought to the table in individual bowls for each guest (American service); service staff could pour broth from a sterling pitcher into each guest's bowl at table side (modified Russian service). These are examples of simple ways to make a banquet appear more elegant.

LODGING LANGUAGE

Head table: Special seating at a banquet event reserved for designated guests.

CONTROL OF BEVERAGE FUNCTIONS

Many banquets include the offering of alcoholic beverages. Examples include receptions before an event, wine service during a function, and continuing service of beverages during and after the meal service has concluded. Banquets offer increased opportunities to sell **call brand** or **premium brand** beverages in addition to or in place of the property's **house brand beverages**.

LODGING LANGUAGE

Call brand beverages: High-priced and higher-quality alcoholic beverages sold by name (such as Johnnie Walker Gold Scotch) rather than by type of liquor (scotch) only.

Premium brand beverages: Highest-priced and highest-quality beverages generally available, such as Johnny Walker Black Scotch. Also referred to as "super call."

House brand beverages: Alcoholic beverages sold by type (scotch) rather than by brand that are served when a call or premium brand beverage is not requested, also called "speed-rail," "well," or "pour brand."

There are several common ways that beverages sold at banquet events can be charged for and priced. They can be sold on a per-drink basis at a cash bar where guests desiring beverages pay for them personally. Many events offer hosted (open) bars in which beverages are paid for by the host for all or part of the banquet order.

Still other events have a combination of a cash and open bar where guests are issued drink tickets for complimentary drinks and then can purchase additional beverages. Another variation occurs when drinks are complimentary for a specified time period (e.g., before dinner) and are purchased (cash bar) by guests after that time.

There are a variety of ways that beverage charges can be assessed:

Individual drink price. Cash or a ticket sold for cash is collected when each drink is sold. Alternatively, a manual or electronic tally can be made of the number of each type of drink sold, and the host is charged at an agreed-upon price-per-drink basis at the end of the event.

LABOR CHARGES

Costs for the labor required to produce and serve food is normally included in the banquet charge. Sometimes, especially when the number of guests is small and the variety of services requested is large, additional charges for the following types of labor are assessed. These can include charges for:

- bartenders and barbacks (bartender assistants)
- beverage servers
- cashiers
- security personnel
- valet (parking) staff
- coat room employees

Bottle charge. Often used with an open bar, beverages are charged on a by-bottle basis for each bottle consumed/opened. Normally, every bottle opened is charged for at a full, agreed-upon rate; guests are not allowed to take open bottles away from the hotel.

Per-person charge. This method involves charging a specific price for beverages based upon event attendance. The same number of guests used for the guarantee (discussed earlier) may become the basis for the per-person charge. A deduction from the guarantee is made for minors attending the event because they will not consume alcoholic beverages.

Hourly charge. This method involves charging the host a specific price for each hour of beverage service. To establish the hourly charge, properties must determine the number of guests to be present (the guarantee can be used with adjustment for minors) and then estimate the number of drinks to be consumed per guest for each hour of the event.

Some hotels may charge a **corkage fee** for alcoholic beverages brought into the property by guests for use during an event. Although this is often misunderstood by guests, hotels *do* incur fees when pre-purchased beverages are brought in. The beverages must be served (labor costs are involved) and the bar/dining areas must be cleaned; glasses subject to breakage are used and washed; stir sticks, cocktail napkins, appropriate garnishes, if applicable, and other supplies will also still be necessary.

LODGING LANGUAGE

Corkage fee: A charge assessed when a guest brings a bottle (e.g., of a special wine) to the hotel for consumption at a banquet function or in the hotel's dining room.

Lodging Language

Banquet
Direct Report
Menu Planning
Value (foodservice)
Demographic Factors
Flambé
Ingredients
Theft
Pilferage
Stockout
Issuing
Production
Standardized Recipe
Scratch (food production)
Convenience Food
Make or Buy Analysis
Chained Recipe
Serving
Service (food and beverage)
Place Setting
Line-up (training)
Server Station
Hospitality Suite
Hosted Event
Suggestive Selling
Guest Check Average
Point-of-Sale (POS) system
Catering
Contribution Margin
Guarantee
Hosted Bars
Cash Bars
Banquet Event Order (BEO)
Function Room
Head Table
Call Brand Beverages
Premium Brand Beverages
House Brand Beverages
Corkage Fee

For Discussion

1. Assume that you are the food and beverage manager in a hotel in New York, San Francisco, New Orleans, or Honolulu that attracts guests from all over the world. What menu-planning tactics could you use that recognize the diverse food preferences of the international markets served by your property?
2. Assume that you are interested in a career in a hotel food and beverage operations. What would be the pros and cons of starting work in a smaller full-service hotel? In a larger hotel?
3. Assume that you are a food and beverage director working with the hotel's chef to plan a new menu. You want to add a vegetarian item to the new menu. What information would the chef want from you before implementing such a change?
4. It has been said that a hotelier will pay for food items of the quality purchased even though food items of the same quality are not received. What are some procedures that you as a food service manager would use to help ensure that proper receiving procedures are in use in your hotel?
5. You have learned about several service styles in common use in hotel à la carte dining and banquet operations. How would you determine which style(s) to use for your operation?
6. There are numerous tasks that servers must perform in order to make their guests' dining experience a memorable one. What are some basics you would use as a hotel restaurant manager to train new service staff in the proper way to perform these tasks?
7. Some hotels use dining room servers and room service attendants interchangeably. What special training would a room service attendant need to become an efficient dining room server?
8. Communication problems often impact the effective planning and delivery of banquets. It is natural for marketing and sales department personnel to want to do whatever they can to fill the hotel's guest rooms and public function spaces. It is also natural for food production staff to be concerned about banquet events being sold to guests. What are some types of issues that can cause conflict between personnel in these two hotel departments?
9. The food and beverage department and its housekeeping counterpart employ the vast majority of the employees in a full-service hotel. These departments are very labor-intensive because it is not practical to use technology to replace human workers in these areas. To what extent do you think technology will replace employees in the food and beverage department in the future? Why?
10. Assume that you are an overnight guest eating a hotel's complimentary breakfast the morning of your departure. Assume also that you are a businessperson staying in a five-star hotel about to dine in the property's high-check dining room on the 60th floor of the property. What are some expectations you would have that would be the same for both dining experiences?

Team Activities

TEAM ACTIVITY 1

Today all large hotel organizations use the Internet to advertise products and services to prospective guests. Find the Web sites for several of your favorite full-service hotel organizations. To what extent do they advertise their à la carte dining opportunities? Their room service and banquet operations? Do their advertising messages give any suggestion about the importance their guests place on food and beverage alternatives when making hotel-selection decisions? While reviewing these sites, check out the "employment opportunities" or similar section, and review the types of positions for which the organizations are currently recruiting. Are there position vacancies in food and beverage operations?

TEAM ACTIVITY 2

Visit a full-service hotel in your area and request permission to borrow a menu from the à la carte dining room. Pretend that you are a consultant to the property who has been asked to make improvement suggestions. Carefully study the menu from the perspectives of both the guests and the property managers. What suggestions would you make to improve the effectiveness of the menu?

Chapter

12 Hotel Accounting

Chapter Outline

On-Property Hotel Accounting
- Centralized Accounting Systems
- Decentralized Accounting Systems

Budgeting
- Long-Range Budgets
- Annual Budgets
- Monthly Budgets

Income Control
- Operational Controls
- Cash Control
- Allowances and Adjustments
- Accounts Receivable Control

Expense Control
- Purchasing and Receiving
- Accounts Payable

Financial Reporting
- The Income Statement
- Balance Sheet
- The Statement of Cash Flows

Chapter Overview

An operating hotel generates a tremendous amount of financial data. Every sale of rooms, food, beverages, and other hotel products and services must be recorded. Whether the word used to describe it is sales, income, or revenue, the money paid by guests must be collected and safeguarded, and, as well, the hotel's operating expenses must be carefully recorded, monitored, and managed. Proper accounting involves the maintenance of accurate records for all of a hotel's financial activities.

In a large hotel, a staff member known as the controller is responsible for the accounting function. In such a hotel, the controller may work with a very large staff. In a smaller property, the hotel's general manager may perform all of the duties of the controller. In either case, the hotel will have either a centralized or a decentralized accounting system in place. In this chapter, you will learn about both of these systems, and we will use the term "controller" to refer to the individual responsible for overseeing the hotel's accounting function.

The accounting function actually begins with budgeting. A hotel must be able to estimate the amount of money it will bring in (income) as well as the amount it must spend (expenses) to operate. Budgets are of three basic types. These are long-range budgets, annual budgets, and monthly budgets. Each budget type will be examined in this chapter.

In a hotel, the money to be collected from guests for purchases of rooms and other services must be carefully accounted for. This work must be done on a daily basis because many guests will only stay at the hotel one night. Thus, every morning at departure time, each guest's properly tabulated bill (folio) must be ready for presentation to that guest. In addition, hotels that operate retail outlets, such as restaurants, lounges, banquet facilities, golf courses, and gift shops, must account for their daily sales. All areas of the hotel that collect money must protect these funds from possible theft. In this chapter, you will see how hotels collect and protect their revenues.

In Chapter 4 (Managing Lodging Operations), you learned that control is one of the four major functions of management. It is not surprising, then, that a primary job of the controller is to help control expenses. This is done through careful management of the hotel's purchasing, receiving, and bill-payment processes.

Finally, the financial performance of a hotel is important to those managing the hotel, but it is also important to many individuals and groups outside the hotel. These may include the hotel's owners, investors, stockholders, lenders, or governmental taxing authorities. These audiences all rely on accurate and timely accounting information to make informed financial decisions about the hotel. In this chapter, you will learn about three of the most important financial documents prepared for use by those outside (as well as inside) a property. These documents are the income statement, the balance sheet, and the statement of cash flows.

Chapter Objectives

1. To explain the difference between centralized and decentralized on-property hotel accounting systems.
2. To show how hotels utilize long-range, annual, and monthly budgets to manage their income and expenses.
3. To describe the controls used to manage hotel revenues.
4. To describe the controls used to manage hotel expenses.
5. To explain how income statements, balance sheets, and statements of cash flows are used to report the financial status of a hotel.

ON-PROPERTY HOTEL ACCOUNTING

Professional hotel managers know they will be held accountable for the financial success of their properties. Accounting is simply the method by which a hotel or any organization's financial performance is measured. To be useful, an effective accounting system must allow for the careful recording, summarizing, and analysis of every financial transaction that occurs. When an accounting system works well, hoteliers can use the financial information it generates to make good managerial decisions. When a system works poorly, decision-making is impaired because it is based on inaccurate or incomplete information.

In a hotel, the **controller** is the individual responsible for overseeing the accounting and bookkeeping functions.

LODGING LANGUAGE

Controller: The individual responsible for recording, classifying, and summarizing a hotel's business transactions. In some hotels, this position is referred to as the comptroller.

While accounting and bookkeeping are similar, the purpose of bookkeeping is primarily to *record* and *summarize* financial data. Accounting includes the development of the systems to *collect* and *report* financial information, analyzing this same information, and making finance-related recommendations to assist in managerial decision-making. In many ways, the controller can be considered the hotel's on-property accountant even if the person who performs this function is not a **C.P.A.**

LODGING LANGUAGE

Certified Public Accountant (C.P.A.): An individual designated by the American Institute of Certified Public Accountants as competent in the field of accounting.

In some cases, the financial records of the hotel must be examined and approved by a C.P.A. before owners, investors, creditors, governmental agencies, and other interested parties will accept them as accurate. In very large hotels, the controller is likely to be a C.P.A., but in smaller properties it is more likely that an individual who is not a C.P.A. will be responsible for the bookkeeping and accounting functions.

It would be a mistake to discount the importance of a C.P.A. to some hotels; however, it would be just as big a mistake to assume that only a person who has earned the C.P.A. designation can be an effective controller. This is true because today's accounting systems can be classified as either centralized or decentralized.

Centralized Accounting Systems

In a **centralized accounting** system, the financial data from a hotel is transmitted via computer (e.g., by e-mail, network, and Web page posting) to a central location where it can be recorded and then analyzed by management, or combined with data from other hotel properties for analysis.

LODGING LANGUAGE

Centralized accounting: A financial management system that collects accounting data from individual hotels, and then combines and analyzes the data at a different (central) site.

To illustrate why some hotels operate under a centralized system, assume that you own five hotels in the southeastern United States. Assume also that your office is in the Midwest. If you wanted to know, on a daily basis, what the combined revenue for your five hotels was on the day before, you would want those hotels to have reported their previous day's income sales to your office. For convenience, you would then have the sales revenues of the five hotels added together to yield one number that represented all your hotels' total sales for that day. Centralized accounting is most prevalent in companies that operate several hotels and wish to combine financial data or spread the costs of the company's accounting system over multiple properties.

If a hotel is one of a number of smaller hotels owned or managed by the same company, it is likely to operate under a centralized accounting system. If so, it is also likely

In a centralized accounting system, hotels report financial information to an office not typically located on the hotel property.

that the company, rather than any individual hotel, will employ a C.P.A. for data analysis. Employing one highly trained C.P.A. in a central location is generally more cost-effective than having multiple C.P.A.s in multiple locations.

Decentralized Accounting Systems

In a **decentralized accounting** system, the general manager (smaller property) or the controller (larger property) must take a greater role in the preparation of the hotel's financial documents.

LODGING LANGUAGE

Decentralized accounting: A financial management system that collects accounting data from an individual hotel site and combines and analyzes it at the same site.

If neither the general manager nor the controller is a C.P.A., it is likely that the hotel's owners will, at least annually, employ the services of a C.P.A. to review the work of the on-property controller and give a professional opinion about the reliability of the financial statements he or she has prepared. This review process is called an **audit**.

LODGING LANGUAGE

Audit: An independent verification of financial records.

In some cases, audits of hotel accounting practices are viewed with the same dread as an individual's Internal Revenue income tax audit! That should not be the case. A hotel audit is routinely performed because hotel room nights, the principle saleable product of a hotel, are an extremely perishable commodity that cannot be held and controlled in a normal manner. This is true because unsold room nights disappear at midnight on each day. In addition, normal service to hotel guests includes a wide variety of transactions in which fairly large amounts of cash are handled. Finally, in smaller hotel properties, there is frequently a limited number of employees among whom accounting-related duties can be divided and rotated.

In nearly every case, an audit will uncover areas of financial reporting and control that can be improved. This is to be expected and should not be cause for concern. If the individuals performing the hotel's accounting functions are professionals committed to excellence, the audit is a tremendous opportunity for growth and improvement. Frequent and detailed auditing of hotel records is vital because of the need to establish and maintain sound accounting systems.

In this text, we will examine a decentralized accounting system to illustrate all of the many bookkeeping and accounting functions taking place in a modern hotel. In some ho-

LODGING ONLINE

C.P.A. is a prestigious designation that carries with it significant responsibilities. The American Institute of Certified Public Accountants (AICPA) is the professional association of those who have earned the C.P.A. designation. To view its Web site and read about the C.P.A. code of conduct, go to:

http://www.aicpa.org/

When you arrive, click on "For the Public" tab, then "Code of Conduct."

Why is it important that a hotel's financial records be prepared by a professional with the highest ethical standards?

tels, all, some, or none of these functions may be centralized. It is essential, however, for hoteliers to understand the budgeting, income and expense control, and financial reporting procedures that are required in a professionally managed hotel.

BUDGETING

Just as individuals make purchasing and spending decisions based upon how much money they will earn, hotels too must estimate the amount of revenue they will generate, how much it will cost to generate that revenue, and how extra funds (if any) will be spent or invested. As a result, professionally managed hotels budget for their income (revenues), expenses, and profits.

Some hoteliers may see the budgeting process as difficult and time-consuming. In fact, it need not be either of these. Properly prepared, a budget provides guidance to hotel managers and vital information to others interested in estimates of the hotel's future financial performance. It is crucial tool for effective hotel management.

In a business context, a budget is much more than a plan for spending cash resources. In fact, it is a plan for utilizing resources of all kinds, including cash, tools and materials, and labor, to operate the hotel in the most effective manner. Budgeting is sometimes described as a financial expression of a hotel's overall business strategy. This makes sense when you consider that a business strategy seeks to project where the hotel is going, how it will get there, what it will cost, and what the profit outcome will be if the strategy is implemented successfully. A well-developed budget, however, can do even more than project revenues and expense. If used properly, the budget is an important means of developing internal controls, another function that is critical to the controller's role.

Hotel managers create their budgets, monitor them closely, modify them when necessary, and seek to achieve their desired results. Yet, some controller/general manager teams do a poor job developing budgets because they feel the process is too time-consuming. Developing a dynamic budget does take time, but good budgets assist the hotel in many ways, including:

1. Allowing management to anticipate and prepare for future business conditions.
2. Providing a communication channel that allows the hotel's objectives to be passed along to all of its operating units.
3. Encouraging department managers who have participated in the preparation of the budget to establish their own operating objectives and evaluation techniques and tools.
4. Providing the hotel's managers with reasonable estimates of future expense levels and serving as a tool for determining future room rates and other pricing structures.
5. Helping the controller and the general manager to carry out periodically a self-evaluation of the hotel and its progress toward its financial objectives.
6. Estimating the probable financial returns on their investments for the hotel's owners.

In the hotel industry, operating budgets generally are one of three types:

- Long-range
- Annual
- Monthly

And we will examine each of these.

Long-Range Budgets

A long-range budget is one that encompasses a relatively lengthy period of time, generally from two to five years, or in some cases, even longer. The general manager, with the help of the controller in large properties, prepares the budget, with input from each of the hotel's operating units.

Obviously, with such a long-term outlook, these budgets are subject to changes due to unforeseen circumstances and market forces, but they are useful for long-term planning

Long-range, annual, and monthly budgeting assists managers and owners in predicting the future financial performance of their properties.

as well as for considering the wisdom of debt financing and refinancing, and for scheduling **capital expenditures**.

LODGING LANGUAGE

Capital expenditures: The purchase of equipment, land, buildings, or other assets necessary for the operation of a hotel.

Annual Budgets

In many cases, preparation of a hotel's annual budget consumes a significant amount of time. This is so because in large, multi-unit hotel companies, annual budgets must be produced by the individual hotels, submitted to a central office for review, and then in some cases revised to ensure that they are in keeping with the overall financial objectives and goals of the hotel company. This budget development process can begin as early as June or July for the following year.

As the name implies, annual budgets are developed to coincide with the calendar year. As such, they provide more detail than a long-term budget and are subject to less fluctuation based on unforeseen events. To be effective, annual budgets must be based upon management's best estimate of market conditions, the effectiveness of the sales and marketing team and its annual marketing plan, new hotels that may open in the area, existing hotels that may close, and any other economic factors that could reasonably affect the total revenues generated by the hotel.

Monthly Budgets

The monthly budget is a natural component of the annual budget. In fact, many hotel managers produce their annual budgets by first producing 12 monthly budgets. You might wonder why a hotel with a well-developed annual budget should concern itself with accurate monthly budgets. The importance of the monthly budget, however, can be seen quite clearly in the example of the annual revenue and expenses of a hotel near a ski resort. In each of the winter months, revenues and expenses will probably be much more than one-twelfth of the annual revenue and expense budget. In a like manner, the revenues and expenditures for the summer months will fall far short of one-twelfth the annual budget. If this **seasonal hotel** is to effectively reach the annual targets, great care will need to be taken with each individual month's budget.

ALL IN A DAY'S WORK 12.1

THE SITUATION

"I don't know. It's a good brand, but their location isn't nearly as convenient as ours," said Peggy Richards, the manager of the Homestead Suites Hotel.

"But what will its opening do to our occupancy next year" asked Kevin Gustafson, the hotel's owner. "And how will it affect our ADR?"

Peggy and Kevin were preparing the Homestead's annual operating budget for the coming year. They were attempting to estimate revenues. This year had been a good one; their 100-room hotel had achieved a 70 percent occupancy rate with slightly better than a $78 per room ADR. The result was nearly $3 million in hotel rooms revenue annually. The problem and challenge, they both knew, was that a new competitor was scheduled to open an 80-room franchised property just a quarter of a mile from them on February 1st. While not an all-suite hotel, the new competitor would be offering newly built, large rooms, with high-speed Internet access in each room and a well-marketed frequent-guest program. Peggy and Kevin had already received invitations to the hotel's "Grand Opening" party.

A RESPONSE

Peggy and Kevin are wise to consider the impact of events outside their control when preparing their annual operating budget. New hotel openings, hotel closings, the state of the economy, and the effectiveness of a hotel's sales and marketing plan are all factors that must be considered when preparing a hotel's long-term, annual, and monthly budgets. Additional factors to be considered include planned property upgrades, the franchisor's marketing efforts, and the efforts of the local convention and visitors bureau.

LODGING LANGUAGE

Seasonal hotel: A hotel whose revenue and expenditures vary greatly depending on the time (season) of the year. Examples include hotels near ski resorts, beaches, theme parks, certain tourist areas, sporting venues, and the like.

Many hotels will see some variation in annual sales based on the time of year. As a result, monthly budgets are an excellent managerial tool for helping to determine whether or not the hotel is making progress toward the overall goals developed in the annual budget.

While the complete development of a hotel's operating budget is beyond the scope of this chapter, it is important to understand that a significant part of a hotel's accounting function consists of preparing and monitoring long-range, annual, and monthly budgets that list a hotel's estimated revenues, expenses, and profits.

INCOME CONTROL

One of the most important reasons for a hotel to have an effective accounting system in place is to safeguard the income it earns. When a guest makes a purchase, the money paid to the hotel by the guest must be documented, collected, and safely held until it can be deposited into the hotel's bank account. Prior to that, however, it is necessary to confirm that

LODGING ONLINE

Hospitality Financial and Technology Professionals (HFTP) is the professional association for individuals working in the areas of hotel accounting and technology. To see its Web site and mission statement, go to:

www.hftp.org/

How important do you believe an understanding of accounting principles is in the management of a hotel?

the amount charged to the guest for the purchase was, in fact, the correct amount. An effective hotel accounting system includes the operational controls necessary to ensure that guests (and the hotel) are not defrauded by hotel employees. These same controls also help ensure that guests do not defraud the hotel. In addition, an effective system will include procedures for handling the cash collected on-property, billing guests to whom the hotel has extended credit, and collecting payments from them.

Operational Controls

On a daily basis, the hotel controller must confirm that the previous day's sales were recorded accurately. Recall from Chapter 6 that the previous day's hotel sales are tabulated by the night auditor and that the "end" of the day, (and therefore the beginning of the next day) is not a fixed time. Rather, it is the time at which the night auditor concludes (closes) the night audit. The controller checks the accuracy of the night audit and also makes sure that the night auditor is not defrauding the hotel. These two operational goals are accomplished by the accurate production of the **manager's daily** sales report.

LODGING LANGUAGE

Manager's daily (sales report): A re-cap of the previous day's rooms, food and beverage, and other sales. The manager's daily may include additional hotel operating statistics as requested by the hotel's general manager. Sometimes referred to simply as the "daily."

The daily is prepared from data supplied every night by the PMS (see Chapter 6). In some cases, the PMS may actually produce the first draft or the final version of the daily. The controller uses the nightly data produced by the PMS for a variety of tasks, one of which is the preparation of the daily.

Information that should be contained on the manager's daily includes the following:

For rooms:
- Number of rooms available for sale
- Number of rooms sold
- Total rooms revenue
- Occupancy rate
- ADR
- RevPAR
- Other rooms revenue information desired by the general manager

For foods and beverages:
- Restaurant sales
- Bar/lounge sales
- Meeting room rentals
- Banquet sales
- Other F&B revenue information desired by the general manager

For other income:
- Telephone revenue
- In-room movie revenue
- No-show billings
- Other income categories unique to the property (e.g., spa, resort, or golf fees)

While the report is called the daily, which implies that it contains only one day's information, most controllers increase the value of the daily by including cumulative monthly data totals, as well as individual and cumulative data from the same day in the preceding year. A sample one-page daily for a mid-sized hotel, produced via Excel spreadsheet, could be designed in a manner similar to what is shown in Figure 12.1.

The more detail desired by the manager, the more in-depth will be the manager's daily. Some managers prefer great detail in their daily information about room types sold, number of guaranteed reservations made, cash overage and shortages, or any number of

Manager's Daily Report

THE BEST SLEEP HOTEL — January 15, 20xx

	Today	To Date	Last Year Today	Last Year to Date
Rooms Available	285	4275	285	4275
Rooms Occupied	**191**	**3035**	**180**	
Occ. %	67%	71%	63%	70%
ADR	$ 105.20	$ 103.98	$ 98.99	$ 100.20
RevPar	$ 70.50	$ 73.82	$ 62.52	$ 70.57
Rooms Revenue	**$ 20,093.20**	**$ 315,579.30**	**$ 17,818.20**	**$ 301,702.20**
Food and Beverage				
Banquets	$ 4,550.00	$ 68,250.00	$ -0	$ 71,250.00
Meeting Room Revenue	$ 1,250.00	$ 18,750.00	$ 150.00	$ 19,850.00
A/V Rental	$ 140.00	$ 2,240.00	$ 75.00	$ 2,500.00
Restaurant	$ 650.00	$ 8,450.00	$ 710.00	$ 10,650.00
Total F&B Income	**$ 6,590.00**	**$ 97,690.00**	**‡$ 935.00**	**$ 104,250.00**
Telephone Revenue				
Local Calls	$ 85.00	$ 1,105.00	$ 79.50	$ 1,033.50
Long-Distance Calls	$ 210.00	$ 2,730.00	$ 185.00	$ 2,220.00
Other Income				
Gift shop	$ 231.25	$ 2,312.50	$ 221.00	$ 2,210.00
In-room movie sales	$ 185.00	$ 2,035.00	$ 78.00	$ 1,850.00
Guest Laundry	$ 71.50	$ 858.00	$ 61.50	$ 738.00
No Show revenue	$ 198.50	$ 2,580.50	$ 520.00	$ 3,200.00
Total Daily Revenue	**$ 27,664.45**	**$ 424,890.30**	**$ 19,898.20**	**$ 417,203.70**

FIGURE 12.1 Manager's Daily Report

Properly processing guest payments is one important income control activity.

other types of information that may be helpful in keeping abreast of the hotel's business on a daily basis. When the controller produces the daily, the job is made substantially easier because the PMS system is used to generate some parts or even all of the report.

An additional part of the controller's operational control role is the documentation and verification of the night auditor's report. This report, generated by the night auditor and the PMS, will provide management a complete and detailed breakdown of the previous day's business. Often running 10 or more pages in length, the night audit report is used to verify credit card charges, cash on hand, revenue sales totals, detailed room revenue statistics, and **allowances and adjustments**.

LODGING LANGUAGE

Allowances and adjustments: Reductions in sales revenue credited to guests because of errors in properly recording sales or to satisfy a guest who has experienced property shortcomings.

The night audit report provides a wealth of information on room sales if the controller produces it properly. For example, the information provided by the PMS required to fully understand the sales revenue and RevPAR generated on any given day includes information related to ADR, rooms sold, and market segment. Figure 12.2 details the comprehensive information that can

Manager's Room Revenue Detail Report						
THE BEST SLEEP HOTEL						January 15, 20XX
Rooms Available	285					
Rooms Sold	191					
Occupancy %	67.0%					
	Situation 1 (285 Rooms Available)			Situation 2 (285 Rooms Available)		
Market Mix	**Rooms Sold**	**ADR**	**Total Revenue**	**Rooms Sold**	**ADR**	**Total Revenue**
Transient Guests						
Corporate	25	119	$ 2,975.00	75	119	$ 8,925.00
Leisure	25	139	$ 3,475.00	5	139	$ 695.00
Government	0	0	$ 0.00	15	75	$ 1,125.00
Total Transient Guests	**50**		**$ 6,450.00**	**95**		**$ 10,745.00**
Group Guests						
Corporate	5	105	$ 525.00	60	105	$ 6,300.00
Leisure	40	118	$ 4,720.00	6	118	$ 708.00
Government	5	78	$ 390.00	30	78	$ 2,340.00
Total Group Guests	**50**		**$ 5,635.00**	**96**		**$ 9,348.00**
Tour Guests	91	88	**$ 8,008.00**	0		**0**
TOTAL GUESTS	**191**		**$ 20,093.00**	**191**		**$ 20,093.00**
ADR			$ 105.20			$ 105.20
RevPar			**$ 70.50**			**$ 70.50**

FIGURE 12.2 Two Alternative Guest Profiles/Same RevPar

be provided on guests staying in the hotel. This information is of importance to several of the hotel's operational areas.

As can be seen, the makeup of the guests in the hotel would be very different under these situations. In situation 1, the hotel is filled primarily with people on a tour (91 rooms) and leisure travelers (40 rooms). In the second situation, transient corporate travelers make up the largest portion of guests (75 rooms), followed by corporate travelers staying in a group (60 rooms). There are several reasons for the controller to analyze the night audit report. Two of the most important are information and accuracy. To understand the importance of information, consider again the data in Figure 12.2.

Assume that the management of the Best Sleep Hotel knows, from past records, that the average leisure or tour room sold by the hotel houses 2.2 individuals while each corporate room sold is occupied, on average, by 1.1 persons. Obviously, the demands placed on the hotel's restaurants and recreational facilities will be very different, as will the housekeeping services required by these two groups. Taking all occupied rooms into consideration, the **house count** in the first situation is likely to be nearly twice that of the second situation.

LODGING LANGUAGE

House count: An estimate of the number of actual guests staying in a hotel on a given day.

Because this is true, it is important for management to know not only how many rooms have been sold in the hotel, and the day's RevPAR, but also to what client type the rooms have been sold. It is the role of the controller to provide this information on a consistent basis.

The controller should, on a daily basis, provide the property's management with the following information from the previous day (night audit):

- Rooms available
- Total rooms occupied
- Rooms occupied by guest type
- Occupancy percentage
- Total revenue (sales)
- Total ADR
- ADR by guest type
- Total RevPAR

To the above data may be added any additional decision-making rooms statistics or information required by management. The controller should have the accounting systems in place to verify the accuracy of all the operational information provided and should be prepared to **sign-off** on the accuracy of the night audit.

LODGING LANGUAGE

Sign-off: To verify or approve accuracy of operational information. Used as in: "Ms. Larson, will you sign-off on last night's audit?"

Cash Control

Because the position title of the controller is derived from the word "control," it is not surprising that one of the very most important functions of the controller is the development and maintenance of internal control systems. Hotels and the restaurants often routinely have large amounts of cash, products, and equipment that can, if not carefully controlled, be the subject of fraudulent activities by guests or employees. A good controller carefully develops policies and procedures designed to protect the hotel's assets, including cash.

Any business that routinely collects cash payments from guests must develop a system of safeguarding this important asset. Hotels are no exception. People unfamiliar with the hotel industry often think of "cash" as currency (coins and bills). In today's hotel environment, cash assets in addition to currency include credit and debit card charges, and personal and business checks. The potential to lose these assets to theft, fraud, or outright carelessness always exists. It is the role of the controller, general manager, and the department head of each cash-handling area to develop and enforce a system of checks and balances and controls that will keep these important assets secure.

In many hotels, cash is collected in many other locations in addition to the front office. Restaurants, bars, lounges, parking and vending areas, and gift shops are just a few examples of locations in a typical hotel that routinely process cash sales. In all of these situations, at least one person serves as a cashier/money handler. Bartenders may serve as their own cashiers during an evening shift. Likewise, the individual responsible for replenishing soft drink vending machines serves as a cashier of sorts when cash is removed from the machines. Even if the vending machines are serviced by an outside entity, theft can impact the hotel because commissions paid to the property are typically based upon a percentage of the revenue generated by the machines.

In hotels, cash assets are at greater risk from internal threats than from external ones. While there is always the potential for robbery by non-employees, the greater threat to the security of the hotel's cash assets is the possibility of employee theft or fraud.

Any time a cashier is responsible for the collection of money, there are several areas of potential employee theft or fraud. The cashier may, for example, record a sale, collect payment from a guest but keep the cash. Or the cashier may not record the sale at all and, again, keep the cash.

The methods used by cashiers to defraud guests and/or the hotel are varied and depend to a great degree upon the type of sale that is made. The methods used by a dishonest bartender to steal from the hotel's food and beverage department will be different from those used by a dishonest front office agent. In either case, management must have systems in place to verify the amount of sales made and the cash receipts they produce. An effective, experienced controller is invaluable in designing and establishing these systems.

While thefts of cash (currency) by a cashier are fairly straightforward, some cashiers also have the opportunity to defraud guests who pay by credit card. These too must be guarded against. Some common credit card-related techniques used to defraud guests include:

- Charging a guest's credit card for items not purchased, then removing an amount of money from the cash register equal to the erroneous charge.
- Changing the totals on credit card charges after the guest has left or imprinting additional credit card charges and removing cash from the cash drawer equal to the amount of the fraudulent overcharge
- Misadding legitimate charges to create a higher-than-appropriate total, with the intent of keeping the overcharge. This, of course, can also be done on a cash sale.
- Charging higher-than-authorized prices for cash sales of products or services, recording the proper price, and keeping the overcharge.
- Giving, or selling, the credit card numbers of guests to unauthorized individuals outside the hotel.

The controller's revenue-control programs must be evident in every cash-handling area and on every shift. For example, a bartender working from 5:00 p.m. to 2:00 a.m. and serving as his or her own cashier might record $1,000 in beverage sales during that time period. If that figure is accurate, and there were no errors in handling change, the cash register should contain currency, checks, and bank charges equal to $1,000 plus, of course, the amount of cash in the register at the beginning of the shift (the **shift bank**).

LODGING LANGUAGE

Shift bank: The total amount of currency and coins in a cashier's drawer at the beginning of that cashier's work shift. Used as in: "Let's start the 3:00 p.m. shift at the front desk with a $750 shift bank."

If, in our example, the bartender's drawer contains less than $1,000 plus the amount of the shift bank, it is said to be **short**; if it contains more than $1,000 plus the shift bank, it is said to be **over**.

LODGING LANGUAGE

Short: A situation in which a cashier has less money in the cash drawer than the official sales records plus shift bank indicate should be available. Thus, a cashier with $10 less in the cash drawer than the sales record plus shift bank is said to be $10 short.

Over: A situation in which a cashier has more money in the cash drawer than the official sales records plus shift bank indicate. Thus, a cashier with $10 more in the cash drawer than the sales record plus shift bank is said to be $10 over.

Overages and shortages should be monitored by the controller, and when excessive, should be brought to the immediate attention of the appropriate manager for corrective action. Cashiers rarely steal large sums of money directly from the cash drawer because such theft is easily detected, but management should make it a policy to monitor cash overages and shortages on a daily basis. Some inexperienced managers believe that only cash shortages, but not overages, need to be investigated. This is not the case. Consistent cash overages as well as shortages may be an indication of employee theft or carelessness and must be investigated.

A dishonest cashier is sometimes able to avoid being short and still defraud the hotel. If, for example, the cash register has a void (erase) key, a dishonest cashier could enter a sales amount, collect for it, and then void the sale after the guest has departed. In this way, total sales would equal the amount in the cash drawer at the end of the shift. If the cashier then destroys the records involved with this sale, the cash register's total sales figure and the cash drawer will balance. To prevent this, management should insist that all cash register voids be performed by a supervisor or at least be individually authorized by management. In addition, because today's computerized cash register equipment records the number, individual, and time at which cashier voids are performed, these controls should also be monitored.

Another method of hotel cashier theft involves the manipulation of reduced-price or complimentary rooms or products. Assume, for example, that at the Best Sleep Hotel, the sales and marketing team has produced and distributed a large number of guest coupons good for 50 percent off a guest's night stay. If the front office cashier has access to these coupons, it is possible to collect the full charge from a guest without a coupon and then add the coupon to the cash drawer while simultaneously removing sales revenue equal to the value of the coupon. A variation is for the cashier to declare a room to be complimentary *after* the guest has paid the bill. In cases like this, the front office agent would revise the records in the PMS to indicate that the room was a comp, and then remove revenue from the cash drawer in an amount equal to the comped room.

These kinds of fraud can be prevented by denying cashiers access to unredeemed cash-value coupons issued by the hotel, and by requiring special authorization from management to comp rooms. While the scenarios presented above do not list all the possible methods of revenue theft and fraud, it should be clear from this discussion that managers must have a complete revenue security system in order to be certain that all the sales revenue generated by the services and products sold by the hotel finds its way into the hotel's bank account.

It is important to evaluate regularly the cash-control systems in place on the property. This includes a through evaluation of:

- Cashier training programs
- Revenue recording systems and procedures
- Cash overage and shortage monitoring tactics
- Enforcement of employee disciplinary procedures for non-compliance with required procedures

Some cashiers find the theft of cash is very tempting. Today's sophisticated cash management systems make it easier than ever to detect cashier theft, but an effective control system is still critical to the process.

Allowances and Adjustments

In a hotel, the issue of controlling allowances and adjustments is related to that of cash control. Recall that an allowance or adjustment is a reduction in a guest's bill resulting from a billing error or from a significant shortcoming in the product or services sold by the hotel. For example, a guest who complains upon departure that the room air conditioner was so loud it was impossible to sleep, might, depending upon hotel policy, receive an allowance (adjustment) on the bill of a specific dollar amount. The guest would pay the reduced amount, and the cashier's drawer would balance because a record of the allowance would be made to explain the reduction in revenues. Similarly, a guest who checked in and was billed during the night audit at a nightly room rate of $99, but whose company had, in fact, previously negotiated a rate of $79 per night would have $20 adjusted off his or her folio when the error was discovered. The importance of a controller maintaining a detailed daily listing of any allowances or adjustments vouchers created by the managers or employees of the hotel is clear.

Vouchers are important because they help to balance actual revenue collected with monies previously billed to guests. From the perspective of the hotel's operating managers, however, vouchers are also important because they can identify shortcomings in hotel services, processes, and procedures that must be addressed, corrected and/or improved. Figure 12.3 shows an allowance and adjustment form used by a typical hotel.

(1) ALLOWANCE/ADJUSTMENT No 348685		
NAME (3)	DATE (2) 20 ROOM OR ACCT. NO. (4)	
EXPLANATION (5)		
X (6) SIGNATURE	11-09-0199 (7)	

FIGURE 12.3 Allowance and Adjustment Voucher

Note that the form has:

1. A sequence number for control purposes.
2. A space for the date the voucher is used.
3. A space for the name of the guest(s) for whom the adjustment was made.
4. A space for the guest's identifying room number or account.
5. A space for an explanation of the event or circumstances that justified issuing an adjustment.
6. A space for the initials or signature of the employee issuing the adjustment.
7. An identification number for reordering purposes.

In a small property, each of these vouchers would be tabulated and reviewed for accuracy by the controller or by the general manager. In a larger property, the information on the vouchers might be combined electronically and a summary of the information they contain would be passed on to the front office manager or employee charged with monitoring this aspect of the accounting system.

The importance of reviewing these allowance and adjustment vouchers regularly becomes evident when you understand that there are three fundamental situations that could result in the completion of an allowance and adjustment voucher.

1. ***Employee error in charges.*** Despite appropriate training, employees can sometimes make errors in the amount they charge guests. This problem can range from charging guests the wrong room rate for their stay, to charging guest "A" for services actually used by guest "B". When the error is discovered, guest A's folio (bill) must be adjusted to reflect the correct charge. Assume, for example, that Mr. and Mrs. York, staying in room 417 on a Saturday night, each have a drink in the hotel lounge. They sign the guest check charging the drinks to their room, but the bartender mistakenly charges the drinks to the guest in room 471. The Yorks check out on Sunday morning. On the following Monday, the guest staying in 471 approaches the front office to check out. Upon reviewing the bill, the guest in room 471 will refuse to pay the incorrect charge. At that point, an allowance and adjustment voucher, removing the drink charges, must be prepared. In such a case, it may not be possible to collect on the charges originally incurred by the Yorks (remember that they left the hotel on the previous morning). Shortcomings in employee training programs, cash sales systems, or guest services techniques may become clear to the hotel's managers if a pattern of employee error is made apparent through the review of allowance and adjustment vouchers.

2. ***Hotel-related problems.*** Despite the best efforts of the hotel's management and staff, some guests will still experience problems with the hotel's facilities or guest services. For example, an ice machine on a particular floor may, on a given day, have stopped working and, before it could be repaired by the hotel, inconvenienced a guest who had to walk to another section of the hotel for ice. Or, unfortunately, a hotel employee may not have been as courteous to a guest as desired, thus offending the guest. In both of these cases, and more, a guest may upon departure request (or demand!) a reduction in the bill. In these situations, an allowance or adjustment in the bill may need to be made, and the voucher would be filled out. The importance of such vouchers being seen by the hotel's managers on a daily basis is self-evident. Changes may be required in equipment inspection programs, guest service training, or a variety of other areas where management intervention is critical to correct recurring problems.
3. ***Guest-related problems.*** In some cases, it is the presence of other guests, rather than the hotel, that causes a particular guest to have an unpleasant experience at the hotel. Complaints ranging from excessive noise in adjacent rooms to rowdy guest behavior in public spaces can make some guests feel they should be compensated for the unpleasantness of their experience. If, in the opinion of the appropriate hotel staff member (front office agent, front office manager, or **MOD**), an adjustment to the guest's bill is warranted and the allowance and adjustment voucher would be completed.

LODGING LANGUAGE

Manager on Duty (MOD): The individual on the hotel property responsible for making any managerial decisions required during the period he or she is MOD.

The hotel's general manager would, of course, want to be made aware of all such incidents on a daily basis. Certainly the general manager would want to take corrective action to:

a. Eliminate the source of the guest disturbance
b. Compensate affected guests appropriately
c. Review and retrain employees about all guest disturbance-related policies

The affected guests are likely to contact the general manager, the hotel's owners, or the franchise brand organization with the same complaint. If management is unaware of problems on the property, corrective action cannot be taken. For that reason, the controller should share allowance and adjustment vouchers information with the appropriate managers every day.

The total dollar amount of allowances and adjustments compared to total overall rooms revenue can be tracked on a monthly basis using the following formula:

$$\frac{\text{Total Monthly Allowances and Adjustments}}{\text{Total Room Revenue}} = \text{Room Allowance and Adjustment \%}$$

This percentage will vary based on the age of the hotel, the quality of staff and training programs, and even the type of guest typically served. Percentages ranging from 0 percent to 3 percent of total room revenue are most common.

Accounts Receivable Control

In some cases, a hotel's actual client will be a company or organization rather than an individual guest. For example, if a large insurance company employed 50 staff members and arranged to hold its annual staff training session at a hotel, the company itself would make the 50 required guest room reservations and would agree to pay for the charges. In a situation of this kind, the insurance company is likely to request that the hotel send it a bill for all the room charges incurred during the training session. If the hotel agrees to do so, it will have agreed to sell the rooms to the insurance company on credit.

When a hotel elects to extend credit to a guest, it creates a direct bill account and then, as the guest incurs charges, periodically prepares an invoice and sends it to the guest. This direct guest billing may occur on the same day the guest incurs the charge, at the end of each month, quarterly, or at any mutually agreed-upon time. When a hotel extends credit to guests, the total dollar amount of the outstanding charges owed to the hotel by these guests is called the hotel's **accounts receivable (AR)**.

LODGING LANGUAGE

Accounts receivable (AR): Money owed to the hotel because of sales made on credit. Sometimes referred to as "AR."

There are many reasons, including guest preference, why a hotel might decide to extend credit to some guests. In all cases, however, it is the controller's job to establish:

1. Which guests will be allowed to purchase good and services on credit?
2. What are the payment terms that will be enforced?
3. Is there a maximum amount the guest is allowed to charge?
4. How promptly will the guests receive their bills?
5. What is the total amount owed to the hotel, and what is the length of time the monies have been owed?

The creditworthiness of guests is frequently debated between the sales and marketing team and the controller. In most cases, the sales and marketing staff will encourage the controller to extend credit to complete the sale while the controller often takes a more conservative view and may suggest that the hotel deny or restrict the amount of credit offered to the same potential guests. A good controller working with the general manager will establish a credit policy that maximizes the number of guests electing to do business with the hotel while minimizing the hotel's risk of creating uncollectable accounts receivable.

To assist in determining which guests should be able to buy on credit, a direct bill application for credit will be completed by the guest, reviewed by the controller or appropriate staff member, and then approved or passed on to the general manager for final approval or denial. Figure 12.4 is an example of a direct bill application.

To learn the reasons why a hotel would extend credit to a guest organization, consider the case of Rae Dopson, president of Dopson Construction, a mid-sized road construction firm. Rae's company has been awarded a state contract to construct two miles of new highway near the Best Sleep Hotel. The job is a big one and will last many months. It will involve the use of dozens of workers, each of whom will require Monday through Thursday night lodging near the worksite. Since the lodging of its workers will be an expense of Dopson Construction, it faces the alternatives of either (1) allowing its workers to stay at hotels of their own choosing and then reimbursing them for their lodging expenses, or (2) negotiating with a single hotel to place all of its lodging business at that property, and then request that the hotel bill the company directly for all its lodging expenses. Clearly, it is in the best interest of both the hotel and this company to select the second alternative. The bookkeeping of the construction company will be simplified if it is awarded direct bill status, and the construction company will also be able to negotiate a better nightly rate from the hotel because it can guarantee a predetermined number of room nights. The hotel also benefits from guaranteed business and simplified billing. Other hotels that desire the business from Dopson Construction will likely compete for it, in part, by offering Rae's company direct bill status and a negotiated rate.

After a determination has been made that credit terms will be extended, it is the responsibility of the controller's office to bill guests promptly. It is also the controller's job to monitor accounts receivable and keep the hotel's managers informed as to their status. This is done by the preparation of an **accounts receivable aging** report.

Best Sleep Hotel

Application for Direct Billing

Date: ____________ ***Federal ID #*** ____________

Company/Organization: ____________

Division/Department: ____________

Mailing Address: ____________

Street Address *Suite #*

____

City *State* *ZipCode*

____

(Area Code) Phone Number *(Area Code) Fax Number*

BILLING ADDRESS: ____________

(if different from above) ***(Name of Invoice Recipient–Attention to)***

____

Street (PO Box #) Suite #

____

City State Zip Code

List of those persons entitled to authorize (call in reservation):

1. ____________ ____________
   Full Name **Title**
2. ____________ ____________
   Full Name **Title**
3. ____________ ____________
   Full Name **Title**

Please circle the charges employees are authorized to bill. Circle all that apply:

Room & Tax only	*Phone*	*Restaurant Bills*
All Charges	*Movies*	*Banquet/Meeting Charges*

Credit References:

1. ____________
   Hotel Name
   ____
   Phone Number
2. ____________
   Hotel Name
   ____
   Phone Number
3. ____________
   Other
   ____
   Phone Number

FIGURE 12.4 Direct Bill Application

Company Bank:

Bank Name: ______________________ Account Type: ______________________

Account Number: ____

At least three credit references and at least one company bank are **required** to complete this application. At least two of the references must be hotel references, while the third may be a company with whom you have a billing history.

If for some reason the application cannot be completed with the requested information, please contact the Accounts Receivable Department of the Best Sleep Hotel.

Please allow at least 15 days for proper processing and approvals.
*Applications must be approved **before** any direct billing may take place. You will be contacted by mail about your approval status.*

By signing this document, I allow the creditors and bank listed above to release to the Best Sleep Hotel all necessary information for the proper processing and approval of this application. I understand that all accumulated charges are submitted to the accounting department upon the completion of each authorized function/stay. I also understand that payment is due within 30 days from the date of the invoice. I further understand that it is my company's responsibility to keep the list of authorized personnel updated and current to avoid improper or unauthorized usage of this direct bill account, and may do so by requesting an authorization/status change form from the Accounts Receivable Department of the Best Sleep Hotel.

Signature of Applicant: ______________________ Date: ______________

For Company Use Only:

Recommendation of Controller ____

Approved By

Signature: ______________________ *Date:* ______________

FIGURE 12.4 (*continued*)

LODGING LANGUAGE

Accounts receivable aging: A process for determining the average length of time money is owed to a hotel because of a credit sale.

Figure 12.5 shows an example of an accounts receivable aging report for a hotel with $100,000 in outstanding accounts receivable.

Best Sleep Hotel: Accounts Receivable Aging Report For January, 200X
Total Amount Receivable $100,000.00

	Number of Days Past Due			
	Less than 30	**30–59**	**60–89**	**90+**
	$ 50,000			
		$ 30,000		
			$ 15,000	
				$ 5,000
Total	$ 50,000	$ 30,000	$ 15,000	$ 5,000
% of Total	50%	30%	15%	5%

FIGURE 12.5 Accounts Receivable Aging Report

1. All clients allowed direct bill privileges have a properly completed and approved direct bill application on file.
2. All direct bills are processed and mailed within three days of the guest's departure.
3. All direct bill clients have two files (paper or electronic). One file contains outstanding invoices; the other contains paid invoices.
4. Payments made by guests on their folio balances are recorded with copies of checks stapled to the front of the folio.
5. An accounts receivable aging report is prepared monthly.
6. The balance due to the hotel on the aging report matches the total uncollected amount charged to guests.
7. Monthly credit meetings are held with the sales and marketing team to communicate current credit policies.
8. Additional credit is denied to direct bill guests who exceed established payment deadlines.
9. Critically overdue accounts are given to a collections attorney.
10. **Write-offs**, if any, are approved by management and recorded.

FIGURE 12.6 Ten Key Elements for Accounts Receivable Management

Figure 12.5 shows that the total amount owed to the hotel is $100,000. This amount can be broken down into four distinct time periods. One half of the total accounts receivable ($50,000) is owed to the hotel by guests who received their bills 30 or fewer days ago while 5 percent ($5,000) is due from guests who have had more than 90 days to pay their bills. As a general rule, as the age of an account receivable increases, the likelihood of its being collected decreases. Also, as the total percentage of accounts receivable 90 days or older increases, the likelihood of collecting on these receivables decreases.

As a receivable account ages, an effective controller will contact the guest to find out whether a problem in billing, documentation, or some other issue is delaying payment to the hotel. In severe cases of non-payment, the guest's direct billing status could be revoked, and the hotel would undertake collection efforts and **write-off** any account deemed to be uncollectable.

The extension of credit and the collection of accounts receivable is an important component of the hotel's income control system. Figure 12.6 lists 10 key elements that should be present in any controller's accounts receivable management system.

LODGING LANGUAGE

Write-off: A guest's direct bill that is considered uncollectible by management and as a result is subtracted from the hotel's accounts receivable total.

EXPENSE CONTROL

It is important to exercise complete control over a hotel's income, and it is just as important to maintain strict control over expenses. To operate properly, a hotel will spend money on staff, supplies, advertising, insurance, taxes, and a variety of other items. It is the job of the controller to see that the hotel pays its bills and maintains accurate records of doing so. Typically, the individual in charge of a specific area within the hotel will make the purchasing decisions for that area. For example, the front office manager may decide where to buy the electronic key cards used at the front desk and place an order for them. The key card vendor will ship the cards along with an invoice for their payment to the hotel. The payment made for the key cards and the recording of that payment will be the responsibility of the controller. Thus, the controller plays a role in the purchasing and receiving of hotel supplies as well as in the overall management of the hotel's **accounts payable (AP)**.

LODGING LANGUAGE

Accounts payable (AP): The sum total of all invoices owed by the hotel to its vendors for credit purchases made by the hotel. Also called "AP."

Accounts payables (AP) management is a very important accounting activity because it ensures vendors are properly paid for the goods and services they deliver.

Purchasing and Receiving

Perhaps the most important role the controller can play in the purchasing and receiving process is that of making sure that vendors are only paid for goods and services actually received. In some cases, the process is relatively easy. When a delivery of coffee is made by a coffee vendor, for example, it is a straightforward process to count the number of cases delivered and verify that the product delivered is the product ordered and that the price matches that which was agreed upon. In other instances, the process of verification is more difficult.

For example, a lawn service invoice may include charges for lawn mowing, edging, and chemical weed treatment. Both the quality of the work done (mowing and edging) and confirmation that it was, in fact, done (chemical weed treatment) must be verified by the person at the hotel who authorized the work. Obviously, the invoice should be paid if the services have been performed. However, payment should be withheld if all services have not been performed, or were not completed at the agreed-upon quality level. Thus, the controller should pay only those vendors who have delivered the hotel's authorized goods and services at the preauthorized price, and in the manner agreed upon by both the hotel and the vendor.

Before an accounts payable invoice is paid, the controller should have a system in place that verifies the terms of the sale, the product prices quoted by the vendor, and a list of the products received by the hotel so that these can be checked against actual vendor's invoices. When a hotel purchases services, it must have a payment system in place to confirm that a member(s) of the property management team has:

- Preauthorized the work to be done.
- Confirmed the cost of the work to be done.
- Verified that the work has been satisfactorily completed before payment is made.

Accounts Payable

Just as a hotel will sell to some of its guests on a credit basis, many suppliers and service companies provide goods and services to the hotel on a credit basis. The hotel is billed by these vendors according to credit terms that have been pre-established. For example, a vendor for dairy products may deliver fresh milk daily to the hotel. Obviously, it makes

LODGING ONLINE

To view the features of a Web-based software program that includes modules on accounts payable, go to:

www.netsuite.com

When you arrive, enter "Accounts payable" in the search window.

What would be some advantages to a hotel of using the Web for storage of its AP records? What would be some disadvantages?

little sense to pay that vendor 30 times per month for the milk products delivered. Typically, a vendor such as this would establish the creditworthiness of the hotel and then send the hotel an invoice on a weekly, biweekly, or monthly basis. The charges for goods and services used by the hotel, and invoiced by the vendor but not yet paid by the hotel make up the hotel's accounts payable.

There are four major areas of concern to controllers establishing an effective accounts payable management system. These are:

Payment of Proper Amounts: Whatever their level of skill and experience, employees sometimes make mistakes in paying invoices. Data entry errors may be commonplace unless the controller has established solid procedures to ensure that legitimate invoices are paid only for the amount actually due. In a well-managed hotel, invoices and payments for invoices are checked for errors by at least two individuals. Software developed to match invoice numbers against hotel check numbers is invaluable in this process. Such software is used to help ensure that accounts payable are processed only for the actual amount of the invoices due.

Payments Made in a Timely Manner: In addition to paying the right amount, an effective controller understands that there is a right time to pay each invoice. Some hotels gain a reputation with their suppliers for paying invoices very promptly. This can be good, but it is important to know that maintaining cash in the hotel's cash accounts is also valuable. An effective controller maintains good relations with vendors, many of whom are likely to be local businesses such as plumbers, electricians, and food vendors, all of whom are important for the hotel's continued success.

Customers who pay their bills slowly are likely to be serviced slowly by their vendors. In fact, prompt payment of invoices is so important to many smaller businesses providing goods and services to a hotel that better purchase prices and delivery terms can often be negotiated if the hotel has a reputation for paying its bills on time. Some vendors will offer the hotel the choice of paying less than the full invoice (discounts for on-time payments) if it pays promptly. In general, an effective controller should take advantage, whenever possible, of discounts offered by vendors for prompt payment. Some vendors will often give a discount of 1–5 percent of the invoice price if a bill is paid within a specific time period. The controller should seize every opportunity to build positive vendor relations and lower costs by managing the accounts payable process professionally.

Payment Records Properly Maintained: While it may seem fairly simple to ensure that each accounts payable invoice is paid only once, that is not, in fact, the case. Careful attention to detail is needed to make sure that invoices are paid and recorded properly. An effective controller creates a system whereby total payments to vendors match vendor-submitted invoice totals, with no overpayments or underpayments.

Payment Totals Assigned to Proper Department or Area: It is important for the controller to pay the hotel's bills, but it is equally important to know which area within the hotel has incurred a given expense. For example, a general manager may want to know how much money is being spent on plumbing repairs for a given month or year. Obviously then, the controller must keep a record of how much money is being spent by the maintenance department for plumbing parts and labor for the requested time period. To do so, controllers use a system of **coding** to assign actual costs to predetermined areas within the hotel.

LODGING LANGUAGE

Coding: The process of assigning incurred costs to predetermined cost centers or categories.

For example, the maintenance department will certainly be interested in its total expenditures for a month. The expenditure breakdown in Figure 12.7 shows where the money in the maintenance department is being spent and where it was over budget in the month of January. Controllers managing the reporting of expenses would assign a code to each expense subcategory and then record any expense payments made within the category. Note that each expense subcategory has been developed to help managers better understand the property's total operations and maintenance expenditures.

An effective controller will work with the employees involved in the purchasing process to code the hotel's expenses to the correct expense categories so that they can be accurately analyzed. Departmental expense categories can be developed by an individual hotel or a hotel company operating multiple hotels. In all cases, however, it is the role of the controller to implement a properly functioning expense coding system.

	Actual	**Budgeted**
Payroll and Related		
Chief Engineer	$ 4,444	$ 4,444
Engineer Assistants	8,450	9,000
Benefit Allocation	3,520	3,700
Total Payroll	16,414	17,144
Expenses		
Computer Equipment	425	500
Equipment Rental	1,000	0
Electrical & Mechanical Equipment	2,520	2,000
Elevators	600	580
Elevator Repairs	200	0
Engineering Supplies	250	300
Floor Covering	0	250
Furniture	0	1,000
Grounds	850	250
HVAC (heating/ventilation and air conditioning)	2,800	3,000
Kitchen Equipment	150	500
Laundry Equipment	0	400
Light Bulbs	250	200
Maintenance Contracts	2,500	2,500
Operating Supplies	185	300
Painting & Decorating	270	500
Parking Lot	1,000	200
Pest Control	350	500
Plants & Interior	280	300
Plumbing & Heating	1,585	500
Refrigeration & A/C	1,500	1,600
Signage Repair	0	0
Snow Removal	1,000	1,000
Swimming Pool	3,500	3,000
Travel & Entertainment	1,600	1,000
Telephone	150	200
Trash Removal	450	425
Uniforms	280	300
Total Expenses	$ 23,695	$ 21,275
Total Prop. Ops. & Maintenance	**$ 40,109**	**$ 38,419**

FIGURE 12.7 Best Sleep Hotel: Property Operations and Maintenance Expenditures for January

LODGING GOES GREEN!

Some hoteliers think green with regard to their operating departments but think less about greening in areas such as the controller's office. The fact is that the office environment offers many great opportunities to go green and save. For environmental conservation and cost savings, hoteliers can try these green office tips:

1. Use recycled paper products throughout the office. Separate waste paper and take it to the local recycling center.
2. When purging files or documents, use a shredder and place the shredded paper in the paper recycling container.
3. Refill or recycle ink and toner cartridges. When possible, purchase laser printers. These use less toner and no ink.
4. Use bio-degradable trash bags. The small added expense is worth it for the planet.
5. Use only rechargeable batteries in battery-powered devices. Regular batteries go to landfills and pollute the ground.
6. Turn off monitors. Simply turning off the monitor when not in use reduces the energy required by computer by about two-thirds.
7. Plug all electronics into a power strip, and switch it off before leaving the office for the day.
8. Set computers to go to sleep automatically during short breaks. This can cut energy use by 70 percent.
9. Unplug chargers when not in use. Mobile phone and Blackberry chargers continue to charge even when not connected to the device, using up to 95 percent of the power they use when the device is actually plugged in.
10. Program the fax machine so that it does not automatically print out a confirmation report for every fax. Better yet, use a fax modem (electronic fax) instead of a regular fax machine.

These are just a few green office tips. With a bit of innovation and creativity, a controller's office can implement many ways to go green and save money.

ALL IN A DAY'S WORK 12.2

THE SITUATION

"I know you signed off on it, but I'm just not comfortable processing payment on this one," said Kathy Waldo, "I need better back-up." Kathy, the general manager of the 65-room Best Rest Hotel, handed the invoice from Pittsburg Plow, the hotel's snow removal and parking lot salting company, back to Ron. Ron was the head of maintenance and the person responsible for ensuring that the hotel's parking areas remained free of ice and snow in the winter. The invoice from Pittsburg Plow was for five parking lot saltings during December. It was now January, and Ron had submitted the Pittsburg Plow invoice he had received for December services.

The single-page invoice simply stated:

"Best Rest Hotel: December Saltings: 5 @ at $180.00 = Total due $900.00"

"How do you know there were five?" Kathy asked Ron. "And when were they? How do we know there weren't three or four, or just one?"

"I'm just not sure," replied Ron, "I'm not here 24/7. And sometimes they come in the middle of the night. But I do remember seeing the salt truck here at least once or twice last month."

A RESPONSE

Kathy is correct to want more information prior to processing this invoice. The hotel does not seem to have the kind of accounting systems in place that can verify whether it has received and can document the services for which it is billed.

A solid system of services verification must be implemented to protect the hotel from fraudulent vendor billings for services such as salting, snow plowing, lawn care, fertilization of plants, and window washing in which the work may be done in a manner, or at times, not easily confirmed.

These systems can be as simple as having the vendor sign in at the front desk when working during off-hours, or as direct as requiring the vendor to make telephone contact with the appropriate hotel staff member when the work is started and/or has been completed. In all cases, however, it is unacceptable to pay a vendor for services when it is not clear whether the services were actually performed.

Working together, the general manager, the head of maintenance and the hotel's salt/plow vendor should work out a system to verify the quality and quantity of work performed. Then the appropriate hotel staff member can sign off on the payment (invoice) for that work. If this cannot be achieved with Pittsburg Plow, a new vendor should be selected.

FINANCIAL REPORTING

In addition to producing budgets, safeguarding income, and managing expenses, the controller in a hotel is also responsible for preparing or supplying the information to prepare the accounting documents known as the **financial statements** that provide an overview of the hotel's fiscal standing.

LODGING LANGUAGE

Financial statements: Financial summaries of a hotel's accounting information. Also called the hotel's "financials."

It is important that these financials accurately reflect the true fiscal health of the business. If a hotel's financial statements *overstate* its economic condition, potential buyers may be misled into thinking the hotel is worth more than it is, and thus might overpay to acquire it. Potential lenders to the hotel, in the same situation, may feel that the hotel could repay money loaned to it when, in fact, the hotel will not likely be able to do so.

Alternatively, if a hotel's financials inaccurately *understate* the value or economic strength of the property, its owners may not be able to achieve the sales price they want when they are ready to sell. Moreover, a lender may not loan money to the hotel even though the hotel's true financial condition would indicate that it could easily repay any loans it obtained.

Business accounting is a dynamic professional field that is constantly being revised and improved by those who work in it. As in nearly all professional fields, there can be real differences of opinion as to how accounting is best done. To ensure that all accountants prepare accurate financial statements and that others in business can easily read and understand the financial statements, accountants follow a set of generally accepted accounting principles known as **GAAP**.

LODGING LANGUAGE

Generally Accepted Accounting Principles (GAAP): Techniques, methods, and procedures utilized by all accountants in the preparation of financial statements.

As the hotel's accountant, the controller must also follow the GAAP. Even when the role of the on-property controller is simply to provide financial information to a centralized accounting system or to a C.P.A. retained by the hotel, the financial information reported must present a fair and accurate picture of the hotel's true financial position. While the hotel industry has not experienced blatant financial fraud on the magnitude of the Enron, WorldCom, and other highly publicized debacles of the 2000s, the experiences of these companies, and the consequences for their financial officers, point to the importance of honesty in reporting financial information.

Accuracy and honesty are important when the controller assists in preparing a budget that attempts to forecast a hotel's future financial performance. In addition to the budget, there are three key financial documents that look to the hotel's past accomplishments and present financial condition. These statements, each of which should be prepared monthly, are the:

- Income statement
- Balance sheet
- Statement of cash flows (SCF)

The Income Statement

The income statement is known by a variety of names. Technically, it is known as the "statement of income and expense." It is sometimes better known, however, as the profit and loss statement, or, even more simply, as the **P&L**.

Among the most important financial documents are income statements, balance sheets, and statements of cash flows.

LODGING LANGUAGE

Profit and Loss statement (P&L): The P&L records total hotel revenues and expenses for a specific time period. Same as the Statement of Income and Expense or Income Statement.

The P&L, when properly prepared, lists the hotel's income (sales revenue) from all its income-producing areas (such as food and beverage, meeting space, telephone charges, and movie rentals), all the expenses required to operate the hotel, **GOP**, and **fixed charges** for a specific time period. This specific time period is typically a month, **fiscal quarter**, or year.

LODGING LANGUAGE

Fixed charges: The expenses incurred in the purchase and occupation of the hotel. These include rent, property taxes, insurance, interest, and depreciation and amortization.

Fiscal quarter: Any 3-month period within the 12-month period that makes up a company's operating year. For example, January, February, and March would make up the first fiscal quarter of an operating year that began on January 1 and ended on December 31.

It is beyond the scope of this text to discuss fully the preparation and analysis of the income statement. It is important to know, however, that a competent controller will produce an accurate income statement in a timeframe that the hotel's owners and the property general manager find helpful for the proper management of the hotel.

LODGING ONLINE

To be of most value, a hotel's income statements must conform to industry standards. These standards are regularly reviewed and improved. To view a copy of the most current version of the Uniform System of Accounts for Hotels, go to:

www.amazon.com/

Why is it important that a hotel's financial statements always be prepared in a consistent manner?

This Period's Actual		
		Revenues
	Less	Direct operating expense
	Equals	Departmental Operating income
	Less	Overhead expense
	Equals	Net Income (GOP)
	Less	Fixed expense
	Equals	Income before taxes

FIGURE 12.8 Income Statement Information

Figure 12.8 lists the type of information commonly detailed on a hotel income statement and the format controllers use to prepare them.

With the information shown in Figure 12.8, the hotel's owners and managers can evaluate and determine answers to the following types of questions:

- How well did the hotel perform during this time period?
- How well did the hotel perform compared to its performance estimate (budget)?
- Where did the estimates vary significantly from actual performance?
- How well did the hotel perform compared to the same period last year?
- Where did any significant financial changes from the previous time period occur?

It is easy to see that the Controller who supplies the information found on a hotel's income statement provides an important benefit to those operating the hotel.

Balance Sheet

An income statement tells the general manager whether the month or other accounting period summarized has been a profitable one, but it is the balance sheet that provides a point-in-time statement about the overall financial position of the hotel. The balance sheet has often been described as a "snapshot" of the financial health of a hotel. This analogy is a good one because the balance sheet captures the financial condition of the hotel on the day the document is produced. It does not tell how profitable the hotel was in a prior accounting period, or how profitable the hotel may be in the future, but it can be compared to previous or later snapshots to determine changes in the hotel's financial condition.

The format of the balance sheet is really rather simple. First, it lists the hotel's assets (what the hotel owns), then its liabilities, (what it owes), and finally the difference between what is owned and what is owed (the owner's equity).

The assets owned by a hotel typically include such items as cash, monies owed to it by others (accounts receivable), the value of items in inventory (food, beverages, cleaning supplies, linens and the like), and **prepaid expenses**.

LODGING LANGUAGE

Prepaid expenses: Expenditures made for items purchased prior to the accounting period in which the items' actual expense is incurred.

LODGING ONLINE

Learning to read a balance sheet is an important managerial skill. To find articles that may help you learn this skill, go to:

www.hotelbusiness.com/

Why would the ability to read a balance sheet be an important managerial skill?

Assets		
Cash	$ 75,000	
Accounts receivable	50,000	
Inventories on-hand	25,000	
Prepaid expenses	10,000	
Total Assets		$ 160,000
Property and equipment	$ 7,000,000	
(Less accumulated depreciation)	500,000	
Net property and equipment		6,500,000
Total Assets		**$ 6,660,000**
Liabilities and Owners' Equity		
Current liabilities		
Accounts payable	$ 75,000	
Wages payable	25,000	
Total current liabilities	$ 100,000	
Long-term liabilities		
Mortgage payable	$ 6,300,000	
Total Liabilities		**$ 6,400,000**
Owners' equity		260,000
Total Liabilities and Owner's Equity		**$ 6,660,000**

FIGURE 12.9 Simplified Balance Sheet for the Best Sleep Hotel as of January 1, 20xx

The asset portion of the balance sheet also lists the value of the hotel's property and equipment (fixed assets), less any accumulated depreciation. Recall from Chapter 2 that depreciation reflects the reduction in the value of an asset as it wears out.

The liabilities section of the balance sheet includes current liabilities, generally defined as debts that will be paid within one year, and long-term liabilities, which are debts that will be paid in a time period longer than the next 12 months. Thus, for example, an invoice for dairy products that is due and payable on the day the balance sheet is produced would be considered a current liability. By contrast, the amount remaining to be paid on the hotel's 20-year mortgage would, on the same date, be classified as a long-term liability.

The difference between what a hotel owns (assets) and what it owes (liabilities) represents the property owner's equity in the hotel. Figure 12.9 represents a sample balance sheet for the Best Sleep Hotel.

The information presented by the balance sheet is important, and it should be prepared as often, and in as timely a manner, as the income statement. The balance sheet is especially useful when a specific time period (e.g., the end of the current year) is compared to an earlier time period (e.g., the end of the preceding year). The balance sheet's "point-in-time" perspective makes it a useful tool for management in the analysis of the overall financial health of the hotel.

Although little seems to have been written on this issue, it is important to realize that balance sheets may have significant limitations, especially in the hotel industry. A complete discussion of the balance sheet's limitations will be found in any fundamental accounting text. What is of most significance here is the fact that the assets listed on the balance sheet do not take into account the relative value, or worth, of the hotel employees who are actually operating the hotel.

Hotel companies are fond of saying that people (their staff) are their most important assets, but the value of experienced, well-trained staff members is not quantified on the balance sheet. To clarify this very important concept, assume that you are the general manager of a hotel and are considering a $1,000 expenditure for your sales and marketing team. You can spend the $1,000 either to replace an aging computer used by the sales staff or to send the sales and marketing team to a one-day training class to learn more about Microsoft Word and Excel, the software programs used at your property for producing sales contracts and guest invoices.

If you purchase the computer, the value of the assets (property and equipment) on your balance sheet will increase, but if you instead elect to "invest" in your staff by choosing the training program, no such increase will occur even though it is likely that the training class, rather than a single computer, could make a much greater difference in the effectiveness, efficiency, accuracy, and "worth" of the hotel's sales and marketing team. Experienced hoteliers recognize both the value and the limitations of the balance sheet when reviewing it.

The Statement of Cash Flows

Controllers produce or help to produce a hotel's income statement and balance sheet. As you have seen, the income statement details the financial performance of the hotel during a specified time period, whereas the balance sheet shows the hotel's financial position at a point in time. These two documents are extremely useful to management, but there is a third and equally important financial summary that should be produced by the hotel's accountant. That summary is the statement of cash flows.

The statement of cash flows provides answers to the following types of questions that cannot be answered by either the income statement or the balance sheet:

- How much cash was provided by the hotel's operation during the accounting period?
- What was the hotel's level of spending for building improvements for the period?
- How much long-term debt did the hotel add (or reduce) during the period?
- Will cash be sufficient in the near future, or will short-term borrowing be required?

In the hotel business, "Cash is King." Savvy hoteliers who make this statement know it is critical not only for a hotel to be profitable, but also for it to maintain its **solvency**.

LODGING LANGUAGE

Solvency: The ability of a hotel to pay its debts as they come due.

The statement of cash flows shows the effects on cash of the hotel's operating, investing, and financing activities. A simplified illustration will clarify the importance of the statement of cash flows. Assume that a hotel's income statement shows sales revenue of $200,000 for the month. Assume also that the hotel shows a profit (income before taxes) of $50,000 for that month. All may seem well until it is realized that $100,000 of the monthly sales were made to a guest to whom the hotel has extended credit. Thus, the income statement may show the hotel has made $50,000 for the month, but that money is not yet on deposit in the hotel's bank accounts and is not available to help pay the hotel's debts (and in fact, the hotel has been required to use $50,000 of its own cash or credit to finance the operation of the property until the $100,000 is collected from the guest). As you can see, it is important to be profitable, but it is equally important to know how many dollars are in the hotel's bank account and in its accounts receivables.

In addition to credit sales, the general manager must be aware of the hotel's own short- and long-term cash needs if the hotel is to remain solvent. Since the cash standing of a hotel is vital, a statement of cash flows detailing that standing should be produced just as frequently as is the income statement and the balance sheet. In fact, the Financial Accounting Standards Board (FASB), the organization responsible for making accounting rules, has since 1988, required that the statement of cash flows be included with other financial statements (balance sheet and income statement) when these are issued to external users.

Lodging Language

Controller
Certified Public Accountant (C.P.A.)
Centralized Accounting
Decentralized Accounting
Audit
Capital Expenditure
Seasonal Hotel
Manager's Daily (sales report)
Allowances and Adjustments
House Count
Sign-off
Shift Bank
Short
Over
Manager on Duty (MOD)
Accounts Receivable (AR)

Accounts Receivable Aging
Write-off
Accounts Payable (AP)
Coding
Financial Statements
Generally Accepted Accounting Principles (GAAP)
Profit and Loss Statement (P&L)
Fixed Charges
Fiscal Quarter
Prepaid Expense
Solvency

For Discussion

1. Identify two advantages of using a centralized accounting system in a hotel, as well as two disadvantages of such a system.
2. Identify two advantages of using a decentralized accounting system in a hotel, as well as two disadvantages of such a system.
3. Budgets may be affected by a variety of external events that are unforeseen by management. Identify three such events that could affect a hotel's long-term budget. Identify three events that could affect its annual budget.
4. While many hotels employ progressive discipline programs, theft is usually grounds for immediate termination. Would you implement an immediate termination policy at your hotel, or would you give a second chance to a cashier caught stealing? Why? What factor(s) would influence your decision?
5. One important decision that must sometimes be made by a hotel pertains to when to deny credit to a client or guest formerly allowed to charge purchases. What factors would influence your decision to deny future credit to a current client whose direct bill account was past due?
6. In some hotels, management has determined that any purchase made by a hotel staff member above an established dollar amount must be preapproved by the hotel's general manager or controller. Identify five factors that you would want to address in such a policy. How would this policy affect accounting procedures in the hotel?
7. Hotel controllers generally rely upon other managers in a hotel to verify many of the invoices submitted for payment. Assume that you are serving in the role of hotel controller and suspect a manager of submitting falsified invoices for the purpose of defrauding the hotel. Outline a procedure you would implement to prevent such abuse.
8. Some hoteliers believe that a hotel's balance sheet is the best indicator of its economic health while others point to the income statement as the better measure of financial strength. Which document do you believe is most important? Give two reasons to support your answer.
9. The independent verification of financial information in a hotel is an important way to help prevent employee fraud. How often do you believe a controller's own work should be audited? What factors would influence your decision?
10. Assume that you are a banker asked to lend money to an operating hotel. Identify three pieces of financial information you would want to see before making the loan. How important would it be to you that the data submitted was independently verified as accurate?

Team Activities

TEAM ACTIVITY 1

Identify the person responsible for the duties of controller at a nearby hotel. Ask that person to answer the following questions. Have the team report the answers to the class.

In your hotel:

1. What is your greatest budgeting challenge?
2. What is your greatest income control challenge?
3. What is your greatest expense control challenge?
4. What is your greatest overall accounting challenge?

TEAM ACTIVITY 2

Assume that a potential client's meeting planners have applied for direct bill status at your hotel. They will agree to do business with your property only if they can purchase on credit. Your team must decide whether the client will be granted credit. Identify the client-related factors you would consider prior to granting this client a line of credit. Identify also the specific terms under which you would be willing to allow the potential client to buy on credit.

Chapter

13

Safety and Security

Chapter Outline

Chapter Overview

Hotel guests depend upon the hotel to maintain an environment in which they will be as safe as possible. Guests, however, are not the only people concerned about safety. Employees count on the hotel to provide working conditions that allow them to do their jobs free from concerns about unnecessary risks. The owners of a hotel want its managers to develop practices and procedures that will safeguard the hotel's assets and minimize the owner's legal liability. In addition, there are governmental agencies at all levels that are charged with monitoring the safety-related efforts of hotels.

The hotel industry is committed to safety. To achieve this goal, it relies upon a variety of internal security–oriented tools, including recodable locks, alarm systems, surveillance systems, and emergency plans that can be used to reduce safety and security risks. In this chapter, you will learn about all of these. You will also learn how external resources, such as local law enforcement personnel and the hotel's insurers, help properties to be safe and secure.

Depending on their location and the services offered, some hotels have unique safety and security issues. These include protecting guests in swimming pool areas, spas, exercise areas, and, in many cases, parking lots. While hoteliers cannot guarantee their guests' safety, they have a responsibility to exercise reasonable care in protecting the welfare of guests. In this chapter, you will learn how hotels can meet the reasonable-care standard.

Threats to the security of hotel assets can come from both internal and external sources. To protect assets adequately, programs must be in place to guard against threats of both types. In this chapter, you will learn about ways to reduce the chances of incurring losses due to dishonest guests and employees. In some cases, safety and security threats are unique to specific hotel departments. For example, in the front office, cash is routinely kept on hand and must be safeguarded while the housekeeping department must control theft of room supplies and furnishings by both employees and guests. This chapter examines in detail the important and specific security concerns of the front office, housekeeping, food and beverage, sales and marketing, and maintenance and engineering departments.

Even in the best managed properties, the risk of a safety- or security-related crisis is real, and all hotel employees must know how to respond. In this chapter, you will learn how a hotel's crisis management plan can help address the many concerns that can arise when a hotel faces or experiences a severe safety or security threat.

Chapter Objectives

1. To stress the importance of keeping hotel guests and employees safe.
2. To identify a variety of internal and external resources available to help hoteliers meet their safety and security goals.
3. To describe to you safety threats that are unique to the hotel industry.
4. To stress the importance of property security.
5. To identify internal, external, and area-specific threats to hotel security.

THE IMPORTANCE OF SAFETY

Regardless of the size of the hotel, all of its employees must be concerned about **safety** and **security**.

LODGING LANGUAGE

Safety: Protection of an individual's physical well-being and health.

Security: Protection of an individual's or business's property and other assets.

Concern for the safety of guests and the security of their possessions is not merely good business; it is also a legal responsibility of the hotel's ownership and becomes an important responsibility of each hotel staff member. Employees and other non-guests visiting the hotel also have a legal right to expect their health and well-being to be protected by management.

Legal Liability for Guest and Employee Safety

Since the earliest days of travel, hotel guests have been rightfully concerned about their safety, especially when they were sleeping. Innkeepers and hoteliers responded to these concerns by striving to provide a safe haven for travelers. In addition to the good intentions of hotel managers, however, there are specific laws that require those who operate hotels to provide the traveling public with a safe and secure environment. These laws, however, do not hold hotels directly responsible for everything that could happen to guests during their stay.

For example, a guest may slip and fall in a bathtub. The hotel will not be held responsible for any resulting injuries if it is determined that it has exercised **reasonable care** in the manner in which it provides and maintains its bathtubs.

LODGING LANGUAGE

Reasonable care: A legal concept identifying the amount of care a reasonably prudent person would exercise in a specific situation.

Assume, however, that the hotel had purchased bathtubs with surfaces that were well-known to become extraordinarily slippery when wet. Assume also that many guests had slipped and fallen in the tubs and that management knew about these instances. In addition, assume that the hotel's franchisor, on several occasions when the hotel was inspected, had advised the hotel's owners to install slip-resistant materials on the floor of the tubs to reduce the chances of injury. If, in the face of this information, the hotel's

Correctly programmed key cards and properly working door locks are a few examples of important safety and security controls.

owners refused to install the non-slip surfaces, they would, in all likelihood, be held liable, to some degree (see Chapter 2) for the guest's fall if a lawsuit was filed.

As an hotelier, it is important to remember that the legal standard of reasonable care means that you must operate your hotel with a degree of care equal to that of other reasonable persons (i.e., reasonable hoteliers). For example, if you know, or should have known, about a threat to the safety of your guests, it is reasonable to assume that you would either immediately eliminate the threat or clearly inform your guests of it. Not doing so would indicate that you exhibited an absence of reasonable care for the safety of your guests.

If a threat to guest safety results in loss or injury, and it is determined that the hotel did not exercise reasonable care in regard to that threat, the hotel may be held wholly or partially liable for the resulting loss or injury. If a hotel is found to be liable for injuries to a guest or employee, it will likely have to bear the cost of that liability. For example, assume that a hotel manager knew about a defective lock on a guest room door but did not authorize an immediate repair. Subsequently a guest rented the room with the defective lock and was robbed and assaulted by an assailant who obtained unlawful entry to the room through the door with the defective lock. In this case, it is highly likely that an attorney hired by the guest to seek **damages** against the hotel would be successful. In this hypothetical case, the damages could include **compensatory damages** and possibly even **punitive damages**.

LODGING LANGUAGE

Damages: The actual amount of losses or costs incurred due to the wrongful act of a liable party.

Compensatory damages: A monetary amount intended to compensate injured parties for actual losses or damage they have incurred. This typically includes such items as medical bills and lost wages. Also known as "actual damages."

Punitive damages: A monetary amount assessed to punish liable parties and to serve as an example to the liable party as well as others not to commit the wrongful act in the future.

These damages could result in extremely large amounts of money the hotel would be required to pay the injured guest—costs that could have been avoided had the guest room lock been repaired, as it should have been, in a timely manner.

It is important to note that hoteliers do not do their job of maintaining a safe property properly simply to avoid paying damages. A demonstrated concern for guest safety is

LODGING ONLINE

Some hoteliers take the issues of guest safety and security so seriously that they have established separate trade associations designed to assist one another's safety efforts. Canadian hoteliers are leaders in this area. To view the Web site of the Alberta Hotel Safety Association (AHSA), go to:

www.albertahotelsafety.com

How important to you is safety when you choose a hotel?

not merely a good business practice; it is also the right thing to do. Guest safety is an important part of every hotel employee's job, and it is the job of the hotel's managers to make sure that employees, as well as guests, are safe while on the property.

Hotel Responsibility for Guest Safety

You have learned that a hotel can be held legally responsible for the results of injury to guests (and employees) if it does not exercise reasonable care. To demonstrate reasonable care, a hotel must address three main issues. These are:

1. The hotel's facility
2. The hotel's staff
3. Policies and procedures implemented by the hotel

Each of these plays an important part in the safety and security of overnight guests and those who work in or visit a hotel.

FACILITY

Every hotel offers different products and services to guests in a variety of different locations and settings. Each hotel, however, should be as safe as possible. This is not to imply that accidents cannot happen, but rather that the management and staff of the hotel should develop and maintain an active **threat analysis** program.

LODGING LANGUAGE

Threat analysis: A systematic procedure designed to identify and eliminate identifiable safety risks.

A threat analysis program is an organized procedure by which a hotel facility is assessed for possible hazards. For example, in a hotel with a parking lot, the lights in the parking area should be periodically checked to see if they are functioning properly. If it is discovered that they are not working properly, they pose a potential safety hazard and that hazard must be eliminated by repairing the lights.

In some cases, it may not be possible to completely eliminate a safety risk. When this is the case, reasonable care demands that guests *must* be informed of the risk. For example, most observers would agree that entering a hotel's swimming pool without a lifeguard present presents a risk to safety. However, most hotels with swimming pools do not employ a full-time lifeguard during the time the pool is open for use by guests.

In this case, the known risk (absence of a life guard) must be communicated to guests. Signage can be developed to communicate the risk. Possible wording alternatives, posted in the pool area in the language(s) of guests, and in a highly visible location, might include:

- Swim At Your Own Risk
- No Lifeguard On Duty
- Adult Swimmers Only

- Children Must Be Supervised By An Adult
- Children Under the Age of 16 Must Be Supervised by an Adult
- No Running or Diving

Note that each of these statements seeks to inform swimmers about risks related to swimming in an area without a lifeguard present. In most cases, if no lifeguard is present during most of the time a hotel's pool is open, the hotel's **insurer** would provide or suggest the actual language to be used to inform swimmers of their safety risk.

LODGING LANGUAGE

Insurer: The entity providing insurance coverage to a business.

Additional steps that can be taken in a threat analysis program are to prohibit behavior by guests and others that could pose a threat to safety. For example, a hotel might establish and enforce a policy prohibiting the use of glassware (glass bottles or drinking glasses) in a pool area. It would do so to eliminate the threat to safety that could come from broken, and thus nearly invisible, glass fragments in a pool area where people are likely to be bare-footed.

Each hotel facility will have its own safety issues; however, three steps are important parts of an effective threat analysis program and can help to demonstrate a hotel's commitment to using reasonable care to protect guests from harm. These three steps include:

Identifying and removing known threats to safety

Informing guests about any remaining safety threats

Prohibiting behavior that is known to create safety threats

STAFF TRAINING

It takes the effort of every employee in the hotel to eliminate, to the greatest degree possible, threats to the safety and security of guests and their property. In larger hotels, there may be a full-time director of safety and security and a staff of departmental employees who routinely patrol the hotel's grounds, make safety and security checks, and direct the hotel's safety programs. In other cases, the hotel may contract with a private security firm to provide security services. In still other cases, off-duty police may be hired to assist with the hotel's security efforts. However, even in the smallest of limited-service hotels, all employees need to be trained in security and safety methods.

Training employees to protect guests and themselves and to assist with the hotel's security efforts is an ongoing process. One way to view the safety-training needs of employees is to think about the training required by all employees and the training essential only to members of a specific department. For example, teaching all employees to promptly report any unauthorized or suspicious person found loitering in the hotel's parking lot is appropriate, whereas training about the safe handling of food would be appropriate only for those employed in the food and beverage department.

Specific hotels or hotel companies develop and implement many detailed safety-training programs. In addition, excellent training materials related to safety and security are developed and continually updated by the Educational Institute of the American Hotel & Lodging Association (E.I.). These materials are made available to hotels at a very reasonable cost.

In most limited-service hotels, safety and security is not a completely separate department. Instead, safety and security programs are administered within each hotel department and are overseen by the general manager or a designated **safety and security committee**.

LODGING LANGUAGE

Safety and Security committee: An interdepartmental task force consisting of hotel managers, supervisors, and hourly-paid employees responsible for monitoring and refining a hotel's safety and security efforts.

LODGING ONLINE

The Educational Institute (E.I.) offers a variety of safety- and security-related training products suitable for all of a hotel's employees and other programs that are departmental-specific. In addition, E.I. offers a self-paced training program leading to the Certified Lodging Security Officer designation (CLSO). To learn about that program and others, go to:

www.ei-ahla.org/

When you arrive, enter "Safety and Security" in the search field.

Do you think every hotel should have a CLSO on its staff?

Many hotels find that maintaining an effective safety and security committee is preferable to a separate safety and security department because the very operation of interdepartmental committee reinforces the message that guest safety and hotel security is the responsibility of every one of its managers, supervisors, and employees.

Regardless of the size or organizational structure of the hotel's safety and security efforts, the training of employees is a key component of any effective program.

Managers are not the only persons interested in the safety of a hotel's employees. In 1970, the federal government passed the Occupational Safety and Health Act, which created, within the Department of Labor, the Occupational Safety and Health Administration **(OSHA)**.

LODGING LANGUAGE

Occupational Safety and Health Administration (OSHA): A federal agency established in 1970 that is responsible for developing and enforcing regulations to help ensure safe and healthful working conditions.

The purpose of the Occupational Safety and Health Act is to bring about safe and healthful working conditions. OSHA has been very aggressive in enforcing the rights of workers. Together with its state-level partners, OSHA has more than 2,000 inspectors and additional complaint-discrimination investigators, engineers, physicians, educators, standards writers, and other technical and support personnel located in over 200 offices throughout the country. This staff establishes and enforces protective standards, and assists employers and employees through technical assistance and consultation programs.

All hotels are legally required to comply with the extensive safety practices, equipment specifications, and employee communication procedures mandated by OSHA. Among other mandates, the OSHA requirements call upon employers to:

- Provide a safe workplace for employees by complying with OSHA safety and health standards
- Provide workers with needed tools and equipment that meet OSHA specifications for health and safety
- Establish training programs for employees who operate potentially dangerous equipment
- Report to OSHA immediately (within 8 hours) any worksite accident that results in a fatality or requires the hospitalization of three or more employees
- Maintain the "OSHA 300" form (an on-site record of work-related injuries or illnesses) and keep it available for inspection for a period of five years
- Display OSHA notices about employee rights and safety in prominent places within the hotel
- Provide all employees access to the Material Safety Data Sheets (MSDS) that provide information about the dangerous chemicals they may be handling during work (see Chapter 8)
- Offer no-cost hepatitis-B vaccinations for employees who may have come in contact with blood or other body fluids

LODGING ONLINE

OSHA maintains an active Web site with valuable information that can be easily accessed. To stay current on OSHA regulations and enforcement programs, visit and bookmark:

www.osha.gov/

How do you think hotel managers can best keep up with changing OSHA requirements?

OSHA inspectors have the legal authority to inspect a hotel to see whether it is in compliance with their regulations. When OSHA was established, few businesses viewed it as a partner in their worker-safety efforts. Today, astute hoteliers recognize that compliance with OSHA standards results in fewer accidents, lower insurance costs, and a healthier workforce.

In addition to OSHA, hotel operators may find that there are state and local laws regarding employee safety that also must be followed. In some cases, a state or local governmental agency may share responsibility for enforcing employee and guest safety-related issues. For example, in most cities, the local fire department will be responsible for ensuring that locally required fire-suppression systems are in place and operational.

POLICIES AND PROCEDURES

The specific safety and security policies and procedures that are best for an individual hotel will vary based upon its size, location, physical layout, and the guest amenities offered. In all cases, however, written policies and procedures help inform all hotel employees of what is expected when responding to safety and security threats. While a text or a legal manual can identify the importance of standardized policies and procedures, each hotel must consider its own property-specific threats, concerns, and solutions. These solutions, formalized in writing and consistently followed by every employee, will go a long way toward confirming that the hotel consistently demonstrates reasonable care.

SAFETY RESOURCES

Fortunately, hoteliers have a number of resources at their disposal as they seek to create lodging environments that are safe and secure. In this section, we will examine some of the most important of these.

Internal Resources

Internal safety and security systems have advanced rapidly in the lodging industry. Among the most important internal tools available to hoteliers are:

- Recodable locks
- Alarm systems
- Surveillance systems
- Emergency plans

The appropriate selection and use of these tools depends upon the safety and security needs of the individual hotel.

RECODABLE LOCKS

The purchase and use of a **recodable locking system** by a hotel was once such a significant event that the hotel could actually market its use of such locks to potential guests. Today, recodable locks are the industry standard, and no hotel should operate without them.

The effective use of industry standard safety resources can greatly reduce the likelihood of legal action taken against a hotel.

ALL IN A DAY'S WORK 13.1

THE SITUATION

J.D. Ojisima, the general manager of the hotel, walked quickly to the hotel's pool area.

"There are an awful lot of kids and only one adult down at the pool," was the statement made a few minutes earlier to the front office manager by a housekeeper, who had gone to the pool area to replenish the towel supply. All housekeepers in the hotel had been trained to report any activity that could possibly be considered dangerous, and this housekeeper had performed well.

Because she could not leave the front office area unattended, the front office manager had called J.D. to ask for assistance.

"What's the problem?" stated the guest when J.D. arrived at the pool. "I rented a room at this hotel to hold my son's eleventh birthday party. These are his friends. Are you saying we are not allowed to invite friends to visit when we are registered guests in your hotel?"

J.D. quickly counted more than 25 children attending the swim party at the pool and only one adult: the father who had rented the single sleeping room for the party.

A RESPONSE

Here is a case where facilities, staff, policies, and procedures must all play a part in how the hotel responds to a safety threat. Children should be able to use a hotel's pool with adult supervision. In this case, however, most reasonable people would doubt whether one adult can effectively supervise 25 young children. Generally, J.D.'s first responsibility would be to satisfy the guest. In this case, however, the greater responsibility is to safeguard the children and the hotel. As a result, J.D. must act decisively to remove this safety threat, even if it means upsetting the guest. If no additional adults are present to help with supervision, J.D. should act to remove enough of the young swimmers from the water to ensure the safety of all.

In the future, J.D. should address and formulate a written policy (if one does not currently exist) regarding the issue of the friends of registered guests and their permitted use (or nonuse) of hotel swim facilities as well as a reasonable adult/ child supervision ratio that can be consistently enforced by all hotel employees.

LODGING LANGUAGE

Recodable locking system: A hotel guest room locking system designed so that when guests insert their "key" (typically an electromagnetic card, but increasingly an electronic chip or password) into the guest room locking device for the first time, the lock is immediately recoded, canceling entry authorization from the previous guest's key.

Most recodable locking systems in use today are independent and stand-alone; that is, no wiring to a central computer or PMS is required. Except in life-threatening emergencies, only standard magnetic strip cards issued to guests or hotel staff will open the lock. This means that the hotel's entire room security system is controlled by software programmed into the individual locks, which are activated by **keycards** coded by a card-issuing computer.

LODGING LANGUAGE

Keycard: The electromagnetic card used in a recodable locking system.

Keycards are time-sensitive and can typically be issued up to 12 months in advance. Thus, individuals or groups can be sent room keys to speed registration when reservations are confirmed.

In a recodable locking system, each lock contains a card reader and electronic lock control module connected to a motor-actuated lock mechanism. Standard AA alkaline batteries or a wireless signal activate the lock. A warning light, visible only to staff, warns when the batteries are in need of replacement. When a guest inserts the keycard (or in a radio frequency-based or wireless system types in a password) for the first time, the lock is immediately recoded, thereby canceling entry authorization for the previous

LODGING ONLINE

To view the operational features of two of the lodging industry's most popular recodable locking systems, go to:

www.onity.com/ or:

www.saflok.com/

How important do you think room security is to the average hotel guest? Is anything more important?

guest. Multiple keycards can be issued to the same guest. In addition to guest rooms and exterior doors, recodable locks can be used to limit guest access to designated areas, such as special elevator floors, swimming pools, spas, exercise rooms, and reserved breakfast or bar areas. They can also limit employee access to specified storage areas within the hotel.

The safety and security challenge for the individuals managing a recodable lock system is to ensure that front office agents do not issue keys to individuals not properly registered in the guest room. For example, assume the (very common) situation where a guest approaches a front office agent and states, "I have misplaced my room key. Can you please give me another?" In a hotel that is exercising reasonable care in its issuance of duplicate room keys, the hotel staff member responding to the guest must:

- Be trained to issue duplicate keys only to confirmed registered guests.
- Maintain an accurate data system that identifies registered guests and their assigned room numbers.

Because guest rooms must be regularly cleaned and maintained, management issues master keycards to hotel employees who need them. With today's recodable lock systems, an electronic record is kept of all keycards used in the lock for a specific period of time. As a result, should the need arise, management can determine whose keycard was used to open a lock and at what day and time the key was used. The use of recodable locks not only reduces the possibility that guests can be victimized in their room by someone who had rented the same room on a previous night, they also help reduce the incidence of employee theft from rooms.

ALARM SYSTEMS

Alarms of many types are used in the hotel industry. They can be either audible or silent. Audible alarms typically consist of high-pitched buzzers, bells, or other noises. Alarm devices, whether audible or silent, normally consist of electrical connections, photoelectric light beams, seismic detectors, infrared beams, magnetic contacts, or radio frequency (RF) fields that, when activated, create the alarm.

Alarms many be classified as either an **internal alarm** or a **contact alarm**.

LODGING LANGUAGE

Internal alarm: A warning system that notifies an area within the hotel if the alarm is activated.

Contact alarm: A warning system that notifies (contacts) an external entity, such as the fire or police department, if the alarm is activated.

Internal alarms generally are designed to serve as a deterrent to criminal or mischievous activity. For example, a warning buzzer on a hotel's fire exit door would typically be wired only to notify hotel personnel if the door was used. In a like manner, an alarm on a liquor storeroom door might serve to notify a manager or the food and beverage director. Conversely, an alarm activated by a front office agent during or after an armed robbery would most likely be wired directly to the local police department for the purpose of contacting them immediately.

Some important areas that may be protected by internal alarms include:

- Storage areas
- Hotel facilities such as pools, spa, and exercise areas
- Hotel grounds and the property perimeter

Some important areas that are more likely to be protected by contact alarms include:

- The front office
- Food and beverage cashier stations
- The controller's office

Hotel fire alarms are so important that they are mandated by federal law and local building codes. Good hotels have these devices wired as both internal and contact alarms. Remember that in case of a fire, hotel employees, guests, and the fire department would all need to be made aware of the danger. Thus, heat or smoke detectors in a guest room should set off an internal alarm that would be heard by the guest in the room as well as by the staff at the front office and should be checked immediately by the appropriate hotel employee. By contrast, a fire alarm activated in a public area may result in an automatic contact and summons of firefighters because the alarm was wired directly to the local fire department.

The hotel staff responsible for doing so should periodically and frequently check all alarms for proper operation. This is necessary because a hotel with a non-functioning alarm system will have great difficulty demonstrating that it exercised reasonable care toward employee and guest safety should the need ever arise. An effective and comprehensive alarm system is an invaluable tool in every hotel's complete safety and security efforts.

SURVEILLANCE SYSTEMS

Properly implemented, electronic surveillance can play a major role in a hotel's safety and security programs. Surveillance is generally done in one of two ways. The first involves simply recording the activity within an area of the hotel. Thus, for example, a hotel could set up a digital camera that records the activity outside a liquor storeroom. Then, if the storeroom was broken into on a given night, a record of the break-in would exist that could be useful in identifying the thieves. Surveillance systems are most frequently used to record activity at the front office, near entrances and exits, in parking areas, and near cashiers.

Some hotels use **closed-circuit television (CCTV)** as a tool in their safety and security programs.

LODGING LANGUAGE

Closed-circuit television (CCTV): A camera and monitor system that displays, in real time, the activity within the camera's field of vision. A CCTV consisting of several cameras and screens showing the camera's fields of vision may be monitored in a single location.

The potential uses of CCTV in a hotel are many. CCTV can be used, for example, in a multiple-entry property where management desires to monitor activity outside each entrance. To be most effective, a CCTV system must be monitored. Viewing monitors are typically placed in a central location and viewed by an assigned employee who is trained to respond appropriately to activities seen on the monitor. For example, if an outside entrance is being monitored, and the monitor shows that a break-in is being attempted, the employee may be trained to summon the local police. Some hotels that use CCTV also have an intercom in the area being monitored, thus extending the effectiveness of the employee monitoring the system by making it possible to talk with anyone observed in the monitored area. States generally mandate the use of CCTV to improve security in casino hotels.

Some hotel managers attempt to create the illusion of having a CCTV system in place, when, in fact, the cameras are not operating as cameras or the monitors are not constantly monitored. This is typically done in an effort to save money on the cost of operating the

CCTV system. The rationale is that the mere presence of the cameras will deter criminals since they will not realize that they are not actually being observed. The courts and juries have found, however, that this approach does not establish reasonable security care by a hotel because victims may mistakenly think that help is on the way (because they believe their situation is being monitored) and base their behavior on that belief. No help is likely to arrive if the monitors are not being viewed. Hotel managers who wish to operate an unmonitored CCTV should consult with both their insurers and their legal counsel before implementing such an approach.

EMERGENCY PLANS

Despite a hotel staff's best efforts, safety and security emergencies will occur. When they do, the hotel must be ready to respond appropriately. Pre-planning is the very best tool available to managers concerned with safety and security. In unforeseen emergencies, it may not be possible to determine the proper response until the actual event occurs. But in the case of crises that are foreseeable (such as severe weather storms or power outages), some of the actions a hotel must be prepared to take will be quite similar, if not the same, in each crisis.

LODGING LANGUAGE

Emergency plan: A document describing a hotel's predetermined, intended response to a safety/security threat it may encounter.

An emergency plan is, quite simply, the identification of a potential threat to the safety and/or security of the hotel as well as the hotel's planned response to the threat. For example, an emergency plan for a hotel near a heavily wooded area might include an evacuation plan to be implemented in case of a forest fire. A hotel on a Florida coast might include in its emergency plan a method of evacuating the hotel in the event of an impending hurricane.

Responses to events such as the following are included in most hotels' emergency plans:

- Fire
- Flood
- Power outages
- Severely inclement weather (e.g., hurricane, snow storm, tornado)
- Robbery
- Death or injury to a guest or employee
- Intense negative publicity by the media

In all of the above cases, the hotel's management and employees may be called upon to react quickly. The emergency plan prepares them to do so. This can be accomplished because many crises share similar characteristics that can, to some degree, be controlled by pre-planning: These characteristics include:

- Extreme importance
- Disruption of normal business
- Potential for human suffering
- Property damage
- Financial loss
- Potential scrutiny by the media
- Threat to the reputation or health of the business

An emergency plan must be a written document. This is important because it must identify precisely what is expected of management and employees in times of crisis. In addition, if the hotel becomes subject to a lawsuit as a result of the crisis, a written emergency plan can help show that it exercised reasonable care in preparing for the crisis.

An emergency plan should be kept simple because it will likely be implemented only in a time of heightened stress. A clearly developed emergency plan should include, for each crisis identified:

- The type of crisis
- Who should be told when the crisis occurs (include telephone or pager numbers)
- What should be done (and who should do it) in the event the crisis occurs
- Who should be informed of the results or impact of the crisis when it is over

Plans for managing an emergency should be developed by the hotel's top-level managers with input from other staff members as applicable. Representatives of insurance companies and local fire/police departments can also provide useful information. Large hotels typically have a security department whose personnel would be involved in implementing emergency plans. Managers of small, limited-service properties must include these responsibilities as an integral part of their jobs. Regardless of hotel size, however, plans must be in place that indicate, for every emergency that can reasonably be anticipated, what exactly must be done and who exactly is responsible for doing it.

The actual plan should be reviewed frequently by management and should be shared with employees so that they know what to do during the emergency. Where practical, hotels should practice the implementation of their plan. By doing so, they demonstrate strongly their commitment to ensuring the safety and security of the hotel and everyone in it.

External Resources

Hoteliers are not alone in their efforts to provide for guest safety. Local law enforcement officials also are charged with maintaining individual safety and community security. They are natural allies of hoteliers. In addition, the hotel's insurers have a deep-seated interest in the safety and security efforts of the hotel's owner and staff. These two resources are readily available to hoteliers and should be utilized to the greatest extent possible.

LOCAL LAW ENFORCEMENT

Hotel employees can and should be well-trained, but their safety and security efforts will be improved tremendously when the hotel's managers establish and maintain an excellent relationship with local law enforcement professionals. Hotel general managers should personally know the individual(s) responsible for law enforcement in the area where their hotel is located. Local law enforcement officials can advise and assist managers and, in many cases, provide no-cost safety and security training for the hotel's employees. In addition, they can advise hoteliers about the best procedures and processes to be used in working together to remove unruly guests from the hotel, an event that, unfortunately, does occur in even the best managed properties.

In many communities, a general manager can request a property safety and security review from the local police. This will likely result in the identification of specific steps the hotel can take to reduce safety and security threats as well as actions it can take to make improvements. Good managers make it a point to meet frequently with local police because they are an important source of information and assistance.

PROPERTY INSURERS

Risk is inherent in running any business, and hotels are no exception. Hotels seek protection from risk by purchasing insurance. Doing so makes good financial sense. Some types of insurance coverage may be required by law (such as **workers' compensation**). Other insurance is required by the hotel's lenders (when the hotel has been purchased with borrowed money) to protect their financial interest in the property.

LODGING LANGUAGE

Workers' Compensation: An insurance program designed to assist individuals who are victims of a work-related injury or illness.

When assessing risk, and before selling insurance to a business, an insurance company predicts the average number of times the risk is likely to result in actual loss or damage. The average monetary value of the loss is then established. The **premiums** (fees) for the insurance to protect against the loss are then determined.

LODGING LANGUAGE

Premiums: The fees paid for insurance.

These fees must be low enough to attract those who want to buy the insurance, but high enough to support the number of losses that is likely to be incurred by the insurer.

The fewer the number of **claims** (potential losses), workers injured, and lawsuits that result from safety- and security-related incidents, the lower the risk that the insurance company will have to compensate those who are insured for their losses.

LODGING LANGUAGE

Claim (insurance): A demand for compensation as the result of loss, injury, or damage.

When there are few claims, the premiums charged for insurance are lower. As a result, it is in the best interest of hotels (because they want to minimize the insurance premiums they pay) and of their insurers (because they want to avoid paying claims) to minimize the number of losses incurred. Because this is so, insurers should partner with hoteliers in finding ways to reduce accidents and other sources of potential loss or damage. Just as a hotel's managers should know and work cooperatively with local law enforcement officers, the hotel's insurance companies should be consulted on a regular basis to identify policies, procedures, and actions that can be taken to reduce potential claims by improving the property's safety and security.

SPECIAL SAFETY–RELATED THREATS

Every business has unique threats to safety and security, and hotels are no exception. These unique threats often require extra caution or effort on the part of the hotel's staff. For many hotels, four of the most important of these areas of special concern are swimming pools, spas, exercise facilities, and parking lots.

Swimming Pools

Hotel swimming pools are exceptionally popular although they are typically used by only a small percentage of hotel guests. Consistently, in opinion polls regarding desirable services, travelers rank the presence of a swimming pool near the top of the list of hotel amenities that influence their hotel selection. The potential legal liability resulting from accidental slipping, diving, or even drowning, however, requires that the individual(s) responsible for taking care of the pool area be extraordinarily vigilant in enforcing pool safety procedures.

It is not possible to avoid every possible accident in a pool area. It is possible, however, to minimize the chances for accidents. Figure 13.1 lists 10 key practices that affect swimming pool safety and legal liability. They should be reviewed on a monthly basis with affected employees to ensure consistent compliance.

Most hotels do not employ full-time lifeguards at their pools. If lifeguards are provided, they must know effective surveillance, rescue procedures, and techniques specific to the facility they are protecting. When groups (especially children) are using a pool, it is the responsibility of the group leaders to provide supervision, regardless of whether lifeguards are provided.

Swimming pools pose a significant safety threat, and managers should take every precaution available to minimize those threats.

1. Post the pool's operating hours and open the pool to guests only during those hours.
2. Clearly mark the depths of pools accurately the on sides and ends and in both metric measure and feet/inches.
3. Ensure that the pool and pool area are properly illuminated and that any electrical components are regularly inspected and maintained to comply with local electrical codes.
4. Install self-closing and self-latching and/or locking gates to prevent unauthorized access to the pool area. If possible, lock the entrance to the pool with a recodable lock.
5. Have appropriate life-saving equipment on hand and easily accessible as well as at least one cardiopulmonary resuscitation (CPR) certified employee on duty at all times the pool is opened.
6. Allow pool use only by registered guests and specifically authorized others.
7. Contact the hotel's insurer to determine the number, placement, and content of necessary pool warning signs.
8. Post all pool policy and information signs in the language(s) of guests. Enforce the policies at all times.
9. Provide an emergency telephone in the pool area that rings directly either to the front desk or to 911 depending on the preference of the hotel's insurer.
10. Carefully document all activities related to pool maintenance, local ordinance compliance, and operating policy enforcement.

FIGURE 13.1 Swimming Pool Safety

When lifeguard services are not provided, the group should be advised that there are no lifeguards on duty and that its leaders must provide stringent and effective surveillance and supervision while the participants are in, on, and around the water. The hotel should provide the group leaders with specific supervisory and safety guidelines to be followed while the pool is in use. This can be done verbally or by use of a written "Pool Rules" fact sheet. The hotel's staff should continuously assess the numbers of guests in, on, and around the water to determine how many adults are needed to ensure the safety of the group members.

Spas

Hotels that have common area spas, whirlpools, or hot tubs face special safety and liability concerns. While spas are popular, they can be dangerous to young children, the elderly, intoxicated individuals, and people taking special medications. As with pools, it may be impossible to prevent all possible accidents, but the practices listed in Figure 13.2 can go a long way toward improving guest safety and minimizing the legal liability of the hotel. Management should review these practices with staff on a monthly basis to ensure compliance.

1. Inspect and document the inspection of spa drain covers on a daily basis.
2. Post all spa policies signs in the language(s) of guests.
3. Install a thermometer and check the spa temperature frequently; recording your readings. A range not to exceed 102–105 degrees Fahrenheit (38.9–40.6 degrees Celsius) is recommended.
4. Display spa temperatures in a manner that is easily readable by guests.
5. Clearly mark the depths of the spa in both metric measures and feet/inches.
6. Do not allow the consumption of alcohol while using the spa.
7. Install non-slip flooring surfaces around the spa and provide stairs/ladders for entry and exit.
8. Prohibit spa use by children and non-guests.
9. Provide an emergency telephone in the spa area that rings directly either to the front desk or to 911 depending on the preference of the hotel's insurer.
10. Carefully document all activities related to spa maintenance, local ordinance compliance, and operating policy enforcement.

FIGURE 13.2 Spa Safety

Exercise Facilities

Many hotels offer their guests the use of a fitness center or exercise room. These areas typically contain a variety of types and kinds of exercise equipment. In most cases, these rooms are not staffed by the hotel on a full-time basis. The rooms do, however, require regular attention. Hotel staff should pick up hazardous items (e.g., towels and weights) that might litter the floor and cause falls, and they should monitor exercise equipment for malfunctions or breakage and remove or immediately repair any machine that is broken or unsafe.

Statistics provided by insurers indicate that treadmills are, by far, the most dangerous apparatus in an exercise room. Even an experienced user can slip, trip, or lose balance on a treadmill. Falls from treadmills can cause serious physical harm, including broken limbs, concussions, and other serious injuries. Accidents are not the only safety risk. Equipment can easily transmit bacteria and other germs. Hoteliers operating exercise facilities must do their best to create a safe and secure exercise environment. One way to do so is by the use of posted signs.

Signs act as a constant reminder of the dangers inherent to exercise facilities. In general, signs can be classified into four types:

Policy Signs. Signs stating rules and regulations involving the use of the facility.

Warning Signs. Signs stating specific risks in an area of the facility or with a particular piece of equipment.

Directional Signs. Signs indicating entrances, exits, fire evacuation plans, and other safety information.

Emergency Signs. Signs indicating where various emergency items are stationed, such as fire extinguishers, first aid kits, and telephones.

Signs in the exercise room (as well as in other areas where safety communications are important) should be made of durable material that will hold up well. They should be made using letters of a size that is easy to read from at least 5 to 10 feet away. Signs should be printed in bright colors that will attract the reader's attention (signs with a white background and colored letters are the best) and should be placed from four feet to six feet from the floor for easy viewing. Computer printouts and handwritten signs can act as temporary or emergency communication devices but should be avoided in most cases.

Parking Areas

Many hotels have parking areas for guest vehicles. While hotels do not insure the vehicles parked in their lots, they are responsible for providing reasonable care in the protection of vehicles and guests using the lots. Figure 13.3 lists 10 key practices that affect the safety of parking areas. They should be reviewed on a monthly basis to ensure compliance.

1. Inspect parking lot lighting on a daily basis. Arrange for replacement of burned-out lights immediately.
2. Inspect parking lot surfaces daily and arrange for pavement patches immediately if they threaten guest safety. Keep surfaces free of ice and snow in inclement weather.
3. Ensure that parking lot stripes and directional signs are easily seen to avoid pedestrian/vehicle accidents.
4. Post easily readable signs in the parking lot reminding guests not to leave valuables in their vehicles.
5. If valet parking is provided, document the training of all drivers employed.
6. Require guests to identify their vehicles by license number or make/color upon check-in.
7. Keep landscaping around parking lots well trimmed to avoid dangerous areas that may provide hiding places for individuals who could threaten guest safety or property security.
8. If possible, arrange for regular and frequent parking lot drive-through patrols by local law enforcement officials.
9. Arrange for daily daytime and nighttime walk-through patrols by hotel staff.
10. Use a manager's daily log to document parking lot maintenance procedures.

FIGURE 13.3 Parking Lot Safety

Best Sleep Hotel

Performed by: ____
Date of Inspection: ____________________ Time of Inspection: ____________________

To ensure the integrity of your walk-through, this checklist should be completed in sequence as it appears.

As appropriate, a check must be placed in the "yes" or "no" column to the right of this paper. If "no" is required, please indicate the problem in the "comments" section. If a work order is submitted, note the work order number in the "comments" section.

ITEM	YES	NO	COMMENTS
Outdoor parking lot is well-lighted.	❑	❑	
Outdoor parking lot is free of trash and debris.	❑	❑	
Painted stripes are easily seen and in good condition.	❑	❑	
Directional signs are posted in conspicuous locations.	❑	❑	
Lot is patrolled at irregular intervals.	❑	❑	
All entrance gates are locked after 8:00 p.m. with the exception of the main entrance.	❑	❑	
Emergency call boxes are located throughout the parking lot and are functioning properly.	❑	❑	
Closed circuit cameras function properly and send clear images to security.	❑	❑	
Gangs or vagrants are noticed and reported to police.	❑	❑	
Cars are checked for length of stay; (note cars that are covered with tarp or excessive dirt).	❑	❑	
Security is aware of long-term stay automobiles.	❑	❑	
Correct percentage of Americans with Disabilities Act (ADA) parking is available and well-marked.	❑	❑	
Grass areas and bushes are well-maintained.	❑	❑	
Bushes and plants are trimmed and away from entrance doors.	❑	❑	
Walkways are well-lighted.	❑	❑	
Walkways are free of trip hazards	❑	❑	
Outside entrances are free of trash and debris	❑	❑	
All external doors leading to the inside are closed, locked and card accessible.	❑	❑	
Key card readers work properly at each entrance.	❑	❑	
All entrances are well-lighted.	❑	❑	
All entrances are secured.	❑	❑	
Directional signage at each entrance is compatible with ADA requirements.	❑	❑	
Outdoor ADA requirements are met regarding wheelchair ramps.	❑	❑	
Other:	❑	❑	
Other:	❑	❑	
Other:	❑	❑	

FIGURE 13.4 MOD Checklist for Parking Areas

The hotel's manager on duty (MOD) should be assigned, as part of his or her daily responsibilities, to conduct a walk-around of the parking area as part of the hotel's overall safety and security program. This walk-around also should be documented. Figure 13.4 is an example of a manager on duty checklist related to parking areas in a hotel.

Despite a hotel's best safety-related efforts, accidents can and will happen. When they do, an **incident report** must be prepared to document the "who, what, when, where, how" as well as the hotel's response to the accident or injury. Figure 13.5 is an example of an incident report used in a hotel.

LODGING LANGUAGE

Incident report: A document prepared to record the details of an accident, injury, or disturbance and the hotel's response to it.

Incident Report

Hutchinson Hotel and Ocean Suites
Sweet Water, FL 10065

Complainant

Last Name ________________ First Name ________________ Initial ____________
Address ________________ City ______________ State ____________ Zip __________
Home Telephone ______________ Business Telephone _____________ E-mail: ___________

Type of Incident

Injury _____ Theft _____ Accident _____ Property Damage _____ Other _____

Injury

First aid given? Yes _____ No _____ First aid refused? Yes _____ No _____
EMS called? Yes _____ No _____ Taken to emergency? Yes _____ No _____
Type of injury ____

Detail of Incident

____
____
(Write on back if necessary)

Property and Value

Damaged/Missing Item(s) Estimated Value
__________________________ __________________________
__________________________ __________________________
(Write on back if necessary)

Room Entry (only if applicable)

Room Number: ________ Entered by: ________________ Witnessed by: ________________
Room entered? Y ____ N ____ Time ____ Door locked? Y ____ N ____ Door chained? Y ____ N ____

Police Response to the Incident

Police Officer: ________________ Shield # ________________ Report # ________________
Arrest made? Y _____ N _____ Citation issued? Y _____ N _____ Warning issued Y _____ N _____

Witnesses to the Incident

1. Name: ________________________________ Telephone: ________________
   Address: ______________________ City ______________ State ____________
2. Name: ________________________ Telephone: ________________________
   Address: ______________________ City ______________ State ____________
   Comments: ____
   ____
   ____
   Report Prepared by ________________________ Date ________________________

FIGURE 13.5 Hotel Incident Report

An incident record should be prepared whenever a guest or employee suffers an accident or injury (a safety-related event) as well as when there has been a loss or damage to property (a security-related event). Other examples of safety-related documentation that should be maintained by the hotel include minutes from safety and security committee meetings, general staff meeting notes relevant to safety issues, records of employee training related to safety and security, and safety seminars attended or certifications acquired by employees.

PROTECTING PROPERTY FROM SECURITY THREATS

As you learned earlier in this chapter, safety-related programs are designed to keep people safe from harm, and security-related efforts are directed toward the protection of property from the threat of theft or damage. The safety of people is always more important than the security of property. Good hoteliers know, however, that they must use sound judgment and establish effective programs to protect the personal assets of guests as well as the assets of the hotel itself. Not to do so would be a disservice to the traveler and the hotel's owners.

Threats to the security of assets can come from individuals inside the hotel (internal threats) or outside the hotel (external threats). In both cases, these individuals seek to steal or damage property that rightfully belongs to the hotel's guests, employees, or owners. Effective hoteliers design, implement, and monitor security programs that reduce, to the greatest extent possible, the internal and external threats to asset security. In addition, hoteliers must know about the unique and specific threats to asset security that exist in individual hotel departments. It is not possible to eliminate all potential for property loss or damage. However, knowledge of specific lodging industry threats to security, as well as implementation of activities developed to minimize the impact of these threats, can help hoteliers show evidence of the reasonable care the law requires them to demonstrate.

Internal Threats

Sometimes employees steal assets owned by guests or by the hotel. When it is clear that an employee is involved in such activity, the response of management should be appropriate and, above all else, consistent. Some hotels include a phrase in their employee handbook warning that theft will be grounds for dismissal. When the theft or loss of property involves significant amounts of money, the hotel may pursue the filing of criminal charges against the employee. Regardless of the approach used, it should be applied equally to all employees and at all levels.

Consider what happens, for example, when a supervisor or manager involved in criminal activity is caught but then allowed to resign while in the same hotel, an hourly employee caught in the same activity is fired and/or prosecuted. This would leave the hotel open to charges of discrimination or unfair labor practices against which it may be difficult to defend. It also sends the hotel's employees a mixed message about management's view of theft.

Towels are one of the most common targets for guest pilferage.

ALL IN A DAY'S WORK 13.2

THE SITUATION

RING!!!!!!! RING!!!!!!! RING!!!!!!! RING!!!!!!!

The telephone woke Dale Parrot, the front office manager at the Better Inn and Suites hotel, from a deep sleep. It was 3:00 a.m. on Sunday morning.

"Mr. Parrot," said Shingi Rukuni, the night auditor and only employee on duty at the hotel, "Room 219 is having a really loud party. I'm getting lots of guest complaints from rooms located near theirs."

"Did you call the room and ask them to hold it down?" asked Dale.

"Yes, I did," replied Shingi. "I called them at 10:00 p.m., when the party started, then again at 1:30 a.m., 2:15, and 2:45, when the complaints really started coming in. They just stop for a couple minutes, then start right up again. I think they're drunk. I don't know what to do next!"

A RESPONSE

Surprisingly, the real problem in this case is not *the noise coming from room 219. Unruly guests are a fact of life in most hotels. The auditor's uncertainty about what to do about it indicates a lack of training by the front office management staff or a lack of direction from the hotel's general manager and suggests that a training deficiency is this hotel's larger problem. Whatever the hotel's policy toward unruly guests (number of specific warnings before the guest is asked to leave or is escorted off the property by local law enforcement officials), it should be documented, clearly communicated, and then followed. The comfort and safety of all the hotel's guests must be considered as should the latitude allowed for "partiers" before the hotel's forced-removal policy is established.*

If the hotel wishes to communicate to employees that theft of all types will be dealt with swiftly and consistently, it must treat internal threats to property security just as seriously as the threats posed by non-employees. A hotel faces two basic types of internal asset threats: those related to cash and those related to other assets.

THREATS TO CASH

In many cases, when hoteliers consider employee theft, they think of employees stealing money. **Embezzlement** is a potential problem in hotels, but using procedures and policies designed to prevent it can minimize its likelihood.

LODGING LANGUAGE

Embezzlement: The theft of a company's financial assets by an employee.

Some hotels are so concerned about employee theft that they **bond** employees who are in a position to embezzle funds.

LODGING LANGUAGE

Bond(ing): Purchasing an insurance policy to protect against the possibility that an employee will steal.

There are many ways that employees can defraud their employers of cash, and managers must stay current in the areas of cost- and revenue-control systems. Good financial controls based on solid control principles go a long way toward reducing employee theft. Of particular importance are controls related to cashiering positions because cashiers can commit fraud in a variety of ways. Typical methods of **fraud** related to cashiering include:

- Charging guests for items not purchased, then keeping the overcharge
- Changing the totals on credit card charges after the guest has left or imprinting additional credit card charges and pocketing the cash difference
- Misadding legitimate charges to create a higher-than-appropriate total with the intent of keeping the overcharge

- Purposely short-changing guests when giving back change and then removing the extra change from the cash drawer
- Voiding legitimate sales as mistakes and keeping the cash amount of the legitimate sale
- Charging higher-than-appropriate prices for hotel goods or services and then recording the sale at the proper price while keeping the overcharge

LODGING LANGUAGE

Fraud: The intentional use of deceit, trickery, or other dishonest methods to take another's money or property.

In addition to cashier theft that can affect the hotel or hotel guests, employees can steal cash in the accounts-payable area by paying the hotel's bills in such a way as to funnel money to the embezzling employee or in the accounts-receivable area by fraudulently diverting funds intended for the hotel to the embezzling employee. The responsibility for preventing the theft of hotel funds falls to the controller (or general manager) and each hotel department head involved in the handling of cash.

THREATS TO OTHER ASSETS

Cash is not the only hotel asset that can be stolen by employees. In fact, the number and type of assets that can be unlawfully taken by employees is large. Those responsible for a hotel's asset security often find it helpful to create programs designed to protect the three non-cash assets most subject to employee theft. These three loss areas involve the stealing of time, company property, and services.

It may seem strange to consider time a hotel asset, yet it is the asset most easily taken by employees. In nearly all cases, employees are paid for their work by the hour or, as in the case of salaried individuals, by the week or month. In effect, the hotel is exchanging one asset (cash), for another (employee time). When an employee takes a hotel's money but does not respond by giving the hotel the time agreed upon, the hotel loses. The theft of time can consist of employees fraudulently filling out time sheets or punching time cards. In some large hotels, particularly those with weak supervision programs, theft of time may result from employees simply disappearing for some time with the result that work they should have performed is not completed.

The best way to prevent theft of time by employees is to have strong controls in place with regard to time cards. To help in this area, hotels are increasingly issuing individual employee swipe cards to reduce the chances of "buddy punching," the practice of one employee fraudulently checking (punching) another employee in or out.

Managers must be vigilant when considering plans to reduce employee theft that involves lack of productivity. This can be challenging, especially in large properties. Good supervision, however, and a realistic workload for each employee on a work schedule that is reviewed daily will help to improve the hotel's ability to detect such theft.

Company property can disappear through the actions of employees as easily as through those of guests. In fact, employees usually know which assets management has neglected to protect as well as it should. From food in a food storage area to zippered laundry bags in housekeeping, employees often find that the physical assets of a hotel are of a type they could use personally. That makes these items very susceptible to employee theft. The best approach to preventing the theft of company property involves:

- ✔ Carefully screening employees prior to hiring them
- ✔ Reducing the chances for theft through the use of effective recodable locks, inventory systems, and other security measures
- ✔ Informing managers and employees of the penalty for theft
- ✔ Treating all proven cases of similar theft in a similar manner

It is unlikely, even with the best controls, that all employee theft in a hotel can be eliminated. There are simply too many opportunities for dishonest employees to take advantage of their access to the hotel's physical resources. Effective employee screening, however, and the creation of an environment that discourages stealing and consistently disciplines, terminates, or prosecutes employees for known cases of theft will help reduce the problem.

Some employees steal company property, and others steal services provided by the hotel. In many ways, this type of theft is harder to detect than the theft of company property. For example, assume that a front office supervisor, working late at night, spends an hour or more per day making a long-distance call to his girlfriend who lives several states away. This inappropriate use of hotel assets will result in the hotel's incurring a larger-than-necessary long-distance telephone bill for the month as well as experiencing the theft of time discussed earlier. This theft of services may go undetected unless someone at the property is monitoring the long-distance telephone bills generated by each administrative telephone extension number. In-room movies and games, telephone tolls, printing, copy, and faxing services are among the services susceptible to employee theft. Proper managerial controls must be in place to minimize, to the greatest degree possible, the chances for loss of hotel services.

External Threats

Since hotels are open 24/7, they are susceptible to asset threats any time of the day or night. Guests or non-guests can pose these threats. As is the case when protecting assets from threats posed by employees, hoteliers protecting hotel assets from the illegal activities of non-employees must be aware of, and guard against, threats to cash and non-cash assets.

THREATS TO CASH

Nearly all hotels keep some money on the property at all times. Because that is true, and because many hotels are laid out in a way that offers thieves the chance to make a rapid getaway by automobile, hotel staff members can sometimes be confronted by armed or unarmed robbers. Preventing such robberies is best achieved by management working with the hotel staff and local law enforcement officials to identify and minimize the opportunities for thieves to rob the hotel.

It is important for hoteliers to understand that a robbery is *not* an occasion to protect cash assets. A robbery is a time to protect staff! In the event of a robbery, the hotel staff member(s) involved should obey the robber's demands and make no movements that might be perceived by the robber as an attempt to stop the crime. Employees should do *nothing* that could risk or jeopardize their lives. Employees can, of course, be trained to observe the robber carefully for the purpose of later recalling physical characteristics, such as height, weight, color and length of hair, color of eyes, mustaches or beards, tattoos, accents, or other identifying characteristics. During a robbery, complying with the robber's demands and observation of the robber should be the employee's only concern.

To help apprehend robbers, many managers install a contact alarm system in their cashier's cash drawers. This alarm is activated when a predetermined bill or packet of bills is removed from the cash drawer. The alarm is wired to summon local law enforcement officers trained to deal with robbery-in-progress situations. If no such alarm is in place, an employee who is robbed should, at the earliest safe opportunity, contact local law enforcement officials as well as others indicated in the robbery section of the hotel's emergency plan.

THREATS TO OTHER ASSETS

Robbers steal from hotels, but so do guests. In fact, guests are much greater threats than robbers to the non-cash assets of hotels. Most often, the targets of guests are not cash but the products and services the hotel sells. Every experienced hotel manager has a "you won't believe this one" story about a guest who removed (or tried to remove!) a significant asset from a hotel illegally. From furniture, television sets, and artwork to minor items such as towels, robes, bed linens, and in-room clock radios, guest theft costs hotels millions of dollars annually in lost assets.

The reality for most guest theft, however, is that it is simply recognized as a cost of doing business. It makes little sense, for example, to accuse a guest of stealing a wooden clothes hanger (even if the hanger was, in fact, stolen by the guest) and then attempt to charge the guest for the item.

Some hotel managers place small signs in guest rooms offering to sell guests those items that frequently disappear. Other managers, in an effort to deter theft, word guest room signs in such a way as to imply that a room attendant will be held financially responsible for any loss of guest room items. Whether managers use these in-room signs (neither of which is recommended by the authors) or other less obtrusive approaches, guests and visitors to a hotel represent a significant threat to asset security. Therefore, it is good business practice to take precautions designed to reduce theft. To that end, security-conscious hoteliers:

- Hang all artwork in lobbies and guest rooms with lockdown-style hangers
- Avoid placing valuable decorations and décor pieces in areas where guests can easily take them
- Train room attendants to alert management if excessive amounts of terry cloth products or in-room items are missing from stay-over rooms
- Bolt televisions and in-room computers securely to guest room furniture
- Train all employees to be alert regarding the loss of hotel property and to report any suspicious activity they encounter

It is important to remember that theft of services by guests can happen just as easily as the theft of physical assets, and proper controls must be in place to prevent these occurrences. Just as nearly all retail stores endure losses from shoplifters, hotels lose items to guest pilferage. However, retail stores and their hotel counterparts must diligently seek to limit the losses caused by theft through the implementation of policies and procedures designed to reduce such losses.

Area-Specific Threats

Threats to a hotel's assets can occur at any time and in any department. Some departments, however, by the nature of their operation, are subject to specific security threats of which hoteliers should be especially aware. These include the front office, housekeeping, food and beverage, sales and marketing, and maintenance departments.

FRONT OFFICE

In addition to the threats to cash posed by employee theft or robbery, the largest area of concern at the front desk is the fraudulent selling of rooms. Consider, for example, the night auditor who checks a guest into the hotel very late at night. The guest states that he or she only needs the room for a few hours to get some sleep before continuing on their travel. The auditor collects the guest's payment in cash at the time of arrival, but later reduces the day's room revenue by the same amount, stating that the guest was unhappy with the room, left early, and the guest's cash was refunded. Obviously, this could have happened. On the other hand, it is also possible that the guest stayed for the short time indicated at arrival and the auditor has defrauded the hotel of one night's room revenue.

Alternatively, assume that a front office agent simply gives the key to a vacant guest room to a friend or relative and collects no room revenue from that individual. The room, of course, must be cleaned the next day by the housekeeping staff. Again in this case, the hotel has been defrauded of its rightful room revenue. The hotel's managers must have systems in place that daily compare rooms cleaned with rooms actually sold to minimize the chances for employee fraud at the front desk.

HOUSEKEEPING

Managers in the housekeeping department must be aware of two distinctly different security issues. The first is the theft of housekeeping supplies, such as in-room amenities, towels, and sheets. Thefts such as these can, of course, be committed either by guests or by employees. While it is virtually impossible to stop all theft of minor amenities and in-room items, proper controls and systems should be in place to detect and respond to significant thefts of this type.

The second and much more sensitive housekeeping issue involves theft from guest rooms by room attendants or other employees. When guests travel, they often keep valuables in their rooms. This is true despite the recommended use of safety-deposit boxes for such items.

If a guest claims that there has been a theft from his or her room, managers must consider four possible scenarios:

1. The guest has made an honest mistake and the item(s) reported stolen has simply been misplaced by the guest
2. The guest is attempting to defraud the hotel because the item was not stolen
3. The theft was committed, but by another hotel guest
4. A hotel employee committed the theft

Obviously, the management of the hotel must be very careful in such situations. If, upon inquiry, management believes that a theft has in fact occurred, it is the best policy to report the incident to local law enforcement officials who are trained to investigate the crime.

FOOD AND BEVERAGE

Because food and beverage items can be used by virtually everyone, they are a common target for theft. Guests may take silverware and glassware as mementos of their stay, and employees may pilfer the same items for their own homes. More significantly, however, employees who purchase products for the food and beverage department may defraud the hotel by accepting kickbacks from vendors or by purchasing and then stealing food and beverage items intended for the hotel. It is in the development of systems and procedures to reduce the threat of this type of fraud about which hotel managers must be extremely vigilant.

SALES AND MARKETING

Sales and marketing staff are frequently responsible for preventing fraudulent behavior directed at the hotel by unscrupulous individuals. Very often, this takes the form of outside parties billing the hotel for marketing services that were not rendered or were not requested. Typically, this scam takes the form of an official-looking invoice arriving in the sales and marketing department by mail or fax. The invoice states that the hotel owes money for its listing in a published directory of hotels targeted toward a specific group, such as government employees. The invoice will also likely state that the hotel must pay promptly to avoid being dropped from the directory. In fact, however, the directory does not even exist. Those responsible for sending the invoice hope that the hotel will pay the invoice without investigation. This scam and others of a similar nature are common, and hotels that do not have sufficient control of their accounts-payable system may fall prey to them.

It may seem unusual to consider sales and marketing employees themselves as a source of fraud; however, due to the nature of their interaction with clients, threats to asset security do exist. Some of these threats take the form of irregularities with expense accounts. Misstating mileage traveled, clients entertained, or sales trips taken can cause the expense account expenditures of sales staff to be overstated, and as a result their reimbursements will be too high. To combat such potential problems, the hotel must have a good check-and-balance system that requires documentation of sales expenses and routine audits of reimbursements.

MAINTENANCE

A unique problem in the maintenance department relates to the loss of small but sometimes expensive hand tools and supplies. It is important to remember that the types of items typically used in a hotel's repair shop are the same items employees and guests would use to do repairs in their own homes. Thus, portable hand drills, electric saws, wrenches, and the like can easily turn up missing if they are not carefully controlled.

It might seem as if this would be an easy problem to alleviate. In fact, taking an inventory of small hand tools like pliers or screwdrivers on a monthly basis is time-consuming and is often not done. When this is the case, dishonest employees know that they can take small items without much fear of detection. In addition, tools left at a worksite in the hotel during meals or other breaks can, if unsecured, be stolen by guests or others in the hotel. To prevent either of these problems, small hand tools should always be inventoried monthly to determine losses, if any. In addition, hand tools should never be left unattended

LODGING GOES GREEN!

The world's largest hotel chains have been meeting regularly to discuss international guiding principles for sustainable tourism, safety, hotel design, and development. Accor, Carlson, Four Seasons, Hilton, InterContinental, Marriott, Rezidor SAS, Starwood Hotels & Resorts Worldwide Inc. and TAJ Hotels, Resorts and Palaces have actively supported the development of these guiding principles.

There is an increasing realization that the hospitality industry should be leaders in the effort. In fact, there is an overwhelming case for hotels to be designed and operated according to sustainable principles. As well as the need to preserve the environment and avoid wastage of resources, businesses are increasingly realizing that a more sustainable approach means a longer-term and more profitable business environment.

The London-based International Tourism Partnership (ITP) (www.tourismpartnership.org) is a membership organization of leading companies from the travel and tourism industry. Its aim is to provide the hotel, travel and tourism industry with the knowledge and ability to develop practical solutions for more responsible business.

in a public area of the hotel. The temptation for theft and potential for loss are too great. While it may inconvenience the department, the head of the maintenance department may consider requiring a **sign-in/sign-out program** for all tools if regular inventories indicate that theft is a significant problem.

LODGING LANGUAGE

Sign-in/Sign-out Program: A system in which employees taking responsibility for hotel assets (such as hand tools, power equipment, or keys to secured areas) must document their responsibility by placing their signature and the date on a form recording their possession (sign-out) and return (sign-in) of the item.

HOTELS AND GLOBAL TERRORISM

The events of September 11, 2001, brought home to hoteliers and to all Americans the very real threat of terrorist attacks. Globally, hotels have increasingly become a target of terrorist attacks. The reasons why hotels are targeted are varied but include the fact that they are often considered by terrorists as symbols of the affluence and influence of Western-culture. Hotel guests usually represent precisely the kind of people terrorist seeks to eliminate, including foreign diplomats, businesspeople, wealthy tourists, and local elites.

Unlike many other potential attack sites (such as foreign embassies or military instillations), hotels generally are unguarded; have multiple points of entry; and have a constant flow of traffic, including hotel guests, employees, and delivery personnel. As a result, hotels are relatively easy to enter without attracting undue attention.

Because hotels are often pictured on the Internet, their physical layout (including precise locations of entrances, exits, and atriums) is easy to determine prior to an attack. As well, because of their high visibility, terrorists can be assured of a great deal of international media attention when hotels are targeted.

The likelihood that a single hotel will be terrorism target is small, but it increases with its size, location, ownership, and symbolic importance. Because the threat of a terrorist attack is real, managers in all properties should be concerned and assess their security procedures so as to take practical steps to protect lives in the event of an intentional explosion, fire, or other disaster, possibly even including the use of biological or chemical weapons. Hoteliers whose properties are at a high risk of terrorist attack must exercise special vigilance. While it may not be possible to prevent all possible attacks, hoteliers can take positive steps to minimize their risk. These include:

- The proper maintenance of existing security and safety equipment/procedures. For example, if surveillance equipment is in current use, it should be properly maintained, and information about building-evacuation procedures should be an integral part of new employee training.
- Careful consideration of potential vulnerability. As the possibility of a terrorist attack increases, so should the precautions taken to address it.
- Controlled access to nonpublic areas of the property.
- The screening (background checks) of employee applicants in accordance with applicable laws.
- Management training that addresses information to yield an awareness of the terrorist threat, the importance of remaining diligent, and the need to be prepared and to keep emergency plans current.
- Regular participation in "best practices" discussions with hoteliers who face similar threats and with local law enforcement officials who can provide guidance.

Since September 2001, the U.S. Congress has enacted many bills related to homeland security. In many cases, these bills affect the hotel industry. It is likely that more hotel-related legislation involving fire safety, emergency/crisis planning, and the prevention of terrorist acts will be passed at the federal or even state level. As a result, professionals in the hotel industry should carefully monitor developments in these important areas.

Lodging Language

Safety
Security
Reasonable Care
Damages
Compensatory Damages
Punitive Damages
Threat Analysis
Insurer
Safety and Security Committee
Occupational Safety and Health Administration (OSHA)
Recodable Locking System
Keycard
Internal Alarm
Contact Alarm
Closed-Circuit Television (CCTV)
Emergency Plan
Workers' Compensation
Premiums
Claim (Insurance)
Incident Report
Embezzlement
Bond(ing)
Fraud
Sign-in/Sign-out Program

For Discussion

1. As you have learned, safety and security are the responsibility of all hotel employees. In some hotels, however, there is a security department with its own full- and part-time employees. List three factors that might cause the management of a hotel to employ designated security staff on a regular basis.
2. Guest safety is a primary concern of all effective hotel managers. What steps can you take to ensure that all of the hotel's employees share your concern for guest safety? Identify at least three specific activities.
3. Material Safety Data Sheets are a valuable source of safety-related information for workers. In most cases, however, these documents are provided only in English and Spanish. Increasingly, the hotel industry employs individuals whose native language is neither of these. Assume that your hotel employs 25 such individuals speaking five different languages. How would you help ensure the safety of these workers with regard to handling chemicals and other toxic materials?
4. Good relations with local law enforcement officials are extremely helpful to a hotel. What are two specific activities the managers of a hotel can undertake to build positive relations with the local police?
5. Some hotel managers believe that uniformed security personnel in the hotel increase the comfort level of guests in the same manner as would uniformed police officers. Other managers feel that uniformed security personnel increase guests' concern about security and their own safety and thus have a negative effect. If it were your decision, would you put your security force in police-style uniforms or uniforms that blend with your clientele? What factors would influence your decision-making?
6. Swimming pool safety is always a concern for hoteliers. Do you believe that there should be a hotel policy limiting the number of additional guests that a registered hotel guest can invite to swim at a hotel pool, or should pools be reserved for registered guests only? What factors would influence your decision?
7. Good recordkeeping is an important part of a hotel's safety and security efforts. Identify three reasons why this is so.
8. Guests with physical limitations related to their movement, hearing, or sight present special safety concerns for a hotel. This is especially true in times of emergency. What are some steps hoteliers can take to ensure that such guests receive needed assistance in case of a hotel emergency, such as a fire or other situation requiring a forced evacuation?

9. Assume that your hotel's housekeeping department is experiencing periodic losses of products that you believe are due to employee theft. As a general manager, what specific steps would you suggest be taken to address this issue?

10. Pilferage of hotel assets by employees is common in the hotel industry. Would you recommend terminating a good hotel employee proven to have pilfered a bar of soap from a room attendant's cart? Why or why not?

Team Activities

TEAM ACTIVITY 1

The text indicated that the three major areas of concern for hoteliers seeking to demonstrate that they exercise reasonable care are related to:

- The hotel's physical facilities
- The hotel's staff
- Policies and procedures implemented by the hotel

While all of these are important, which does your team believe is *most* important? Why?

TEAM ACTIVITY 2

On Thanksgiving Day 2008, the world looked on in horror as terrorists armed with assault rifles, submachine guns, and hand grenades attacked Mumbai, India's financial and entertainment capital for nearly three days (November 26–29). The final result was 166 people killed. Among the direct targets were two of the city's most famous 5-star hotels: the Taj Mahal Palace and Tower and the Oberoi Trident complex. Western tourists and businesspeople especially were singled out for attack. The final death toll included 28 foreign nationals from 10 countries, 6 of which were Americans.

Use the Internet (Wikipedia.org) to familiarize your team with the November 28, 2008, attack on Mumbai. Next, assume that your team is operating a large hotel in a major metropolitan area such as New York, London, Paris or Mumbai. What are three concrete actions you could employ to reduce the threat to your guests and property that could result from your hotel being targeted by terrorists?

Chapter

14

Careers in the Lodging Industry

Chapter Outline

Chapter Overview

You have been studying about the lodging industry. This may have prompted you to think that a career in the lodging industry would be a good one for you. How do you plan a career that may last 40 years or longer? Fortunately, there are some basic principles and procedures that are useful in evaluating professional employment alternatives, and you will learn about them in this chapter.

It will be exciting to accept your first full-time professional position. Where do you obtain the information needed to make this important employment decision? What concerns will prospective employers have? What factors in the employer-selection process should be important to you? We will also answer these questions in this chapter.

After you have secured your new professional position, it will be necessary to master a number of important workplace skills. What are they? The first days on the job will be critical because you will be forming an impression of your new employer and the organization you have chosen will be learning about you. At this point, you will begin to realize what you need to know, and, as well, you are likely to discover that your learning will never end.

Do you want to work for yourself or for someone else? Do you want to work in this country or around the globe? We'll also address these issues in this chapter.

Your future will be exciting. You have already begun preparing for it, and your experiences after graduation will have a significant influence on your career. If you plan to make the lodging industry your professional home, this chapter should be of extra-special interest to you, so let's begin.

Chapter Objectives

1. To provide an overview of initial career-planning steps.
2. To examine careers in alternative types of lodging organizations.
3. To review the tactics that can help you secure your first full-time professional position in the lodging industry.
4. To explain to you the tactics that will help you succeed at work.
5. To contrast career opportunities in domestic and international hotel positions.

It is a good idea to reflect on your personal attributes to determine the best career path for you in the hospitality industry.

PLANNING A CAREER IN HOSPITALITY

Many people use a daily schedule to help keep them organized.[1] They prioritize important activities and pay attention to projects with deadlines. Activities can be added, deleted, or changed to help keep the schedule current. While nothing in the future is "cast in stone," schedule planners try to control or, at least, to influence it.

Career planning is similar, in many ways, to planning a daily schedule. The purpose is the same (to keep organized and to manage deadlines). Changes are made to keep the schedule (career plan) current as priorities and circumstances change. Many things can affect the plan, but constant efforts are made to manage it. The recognition that careers should be planned and not left to chance alone is a critical first step in efforts to do all you possibly can to control your own professional future.

Career-Planning Steps

An overview of the career-planning process is presented in Figure 14.1

Recognizing the need for career planning is the first step noted in Figure 14.1. This should be followed by exploring your personal interests, skills, values, and even personality. The results of this analysis should drive the remainder of your career planning process. Knowing about as many employment alternatives as possible will help you select your preferred industry (hospitality), segment (such as lodging or club management), specific organization, and

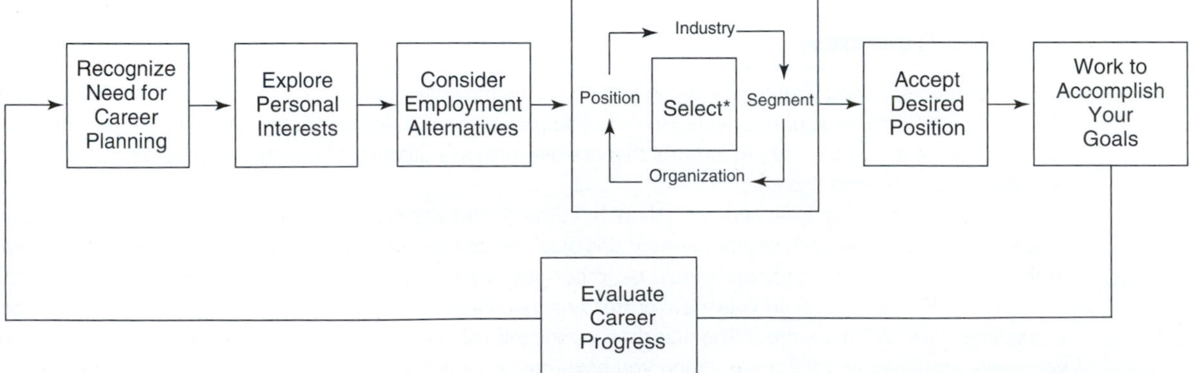

*Note: The process of selecting the area of work is *not* sequential (first industry, then segment, then organization, then position). Rather, it is simultaneous; one considers each of these factors in a personal order of preference. One person, for example, may think first of a position (general manager) and then consider the industry, segment, and organization. Another person may think first about segment (hotel) and then consider the organization and/or the position.

FIGURE 14.1 Steps in Career Planning

[1]This chapter is loosely based on Chapters 31–35 in Jack Ninemeier and Joe Perdue, *Discovering Hospitality and Tourism: The World's Greatest Industry* (Copyright © 2008, 2005 by Pearson Education, Inc., Upper Saddle River, New Jersey 07458).

LODGING ONLINE

Hospitality careers (Hcareers) is the leading job posting site for the hospitality industry. To view the types of opportunities listed on its web page, go to:

www.hcareers.com/

If you were looking for a management position, would you post your resume on a site such as this one?

position for the first step in your career. After you have accepted an initial position, it is important to work hard to attain the goals that prompted you to take the job.

Figure 14.1 also illustrates that your career progress should be continually evaluated because the career-planning process will continue as you assess new opportunities and alternatives as they are presented to you.

Enrolling in a hospitality management education program is an important first step in career planning. The courses you take, your internships, and your job experiences will all reinforce your initial decision to choose the hospitality industry as your professional home. After you have done so, your career-planning priorities will shift to issues concerning your desired industry segment, organization, and position. Even if you have not yet decided to make your career in the hospitality industry, questions such as "What do I want do in my career?" or "In what industry do I wish to work?" must still be answered, and doing so will utilize the same decision-making process.

Assessing Personal Interests

How can you find a career you will really enjoy? The best way is to consider carefully what you like to do and then to find a career that permits you to do what you like to do.

Can you imagine professional athletes practicing many hours every day to become better at a sporting skill that is not of interest to them? How about a chef developing new recipes or a hotel's general manager making important decisions about many challenges and opportunities every day when they really don't care about their jobs? There may be some athletes, chefs, and general managers who truly do not like what they do. However, their counterparts who continually find pride and joy in their work will be much happier because they take pleasure in the time they spend in this important part of their lives.

Figure 14.2 illustrates the effects of finding fulfillment on the job. Look at it and ask yourself, "Which do I prefer?" When you have a passion for your job, there is likely to be contentment and an interest in succeeding. This typically yields success in the position and leads to a rewarding career and increased job satisfaction.

Contrast this with the attitude of those people doing a job "because they have to." If you have no interest in or, even worse, truly dislike your job, you will not find

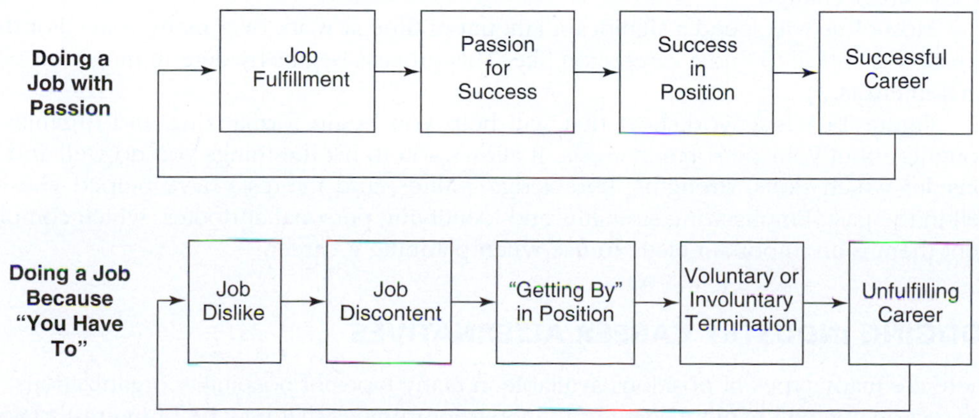

FIGURE 14.2 Finding Fulfillment on the Job

PART I

List those things you do well (your strengths):

1. ____

2. ____

3. ____

PART II

Personal Attributes (Characteristics)	How Does This Attribute Help You Do Well?
What are your greatest skills?	
What are your greatest strengths?	
About what do you have the greatest knowledge?	
For what do you have the greatest aptitudes (natural abilities)?	
What things in life do you most highly value?	
What are your interests? (What do you most like to do?)	

FIGURE 14.3 What Are Your Personal Interests?

contentment in it and, as a result, will not do it well. You may attempt to just "get by" while meeting only the minimal expectations of your employer. This type of attitude does not lead to success and will generally lead to an unfulfilling career. This can become a cyclical process leading to further dislike and disinterest and, eventually, to a job or career change.

Most of us will spend a significant amount of time at work over many years. For that reason, it is critical to find a career you like. This process begins by determining your personal interests.

Figure 14.3 is a worksheet that will help you begin formalizing and organizing thoughts about your personal interests. It allows you to list the things you do well and to consider which skills, strengths, knowledge, values, and interests have helped you do well in the past. Emphasizing strengths and identifying personal attributes, which complement them is an important tactic to use when planning a career.

LODGING INDUSTRY CAREER ALTERNATIVES

There are many types of positions available in many types of hospitality organizations. In this section, we will explore some of the job opportunities that may be of interest to you.

The lodging industry offers lots of exciting opportunities, it is up to you to decide which personal goals you want to pursue.

Independent Hotel or Multi-Unit Organization?

Is it better to begin or to continue your career in the hotel industry by working in a single property owned by an independent hotelier or by working for a hotel organization that owns or manages many hotels? Not surprisingly, the answer is "It depends," and the primary consideration is you and your own personal interests.

PERCEPTIONS AND REALITY

Many hospitality students maintain that they are "people persons" and state that this is what excites them about the hospitality industry. They want to work in organizations that serve people (guests) and that need people (staff) to serve them. However, it is important to recognize that there are many parts of a hotel manager's job that do not relate directly to people. These include activities relating to financial planning, laws and regulations, insurance and risk management, and technology planning to name just a few. If working with people is indeed the highest-priority factor in your career-selection decision, there are some positions in the hotel industry that may not be right for you.

Another stereotype involves thinking about the industry relative to starched white tablecloths and beautiful table appointments (in hotel restaurants) and beautiful atriums and other architectural wonders (in the lobbies of hotels). These amenities are designed into the environment so that guests can enjoy them. However, much of a professional hotelier's job will be performed behind the scenes in offices that look similar to those in any other business and in kitchens, laundry rooms, and other work areas where the environment is usually much less attractive and inviting. As well, you are likely to spend time in corridors, parking lots, meeting rooms, and numerous other spaces as you "manage by walking around."

The hotel industry can be a great business and provide rewarding careers for people who enjoy it. If you learn as much as you can about it before making your employment decisions, your decisions will be good ones.

In this section, we will illustrate parts of the career-planning process by examining the approaches used by Contina and Ellis as they evaluate the type of employer for whom they want to work. They are both about to graduate from a two-year community college program located in the suburbs of a large city and are interested in the hotel industry. Both have thoughts about the factors that may impact their employment decisions:

Factor	Contina	Ellis
Preferred location	Local area	Anywhere; no preference
Additional hospitality education	No (not now)	Maybe
Good on-job technical training	Yes	Yes
Career that will always have day-to-day operating responsibilities	Yes	No
Access to technical help when working through decisions	No (wants to be "in charge")	Yes (concerned about the impact of a bad decision)
Desired job flexibility	Wants to grow within a position	Wants to "keep options open"
Compensation (salary and benefits)	"Better-than-average"	"Better-than-average"

Let's examine what Contina and Ellis think about each factor and how they can use their personal viewpoints to help them focus on a specific type of hotel employer.

Preferred Location Contina will probably discover there are several hotels in her metropolitan area that are operated by independents and national, regional, or even local contract management companies. The availability of positions in the area is important because she does not want to relocate. Ellis has no preference about where he goes after graduation. He likes his community but has also traveled enough to know that there are many places around the country and the world where he would enjoy living and working.

Additional Hospitality Education Both Contina and Ellis recognize the need to become proficient in their first job before exploring the possibilities of additional hospitality education. Contina does not desire further hospitality education now; she may take some classes later. Ellis is potentially interested in additional education sometime. He knows about traditional **distance learning courses** and Internet-based alternatives to continue his education. However, he would like to live and work in a community where a traditional **residential education program** is available.

LODGING LANGUAGE

Distance learning courses: Formal education (training) programs that are available to students or trainees in remote locations.

LODGING LANGUAGE

Residential education programs: Formal education (training) programs that are available to students or trainees at a specific geographic location.

Good On-Job Technical Training Both Contina and Ellis recognize the need for good technical training in their new position to supplement the very useful and practical knowledge learned in their formal education.

Operating Responsibilities Contina thinks she would like a job with day-to-day managerial responsibilities involving guests and employees. Ellis knows that he will need to spend several (or more) years in a career of progressively more responsible operating duties. However, at some point he wants to be more removed from the day-to-day operations of the hotel and become more involved with the development of new hotel properties.

Access to Technical Help Contina is a "take charge" person who will know when she needs technical help (e.g., to improve a guest check-in process or a housekeeping procedure). She wants a position where she can be fully responsible and accountable. Ellis also likes to make decisions. However, he would like to get all available information from all possible sources before making high-priority decisions.

Job Flexibility Contina wants to find the right organization, be promoted within it, and enjoy the more structured routine it provides. Ellis wants to keep his options open. A different position in a new organization located in a different city would be a challenge he might accept.

Fair Compensation Both Contina and Ellis want fair compensation based upon the value they bring to their employer.

Let's consider what we have learned about Contina and Ellis to consider whether an independent or multi-unit hotel organization might be best for them.

Figure 14.4 identifies some of the pros and cons of positions in these organizations relative to the factors presented.

	Independent Hotel	Multi-Unit Hotel Organization
• Preferred Location	Independent hotels are typically located in only one area.	A multi-unit hotel organization typically has properties in numerous locations.
• Additional Hospitality Education	Must determine whether tuition is a fringe benefit; if residential education is desired, the hotel must be located near a school/college campus.	Large multi-unit hotel companies provide educational benefits; if residential hospitality education is desired, it may be possible to transfer to a desired location.
• Wants Good On-Job Technical Training	Training quality depends upon programs established by the hotel and, perhaps, upon whether unforeseen problems arise which reduce training time.	Large multi-unit organizations have structured training programs and resources and may be able to train new employees in units with different challenges.
• Career with Day-to-Day Operating Responsibilities	Top-level managerial positions in independent hotels have daily operating responsibilities.	Higher-level managerial positions often involve multi-unit responsibilities; these managers supervise other managers who are responsible for day-to-day operations in specific hotels.
• Access to Technical Help	The manager in an independent hotel is the "expert." It is only when specialized expertise is needed that external (consulting) help is solicited.	Large multi-unit hotel companies have headquarters-level specialists in many areas of operations that can help managers in individual hotels.
• Job Flexibility (position responsibility)	A career in an independent hotel means working in the same location and building.	A career in numerous locations and in many types of hotel properties is possible.
• Compensation (salary and benefits)	Compensation (starting pay) is typically slightly less than that paid by a multi-unit hotel company.	Compensation (starting pay) from a multi-unit hotel company is typically slightly higher than in independent hotels.

FIGURE 14.4 Pros and Cons of Positions in Independent and Multi-Unit Hotel Organizations

Let's see how Contina and Ellis might personally evaluate the factors in Figure 14.4.

Preferred Location Employment with an independent hotel dictates the location of employment. Those who desire geographic moves may prefer a contract management company.

Additional Hospitality Education Tuition assistance is a benefit offered by many independent and multi-unit hotel companies. If a traditional education on a campus is desired, the independent hotel must be within commuting distance of the campus. By contrast, a multi-unit hotel company has numerous locations.

On-Job Technical Training The quality of initial orientation and training in an independent hotel depends upon the property. Most multi-unit hotel companies provide structured training and educational opportunities for new managers.

Day-to-Day Responsibilities Managers in most independent hotels have day-to-day operating responsibilities. Top-level managers are either directly responsible for or supervise managers with direct operating concerns. Higher-level managers in multi-unit hotel companies may supervise hotel managers who, in turn, are responsible for daily operating activities in their properties.

Technical Help The independent hotel manager is the property's expert on all of the highly specialized and technical fields applicable to property management. By contrast, unit managers in multi-unit companies often have external technical expertise available that can provide additional assistance.

Job Flexibility (position responsibility) Managers with multi-unit hotel companies often have more flexibility in position, industry segment, and in location compared to their independent property counterparts.

Compensation (salary and benefits) Independent and multi-unit hotel companies are concerned about compensation and recognize it to be an important recruitment incentive. Thus pay for beginning managerial positions must be competitive. However, managers in upper-level positions tend to receive higher compensation in multi-unit organizations because their responsibilities, measured in terms of dollars of business volume, are greater than for their counterparts in independent hotels.

While there are many factors to consider, and we have noted only some of the most important ones in the preceding discussion, it appears that Contina will want to pursue a position with an independent hotel, whereas Ellis will probably seek an initial career position with a multi-unit hotel organization.

Large or Small Hotel Company?

What are the pros and cons of managing in a large or small hotel company?

The advantages to accepting a management position with a large hotel company include:

Greater opportunities to advance and relocate: It may even be possible to transfer to other locations worldwide.

Prestige associated with a well-recognized name: Large organizations are often better known than their smaller counterparts.

Less employment risk: Many people believe that there is greater job security within a larger company.

Compensation and benefits: Managers in larger organizations may have the long-term ability to earn more because promotion opportunities within their company may be greater than in smaller organizations.

Legal protection: Larger companies may provide employees with greater job security because of greater adherence to written policies and procedures that may include the right to appeal arbitrary decisions related to termination.

Training: The training offered in larger hotel companies is often more structured and effective and is enhanced by dollars allocated specifically for training purposes.

Possible disadvantages to managing in large hotel companies may include:

Less control over one's work: Strategies may be set for the whole organization, and employees may have fewer opportunities to contribute ideas.

Anonymity: Some people believe that they can become "lost" because they are just a number in a larger organization. This is similar to how some students feel about colleges or universities with very large enrollments.

Less access to senior executives: When you work for a large organization, you may rarely see the highest-level managers and may never actually see the company owners.

While larger companies present real career-related advantages, there are also advantages to a managerial position with small hotel companies, such as a single property owned by an individual or a management company operating a small number of hotels in a local or regional area. Some of these advantages include:

- Employees get to know each other well and there can be a sense of teamwork that may be less common in large companies.
- Employees have a greater variety of duties. They often have more control over their work and can make a greater contribution to the company's short- and long-term strategies.
- Executives in small companies tend to be approachable and available to all employees.
- Employees may have broader responsibilities and be less limited by their job title or job description.
- More company-wide involvement. One is more likely to be involved in the entire organization rather than in a specific department or property.
- Less bureaucracy (rules and regulations).
- The best small companies do not always stay small. Small organizations offer the potential of a job that can grow as the company grows and the opportunity to be part of building a business.

Potential disadvantages of management positions within small companies could include:

- Limited benefits. Many small companies do not offer the same health and retirement benefits as larger organizations.
- Smaller hotel companies often provide less overall training, and highly structured training programs are relatively rare.
- Fewer opportunities for promotion. There are, by definition, fewer positions in small companies that limit one's advancement.

In the United States, most new job growth comes from small businesses. The hotel and hospitality industry readily lends itself to entrepreneurs beginning a new business and enjoying the success that it can bring. The ability to achieve individual hotel ownership is an exciting prospect that we will examine fully later in this chapter.

Franchisor or Operating Company?

What are the employment opportunities available from franchisors? As you have learned, franchisors do not typically operate hotels. Franchise companies, however, employ many hospitality professionals. These jobs often pay well and can be very exciting. Among the varied employment opportunities offered by franchisors are positions in:

Franchise Sales One of the most important positions in a franchise company is that of a franchise sales representative. These individuals work with hotel developers and seek to persuade them to build hotels with the brand name they represent. They also work with the owners of existing hotels to convert these hotels to the brand(s) represented by the salesperson. Franchise sales staff may represent one or more of the franchisor's hotel brands and may oversee regions as small as one state or as large as the entire country. In addition, because many brands are franchised outside of the United States, the opportunity exists for international sales positions.

Field Support Each franchisor offers consultative support to its franchisees. The franchise services director (FSD) represents the franchisor at the individual hotel level. This person serves an important role as an on-site sales and operations adviser and helper. He or she normally visit each hotel within an assigned area of responsibility one or more times per month. The best franchise services directors are strongly committed to the success of the franchisees in their assigned territories, and they are knowledgeable and able to provide a real service to those who operate hotels.

Marketing Services Hotel owners look to their franchise company for assistance in selling hotel rooms. This is the primary responsibility of a franchisor's marketing services department. From designing and implementing national advertising to advising an individual hotelier about a Web site design, employees working in this area of a franchise company are creative and talented marketing specialists. Not surprisingly, these corporate jobs are among a franchisor's highest-paying and most visible ones.

Reservation Data Management Managing the data required to operate a franchise company is an almost overwhelming task. With thousands of hotels, offering hundreds of different room types at dozens of different rate structures, simply keeping track of which hotel is selling what room at what price is a complex endeavor. Yet, this must be done and done well if rooms are to be marketed over the many distribution channels offering hotel rooms for sale (e.g., the Internet, toll-free call centers, and the individual property). The data management department of a franchisor is inevitably very large, and it seeks talented individuals who are detail-oriented. These positions are normally based at a franchisor's corporate headquarters and can provide an excellent opportunity for career growth.

Training Services The top franchisors know that it is in their own best interests to have highly trained staff members working in their branded properties. As a result, each franchisor employs a group responsible for providing this training. These professionals design and deliver training in the form of seminars and workshop sessions. The sessions are held around the country to maximize the number of attendees. The instructors who conduct the franchisor-sponsored seminars and training sessions are among the hotel industry's brightest and most outgoing individuals.

Large franchisors such as Wyndham, Hilton, Marriott, Choice, and Best Western provide individual hoteliers with opportunities for real career growth, even though their employees will not manage hotels. While there are only a few large franchise companies, they all maintain national offices as well as regional offices that must be staffed with skilled employees.

Employees of companies that actually operate franchised hotels will find that they interact often with representatives from the franchise company. In most cases, these interactions are positive, but even in the hotel business there are inevitably areas of potential conflict between a franchisor and its franchisees. Franchisors and those working for them provide guidance and assistance to hotel operators, but they do not assume financial responsibility for the operating results of franchisees. Interestingly, this is one of the greatest advantages as well as a disadvantage of seeking employment with a hotel franchise company.

Profit or Non-Profit?

While the majority of students will go to work in the private or for-profit sector of the lodging industry, there are many hospitality-related jobs in the non-profit sector. Positions in non-profit organizations have traditionally paid less than their for-profit counterparts. Alternatively, however, the non-profit sector has been noted for its job stability and strong benefit packages as well as the sense of personal achievement that many of its jobs provide.

What types of non-profit organizations hire hoteliers? The following partial list will help you understand why individuals with training in the lodging industry are highly valued by non-profit organizations.

Convention and Visitors Bureaus (CVBs) As you have learned in this book, the goal of a convention and visitors bureau (CVB) is to promote travel to the geographic area it represents. The skills needed for many CVB positions (e.g., good verbal and written communications skills and marketing abilities) are the same, in

LODGING ONLINE

The Destination Marketing Association International (formerly the International Association of Convention and Visitor Bureaus) is the professional association for those working in CVBs. It offers its members social networking and professional development opportunities. To view its Web site, go to:

www.destinationmarketing.org/

What is the name and location of the CVB that represents your own local area?

many respects, as those required for effective hoteliers. In addition, a thorough knowledge of how the lodging industry works gives CVB staff members an extra edge over their peers without a lodging background.

In addition to professionals working in positions related to marketing the services and attractions available in their area, CVBs often employ event planners. These professionals offer assistance to other event planners for organizations located outside of the geographic region who are interested in holding their events in the local area. The CVB staff members use their extensive knowledge of the city or local area to make recommendations to assist out-of-town event planners with their meetings or tours.

For example, if a meeting planner's event is to have a Hawaiian theme, the CVB-employed event planner would be able to put the out-of-town event planner in contact with local caterers that specialize in Hawaiian food, a party supply company that can supply Hawaiian decorations, perhaps identify a professional ukulele player, and make suggestions regarding a local hotel or restaurant whose interior decor is most suitable for creating a Hawaiian-like atmosphere for the event.

Chambers of Commerce. Chambers of commerce, like CVBs, seek to advance the interests of their geographic areas. While CVBs promote tourism, chambers promote their areas as good places to establish and grow businesses. To do so, they employ a variety of skilled staff members, including people with a solid understanding of the hospitality industry. These individuals plan and execute special events, may be involved in charitable fund-raising, and use their business skills to help others in the local business community to prosper.

Association Meeting Planner There are more than 35,000 trade, professional, charitable, and other non-profit associations in the United States alone. The category of an association dictates, in many ways, its goals. Nearly all associations, however, meet on a local, regional, and/or national basis. These meetings may be held to disseminate information, provide training, or simply serve the social interests of the association's membership. For nearly all the meetings held, a representative from the association will secure sleeping rooms, meeting space, and meals from the hoteliers in the meeting site. Clearly, a good understanding of how hotels operate provides these professional meeting planners with many of the tools required to be successful in their jobs.

LODGING ONLINE

The American Society of Association Executives (ASAE) is the professional association for those who manage associations. It provides its members with a variety of services, including information related to job openings. Visit the ASAE and its Center for Professional Leadership Web site at

www.asaecenter.org/

When you arrive click, "Career" to see its current job postings.

Where is the location of your state or regional chapter of the ASAE?

LODGING GOES GREEN!

You do not have to graduate before you can begin undertaking environmentally friendly efforts. You can join thousands of other students and schools by starting right now. In an effort aimed at identifying environmentally (Green) programs at universities and colleges across the country, The Princeton Review, in partnership with the U.S. Green Building Council (USGBC), released "*The Princeton Review's Guide to 286 Green Colleges.*"

The guide is based on a survey of hundreds of colleges and universities across the United States. The survey looked at the following: building certification using USGBC's LEED green building certification program, environmental literacy programs, available courses, formal sustainability committees, use of renewable energy resources, and recycling and conservation programs.

The Princeton Review published Green Rating scores for 697 schools in its online college profiles and/or annual college guidebooks. The Review chose to recognize the outstanding commitment of 286 schools whose sustainability programs were judged to be outstanding.

If you are committed to helping others see that "it's easy being green," now is the best time to start, even if you are still in school!

YOUR FIRST FULL-TIME PROFESSIONAL POSITION

Assume that you have decided to make your professional home in the lodging industry. Where should you start your job search? There are many sources of information about hotel companies where you can obtain background information about potential employers. In addition, you should know about concerns that prospective employers commonly have when they recruit job applicants. You too will likely have some concerns. All of these are the topics of this section.

Collecting Information

You should obtain as much information as possible about those hotel companies you consider potential employers. Some of the ways you can do that include networking and research.

NETWORKING: There are numerous ways to gain contacts that can provide information about possible hotel employers. Talk with:

Classmates. Some of your peers may have worked for companies as they completed internships and/or to earn money while in school.

Faculty members. The faculty who teach hospitality-related courses in your school may have contacts (their own networks) that can help with your job search.

Campus recruiters. Representatives of hotel companies may visit schools and participate in **career fairs** sponsored by educational institutions.

LODGING LANGUAGE

Career fair: Trade show–type events that allow prospective job applicants to meet recruiters representing multiple employers in one location during a specified time period.

School alumni. Graduates of your school may hold positions in companies in which you are interested.

Your family and friends. In many cases, this can be one of the best sources of information about potential employers.

RESEARCH: Your own use of the following can help:

The Internet. All hotel organizations have Web sites that provide information about their company; increasingly, they also have an "employment opportunities" section on the site. Professional and trade associations also feature employer information and job boards.

LODGING ONLINE

All of the large-circulation trade journals applicable to the hotel industry have Web sites; here are some of the largest and their web addresses:

Hotel and Motel Management	www.hotelworldnetwork.com/
Hotel Business	www.hotelbusiness.com/
Lodging	www.lodgingmagazine.com/

Check out these Web sites. While reviewing them, look for employment opportunities advertised on these sites.

In what area of the country would you most like to work?

Trade publications. Numerous trade magazines feature articles about current events, prominent organizations, and related information about the hotel industry. These may be available in hard copy or in electronic form.

Organization-specific information. Some companies (especially multi-unit lodging companies) have printed information available that reviews important employment information.

Other written information. Annual reports from hotel organizations, recruitment brochures, and class handouts can help you learn about prospective employers.

Career centers. Some colleges and universities offer resources to help students learn about prospective employers. They may have written information and may also compile invaluable feedback about positions accepted by past graduates.

Important Concerns: Prospective Employers

Hotel employers look for managers who can "think outside of the box" and have flexible skills. While some positions will require specialized skills or training, in nearly all cases an employer's preferred candidates will possess:

- effective communication skills
- computer aptitude
- leadership and organizational traits
- teamwork abilities
- interpersonal (between-people) skills
- personal accountability
- problem-solving/decision-making skills
- enthusiasm (enthusiastic personality)
- a professional appearance

STARTING POSITIONS

Many students begin their hospitality careers as management trainees. They rotate through a planned sequence of positions and begin to master a set of skills that their employer believes are necessary for them to become a qualified manager. They learn basics about responsibilities and tasks in various positions in each department. They also begin to learn about the organizational culture, the relationship of each department to the others, and the managerial challenges and operating procedures of each department.

Many students negotiate an agreement before employment that states they will begin working in a mutually agreeable position after successful completion of the management training program. This will be the beginning of a career track that will take them, initially, up the ladder within the organization.

Some students, especially those who have completed internships or who have work experience with an employer, may not need to participate in this rotating management training, or it might be shortened. These experienced students can, instead, move more directly and quickly into the managerial position they have secured.

ALL IN A DAY'S WORK 14.1

THE SITUATION

"I don't know . . . he just looked . . . funny," said Noel Larsen, front office manager at the Quality Place Suites.

"What do you mean," asked Dan the hotel's GM.

"Well, the tattoos for one thing. I guess I'm not used to them," said Noel.

"I know what you mean. . . . I'm not so sure I understand the whole tattoo thing either. But what did you think about his personality?" asked Dan.

"That was great," said Cindy. "And his resume looked really good. The piercings were another thing . . . I'm just not sure how our guests will react with him working at the front desk."

A RESPONSE

Personal appearance issues are some of the trickiest faced by managers. Policies and hiring practices related to allowable hairstyles, visible body piercings and tattoos, personal grooming, and even dress related to a candidate's religious practices must be carefully implemented to ensure that they are fair to prospective employees and to employers.

A good rule of thumb for employers is that only those personal characteristics directly related to the ability to do a job effectively should be considered when assessing a job candidate's potential to be an effective employee. Also, it is important to remember that, in the United States, it is not lawful to discriminate against potential job holders based on protected characteristics such as gender, race, or religion when making hiring decisions.

As a potential job candidate, it is important to remember that all businesses will want their employees to look and act professionally at all times. How a potential employee acts and presents himself or herself during an interview gives a preview of what the employer can expect in the future and thus can certainly affect hiring decisions.

Recruiters working for hotel organizations typically mention several things that hospitality students should avoid as they search for a professional position. These include:

- Developing an overly detailed resume
- Sending a resume to an organization without first learning as much as possible about it
- Being dishonest and/or overstating their experience
- Applying for a management position at a property that is part of a multi-unit organization without determining whether the resume should be sent to a human resources official at corporate headquarters

You should always maintain a professional attitude and appearance while searching for a position in the hospitality industry.

Tactics that should be used when searching for a professional position include:

- Develop a well-prepared resume using facts that will interest prospective employers and sell oneself
- If possible, getting to know recruiters representing organizations in which they are interested. Ask questions and recall that a recruiter can be a good mentor
- Avoid using a search firm to distribute resumes. Instead, consider sending e-mail resumes directly to the individual responsible for making the hiring decision
- Practice interviewing (and then practice some more!)

Employers typically state their desire for a total package of knowledge, skills, and aptitudes. They mention critical thinking, intelligence, common sense, and a willingness to learn quickly and continuously. Figure 14.5 shows a ranking of key candidate characteristics that are important to many employers.

It should be noted that potential employers responding to a generic survey (not a hospitality-specific survey) provided the data presented in Figure 14.5. Many in the hospitality industry would agree, however, that one's academic major, leadership (effective use of interpersonal and communication skills), and a basic grasp of technology are very important. They would likewise agree that grade point average (GPA) while somewhat important, is not as important as several of the other factors noted by these employers.

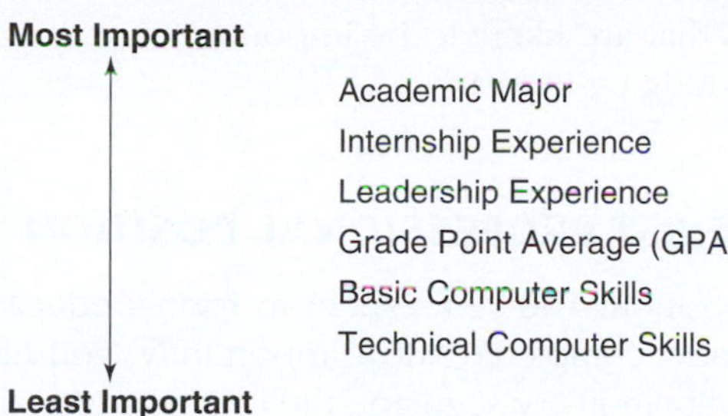

FIGURE 14.5 What's Important to Employers?

Important Concerns: Prospective Employees

Now that you have learned something about the factors that will likely be of concern to employers, let's review some issues that should concern you as a prospective employee.

There are numerous factors to consider as you evaluate professional employment alternatives. Figure 14.6 presents a checklist for assessing employment alternatives that

FACTOR	IMPORTANCE TO ME			
	SIGNIFICANT	VERY	SOMEWHAT	NONE
General				
Relevance of your education	❑	❑	❑	❑
Location	❑	❑	❑	❑
Physical demands	❑	❑	❑	❑
Your aptitude to do required work	❑	❑	❑	❑
Total compensation	❑	❑	❑	❑
Your interest in doing the work	❑	❑	❑	❑
Future of organization	❑	❑	❑	❑
Daily work hours	❑	❑	❑	❑
Weekly work hours	❑	❑	❑	❑
Workplace environment	❑	❑	❑	❑
Location				
Cost of living	❑	❑	❑	❑
Friends/family	❑	❑	❑	❑
Moving expenses	❑	❑	❑	❑
Recreational opportunities	❑	❑	❑	❑
Travel requirements	❑	❑	❑	❑
Position				
Level of responsibility	❑	❑	❑	❑
Quality of training	❑	❑	❑	❑
Challenges	❑	❑	❑	❑
Mentor available	❑	❑	❑	❑
Advancement	❑	❑	❑	❑
Transfer of knowledge/skills to other positions	❑	❑	❑	❑
Company				
Culture	❑	❑	❑	❑
Reputation	❑	❑	❑	❑
Mission	❑	❑	❑	❑
Job security	❑	❑	❑	❑
Management quality	❑	❑	❑	❑
Support for additional education	❑	❑	❑	❑
Compensation				
Salary	❑	❑	❑	❑
Bonus	❑	❑	❑	❑
Health insurance	❑	❑	❑	❑
Life insurance	❑	❑	❑	❑
Vacations/holidays	❑	❑	❑	❑
Sick leave	❑	❑	❑	❑
Pension	❑	❑	❑	❑
Retirement	❑	❑	❑	❑
Profit-sharing	❑	❑	❑	❑
Overtime	❑	❑	❑	❑
Stock options	❑	❑	❑	❑
Pre-tax accounts (health and child care)	❑	❑	❑	❑
Relocation expenses	❑	❑	❑	❑

FIGURE 14.6 Checklist for Evaluating Employment Alternatives

identifies basic concerns that are likely to be important to you as you consider your employment options in the lodging industry.

SUCCESS IN YOUR FIRST PROFESSIONAL POSITION

Your first professional position! The years spent in formal education, the part-time jobs, and the internships are now completed. Most importantly, you have made important decisions about the hospitality industry segment, the organization, and the position you will hold to begin your career.

What's next? The rest of your life—much of which will be spent working and, most likely, working for a variety of employers in a variety of positions. The time to begin thinking about your professional career is now, and many of your thoughts should relate to your first position. In this section, we will discuss success tactics helpful during your first days on the job and the need for ongoing professional development.

Success Tactics

Many hospitality management graduates begin their careers in a management training program. The best training programs identify the skills to be learned, and job descriptions (see Chapter 5) will be available to indicate the tasks a trainee must know and be able to do in the position assigned after the training is completed.

Hotel managers, from entry-level supervisors to those at the highest organizational level, must perform their jobs well. While their specific duties will vary by position, Figure 14.7 identifies and provides examples of some basic management competencies. The hospitality industry is a people business, so you will see the emphasis on people with competencies relating to interaction with others, effective communication, and understanding organizations.

Note also the emphasis on basic managerial competencies, including those relating to making decisions, using technology, managing resources, and utilizing information. As well, a manager must have appropriate personal qualities to be effective. This is increasingly gaining importance as managers serve more as team leaders and less as people who are simply bossing others around.

Figure 14.8 further illustrates the importance of human relations competencies. Note that supervisors require significant technical skills, while their top-level manager counterparts utilize more conceptual skills. However, human relations skills are an integral part of a manager's job at all organizational levels.

Competency	Example
• Interact with others	• Facilitate the work of employees; interact with guests
• Effective communicator	• Write letters and memos; speak in public; talk with employees, peers, bosses, and guests
• Make decisions	• Solve problems; think creatively; analyze alternatives
• Use technology	• Apply technology to collect/analyze information and to communicate with others
• Manage resources	• Maximize the use of limited resources to attain objectives
• Understand organizations	• Know and use information about how business, social, and political systems work
• Utilize information	• Collect, organize, and study necessary data as needed for effective management
• Basic skills	• Read, write, speak, listen, and use mathematics and science-related abilities
• Personal qualities	• Integrity, time- and self-management, social skills, and respect for oneself and others

FIGURE 14.7 Basic On-Job Management Competencies

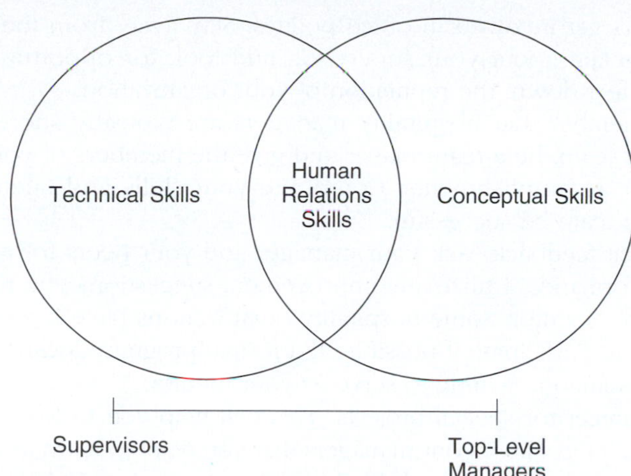

FIGURE 14.8 Human Relations Competencies Are Important

First Days on the Job

When you take your first full-time position, you will have been hired to add value to your employing organization. What you provide should be worth more to the company than what it pays for your services. It is your output (work performance), not your input (education and years of experience), that will be most important to your employer.

You can use a number of tactics to help you begin the right relationship with your employer. These same tactics should be consistently applied in all the positions you will hold throughout your career:

- Dress the way you are expected to dress. If there is a uniform requirement, comply with it. Remember that clean and pressed clothes help you project a professional attitude. Managerial positions often require professional business attire that you must provide. Begin to invest in good-quality conservative attire so that you can develop a professional wardrobe over time.
- Develop a system that will help you remember the names of those you meet. You may need to write names down, or perhaps you can use a system that helps you relate a name to something else. Whatever method you choose, the ability to recall the names of those you meet is an important trait.
- Observe your own supervisor and others who are successful in the company. What do they seem to have in common? What can you learn from them to help in your own performance? If it is someone you admire, consider asking him or her to serve as your mentor.
- Use a personal time planner. At the end of the day, think about what you need to accomplish tomorrow. Alternatively, at the beginning of the day, think about your plans for that day.
- Be punctual.
- Don't get into a routine; make sure that you are always doing whatever is the highest priority.
- Be friendly; say "Hello, how are you?" or a similar greeting because you are genuinely interested in the person to whom you are speaking.
- With one mouth and two ears, listen more than you talk!
- Be quick to praise others when they have earned your praise.
- Practice conflict resolution to avoid confrontations.
- Look for solutions rather than for problems. Remember the old saying: "If you are not part of the solution, you are part of the problem!"
- Remember that neither life nor what happens to you on the job always seems fair. Over time, however, people are most often rewarded according to the extent of their efforts.

Paying attention to detail and consistently providing quality guest service will guarantee you success in the hospitality industry.

- Don't get involved in office politics. Stay away from the grapevine, don't complain about your supervisor, and look for opportunities to build up, not tear down, the reputation of your organization.
- Remember that hospitality managers are typically successful because of their team; be a team player and give the members of your team credit for their accomplishments. Contribute your skills and talents freely to help your team be successful.
- Solicit feedback. Ask your manager and your peers for advice about your performance. Utilize any improvement suggestions you receive.
- Find a mentor. Some hospitality organizations have formal mentoring programs. Participate if possible. If a formal program doesn't exist, try to identify someone willing to serve as your mentor.
- Volunteer for special projects. This will help you to learn more and, at the same time, show your managers that you want to learn as much as possible.
- Recognize that you will likely work extra hours; 50-hour work weeks are not uncommon, especially early in hospitality careers. Long hours and hard work are typical in entry-level managerial positions in all industries including hospitality.
- Meet fellow employees from outside your department. Networking can be a very effective tactic to learn about an organization and advance in one's career.
- Think about the present and the future. Work hard to succeed in your first position, but recognize that it is a first step in what will be, hopefully, a long and rewarding career.
- Keep alert to job openings within your company. Even though you have carefully considered your career, positions may become available that provide educational and professional advancement opportunities. Most companies prefer to **promote from within**. Pay attention to the requirements for these positions and carefully evaluate them for growth potential.
- Have fun at work. Enjoy what you do.

LODGING LANGUAGE

Promote From Within: The concept that a company offers higher-level positions to its existing employees before seeking external candidates when these positions must be filled.

LODGING LANGUAGE

Ethics: A person's beliefs about what is right or wrong.

A WORD ABOUT WORK ETHICS

The concept of **ethics** refers to a person's perception of what is right and wrong. Ethical behavior is influenced by such factors as one's cultural background, religious views, professional training, and personal moral code.

Hotel managers in every position from beginning supervisor to top-level chief executive officer (CEO) must be ethical. When considering alternative courses of action, it is helpful to ask such questions as:

- Is the alternative legal?
- Would the alternative hurt anyone if it were implemented?
- Is the alternative fair?
- Is the alternative the right and honest thing to do?
- Would I be willing to publicly announce the alternative I select?
- Would my organization be improved if everyone utilized the alternative?

Some hospitality organizations have a **code of ethics**, which summarizes the acceptable philosophy about ethics and frequently includes policies to be utilized to help ensure that ethical decisions are made.

LODGING LANGUAGE

Code of Ethics: A statement adopted by an organization that outlines policies developed to guide the making of ethical decisions.

Ongoing Professional Development

Your first position is the first step in your career. However, professional development activities will be valuable to you throughout your career. Some hospitality management graduates may think, "*My education in the hospitality industry is over; everything else I need to learn will now come from experience.*" They are partially correct because experience can be a good teacher. However, in the fast-changing hospitality industry, a mix of additional education along with experience is necessary if you seek to advance up the career ladder.

For example, few hotel managers educated as recently as the 1980s were taught anything about the Internet. Today's hotel managers must be very familiar with the Internet, with high-speed Internet access terminology, and with the technological means required to deliver dependable Internet service to hotel guest rooms, meeting rooms, and administrative offices. Hoteliers who have acquired this information have done so through reading and studying.

Figure 14.9 notes some common professional-development opportunities. Some occur on the job as one gains experience in a specific position. Others occur during activities such as group training on specific topics, **job rotation**, and **job enlargement**.

LODGING LANGUAGE

Job rotation: A systematic plan to move employees into different positions so that they acquire the knowledge/skills required to be effective in these positions.

Job enlargement: The act of including additional tasks/assignments in one's position to provide more opportunities to learn how the position relates to others.

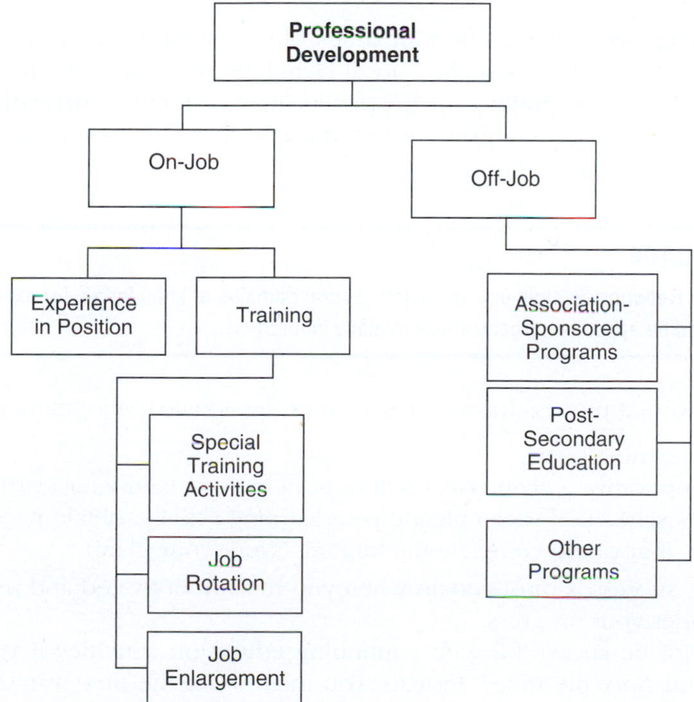

FIGURE 14.9 Professional Development Opportunities

SUGGESTIONS FOR SHORT-TERM CAREER PLANNING

- Think about the tasks in your present position you could do better. You will probably recognize them, or you may receive formal feedback during performance reviews and informal feedback from your own supervisor's coaching comments. Learn more about the knowledge and skills required to perform these tasks.
- If you have a mentor, he/she can be a ready source of professional-development alternatives.
- Try to objectively assess your strengths and weaknesses relative to your longer-term career plans.
- Think about your likes and dislikes. They will influence your career plans and the activities you undertake to move toward career goals.
- Establish professional-development priorities. You may decide to first develop knowledge and skills in areas that will help with promotion. Alternatively, you may focus on your strengths (to become stronger) or weaknesses (to raise them to a par with your other competencies).

Other professional-development opportunities arise from off-site job sources. These include:

Association-sponsored programs. Professional associations such as the American Hotel & Lodging Association, the Asian American Hotel Owners Association, and the National Restaurant Association consider professional development for members to be a high-priority responsibility. Programs are often available at national- and state-level conferences, through independent learning, and from resources available for self-study.

Post-secondary educational programs. Educational institutions frequently offer programs on management topics applicable to the hotel industry. Generic programs may be offered, or programs may be developed for a specific organization. Programs are increasingly available online for anyone in any place at any time. If you want to advance, additional formal education may help you to attain a senior managerial position.

Other programs. For-profit companies offer a wide range of programs, as do community-based groups such as local chambers of commerce and governmental agencies. Since the practice of hospitality management is **interdisciplinary**, a widely diverse range of subject matter is useful for study as part of a professional development program.

LODGING LANGUAGE

Interdisciplinary: Between disciplines—involving several domains of knowledge; for example, basic business principles can be applied in organizations in many industries.

Figure 14.10 shows a process for working your professional-development plan:

- Establish learning goals.
- Identify supportive activities that will most help you attain your learning goals.
- Establish a schedule for completing your learning activity, obtain necessary training resources, if any, and complete the training (work your plan!).

Along the way, success is most certain when you remain motivated and remove any obstacles that hinder your progress.

You cannot be successful with continuing education activities if you plan to do them "when you *have* the time." Instead, you must *make* the time, establish a priority, and allocate your time (always a precious resource). Some hotel employers provide compensated time off or other financial assistance to help their staff members complete

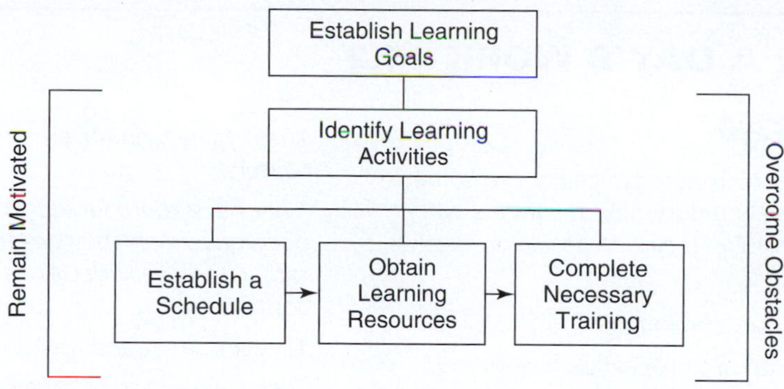

FIGURE 14.10 Working Your Professional Development Plan

LODGING ONLINE

Check out the extensive array of professional-development resources available from the Educational Institute of the American Hotel & Lodging Association (EI of AH&LA) at:

http://www.ahlei.org/

Why is it important for an hotelier to continue learning throughout his or her career?

relevant training and education; others do not. Either way, the drive to do better in your position and to move forward in your career will be an important part of your own professional-development program.

ENTREPRENEUR OR INTRAPRENEUR?

The hotel industry provides many examples of people with great ideas who built them into very large and successful businesses. In Chapter 1, you learned about Kemmons Wilson and the Holiday Inns chain. Willard Marriott's small diner in Washington, D.C. was the forerunner of today's Marriott Corporation. The list of success stories is a long one. Unfortunately, there are also stories about people with many years of hotel industry experience and seemingly great ideas who were not as successful.

Definitions

An **entrepreneur** is a person who assumes the risk of owning and operating a business in exchange for the financial and other rewards it may produce. By contrast, an **intrapreneur** is a person employed by an organization and whose compensation is based, at least in part, upon the success of the area for which he or she has responsibility.

LODGING LANGUAGE

Entrepreneur: A person who assumes the risk of owning and operating a business in exchange for the financial and other rewards it may produce.

Intrapreneur: A person employed by an organization whose compensation is based, at least in part, upon the financial success of the unit for which he/she has responsibility.

Entrepreneurs start their own businesses. Perhaps, for example, a person has worked in the hotel industry for many years and has also accumulated or gained access to the capital resources needed to buy a lodging business. Alternatively, a person may have grown up in a family-owned lodging operation and has the opportunity to take it over. Some entrepreneurs are satisfied when their business provides for their immediate

ALL IN A DAY'S WORK 14.2

THE SITUATION

Hotel industry recruiters typically note some characteristics shared by new managers who are ***not*** successful in their first positions. These include:

- They lack commitment.
- They do not take criticism well.
- They lack initiative.
- They have poor follow-through.
- They lack courage.
- They have problems with the lifestyle of the hotel business.

A RESPONSE

Recruiters also note some of the characteristics that are shared by new managers who are successful. These include:

They have initiative; they are self-starters.

They have the courage to make tough decisions when they are the right ones rather than easy decisions just to avoid conflict.

They are smart and friendly.

They have a passion for all aspects of the business.

They have a drive to get better every day.

They seek additional responsibilities.

They pay attention to details.

wants and needs. Others are challenged to learn whether their success in one hotel can be extended to more hotels. Then, sustained business growth rather than profitability of a single operation becomes a goal.

The concept of intrapreneurship, by contrast, can be more difficult to understand. Intrapreneurs are persons with entrepreneurial talent who do not want to start their own business. They work best in organizations that give them responsibility for a specific and defined part of the enterprise. Consider, for example, a general manager of one hotel in a multi-unit organization. The manager may be compensated, in part, by a profit-sharing plan based upon the property's financial success. Within limitations imposed by the organization, the general manager can implement programs designed to reduce expenses and to increase revenues. In so doing, he or she can directly share in the profits generated by the successful business.

In the example cited, the general manager was involved as an intrapreneur in revenue-producing activities. However, this is not always necessary. Managers responsible for housekeeping, the front office, or security may make decisions leading to cost reductions, and their compensation can, at least in part, be based upon their ability to do so.

Tactics of Successful Intrapreneurs

Intrapreneurs use a process of risk-taking and innovation similar to the one utilized by their entrepreneurial counterparts. Some hospitality organizations encourage intrapreneurship, and there are relationships between general managers and **subordinates** in

DO WHAT YOU LIKE TO DO

Successful entrepreneurs and intrapreneurs have at least one thing in common: they don't consider their job to be work. The goal of having fun at and looking forward to one's job is admirable. As one thinks about the time spent in a career, the old saying "Life is short; have fun at work!" becomes meaningful.

It is very important to enjoy what you do. Entrepreneurial and intrapreneurial positions in the hotel industry allow this to happen. Positions in the industry become even more meaningful when you consider that while enjoying work, you can also help hotel guests enjoy their travel experiences.

which empowerment allows this to happen. Businesses that encourage intrapreneurs generally have four traits:

- They have a realistic vision that is widely understood by and shared with staff members.
- They recruit staff members with entrepreneurial talents and abilities.
- They emphasize teamwork.
- They reward success and do not punish their personnel for creative efforts designed to improve the organization even if the efforts are unsuccessful.

LODGING LANGUAGE

Subordinates: Employees whose work is directly supervised or controlled by an individual of higher rank or position.

Many managers working for hotel companies have opportunities to think and act like an entrepreneur. They can:

Dream/think about ideas to improve the operation. Questions such as "How would I do this if it were my business?" may provide answers that can be implemented.

Obtain ideas from others. Those performing specific work tasks may have improvement ideas. As these ideas are implemented, feelings of accomplishment like those enjoyed by entrepreneurs can also be enjoyed by the hotel's employees.

Take ownership in ideas. Intrapreneurs can explain and defend why something new should be tried. They should be open for feedback about potential challenges, which can arise and why modifications of initial ideas will be helpful.

Know what to do when. They recognize when they need to obtain approval and when they can experiment with existing procedures.

Try new ideas. The fact that something has never been done before or was done yesterday without success doesn't mean that the time isn't right today for another attempt (especially if updated techniques are used).

Look for short-term successes. For example, successful intrapreneurs know the advantage of changing procedures to improve specific products and service tactics.

Understand the organization. They know its expectations and limitations.

Encourage open discussions. They invite discussion with team members, including peers and others within the hotel.

Build a coalition of supporters. They seek support from fellow employees who have similar goals.

Be persistent. They recognize that success frequently correlates with revisions to plans that originally failed.

Recognize the importance of teamwork. They work together with others to create visions of improvement that can involve and inspire others.

Keep their bosses informed. The best surprise is no surprise! Input from supervisors with access to "big picture" ideas and information can be helpful as improvement efforts are planned.

DOMESTIC AND GLOBAL HOTEL POSITIONS

Living and working in paradise! Always warm weather, close to the ocean, palm trees and beautiful scenery, and a lifestyle that will be the envy of your friends and family! Is this what comes to mind when you first think about an island in the North or South Pacific?

Now think about a traditional job and the resulting personal life you would experience in a city far away in Southeast Asia, South America, or Europe. Each of these locations would also offer professional experiences that would be vastly different from what you would typically experience in a job in the United States.

SUCCESSFUL INTRAPRENEURS SHARE COMMON TRAITS

- They are driven by a vision for a better way of doing things and have the desire to implement better ways of doing things.
- They consider risks and assess ways to manage them.
- They are consistent and recognize that purposeful change takes time.
- They use careful analysis when information is available, and intuition influenced by knowledge and experience when it is not.
- They are honest and share good and bad results with others.
- They are willing to do the work necessary to further their ideas.
- They share credit with their teams.
- They keep the best interests of their hotel and its guests in the forefront of decision-making.
- They stick to their goals but are realistic about the best tactics to attain them.
- They have a clear vision about what must be done.
- It should come as no surprise that the traits of successful intrapreneurs are very similar to those of successful entrepreneurs!

You have learned that people from around the world increasingly travel and require lodging and food services as they do so. Since people travel everywhere, hotels need to be everywhere to provide travelers with the services and products they require. Employment opportunities in the hotel industry are available around the world. Positions outside of one's country can be especially rewarding and personally enjoyable. However, they can also lead to professional and personal frustration! Because that is true, a decision to seek employment in the international hotel industry must be the result of careful study.

Working in Another Country

Very large American-owned hotel organizations own and can operate properties in the United States and throughout the world. Large hotel organizations owned by Asians, Europeans, and people of other nationalities own and can operate properties in the United States and other regions of the world. It is, therefore, increasingly true that promotions within a multi-unit organization may involve relocating around the country and even to other parts of the world. What should one consider when making a decision about whether to become an **expatriate** hotel manager?

The hospitality industry offers many global and domestic opportunities to choose from.

LODGING ONLINE

Marriott is one of several American hotel companies with properties worldwide. To see where it operates hotels, go to:

www.marriott.com/

When you arrive, select "Country" to see a list of the countries where Marriott hotels are located.

Would you consider a five-year assignment in a foreign country? A one-year assignment?

LODGING LANGUAGE

Expatriate: A citizen of one country who is employed in another country. Example: a United States citizen working in Asia would be considered an expatriate by his/her Asian counterparts.

Anyone considering work in a foreign country must take several things into account including:

The Political Environment. The United States is incredibly fortunate to have a stable and long-standing legal and political system. Political evolution is slow, and changes are made in a democratic manner. This is not the case everywhere. Governmental structures are much less stable in some countries. This can result in societal turmoil, overnight changes in leadership, laws, and travel restrictions, and the potential for personal harm. The decision about managing a hotel and protecting oneself and one's family in these environments generally signals a "don't go!" for most persons. Fortunately, in many countries, while the legal/political environment is different from that in the United States, opportunities for professional success and personal enjoyment do exist.

Economic Issues. The cost of doing business and living in other countries can be a concern. Diverse tax laws have an obvious effect on business decisions. Currency **exchange rates** impact business and personal decisions.

LODGING LANGUAGE

Exchange rate: The rate at which the money of one country is traded (exchanged) for the money of another country.

Expatriate hotel managers have an advantage when, for example, they are paid a competitive salary in dollars but work in a country where the dollar purchases significantly more than it would in the United States.

Cultural Environment. People living in a country share a **national culture** of values and attitudes that influences their behavior and shapes their beliefs about what is important. In order to work in another country successfully, it is advisable to learn about and become sensitive to its culture.

LODGING LANGUAGE

National culture: The values and attitudes shared by citizens of a specific country that impact their behavior and shape their beliefs about what is important.

National culture can have a significant impact on how employees view their work and one other. Differences between people from different countries relative to how to they treat each other, behave, compete, and value punctuality (being on time for meetings and appointments) are examples of issues that can significantly affect one's attitudes about and ability to work and live in another country.

Expatriates working in a country with a national culture similar to their own are less likely to suffer from **culture shock** than will their counterparts relocating to a country with a more diverse culture. For example, managers originally working in a large city in the United States, and then moving to a large city in Western Europe, would likely feel more at home than would those managers moving to a very rural part of a third-world country.

LODGING LANGUAGE

Culture shock: The feeling of disorientation, confusion, and changes in emotions created when one visits or lives in a different culture.

Success Factors in Global Assignments

Figure 14.11 identifies the key factors that influence whether expatriate managers are successful.

Figure 14.11 is a self-test that may be of interest if you are considering a global assignment. Some (but not all) of these factors are easy to assess.

A person who does not adapt well to change is more likely to have difficulty adjusting to work and living in another culture.

Someone who desires an expatriate position will be happier than others who take the position only for the sake of career advancement.

Expatriates with an understanding of the host country's national culture will know what they are getting into; fewer surprises are likely which may detract from their continued interest in living/working there.

Persons with the knowledge/skills required for successful job performance will feel less stress on the job (and about job security) than those who do not have the necessary job knowledge/skills.

Check (✓) one box for each factor noted below.

FACTOR	NO	MAYBE (A LITTLE)	YES
You are able to adapt to change.	❑	❑	❑
You want to live in another country.	❑	❑	❑
You understand the country's national culture.	❑	❑	❑
You know the country's language.	❑	❑	❑
You have the knowledge/skill needed for successful job performance.	❑	❑	❑
You have the necessary human relations abilities to manage employees with backgrounds significantly different than yours.	❑	❑	❑
You have previous experience(s) working or living in another country.	❑	❑	❑
Your family will support the decision to accept a global assignment and to adapt to life in another country.	❑	❑	❑
You have positive reasons (motivations) which influence your interest in a global assignment.	❑	❑	❑
You have reasonable expectations about the experiences you will have.	❑	❑	❑
You are willing to listen to and try to understand the perspectives of others.	❑	❑	❑

FIGURE 14.11 Checklist of Factors Important to Expatriate Success

WHAT TIME IS IT ANYWAY?

Americans typically value punctuality. For example, if they have an appointment at 11:00 a.m., most of them make every effort to be where they need to be at 11:00 a.m. By contrast, the concept of 11:00 in the morning can mean something entirely different to people in other countries. For example, in some South Pacific Islands, 11:00 in the morning means anytime during the hour of 11:00 in the morning. Therefore, if a person arrives at an 11:00 meeting at 11:50 a.m. or even 11:59 a.m., attendees will be on time for an 11:00 a.m. meeting. Equally frustrating for some expatriate managers from the United States is that the meeting itself, which was scheduled to convene at 11:00 a.m., may not actually begin until 11:30 a.m., 11:45 a.m. or even later!

Interactions with people on and off the job are likely to be a significant factor in whether an expatriate position is successful. Hotel professionals typically think of themselves as people persons; however, they must be effective not only when interacting with fellow workers in their organizations but with their neighbors where they live while in the host country.

Managers with previous experience in another country are likely to know what they are getting into, and their positive attitude and previous professional and personal experiences will be helpful.

Whether family members are interested in relocating and their general support of the decision are significant concerns that will impact the success of the global assignment.

One's motivation to accept an international assignment is important. Consider the manager who volunteers for reasons of personal and professional growth and "adventure," and another manager who is told that it is a good career move.

Expectations about a global assignment must be reasonable. Effective transition training help the manager to realize what working and living in another country will really involve.

The ability to listen and attempt to understand the beliefs of others is very important. Expatriate managers are likely to experience ideas expressed by co-workers, employees, and others in the host country which are profoundly different than theirs.

Seldom, if ever, is a global hotel management assignment successful by chance alone. Many factors must be in place for an assignment to be acceptable. When these factors work against the international assignment, they can, at best, cause strain and stress, and at worse can yield very unpleasant professional or personal experiences.

Figure 14.12 reviews the factors that influence the success of managers in global assignments.

Note that Figure 14.12 first addresses the candidate. The types of personal concerns and factors noted here and discussed above are important considerations. The selection process is also an important factor in the success of a global assignment. Until recently, some hotel organizations made international assignments by doing little more than asking the question "Who wants to go?" or by making the statement "You really should go!" Today, however, a more focused and formalized selection process is generally utilized.

Since expatriate assignments often fail because employees or their families have difficulty adjusting, their level of **cross-cultural adaptability** becomes important.

LODGING LANGUAGE

Cross-cultural adaptability: The extent to which a person can adjust (adapt) to another culture.

The extent to which one can readily adapt to a new culture can be assessed by:

- Administering cross-cultural assessment tools to the employee/spouse/family to assess attitudes and attributes that are important for adjustment.

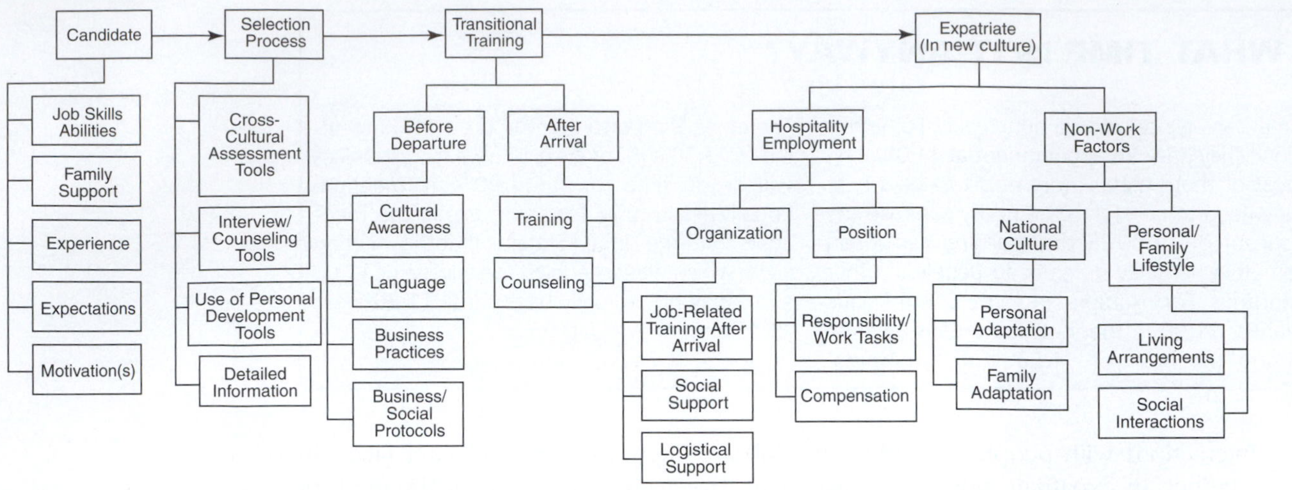

FIGURE 14.12 Factors Influencing Success of Global Assignments

- Interviewing and counseling sessions to further explore the potential for cultural adjustment.
- Considering the availability and quality of cross-cultural support programs provided by the employer.
- Providing detailed information to help the staff member understand the international assignment and adapt to day-day life in the host country.

Figure 14.12 indicates that transitional training is also important. Employees selected for international assignments will, ideally, receive training before they depart. Examples of topics for which training should be provided include:

Cultural Awareness. To teach them how the national culture affects work relations, and how teamwork and productivity can be enhanced when working with staff members from that culture.

Language Training. English is widely spoken in many countries (at least in the world of business). However, expatriates must also live in the community where a foreign language may be commonly spoken and thus they will likely need to acquire basic language fluency to enjoy their lives off the job.

Business Practices. Changes in basic business practices may be necessary, including information about applicable laws, tax issues, and the availability of required resources.

Business and Social Protocols. The specific do's and don'ts of business and social practices in other countries vary and they must be learned.

Transitional training after arrival in the new country is very helpful. This can be provided several weeks after the expatriate manager arrives. Managers and their families will have had an opportunity to experience the new environment and to interact with local citizens, and they may be seeking answers to numerous questions. Their beginning efforts at becoming culturally aware can form the foundation for training and counseling that will make their foreign assignment more enjoyable and rewarding.

Several factors influence the success of a global assignment after the expatriate has arrived in the country. These are:

Hospitality Employment. This includes the organization's job-related training after arrival, social support when on and off the job, and logistical support (e.g., information about which are the best schools for one's children). The position itself, including for example, specific job responsibilities and compensation

LODGING ONLINE

Those working in the hospitality field can join the professional trade associations located in their own countries but may also consider becoming active in the Paris-based International Hotel and Restaurant Association. To examine an overview of this association's goals and activities, go to:

www.ih-ra.com/

What are the advantages or disadvantages of joining an international association of hoteliers who shared your same managerial interest areas?

are important. Other benefits for expatriates may include extended annual leave, travel reimbursements to and from the host country, educational expense reimbursements for family members, costs of moving household belongs to and from the host country, and insurance or reimbursements for emergency travel costs.

Non-Work Factors. Expatriates and their families must adapt to the host country's culture. The personal and family lifestyle that is enjoyed will influence the assignment's success. For example, the expatriate's living arrangements, including transportation to and from work and the numerous non-work social interactions, will impact willingness to continue the assignment.

The hotel industry is an exciting one wherever you may work and whatever position you may hold. Hoteliers who strive to excel and who continue to learn throughout their careers will meet with great professional and personal success and satisfaction.

Lodging Language

Distance Learning Courses
Residential Education Programs
Career Fairs
Promote from Within
Ethics
Code of Ethics
Job Rotation
Job Enlargement
Interdisciplinary
Entrepreneur
Intrapreneur
Subordinates
Expatriate
Exchange Rate
National Culture
Culture Shock
Cross-Cultural Adaptability

For Discussion

1. Give three specific examples (one each) of questions you can ask faculty members, campus recruiters, and school alumni to gain information you could use to identify potential future employers.
2. What do you think would be the single biggest advantage and disadvantage to working with a large organization? A small organization?
3. If you were a recruiter for a hotel organization, what would be among the most important factors you would consider as you recruited management trainee applicants?
4. What will be your two most important concerns as you evaluate alternative job offers? Why are these factors most important to you?
5. Some graduating students view starting salary as more important than benefits when selecting their initial employer? Others view benefits as more important. What factors do you think impact these alternate views?
6. What risks would be of most concern to you if you were thinking about starting your own business?
7. Assume that you are a department head in a lodging organization that believes in and practices intrapreneurship. What percentage of your total compensation would ideally be based upon your ability to attain predetermined goals? How much discretion would you want in making decisions under this ideal situation?
8. How do you think the national culture of a host country impacts the management of hotels in that country? Give two specific examples.
9. What would be some of the biggest challenges in your professional and work lives if you were an expatriate managing a hotel in a country whose language you were fluent in? If you were not fluent in the country's language?
10. Would you be willing to manage a hotel in another country? Why or why not?

Team Activities

TEAM ACTIVITY 1

The chapter provides examples of competencies that are necessary for job success. Identify three of the competencies you feel are most important. For each of these:

1. Cite an additional example of how the competency would be used.
2. Provide an example of a hotel problem that can occur if the competency has not been mastered.

TEAM ACTIVITY 2

Review the section of the chapter that addresses international job placement. Consider five things your team feels would be important to know about a host country before agreeing to accept a job there (e.g., the educational system in place or the religious tolerance practiced). Explain how you would go about obtaining relevant information about each of these five topics.

Chapter

15

The Front Office Management Simulation (FOMS)

Chapter Outline

Chapter Overview

In many cases, the skills needed by those who are learning to be hospitality managers can be readily practiced. To cite just one example, in the area of Food and Beverage management, the knowledge and skill required to properly set a dining room table can be easily practiced in a real or simulated dining room. Not all of the important skills hospitality managers must acquire, however, can be easily simulated.

For example, many of the skills that must be learned by those who will manage the front office in a hotel must be acquired and should be practiced, but, until the introduction of the Front Office Management Simulation (FOMS), doing so in a classroom setting has been problematic. This was true because few hospitality programs have fully functional simulated front desk areas, and fewer still have operating hotels that allow students to gain hands-on experience performing such critical front office tasks as:

- Forecasting demand for rooms
- Making guest reservations
- Checking guests in to the hotel (assigning guests to rooms)
- Posting charges to guest folios
- Checking guests out of the hotel (collecting guest payments)
- Balancing ledgers (guest ledgers and city ledgers)

With the 2011 publication by Pearson Higher Education of the FOMS program (*ISBN 10: 0135107385*), many of the critical skills that must be mastered by front office managers can now be practiced in a simulated, but very realistic, setting. The FOMS program is effective and fun to use. Even more importantly, it gives students the hands-on experience they must have to understand the use and complexity of today's modern hotel property management systems.

Use of FOMS with this textbook is optional. This chapter has been included in the book to provide information and guidance to those instructors and students electing to use FOMS.

It is important to note that access to FOMS also includes a "Help Sheet" designed to assist users in navigating FOMS, and under the "Instructor's Resources" tab in FOMS there is an "Instructor's Guide" detailing the pedagogical approach used in the development of FOMS, as well tips for using it in the classroom.

FOMS is fun for students, and instructors have found its Web-based access and grading easy to administer. In this chapter, you will learn about the various lessons found in FOMS as well as how the program's lessons can best be used to maximize their effectiveness in learning critical front office management skills.

Chapter Objectives

1. To explain the need for an effective front office management training tool and how the Pearson Higher Education Front Office Management Simulation (FOMS) fills that need.
2. To describe the Revenue Management-related content of Lessons 1 and 2 in FOMS.
3. To describe the Reservation Management-related content of Lessons 3 through 5 in FOMS.
4. To describe the Guest Stay Information-related content of Lessons 6 and 7 in FOMS.
5. To describe the Guest Departure and Payment-related content of Lessons 8 and 9 in FOMS.
6. To describe the Accounting and Financial Summaries-related content in Lessons 10 through 12 in FOMS.

FRONT OFFICE MANAGEMENT TRAINING CHALLENGES

Most hospitality education programs have one or more courses in "Front Office Management" or "Hotel Operations." Typically these courses include detailed explanations of how a hotel's front office department operates and how its important guest-related data is generated and managed.

Twenty years ago, it was fairly effective to use basic forms and visual illustrations of the reports utilized at the front office to help students learn about the kinds of management activities that occurred there. Today, however, the operation of the front office in all but the very smallest of hotels is highly (nearly 100 percent) automated. Traditional paper forms, charts, and graphs that were completed and analyzed by hospitality students in the past have been replaced with databases so advanced that front office managers (FOMs) now do different things (not just do things differently) when they actually manage their front office.

It is not just the Internet that has changed how hotels operate; rather, it is how hotels use their property management system (PMS) to interface with the Internet, as well as the myriad of other external and internal revenue-generating sources and the numerous data collection points that must be managed.

The ability of hospitality management graduates to effectively understand and use computerized front office systems is now assumed, yet in many cases, hospitality students have not been well-prepared for assuming front office management responsibilities. This is because those who have not held a job at a hotel's front desk would not have any hands-on experience operating these advanced technology systems.

To complicate matters further, it is a simple fact that, when they graduate, hospitality students find that each major hotel company has specially designed and continually updated software to operate its own increasingly complex PMS. As a result, it is not really possible for any instructor in a hospitality management program to easily teach students how to use all of the literally dozens of such property management systems currently on the market and in use.

Even if an instructor had access to all the software packages available, the full complexity of their operation is not mastered in one or two college class periods. Most FOMs who hire inexperienced staff allow those new front office employees at least two or more 40-hour weeks to familiarize themselves, even at a basic level, with the specific PMS used at their hotels. Clearly, it is not possible for hospitality instructors to teach their students how to operate each of the many property management systems in use today, yet the principles of *how* they operate can be taught.

Faced with all of these challenges in the past, many instructors were utilizing a "paper and pencil" approach to teaching front office systems. Today, those paper-based systems are clearly obsolete; however, prior to the 2011 release of Pearson Higher Education Front Office Management Simulation (FOMS), no cost-effective computer-based tool had been developed to assist instructors in helping their students learn and practice the important tasks that are undertaken at a modern hotel's Front Desk.

FOMS (Second Edition) is the first Web-based tool designed to address the front office training challenges faced by hospitality instructors and students, and it represents a huge step forward in front office training. This exciting simulation product, classroom-tested by thousands of hospitality students worldwide, has proven to be extremely effective at solving the hospitality instructor's (and their students') front office management and PMS training dilemma.

THE FRONT OFFICE MANAGEMENT SIMULATION (FOMS)

Those hospitality instructors who have chosen to integrate the FOMS program into their lodging-related courses will find the information in this chapter helpful both to themselves and to their students. This is so because the chapter includes important:

- Information for the Instructor
- Information for the Student

Information for the Instructor

It is important to recognize that individual lessons in the FOMS program have been designed to work well whether they are assigned throughout the semester or near the semester's end. In either case, it is important to know that the FOMS Instructor's Resources (available online) includes:

- An overview of each simulation lesson
- A description of the importance of the lesson topic
- Extensive teaching notes for each of the lessons
- Complete "Answer Sheets" for each lesson
- An automated grade book to record student progress as lessons are completed

There are five major topic areas and 12 lessons addressed in FOMS. These are:

Topic Area	Lessons
1. Revenue Management	1–2
2. Reservation Management	3–5
3. Guest Stay Information	6–7
4. Guest Departure and Payment	8–9
5. Accounting and Financial Summaries	10–12

Each lesson has two parts (Main and Advanced), thus creating a total of 24 unique learning activities.

FOMS was developed by a team of experienced hospitality management educators, currently practicing hotel front office professionals, specialists in revenue management, the most advanced of computer graphic design specialists, and the educational experts at Pearson Higher Education.

Each lesson has been extensively field-tested with hospitality students at a variety of educational institutions. The lessons are designed to appeal directly to the desire of today's student to receive immediate feedback and to engage in interactive learning activities.

This self-paced simulation lessons can be completed in a classroom computer laboratory or by individual students using their own computers. Instructors may, of course, make use of all the lessons in FOMS or any desired number of individual lessons.

Information for the Student

FOMS was designed to be challenging and fun to use. It is an exciting way to practice the skills and teach the management concepts used in an operating hotel's front office.

The activities in FOMS take place in the hypothetical Hutchinson Hotel and Ocean Suites, a full-service hotel property where you have just been hired as part of the front office management team. As a new employee, there is much for you to learn! To begin, you will log in to FOMS' Web site using the following information:

- Go to http://frontoffice.pearsoncmg.com/index.php
- User name—(enter your user name)
- Password—(enter your password)

You will do this on a screen similar to the one shown in Figure 15.1.

After you have successfully logged in, click the FOM Application tab.

To run the FOM application, you may be asked to allow pop-ups. If so, select either:

1. Temporarily Allow Pop-ups or
2. Always Allow Pop-ups from This Site.

The simulation's main menu lists the lessons (Figure 15.2) you can choose to complete.

Individual lesson lengths have been designed to range from 10 to 60 minutes. The time it will actually take you to complete each of the lessons will vary based upon your background and experience.

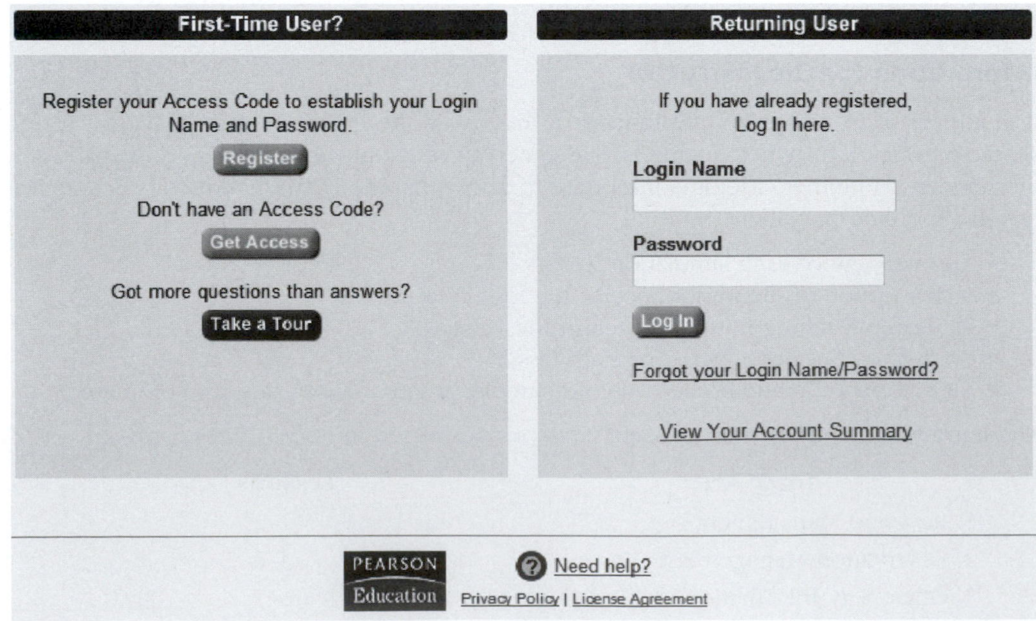

FIGURE 15.1 FOMS User Login Screen

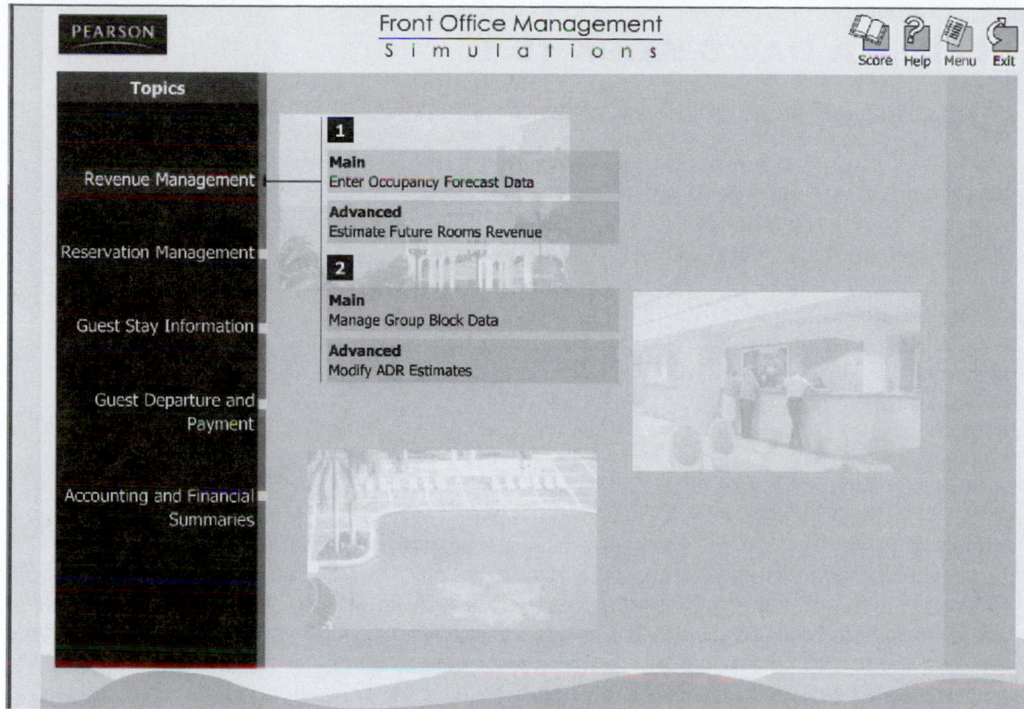

FIGURE 15.2 FOMS Lesson Listing Screen

Using FOMS is easy, especially when you review the "FOM Help" tab (posted online) prior to beginning. You should also know that FOMS will automatically record your lesson progress in a format (an electronic grade book) that can be easily viewed by your instructor.

When you have successfully completed each of the **simulation's** lessons, you will be able to answer an enthusiastic **YES!** to each of the following questions:

- Do you have significant hands-on experience using a PMS to make individual hotel reservations?
- Can you utilize rooms revenue forecast data to determine the best room rate strategy to use on targeted future dates?
- Do you have experience updating guest room status in a PMS?
- Do you know the alternative room assignment strategies to use when arriving guests simply cannot be assigned immediately to their initially requested room types?
- Can you balance a hotel shift report?
- Can you create a housekeeper's work schedule based on known occupancy levels?
- Do you have experience in posting charges to guest folios?
- Do you have experience determining when, and by how much, guest folios should be adjusted in response to guest complaints?
- Can you properly adjust charges on a guest folio when it is necessary to do so?
- Have you worked with, and understand how to balance and reconcile Guest and City ledgers?
- Can you read a real Manager's Daily statistics report?
- Do you understand a "Competitive Set" and how to compare your hotel's performance to it?

LODGING LANGUAGE

Simulation (training): The imitation of a human activity designed to improve a trainees' ability to respond to the real activity. Examples include flight simulators (to train airline pilots), medical emergency response simulators (to train physicians), and FOMS (to train hotel front office managers).

ALL IN A DAY'S WORK 15.1

THE SITUATION

"We didn't cover that in class," said Austin Rodgers, the newly appointed front office supervisor at the Plaza Place hotel. Austin was a recent hospitality management school graduate who was delighted to have landed his first job on the management team at the Plaza Place.

"What do you mean you didn't cover reservations?" said Dale, one of the hotel's most experienced front desk agents and a person who had quickly become one of Austin's best friends at work.

Austin had just taken a phone call at the hotel's front desk. It was from a guest who wanted to make a change in their requested room type for a stay that was to occur six months in the future. Austin had needed to call Dale over to find the reservation in the hotel's database and to make the requested change to it. Dale easily retrieved the reservation and made the change.

"Well, we talked about the information contained in a reservation, of course. And why each piece was important . . . but we didn't actually practice making reservations. We didn't have a way to do that. Besides, there were 75 students in my Hotel Operations class. It would have been really hard for our Professor to grade 75 students on only one reservation let alone if each student attempted to make 5 or 10 each."

"Well, come over here college boy," Dale teased, "let me show you how our PMS is set up and what you need to do to recall a reservation . . . and to make a new one!"

A RESPONSE

Nearly every hospitality management educator would agree that it is good for their students who will work in the food service industry to have received practical training in laboratory classes when studying their field.

As a result, hands-on classes in food chemistry, quantity food production, and quality service management are common within the plans of study for both two- and four-year hospitality management programs. In the past, however, providing hospitality management students hands-on training for many hotel-related skills has been more difficult. The Pearson Higher Education FOMS was designed to directly address this training dilemma and minimize the number of situations such as the one described in this mini-case.

JUST WHAT IS A TRAINING SIMULATION?

LIVE OR VIRTUAL?

Simulations are imitations of reality. To be effective, they often address one part of reality at the expense of other parts. For example, to simulate driving a car, the simulation creator must provide a real steering device (usually a wheel or buttons on a controller) but will not likely provide a duplication of the car's back seat or exhaust system. Those car components, while certainly existing in a "real" car, are simply not required when simulating the driving experience. Good training simulations duplicate what trainees need most while leaving out unneeded information and activities.

Training simulations can be thought of as one of two types: live or virtual.

Live training simulations typically involve humans and activities in a setting designed to duplicate, as realistically as possible, what trainees would do in a specific situation. For an example, think of yourself role-playing in a mock job interview setting, or think *war games* with real-life soldiers or sailors simulating the things they would do in a "real" war. Similarly, think firefighters responding (in real time and with real equipment) to a fire that has been intentionally set for the express purpose of allowing them to practice their response to fires.

Unlike live simulations, virtual simulations involve humans and/or equipment in a setting they can control directly. In these types of simulations, time progresses in steps that are controlled, to some degree, by the simulation's user, allowing him or her to spend the amount of time on an activity that best addresses his or her skill level (think, for example, about the amount of time required by different skilled players to reach advanced levels of a popular video game). A race car or flight simulator falls into this virtual simulation category. So does FOMS. FOMS was designed as a virtual simulation, imitating the kinds of tasks undertaken in a hotel's front office and at its front desk.

A simulator designed may use any combination of sound and sight to make you feel that you are experiencing an actual situation. Some simulations seek to provide an extremely high degree of reality. For example, consider race car arcade games. The booths containing such games typically have a steering wheel, stick shift, gas and brake pedals, and a display monitor. You use these devices to "drive" your "race car" along the track and through changing scenery displayed on the monitor. As you drive, you hear the engine rumble, the brakes squeal, and the metal crunch if you crash. Some booths even use movement to create sensations of acceleration, deceleration, and turning. The sights, sounds, and feel of the game booth combine to create, or simulate, the experience of driving a car in a race. It is easy to see that the cost of producing simulations increases in direct proportion to the amount of "realism" provided in the simulation. Thus, one important task of a simulation producer is the proper balance of "realism" with "cost." When designing training simulations for use by college students, concern for cost is of special importance.

SIMULATION DESIGN

Many people first think of "flight simulators" or "driving simulators" when they hear the term "simulation." But simulation is actually a much broader concept. Because they recreate experiences, simulations hold great potential for training people for almost any situation. Education researchers have, in fact, determined that most people, especially adults, learn better by experience than through reading or lectures. In many cases, simulated experiences can be just as valuable a training tool as the real thing. But building effective simulations is not easy. Creating fun-to-use simulations that *accurately* answer such questions as *"If I do this, what happens then?"* is, however, an expensive, demanding, and time-consuming process.

It is important to understand that simulation designers do not typically produce computer hardware. Instead, those educators designing simulation lessons use sound pedagogy, existing computer technology, and creative software programming to create effective training experiences. While it is not often mentioned, human testing of a simulation is also crucial to the simulation's ultimate effectiveness. The 24 FOMS simulations have been extensively field tested (on more than 4,000 hospitality students) and carefully revised and improved to make it the best, most *realistic* and, just as importantly, fun-to-use front office management simulation product available.

If you understand the career placement advantages you will enjoy after you have successfully completed FOMS, then you are ready to begin learning more about it.

REVENUE MANAGEMENT LESSONS

In Chapter 6, you learned that an effective PMS includes revenue management (RM)-related components. These RM-related programs help the hotel forecast room demand and establish appropriate rooms pricing. Some property management systems have very sophisticated and detailed RM features while other systems take a less complex approach.

FOMS lessons 1 and 2 were designed to familiarize you with some of the most important RM-related procedures undertaken at a well-managed hotel's front office.

Four simulations have been designed to directly address RM-related issues. These are:

- Lesson 1: Main: Enter Occupancy Forecast Data
- Lesson 1: Advanced: Estimate Future Rooms Revenue
- Lesson 2: Main: Manage Group Block Data
- Lesson 2: Advanced: Modify ADR Estimates

Lesson 1: Main: Enter Occupancy Forecast Data

In this lesson, you will learn how to read and modify a hotel's rooms demand **forecast**. This is the forecast that tells hotel FOMs how many guests will be staying at their hotels on specific dates in the future.

LODGING LANGUAGE

Forecast (rooms): An estimate of the number and type of rooms to be sold on specific future dates. Also referred to as a "demand" forecast or "occupancy" forecast.

Guest demand for hotel rooms often affects the rate hoteliers charge for their rooms during a specific period of time or season.

Managing a rooms forecast, however, involves more than merely estimating the number of rooms that will be sold. Hoteliers use forecasts to:

1. Generate an estimate of room demand
2. Establish initial selling prices
3. Monitor events likely to affect room sales
4. Modify (increase or decrease) room rates if appropriate

Initially developing and then managing a hotel's room rate strategy is a critical part of any hotel's revenue management efforts. Because that is so, this simulation has been designed to help you better understand room demand forecasts and how they are developed. It also will help you see directly the relationship between increases and decreases in room demand and changes in forecasted revenues.

When you successfully complete this lesson, you will have correctly entered into a 14-day rooms forecast, all of the information from six occupancy forecast altering events.

Lesson 1: Advanced: Estimate Future Rooms Revenue

In this lesson, you will learn how to interpret data found on a 14-day rooms forecast and then, based upon pre-established room rate strategies, apply a strategy to create a **revenue forecast** for the dates included in the rooms forecast.

LODGING LANGUAGE

Forecast (revenue): An estimate of the rooms revenue to be achieved on specific future dates.

Occupancy forecasts estimate the number of rooms to be sold on future date(s) while revenue forecasts estimate the amount of income a hotel will generate on those dates. In this lesson, you will see clearly how increased levels of forecasted room demand typically result in the implementation of revenue management strategies designed to increase the estimate of ADR levels at which remaining rooms will be sold. This is important because, in most cases, increased room demand levels will result in higher rates at which guest rooms are to be sold, and thus higher ADRs estimates for days with higher demand for rooms.

While later lessons will delve more deeply into revenue management practices, philosophy, and room rate determination, this lesson shows how room demand affects estimated rates achieved. This simulation lesson was developed to help you recognize that a *decrease* in rooms remaining to be sold will typically result in *increased* room rates charged and thus increased room revenue forecasts (because rooms will likely be sold at higher average rates during periods of higher room demand).

When you have successfully completed this lesson, you will have correctly adjusted the ADR estimates on five different dates in a 14-day forecast.

Lesson 2: Main: Manage Group Block Data

In this lesson, you learn how to modify an occupancy forecast by entering information about group room sales into the forecast. This lesson was designed to reinforce the concept that guest rooms that have been blocked for a group, but not sold, still reduce the number of guest rooms available to sell.

Chapter 7 describes group room sales and the process FOMs use to block rooms for groups. "Group Block" rooms are those which the hotel has held, or removed from general sale, for a group, but which have not yet been reserved by individual guests. There are a number of reasons a hotel would choose to block rooms for a group. In this lesson, you will learn about some of those reasons as well as how group block rooms affect the number of rooms a hotel has available to sell.

While the definition of precisely what constitutes a "group" (vs. transient) room can vary somewhat across different hotels, this lesson carefully identifies group rooms as they are defined by the management of the Hutchinson hotel. When you have successfully completed this lesson, you will have correctly entered all of the information related to five of this hotel's group blocks and will see how the number of group block rooms directly affects Total Available (rooms for sale), as well as other important hotel operating statistics.

Lesson 2: Advanced: Modify ADR Estimates

In this lesson, you will learn how to develop an accurate rooms revenue forecast after you have modified ADR estimates based upon total room demand.

In a previous lesson (Lesson 1 Main), you learned how to modify a rooms revenue forecast based upon events that affected the number of guest rooms sold on specific days. In this lesson, you will see how group block rooms held (but not sold) can also affect the FOM's decision-making.

The principles of revenue management indicate that, as demand for guest rooms increases, hoteliers typically are able to increase their room rates and thus increase their total room revenue. In this lesson, you will identify the number of "Total Available" (to be sold) rooms for five specific dates in the future and then use a pre-determined ADR estimate (based on rooms demand levels) to modify the revenue estimated to be achieved on those dates.

To complete this lesson, you will, on the 10 dates for which an estimate is requested, correctly enter the data called for by the ADR strategy. The result will be the creation of an accurate and up-to-date rooms revenue forecast.

LODGING ONLINE

The importance of effective revenue management systems is increasingly recognized. To see one such company's innovative approach to revenue management, go to:

www.buckhiester.com

When you arrive at the site, click on "Myths vs. Reality" to learn more about the complex but fascinating topic of revenue management in the lodging industry.

RESERVATION MANAGEMENT LESSONS

One of the most important features of a hotel's PMS is its ability to maintain accurate information about guests. This includes information about guests who will be coming to the hotel, those who are in the hotel, and those who have stayed at the hotel in the past.

Gathering information about guests who will be coming to the hotel in the future is a major function of the reservations module contained in a PMS system and that function is the focus of this lesson group. The reservation management-related lessons in FOMS are important because they demonstrate:

- The importance of accuracy when creating a guest's reservation
- The importance of accuracy when modifying an existing reservation
- How group reservations are made
- How and why group reservations are modified
- How the number of reservations made affects revenue management decisions
- How the number of reservations made affects prices charged for rooms in the future

Six simulations in FOMS were designed to address important reservations-related skills that must be learned and concepts that must be understood. These are:

- Lesson 3: Main: Make Individual Room Reservations
- Lesson 3: Advanced: Modify Individual Room Reservations
- Lesson 4: Main: Make Group "Master" Reservations
- Lesson 4: Advanced: Modify Group "Master" Reservations
- Lesson 5: Main: Learn Revenue Management Principles
- Lesson 5: Advanced: Determine Room Rates to Be Charged

Lesson 3: Main: Make Individual Room Reservations

In this lesson, you will learn and extensively practice the procedures front office agents use when making guest room reservations. The guest room reservation process is an important skill that every hotelier assigned to a hotel's front office simply must master.

In some cases, reservations are made by telephone, and the hotel's reservation representative has the opportunity to carefully ask the guest to provide the information necessary to complete a reservation. In other situations, guest-related information is submitted via letter, fax, text message, tweet, or e-mail.

When front office agents are able to enter guest data in a PMS quickly, they will have more time available for quality guest interaction.

In this simulation, you will make ten reservations in the PMS simulator based upon guest information supplied from the simulator's Lesson 3 data bank. Each reservation has been carefully designed to ensure that when you have successfully completed the lesson, you will recognize the critical nature of the following reservation-related skills:

- Properly spelling complex names
- Recording of Travel Agent (TA) information
- Placement of reservations in a group block
- Making "notes" entries for special guest requests
- Guaranteeing rooms to direct bill accounts
- Assigning the proper room rate based upon specific guest characteristics such as company affiliation
- Recognition of the special importance of carefully recording arrival and departure dates of international guests

When you have successfully completed this lesson, you will have correctly entered into the PMS simulator all of the information from ten reservation requests sent to your hotel, thus creating ten individual guest reservations. In this lesson, accuracy in data entry is critical!

Lesson 3: Advanced: Modify Individual Room Reservations

Because their travel plans can change, guests who have made their lodging reservations previously may sometimes find that they need to modify them. In this lesson, you will learn and practice the proper procedures for retrieving an existing reservation from the PMS and then modifying or canceling that reservation.

In some cases, reservation modifications or cancellations are made by telephone, and the hotel's reservation representative has the opportunity to carefully ask the guest to provide the information necessary to change, complete, or even cancel that reservation. In other situations, revised guest information may be submitted electronically.

In this simulation, you will be assigned the task of revising or canceling five reservations in the PMS simulator based upon information supplied to you. In addition to learning the process by which a PMS actually changes a reservation, in this lesson you will learn:

- How to change a guest's arrival date
- How to change a guest's requested room type
- How to change the form of payment on a reservation
- How to extend the length of a reservation
- How to cancel a reservation

To begin the lesson, you will access reservations previously made (from Lesson 3 Main). You will have successfully completed this lesson when you have correctly entered all of the information from the five reservation modification or cancellation requests sent to your hotel.

Lesson 4: Main: Make Group "Master" Reservations

Group room reservations are maintained differently in a hotel's PMS than are individual room reservations. First, a "master" reservation must be established that identifies the group, the date(s) they are staying, the rate(s) group members will pay, and the cut-off dates associated with the group master, as well as any other reservation-related information unique to the group. In this lesson, you will learn and practice making a **group master** reservation in a PMS.

LODGING LANGUAGE

Group Master (reservation): The reservation information related to creating a group block, including information such as rates to be paid, cut-off dates, and the group's contact person as well as other information specific to that group.

In Lesson 2 Main of FOMS, you learned that a *group block* reservation is defined as one in which a hotel's guest rooms are reserved as a *group* or *block*. In most PMSs, blocked rooms are not considered sold until they are individually reserved by guests or rooming lists are sent in by the group's point of contact. Ultimately, blocked rooms are picked up or assigned to individual guests through the standard reservation process you learned in FOMS Lesson 3 Main.

In this lesson, you will learn how to initially establish a group's "master" reservation, from which the group's individual reservations will, in the future, be made. In this lesson, you create group master reservations, thus creating group room blocks.

The reasons hotels choose to block group rooms for groups vary, and several of those are illustrated in this lesson. As you complete the lesson, you will come to recognize key components of a group master reservation. These include:

- The group's name
- The group's contact person(s)
- The group's contact information (i.e., address, telephone number, fax number, e-mail address)
- The group's arrival date
- The group's departure date
- The date the group's blocked rooms will be released for public sale if not picked up
- The payment method to be utilized
- The reservation method
- The room types requested
- The room rates to be charged
- The group's assigned account number

In this simulation, you will be assigned the task of making five group master reservations. You will have successfully completed this lesson when you have correctly entered all of the information for the five requested group reservations.

Lesson 4: Advanced: Modify Group "Master" Reservations

Just as circumstances can change for individual travelers and, as a result, changes must be made to their individual reservations, group reservations are also subject to change. In this lesson, you will learn and practice the proper procedures for retrieving from the PMS, and then modifying, group block "master" reservations.

In this simulation, you will be assigned the task of modifying five group master reservations in the PMS simulator based upon information supplied to you from a variety of sources. In addition to learning the process by which a PMS actually records changes in a group master reservation, it is important to realize that each group master modification presented in this lesson has been carefully designed to ensure that, when the lesson is complete, you will have learned how to:

- Change the contact person associated with a group block master
- Change the room types requested in a group block
- Change the group rate to match any new room types requested
- Change the room release (cut-off) date associated with a group block master reservation
- Increase the number of days and the number of rooms requested in a group block
- Reduce the number of rooms requested in a group block

You will have successfully completed this lesson when you have correctly modified five of the hotel's existing group master reservations.

Lesson 5: Main: Learn Revenue Management Principles

The number of reservations made, and group blocks created, directly impacts the revenue management decisions made by hoteliers. In Lesson 2 Advanced, you learned that increased

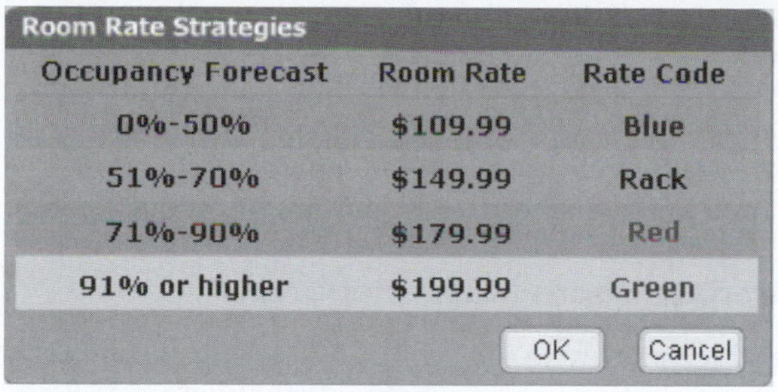

Occupancy Forecast	Room Rate	Rate Code
0%-50%	$109.99	Blue
51%-70%	$149.99	Rack
71%-90%	$179.99	Red
91% or higher	$199.99	Green

FIGURE 15.3 Color-Coded Room Rate Strategy

demand for rooms typically results in increases in the size of room revenue forecasts. In this lesson, you will learn about some of the important principles of revenue management utilized by hoteliers when determining the rates they will actually charge for their rooms.

Hoteliers seeking to optimize room revenue utilize information from a variety of sources before they determine the room rates they will charge. In this lesson, you will learn how and why hoteliers use demand for rooms (measured by the number of reservations made for a future date) to determine their room rates for any rooms remaining unsold. You will learn about these by first reading, and then answering five questions about, each of the following topics:

- Room rate economics
- Revenue (yield) management
- Variable rate strategies

You will have successfully completed this lesson when you have correctly answered the questions posed to you in each of the three topic area quizzes that address the issues presented in the lesson.

Lesson 5: Advanced: Determine Room Rates to Be Charged

In this simulation, you will apply what you learned in Lesson 5 Main to modify room rates your hotel will charge on future selected dates, based upon the room demand levels forecasted for those dates. This simulation was designed to teach you the important relationship between accurate room demand forecasts and the optimization of room rates.

Hoteliers who seek to optimize room revenue must ensure that the rooms they are selling are sold at rates consistent with the room rate strategies developed by their property's revenue managers. These, of course, will vary based upon the revenue goals of each individual hotel's revenue management team.

In this lesson, you will receive information from the hotel's GM about ten future dates in which the GM wishes to adjust the room rates charged based upon room demand forecasted on those dates. To complete the lesson, you will utilize the color-coded room rate strategy shown in Figure 15.3.

You will have successfully completed this lesson when you have utilized the color-coded *Room Rate Strategies* to correctly modify the room rates to be charged on those dates identified by the hotel's GM.

GUEST STAY INFORMATION LESSONS

One of the most important functions of a hotel's front office is that of maintaining accurate information about the condition, or status, of the hotel's individual guest rooms and the guests who occupy them. In this series of simulations, you will learn how FOMs use the PMS to create updated room status reports (described in Chapter 8) and how to ensure that enough room attendants have been scheduled to properly clean all of the guest rooms that need cleaning. Additional simulations in this section address what front desk agents do when guests arrive at the hotel for check-in and what to do when the room type requested by guests is not available for them at the time of arrival.

Four simulation exercises have been developed for this section. These are:

- Lesson 6: Main: Update Room Status Reports
- Lesson 6: Advanced: Schedule Room Attendants
- Lesson 7: Main: Assign Guests to Specific Rooms
- Lesson 7: Advanced: Make Alternate Room Assignments

Lesson 6: Main: Update Room Status Reports

In this lesson, you will learn how to read a housekeeping report and use the information in it to update guest room status within your hotel's PMS. One of the most important tasks accomplished by a modern PMS system is accurately maintaining the status of a hotel's guest rooms. This is critical because newly arriving hotel guests should never be assigned to rooms that have not been properly cleaned or that have already been assigned to, or are occupied by, other guests.

Information in the PMS must be manually updated when guest rooms have been cleaned. The methods used in hotels to communicate this information from the housekeeping department to those staff working at the front desk can vary. In some cases, the information is relayed to the front desk in person while in other cases the information is updated electronically by a member of the housekeeping staff. In all cases, however, accurate information about a room's status must be continually communicated to those responsible for updating the PMS.

In this lesson, you will read a Housekeeper's report about the updated room status of 20 selected guest rooms and use that information to accurately input the correct status of the 20 guest rooms in the PMS. You will have successfully completed this lesson when you have correctly updated the room status of all 20 rooms.

Lesson 6: Advanced: Schedule Room Attendants

Employee scheduling is one feature built into many of the PMSs in use today. In this lesson, you will learn how that feature can be used effectively. To do that, you will review a selected day's rooms sales forecast and, based upon pre-established standards for the amount of time required to clean various types of rooms, create a work schedule detailing the number of room attendant hours that will be needed to fully staff that date.

To complete this lesson, you will calculate the number of rooms that require cleaning in each of five different categories corresponding to this hotel's five different room types. The standard time required to clean each of the differently configured rooms varies (e.g., the time to clean a standard room vs. the time required to clean a suite), so timing must be considered as the work schedule is developed.

You will have successfully completed this lesson when you have correctly tabulated the number of room attendant hours that will be required to clean all the rooms forecasted to need cleaning on the date identified in the lesson.

Lesson 7: Main: Assign Guests to Specific Rooms

In this lesson, you will learn how to assign arriving guests to their requested room types. Recall that, where they have a choice, guests request a specific room type (e.g., King or Double, Smoking or Non-smoking) when making their reservations. Upon arrival, guests should be assigned to a clean and vacant room of the type requested on their original reservation (see FOMS Lesson 3 Main: Make Individual Room Reservations).

It is important to understand that hotels can choose different methods of assigning guests to specific guest rooms. For example, guests could be assigned a specific room at the time their reservations are made. This is an effective method for groups that submit rooming lists because all of the reservations are made at one time and groups may want to have their rooms located near each other. Alternatively, a hotel may determine that it is best to assign guests to their requested rooms on the *day* of their arrival, but prior to their actual *time* of their arrival.

In this simulation, you will assign guests to their rooms at the time of the guest's arrival. To do so, the PMS must be used to identify exactly which room the arriving guest will

LODGING GOES GREEN!

Conservation efforts in the lodging industry can range from the very visible and operationally significant (such as changing guestroom bedding only upon guest request) to the nearly invisible (such as utilizing training programs delivered and maintained via computer rather than by paper and pencil).

FOMS was designed to be a paperless training program. The advantages of going "paperless" when developing training programs are many. They include the elimination of filing cabinets for the storage of educational materials and trainee results, reduced supplies expense, faster access to files and information, elimination of lost files, elimination of lost documents from within an employee's personal file, and reclaimed office space, to name only a few such advantages.

Like many Green efforts, however, there are challenges with converting to paperless training. In the first days (1–30 days) of a conversion to paperless training, there is little or no information in the system, so there is a great deal of activity in file setup, with few readily apparent benefits. In days 31–60, familiarity grows, routines are established, and early benefits are now realized. In the third and fourth months and beyond, the needed information is in the system, database searches yield results, training records are well organized, targeted training dates permit training prioritization, and the advantages of the paperless process become more evident.

Understanding that it may take a few months for the benefits of programs (such as FOMS) to become fully apparent is important. While it may take some time for that message to be heard by training-oriented hoteliers, it is clear that, *over time,* the advantages of paperless training are unparalleled.

occupy. This lesson contains scenarios consisting of conversations between hotel staff and five different arriving guests.

You will have successfully completed this lesson when each of the five arriving guests has been assigned to a "Ready-to-sell" room of the specific room type requested by the guest when his or her reservation was originally made.

Lesson 7: Advanced: Make Alternate Room Assignments

In Lesson 7 Main, you learned how to use the PMS to assign guests (upon their arrival at the hotel) to the room type requested on their advanced reservation. In this lesson, you will practice the techniques front office agents use to assign arriving guests to "Ready and Vacant" rooms when the room type originally requested on the guest's reservation is *not* available at the time of the guest's arrival.

In this simulation, you will be presented with five different guest interaction scenarios. In each case, the arriving guests cannot be assigned to their originally requested room type because a "Ready and Vacant" room of that type is not available at the time of arrival. You will choose from three alterative courses of action that could be taken to satisfy these arriving guests.

You will have successfully completed this lesson when you have selected an appropriate course of action for each of the five guest's interaction scenarios presented in the simulation.

GUEST DEPARTURE AND PAYMENT

Keeping track of the amount of money guests owe the hotel is a critical PMS function. Front office agents, as well as hotel night auditors, must know how to post, or record, charges to a guest's folio. In addition, they must know how to accept guest payments and record the payments in the PMS when guests depart.

In this series of lesson, you will learn how to post charges, modify charges, and record guest payments. In addition, you will choose the front office agent's appropriate response to guests who question or protest one or more of the charges on their folios.

Guest departure is a good time to ensure all charges are posted and paid for correctly as well as seek future reservations from departing guests.

Four simulation exercises have been developed for this section. These are:

- Lesson 8: Main: Post Folio Charges
- Lesson 8: Advanced: Adjust Folio Charges
- Lesson 9: Main: Split Charges and Close Folios
- Lesson 9: Advanced: Manage Payment Disputes

Lesson 8: Main: Post Folio Charges

In this lesson, you will learn how a front office staff keeps in-house guests' financial records up-to-date by posting (recording) transactions on the guests' folios. Proper record-keeping is very important for any hotel because a guest can elect to check out at any moment. When they do, their folios must be up-to-date.

In this lesson, you will learn the steps involved in recording guest charges. These include identifying the guest who is to be charged, selecting the type of charge to be made, and identifying the amount of the charge. While many folio charges are posted by a hotel's night auditor, there are various reasons office agents must know how to manually post charges to guest folios. These can include:

- Miscellaneous charges for guests who, upon check-out, state they wish to purchase a bathrobe, pillow, or other room amenity
- Movie or other charges that are not interfaced and thus must be manually posted
- Restaurant charges that have not posted automatically
- Copy charges for guests attending a meeting
- Partial room charges for guests who have stayed in their rooms later than the hotel's normally allowed check-out time.

You will have successfully completed this lesson when you have correctly posted the charges to five different guest folios.

Lesson 8: Advanced: Adjust Folio Charges

In the previous lesson, you learned how to manually post charges to guests' folios. In this lesson, you will learn how to manually adjust (deduct) charges from guests' folios. Learning how to adjust charges from a guest's folio is just as important as learning how to post charges to folios. This is so because there are a variety of reasons why it may be necessary to adjust charges from a guests' folio. These include events such as the previous posting of an incorrect room rate, resolving guest satisfaction issues, and other circumstances that legitimately warrant a reduction in a guest's charges.

In this lesson, you will learn how to use the PMS to identify the guest whose folio is to be adjusted, retrieve the guest's folio by referring to a list of *In-House* guests, and then select the appropriate guest folio. After selecting the proper folio, you will enter the correct amount of the adjustment. In this lesson, you will also come to understand that changes to room rate and other charges will result in changes to any state sales tax or city assessment taxes associated with the rate. While the amount of taxes charged to guests varies by locale, it does not alter the fact that changes in room charges will result in changes to the amount of tax that should be collected.

You will have successfully completed this lesson when each of five guests' folios has had their balances due adjusted properly.

Lesson 9: Main: Split Charges and Close Folios

Anyone who has ever been employed as a wait person or even who has dined out with friends is familiar with the challenges that occur when one bill must be split among several guests. The same challenges exist in the lodging industry. In many cases, guests sharing rooms will want to pay their own fair share of the room's charges at the time of departure. In other cases, guests may be allowed to charge some items (such as the cost of their rooms) to one payment source while other charges (e.g., alcoholic beverages or movie charges) must be paid for separately and from a different payment source.

In this lesson, you will learn how to close, or accept full payment for, guest folios and split guest charges among various hotel accounts when checking guests out of the hotel. In this simulation, you will be presented with five different scenarios designed to teach you how to split charges and **close**, or bring to a zero balance, a guest's folio.

LODGING LANGUAGE

Close (folio): To bring to zero the balance due on a hotel guest's folio.

A closed folio is created when a registered guest does not owe money to hotel and the hotel does not owe money to the guest. Thus, a folio will have a zero balance when it is properly closed. To change a folio from one with an amount due to the hotel or guest to one with a zero balance, a payment or an adjustment must be recorded in the PMS.

Some guests may elect to utilize two, three, or even more different payment methods when closing their accounts. These payment methods may include direct billing to pre-established accounts and the use of debit cards, cash, checks, or credit cards.

In this lesson, you will learn how to identify those guests who want to close their folios, retrieve the guest's folio by referring to a list of *In-House* guests, locate and select the correct transaction code to be used to close the folio, and finally you will enter the amount required to properly close the guest's folio.

In this simulation, when a posting is made to a *Room Charge,* the State Taxes (8 percent) and the City Assessments (5 percent) are automatically posted. It is also true that, in PMSs, when an adjustment is made to a *Room Charge,* the State Taxes (8 percent) and the City Assessments (5 percent) are automatically adjusted or removed from the bill. This is consistent with the manner in which a modern PMS is programmed.

You will have successfully completed this lesson when each of five guests is properly charged and their folios have been closed.

Lesson 9: Advanced: Manage Payment Disputes

In this lesson, you will learn about the techniques used, and actions front office agents should take, when they encounter guests who dispute all or parts of the charges that appear on their folios. In this simulation, you will be presented with five guests who question the accuracy of their folio charges. In each case, you will choose your response to

ALL IN A DAY'S WORK 15.2

THE SITUATION

"When will the new system be rolled out?" asked Dipan Patel, owner of the Best Sleep hotel.

"Our target date to cut over to the new PMS is October 1," replied Jim Pratt, Regional Franchise Services Director for Select Hotels International, the franchisor of the Sleep Well brand.

"That's less than four weeks from now," replied Dipan, "I want to make sure our desk agents are ready to make the switch. I know Select has the IT people needed to make the conversion, but what is the company's plan for providing us with the training materials we will need to make sure our desk agents are ready for the change over?"

"We've thought of that," replied Jim, "a simulated version of the new system, with an active training module, will be on-line next week. Your people can practice and learn on it prior to the cut-over. Are you familiar with that kind of training system?"

A RESPONSE

Operating hotels face many of the same challenges as hospitality instructors do. Because staff at a hotel's front desk can turn over rapidly, there is a need for continual PMS training, yet the disadvantages of using "real customers' to train inexperienced workers are real.

Few potential guests, for example, will exhibit the patience required to wait as desk agents learn how to make their very first few reservations, nor will guests easily tolerate mistakes new front office agents will inevitably make as those agents learn how to post and adjust charges to guests' folios.

For most franchisors and makers of property management systems, the solution to this training dilemma is the creation of a simulated PMS environment. Typically titled the "Training" or "Practice" mode, this simulation of their proprietary PMS is designed in a manner very similar to that of FOMS. If Dipan had encountered and used Pearson's FOMS in his own hospitality management studies, his answer to Jim would be an enthusiastic "Yes! . . . Yes I am!"

the guest from three presented alternatives. After you have selected a response, the simulation will identify your answer as either "Best," "Acceptable," or "Poor."

As you proceed through this lesson, you should pay close attention to:

- The actual cause of the guest's payment dispute
- The alternative solutions available to you
- The fairness, to the guest, of each proposed solution
- The fairness, to the hotel, of each proposed solution
- The cost, to the hotel, of each proposed solution
- The long-term impact the solution will have on the guest's feelings toward the hotel

You will have successfully completed this lesson when acceptable solutions to each of the five guest's folio issues in the lesson have been chosen.

ACCOUNTING AND FINANCIAL SUMMARIES

Many of a hotel's important financial records are maintained in their PMS. These records must be carefully and accurately maintained because the information contained in them will be used in preparation of the hotel's major financial summaries, including its Statement of Income and Expense (P&L), Statement of Cash Flows, and Balance Sheet.

Because a hotel's FOM is responsible for maintaining accurate financial records, their front office agents must understand how to use the financial information-related portions of the PMS. In most hotels, this also includes the production of a daily summary of financial results (the **Manager's Daily**) prepared for the property's upper-level managers.

In this section of FOMS, you will learn how financial records are maintained in a PMS as well as how a Manager's Daily is prepared.

LODGING LANGUAGE

Manager's Daily: A summary of a hotel's daily revenue generation that can include additional operating data as requested by the property's general manager.

The final exercise in FOMS relates to the question of a hotel's operating effectiveness. To understand the purpose of the final lesson, it is important to know that hotel managers are keenly interested in the performance of their hotel relative to their direct competitors. In Chapter 7, you learned that hotels identify a group of hotels (their competitive set) against which they measure their own performance. In this last lesson, you will learn how hoteliers interpret the results of a competitive set analysis.

To achieve all of its goals, six simulation exercises have been developed for this final FOMS section. These are:

- Lesson 10: Main: Balance and Close Out a Shift
- Lesson 10: Advanced: Balance a Full Day's Shift Reports
- Lesson 11: Main: Reconcile a Guest Ledger
- Lesson 11: Advanced: Reconcile a City Ledger
- Lesson 12: Main: Complete a Manager's Daily
- Lesson 12: Advanced: Assess Competitive Set Data

Lesson 10: Main: Balance and Close Out a Shift

In previous FOMS lessons, you learned how to record guest payments and adjustments, split guest charges, and close guest folios. In this lesson, you will learn how to sum each of these transaction types to balance and close a single work shift, thus generating an accurate shift report. A **shift report** is simply an accurate summarization of every folio transaction completed during a pre-determined time period.

LODGING LANGUAGE

Shift report (front desk): A summary of all folio and other financial transactions completed at a hotel's front office during a pre-determined time period (typically eight hours).

In most hotels, work shifts consist of the following hours:

1st Shift	7:00 a.m. to 3:00 p.m.
2nd Shift	3:00 p.m. to 11:00 p.m.
3rd Shift	11:00 p.m. to 7:00 a.m.

In most modern PMSs, the process of summarizing each folio transaction is automatic. A manual *double check* is most often performed, however, to ensure that every transaction recorded on guest folios has been performed properly. Examples of transactions are payments of a variety of types, including cash, check, debit card, and credit card.

Folio adjustments prior to guest payment and departure can include those types of events presented in Lesson 9 Advanced: Guest Payment Disputes. Other transaction groups include room charges, charges for telephone calls, and other purchases you learned about in Lesson 8 Main; Post Folio Charges.

In this lesson, you will learn to balance a single shift and create an accurate shift report for it. A shift is considered In-Balance when the guest payments recorded during the shift equal the amount of money (including checks, credit and debit cards, and other payment forms) actually collected by the hotel's front desk.

If the payments recorded do not equal the amount of money collected, the shift is considered to be Out-of-Balance and must be corrected. This is not uncommon. An Out-of-Balance shift is corrected by manually checking each transaction within the specific transaction group (e.g. all Visa charges, all cash charges, or all room adjustments) to locate the error. One goal of this lesson is to teach you how to make the proper adjustments to an Out-of-Balance shift report. You will have successfully completed this lesson when you have created an accurate and In-Balance shift report.

Lesson 10: Advanced: Balance a Full Day's Shift Reports

In the previous lesson, you learned to balance and close a single shift. In this lesson, you will learn how front office agents balance and summarize a full day's financial transactions, thus generating a Full Day's Shift Report.

The number of daily financial transactions that take place at a hotel's front desk is considerable. A summary of all these transactions is, in most cases, performed during the Night Audit (see Chapter 6). The Night Audit is the summarization of a single day's financial information, including daily sales postings and payment transactions. As its name suggests, the Night Audit usually takes place during the late night or early morning hours when the hotel employee performing the night audit will have the least number of interruptions.

Along with summarizing the day's statistical and financial information, the Night Auditor's responsibilities typically include preparing other useful information such as arrival lists, departure lists, forecasted sales levels, and housekeeping reports that will be utilized in the coming day. This lesson addresses the portion of the Night Audit that relates to the summarization of shift reports. You have successfully completed this lesson when the shift reports included in it are combined and are In-Balance.

Lesson 11: Main: Reconcile a Guest Ledger

In this lesson, you will learn how a hotel's **Guest Ledger** accurately maintains the purchases and payment transactions of its registered guests.

LODGING LANGUAGE

Guest Ledger: The set of accounts used to record charges to, and payments from, a hotel's registered guests. Also called a "Front office ledger" or "Rooms ledger."

The Guest Ledger is prepared using the following accounting formula:

Sales = (Guest Payments + Guest Accounts Receivable) − Advanced Deposits

In previous lessons, you learned that individual guest charges and payments are maintained on guest folios. The guest ledger is simply the sum of all guest folios.

In this lesson, you will enter information about guest-initiated purchases and payments directly into the appropriate section of the guest ledger formula and see the affects of these entries. The entries presented represent 10 different, but very common, guest charge and payment scenarios. You will have successfully completed this lesson when you have correctly entered the information described in all 10 of the guest ledger-related financial transactions.

Lesson 11: Advanced: Reconcile a City Ledger

In this lesson, you will learn how a hotel's **City Ledger** accurately maintains records of its non-registered guests' purchases and payment transactions.

LODGING LANGUAGE

City Ledger: The set of accounts used to record charges to and payments from a hotel's nonregistered guests (e.g., food or beverage purchases made by a person who is not a registered guest of the hotel).

The City Ledger is the name of the system hotel accountants use for recording the purchases and payments made by non-registered guests. The City Ledger is prepared using the following accounting formula:

Sales = (Guest Payments + Guest Accounts Receivable) − Advanced Deposits

There are many reasons why individuals who are not staying in a hotel make purchases. Examples include local residents who eat in the hotel's restaurant or drink in its lounge, as well as those who schedule conferences or banquets that utilize the hotel's meeting space.

In this lesson, you will make accounting entries needed to update the hotel's city ledger.

The entries relate to five very common, non-registered guest charge and payment scenarios. You will have successfully completed this lesson when you have correctly entered, in the proper portion of the city ledger, the financial information related to all five of the events described in these scenarios.

Lesson 12: Main: Complete a Manager's Daily

In this lesson, you will show that you can apply what you have learned about hotel operations by inserting missing data into a *Manager's Daily* report. In this lesson, you will be presented with an incomplete Manager's Daily report. Applying what you have learned in this book about hotel operations will allow you to fill in correctly the missing parts of the Manager's Daily.

This lesson also reinforces the importance of the information contained in management reports produced by a hotel's front office because this report is representative of the type of reports commonly generated by a hotel's PMS. You will have successfully completed this lesson when you have correctly entered, into the Manager's Daily, five pieces of missing data.

Lesson 12: Advanced: Assess Competitive Set Data

In this final FOMS lesson, you will learn about, and demonstrate your understanding of, the following concepts:

- Competitive Sets
- ADR Index
- Occupancy Index
- RevPAR Index

This lesson is among the most challenging lessons in FOMS. In it you will be presented with information about *Competitive Sets*, the term hoteliers use to describe those hotels with which their own hotels directly compete.

Competitive Sets, or "Comp sets" as they are frequently called, are important because they allow hoteliers to benchmark their own performance against that of other properties. These comparisons are calculated and compared in the form of a performance index.

In this lesson, you will learn how to calculate and assess three types of performance indexes. These are:

ADR Index

Occupancy Index

RevPAR Index

Indexes such as these are important to know about because they compare operating performance information taken from one hotel with similar information taken from competing hotels.

In this lesson, you will learn about these three key indexes by reading relevant information presented about each one. You will finish this lesson (and the entire FOMS program) by providing the correct answers to three five-item quizzes that directly address these three importance indexes.

FOMS COMPLETION

When you have successfully completed the Pearson Higher Education FOMS, you will have demonstrated that you understand a great deal about the management of a modern hotel's front office.

You have demonstrated ability in:	By Completing FOMS Lesson(s):
1. Assessing occupancy trends from PMS data	Lesson 1: Main: Enter Occupancy Forecast Data Lesson 1: Advanced: Estimate Future Rooms Revenue Lesson 2: Main: Manage Group Block Data Lesson 2: Advanced: Modify ADR Estimates
2. Making guest room reservations	Lesson 3: Main: Make Individual Room Reservations
3. Changing and canceling guest room reservations	Lesson 3: Advanced: Modify Individual Room Reservations
4. Retrieving reservations from arrival lists and making guest room assignments	Lesson 7: Main: Assign Guests to Specific Rooms Lesson 7: Advanced: Make Alternate Room Assignments
5. Making and modifying group reservations from blocks	Lesson 4: Main: Make Group Master Reservations Lesson 4: Advanced: Modify Group Master Reservations
6. Posting charges to guest folios	Lesson 8: Main: Post Folio Charges
7. Resolving guest payment disputes	Lesson 9: Advanced: Manage Guest Payment Disputes
8. Adjusting guest folio charges	Lesson 8: Advanced: Adjust Folio Charges
9. Closing guest folios and payment posting	Lesson 9: Main: Split Charges and Close Folios
10. Completing shift reports	Lesson 10: Main: Balance and Close Out a Shift Lesson 10: Advanced: Balance a Full Day's Shift Reports:
11. Reconciling guest and city ledgers	Lesson 11: Main: Reconcile a Guest Ledger Lesson 11: Advanced: Reconcile a City Ledger
12. Completing a Manager's Daily	Lesson 12: Main: Complete a Manager's Daily
13. Assessing competitive set performance	Lesson 12: Advanced: Assess Competitive Set Data

FIGURE 15.4 Summary of FOMS Completion Abilities

Figure 15.4 lists some of the abilities you now possess due to your completion of FOMS as well as the specific lessons in which you gained that ability. FOMS completion is a significant achievement and is worthy of listing on your resume by including wording similar to the following:

- *Successfully completed the Pearson Higher Education Front Office Management Simulation (FOMS) training program.*

If you have now completed FOMS, congratulations on a job well done!

Lodging Language

Simulation (training)
Forecast (rooms)
Forecast (revenue)
Group Master (reservation)
Close (folio)
Manager's Daily
Shift report (front desk)
Guest Ledger
City Ledger

For Discussion

1. You have used simulation exercises to learn important front office management skills. What are other areas within a hospitality operation for which you think simulations would be a good way to provide employee training? Give three specific examples.
2. Do you think the use of training simulations for the hospitality industry will increase in the future? Explain your answer.
3. What are three reasons hotels operate better when FOMs produce timely and accurate rooms demand forecasts?
4. How do rooms demand forecasts affect the selling prices of a lodging operation's guest rooms?
5. Some hotels allow guests to cancel room reservations at the last minute and without penalty if a personal emergency arises. Would you implement such a policy? If so, how could

you protect your hotel from unscrupulous guests seeking to defraud your hotel by falsifying the reason for their last-minute cancellation?

6. Assume that you are a hotelier who has a group booked at your hotel. The group has picked up all of its originally requested rooms and is now requesting additional rooms at the same reduced rates you originally agreed to when their group rooms contract was signed. You do have rooms available to fulfill the group's new request, but you know those remaining rooms could now be sold to the general public at rates much higher than those being paid by the group. What factors would you consider prior to granting, or not granting, this group's request for additional rooms?

7. Some hotels state that they guarantee room availability (but not room *type* availability) when a guest arrives with a guaranteed reservation. Name one advantage of such an approach. Name one disadvantage.

8. Some hotels' FOMs authorize their front office agents to adjust room charges up to the amount of a guest's total charges for their stay. Other FOMs limit the dollar amount of adjustment that can be made without first seeking approval from a supervisor. What would be the advantages to the hotel of each approach? Which approach would you prefer to take if you were serving as FOM of a hotel?

9. Staffing the night auditor's position in a hotel can sometimes be a real challenge. Why do you think it is most often harder to find qualified night auditors than it is to find qualified front office agents working other shifts?

10. Now that you have completed all of the FOMS lessons, would you recommend its use to other students? Give specific examples to support your answer.

Team Activities

TEAM ACTIVITY 1

The front office training methods used by hotels to develop effective front office agents can vary greatly. Identify one type of hotel (e.g., full-service, limited-service, extended stay, and economy) in your area, and contact one of the property's front office managers to determine:

- Who trains new front office agents at that hotel?
- What training tools are used to train the new agents?
- How much training (in hours) would a new agent receive prior to working alone at the desk?
- What training challenges do the front office managers at that property commonly experience?
- How would your team suggest those challenges best be addressed?

TEAM ACTIVITY 2

In this activity, teams are assigned the task of carefully considering the content in specifically assigned FOMS lessons. Each team should assume that a student in the class has successfully completed the assigned lessons. Using the information in Figure 15.4 as a guide, create one *new* bullet point that could be utilized on a student's resume for each lesson assigned to the team.

Be imaginative, yet realistic, in creating the new bullet points that will demonstrate to potential employers the understanding each team member has gained through successful completion of the FOMS program.

GLOSSARY

A la carte A menu that lists its dishes separately and individually priced.

Abandoned Property Items the owner has intentionally left behind. Common examples include newspapers, magazines, foods and beverages.

Accountability An obligation created when a person is delegated duties/responsibilities by higher levels of management.

Accounts Payable (AP) The sum total of all invoices owed by the hotel to its vendors for credit purchases made by the hotel. Also called "AP."

Accounts Receivable (AR) Money owed to the hotel because of sales made on credit. Sometimes referred to as "AR."

Accounts Receivable Aging A process for determining the average length of time money is owed to a hotel because of a credit sale.

Accrual Accounting System An accounting system that matches expenses incurred with revenues generated. In an accrual system, revenue is considered to be earned when products/services are provided (not when money paid for them is received); expenses are incurred when products, labor, and other costs are expended to generate revenue (not when the expenses are paid).

Advertising Information about a hotel that the hotel pays a fee to distribute.

Agitation (washing machine) Movement of the washing machine resulting in friction as fabrics rub against each other.

Air Handler The fans and mechanical systems required to move air through ducts and to vents.

Allowances and Adjustments Reductions in sales revenue credited to guests because of errors in properly recording sales or to satisfy a guest who has experienced property shortcomings.

Amenities Hotel products and services designed to attract guests. Examples include Internet access and copying services, in-room hair dryers, irons, ironing boards, and microwave ovens, as well as indoor pools, exercise rooms, and in-room movies.

Appreciation The increase, over time, in the value of an asset. The amount of the increased value is not taxed unless the asset changes hands (is sold).

Asian American Hotel Owners Association (AAHOA) Association of hotel owners who, through an exchange of ideas, seek to promote professionalism and excellence in hotel ownership.

Asset The resources owned by an organization. These include cash, accounts receivable, inventories, goodwill, furniture, fixtures, equipment, buildings, and real estate.

Atrium A large, open central space used by some hotels for registration, lobby, retail sales, and food services, among other purposes.

Attrition The difference between the original request of group rooms and the actual pickup of a group. For example, a group might reserve 100 rooms but actually use only 50 rooms. Because the room rate quoted to the group was based upon the revenue generated from the 100 rooms, the hotel's standard group contract may require, in such a case, that the group pay a penalty for its failure to purchase the number of rooms it originally agreed to purchase.

At-will employment The employment relationship that exists when employers can hire any employee they choose and dismiss an employee with or without cause at any time. Employees can also elect to work for the employer or to terminate the relationship anytime they desire to do so.

Audit An independent verification of financial records.

Authority The power or right to direct the activities of others and to enforce compliance.

Authorize To validate or confirm. When used in reference to a credit card offered by a guest at the time of check-in, the term "authorize" refers to the office agent's validation of the card. A hotel's front office validation means: (A) The card is being used legally. (B) The card has sufficient credit remaining to pay for the guest's estimated charges. (C) A hold for a dollar amount determined by front office policy has been placed on the card to ensure the hotel's payment.

Autocratic Leadership Style Leadership approach that emphasizes a "do it my way or else!" philosophy.

Average Daily Rate (ADR) The average (mean) selling price of all guest rooms in a hotel, city, or country for a specific period of time.

Back-up Generator Equipment used to make limited amounts of electricity onsite; utilized in times of power failure or when the hotel experiences low supply from the usual provider of electricity.

Back-up System Redundant hardware and/or software operated in parallel to the system it serves. Used in times of failure or power outages, such systems are often operated on batteries. For example, a back-up system to the hotel's PMS would enable continued operation even in the event of a power failure.

Ballast The device in an electric discharge lamp that starts, stops, and controls the electrical current to the light.

Banquet A food event held in a hotel's privately reserved function room.

Banquet Event Order (BEO) A form used by sales and food service personnel to detail all the requirements for a banquet event. Information provided by the client is summarized on the form, and it becomes the basis for the formal contract between the client and the hotel.

Bed and Breakfast Inns Very small properties (one to several guest rooms) owned or managed by persons living onsite; these businesses typically offer one meal a day; also called B&B.

Benchmark The search for best practices and an understanding about how they are achieved in efforts to determine how well a hospitality organization is doing.

Bid An offer by a hotel to supply sleeping rooms, meeting space, food and beverages, or other services to a potential client at a stated price. If the bid is accepted, the hotel will issue the client a contract detailing the agreement made between the hotel and the client.

Biohazard Waste Bag A specially marked plastic bag used in hotels. Laundry items that are stained with blood or bodily fluids and thus need special handling are put into these bags for transport to the OPL.

Black-out Date Specific day(s) when the hotel is sold out and/or is not accepting normal reservations.

Block Rooms reserved exclusively for members of a specific group. Used as in, "We need to create a block of 50 rooms for May 10th and 11th for the Society of Antique Furniture Appraisers."

Blood-borne Pathogen Any microorganism or virus that is carried by blood and that can cause a disease.

Body Language The concept that one communicates by the way one's arms, hands, and/or legs are positioned during a conversation or presentation.

Bonafide Occupational Qualification (BOQ) The skills and knowledge to perform a job that are necessary to safely and adequately perform all the tasks required by the job.

Bond(ing) Purchasing an insurance policy to protect against the possibility that an employee will steal.

Booking A confirmed sale, such as a reservation (individual or group) or an event. Used as in: "What is the current level of group bookings for the month?" or "How many out-of-state tour buses did Monica book last month?"

Brand The name of a specific hotel group. For example, Holiday Inn and Comfort Inn are two different brands. Additional examples of brands include Hyatt, Hampton Inn, Super 8, and Radisson.

Brand Standard A hotel service or feature that must be offered by any property entering or remaining in a specific hotel brand. Used, for example, in: "The franchisor has determined that free wireless internet access in all guest rooms will become a new brand standard effective on January 1st. next year."

Bureaucratic Leadership Style Leadership approach that emphasizes a "do it by the book" philosophy.

Buy-out An arrangement in which both parties to a contract agree to end the contract early as a result of one party paying the other the agreed-upon financial compensation.

Calibration The adjustment of equipment to maximize its effectiveness and operational efficiency.

Call Accounting The system used by a hotel to document and charge guests for the use of their in-room telephones.

Call Brand Beverages High-priced and higher-quality alcoholic beverages sold by name (such as Johnnie Walker Gold Scotch) rather than by type of liquor (scotch) only.

Camps/Parks Lodges Sleeping facilities in national, state, or other parks and recreational areas that accommodate visitors to these areas.

Cancellation Number A series of numbers and/or letters that serve to identify the cancellation of a specific hotel reservation.

Capital Expenditures The purchase of equipment, land, buildings, or other assets necessary for the operation of a hotel.

Career Fair Trade show–type events which allow prospective job applicants to meet recruiters representing multiple employers in one location during a specified time period.

Career ladder A plan that projects successively more responsible positions within an organization or an industry. Career ladders allow one to plan and schedule developmental activities necessary to assume more responsible positions.

Case Goods Non-upholstered furniture such as guest room dressers, tables, end tables, desks and the like.

Cash Accounting System An accounting system that considers revenue to be earned when it is received and expenses to be incurred when they are paid.

Cash Bar A beverage service alternative where guests desiring beverages during a banquet function pay for them personally.

Casino A business operation that offers table and card games along with (usually) slot operations and other games of skill or chance and amenities that are marketed to customers seeking gaming activities and entertainment. Many casinos offer lodging accommodations for their visitors.

Catering The process of selling a banquet event.

Central Reservation System (CRS) The industry term for the computerized program used to record guest room reservations.

Centralized Accounting A financial management system that collects accounting data from individual hotels, and then combines and analyzes the data at a different (central) site.

Centralized Purchasing A purchasing system in which participating properties develop common purchase requirements and combine purchase quantities. Suppliers frequently lower the price per purchase unit (per pound or per gallon, for example) as the quantities of items to be purchased increase.

Certified Public Accountant (C.P.A.) An individual designated by the American Institute of Certified Public Accountants as competent in the field of accounting.

CFL Short for "Compact Fluorescent Light." An alternative light source that uses less energy and lasts longer than incandescent light.

Chain The hotels operated by a group of franchisees who have all franchised the same hotel brand name. Also called a "brand" or "flag."

Chained Recipe A recipe for an item such as a sauce that is itself an ingredient in another recipe (such as a pasta dish).

Chamber of Commerce An organization whose goal is the advancement of all business interests within a community or larger business region. Sometimes called "the chamber" for short.

Charter A form of transportation rented exclusively for a specific group of travelers. Planes and buses are often chartered for group travel.

Chief Engineer The employee responsible for the management of a hotel's maintenance department. Sometimes referred to as "maintenance chief."

City Ledger The set of accounts used to record charges to and payments from a hotel's nonregistered guests (e.g., food or beverage purchases made by a person who is not a registered guest of the hotel).

Claim (Insurance) A demand for compensation as the result of loss, injury, or damage.

Close (folio) To bring to zero the balance due on a hotel guest's folio.

Closed-Circuit Television (CCTV) A camera and monitor system that displays, in real time, the activity within the camera's field of vision. A CCTV consisting of several cameras and screens showing the camera's fields of vision may be monitored in a single location.

Code of Ethics A statement adopted by an organization that outlines policies developed to guide the making of ethical decisions.

Coding The process of assigning incurred costs to predetermined cost centers or categories.

Cold Calling Making telephone contact with or an in person sales visit to, a potential client without having previously set an appointment to do so.

Commodity A commonly available and most often unspecialized product.

Comp Short for "complimentary" or "no-charge" for products or services. Rooms, food, beverages, or other services may be given to guests by management if, in their opinion, the "comp" is in the best interests of the hotel.

Compensatory Damages A monetary amount intended to compensate injured parties for actual losses or damage they have incurred. This typically includes such items as medical bills and lost wages. Also known as "actual damages."

Competitive Set The group of competing hotels to which an individual hotel's operating performance is compared. Sometimes referred to as a "Comp Set."

Conference Center A specialized hospitality operation specifically designed for and dedicated to the needs of small- and medium-sized meetings of 20 to 100 people.

Confirmation Number A series of numbers and/or letters that serve to identify a specific hotel reservation.

Consortia Groups of hotel service buyers organized for the purpose of reducing their clients' travel-related costs. A single such group is a consortium.

Contact Alarm A warning system that notifies (contacts) an external entity, such as the fire or police department, if the alarm is activated.

Continental Breakfast A simple breakfast consisting of fruit juice or fruit, coffee, and toast or a pastry.

Continuous Quality Improvement (CQI) Ongoing efforts within a hospitality operation to better meet (or exceed) guest expectations and to define ways to perform work with better, less costly, and faster methods.

Contract rate A fixed term room rate that is agreed to in advance and for the length of the contract agreement.

Contribution Margin The amount of revenue remaining from food revenue after the cost of the food used to generate the sale is paid for.

Controller The individual responsible for recording, classifying, and summarizing a hotel's business transactions. In some hotels, this position is referred to as the comptroller.

Controlling The process of comparing actual results to planned results and taking corrective action as needed.

Convenience Food Food or beverage products that have some labor "built in" that otherwise would have to be added onsite. For example, a minestrone soup may be purchased pre-made in a frozen or canned form.

Convention and Visitors Bureau (CVB) An organization, generally funded by taxes levied on overnight hotel guests, which seeks to increase the number of visitors to the area it represents. Also called the "CVB" for short.

Convention Hotel A lodging property with extensive and flexible meeting and exhibition spaces that markets to associations, corporations, and other groups bringing people together for meetings.

Conversion The changing of a hotel from one brand to another. Also known as "re-flagging."

Corkage Fee A charge assessed when a guest brings a bottle (e.g., of a special wine) to the hotel for consumption at a banquet function or in the hotel's dining room.

Corporate Rate The special rate a hotel charges to its typical business traveler. For example, a rate that is 5–20 percent below the hotel's rack rate might be designated as the hotel's corporate rate.

Cost Per Occupied Room (CPOR) Total costs incurred for an item or area, divided by the number of rooms occupied in the hotel for the time period examined.

Cross-Cultural Adaptability The extent to which a person can adjust (adapt) to another culture.

Cross-Functional Teams A group of employees from each department within the hospitality operation who work together to resolve operating problems.

Cruise Ship A passenger vessel designed to provide leisure experiences for people on vacation at sea.

Culture Shock The feeling of disorientation, confusion, and changes in emotions created when one visits or lives in a different culture.

Curb Appeal The initial visual impression the hotel's parking areas, grounds, and external buildings create for an arriving guest.

Damages The actual amount of losses or costs incurred due to the wrongful act of a liable party.

Decentralized Accounting A financial management system that collects accounting data from an individual hotel site and combines and analyzes it at the same site.

Deep Cleaning Intensive cleaning of a guest room. Typically includes thorough cleaning of such items as drapes, lamp shades, carpets, furniture, and walls. Regularly scheduled deep cleaning of guest rooms is one mark of an effective housekeeping department.

Delivery Invoice A statement from the supplier that accompanies product delivery and provides information to establish the amount of money due to the supplier. This information includes name of product, quantity, and price, and must be signed by a hotel representative to confirm that the products were delivered.

Deluxe Hot Breakfast A breakfast with hot food choices offered by a limited-service hotel.

Demand Generator An organization, entity, or location that creates a significant need for hotel services. Examples in a community include large businesses, tourist sites, sports teams, educational facilities, and manufacturing plants.

Democratic Leadership Style Leadership approach that emphasizes a "let's work together and determine the best way to do it" philosophy.

Demographic Factors Characteristics such as age, marital status, gender, ethnicity, and occupation that help to describe or classify a person as a member of a group.

Depreciation The reduction in the value of an asset as it wears out. This non-cash expense is often termed a "tax write-off" because the decline in the value of the asset is tax deductible.

Depressed Market A hotel market area where occupancy rates and/or ADRs are significantly below their historical levels.

Direct Bill A financial arrangement whereby a guest is allowed to purchase hotel services and products on credit terms.

Direct Mail The process of sending an advertisement to clients by U.S. mail service. The total cost of a direct mail piece includes the expenditures for the advertisement's design, printing, and mailing.

Direct Report An employee over whom a supervisor has immediate authority. For example, a sous chef is a direct report of the executive chef.

Directing The process of supervising staff members in the workplace.

Director of Sales and Marketing (DOSM) The person responsible for leading a hotel's marketing efforts. Job title variations include DOS (director of sales) and DOM (director of marketing).

Discipline Corrective actions designed to encourage employees to follow established policies, rules, and regulations.

Distance Learning Courses Formal education (training) programs that are available to students or trainees in remote locations.

Diversity The range of differences in attitudes, values, and behaviors of employees relative to gender, race, age, ethnicity, physical ability, and other personal characteristics.

Drop In A potential buyer of a significant number of rooms or hotel services who arrives at the hotel without an appointment.

Duct A passageway, usually built of sheet metal that allows fresh, cold, or warm air to be directed to various parts of a building.

Electric Discharge Lamp A lamp in which light is generated by passing electrical current through a space filled with a special combination of gases. Examples include fluorescent, mercury vapor, metal halide, and sodium.

Embezzlement The theft of a company's financial assets by an employee.

Emergency Maintenance Maintenance activities performed in response to an urgent situation.

Emergency Plan A document describing a hotel's predetermined, intended response to a safety/security threat it may encounter.

Employee handbook Written policies and procedures related to employment at the hotel; sometimes called an "employee manual."

Employee-to-Guest Ratio The number of employees relative to the number of guests. In the lodging industry, this is typically expressed in terms of employees per room; a 500-room luxury, full-service property may have 500 employees: a 1:1 employee-to-guest ratio. A 100-room limited-service property may have 25 employees: a 1:4 employee-to-guest ratio.

Employer of Choice The concept that the hospitality operation is a preferred place of employment in the community for applicants who have alternative employment opportunities.

Empowerment The act of granting authority to employees to make key decisions within their areas of responsibility.

Energy Management Specific engineering, maintenance, and facility-design policies and activities intended to control and reduce energy usage.

Engineering Designing and operating a building to ensure a safe and comfortable atmosphere.

Entrepreneur A person who assumes the risk of owning and operating a business in exchange for the financial and other rewards it may produce.

Entry-level Employees Staff members working in positions that require little previous experience and who do not direct the work of other staff members. Sometimes called "hourly" employees.

Ethics A person's beliefs about what is right or wrong.

Exchange Rate The rate at which the money of one country is traded (exchanged) for the money of another country.

Executive Housekeeper The individual responsible for the management and operation of a hotel's housekeeping department.

Expatriate A citizen of one country who is employed in another country. Example: a United States citizen working in Asia would be considered an expatriate by his/her Asian counterparts.

Extended-Stay Hotel A moderately priced, limited-service hotel marketing to guests desiring accommodation for extended time periods (generally one week or longer).

External recruiting Tactics designed to attract persons who are not current hotel employees for vacant positions at a property.

Federal Trade Commission (FTC) Government agency that enforces federal antitrust and consumer protection laws. It also seeks to ensure that the nation's business markets function competitively and are free of undue restrictions caused by acts or practices that are unfair or deceptive.

FF&E The furniture, fixtures, and equipment used by a hotel to service its guests.

FF&E Reserve Funds set aside by ownership today for the future "furniture, fixture, and equipment" replacement needs of a hotel.

Financial Statements Financial summaries of a hotel's accounting information. Also called the hotel's "financials."

Finger Foods Small sandwiches, salty snacks, sliced vegetables, cubed cheese and other foods that do not require flatware or other service items for guest consumption.

First-tier Management companies that operate hotels for owners using the management company's trade name as the hotel brand. Hyatt, Hilton, and Sheraton are examples.

Fiscal Quarter Any three-month period within the 12-month period that makes up a company's operating year. For example, January, February, and March would make up the first fiscal quarter of an operating year that began on January 1st and ended on December 31st.

Fixed Charges The expenses incurred in the purchase and occupation of the hotel. These include rent, property taxes, insurance, interest, and depreciation and amortization.

Flambé A cooking procedure in which alcohol (ethanol) is added to a hot pan to create a burst of flames.

Folio Detailed list of a hotel guest's room charges as well as other charges authorized by the guest or legally imposed by the hotel.

FOM The hotel industry term for a front office manager.

Food Cost per Guest (Limited-Service Hotels) The average amount expended for breakfast for each guest served. Food Cost per Guest is calculated as: Total Breakfast Food Cost (÷) Number of Guests Served = Food Cost Per Guest

Foot-candle A measure of illumination. One foot-candle equals one lumen per square foot.

Forecast (revenue) An estimate of the rooms revenue to be achieved on specific future dates.

Forecast (rooms) An estimate of the number and type of rooms to be sold on specific future dates. Also referred to as a "demand" forecast or "occupancy" forecast.

Franchise An arrangement whereby one party (the franchisor) allows another party to use its logo, brand name, systems, and resources in exchange for a fee.

Franchise Agreement A legal contract between a hotel's owners (the franchisee) and the brand managers (the franchisor) that describes the duties and responsibilities of each in the franchise relationship.

Franchise Offering circular (FOC) Franchise disclosure document prepared by a franchisor and registered and filed with the state governmental agency responsible for administering franchise relationships.

Franchise Service Director (FSD) The representative of a franchise brand who interacts directly with a hotel franchisee. Different brands may title this important position somewhat differently, but each will have a comparable position.

Franchisee An individual or company that buys, under specific terms and conditions, the right to use a brand name for a fixed period of time and at an agreed-upon price.

Franchisor An organization that manages a brand and sells the right to use the brand name.

Fraud The intentional use of deceit, trickery, or other dishonest methods to take another's money or property.

Frequent Guest Program A promotional effort administered by a hotel brand that rewards travelers every time they choose to stay at the brand's affiliated hotels. Typical rewards include free-night stays, room upgrades, and complimentary hotel services.

Front Desk The area within the hotel used for guest registration and payment.

Front Office The department within the hotel responsible for guest reservations, registration, service, and payment.

Full-Service Hotel A lodging facility that offers complete food and beverage services.

Function Room A designated hotel space that can accommodate different types of special events.

General Manager (GM) The traditional title of the individual at a hotel property who is responsible for final decision-making regarding property-specific operating policies and procedures. Also, the leader of the hotel's management team.

Generally Accepted Accounting Principles (GAAP) Techniques, methods, and procedures utilized by all accountants in the preparation of financial statements.

GFI Outlet Short for "Ground Fault Interrupter" outlet. This special electrical outlet is designed to interrupt power (by "tripping" or "blowing") before significant damage can be done to a building's wiring system. These outlets are most commonly installed in the bathroom or vanity areas of a hotel room, where high-voltage usage (such as high wattage hairdryers) or high moisture levels can cause electrical power interruptions.

Global Distribution System (GDS) Commonly referred to as the GDS, this computer system connects travel professionals worldwide for the purpose of reserving hotel rooms for their clients.

GOPPAR The amount of profit made from room sales divided by the number of rooms available to sell.

Gross Operating Profit (GOP) The amount of revenue generated in a defined time period minus its management controllable expenses for that same period.

Group Contract A legal document used to summarize the agreement between a hotel and its group client.

Group Master (reservation): The reservation information related to creating a group block, including information such as rates to be paid, cut-off dates, and the group's contact person as well as other information specific to that group.

Group Rate Special discounted room rates given to customers who agree to buy a large number of room nights for their group. In smaller hotels, any customer buying 10 or more room nights would likely qualify for a group rate. In larger hotels, the number of rooms required to qualify can vary to a greater number.

Guarantee A contractual agreement about the number of meals to be provided at a banquet event. The event's sponsor agrees to pay for the number of guests served or the guarantee, whichever is greater.

Guest Check Average The average amount spent by a guest for a room service or dining room order. The formula for calculating Guest Check Average is: Total Revenue ÷ Total Number of Guests Served = Guest Check Average.

Guest History Information related to the past stay(s) of one guest

Guest Ledger The set of accounts used to record charges to, and payments from, a hotel's registered guests. Also called a "front office ledger" or "rooms ledger."

Guided Tour A group tour package that includes the services of one or more tour guides.

Head Table Special seating at a banquet event reserved for designated guests.

Health hazard Aspects of the workplace that can lead to a decline in an employee's health. Examples include stressful working conditions and exposure to toxic chemicals.

Historical Data Information related to the stays of past guests. Collectively, this information details the history of all past hotel guests.

Hospitality industry Organizations that provide lodging accommodations and food services for people when they are away from home.

Hospitality Suite A guest room rented by a supplier/vendor, usually during a convention/conference, to provide complimentary food and/or beverages to invited guests.

Hosted Bar A beverage service alternative in which the host of a function pays for beverages during all or part of the banquet event. Also known as an "open bar."

Hosted Event Functions that are complimentary for invited guests; costs are borne by the event's sponsor. A hosted bar may offer free beverages to wedding party guests, and a corporate sponsor may pay for a hosted reception in a hospitality suite.

Hotel An establishment that provides sleeping rooms as well as various services to the traveling public.

Hotel Shuttle A vehicle used by a hotel to transport guests to and from such destinations as airports, restaurants, and shopping.

Hotelier The owner/manager of one or more hotels.

House Brand Beverages Alcoholic beverages sold by type (scotch) rather than by brand that are served when a call or premium brand beverage is not requested; also called "speed-rail," "well," or "pour brand."

House Count An estimate of the number of actual guests staying in a hotel on a given day.

Houseperson Housekeeping employee responsible for assisting room attendants with their work.

Hub Typically, a big-city airport within a short driving distance of a very large population center. These mega-airports are used to economically connect travelers with flights to their desired departure and arrival cities.

Human resources (department) The functional area in a hotel with the responsibility to assist managers in other departments with human resources concerns, including recruitment, selection, orientation, training, compensation, legal, safety and health, and a wide range of other specialized tasks. Also known as "HR."

HVAC Industry shorthand term for "heating, ventilating, and air-conditioning."

Incandescent Lamp A lamp in which a filament inside the lamp's bulb is heated by electrical current to produce light.

Incident Report A document prepared to record the details of an accident, injury, or disturbance and the hotel's response to it.

Inclusive A single price that includes all charges.

Ingredients Individual components of a food or beverage recipe.

Inspector (Inspectress) Employee responsible for physically checking the room status of guest rooms and performing other tasks as assigned by the executive housekeeper.

Insurer The entity providing insurance coverage to a business.

Interdisciplinary Between disciplines—involving several domains of knowledge; for example, basic business principles can be applied in organizations in all industries.

Interface The process in which one data-generating system automatically shares all or part of its information with another system.

Internal Alarm A warning system that notifies an area within the hotel if the alarm is activated.

Internal recruiting Tactics to identify and attract staff members who are currently employed at the hotel for vacancies that represent promotions or transfers to other positions.

Intrapreneur A person employed by an organization whose compensation is based, at least in part, upon the financial success of the unit for which he/she has responsibility.

Issuing The process of moving stored products to the place of production.

Job description A list of tasks that an employee working in a specific position must be able to effectively perform.

Job Enlargement The act of including additional tasks/assignments in one's position to provide more opportunities to learn how the position relates to others.

Job Rotation A systematic plan to move employees into different positions so that they acquire the knowledge/skills required to be effective in these positions.

Job specification A list of personal qualities or characteristic necessary for successful job performance.

Job Task An activity that an employee working in a specific position must know how and be able to do. For example, a front office agent in a hotel must be able to properly check-in an arriving guest.

Keycard The electromagnetic card used in a recodable locking system.

Laissez-faire Leadership Style Leadership approach that emphasizes a "do it the way you feel it can best be done" approach.

Last-call Notice given to guests that service will end at a specified time. For example, guests in a hotel bar may be notified 20 minutes before closing time that last drink orders must be placed, and guests in a lobby breakfast service may be informed that service will end in 10 minutes.

Laundry Par Levels The amount of laundry in use, in process, and in storage.

Lead Information about a transient or group rooms prospect who is likely to buy products and services from the hotel.

Leadership Accomplishing goals by working with others while, at the same time, gaining their respect, loyalty, competence, and enthusiastic cooperation.

LEED Short for "Leadership in Energy and Environmental Design." LEED promotes practical and measurable green building design, construction, operations and maintenance solutions.

Liable Legally bound to compensate for injury or loss.

Licensing Formal authorization to practice a profession that is granted by a governmental agency.

Limited-Service Hotel A lodging facility that offers no, or very restricted, food and beverage services. Also known as a "select service hotel."

Line of Authority A direct superior-subordinate relationship in which one person (the superior) is completely responsible for directing and exercising control over the actions of another (the subordinate).

Line-Level Employees whose jobs are non-supervisory. These are typically positions where the employee is paid a per-hour wage (not a salary) and performs a recurring and specific task for the hotel. Sometimes referred to as an "hourly" employee.

Linen Generic term for the guest room sheets and pillowcases (and food and beverage department tablecloths and napkins) washed and dried in the laundry area.

Line-up (training) A brief informational training session held before the work shift begins.

Link Short for *Hyperlink*. A relationship between two Web sites. If a Web site chooses to link itself with another Web site, the link, when activated, will direct the user to the linked Web page. An external link leads to a Web page other than the current one; an internal link leads to another section of the current Web site.

Lobby Food Services Food services offered in a limited-service hotel's atrium or lobby area.

Lodging Industry All the businesses that provide overnight accommodations for guests.

Long-Range Goals Goals that are to be achieved over an extended period (usually longer than one year). Sometimes called "long-term goals."

Lost Property Items the owner has unintentionally left behind and then forgotten. Common examples include robes, slippers, hairdryers, and cosmetics.

Maintenance The activities required to keep a building and its contents in good repair. Also, the department or area of a hotel responsible for these activities.

Maintenance Chief The employee responsible for the management of a hotel's maintenance department. Sometimes referred to as "chief engineer."

Make or Buy Analysis The process of considering quality, costs, and other factors in scratch production and convenience food alternatives to determine which form is best for the operation.

Malcolm-Baldridge National Quality Award Award granted to U.S. businesses that demonstrate successful quality-related strategies relating to leadership, information/analysis, strategic planning, human resource development/management, process management, business results, and customer focus/satisfaction.

Management The coordination of individual efforts to achieve established goals.

Management Company An organization that operates a hotel for a fee. Sometimes called a "contract company."

Management Contract An agreement between a hotel's owners and a hotel management company under which, for a fee, the management company operates the hotel. Also sometimes called a "management agreement," or an "operating agreement."

Manager A staff member who directs the work of supervisors.

Manager on Duty (MOD) The individual on the hotel property responsible for making any managerial decisions required during the period he or she is MOD.

Manager's Daily (FOMS) A summary of a hotel's daily revenue generation that can include additional operating data as requested by the property's general manager.

Manager's Daily (sales report) A re-cap of the previous day's rooms, food and beverage, and other sales. The manager's daily may include additional hotel operating statistics as requested by the hotel's general manager. Sometimes referred to simply as the "daily."

Manager's Reception A time, usually during the late afternoon/early evening, when complimentary foods and beverages are offered to guests of limited-service properties.

Market The potential customers for a business's products and services.

Market Share The percentage of a total market (typically measured in dollars spent) captured by a property. For example, a hotel generating $200,000 in guest room rental in a market where travelers spend $1,000,000 per year would have a 20 percent market share ($200,000/$1,000,000 = 20%).

Marketing Activities directly related to increasing a potential guest's awareness of a hotel.

Marketing Plan A calendar of specific activities designed to meet the hotel's revenue goals.

Mark-up A fee added to a supplier's charges that the hotel bills a guest or group to compensate for value added by the hotel.

Material Safety Data Sheets (MSDS) Written statements describing the potential hazards of, and best ways to handle, chemicals or toxic substances. An MSDS is provided to the buyer by the manufacturer of the chemical or toxic substance used by the hotel and must be posted and made available in a place where it is easily accessible to those who will actually handle the product.

Meeting Planner A professional employed by a group to negotiate the group's contract with a hotel.

Mentor To serve as a personal teacher. Also known as a guide or coach.

Menu Planning The process of determining which food and beverage items will most please the guests while meeting established cost objectives.

Minimum wage The lowest amount of compensation that an employer may pay to an employee covered by the FLSA or applicable state law. Most hotel employees are covered by minimum wage provisions; however, exceptions can include youthful employees being paid a training wage for the first 90 days of employment and tipped employees (if reported tips plus wages received at least equal the minimum wage).

Minutes Per Room (guest room cleaning) The average number of minutes required to clean a guest room.

Mislaid Property Items the owner has unintentionally left behind. Common examples include laptop computers, jewelry, and clothing.

Mission Statement A planning tool that broadly identifies what a hospitality operation would like to accomplish and how it will accomplish it.

Moments of Truth Any (and every) time a guest has an opportunity to form an impression about the hospitality organization. Moments of truth can be positive or negative.

Motivation An internal force that drives employees to do something to reach a goal.

National Culture The values or attitudes shared by citizens of a specific country that impact their behavior and shape their beliefs about what is important.

Negotiated rate An agreed upon rate that is offered by a hotel but is subject to room availability. Also referred to as a volume rate or volume discount rate.

Networking The development of personal relationships for a business-related purpose. For example, an area's chamber of commerce–sponsored breakfast open to all community business leaders interested in improving local traffic conditions would be a networking opportunity for a member of a hotel's sales team.

Night Audit The process of reviewing for accuracy and completeness the accounting transactions from one day to conclude, or "close," that day's sales information in preparation for recording the transactions of the next day

Night Auditor The individual who performs the daily review of all the financial transactions with hotel guests recorded by the front office

No-show A guest who makes a room reservation but fails to cancel it or does not arrive at the hotel on the date of the confirmed reservation. (See Figure 6.2)

Occupancy Rate The ratio of guest rooms sold (or given away) to the number of guest rooms available for sale in a given time period and expressed as a percentage.

Occupational Safety and Health Administration (OSHA) A federal agency established in 1970 and that is responsible for developing and enforcing regulations to help ensure safe and healthful working conditions.

On-line Travel Agent (OTA) An organization that provides travel booking services on the Internet.

On-premise laundry (OPL) The area within the hotel where the cleaning of fabrics takes place.

Organizational Chart A visual portrayal of the jobs and positions of authority within an organization.

Organizing Actions designed to bring together and arrange the resources of a group to help it achieve its goals.

Orientation The process of providing basic information about the hotel which must be known by all of its employees.

Outsource To obtain labor or parts from an outside provider. Typically done to reduce costs or obtain specialized expertise.

Over A situation in which a cashier has more money in the cash drawer than the official sales records plus shift bank indicate. Thus, a cashier with $10 more in the cash drawer than the sales record plus shift bank is said to be $10 over.

Overbook(ed) A situation in which the hotel has more confirmed guest reservations than it has rooms available to lodge those guests. Sometimes referred to as "oversold."

Overtime The number of hours of work after which an employee must receive a pay premium (generally one and one-half times the normal hourly rate).

Owner/Operator A hotel investor who also manages (operates) the hotel.

Ozone System (laundry) A method of processing laundry that utilizes ozonated cold water rather than hot water to clean and sanitize laundry items.

Package A group of travel services, such as hotel rooms, meals, and airfare, sold for one price. For example, a Valentine's Day Getaway package to Las Vegas suggested by a travel agent might include airfare, lodging, meals, and show tickets for two people at an all-inclusive price.

Par Inventory System A system of managing purchasing and inventory levels based upon the requirement that a specified quantity of product be available in inventory. For example, if a par for five cases of disposable coffee cups is established, the quantity necessary to bring the inventory level back to five cases is ordered whenever coffee cups are purchased.

Participative Management A leadership style that emphasizes seeking out and considering group input before making decisions that affect the group.

PBX Short for "Private Branch Exchange." The system within the hotel used to process incoming, internal, and outgoing telephone calls.

Per Diem A daily, fixed amount paid for a traveler's expenses. Established by companies, government agencies, or other entities, the per diem amount for a traveler will be based upon the costs associated with the area to which the individual travels. For example, the per diem for food and lodging for a traveler spending the night in New York City will be higher than for a traveler spending the night in a less expensive area of the country.

Performance appraisal A periodic formal evaluation of an employee's job performance, including a discussion of professional development goals; also called "performance evaluation."

Pickup The actual number of rooms purchased by a client in a specific time period. Used as in: "What was the Florida Furniture Society's total room pick-up last week?"

Pilferage Stealing small quantities of something over a period of time; for example, a thief might steal one bottle from a case of liquor.

Pilot Light A small permanent flame used to ignite gas at a burner.

Place Setting The arrangement of plates, glasses, knives, forks, and spoons (flatware), and other service items on a dining table for one guest.

Planning The process of considering the future and establishing goals for an organization.

PM (Preventive Maintenance) Program A specific inspection and activities schedule designed to minimize maintenance-related costs and to prolong the life of equipment by preventing small problems before they become larger ones.

PM Checklist A tool developed to identify all the critical areas that should be inspected during a PM review of a room, area, or piece of equipment.

Point-of-Sale (POS) system A computer system that maintains a record of guests' food and beverage purchases and payments.

POM Short for "property operation and maintenance." The term is taken from the Uniform System of Accounts for Hotels and refers to the segment of the income statement that details the costs of operating the maintenance department.

Post To enter a guest's charges into the PMS to create a permanent record of the sale. Used as in "Please post this meeting room charge to Mr. Walker's folio."

Premium Brand Beverages Highest-priced and highest-quality beverages generally available, such as "Johnnie Walker Scotch." Also referred to as "super call."

Premiums The fees paid for insurance.

Pre-paid Expense Expenditures made for items prior to the accounting period in which the items' actual expense is incurred.

Preventive Maintenance Maintenance activities designed to minimize maintenance costs and prolong the life of equipment.

Private Clubs Membership organizations not open to the public that exist for people enjoying common interests. Examples include country (golf) clubs, city clubs, university clubs, yacht clubs, and military clubs. Some private clubs offer sleeping rooms for members and guests.

Product Usage Report A report detailing the amount of an inventoried item used by a hotel in a specified time period (week, month, quarter, or year).

Production All of the cooking and preparation processes used to ready products for consumption.

Professional Development The process by which hoteliers continue to improve their knowledge and skills.

Professionals People working in an occupation that requires extensive knowledge and skills in a specialized body of knowledge.

Profit The money remaining after all the expenses of operating a business have been paid.

Profit and Loss statement (P&L) The P&L records total hotel revenues and expenses for a specific time period. Same as the statement of income and expense.

Progressive disciplinary program A carefully planned series of corrective actions, each increasing in its severity and designed to encourage employees to follow established policies, rules, and regulations.

Promote from Within The concept that a company offers higher-level positions to its existing employees before seeking external candidates when these positions must be filled.

Property Management System (PMS) The industry term for the computerized system used to record guest reservations, financial information and other data related to the operation of a hotel's front office.

Public Space Areas within the hotel that can be freely accessed by guests and visitors. Examples include lobby areas, public restrooms, corridors, and stairwells.

Publicity Information about a hotel that is distributed by the media but for which the hotel does not pay a fee.

Punitive Damages A monetary amount assessed to punish liable parties and to serve as an example to the liable party as well as others not to commit the wrongful act in the future.

Quality The consistent delivery of products and services according to expected standards.

Quality Inspection Scores Sometimes called Quality Assurance (QA) scores, these scores are the result of annual (or more frequent) inspections conducted by a franchise company to ensure that franchisor-mandated standards are being met by the franchisee. In some cases, management companies or the property itself may also establish internal inspection systems. In general, however, it is the franchise company's quality inspection score that is used as a measure of the effectiveness of the general manager, the hotel's management team, and the owner's financial commitment to the property.

Rack Rate The price at which a hotel sells its rooms when no discounts of any kind are offered to the guest. Often shortened to "rack."

Reasonable Care A legal concept identifying the amount of care a reasonably prudent person would exercise in a specific situation.

Receiving (Foodservice) The point at which ownership of products being purchased transfers from the seller (supplier) to the hospitality operation.

Recodable Locking System A hotel guest room locking system designed so that when guests insert their "key" (typically an electromagnetic card, but increasingly a password) into the guest room locking device for the first time, the lock is immediately recoded, canceling entry authorization from the previous guest's key.

Recruitment Activities designed to attract qualified applicants for the hotel's vacant management and non-management positions.

Regional Manager The individual responsible for the operation of multiple hotels in a designated geographic area. In some companies, the person's title may be area or district manager.

Registration Acceptance for one to work within a profession that is (typically) granted by a nongovernmental agency such as an association.

Registration (Reg) Card A document that provides details such as guest's name, arrival date, rate to be paid, departure date, and other information related to the guest's stay. In conversation, most often shortened to "reg" card, as in: "Where is the signed Reg card for room 417?"

Reinforcement (training) Use of encouraging words and actions that re-emphasize the proper way to do a job task.

Repeat Business Guests who return to the property for additional visits after their first visit.

Replace as Needed A parts or equipment replacement plan that delays installing a new part until the original part fails or is near failure. For example, most chief engineers would use a replace-as-needed plan in the maintenance of refrigeration compressors or water pumps.

Repossession The taking back of a property by a seller or lender, usually in response to non-payment by the buyer.

Residential Education Programs Formal education (training) programs that are available to students or trainees at a specific geographic location.

Resort A full-service hotel with additional attractions that make it a primary destination for travelers.

Restoration Returning an older hotel building to its original, or better than original, condition.

Return On Investment (ROI) The percentage rate of financial return achieved on the money invested in a hotel property.

Revenue Management (RM) The process and procedures used to optimize RevPAR.

Revenue Manager An individual whose major task consists of forecasting room demand so that the hotel can maximize RevPAR. In larger hotels, this will be a full-time position. In a smaller, limited-service property, the general manager or front office manager will have this responsibility.

Revenue Per Available Room (RevPAR) The average revenue generated by each guest room available during a specific time period. RevPAR combines the information from ADR and occupancy rate into a single measure.

Room Attendant Employee responsible for cleaning guest rooms. Also referred to as "housekeeper." Sometimes called "maids" by guests, but that term is *never* used by professional hoteliers.

Room Attendant Cart A wheeled cart that contains all of the items needed to properly and safely clean and restock a guest room. Also referred to as a "room attendant's cleaning cart or a housekeeping cart."

Room Mix The ratio of room types in a hotel. For example, the number of double-bedded rooms compared to king-bedded rooms, the number of smoking-permitted rooms to no-smoking rooms, or the number of suites compared to standard rooms.

Room Night The number of rooms used times the number of nights they are sold. For example, a guest who reserves two rooms for five nights each has made a reservation for 10 room nights (2 rooms × 5 nights = 10 room nights).

Room Service The delivery of food and beverages to a hotel guest's sleeping room.

Room Status The up-to-date (actual) condition of each of the hotel's guest rooms (e.g., occupied, vacant, or dirty.)

Room Type Specific configurations of guest rooms. For example, king-sized bed vs. double-sized bed, or parlor suite vs. standard sleeping room. Commonly abbreviated (K for king, D for double bed, etc.), reserving of the proper room type is often as important to guests as whether the hotel, in fact, has a room available for them

Routine Maintenance Maintenance activities that must be performed on a continual (ongoing) basis.

Safety Protection of an individual's physical well-being and health.

Safety and Security Committee An interdepartmental task force consisting of hotel managers, supervisors, and hourly-paid employees responsible for monitoring and refining a hotel's safety and security efforts.

Safety hazard Conditions in the workplace that can cause immediate harm. Examples include unsafe equipment, accidents, and the improper use of chemicals.

Sales Activities directly related to a client's purchase (booking) of hotel rooms or services.

Sales and Marketing Committee The team of employees responsible for coordinating the hotel's sales and marketing efforts.

Sales Call A pre-arranged meeting held for the purpose of explaining and selling the hotel's products and services.

Scratch (food production) The use of basic ingredients to make items for sale. For example, a minestrone soup may be made onsite with fresh vegetables, meat, and other ingredients.

Seasonal Hotel A hotel whose revenue and expenditures vary greatly depending on the time (season) of the year. Examples include hotels near ski resorts, beaches, theme parks, certain tourist areas, sporting venues, and the like.

Second-tier Management companies that operate hotels for owners and do not use the management company name as part of the hotel name. American General Hospitality, Summit Hotel Management, and Winegardner and Hammons are examples.

Security Protection of an individual's or business's property or assets.

Selection The process of evaluating job applicants to determine who is most qualified for and likely to be successful in a vacant position.

Sell-out (1) A situation in which all available rooms are sold. A hotel, area, or entire city may, if demand is strong enough, sell out. (2) A period of time in which management must attempt to optimize ADR.

Server Station An area of the dining room where all tables and booths have been assigned to a specific server.

Service (Food and Beverage) The process of transferring food and beverage products from wait staff to the guests.

Service (Guest) The process of helping guests by addressing their wants and needs with respect and dignity and in a timely manner.

Serving The process of moving prepared food or beverage items from production staff to service personnel.

Shift Bank The total amount of currency and coins in a cashier's drawer at the beginning of that cashier's work shift. Used as in: "Let's start the 3:00 p.m. shift at the front desk with a $750 shift bank."

Shift report (front desk) A summary of all folio and other financial transactions completed at a hotel's front office during a pre-determined time period (typically 8 hours).

Short A situation in which a cashier has less money in the cash drawer than the official sales records plus shift bank indicate should be available. Thus, a cashier with $10 less in the cash drawer than the sales record plus shift bank is said to be $10 short.

Short-Range Goals Goals that are to be achieved in the very near future (usually less than one year). Sometimes called "short-term goals."

Signature Items Food or beverage products produced by a hospitality operation that are unique to the property and that the general public associates with it.

Sign-in/Sign-out Program A system in which employees taking responsibility for hotel assets (such as hand tools, power equipment, or keys to secured areas) must document their responsibility by placing their signature and the date on a form recording their possession (sign-out) and return (sign-in) of the item.

Sign-off To verify or approve accuracy of operational information. Used as in: "Ms. Larson, will you sign-off on last night's audit?"

Simulation (training) The imitation of a human activity designed to improve a trainees' ability to respond to the real activity. Examples include flight simulators (to train airline pilots), medical emergency response simulators (to train physicians) and FOMS (to train hotel front office managers).

Site Tour A potential customer's physical visit to a hotel that is hosted by a member of the hotel's staff.

SMERF Short for "Social, Military, Educational, Religious, or Fraternal groups" and organizations.

Solvency The ability of a hotel to pay its debts as they come due.

Source Reduction Efforts by product manufacturers to design and ship products in a way that minimizes packaging waste resulting from the product's shipment to a hotel.

Standardized Recipes A written explanation about how a food or beverage item should be prepared. It lists the quantity of each ingredient, preparation techniques, portion size and other information production personnel need to ensure that the item is always prepared in the same way.

STAR Report Short for the "Smith Travel Accommodations Report." Produced by the Smith Travel Research (STR) company, this report is used to compare a hotel's sales results to those of its selected competitor.

Stay-over A guest who is *not* scheduled to check out of the hotel on the day his or her room status is assessed. That is, the guest will be staying at least one more day.

Stockout The condition that arises when a food/beverage item needed for production is not available onsite.

Subordinates Employees whose work is directly supervised or controlled by an individual of higher rank or position.

Suggestive Selling Information suggested by an order taker (in a room service operation) or by a server (in an à la carte dining operation) to encourage guests to purchase additional items or higher priced items they might otherwise not have ordered. This is commonly referred to as *up-selling.*

Supervisor A staff member who directs the work of line-level (non-supervisory) employees.

System-wide The term used to describe a characteristic of all hotels within a single brand. Used, for example, in: "Last year, the system-wide ADR for our brand was $99.50."

Team A group of individuals who work together and set the goals of the group above their own.

Terry Generic term for the bath towels, bath mats, hand towels, and wash cloths washed and dried in the laundry area.

Theft Stealing all of something at one time; for example, a thief might steal a case of liquor.

Third Party Liability A legal concept that can hold the provider of alcoholic beverages responsible for the acts of those who have consumed the alcohol. Also referred to as "dram shop" legislation.

Threat Analysis A systematic procedure designed to identify and eliminate identifiable safety risks.

Timeshare A lodging property that sells its rooms to guests for use during a specific time period each year; also called vacation ownership property.

Total Replacement A parts or equipment replacement plan that involves installing new or substitute parts based on a predetermined schedule. For example, most chief engineers would use a total replacement approach to the maintenance of light bulbs in high-rise exterior highway signs.

Tour Operator A company or individual that plans and markets travel packages.

Tourist A person who travels for pleasure.

Track To maintain extensive information on a specific type of traveler. For example, a hotel may wish to track the ADR, rooms used, and arrival patterns of transient military travelers to learn more about this specific type of traveler.

Trade show An industry-specific event that allows suppliers to an industry to interact with, educate, and sell to individuals who are part of the industry; also called an exhibition.

Transient Individual guests who are not part of a group or tour booking. Transient guests can be further subdivided by traveler demographics to obtain more detailed information about the type of guest staying in the hotel (e.g., corporate, leisure, and government).

Travel Agent A professional who assists clients in planning and purchasing travel.

Turnover (employee) The replacement of employees needed in an organization or a position as other staff members leave.

Turnover Rate A measure of the proportion of a work force that is replaced during a designated time period (month, quarter, or year). It can be calculated as: Number of Employees Separated (÷) Number of Employees in the Workforce = Turnover Rate.

Upselling Tactics used to increase the hotel's average daily rate (ADR) by encouraging guests to reserve higher-priced rooms with better or more amenities than are provided with lower-priced rooms (e.g., view, complimentary breakfast and newspaper, increased square footage).

User Generated Content (UGC) site A Web site designed to host forums, blogs, or other reviewer submitted information allowing those seeking information to read the comments of other consumers prior to making their buying decisions. UGC sites are sometimes referred to as Web 2.0

Value The relationship between price paid and the quality of the products and services received.

Value (Foodservice) The guest's perception of the selling price of a menu item relative to the quality of the menu item, service, and dining experience received.

Value (Lodging Accommodations) The price paid to rent a room relative to the quality of the room and services received.

Vendors Those who sell products and services to hoteliers.

Walked A situation in which a guest with a reservation is relocated from the reserved hotel to another hotel because no room was available at the reserved hotel.

Walk-in A guest seeking a room who arrives at the hotel without an advance reservation.

Word of Mouth Advertising The favorable or unfavorable comments made when previous guests of a hospitality operation tell others about their experiences.

Work Order A form used to initiate and document a request for maintenance. Also referred to as a "maintenance request."

Workers' Compensation An insurance program designed to assist individuals who are victims of a work-related injury or illness.

Wow Factor The feeling guests have when they experience an unanticipated and positive "extra" as they interact with a hospitality operation.

Write-off A guest's direct bill that is considered uncollectible by management and as a result is subtracted from the hotel's accounts receivable total.

Zero Defects A goal of no guest-related complaints established when guest service processes are implemented.

INDEX

D

E

I

J

K

L

M

Q

R

S

T

U

V

W

Z